TAKING SIDES

Clashing Views on Controversial

Political Issues

THIRTEENTH EDITION

Selected, Edited, and with Introductions by

George McKenna
City College, City University of New York

and

Stanley Feingold

McGraw-Hill/Dushkin
A Division of The McGraw-Hill Companies

Photo Acknowledgment
Cover image: © 2003 by PhotoDisc, Inc.

Cover Art Acknowledgment
Charles Vitelli

Copyright © 2004 by McGraw-Hill/Dushkin,
A Division of The McGraw-Hill Companies, Inc., Guilford, Connecticut 06437

Copyright law prohibits the reproduction, storage, or transmission in any form by any means of any
portion of this publication without the express written permission of McGraw-Hill/Dushkin and of
the copyright holder (if different) of the part of the publication to be reproduced. The Guidelines for
Classroom Copying endorsed by Congress explicitly state that unauthorized copying may not be
used to create, to replace, or to substitute for anthologies, compilations, or collective works.

Taking Sides ® is a registered trademark of McGraw-Hill/Dushkin

Manufactured in the United States of America

Thirteenth Edition

123456789BAHBAH6543

Library of Congress Cataloging-in-Publication Data
Main entry under title:
Taking sides: clashing views on controversial political issues/selected, edited, and with
introductions by George McKenna and Stanley Feingold.—13th ed.
Includes bibliographical references and index.
1. United States—Politics and government—1945–. I. McKenna, George, comp.
II. Feingold, Stanley, comp.
320'.973
0-07-293307-0
ISSN: 1080-580X

Printed on Recycled Paper

Dedication

In memory of Hillman M. Bishop and Samuel Hendel, masters of an art often neglected by college teachers: teaching.

Preface

Dialogue means two people talking to the same issue. This is not as easy as it sounds. Play back the next debate between the talking heads you see on television. Listen to them try to persuade each other—actually, the TV audience —of the truth of their own views and of the irrationality of their opponents' views.

What is likely to happen? At the outset, they will probably fail to define the issue with enough clarity and objectivity to make it clear exactly what it is that they are disputing. As the philosopher Alasdair MacIntyre has put it, the most passionate pro and con arguments are often "incommensurable"—they sail past each other because the two sides are talking about different things. As arguments proceed, both sides tend to employ vague, emotion-laden terms without spelling out the uses to which the terms are put. When the heat is on, they may resort to shouting epithets at one another, and the hoped-for meeting of minds will give way to the scoring of political points and the reinforcement of existing prejudices. For example, when the discussion of affirmative action comes down to both sides accusing the other of "racism," or when the controversy over abortion degenerates into taunts and name-calling, then no one really listens and learns from the other side.

It is our conviction that people *can* learn from the other side, no matter how sharply opposed it is to their own cherished viewpoint. Sometimes, after listening to others, we change our view entirely. But in most cases, we either incorporate some elements of the opposing view—thus making our own richer —or else learn how to answer the objections to our viewpoint. Either way, we gain from the experience. For these reasons we believe that encouraging dialogue between opposed positions is the most certain way of enhancing public understanding.

The purpose of this 13th edition of *Taking Sides* is to continue to work toward the revival of political dialogue in America. As we have done in the past 12 editions, we examine leading issues in American politics from the perspective of sharply opposed points of view. We have tried to select authors who argue their points vigorously but in such a way as to enhance our understanding of the issue.

We hope that the reader who confronts lively and thoughtful statements on vital issues will be stimulated to ask some of the critical questions about American politics. What are the highest-priority issues with which government must deal today? What positions should be taken on these issues? What should be the attitude of Americans toward their government? Our conviction is that a healthy, stable democracy requires a citizenry that considers these questions and participates, however indirectly, in answering them. The alternative is apathy, passivity, and, sooner or later, the rule of tyrants.

Plan of the book   Each issue has an issue *introduction,* which sets the stage for the debate as it is argued in the YES and NO selections. Each issue concludes with a *postscript* that makes some final observations and points the way to other questions related to the issue. In reading the issue and forming your own opinions you should not feel confined to adopt one or the other of the positions presented. There are positions in between the given views or totally outside them, and the *suggestions for further reading* that appear in each issue postscript should help you find resources to continue your study of the subject. We have also provided relevant Internet site addresses (URLs) on the *On the Internet* page that accompanies each part opener. At the back of the book is a listing of all the *contributors to this volume,* which will give you information on the political scientists and commentators whose views are debated here.

Changes to this edition   Over the past quarter century *Taking Sides* has undergone extensive changes and improvements, and we are particularly proud of this 13th edition. There are seven new issues in this volume, more than we have ever added during a revision: *Do the Media Have a Liberal Bias?* (Issue 4); *Should the Electoral College Be Abolished?* (Issue 6); *Was* Bush v. Gore *Correctly Decided?* (Issue 7); *Is America's War on Terrorism Justified?* (Issue 17); *Is Free Trade Fair Trade?* (Issue 18); *Must America Exercise World Leadership?* (Issue 19); and *Should Terrorist Suspects Be Tried by Military Tribunals?* (Issue 20). In addition, for seven of the issues that were carried over from the previous edition (democracy for every country, campaign spending, gun control, affirmative action, abortion, taxes, and immigration), we have freshened up the debate by changing one or both of the selections. All told, 24 of the selections in this edition are new—more than half the book.

   We worked hard on what we hope will be a truly memorable 13th edition, and we think you will like the result. Let us know what you think by writing to us care of McGraw-Hill/Dushkin, 530 Old Whitfield Street, Guilford, CT 06437 or e-mailing us at GMcK1320@aol.com or stanleyfeingold@mindspring.com. Suggestions for further improvements are most welcome!

A word to the instructor   An *Instructor's Manual With Test Questions* (multiple-choice and essay) is available through the publisher for the instructor using *Taking Sides* in the classroom. A general guidebook, *Using Taking Sides in the Classroom,* which discusses methods and techniques for integrating the pro-con approach into any classroom setting, is also available. An online version of *Using Taking Sides in the Classroom* and a correspondence service for *Taking Sides* adopters can be found at http://www.dushkin.com/usingts/.

   Taking Sides: Clashing Views on Controversial Political Issues is only one title in the Taking Sides series. If you are interested in seeing the table of contents for any of the other titles, please visit the Taking Sides Web site at http://www.dushkin.com/takingsides/.

Acknowledgments   We are grateful to Laura McKenna for her help and suggestions in preparing this edition. Thanks also to the reference departments of

City College's Morris Raphael Cohen Library and the public library of Tenafly, New Jersey—especially to Agnes Kolben.

We also appreciate the spontaneous letters from instructors and students who wrote to us with comments and observations. Many thanks to Ted Knight, list manager of the Taking Sides series, for his able editorial assistance; to David Brackley, senior developmental editor; and to Rose Gleich, administrative assistant. Needless to say, the responsibility for any errors of fact or judgment rests with us.

George McKenna
City College, City University of New York
Stanley Feingold

Contents In Brief

Contents

Professor of political science Michael McFaul argues that the conditions exist to increase the number of democratic nations and that the United States can and should use its power to encourage and support liberty and democracy in nations that have never before enjoyed freedom. Foreign correspondent Robert D. Kaplan contends that not all nations have the conditions in which democracy can thrive, that some nations prosper without it, and that democracy may be less important in the future.

Professor of political science Samuel L. Popkin argues that presidential election campaigns perform a unique and essential service in informing and unifying the American people. Political scientist Anthony King contends that American officeholders spend too much time and effort running for office, which detracts from their responsibility to provide good government.

Paul D. Wellstone, a Democratic senator from Minnesota, argues that the new campaign spending reform legislation constitutes an "enormous step forward" in lessening the undue power of wealthy special interests in U.S. elections. John Samples, director of the Cato Institute's Center for Representative Government, predicts that the new campaign finance law will reduce voter turnout, make it more difficult for challengers to win against incumbents, and stifle free speech.

Reporter Bernard Goldberg cites studies of journalists' attitudes and recalls some of his own experiences at CBS News to show that the culture of the news media is hostile to conservatism. Radio talk show host Jim Hightower cites a number of examples indicating that there is in fact a paucity of "actual liberals, much less progressive populists," with access to a national audience to counter the many conservative voices in the media.

PART 2   THE INSTITUTIONS OF GOVERNMENT   81

Supreme Court chief justice William H. Rehnquist argues that Congress cannot regulate activities within a state that are not economic and do not substantially affect commerce among the states. Supreme Court justice Stephen G. Breyer upholds the right of Congress to regulate activities within a state if Congress has a rational basis for believing that it affects the exercise of congressional power.

Freelance writer Daniel Lazare argues that the electoral college is an undemocratic institution that no longer serves to democratically choose a president. Richard A. Posner, a judge and a legal scholar, sees more difficulties in abolishing the electoral college than in retaining it, and he maintains that the U.S. Supreme Court has the right to ensure that the casting of a state's electoral vote conforms with that state's laws.

Former judge Robert H. Bork contends that, in denying the effort of the Florida Supreme Court to rewrite the Florida election law, the U.S. Supreme Court correctly prevented Al Gore from overturning George W. Bush's narrow victory in the 2000 presidential election. Professor of jurisprudence Cass R. Sunstein concludes that the intervention of the U.S. Supreme Court to halt the vote recount in contested Florida districts lacked precedent, was unprincipled, and raised questions regarding the denial of equal protection, which the Court was unwilling to confront.

Essayist Robert W. Lee argues that capital punishment is the only fair way for society to respond to certain heinous crimes. Law professor Eric M. Freedman contends that the death penalty does not reduce crime but does reduce public safety and carries the risk of innocent people being executed.

Writer Carl T. Bogus argues that even local gun control laws will reduce the number of gun-related crimes. Social analyst John R. Lott, Jr., argues that giving law-abiding citizens the right to carry concealed handguns deters street crime.

Mary Frances Berry, chair of the U.S. Civil Rights Commission, contends that affirmative action is needed because minorities have suffered so much negative action throughout American history. Columnist Linda Chavez argues that racial preferences create a surface appearance of progress while destroying the substance of minority achievement.

Law professor Charles R. Lawrence III asserts that speech should be impermissible when, going beyond insult, it inflicts injury on its victims. Author Jonathan Rauch maintains that there can be no genuine freedom of expression unless it includes the freedom to offend those who oppose the expressed opinion.

Legal philosopher Robert P. George asserts that, since each of us was a human being from conception, abortion is a form of homicide and should be banned. Writer Mary Gordon maintains that having an abortion is a moral choice that women are capable of making for themselves and that aborting a fetus is not killing a person.

Wall Street Journal editorial writer Amity Shlaes maintains that the federal income tax is too high, too complex, and unfair in withholding income from wage earners. Philosophy professors Liam Murphy and Thomas Nagel contend that the issue of tax fairness is misunderstood because, contrary to what most people believe, taxes do not take one's property but, in fact, help to establish property rights.

Economist Paul Krugman maintains that corporate greed, the decline of organized labor, and changes in production have contributed to a sharp increase in social and economic inequality in America. Christopher C. DeMuth, president of the American Enterprise Institute, asserts that Americans have achieved an impressive level of wealth and equality and that a changing economy ensures even more opportunities.

PART 4   AMERICA AND THE WORLD   269

Political science professor Lucian W. Pye warns that China is not to be trusted in its economic and political dealings with the United States and other nations. Chinese studies professor David M. Lampton maintains that popular assumptions about China's military, political, and economic objectives are wrong and should be corrected.

Political commentator Patrick J. Buchanan argues that large-scale, uncontrolled immigration has increased America's social and economic problems and deprived it of the shared values and common language that define a united people. Daniel T. Griswold, associate director of the Cato Institute's Center for Trade Policy Studies, contends that immigration gives America an economic edge, does not drain government finances, and is not remarkably high compared with past eras.

Editor Norman Podhoretz maintains that America must not only eliminate the Al Qaeda network terrorists but also overthrow state regimes that sponsor terrorism. Editor Thomas Harrison argues that America's war on terrorism is simply an attempt to preserve an oppressive status quo and that the only way to eliminate terrorism is to form a third party that seeks a more democratic and egalitarian world.

Issue 18.   Is Free Trade Fair Trade?   336

Professor of economics Douglas A. Irwin asserts that all countries benefit from free trade because it promotes efficiency, spurs production, and results in better goods at lower prices. David Morris, vice president of the Institute for Local Self-Reliance, argues that free trade is undesirable because it widens the standard-of-living gap between rich and poor nations.

Issue 19.   Must America Exercise World Leadership?   356

William Kristol, editor of *The Weekly Standard,* and Robert Kagan, a senior associate at the Carnegie Endowment for International Peace, maintain that America must exercise a role of world preeminence to shape the international environment in order to protect American interests. Benjamin Schwarz, a correspondent for *The Atlantic Monthly,* and Christopher Layne, a MacArthur Fellow in Peace and International Security Studies, conclude that it is burdensome, risky, and ultimately futile for America to attempt to preserve its status as the only great power.

Issue 20.   Should Terrorist Suspects Be Tried by Military Tribunals?   382

Ambassador Pierre-Richard Prosper defends military tribunals as consistent with established law and as necessary to protect American jurors and court personnel from an international terror network. Aryeh Neier, of the American Civil Liberties Union, contends that the proposed military tribunals would deprive defendants of essential rights guaranteed under both American and international law.

Introduction

Labels and Alignments in American Politics

George McKenna

Stanley Feingold

Like a giant tidal wave crashing ashore, the September 11, 2001, attacks on the United States seemed to wash away some of America's most recognizable political landmarks. Suddenly, America's competing political parties, interest groups, and ideologies—whose outlines had been prominent in congressional debates, political campaigns, and media talk shows—seemed irrelevant. In the face of these murderous attacks, who cared about petty political differences? In the most remarkable display of national unity since Pearl Harbor, Congress, with only one dissent, voted to authorize President George W. Bush to use "all necessary and appropriate force" against those he considered responsible for the attacks and even those nations harboring them. On September 20 some of Bush's harshest congressional critics were on their feet cheering his dramatic speech before a special joint session of Congress. As the Republican president left the chamber, he approached the Democratic Senate majority leader, Tom Daschle, and in a moment the two were locked in a fervent embrace. The act symbolized the embrace of all Americans at that moment. Democrats, Republicans, liberals, conservatives, moderates, radicals—none of these labels seemed to matter anymore: all Americans were in the trenches together.

But even the mightiest tidal wave must recede at some point. When it does, some of the features of the old landscape may start to reappear. Very gradually, something like this happened in America between the fall of 2001 and the summer of 2002. Some Democrats who had assured the president that he could count on their total support in the war now began to question the way the war was going. Some Republicans who had assured their Democratic brethren that the war effort would be bipartisan now began talking as if their party had a monopoly on patriotism. And on domestic issues the two parties were even more clearly divided, as the old battles over Social Security, the environment, taxes, welfare, and other divisive issues resumed.

Some deplore this reemergence of "partisan wrangling." We regard it as the inevitable expression of political differences. Americans vote for different political parties because, however loosely, American parties help to give expression to competing ideologies embraced by Americans. In this introduction we shall attempt to explore these ideologies, put some labels on them—labels such as *liberal, conservative, moderate, extremist,* and *pluralist*—and see how they fit the issue positions presented in this book. We have sought to do our labeling gently and tentatively, not only because Americans generally shy away from political labels but also because, as we shall see, the meanings of some of these terms appear to have shifted over the past two and a half centuries.

Liberals Versus Conservatives: an Overview

Let us examine, very briefly, the historical evolution of the terms *liberalism* and *conservatism.* By examining the roots of these terms, we can see how these philosophies have adapted themselves to changing times. In that way, we can avoid using the terms rigidly, without reference to the particular contexts in which liberalism and conservatism have operated over the past two centuries.

Classical Liberalism

The classical root of the term *liberalism* is the Latin word *libertas,* meaning "liberty" or "freedom." In the early nineteenth century, liberals dedicated themselves to freeing individuals from all unnecessary and oppressive obligations to authority—whether the authority came from the church or the state. They opposed the licensing and censorship of the press, the punishment of heresy, the establishment of religion, and any attempt to dictate orthodoxy in matters of opinion. In economics, liberals opposed state monopolies and other constraints upon competition between private businesses. At this point in its development, liberalism defined freedom primarily in terms of freedom *from.* It appropriated the French term *laissez-faire,* which literally means "leave to be." Leave people alone! That was the spirit of liberalism in its early days. It wanted government to stay out of people's lives and to play a modest role in general. Thomas Jefferson summed up this concept when he said, "I am no friend of energetic government. It is always oppressive."

Despite their suspicion of government, classical liberals invested high hopes in the political process. By and large, they were great believers in democracy. They believed in widening suffrage to include every white male, and some of them were prepared to enfranchise women and blacks as well. Although liberals occasionally worried about "the tyranny of the majority," they were more prepared to trust the masses than to trust a permanent, entrenched elite. Liberal social policy was dedicated to fulfilling human potential and was based on the assumption that this often-hidden potential is enormous. Human beings, liberals argued, were basically good and reasonable. Evil and irrationality were believed to be caused by "outside" influences; they were the result of a bad social environment. A liberal commonwealth, therefore, was one that would remove the hindrances to the full flowering of the human personality.

The basic vision of liberalism has not changed since the nineteenth century. What has changed is the way it is applied to modern society. In that respect, liberalism has changed dramatically. Today, instead of regarding government with suspicion, liberals welcome government as an instrument to serve the people. The change in philosophy began in the latter years of the nine-teenth century, when businesses—once small, independent operations—began to grow into giant structures that overwhelmed individuals and sometimes even overshadowed the state in power and wealth. At that time, liberals began recon-sidering their commitment to the *laissez-faire* philosophy. If the state can be an oppressor, asked liberals, can't big business also oppress people? By then, many were convinced that commercial and industrial monopolies were crushing the souls and bodies of the working classes. The state, formerly the villain, now was viewed by liberals as a potential savior. The concept of freedom was trans-formed into something more than a negative freedom *from;* the term began to take on a positive meaning. It meant "realizing one's full potential." Toward this end, liberals believed, the state could prove to be a valuable instrument. It could educate children, protect the health and safety of workers, help people through hard times, promote a healthy economy, and—when necessary—force business to act more humanely and responsibly. Thus was born the movement that culminated in New Deal liberalism.

New Deal Liberalism

In the United States, the argument in favor of state intervention did not win an enduring majority constituency until after the Great Depression of the 1930s began to be felt deeply. The disastrous effects of a depression that left a quarter of the workforce unemployed opened the way to a new administration—and a promise. "I pledge you, I pledge myself," Franklin D. Roosevelt said when ac-cepting the Democratic nomination in 1932, "to a new deal for the American people." Roosevelt's New Deal was an attempt to effect relief and recovery from the Depression; it employed a variety of means, including welfare programs, public works, and business regulation—most of which involved government in-tervention in the economy. The New Deal liberalism relied on government to liberate people from poverty, oppression, and economic exploitation. At the same time, the New Dealers claimed to be as zealous as the classical liberals in defending political and civil liberties.

The common element in *laissez-faire* liberalism and welfare-state liber-alism is their dedication to the goal of realizing the full potential of each individual. Some still questioned whether this is best done by minimizing state involvement or whether it sometimes requires an activist state. The New Deal-ers took the latter view, though they prided themselves on being pragmatic and experimental about their activism. During the heyday of the New Deal, a wide variety of programs were tried and—if found wanting—abandoned. All decent means should be tried, they believed, even if it meant dilution of ideological purity. The Roosevelt administration, for example, denounced bankers and busi-nessmen in campaign rhetoric but worked very closely with them while trying to extricate the nation from the Depression. This set a pattern of pragmatism that New Dealers from Harry Truman to Lyndon Johnson emulated.

Progressive Liberalism

Progressive liberalism emerged in the late 1960s and early 1970s as a more militant and uncompromising movement than the New Deal had ever been. Its roots go back to the New Left student movement of the early 1960s. New Left students went to the South to participate in civil rights demonstrations, and many of them were bloodied in confrontations with southern police; by the mid-1960s they were confronting the authorities in the North over issues like poverty and the Vietnam War. By the end of the decade, the New Left had fragmented into a variety of factions and had lost much of its vitality, but a somewhat more respectable version of it appeared as the New Politics movement. Many New Politics crusaders were former New Leftists who had traded their jeans for coats and ties; they tried to work within the system instead of always confronting it. Even so, they retained some of the spirit of the New Left. The civil rights slogan "Freedom Now" expressed the mood of the New Politics. The young university graduates who filled its ranks had come from an environment where "nonnegotiable" demands were issued to college deans by leaders of sit-in protests. There was more than youthful arrogance in the New Politics movement, however; there was a pervasive belief that America had lost, had compromised away, much of its idealism. The New Politics liberals sought to recover some of that spirit by linking up with an older tradition of militant reform, which went back to the time of the Revolution. These new liberals saw themselves as the authentic heirs of Thomas Paine and Henry David Thoreau, of the abolitionists, the radical populists, the suffragettes, and the great progressive reformers of the early twentieth century.

While New Deal liberals concentrated almost exclusively on bread-and-butter issues such as unemployment and poverty, the New Politics liberals introduced what came to be known as social issues into the political arena. These included: the repeal of laws against abortion, the liberalization of laws against homosexuality and pornography, the establishment of affirmative action programs to ensure increased hiring of minorities and women, and the passage of the Equal Rights Amendment. In foreign policy, too, New Politics liberals departed from the New Deal agenda. Because they had keener memories of the unpopular and (for them) unjustified war in Vietnam than of World War II, they became doves, in contrast to the general hawkishness of the New Dealers. They were skeptical of any claim that the United States must be the leader of the free world or, indeed, that it had any special mission in the world; some were convinced that America was already in decline and must learn to adjust accordingly. The real danger, they argued, came not from the Soviet Union but from the mad pace of America's arms race with the Soviets, which, as they saw it, could bankrupt the country, starve its social programs, and culminate in a nuclear Armageddon.

New Politics liberals were heavily represented at the 1972 Democratic national convention, which nominated South Dakota senator George McGovern for president. By the 1980s the New Politics movement was no longer new, and many of its adherents preferred to be called progressives. By this time their critics had another name for them: radicals. The critics saw their positions as inimical to the interests of the United States, destructive of the family, and fundamentally at odds with the views of most Americans. The adversaries of the progressives were not only conservatives but many New Deal liberals, who openly scorned the McGovernites.

This split still exists within the Democratic party, though it is now more skillfully managed by party leaders. In 1988 the Democrats paired Michael Dukakis, whose Massachusetts supporters were generally on the progressive side of the party, with New Dealer Lloyd Bentsen as the presidential and vice-presidential candidates, respectively. In 1992 the Democrats won the presidency with Arkansas governor Bill Clinton, whose record as governor seemed to put him in the moderate-to-conservative camp, and Tennessee senator Albert Gore, whose position on environmental issues could probably be considered quite liberal but whose general image was middle-of-the-road. Both candidates had moved toward liberal positions on the issues of gay rights and abortion. By 1994 Clinton was perceived by many Americans as being "too liberal," which some speculate may have been a factor in the defeat of Democrats in the congressional elections that year. Clinton immediately sought to shake off that perception, positioning himself as a "moderate" between extremes and casting the Republicans as an "extremist" party. (These two terms will be examined presently.)

Conservatism

Like liberalism, conservatism has undergone historical transformation in America. Just as early liberals (represented by Thomas Jefferson) espoused less government, early conservatives (whose earliest leaders were Alexander Hamilton and John Adams) urged government support of economic enterprise and government intervention on behalf of certain groups. But today, in reaction to the growth of the welfare state, conservatives argue strongly that more government means more unjustified interference in citizens' lives, more bureaucratic regulation of private conduct, more inhibiting control of economic enterprise, more material advantage for the less energetic and less able at the expense of those who are prepared to work harder and better, and, of course, more taxes—taxes that will be taken from those who have earned money and given to those who have not.

Contemporary conservatives are not always opposed to state intervention. They may support larger military expenditures in order to protect society against foreign enemies. They may also allow for some intrusion into private life in order to protect society against internal subversion and would pursue criminal prosecution zealously in order to protect society against domestic violence. The fact is that few conservatives, and perhaps fewer liberals, are absolute with respect to their views about the power of the state. Both are quite prepared to use the state in order to further *their* purposes. It is true that activist presidents such as Franklin Roosevelt and John Kennedy were likely to be classified as liberals. However, Richard Nixon was also an activist, and, although he does not easily fit any classification, he was far closer to conservatism than to liberalism. It is too easy to identify liberalism with statism and conservatism with anti-statism; it is important to remember that it was liberal Jefferson who counseled against "energetic government" and conservative Alexander Hamilton who designed bold powers for the new central government and wrote, "Energy in the executive is a leading character in the definition of good government."

For a time, a movement calling itself *neoconservatism* occupied a kind of intermediate position between New Deal liberalism and conservatism. Composed for the most part of former New Deal Democrats and drawn largely from academic and publishing circles, neoconservatives supported most of the New Deal programs of federal assistance and regulation, but they felt that state intervention had gotten out of hand during the 1960s. In foreign policy, too, they worried about the directions in which the United States was going. In sharp disagreement with progressive liberals, they wanted a tougher stance toward the Soviet Union, fearing that the quest for détente was leading the nation to unilateral disarmament. After the disappearance of the Soviet Union, neoconcervatism itself disappeared—at least as a distinctive strain of conservatism—and most former neoconservatives either resisted all labels or considered themselves simply to be conservatives.

The Religious Right

A more enduring category within the conservative movement is what is often referred to as "the religious right." Termed "the new right" when it first appeared more than 20 years, ago, the religious right is composed of conservative Christians who are concerned not so much about high taxes and government spending as they are about the decline of traditional Judeo-Christian morality, a decline that they attribute in part to certain unwise government policies and judicial decisions. They oppose many of the recent judicial decisions on sociocultural issues such as abortion, school prayer, pornography, and gay rights, and they have been outspoken critics of the Clinton administration, citing everything from President Clinton's views on gays in the military to his sexual behavior while in the White House.

Spokesmen for progressive liberalism and the religous right stand as polar opposites: The former regard abortion as a woman's right; the latter see it as legalized murder. The former tend to regard homosexuality as a lifestyle that needs protection against discrimination; the latter are more likely to see it as a perversion. The former have made an issue of their support for the Equal Rights Amendment; the latter includes large numbers of women who fought against the amendment because they believed it threatened their role identity. The list of issues could go on. The religious right and the progressive liberals are like positive and negative photographs of America's moral landscape. Sociologist James Davison Hunter uses the term *culture wars* to characterize the struggles between these contrary visions of America. For all the differences between progressive liberalism and the religious right, however, their styles are very similar. They are heavily laced with moralistic prose; they tend to equate compromise with selling out; and they claim to represent the best, most authentic traditions of America. This is not to denigrate either movement, for the kinds of issues they address are indeed moral issues, which do not generally admit much compromise. These issues cannot simply be finessed or ignored, despite the efforts of conventional politicians to do so. They must be aired and fought over, which is why we include some of them, such as abortion (Issue 12), in this volume.

Radicals, Reactionaries, and Moderates

The label *reactionary* is almost an insult, and the label *radical* is worn with pride by only a few zealots on the banks of the political mainstream. A reactionary is not a conserver but a backward-mover, dedicated to turning the clock back to better times. Most people suspect that reactionaries would restore us to a time that never was, except in political myth. For many, the repeal of industrialism or universal education (or the entire twentieth century itself) is not a practical, let alone desirable, political program.

Radicalism (literally meaning "from the roots" or "going to the foundation") implies a fundamental reconstruction of the social order. Taken in that sense, it is possible to speak of right-wing radicalism as well as left-wing radicalism—radicalism that would restore or inaugurate a new hierarchical society as well as radicalism that calls for nothing less than an egalitarian society. The term is sometimes used in both of these senses, but most often the word *radicalism* is reserved to characterize more liberal change. While the liberal would effect change through conventional democratic processes, the radical is likely to be skeptical about the ability of the established machinery to bring about the needed change and might be prepared to sacrifice "a little" liberty to bring about a great deal more equality.

Moderate is a highly coveted label in America. Its meaning is not precise, but it carries the connotations of sensible, balanced, and practical. A moderate person is not without principles, but he or she does not allow principles to harden into dogma. The opposite of moderate is *extremist,* a label most American political leaders eschew. Yet there have been notable exceptions. When Arizona senator Barry Goldwater, a conservative Republican, was nominated for president in 1964, he declared, "Extremism in defense of liberty is no vice! ...Moderation in the pursuit of justice is no virtue!" This open embrace of extremism did not help his electoral chances; Goldwater was overwhelmingly defeated. At about the same time, however, another American political leader also embraced a kind of extremism, and with better results. In a famous letter written from a jail cell in Birmingham, Alabama, the Reverend Martin Luther King, Jr., replied to the charge that he was an extremist not by denying it but by distinguishing between different kinds of extremists. The question, he wrote, "is not whether we will be extremist but what kind of extremist will we be. Will we be extremists for hate, or will we be extremists for love?" King aligned himself with the love extremists, in which category he also placed Jesus, St. Paul, and Thomas Jefferson, among others. It was an adroit use of a label that is usually anathema in America.

Pluralism

The principle of pluralism espouses diversity in a society containing many interest groups and in a government containing competing units of power. This implies the widest expression of competing ideas, and in this way, pluralism is in sympathy with an important element of liberalism. However, as James Madison and Alexander Hamilton pointed out when they analyzed the sources of pluralism in their *Federalist* commentaries on the Constitution, this philosophy springs from a profoundly pessimistic view of human nature, and in this respect it more closely resembles conservatism. Madison, possibly the single most influential member of the convention that wrote the Constitution, hoped that in a large and varied nation, no single interest group could control the government. Even if there were a majority interest, it would be unlikely to capture all of the national agencies of government—the House of Representatives, the Senate, the presidency, and the federal judiciary—each of which was chosen in a different way by a different constituency for a different term of office. Moreover, to make certain that no one branch exercised excessive power, each was equipped with "checks and balances" that enabled any agency of national government to curb the powers of the others. The clearest statement of Madison's, and the Constitution's, theory can be found in the 51st paper of the *Federalist*:

> It may be a reflection on human nature that such devices should be necessary to control the abuses of government. But what is government itself, but the greatest of all reflections on human nature? If men were angels, no government would be necessary.

This pluralist position may be analyzed from different perspectives. It is conservative insofar as it rejects simple majority rule; yet it is liberal insofar as it rejects rule by a single elite. It is conservative in its pessimistic appraisal of human nature; yet pluralism's pessimism is also a kind of egalitarianism, holding as it does that no one can be trusted with power and that majority interests no less than minority interests will use power for selfish ends. It is possible to suggest that in America pluralism represents an alternative to both liberalism and conservatism. Pluralism is antimajoritarian and antielitist and combines some elements of both.

Some Applications

Despite our effort to define the principal alignments in American politics, some policy decisions do not fit neatly into these categories. Readers will reach their own conclusions, but we may suggest some alignments to be found here in order to demonstrate the variety of viewpoints.

The conflicts between liberalism and conservatism are expressed in a number of the issues presented in this book. One of the classic splits, and one that revisits an argument famous during the New Deal era, concerns the reach of federal power. The Tenth Amendment states that all powers not delegated to the federal government nor denied to the states "are reserved to the States respectively, or to the people." Yet the federal government passes laws affecting many entities *within* states, from businesses to educational institutions. How can it do that? One of the main "hooks" for federal power within states is the constitutional clause authorizing Congress to regulate commerce "among the several states." The Supreme Court has interpreted the commerce clause to mean that any entity within a state that substantially "affects" interstate commerce can be regulated by the federal government. But how close should the "effect" be? Conservatives insist that the effects on interstate commerce must be quite direct and tangible, while liberals would give Congress more leeway in regulating "intrastate" activities. This liberal/conservative dichotomy is crisply illustrated in the majority opinion versus one of the dissents in the Supreme Court case of *United States v. Lopez* (1995), both of which we present in Issue 5. The immediate question is whether or not the federal government has the authority to ban handguns from the vicinity of public schools, but the larger issue is whether or not the federal government can regulate activities within a state that do not directly and tangibly affect interstate commerce. Liberals say yes, conservatives say no.

The death penalty is another issue dividing liberals and conservatives. Robert Lee's defense of the death penalty (Issue 8) is a classic conservative argument. Like other conservatives, Lee is skeptical of the possibilities of human perfection, and he therefore regards retribution—giving a murderer what he or she "deserves" instead of attempting some sort of "rehabilitation"—as a legitimate goal of punishment. Issue 14, on whether or not the gap between the rich and the poor is increasing, points up another disagreement between liberals and conservatives. Most liberals would agree with Paul Krugman that socioeconomic inequality is increasing and that this undermines the basic tenets of American democracy. Christopher DeMuth, representing the conservative viewpoint, maintains that Americans are becoming more equal and that virtually all people benefit from increased prosperity because it takes place in a free market. Then there is the battle over taxes, the hardiest perennial of all the issues that divide liberals and conservatives. Issue 13 features Amity Shlaes, who advances the conservative argument that "the greedy hand" of government is taking too much from taxpayers, versus Liam Murphy and Thomas Nagel, who reject the idea that the pretax money was "theirs," in any meaningful sense, in the first place. Issue 3, on campaign spending, also divides liberals and conservatives. Senator Paul Wellstone (D-Minnesota) voices the liberal view, which has now become law, that the flow of "soft money" into political campaigns must be stopped, while John Samples, of the Cato Institute, takes a position favored by conservatives when he contends that people have the right to contribute large sums to the candidate or party of their choice. Affirmative action (Issue 10) has become a litmus test of the newer brand of progressive liberalism. The progressives say that it is not enough for the laws of society to be color-blind or gender-blind; they must now reach out to remedy the ills caused by racism and sexism. New Deal liberals, along with conservatives and libertarians, generally oppose affirmative action. One major dispute between liberals and conservatives concerns liberalism itself: whether or not it pervades news coverage in the media. In Issue 4, Bernard Goldberg, a former CBS reporter, takes a position often held by conservatives when he argues that it does. Radio talk show host Jim Hightower argues that, on the contrary, the media are dominated by conservative viewpoints.

This book contains a few arguments that are not easy to categorize. The issue on hate speech (Issue 11) is one. Liberals traditionally have opposed any curbs on free speech, but Charles Lawrence, who would certainly not call himself a conservative, contends that curbs on speech that abuses minorities may be necessary. Opposing him is Jonathan Rauch, who takes the traditional liberal view that we must protect the speech even of those whose ideas we hate. Issue 1, on whether or not liberty and democracy is good for all countries, is also hard to classify. President Woodrow Wilson, a liberal, regarded World War I as a war to "make the world safe for democracy," but some latter-day liberals worry that exporting democracy to the ends of the earth is just as bad as pushing capitalism or other aspects of American life on other peoples. Robert Kaplan, who does not think democracy and civil liberties are good for all countries, is not necessarily a conservative, then, any more than Michael McFaul is a liberal for thinking that they are. Issue 12, on whether or not abortion should be restricted, also eludes easy classification. The pro-choice position, as argued by Mary Gordon, is not a traditional liberal position. Less than a generation ago legalized abortion was opposed by liberals such as Senator Edward Kennedy (D-Massachusetts) and the Reverend Jesse Jackson, and even recently some liberals, such as the late Pennsylvania governor Robert Casey and columnist Nat Hentoff, have opposed it. Nevertheless, most liberals now adopt some version of Gordon's pro-choice views. Opposing Gordon is Robert George, whose argument here might be endorsed by liberals like Hentoff.

Issues 15 and 16 return us to the liberal/conservative arena of debate. Issue 15 revisits the China debate, which periodically surfaces between liberals and conservatives. In 1972 President Nixon astounded friend and foe alike when he visited China and started melting the ice that had frozen the two countries into postures of confrontation. But Nixon was an exception among conservatives. Most have never stopped regarding "Red China" as a menace to world peace and stability. This is the position taken by Lucian Pye, while David Lampton takes a more liberal view in minimizing the danger posed by today's China. In Issue 16, "Should America Restrict Immigration?" Patrick Buchanan worries about the effect of "newcomers" on the U.S. economy and culture, which is not a surprising view for someone who is deeply committed to stability and continuity of culture, as conservatives are. Daniel Griswold argues that America thrives on the energies brought to its shores by immigrants.

Obviously one's position on the issues in this book will be affected by circumstances. However, we would like to think that the essays in this book are durable enough to last through several seasons of events and controversies. We can be certain that the issues will survive. The search for coherence and consistency in the use of political labels underlines the options open to us and reveals their consequences. The result must be more mature judgments about what is best for America. That, of course, is the ultimate aim of public debate and decision making, and it transcends all labels and categories.

On the Internet . . .

The Federal Web Locator

Use this handy site as a launching pad for the Web sites of U.S. federal agencies, departments, and organizations. It is well organized and easy to use for informational and research purposes.

http://www.infoctr.edu/fwl/

The Library of Congress

Examine this Web site to learn about the extensive resource tools, library services/resources, exhibitions, and databases available through the Library of Congress in many different subfields of government studies.

http://www.loc.gov

U.S. Founding Documents

Through this Emory University site you can view scanned originals of the Declaration of Independence, the Constitution, and the Bill of Rights. The transcribed texts are also available, as are the *Federalist Papers*.

http://www.law.emory.edu/FEDERAL/

Hoover Institution Public Policy Inquiry: Campaign Finance

Use this Stanford University site to explore the history of campaign finance as well as the current reforms and proposals for future change.

http://www.campaignfinancesite.org

Poynter.org

This research site of the Poynter Institute, a school for journalists, provides extensive links to information and resources about the media, including media ethics and reportage techniques. Many bibliographies and Web sites are included.

http://www.poynter.org/research/index.htm

The Gallup Organization

Open this Gallup Organization page for links to an extensive archive of public-opinion poll results and special reports on a huge variety of topics related to American society, politics, and government.

http://www.gallup.com

PART 1

Democracy and the American Political Process

*D*emocracy *is derived from two Greek words,* démos *and* kratia, *and means "people's rule." The prerequisites for people's rule are many, including free speech and other liberties, a well-informed citizenry, a fair presentation of differing points of view, and an equal counting of votes. Since these basic prerequisites do not exist in many areas of the world, should America try to export them to other countries? Or would that be futile and ultimately harmful to American interests? At home, Americans must deal with issues concerning their own democracy. Can elections really be fair if money continues to play an important role in campaigns? Does the campaign process really clarify issues, or is it simply noise and hoopla? Are Americans hearing all points of view before they vote, or are news and opinion in the mass media slanted in some direction? If so, in what direction? In this section we try to address these and related issues.*

- Are Liberty and Democracy Good for Every Country?

- Do Political Campaigns Promote Good Government?

- Are the New Limits on Campaign Spending Justified?

- Do the Media Have a Liberal Bias?

ISSUE 1

Are Liberty and Democracy Good for Every Country?

YES: Michael McFaul, from "The Liberty Doctrine," *Policy Review* (April 2002)

NO: Robert D. Kaplan, from "Was Democracy Just a Moment?" *The Atlantic Monthly* (December 1997)

ISSUE SUMMARY

YES: Professor of political science Michael McFaul argues that liberty and democracy are desirable for every country, that the conditions exist to increase the number of democratic nations, and that the United States can and should use its power to encourage and support liberty and democracy in nations that have never before enjoyed freedom.

NO: Foreign correspondent Robert D. Kaplan contends that recent experience demonstrates that not all nations have the conditions in which democracy can thrive, that some nations prosper without it, and that democracy may be less important in the future.

T he most thoughtful advocates of democracy do not claim that it provides a cure for all that ails us. Rather, they argue, it is simply the best way of organizing societies to deal with public issues. Winston Churchill acknowledged that he was not the first to express the sentiment in his famous observation, "No one pretends that democracy is perfect or all-wise. Indeed, it has been said that democracy is the worst form of government except all those other forms that have been tried from time to time."

Writing about the United States more than 150 years ago, Alexis de Tocqueville expressed his belief that the spread of democracy was irresistible, but he also concluded that the American example of the 1830s might not be the best for either America's future or the rest of the world. Tocqueville warned that democracy must "adapt its government to time and place, and to modify it according to men and conditions." With the belief of hindsight and an awareness of the ways in which democracy has developed, we may ask, Can those adaptations and modifications be sufficient to meet the needs of all nations and cultures? Is it possible that democracy is neither inevitable nor desirable at some times, under some circumstances, and in some places?

In the half-century in which the United States feared the spread of communism, domestic critics accused the nation of supporting authoritarian regimes and undermining socialist democracies, all in the name of anticommunism. The history of the post–cold war world is encouraging to those who believe in the triumph of democracy. More than 30 countries—including Spain, Portugal, the Philippines, South Korea, Eastern Europe (including Russia), and many Latin American countries—shifted from authoritarian to democratic systems. By contrast, Freedom House, a private organization that is devoted to the spread of democracy, estimated in 1996 that only one-fifth of the world's population lived in free societies, two-fifths in partly free nations, and another two-fifths in countries that are not free.

Should America seek to export democracy? "The world must be made safe for democracy," was President Woodrow Wilson's plea when he urged Congress to involve the United States in World War I. Since then America has often sought the expansion of democracy, but it has also given military and economic assistance to governments that were undisguisedly antidemocratic. America's foreign policy often hinges on a choice between morality (what's good?) and practicality (what's good for America?). Those who urge American commitment to the spread of democracy argue that the idealistic and pragmatic approaches now coincide because the security of the United States is endangered by the presence of authoritarian regimes.

The United States has committed itself to democratic nation-building in Afghanistan with its promise to provide that devastated nation with $4.5 billion to rebuild after the antidemocratic Taliban was removed from power. The new Afghan leaders responded by agreeing to a political blueprint that called for a transitional government ending in "free and fair elections" within 30 months. Paradoxically, elections encourage conflict, particularly in countries where arms remain widely held. Critics have pointed out that early elections strengthen warlords and other armed people, who will use their weapons to confront opponents and intimidate voters. For example, in Cambodia national elections were held two years after a UN-supervised cease-fire was signed in 1991. Forces under strongman Hun Sen remained armed, and six years later he seized full power in a coup. Early in 2002, as Cambodia prepared to hold its first local elections in decades, 20 opposition candidates and activists were killed, and, using intimidation, Hun Sen's party won control of all but 20 of Cambodia's 1,621 communal councils.

In the first of the following selections, Michael McFaul maintains that no international interest of the United States is greater than its aggressive support for liberty and democracy because, beyond the obvious moral superiority of freedom, American security is most threatened by antidemocratic political systems and the terrorist organizations that they harbor. In the second selection, Robert D. Kaplan suggests that democracy may be rendered irrelevant as a result of the globalization of economic enterprise, culture, electronic communications that transcend all boundaries, and material prosperity that leaves less time and thought for public concerns.

3

Michael McFaul  **YES**

The Liberty Doctrine

The immediate response of President [George W.] Bush and his administration to the September 11, 2001 terrorist attacks against the United States was superb, both purposeful and principled—a military, political, and diplomatic success. But what comes next? In his State of the Union address, Bush suggested specific targets of future phases of the war—the "axis of evil" of Iraq, Iran, and North Korea. But what has been missing in the discussion of the second stage (and perhaps the third, fourth, and fifth stages) of the war on terrorism is an articulation of the general principles that will guide policy in difficult times ahead. The new threat to American national security and the American way of life is no less threatening than such earlier challenges as the defeat of fascism in Europe and imperialism in Japan during World War II, or the containment and ultimate destruction of world communism during the Cold War. A grand vision of the purposes of American power is needed not only to shape strategy, but also to sustain support from the American people and America's allies.

During the twentieth century, the central purpose of American power was to defend against and when possible to destroy tyranny. American presidents have been at their best when they have embraced the mission of defending liberty at home and spreading liberty abroad. This was the task during World War II, and it was again our objective (or should have been the mission) during the Cold War. It must be our mission again. In fact, the war on terrorism is a new variation of the old war against the anti-democratic "isms" of the previous century.

Adherence to a *liberty doctrine* as a guide to American foreign policy means pushing to the top of the agenda the promotion of individual freedoms abroad. The expansion of individual liberty in economic and political affairs in turn stimulates the development and consolidation of democratic regimes. To promote liberty requires first the containment and then the elimination of those forces opposed to liberty, be they individuals, movements, or regimes. Next comes the construction of pro-liberty forces, be they democrats, democratic movements, or democratic institutions. Finally comes the establishment of governments that value and protect the liberty of their own people as the United States does. Obviously, the United States does not have the means to deliver liberty to all subjugated people around the world at the same time. And the spread

From Michael McFaul, "The Liberty Doctrine," *Policy Review*, no. 112 (April 2002). Copyright © 2002 by The Board of Trustees of the Leland Stanford Junior University. Reprinted by permission of *Policy Review*. Notes omitted.

of liberty and democracy will not always be simultaneous. In some places, the promotion of the individual freedoms must come first, democratization second. Nonetheless, the spread of liberty should be the lofty and broad goal that organizes American foreign policy for the coming decades.

By defining the purposes of American power in these terms, American foreign policymakers achieve several objectives not attainable by narrower or less normative doctrines. First, the liberty doctrine, like containment during the Cold War, is useful in clarifying the relationship between often very different policies. Toppling Saddam Hussein does in fact have something in common with providing education to Afghan women, and a liberty doctrine allows us to see it clearly. Second, the liberty doctrine properly defines our new struggle in terms of ideas, individuals, and regimes—not in terms of states. Allies of liberty exist everywhere, most certainly in Iran and even in Iraq. Likewise, not all the enemies of liberty are states; they also include non-governmental organizations like al Qaeda. Third, the liberty doctrine provides a cause that others—allies of the United States as well as states, movements, and individuals not necessarily supportive of all U.S. strategic interests—can support. For example, the Iraqi regime constitutes an immediate threat to American national security but does not pose the same threat to France or Russia. A campaign against Iraq defined in terms of "national interests" means that we will go it alone. A credible campaign for liberty in Iraq, however, may attract a wider coalition. Fourth, the liberty doctrine underscores two phases of engagement with enemy regimes —the destructive phase and the constructive phase. To demonstrate real commitment to this mission of promoting liberty abroad, the United States must also devote substantial rhetorical attention and concrete resources to the constructive phase of the promotion of liberty. If not, we will be waging military campaigns against new tyrannical regimes over and over again....

Knowing the Enemy

Since September 11, many policymakers and commentators have noted the uniqueness and newness of our current era. They are wrong. The intellectual challenge of defining the enemy may not be as difficult as it first looks. During World War II and again during the Cold War, the enemy was clearly those fascist, imperialist, and communist forces that abhorred liberty and aimed to destroy democracy. America's new enemy is cut from the same anti-Western, anti-democratic, anti-liberal cloth.

The decade after the Cold War, like the shorter interregnum between World War II and the Cold War, created at times the illusion of "mission accomplished." For some, the end of communism was the end of history. For others, the collapse of the Soviet Union marked the extinction of the only major threat to American security. Obviously, the euphoria and complacency of the 1990s were misplaced. The absence of communism did not translate automatically and smoothly into the presence of democracy. On the contrary, a decade after the fall of the Berlin Wall and the Soviet Union, democratic regimes are still a minority in the post-communist world. Although democratic victories in the former communist world did reverberate well beyond Europe, the so-called third wave of democracy failed to splash in whole regions, including the Middle East and many other parts of the Muslim world. Nor did the weakening of the Soviet Union and then of Russia enhance U.S. security (American territory was never attacked during the Cold War). The hegemony of balance-of-power theories among American strategic thinkers fueled a false sense of security once the United States became the world's sole superpower....

In the long run, the 1990s should look like the interregnum, while history after September 11 should mark the *return* of a United States engaged in the world with both a moral and self-interested purpose—the purpose of defending and spreading liberty. Defining our international mission in these terms is the best way to frame, sustain support for, and ultimately win the war on terrorism.

As in previous struggles, the essence of the enemy is ideological. Osama bin Laden and his followers do not want territory or treasure. They seek the destruction of liberal democracies and the way of life that these regimes provide. Like communism, extreme versions of Islamic fundamentalism offer followers a comprehensive set of beliefs that explain everything in the world. Communism framed world politics as a Manichean struggle between the forces of good and evil. So too do bin Laden and his ilk, though for them the enemy is modernity in all its variations. Radical communists did not seek a resolution of grievances with the West, a negotiated settlement including such things as Angolan independence and higher wages for West European workers. Rather, the mission was the total destruction of the United States, its allies, and its way of life. Colonialism and "worker exploitation" were *good* for the communist cause. Likewise, those embracing the Islamic totalitarianism propagated by bin Laden have not limited their aims to the creation of a Palestinian state, the removal of U.S. troops from Saudi Arabia, or even the obliteration of Israel. On the contrary, these issues help fuel anti-American mobilization and therefore serve bin Laden's purposes. Their mission is much grander—the destruction of the West. Like some of the early Bolsheviks, bin Laden wants to join a world war between us and them as soon as possible. Bin Laden and his followers hoped that September 11 would spark a global war between Islam and the West....

Knowing the Prescription

... Democracies do not attack each other. This hope from centuries ago about the relationship between domestic regime type and international behavior received empirical validation in the twentieth century. No country's national security has benefited more from the spread of democracy than the United States's. Today, every democracy in the world has cordial relations with the United States. No democracies are enemies of the United States. Not all dictatorships in the world are foes of the United States, but every foe of the United States—Iraq, Iran, Libya, North Korea, Cuba, and (possibly in the future) China— is a dictatorship. With few exceptions, the countries that provide safe haven to non-state enemies of the United States are autocratic regimes. With rare exceptions, the median voter in consolidated democracies pushes extreme elements to the sidelines of the political arena. Democracies also are more transparent, which makes them more predictable and less able to hide hostile activities, such as the production of weapons of mass destruction for non-state actors. Logically, then, the expansion of liberty and democracy around the world is a U.S. national security interest.

The deductive logic of the liberty doctrine is complemented by empirical evidence from the twentieth century. In the first half of the last century, imperial Japan and fascist Germany constituted the greatest threats to U.S. national security. The destruction of these tyrannical regimes *followed by the imposition of democratic regimes* in Germany and Japan helped make these two countries American allies.

In the second half of the past century, Soviet communism and its supporters represented the greatest threat to American national security. The collapse of communism in Eastern Europe and then the Soviet Union has greatly enhanced American national security. The emergence of democracies in eastern Central Europe a decade ago and the fall of dictators in southeastern Europe more recently have radically improved the European security climate, and therefore U.S. national security interests. Without question, however, liberty's expansion produced the greatest payoff for American national security when democratic ideas and practices began to take hold within the Soviet Union and then Russia. So long as unreconstructed communists ruled there, the USSR represented a unique threat to American security. When the communist regime disintegrated and a new democratically oriented regime began to take hold in Russia, this threat to the United States diminished almost overnight.

In spearheading the successful struggle against communism, the United States made mistakes that must be avoided in the new campaign. Oftentimes we confused means and ends, so that all users of violence against non-communist states and actors were considered part of the world communist movement. Not long ago, Nelson Mandela was labeled a "communist terrorist." So too were many anti-colonial movements whose real aim was sovereignty, not world revolution. Distinguishing between those focused on territorial or ethnic disputes and those dedicated to a global messianic mission is critical in the new war. During the battle against communism, we initially treated the entire communist world as monolithic, a mistake we cannot repeat with the Islamic world. The new struggle requires that we embrace and support moderate, pro-democratic Muslim forces. Our overzealous search for enemies from within in the 1950s and its tragic consequences must be remembered and not repeated. One of our great resources in fighting the new war is the testimony of the several million Muslims living in the United States who successfully practice their faith but also live (and thrive) in a secular, democratic state.

The Cold War also diverted the United States into courting almost all anti-communist regimes around the world, be they dictatorships or democracies. Over the years, though, the democracies on this list proved to be the more effective and reliable allies. Not infrequently, ostensible gains from partnerships with autocratic governments and movements—such as the shah in Iran, the Suharto regime in Indonesia, the mujaheddin in Afghanistan, and the apartheid system in South Africa—were more than offset by setbacks to American security and embarrassments to American ideals.

The United States, especially under Ronald Reagan, also supported anti-communist movements and groups that sought to overthrow Soviet puppet regimes. The objective was noble, but the strategy sometimes suffered from two flaws. First, American foreign policymakers devoted real attention and resources to the destruction of communist regimes but failed to follow through with the same level of effort to construct new democratic regimes in the same places. Afghanistan is a perfect example of this failure to follow through. The goal of expanding liberty should have continued in the wake of communism's collapse. Instead, U.S. policymakers were content to try to preserve the new order and abandon those regions and allies important to the struggle against communism but considered marginal to the post–Cold War order. Second, many of these anti-communist allies had dubious democratic credentials. Many failed states dominated by non-democratic forces (who were once American allies) are Cold War legacies that have combined to create a threat to the United States.

After the Cold War, American policymakers (especially during the first Bush administration) also defined a conservative role for the United States in the world. If Reagan purposively sought to revise the world order in place when he became president, Bush and to a lesser extent Clinton sought to preserve the "new world order." This status quo impulse produced successful policies, such as the preservation of Kuwaiti sovereignty. Yet American uneasiness with revolutionary change—even when it was *democratic* change—also allowed some opportunities to be lost. In the Middle East, preserving the status quo meant preserving existing borders (thus the war against Iraq) but also maintaining the balance of power (thus the refusal to dismantle Iraq). On the frontlines of the anti-communist revision, in places like Angola, Pakistan, and Afghanistan, the post–Cold War era brought with it a policy of neglect. In all of these neglected pockets, the result was autocracy at best, failed states in the extreme, but no advancement of liberty.

The next phase of the war on terrorism, therefore, must be the expansion of liberty to these areas. The United States cannot be content with preserving the current order in the international system. Rather, the United States must become once again a revisionist power—a country that seeks to change the international system as a means of enhancing its own national security. Moreover, this mission must be offensive in nature. The United States cannot afford to wait and react to the next attack. Rather, we must seek to isolate and destroy our enemies by eliminating their regimes and safe havens. The ultimate purpose of American power is the creation of an international community of democratic states that encompasses every region of the planet.

It must be remembered that the battle against communism was a worldwide, multifaceted campaign that included military action and deterrence against communist states *and* non-state actors, economic support for countries threatened by communist takeover, and an ideological counteroffensive. The century-long campaign ended only when the war of ideas, not a battle of tanks, was won. We now face a similar long-term, multifaceted struggle. . . .

Priorities . . .

Promoting liberty within the "axis of evil."   Once the contours of our new struggle have been articulated clearly, the next phase of the new war must be the promotion of liberty in those countries that support anti-Western revolutionaries like bin Laden and also are developing weapons of mass destruction. Not coincidentally, these kinds of regimes are also dictatorships. Only one country firmly meets all of these criteria—Iraq. Regime change in Iraq must be the next application of the liberty doctrine. Ultimately, military force will have to be deployed to achieve this outcome. Before doing so, however, U.S. policymakers should declare their commitment to the creation of a democratic regime in Iraq, which could include greater autonomy if not independence for the Kurds in northern Iraq.

The strategies for dealing with Iran and North Korea will have to be different. In Iran, the Bush administration must stop treating the country as a unitary actor and instead recognize and support the allies of liberty there. It is disturbing that the liberalizing forces in Iran have made the tactical decision to avoid commentary on foreign affairs, and therefore do not denounce Iran's support for Hezbollah. At the same time, American officials cannot hold these liberalizing forces in Iran to a standard higher than the one to which they hold Gen. Pervez Musharraf in Pakistan, whose government, after all, sponsored and supported the Taliban regime in Afghanistan and continues to harbor and fund terrorist groups. The same can be said of the Saudi regime, an American ally. Rather, the promotion of liberty in Iran requires new engagement of democrats within the country, in both the state and society. Khatami is not the Gorbachev of the anti-Islamic revolution. Unlike Gorbachev, he does not control the guns. Nor has a Yeltsin-like figure—i.e., someone determined to destroy the ancient regime rather than reform it—yet emerged in Iran. Still, the parallels between the late Soviet period and the current situation in Iran are striking. The analogy suggests a similar strategy for American foreign policy—sustained praise for and encouragement of reformers within the state and quiet support, including material support, for societal actors seeking to change the system altogether.

In North Korea, the problem is Kim Jong Il, a crazy and insecure dictator. The collapse of his regime is more likely to be revolutionary than evolutionary—through a coup or a massive uprising (most likely manifested in its first phase as starving millions crossing the Chinese border). In this situation, the best policy option is full support of South Korean engagement of the North Korean regime. A premium must be placed on people-to-people contacts. Increased knowledge among North Koreans about South Korea's prosperity is surely an effective weapon against Kim Jong Il's regime.

Promoting liberty among friends.   With a few exceptions, U.S. foreign policymakers must promote liberty proactively and aggressively. The experience of democratization, especially in the twentieth century, demonstrates that the earlier an autocratic regime begins to liberalize, the better the chance of a peaceful, evolutionary transition to democracy. Dictators who initiate reform from above can shape the pacts, interim arrangements, and constitutions of the new liberal regime. Those who wait run the risk of guiding regime change when opposition forces have mobilized.

Bush and his administration must take this message to the autocrats who currently consider themselves allies of the United States. Regime liberalization does not mean full-blown democracy overnight. For instance, the ruling elite in Saudi Arabia, Egypt, Kyrgyzstan, and Pakistan might consider the initial step of opening the legislative branch to popular rule while maintaining control of the executive branch. The only policy that cannot be pursued is inaction or the tightening of autocratic rule. Thankfully, the Bush administration has a new role model—Gen. Musharraf in Pakistan—that it can assist and develop. If successful, Musharraf's reforming regime can then serve as an example of the benefits of liberalization for other pro-Western autocrats in the region. . . .

Hope

The battle against communism took more than a century. This new battle against a new "ism" could take longer. Yet the West eventually did win the war against communism, an outcome that few predicted just a few decades ago. Our new war against a new "ism" will be long and difficult. But armed with the proper conceptual framework and grand strategy—the liberty doctrine—it can and will be won.

NO ↵

Robert D. Kaplan

Was Democracy Just a Moment?

In the fourth century A.D. Christianity's conquest of Europe and the Mediterranean world gave rise to the belief that a peaceful era in world politics was at hand, now that a consensus had formed around an ideology that stressed the sanctity of the individual. But Christianity was, of course, not static. It kept evolving, into rites, sects, and "heresies" that were in turn influenced by the geography and cultures of the places where it took root. Meanwhile, the church founded by Saint Peter became a ritualistic and hierarchical organization guilty of long periods of violence and bigotry. This is to say nothing of the evils perpetrated by the Orthodox churches in the East. Christianity made the world not more peaceful or, in practice, more moral but only more complex. Democracy, which is now overtaking the world as Christianity once did, may do the same.

The collapse of communism from internal stresses says nothing about the long-term viability of Western democracy. Marxism's natural death in Eastern Europe is no guarantee that subtler tyrannies do not await us, here and abroad. History has demonstrated that there is no final triumph of reason, whether it goes by the name of Christianity, the Enlightenment, or, now, democracy. To think that democracy as we know it will triumph—or is even here to stay —is itself a form of determinism, driven by our own ethnocentricity. Indeed, those who quote Alexis de Tocqueville in support of democracy's inevitability should pay heed to his observation that Americans, because of their (comparative) equality, exaggerate "the scope of human perfectibility." Despotism, Tocqueville went on, "is more particularly to be feared in democratic ages," because it thrives on the obsession with self and one's own security which equality fosters.

I submit that the democracy we are encouraging in many poor parts of the world is an integral part of a transformation toward new forms of authoritarianism; that democracy in the United States is at greater risk than ever before, and from obscure sources; and that many future regimes, ours especially, could resemble the oligarchies of ancient Athens and Sparta more than they do the current government in Washington. History teaches that it is exactly at such prosperous times as these that we need to maintain a sense of the tragic, however unnecessary it may seem.

From Robert D. Kaplan, "Was Democracy Just a Moment?" *The Atlantic Monthly* (December 1997). Copyright © 1997 by Robert D. Kaplan. Reprinted by permission.

... Those who think that America can establish democracy the world over should heed the words of the late American theologian and political philosopher Reinhold Niebuhr:

> The same strength which has extended our power beyond a continent has also ... brought us into a vast web of history in which other wills, running in oblique or contrasting directions to our own, inevitably hinder or contradict what we most fervently desire. We cannot simply have our way, not even when we believe our way to have the "happiness of mankind" as its promise.

The lesson to draw is not that dictatorship is good and democracy bad but that democracy emerges successfully only as a capstone to other social and economic achievements. In his "Author's introduction" to *Democracy in America,* Tocqueville showed how democracy evolved in the West not through the kind of moral fiat we are trying to impose throughout the world but as an organic outgrowth of development. European society had reached a level of complexity and sophistication at which the aristocracy, so as not to overburden itself, had to confer a measure of equality upon other citizens and allocate some responsibility to them: a structured division of the population into peacefully competing interest groups was necessary if both tyranny and anarchy were to be averted.

The very fact that we retreat to moral arguments—and often moral arguments only—to justify democracy indicates that for many parts of the world the historical and social arguments supporting democracy are just not there....

The demise of the Soviet Union was no reason for us to pressure Rwanda and other countries to form political parties—though that is what our post–Cold War foreign policy has been largely about, even in parts of the world that the Cold War barely touched. The Eastern European countries liberated in 1989 already had, in varying degrees, the historical and social preconditions for both democracy and advanced industrial life: bourgeois traditions, exposure to the Western Enlightenment, high literacy rates, low birth rates, and so on. The post–Cold War effort to bring democracy to those countries has been reasonable. What is less reasonable is to put a gun to the head of the peoples of the developing world and say, in effect, "Behave as if you had experienced the Western Enlightenment to the degree that Poland and the Czech Republic did. Behave as if 95 percent of your population were literate. Behave as if you had no bloody ethnic or regional disputes."

States have never been formed by elections. Geography, settlement patterns, the rise of literate bourgeoisie, and, tragically, ethnic cleansing have formed states. Greece, for instance, is a stable democracy partly because earlier in the century it carried out a relatively benign form of ethnic cleansing—in the form of refugee transfers—which created a monoethnic society. Nonetheless, it took several decades of economic development for Greece finally to put its coups behind it. Democracy often weakens states by necessitating ineffectual compromises and fragile coalition governments in societies where bureaucratic institutions never functioned well to begin with. Because democracy neither forms states nor strengthens them initially, multiparty systems are best suited to nations that already have efficient bureaucracies and a middle class that pays income tax, and where primary issues such as borders and power-sharing have already been resolved, leaving politicians free to bicker about the budget and other secondary matters.

Social stability results from the establishment of a middle class. Not democracies but authoritarian systems, including monarchies, create middle classes—which, having achieved a certain size and self-confidence, revolt against the very dictators who generated their prosperity. This is the pattern today in the Pacific Rim and the southern cone of South America, but not in other parts of Latin America, southern Asia, or sub-Saharan Africa....

Foreign correspondents in sub-Saharan Africa who equate democracy with progress miss this point, ignoring both history and centuries of political philosophy. They seem to think that the choice is between dictators and democrats. But for many places the only choice is between bad dictators and slightly better ones. To force elections on such places may give us some instant gratification. But after a few months or years a bunch of soldiers with grenades will get bored and greedy, and will easily topple their fledgling democracy. As likely as not, the democratic government will be composed of corrupt, bickering, ineffectual politicians whose weak rule never had an institutional base to start with: modern bureaucracies generally require high literacy rates over several generations. Even India, the great exception that proves the rule, has had a mixed record of success as a democracy, with Bihar and other poverty-wracked places remaining in semi-anarchy. Ross Munro, a noted Asia expert, has documented how Chinese autocracy has better prepared China's population for the economic rigors of the post-industrial age than Indian democracy has prepared India's.

Of course, our post–Cold War mission to spread democracy is partly a pose. In Egypt and Saudi Arabia, America's most important allies in the energy-rich Muslim world, our worst nightmare would be free and fair elections, as it would be elsewhere in the Middle East. The end of the Cold War has changed our attitude toward those authoritarian regimes that are not crucial to our interests—but not toward those that are. We praise democracy, and meanwhile we are grateful for an autocrat like King Hussein, and for the fact that the Turkish and Pakistani militaries have always been the real powers behind the "democracies" in their countries. Obviously, democracy in the abstract encompasses undeniably good things such as civil society and a respect for human rights. But as a matter of public policy it has unfortunately come to focus on elections....

The current reality in Singapore and South Africa, for instance, shreds our democratic certainties. Lee Kuan Yew's offensive neo-authoritarianism, in which the state has evolved into a corporation that is paternalistic, meritocratic, and decidedly undemocratic, has forged prosperity from abject poverty. A survey of business executives and economists by the World Economic Forum ranked Singapore No. 1 among the fifty-three most advanced countries appearing on an index of global competitiveness. What is good for business executives is often good for the average citizen: per capita wealth in Singapore is nearly equal to that in Canada, the nation that ranks No. 1 in the world on the United Nations' Human Development Index. When Lee took over Singapore, more than thirty years ago, it was a mosquito-ridden bog filled with slum quarters that frequently lacked both plumbing and electricity. Doesn't liberation from filth and privation count as a human right? Jeffrey Sachs, a professor of international trade at Harvard, writes that "good government" means relative safety from corruption, from breach of contract, from property expropriation, and from bureaucratic inefficiency. Singapore's reputation in these regards is unsurpassed. If Singapore's 2.8 million citizens ever demand democracy, they will just prove the assertion that prosperous middle classes arise under authoritarian regimes before gaining the confidence to dislodge their benefactors. Singapore's success is frightening, yet it must be acknowledged.

Democratic South Africa, meanwhile, has become one of the most violent places on earth that are not war zones, according to the security firm Kroll Associates. The murder rate is six times that in the United States, five times that in Russia. There are ten private-security guards for every policeman. The currency has substantially declined, educated people continue to flee, and international drug cartels have made the country a new transshipment center. Real unemployment is about 33 percent, and is probably much higher among youths. Jobs cannot be created without the cooperation of foreign investors, but assuaging their fear could require the kind of union-busting and police actions that democracy will not permit. The South African military was the power behind the regime in the last decade of apartheid. And it is the military that may yet help to rule South Africa in the future. Like Pakistan but more so, South Africa is destined for a hybrid regime if it is to succeed. The abundant coverage of South Africa's impressive attempts at coming to terms with the crimes of apartheid serves to obscure the country's growing problems. There is a sense of fear in such celebratory, backward-looking coverage, as if writing too much about difficulties in that racially symbolic country would expose the limits of the liberal humanist enterprise worldwide....

"World Government"

Authoritarian or hybrid regimes, no matter how illiberal, will still be treated as legitimate if they can provide security for their subjects and spark economic growth. And they will easily find acceptance in a world driven increasingly by financial markets that know no borders.

For years idealists have dreamed of a "world government." Well, a world government has been emerging—quietly and organically, the way vast developments in history take place. I do not refer to the United Nations, the power of which, almost by definition, affects only the poorest countries. After its peacekeeping failures in Bosnia and Somalia—and its $2 billion failure to make Cambodia democratic—the UN is on its way to becoming a supranational relief agency. Rather, I refer to the increasingly dense ganglia of international corporations and markets that are becoming the unseen arbiters of power in many countries....

Of the world's hundred largest economies, fifty-one are not countries but corporations. While the 200 largest corporations employ less than three fourths of one percent of the world's work force, they account for 28 percent of world economic activity. The 500 largest corporations account for 70 percent of world trade. Corporations are like the feudal domains that evolved into nation-states;

they are nothing less than the vanguard of a new Darwinian organization of politics. Because they are in the forefront of real globalization while the overwhelming majority of the world's inhabitants are still rooted in local terrain, corporations will be free for a few decades to leave behind the social and environmental wreckage they create—abruptly closing a factory here in order to open an unsafe facility with a cheaper work force there. Ultimately, as technological innovations continue to accelerate and the world's middle classes come closer together, corporations may well become more responsible to the cohering global community and less amoral in the course of their evolution toward new political and cultural forms....

The level of social development required by democracy as it is known in the West has existed in only a minority of places—and even there only during certain periods of history. We are entering a troubling transition, and the irony is that while we preach our version of democracy abroad, it slips away from us at home.

The Shrinking Domain of "Politics"

I put special emphasis on corporations because of the true nature of politics: who does and who doesn't have power. To categorize accurately the political system of a given society, one must define the significant elements of power within it. Supreme Court Justice Louis Brandeis knew this instinctively, which is why he railed against corporate monopolies. Of course, the influence that corporations wield over government and the economy is so vast and obvious that the point needs no elaboration. But there are other, more covert forms of emerging corporate power.

The number of residential communities with defended perimeters that have been built by corporations went from 1,000 in the early 1960s to more than 80,000 by the mid-1980s, with continued dramatic increases in the 1990s. ("Gated communities" are not an American invention. They are an import from Latin America, where deep social divisions in places like Rio de Janeiro and Mexico City make them necessary for the middle class.) Then there are malls, with their own rules and security forces, as opposed to public streets; private health clubs as opposed to public playgrounds; incorporated suburbs with strict zoning; and other mundane aspects of daily existence in which—perhaps without realizing it, because the changes have been so gradual—we opt out of the public sphere and the "social contract" for the sake of a protected setting. Dennis Judd, an urban-affairs expert at the University of Missouri at St. Louis, told me recently, "It's nonsense to think that Americans are individualists. Deep down we are a nation of herd animals: micelike conformists who will lay at our doorstep many of our rights if someone tells us that we won't have to worry about crime and our property values are secure. We have always put up with restrictions inside a corporation which we would never put up with in the public sphere. But what many do not realize is that life within some sort of corporation is what the future will increasingly be about." ...

Corporations, which are anchored neither to nations nor to communities, have created strip malls, edge cities, and Disneyesque tourist bubbles. Developments are not necessarily bad: they provide low prices, convenience, efficient work forces, and, in the case of tourist bubbles, safety. We need big corporations. Our society has reached a level of social and technological complexity at which goods and services must be produced for a price and to a standard that smaller businesses cannot manage. We should also recognize, though, that the architectural reconfiguration of our cities and towns has been an undemocratic event—with decisions in effect handed down from above by an assembly of corporate experts.

"The government of man will be replaced by the administration of things," the Enlightenment French philosopher Henri de Saint-Simon prophesied. We should worry that experts will channel our very instincts and thereby control them to some extent. For example, while the government fights drug abuse, often with pathetic results, pharmaceutical corporations have worked *through* the government and political parties to receive sanction for drugs such as stimulants and anti-depressants, whose consciousness-altering effects, it could be argued, are as great as those of outlawed drugs.

The more appliances that middle-class existence requires, the more influence their producers have over the texture of our lives. Of course, the computer in some ways enhances the power of the individual, but it also depletes our individuality. A degree of space and isolation is required for a healthy sense of self, which may be threatened by the constant stream of other people's opinions on computer networks.

Democratic governance, at the federal, state, and local levels, goes on. But its ability to affect our lives is limited. The growing piles of our material possessions make personal life more complex and leave less time for communal matters. And as communities become liberated from geography, as well as more specialized culturally and electronically, they will increasingly fall outside the realm of traditional governance. Democracy loses meaning if both rulers and ruled cease to be part of a community tied to a specific territory. In this historical transition phase, lasting perhaps a century or more, in which globalization has begun but is not complete and loyalties are highly confused, civil society will be harder to maintain. How and when we vote during the next hundred years may be a minor detail for historians....

Umpire Regimes

This rise of corporate power occurs more readily as the masses become more indifferent and the elite less accountable. Material possessions not only focus people toward private and away from communal life but also encourage docility. The more possessions one has, the more compromises one will make to protect them. The ancient Greeks said that the slave is someone who is intent on filling his belly, which can also mean someone who is intent on safeguarding his possessions. Aristophanes and Euripides, the late-eighteenth-century Scottish philosopher Adam Ferguson, and Tocqueville in the nineteenth century all warned that material prosperity would breed servility and withdrawal, turning people into, in Tocqueville's words, "industrious sheep."

... The mood of the Colosseum goes together with the age of the corporation, which offers entertainment in place of values. The Nobel laureate Czeslaw Milosz provides the definitive view on why Americans degrade themselves with mass culture: "Today man believes that there is *nothing* in him, so he accepts *anything,* even if he knows it to be bad, in order to find himself at one with others, in order not to be alone." Of course, it is because people find so little in themselves that they fill their world with celebrities. The masses avoid important national and international news because much of it is tragic, even as they show an unlimited appetite for the details of Princess Diana's death. This willingness to give up self and responsibility is the sine qua non for tyranny....

A continental regime must continue to function, because America's edge in information warfare requires it, both to maintain and to lead a far-flung empire of sorts, as the Athenians did during the Peloponnesian War. But trouble awaits us, if only because the "triumph" of democracy in the developing world will cause great upheavals before many places settle into more practical—and, it is to be hoped, benign—hybrid regimes. In the Middle East, for instance, countries like Syria, Iraq, and the Gulf sheikhdoms—with artificial borders, rising populations, and rising numbers of working-age youths—will not instantly become stable democracies once their absolute dictators and medieval ruling families pass from the scene. As in the early centuries of Christianity, there will be a mess.

Given the surging power of corporations, the gladiator culture of the masses, and the ability of the well-off to be partly disengaged from their own countries, what will democracy under an umpire regime be like?

The Return of Oligarchy?

... [T]he differences between oligarchy and democracy and between ancient democracy and our own could be far subtler than we think. Modern democracy exists within a thin band of social and economic conditions, which include flexible hierarchies that allow people to move up and down the ladder. Instead of clear-cut separations between classes there are many gray shades, with most people bunched in the middle. Democracy is a fraud in many poor countries outside this narrow band: Africans want a better life and instead have been given the right to vote. As new and intimidating forms of economic and social stratification appear in a world based increasingly on the ability to handle and analyze large quantities of information, a new politics might emerge for us, too—less like the kind envisioned by progressive reformers and more like the pragmatic hybrid regimes that are bringing prosperity to developing countries.

... If democracy, the crowning political achievement of the West, is gradually being transfigured, in part because of technology, then the West will suffer the same fate as earlier civilizations.

POSTSCRIPT

Are Liberty and Democracy Good for Every Country?

The questions raised by McFaul and Kaplan are as complex as they are important. At least one prominent American political scientist, Samuel P. Huntington, has shifted his position from a positive view of the likelihood of democratic domination in the future in *The Third Wave: Democratization in the Late Twentieth Century* (University of Oklahoma Press, 1991) to a more negative outlook in *The Clash of Civilizations and the Remaking of the World Order* (Simon & Schuster, 1996). Particularly pertinent at the present time is Huntington's conclusion that Islam has moved in an anti-Western, antidemocratic direction. On the other hand, this trend is not seen in Indonesia, the country with the largest Muslim population. Another analysis that argues that democracy has not established the claim of its ultimate triumph is found in Albert Somit and Steven A. Peterson, *Darwinism, Dominance, and Democracy* (Praeger, 1997).

What if democratic elections resulted in the election of anti-American, anti-Western nationalists and fundamentalists? Those who believe in the spread of liberty and democracy doubt that this could happen if the conditions of freedom have been established. Yet even in Western Europe, with its longer democratic traditions, recent electoral evidence suggests that a significant minority of the electorate might support antidemocratic leaders. In "Democracy for All?" *Commentary* (March 2000), James Q. Wilson concludes that democracies that endure are homogeneous, tend to be isolated, possess widely held private property, and develop traditions of liberty and democracy. Nevertheless, the ethnically diverse United States has succeeded in expanding democratic participation. By contrast, most nondemocratic nations lack most of these characteristics.

It is likely that the rise of global corporations and the worldwide communications made possible by the Internet will diminish the importance of national boundaries and, to a considerable extent, homogenize national and ethnic cultures. Will such changes adversely affect the movement toward democracy? A pessimistic answer is offered by Donald N. Wood in *Post-Intellectualism and the Decline of Democracy: The Failure of Reason and Responsibility in the Twentieth Century* (Praeger, 1997).

President John F. Kennedy's ringing proclamation in 1961 that the United States was ready to "pay any price, bear any burden, meet any hardship, support any friend, oppose any foe, to assure the survival and the success of liberty" suggested that America has a unique role in spreading democracy. Consider the following facts, which are much more evident now than when Kennedy spoke four decades ago: English has become the language that links educated people throughout the world. The United States is the sole military superpower. American movies and music threaten to overwhelm the popular culture of other nations. And, despite the challenge of Japan, America is the world's only information superpower. Perhaps the decline of cultural distinctions and the evolution of a global culture of shared interests is a measure of enhanced communications and understanding. Insofar as this is occurring, it provides for the United States not only an enormous commercial opportunity but also the opportunity to promote liberties identified with democracy.

ISSUE 2

Do Political Campaigns Promote Good Government?

YES: Samuel L. Popkin, from *The Reasoning Voter: Communication and Persuasion in Presidential Campaigns* (University of Chicago Press, 1991)

NO: Anthony King, from "Running Scared," *The Atlantic Monthly* (January 1997)

ISSUE SUMMARY

YES: Professor of political science Samuel L. Popkin argues that presidential election campaigns perform a unique and essential service in informing and unifying the American people.

NO: Political scientist Anthony King contends that American office-holders spend too much time and effort running for office, which detracts from their responsibility to provide good government.

Americans have the opportunity to vote more often to elect more office-holders than the citizens of any other democracy. Many elected officials serve two-year terms (members of the House of Representatives and many local and state officials), some serve four-year terms (the president, vice president, and other state and local officials), and only a few serve as long as six years (members of the Senate). In addition, voters may participate in primary elections to choose the candidates of the major parties for each of these offices. In the case of the presidential nominee, voters may select national convention delegates, whose election will determine who the party's nominee will be.

As a consequence, Americans are engaged in an almost ceaseless political campaign. No sooner is one congressional election over than another one begins. Given the long period required for organization and delegate-seeking prior to a presidential nomination, those who would be their party's nominee are off and running almost as soon as the last election has been decided.

Does this virtually nonstop campaigning serve the interests of American democracy? It surely makes for the most sustained appeal for public support by would-be candidates and those who finally win their party's support. During the height of the campaign season, lavish amounts of television time are bought for candidates' commercials, speeches, and sound bites on evening news broadcasts. Voters who want to learn more about the candidates and their positions can expose themselves to more information than they can absorb in daily newspapers, the news weeklies, talk radio, and C-SPAN. Less-interested adults cannot entirely escape political campaigns by switching their televisions to sitcoms and dramas, because they will be inundated with 30- and 60-second commercials for the candidates.

Yet despite this surfeit of information and advertisement, a smaller proportion of the eligible American electorate votes in presidential elections than did a century ago, and this proportion is smaller than those of other major democracies throughout the world. Just under 50 percent of the eligible electorate voted for president in 1996. An even smaller percentage votes in congressional, state, and local elections.

Declining voter turnout may derive in part from the reduced role of political parties, which once organized community rallies and door-to-door voter solicitation. In other democracies, party committees choose candidates; in the United States, candidates for national, state, and local office seek nomination by voters in primary elections. This diminishes the influence of parties and increases the amount and cost of campaigning. In presidential campaigns, the national party convention used to be an exciting affair in which the delegates actually chose from among competing candidates. As a result of changes in the method of delegate selection, the winning nominee is now known long before the formal decision, and the convention has been reduced to a carefully scripted show. As a result, the television networks have cut back their coverage, and viewer interest has diminished.

Critics argue that television has not only supplanted traditional campaigning but has placed candidates in contrived settings and reduced issues to slogans. Furthermore, long campaigns become negative and candidates attempt to show their opponents in as bad a light as possible. Examples from recent campaigns abound, including mudslinging, character bashing, and the blatant misrepresentation of opponents' records.

Many supporters of the American electoral system believe that more campaigning is needed in order to educate potential voters and to inspire their participation. The campaign serves the invaluable function of illuminating the common interests of varied economic, social, ethnic, and racial groups in America's heterogeneous society. As for low voter turnout, some maintain that this represents satisfaction with the workings of American democracy. That is, if the two major parties do not represent diametrically opposed positions on the gravest issues, it is precisely because most Americans approve of moderate policies and few would be attracted to extreme views.

In the selections that follow, Samuel L. Popkin maintains that campaigns bring together a diverse population and that voters need to see more campaigning and fuller coverage, not less. Anthony King asserts that short terms, weak parties, and expensive campaigns mean that officeholders spend more time and effort running for office than trying to provide good government.

Samuel L. Popkin

 **YES**

The Reasoning Voter

I believe that voter turnout has declined because campaign stimulation, from the media and from personal interaction, is also low and declining, and there is less interaction between the media and the grass-roots, person-to-person aspects of voter mobilization. The lack of campaign stimulation, I suggest, is also responsible for the large turnout gap in this country between educated and uneducated voters.

The social science research shows clear relations between the turnout and social stimulation. Married people of all ages vote more than people of the same age who live alone. And much of the increase in turnout seen over one's life cycle is due to increases in church attendance and community involvement. I believe that in this age of electronic communities, when more people are living alone and fewer people are involved in churches, PTA's, and other local groups, interpersonal social stimulation must be increased if turnout is to increase....

Political parties used to spend a large portion of their resources bringing people to rallies. By promoting the use of political ideas to bridge the gap between the individual "I" and the party "we," they encouraged people to believe that they were "links in the chain" and that the election outcome would depend on what people like themselves chose to do. Today, less money and fewer resources are available for rallies as a part of national campaigns. And parties cannot compensate for this loss with more door-to-door canvassing; in the neighborhoods where it would be safe to walk door-to-door, no one would be home.

Some of the social stimulation that campaigns used to provide in rallies and door-to-door canvassing can still be provided by extensive canvassing. This is still done in Iowa and New Hampshire. These are the first primary states, and candidates have the time and resources to do extensive personal campaigning, and to use campaign organizations to telephone people and discuss the campaigns. In research reported elsewhere, I have analyzed the effect of the social stimulation that occurs in these states. People contacted by one political candidate pay more attention to all the candidates and to the campaign events reported on television and in the papers. As they watch the campaign they become more aware of differences between the candidates. And as they become more aware of the differences, they become more likely to vote.

From Samuel L. Popkin, *The Reasoning Voter: Communication and Persuasion in Presidential Campaigns* (University of Chicago Press, 1991). Copyright © 1991 by Samuel L. Popkin. Reprinted by permission of University of Chicago Press. Notes omitted.

This suggests a surprising conclusion: The best single way to compensate for the declining use of the party as a cue to voting, and for the declining social stimulation to vote at all, might be to increase our spending on campaign activities that stimulate voter involvement. There are daily complaints about the cost of American elections, and certainly the corrosive effects of corporate fundraising cannot be denied; but it is not true that American elections are costly by comparison with those in other countries. Comparisons are difficult, especially since most countries have parliamentary systems, but it is worth noting that reelection campaigns to the Japanese Diet—the equivalent of the U.S. House of Representatives—cost over $1.5 million per seat. That would be equivalent to $3.5 million per congressional reelection campaign, instead of the current U.S. average of about $400,000 (given the fact that Japan has one-half the U.S. population and 512 legislators instead of 435). Although the differences in election systems and rules limit the value of such comparisons, it is food for thought that a country with a self-image so different from America's spends so much more on campaigning.

I believe that voters should be given more to "read" from campaigns and television, and that they need more interpersonal reinforcement of what they "read." Considering the good evidence that campaigns work, I believe that the main trouble lies not with American politicians but in the fact that American campaigns are not effective enough to overcome the increasing lack of social stimulation we find in a country of electronic as well as residential communities. This confronts us with some troubling questions. What kinds of electronic and/or social stimulation are possible today? To what extent can newspaper and television coverage provide the kinds of information citizens need to connect their own concerns with the basic party differences that campaigns try to make paramount? Is there a limit to what electronic and print stimulation can accomplish, so that parties must find a way to restore canvassing and rallies, or can electronic rallies suffice? Does watching a rally on television have the same effect as attending a rally? Could a return to bumper stickers and buttons, which have become far less prominent since campaigns began pouring their limited resources into the media, make a difference by reinforcing commitments and encouraging political discussions?

The problem may also be not simply a *lack* of social stimulation, but the growing *diversity* of social stimulation, and a resulting decline in reinforcement. In 1948, Columbia sociologists collected data about the social milieu of each voter and related the effects of the mass media on the voter to the political influences of family, friends, church, etc. They found that a voter's strength of conviction was related to the political homogeneity of the voter's associates. At that time, most voters belonged to politically homogeneous social groups; the social gulf between the parties was so wide that most voters had no close friends or associates voting differently from them. A decline in the political homogeneity of primary groups would lead to less social reinforcement; since the political cleavage patterns which exist today cut more across social groups, voters are in less homogeneous family, church, and work settings and are getting less uniform reinforcement. Whether there is less overall social stimulation today, or whether there is simply less uniformity of social stimulation, the demands on campaigns to pull segments together and create coalitions are vastly greater today than in the past.

What Television Gives Us

Television is giving us less and less direct communication from our leaders and their political campaigns. Daniel Hallin, examining changes in network news coverage of presidents from 1968 to 1988, has found that the average length of the actual quote from a president on the news has gone from forty-five seconds in 1968 to nine seconds today. Instead of a short introduction from a reporter and a long look at the president, we are given a short introduction from the president and a long look at the reporter.

In the opinion of Peggy Noonan, one of the most distinguished speechwriters of recent years, who wrote many of President Reagan's and President Bush's best speeches, the change from long quotes to sound bites has taken much of the content out of campaigning: "It's a media problem. The young people who do speeches for major politicians, they've heard the whole buzz about sound bites. And now instead of writing... a serious text with serious arguments, they just write sound bite after sound bite." With less serious argument in the news, there is less material for secondary elites and analysts to digest, and less need for candidates to think through their policies.

We also receive less background information about the campaign and less coverage of the day-to-day pageantry—the stump speeches, rallies, and crowds. Moreover, as Paul Weaver has shown, the reporter's analysis concentrates on the horse-race aspect of the campaign and thus downplays the policy stakes involved. To a network reporter, "politics is essentially a game played by individual politicians for personal advancement... the game takes place against a backdrop of governmental institutions, public problems, policy debates, and the like, but these are noteworthy only insofar as they affect, or are used by, players in pursuit of the game's rewards.

As a result of this supposedly critical stance, people are losing the kinds of signals they have always used to read politicians. We see fewer of the kinds of personalized political interactions, including the fun and the pageantry, that help people decide whose side they are on and that help potential leaders assemble coalitions for governing.

Gerald Ford went to a fiesta in San Antonio because he wanted Hispanic voters to see his willingness to visit them on their own ground, and to demonstrate that some of their leaders supported him. He also wanted to remind them of his willingness to deal respectfully with the sovereignty issues raised by the Panama Canal question. But when he bit into an unshucked tamale, these concerns were buried in an avalanche of trivial commentary. Reporters joked that the president was going after the "klutz" vote and talked about "Bozo the Clown." From that moment on, Ford was pictured in the media as laughably uncoordinated. Reporters brought up Lyndon Johnson's contemptuous jibe that Ford "was so dumb he couldn't walk and chew gum at the same time." Jokes circulated that he had played too much football without his helmet. For the rest of the campaign, his every slip was noted on the evening news. Yet the news photos supposedly documenting the president's clumsiness reveal a man of remarkably good balance and body control, given the physical circumstances—not surprising for a man who had been an all-American football player in college and was still, in his sixties, an active downhill skier.

Similarly, during the 1980 campaign, Ronald Reagan visited Dallas and said, in response to a question, that there were "great flaws" in the theory of evolution and that it might be a good idea if the schools taught "creationism" as well. This statement was characterized in the media as the sort of verbal pratfall to be expected from Reagan, and much of the coverage related such gaffes *entirely* to questions about his intellectual capacity, not to the meaning of his appearance or the implications of the appearance for the coalition he was building.

What difference would it have made if press and television reporters had considered these actions by Ford and Reagan as clear and open avowals of sympathy for political causes dear to their hearts? What if Ford's political record on issues dear to Hispanics had been discussed, or if the guest list for the fiesta had been discussed to see which prominent Hispanics were, in fact, endorsing him? The nature of the gathering Reagan attended was noted at the time, but it was never referred to again. It was not until 1984 that Americans uninvolved in religious fundamentalism understood enough about what the Moral Majority stood for to read anything from a politician's embrace of Jerry Falwell, its president, or a religious roundtable such as the one Reagan attended in 1980. By 1988, as more people on the other side of the fundamentalism debates learned what the Moral Majority stood for, the group was disbanded as a political liability.

Television, in other words, is not giving people enough to read about the substance of political coalition building because it ignores many important campaign signals. That rallies and other campaign events are "staged" does not diminish their importance and the legitimate information they can convey to voters. When Richard Nixon met Mao Tse Tung in 1972, the meeting was no less important because it was staged. And when Jesse Jackson praised Lloyd Bentsen by noting the speed with which he could go from biscuits to tacos to caviar, he was acknowledging another fact of great importance: in building coalitions, a candidate must consider the trade-off between offering symbols and making promises.

If politicians cannot show familiarity with people's concerns by properly husking tamales or eating knishes in the right place with the right people, they will have to promise them something. As Jackson noted, the tamales may be better than promises, because promises made to one segment of voters, or one-issue public, will offend other groups and therefore tie the politician's hands in the future policy-making process.

Is it more meaningful when a governor of Georgia hangs a picture of Martin Luther King Jr. in the statehouse, or when a senator or congressman votes for a bill promising full employment? Is it better for a politician to eat a kosher hot dog or to promise never to compromise Israel's borders? When voters are deprived of one shortcut—obvious symbols, for example—obvious promises, for example—instead of turning to more subtle and complicated forms of information.

How good a substitute are electronic tamales for the real thing? Does watching a fiesta provide any of the stimulation to identification and turnout that attendance at a fiesta provides? How long does it take to bring us together, at least in recognizable coalitions? We need not have answers to these questions to see that they speak to the central issue of stimulating turnout and participation in elections in an age of electronic communities. The media *could* provide more of the kinds of information people use to assess candidates and parties. However, I do not know if electronic tamales provide the social stimulation of interacting with others, or the reinforcement of acting with others who agree, and I do not know how much more potent are ideas brought clearly to mind through using them with others. The demands placed on television are greater than the demands ever placed on radio or newspapers because the world is more diverse today and there are more segments which need to be reunited in campaigns.

Objections and Answers

Two notable objections can be made to my suggestions for increasing campaigning and campaign spending. The first is the "spinmaster" objection: contemporary political campaigns are beyond redemption because campaign strategists have become so adept at manipulation that voters can no longer learn what the candidates really stand for or really intend to do. Significantly, this conclusion is supported by two opposing arguments about voter behavior. One objection is that voters are staying home because they have been turned off by fatuous claims and irrelevant advertising. A variant of this is that voters are being manipulated with great success by unscrupulous campaign advertising, so that their votes reflect more concern with Willie Horton* or school prayer or flag burning than with widespread poverty, the banking crisis, or global warming. The second objection is that popular concern with candidates and with government in general has been trivialized, so that candidates fiddle while America burns. In the various versions of this hypothesis, voter turnout is down because today's political contests are waged over small differences on trivial issues. While Eastern Europe plans a future of freedom under eloquent spokesmen like Vaclav Havel, and while Mikhail Gorbachev declares an end to the cold war, releases Eastern Europe from Soviet control, and tries to free his countrymen from the yoke of doctrinaire communism, in America Tweedledum and Tweedledee argue about who loves the flag more while Japan buys Rockefeller Center, banks collapse, and the deficit grows.

Both of these critiques of the contemporary system argue that campaigns themselves are trivial and irrelevant, that campaign advertising and even the candidates' speeches are nothing but self-serving puffery and distortion. This

---

* [Willie Horton, a convicted murderer, escaped a prison furlough approved by then-governor of Massachusetts Michael Dukakis and committed a violent crime. George Bush exploited the incident in his campaign against Dukakis during the 1988 presidential race.—Eds.]

general argument has an aesthetic appeal, especially to better-educated voters and the power elite; campaign commercials remind no one of the Lincoln-Douglas debates, and today's bumper stickers and posters have none of the resonance of the Goddess of Democracy in Tiananmen Square. But elite aesthetics is not the test of this argument; the test is what voters learn from campaigns.

There is ample evidence that voters *do* learn from campaigns. Of course, each campaign tries hard to make its side look better and the other side worse. Despite that, voter perceptions about the candidates and their positions are more accurate. Furthermore, . . . there is no evidence that people learn less from campaigns today than they did in past years. This is a finding to keep in mind at all times, for many of the criticisms of campaigns simplistically assume that because politicians and campaign strategists have manipulative intentions, campaigns necessarily mislead the voter. This assumption is not borne out by the evidence; voters know how to read the media and the politicians better than most media critics acknowledge.

. . . Voters remember past campaigns and presidents, and past failures of performance to match promises. They have a sense of who is with them and who is against them; they make judgments about unfavorable new editorials and advertisements from hostile sources, ignoring some of what is favorable to those they oppose and some of what is unfavorable to those they support. In managing their personal affairs and making decisions about their work, they collect information that they can use as a reality test for campaign claims and media stories. They notice the difference between behavior that has real consequences, on one hand, and mere talk, on the other.

. . . The ability of television news to manipulate voters has been vastly overstated, as one extended example will suggest. In television reporting—but not in the academic literature—it was always assumed before 1984 that winning debates and gaining votes are virtually one and the same. But on Sunday, October 7, 1984, in the first debate between Walter Mondale and Ronald Reagan, this assumption was shown to be flawed. Mondale, generally a dry speaker, was unexpectedly relaxed and articulate, and Reagan, known for his genial and relaxed style, was unexpectedly tense and hesitant. Mondale even threw Reagan off guard by using "There you go again," the jibe Reagan had made famous in his 1980 debate with Jimmy Carter. Immediately after the debate, the CBS News/*New York Times* pollsters phoned a sample of registered voters they had interviewed before the debate, to ask which candidate they were going to vote for and which they thought had done a better job in the debate. Mondale was considered to have "done the best job" by 42 percent to 36 percent, and had gained 3 points in the polls. As a result of similar polls in the next twenty-four hours by other networks and news organizations, the media's main story the rest of the week was of Mondale's upset victory over the president in the debate. Two days later, when another CBS News/*New York Times* poll asked voters about the debate and about their intended vote, Mondale was considered to have "done the best job" not by 42 percent to 36 percent margin of Sunday, but by 65 percent to 17 percent. Media reports, then, claimed that millions of voters had changed their minds about what they themselves had just seen days earlier.

Yet in the three days during which millions changed their minds about who had won the debate, the same poll reported, few if any changed their minds about how they would vote.

This example emphasizes just how complex the effects of television can be. Voters now have opinions about opinions. When asked who won the debate, they may say not what they think personally, but what they have heard that the majority of Americans think. It is easier to change their opinions about what their neighbors think than to change their own opinions. And most important of all, it is clear that they understand the difference between a debater and a president, and that they don't easily change their political views about who they want to run the country simply on the basis of debating skills.

Critics of campaign spinmasters and of television in general are fond of noting that campaigners and politicians intend to manipulate and deceive, but they wrongly credit them with more success than they deserve. As Michael Schudson has noted, in the television age, whenever a president's popularity has been high, it has been attributed to unusual talents for using television to sell his image. He notes, for example, that in 1977 the television critic of the *New York Times* called President Carter "a master of controlled images," and that during the 1976 primaries David Halberstam wrote that Carter "more than any other candidate this year has sensed and adapted to modern communications and national mood.... Watching him again and again on television I was impressed by his sense of pacing, his sense of control, very low key, soft." A few years later this master of images still had the same soft, low-key voice, but now it was interpreted as indicating not quiet strength but weakness and indecision. Gerald Rafshoon, the media man for this "master of television," concluded after the 1980 campaign that all the television time bought for Carter wasn't as useful as three more helicopters (and a successful desert rescue) would have been.

As these examples suggest, media critics are generally guilty of using one of the laziest and easiest information shortcuts of all. Assuming that a popular politician is a good manipulator of the media or that a winner won because of his media style is not different from what voters do when they evaluate presidents by reasoning backward from known results. The media need reform, but so do the media critics. One cannot infer, without astonishing hubris, that the American people have been successfully deceived simply because a politician wanted them to believe his or her version of events. But the media critics who analyze political texts without any reference to the actual impact of the messages do just that.

Negativism and Triviality

Campaigns are often condemned as trivial—as sideshows in which voters amuse themselves by learning about irrelevant differences between candidates who fiddle over minor issues while the country stagnates and inner cities burn—and many assume that the negativism and pettiness of the attacks that candidates make on each other encourage an "a pox on all your houses" attitude. This suggests a plausible hypothesis, which can be given a clean test in a simple experiment. This experiment can be thought of as a "stop and think" experiment because it is a test of what happens if people stop and think about what they know of the candidates and issues in an election and tell someone what they know. First, take a random sample of people across the country and interview them. Ask the people selected what they consider to be the most important issues facing the country, and then ask them where the various candidates stand on these issues. Then ask them to state their likes and dislikes about the candidates' personal qualities and issue stands, and about the state of the country. Second, after the election, find out whether these interviewees were more or less likely to vote than people who were not asked to talk about the campaign. If the people interviewed voted less often than people not interviewed, then there is clear support for the charge that triviality, negativism, and irrelevancy are turning off the American people and suppressing turnout.

In fact, the National Election Studies done by the University of Michigan's Survey Research Center, now the Center for Political Studies, are exactly such an experiment. In every election since 1952, people have been asked what they care about, what the candidates care about, and what they know about the campaign. After the election people have been reinterviewed and asked whether they voted; then the actual voting records have been checked to see whether the respondents did indeed vote.

The results convincingly demolish the triviality and negativism hypothesis. In every election, people who have been interviewed are more likely to vote than other Americans. Indeed, the reason the expensive and difficult procedure of verifying turnout against the voting records was begun in the first place was that the scholars were suspicious because the turnout reported by respondents was so much higher than either the actual turnout of all Americans or the turnout in surveys conducted after the election. So respondents in the national election studies, after seventy minutes of thinking about the candidates, the issues, and the campaign, were both more likely than other people to vote and more likely to try to hide the fact that they did not vote! Further, if people are reinterviewed in later elections, their turnout continues to rise. Still further, while an interview cuts nonvoting in a presidential election by up to 20 percent, an interview in a local primary may cut nonvoting by as much as half.

The rise in no-shows on voting day and the rise of negative campaigning both follow from the rise of candidate-centered elections. When voters do not have information about future policies they extrapolate, or project, from the information they have. As campaigns become more centered on candidates, there is more projection, and hence more negative campaigning. Negative campaigning is designed to provide information that causes voters to stop projecting and to change their beliefs about a candidate's stand on the issues. "Willie Horton . . . was a legitimate issue because it speaks to styles and ways of governance. In that case Dukakis's."

As Noonan has also noted of the 1988 campaign, "There should have been more name-calling, mud slinging and fun. It should have been rock-'em-sock-'em the way great campaigns have been in the past. It was tedious." Campaigns cannot deal with anything substantive if they cannot get the electorate's attention and interest people in listening to their music. Campaigns need to make noise. The tradition of genteel populism in America, and the predictable use of sanitary metaphors to condemn politicians and their modes of communication, says more about the distaste of the people who use the sanitary metaphors for American society than it does about the failing politicians.

The challenge to the future of American campaigns, and hence to American democracy, is how to bring back the excitement and the music in an age of electronic campaigning. Today's campaigns have more to do because an educated, media-centered society is a broadened and segmented electorate which is harder to rally, while today's campaigns have less money and troops with which to fight their battles.

⋅❀⋅

When I first began to work in presidential campaigns I had very different ideas about how to change campaigns and their coverage than I have today. Coverage of rallies and fiestas, I used to think, belonged in the back of the paper along with stories about parties, celebrity fund-raisers, and fad diets. Let the society editor cover banquets and rubber chickens, I thought; the reporters in Washington could analyze the speeches and discuss the policy implications of competing proposals.

I still wish that candidates' proposals and speeches were actually analyzed for their content and implications for our future. I still wish that television told us more about how elites evaluate presidential initiatives than what my neighbors said about them in the next day's polls. However, I now appreciate the intimate relationships between the rallies and governance which escaped me in the past. I now appreciate how hard it is to bring a country together, to gather all the many concerns and interests into a single coalition and hold it together in order to govern.

Campaigns are essential in any society, particularly in a society that is culturally, economically, and socially diverse. If voters look for information about candidates under streetlights, then that is where candidates must campaign, and the only way to improve elections is to add streetlights. Reforms can only make sense if they are consistent with the gut rationality of voters. Ask not for more sobriety and piety from citizens, for they are voters, not judges; offer them instead cues and signals which connect their world with the world of politics.

NO ⬅

Anthony King

Running Scared

To an extent that astonishes a foreigner, modern America is *about* the holding of elections. Americans do not merely have elections on the first Tuesday after the first Monday of November in every year divisible by four. They have elections on the first Tuesday after the first Monday of November in every year divisible by two. In addition, five states have elections in odd-numbered years. Indeed, there is no year in the United States—ever—when a major statewide election is not being held somewhere. To this catalogue of general elections has of course to be added an equally long catalogue of primary elections (for example, forty-three presidential primaries [in 1996]). Moreover, not only do elections occur very frequently in the United States but the number of jobs legally required to be filled by them is enormous—from the presidency of the United States to the post of local consumer advocate in New York. It has been estimated that no fewer than half a million elective offices are filled or waiting to be filled in the United States today.

Americans take the existence of their never-ending election campaign for granted. Some like it, some dislike it, and most are simply bored by it. But they are all conscious of it, in the same way that they are conscious of Mobil, McDonald's, *Larry King Live,* Oprah Winfrey, the Dallas Cowboys, the Ford Motor Company, and all the other symbols and institutions that make up the rich tapestry of American life.

To a visitor to America's shores, however, the never-ending campaign presents a largely unfamiliar spectacle. In other countries election campaigns have both beginnings and ends, and there are even periods, often prolonged periods, when no campaigns take place at all. Other features of American elections are also unfamiliar. In few countries do elections and campaigns cost as much as they do in the United States. In no other country is the role of organized political parties so limited.

America's permanent election campaign, together with other aspects of American electoral politics, has one crucial consequence, little noticed but vitally important for the functioning of American democracy. Quite simply, the American electoral system places politicians in a highly vulnerable position. Individually and collectively they are more vulnerable, more of the time, to the vicissitudes of electoral politics than are the politicians of any other democratic

From Anthony King, "Running Scared," *The Atlantic Monthly* (January 1997). Abridged and reprinted from Anthony King, *Running Scared: Why America's Politicians Campaign Too Much and Govern Too Little* (Martin Kessler Books, 1997). Copyright © 1997 by Anthony King. Reprinted by permission of the author.

country. Because they are more vulnerable, they devote more of their time to electioneering, and their conduct in office is more continuously governed by electoral considerations. I will argue that American politicians' constant and unremitting electoral preoccupations have deleterious consequences for the functioning of the American system. They consume time and scarce resources. Worse, they make it harder than it would otherwise be for the system as a whole to deal with some of America's most pressing problems. Americans often complain that their system is not sufficiently democratic. I will argue that, on the contrary, there is a sense in which the system is too democratic and ought to be made less so. . . .

Fear and Trembling

Politics and government in the United States are marked by the fact that U.S. elected officials in many cases have very short terms of office *and* face the prospect of being defeated in primary elections *and* have to run for office more as individuals than as standard-bearers for their party *and* have continually to raise large sums of money in order to finance their own election campaigns. Some of these factors operate in other countries. There is no other country, however, in which all of them operate, and operate simultaneously. The cumulative consequences, as we shall see, are both pervasive and profound.

The U.S. Constitution sets out in one of its very first sentences that "the House of Representatives shall be composed of members chosen every second year by the people of the several states." When the Founding Fathers decided on such a short term of office for House members, they were setting a precedent that has been followed by no other major democratic country. In Great Britain, France, Italy, and Canada the constitutional or legal maximum for the duration of the lower house of the national legislature is five years. In Germany and Japan the equivalent term is four years. Only in Australia and New Zealand, whose institutions are in some limited respects modeled on those of the United States, are the legal maximums as short as three years. In having two-year terms the United States stands alone.

Members of the Senate are, of course, in a quite different position. Their constitutionally prescribed term of office, six-years, is long by anyone's standards. But senators' six-year terms are not all they seem. In the first place, so pervasive is the electioneering atmosphere that even newly elected senators begin almost at once to lay plans for their re-election campaigns. Senator Daniel Patrick Moynihan, of New York, recalls that when he first came to the Senate, in 1977, his colleagues when they met over lunch or a drink usually talked about politics and policy. Now they talk about almost nothing but the latest opinion polls. In the second place, the fact that under the Constitution the terms of a third of the Senate end every two years means that even if individual senators do not feel themselves to be under continuing electoral pressure, the Senate as a whole does. Despite the Founders' intentions, the Senate's collective electoral sensibilities increasingly resemble those of the House.

Most Americans seem unaware of the fact, but the direct primary—a government-organized popular election to nominate candidates for public office—is, for better or worse, an institution peculiar to the United States. Neither primary elections nor their functional equivalents exist anywhere else in the democratic world. It goes without saying that their effect is to add a further dimension of uncertainty and unpredictability to the world of American elective politicians.

In most other countries the individual holder of public office, so long as he or she is reasonably conscientious and does not gratuitously offend local or regional party opinion, has no real need to worry about renomination. To be sure, cases of parties refusing to renominate incumbent legislators are not unknown in countries such as France, Germany, and Canada, but they are relatively rare and tend to occur under unusual circumstances. The victims are for the most part old, idle, or alcoholic.

The contrast between the rest of the world and the United States could hardly be more striking. In 1979 no fewer than 104 of the 382 incumbent members of the House of Representatives who sought re-election faced primary opposition. In the following three elections the figures were ninety-three out of 398 (1980), ninety-eight out of 393 (1982), and 130 out of 409 (1984). More recently, in 1994, nearly a third of all House incumbents seeking re-election, 121 out of 386, had to face primary opposition, and in the Senate the proportion was even higher: eleven out of twenty-six. Even those incumbents who did not face opposition could seldom be certain in advance that they were not going to. The influence—and the possibility—of primaries is pervasive. As we shall see, the fact that incumbents usually win is neither here nor there.

To frequent elections and primary elections must be added another factor that contributes powerfully to increasing the electoral vulnerability of U.S. politicians: the relative lack of what we might call "party cover." In most democratic countries the fate of most politicians depends not primarily on their own endeavors but on the fate—locally, regionally, or nationally—of their party. If their party does well in an election, so do they. If not, not. The individual politician's interests and those of his party are bound together.

In contrast, America's elective politicians are on their own—not only in relation to politicians in most other countries but also in absolute terms. Party is still a factor in U.S. electoral politics, but it is less so than anywhere else in the democratic world. As a result, American legislators seeking re-election are forced to raise their own profiles, to make their own records, and to fight their own re-election campaigns.

If politicians are so vulnerable electorally, it may be protested, why aren't more of them defeated? In particular, why aren't more incumbent congressmen and senators defeated? The analysis here would seem to imply a very high rate of turnover in Congress, but in fact the rate—at least among incumbents seeking re-election—is notoriously low. How can this argument and the facts of congressional incumbents' electoral success be reconciled?

This objection has to be taken seriously, because the facts on which it is based are substantially correct. The number of incumbent congressmen and senators defeated in either primary or general elections *is* low. But to say that because incumbent members of Congress are seldom defeated, they are not really vulnerable electorally is to miss two crucial points. The first is that precisely because they are vulnerable, they go to prodigious lengths to protect themselves. Like workers in nuclear-power stations, they take the most extreme safety precautions, and the fact that the precautions are almost entirely successful does not make them any less necessary.

Second, congressmen and senators go to inordinate lengths to secure re-election because, although they may objectively be safe (in the view of journalists and academic political scientists), they do not *know* they are safe—and even if they think they are, the price of being wrong is enormous. The probability that anything will go seriously wrong with a nuclear-power station may approach zero, but the stations tend nevertheless to be built away from the centers of large cities. A congressman or a senator may believe that he is reasonably safe, but if he wants to be re-elected, he would be a fool to act on that belief.

How They Came to Be Vulnerable

American politicians run scared—and are right to do so. And they run more scared than the politicians of any other democratic country—again rightly. How did this come to be so?

The short answer is that the American people like it that way. They are, and have been for a very long time, the Western world's hyperdemocrats. They are keener on democracy than almost anyone else and are more determined that democratic norms and practices should pervade every aspect of national life. To explore the implications of this central fact about the United States, and to see how it came to be, we need to examine two different interpretations of the term "democracy." Both have been discussed from time to time by political philosophers, but they have never been codified and they certainly cannot be found written down in a constitution or any other formal statement of political principles. Nevertheless, one or the other underpins the political practice of every democratic country—even if, inevitably, the abstract conception and the day-to-day practice are never perfectly matched.

One of these interpretations might be labeled "division of labor." In this view, there are in any democracy two classes of people—the governors and the governed. The function of the governors is to take decisions on the basis of what they believe to be in the country's best interests and to act on those decisions. If public opinion broadly supports the decisions, that is a welcome bonus. If not, too bad. The views of the people at large are merely one datum among a large number of data that need to be considered. They are not accorded any special status. Politicians in countries that operate within this view can frequently be heard using phrases like "the need for strong leadership" and "the need to take tough decisions." They often take a certain pride in doing what they believe to be right even if the opinion of the majority is opposed to it.

The function of the governed in such a system, if it is a genuine democracy, is very important but strictly limited. It is not to determine public policy or to decide what is the right thing to do. Rather, it is to go to the polls from time to time to choose those who will determine public policy and decide what the right thing is: namely, the governors. The deciding of issues by the electorate is secondary to the election of the individuals who are to do the deciding. The analogy is with choosing a doctor. The patient certainly chooses which doctor to see but does not normally decide (or even try to decide) on the detailed course of treatment. The division of labor is informal but clearly understood.

It is probably fair to say that most of the world's major democracies—Great Britain, France, Germany, Japan—operate on this basis. The voters go to the polls every few years, and in between times it is up to the government of the day to get on with governing. Electing a government and governing are two different businesses. Electioneering is, if anything, to be deplored if it gets in the way of governing.

This is a simplified picture, of course. Democratically elected politicians are ultimately dependent on the electorate, and if at the end of the day the electorate does not like what they are doing, they are dead. Nevertheless, the central point remains. The existing division of labor is broadly accepted.

The other interpretation of democracy, the one dominant in America, might be called the "agency" view, and it is wholly different. According to this view, those who govern a country should function as no more than the agents of the people. The job of the governors is not to act independently and to take whatever decisions they believe to be in the national interest but, rather, to reflect in all their actions the views of the majority of the people, whatever those views may be. Governors are not really governors at all; they are representatives, in the very narrow sense of being in office solely to represent the views of those who sent them there.

In the agency view, representative government of the kind common throughout the democratic world can only be second-best. The ideal system would be one in which there were no politicians or middlemen of any kind and the people governed themselves directly; the political system would take the form of more or less continuous town meetings or referenda, perhaps conducted by means of interactive television. Most Americans, at bottom, would still like to see their country governed by a town meeting.

Why Their Vulnerability Matters

In this political ethos, finding themselves inhabiting a turbulent and torrid electoral environment, most American elective officials respond as might be expected: in an almost Darwinian way. They adapt their behavior—their roll-call votes, their introduction of bills, their committee assignments, their phone calls, their direct-mail letters, their speeches, their press releases, their sound bites, whom they see, how they spend their time, their trips abroad, their trips back home, and frequently their private and families' lives—to their environment: that is, to their primary and overriding need for electoral survival. The effects are felt not only in the lives of individual officeholders and their staffs but also in America's political institutions as a whole and the shape and content of U.S. public policy.

It all begins with officeholders' immediate physical environment: with bricks, mortar, leather, and wood paneling. The number of congressional buildings and the size of congressional staffs have ballooned in recent decades. At the start of the 1960s most members of the House of Representatives contented themselves with a small inner office and an outer office; senators' office suites were not significantly larger. Apart from the Capitol itself, Congress was reasonably comfortably housed in four buildings, known to Washington taxi drivers as the Old and New House and Senate Office Buildings. The designations Old and New cannot be used any longer, however, because there are now so many even newer congressional buildings.

Congressional staffs have grown at roughly the same rate, the new buildings having been built mainly to house the staffs. In 1957 the total number of people employed by members of the House and Senate as personal staff was 3,556. By 1991 the figure had grown to 11,572—a more than threefold increase within the political lifetime of many long-serving members. [In 1996] the total number of people employed by Congress in all capacities, including committee staffs and the staffs of support agencies like the Congressional Research Service, was 32,820, making Congress by far the most heavily staffed legislative branch in the world.

Much of the growth of staff in recent decades has been in response to the growth of national government, to Congress's insistence on strengthening its policymaking role in the aftermath of Vietnam and Watergate, and to decentralization within Congress, which has led subcommittee chairmen and the subcommittees themselves to acquire their own staffs. But there is no doubt that the increase is also in response to congressional incumbents' ever-increasing electoral exposure. Congress itself has become an integral part of America's veritable "elections industry."

One useful measure of the changes that have taken place—and also an important consequence of the changes—is the increased proportion of staff and staff time devoted to constituent service. As recently as 1972 only 1,189 House employees—22.5 percent of House members' personal staffs—were based in home-district offices. By 1992 the number had more than doubled, to 3,128, and the proportion had nearly doubled, to 42.1 percent. On the Senate side there were only 303 state-based staffers in 1972, making up 12.5 percent of senators' personal staffs, but the number had more than quadrupled by 1992 to 1,368, for fully 31.6 percent of the total. Since a significant proportion of the time of Washington-based congressional staffs is also devoted to constituent service, it is a fair guess that more than half of the time of all congressional staffs is now given over to nursing the district or state rather than to legislation and policymaking.

Much constituent service is undoubtedly altruistic, inspired by politicians' sense of duty (and constituents' understandable frustration with an unresponsive bureaucracy); but at the same time nobody doubts that a large proportion of it is aimed at securing re-election. The statistics on the outgoing mail of members of Congress and their use of the franking privilege point in that direction too. Congressional mailings grew enormously in volume from some 100 million pieces a year in the early 1960s to more than 900 million in

1984—nearly five pieces of congressional mail for every adult American. New restrictions on franking introduced in the 1990s have made substantial inroads into that figure, but not surprisingly the volume of mail emanating from both houses of Congress is still invariably higher in election years.

The monetary costs of these increases in voter-oriented congressional activities are high: in addition to being the most heavily staffed legislative branch in the world, Congress is also the most expensive. But there is another, non-monetary cost: the staffs themselves become one of the congressman's or senator's constituencies, requiring management, taking up time, and always being tempted to go into business for themselves. American scholars who have studied the burgeoning of congressional staffs express concern about their cumulative impact on Congress as a deliberative body in which face-to-face communication between members, and between members and their constituents, facilitates both mutual understanding and an understanding of the issues. Largely in response to the requirements of electioneering, more and more congressional business is conducted through dense networks of staffers.

One familiar effect of American politicians' vulnerability is the power it accords to lobbyists and special-interest groups, especially those that can muster large numbers of votes or have large amounts of money to spend on campaigns. Members of Congress walk the electoral world alone. They can be picked off one by one, they know it, and they adjust their behavior accordingly. The power of the American Association of Retired Persons, the National Rifle Association, the banking industry, and the various veterans' lobbies is well known. It derives partly from their routine contributions to campaign funds and the quality of their lobbying activities in Washington, but far more from the votes that the organizations may be able to deliver and from congressmen's and senators' calculations of how the positions they take in the present may affect their chances of re-election in the future—a future that rarely is distant. Might a future challenger be able to use that speech against me? Might I be targeted for defeat by one of the powerful lobbying groups?

A second effect is that American politicians are even more likely than those in other countries to engage in symbolic politics: to use words masquerading as deeds, to take actions that purport to be instrumental but are in fact purely rhetorical. A problem exists; the people demand that it be solved; the politicians cannot solve it and know so; they engage in an elaborate pretense of trying to solve it nevertheless, often at great expense to the taxpayers and almost invariably at a high cost in terms of both the truth and the politicians' own reputations for integrity and effectiveness. The politicians lie in most cases not because they are liars or approve of lying but because the potential electoral costs of not lying are too great.

At one extreme, symbolic politics consists of speechmaking and public position-taking in the absence of any real action or any intention of taking action; casting the right vote is more important than achieving the right outcome. At the other extreme, symbolic politics consists of whole government programs that are ostensibly designed to achieve one set of objectives but are actually designed to achieve other objectives (in some cases simply the re-election of the politicians who can claim credit for them).

Take as an example the crime bills passed by Congress in the 1980s and 1990s, with their mandatory-minimum sentences, their three-strikes-and-you're-out provisions, and their extension of the federal death penalty to fifty new crimes. The anti-drug and anti-crime legislation, by the testimony of judges and legal scholars, has been at best useless and at worst wholly pernicious in its effects, in that it has filled prison cells not with violent criminals but with drug users and low-level drug pushers. As for the death penalty, a simple measure of its sheer irrelevance to the federal government's war on crime is easily provided. The last federal offender to be put to death, Victor H. Feguer, a convicted kidnapper, was hanged in March of 1963. By the end of 1995 no federal offender had been executed for more than thirty years, and hardly any offenders were awaiting execution on death row. The ferocious-seeming federal statutes were almost entirely for show.

The way in which the wars on drugs and crime were fought cannot be understood without taking into account the incessant pressure that elected officeholders felt they were under from the electorate. As one former congressman puts it, "Voters were afraid of criminals, and politicians were afraid of voters." This fear reached panic proportions in election years. Seven of the years from 1981 to 1994 were election years nationwide; seven were not. During those fourteen years Congress passed no fewer than seven major crime bills. Of those seven, six were passed in election years (usually late in the year). That is, there was only one election year in which a major crime bill was *not* passed, and only one nonelection year in which a major crime bill *was* passed.

Another effect of the extreme vulnerability of American politicians is that it is even harder for them than for democratically elected politicians in other countries to take tough decisions: to court unpopularity, to ask for sacrifices, to impose losses, to fly in the face of conventional wisdom—in short, to act in what they believe to be their constituents' interest and the national interest rather than in their own interest. Timothy J. Penny, a Democrat who left the House of Representatives in 1994, put the point starkly, perhaps even too harshly, in *Common Cents* (1995).

> Voters routinely punish lawmakers who try to do unpopular things, who challenge them to face unpleasant truths about the budget, crime, Social Security, or tax policy. Similarly, voters reward politicians for giving them what they want—more spending for popular programs—even if it means wounding the nation in the long run by creating more debt....

What, if Anything, Might Be Done?

Precisely because American politicians are so exposed electorally, they probably have to display—and do display—more political courage more often than the politicians of any other democratic country. The number of political saints and martyrs in the United States is unusually large.

There is, however, no special virtue in a political system that requires large numbers of politicians to run the risk of martyrdom in order to ensure that tough decisions can be taken in a timely manner in the national interest. The number of such decisions that need to be taken is always likely to be large;

human nature being what it is, the supply of would-be martyrs is always likely to be small. On balance it would seem better not to try to eliminate the electoral risks (it can never be done in a democracy) but to reduce somewhat their scale and intensity. There is no reason why the risks run by American politicians should be so much greater than the risks run by elective politicians in other democratic countries.

How, then, might the risks be reduced? What can be done? A number of reforms to the existing system suggest themselves. It may be that none of them is politically feasible—Americans hold tight to the idea of agency democracy —but in principle there should be no bar to any of them. One of the simplest would also be the most radical: to lengthen the terms of members of the House of Representatives from two years to four. The proposal is by no means a new one: at least 123 resolutions bearing on the subject were introduced in Congress in the eighty years from 1885 to 1965, and President Lyndon B. Johnson advocated the change in his State of the Union address in January of 1966.

A congressman participating in a Brookings Institution round table held at about the time of Johnson's message supported the change, saying, "I think that the four years would help you to be a braver congressman, and I think what you need is bravery. I think you need courage." Another congressman on the same occasion cited the example of another bill that he believed had the support of a majority in the House. "That bill is not going to come up this year. You know why it is not coming up? . . . Because four hundred and thirty-five of us have to face election. . . . If we had a four-year term, I am as confident as I can be the bill would have come to the floor and passed."

A similar case could be made for extending the term of senators to eight years, with half the Senate retiring or running for re-election every four years. If the terms of members of both houses were thus extended and made to coincide, the effect in reducing America's never-ending election campaign would be dramatic.

There is much to be said, too, for all the reasons mentioned so far, for scaling down the number of primary elections. They absorb extravagant amounts of time, energy, and money; they serve little democratic purpose; few people bother to vote in them; and they place additional and unnecessary pressure on incumbent officeholders. Since the main disadvantage of primaries is the adverse effect they have on incumbents, any reforms probably ought to be concerned with protecting incumbents' interests.

At the moment, the primary laws make no distinction between situations in which a seat in the House or the Senate is already occupied and situations in which the incumbent is, for whatever reason, standing down. The current laws provide for a primary to be held in either case. An incumbent is therefore treated as though the seat in question were open and he or she were merely one of the candidates for it. A relatively simple reform would be to distinguish between the two situations. If a seat was open, primaries would be held in both parties, as now; but if the incumbent announced that he or she intended to run for re-election, then a primary in his or her party would be held only if large numbers of party supporters were determined to have one—that is, were determined that the incumbent should be ousted. The obvious way to ascertain whether such determination existed would be by means of a petition supervised by the relevant state government and requiring a considerable number of signatures. The possibility of a primary would thus be left open, but those who wanted one would have to show that they were both numerous and serious. A primary would not be held simply because an ambitious, possibly demented, possibly wealthy individual decided to throw his or her hat into the ring.

Any steps to strengthen the parties as institutions would be desirable on the same grounds. Lack of party cover in the United States means that elective officeholders find it hard to take tough decisions partly because they lack safety in numbers. They can seldom, if ever, say to an aggrieved constituent or a political-action committee out for revenge, "I had to vote that way because my party told me to," or even "I had to vote that way because we in my party all agreed that we would." Lack of party cohesion, together with American voters' disposition to vote for the individual rather than the party, means that congressmen and senators are always in danger of being picked off one by one.

Ballot Fatigue

What might be done to give both parties more backbone? Clearly, the parties would be strengthened—and elective officeholders would not need to raise so much money for their own campaigns—if each party organization became a major source of campaign funding. In the unlikely event (against the background of chronic budget deficits) that Congress ever gets around to authorizing the federal funding of congressional election campaigns, a strong case could be made for channeling as much of the money as possible through the parties, and setting aside some of it to cover their administrative and other ongoing costs.

The party organizations and the nexus between parties and their candidates would also be strengthened if it were made easier for ordinary citizens to give money to the parties and for the parties to give money to their candidates. Until 1986, when the program was abolished, tax credits were available for taxpayers who contributed small sums to the political parties. These credits could be restored. Larry J. Sabato, a political scientist at the University of Virginia, has similarly suggested that citizens entitled to a tax refund could be allowed to divert a small part of their refund to the party of their choice. Such measures would not, however, reduce candidates' dependence on donations from wealthy individuals and PACs [political action committees] unless they were accompanied by measures enabling the parties to contribute more generously to their candidates' campaigns. At the moment there are strict legal limits on the amount of money that national or state party organizations can contribute to the campaigns of individual candidates. The limits should be raised (and indexed to inflation). There is even a case for abolishing them altogether.

All that said, there is an even more straightforward way of reducing incumbents' dependence on campaign contributions. At present incumbents have to spend so much time raising funds because the campaigns themselves are so expensive. They could be made cheaper. This, of course, would be one of the effects of making U.S. elections less numerous and less frequent than they are now. Another way to lower the cost of elections would be to provide candidates and parties with free air time on television and radio.

POSTSCRIPT

Do Political Campaigns Promote Good Government?

The right of people to choose their governors is the essence of democracy. In that spirit Popkin argues that Americans need more democracy—that is, more participation by the people, inspired by more campaigning and political education. Roderick P. Hart, in *Campaign Talk: Why Elections Are Good for Us* (Princeton University Press, 2000), endorses the view that campaigns inform us, explain the concerns of others, and encourage voting, or at least a heightened sense of the political world. King vigorously dissents, asserting that America has an excess of democracy and that the burden imposed by so many and so frequent elections is too great and leads to disillusion and nonvoting.

Catherine Shaw, a three-term mayor of Ashland, Oregon, has written an illuminating how-to book on political campaigning entitled *The Campaign Manager: Running and Winning Local Elections,* 2d ed. (Westview Press, 2000). Shaw's book provides some support for those who value campaigns for the information and understanding that they provide for voters as well as for those who bemoan the time and effort it takes to run for office.

In order to stimulate greater voter participation, beginning in 1972 radical reforms were adopted to ensure that the presidential nominees of the two major parties would be those favored by the largest proportion of party members participating in the primaries and caucuses in which the national convention delegates were chosen. The local party organization plays a greatly reduced role because it no longer hand-picks the delegates. The national convention plays a greatly reduced role because it no longer engages in any real deliberation regarding the choice of nominee. For better or worse, the electorate gets the presidential candidate endorsed by the largest number of delegates.

More directly, the people vote in primaries in order to designate candidates for all other elective offices. This means that voters are exposed to more and longer campaigns; they should therefore be motivated and informed both in the long primary campaign before the party choices are made and in the months leading up to the election before the officeholders are chosen.

A classic text that provides an overview of presidential campaigns is Nelson W. Polsby and Aaron Wildavsky, *Presidential Elections: Strategies and Structures of American Politics,* 10th ed. (Chatham House, 2000). Ever since Theodore White began his distinguished series of vivid accounts with *The Making of the President 1960* (Atheneum, 1961), each presidential election has produced a spate of books providing insightful analysis and insider revelations regarding the conduct of the campaign. One of the best is Richard Ben Cramer, *What It Takes: The Way to the White House* (Random House, 1992). In the tradition of White's intimate journalism is Bob Woodward's account of the 1996 presidential campaigns of President Bill Clinton and Senator Bob Dole, *The Choice: How Clinton Won* (Simon & Schuster, 1997).

ISSUE 3

Are the New Limits on Campaign Spending Justified?

YES: Paul D. Wellstone, from Remarks on the Need for Campaign Finance Reform, U.S. Senate (September 9, 1998)

NO: John Samples, from "Making the World Safer for Incumbents: The Consequences of McCain-Feingold-Cochran," *Policy Analysis No. 393* (March 14, 2001)

ISSUE SUMMARY

YES: Paul D. Wellstone, a Democratic senator from Minnesota, argues that the new campaign spending reform legislation constitutes an "enormous step forward" in lessening the undue power of wealthy special interests in U.S. elections.

NO: John Samples, director of the Cato Institute's Center for Representative Government, predicts that the new campaign finance law will reduce voter turnout, make it more difficult for challengers to win against incumbents, and stifle free speech.

The amounts spent on American political campaigns have been rising steadily for decades, but the 2000 race shattered all records. About $3 billion was spent on the presidential and congressional races, another $1 billion on state contests, and perhaps hundreds of millions by outside groups who did not have to account for their expenditures. The fundraising and spending continued during the 2002 election season.

What is wrong with this increased spending? A great deal, say those who believe that rampant spending on political campaigns discourages less-wealthy citizens from seeking office, diverts office-holders from doing their real jobs, gives disproportionate power to special interests, and turns off voters who suspect that money influences policy more than votes do. These were among the principal arguments made by advocates of the campaign finance bill signed into law by President George W. Bush on March 27, 2002. For supporters of the bill, one of the biggest loopholes in the existing system of campaign finance regulation was that it allowed unlimited amounts of "soft money" to flow into campaigns. Soft money is money that is contributed not to individual campaigns but to political parties, ostensibly for the purpose of "party-building" activities, such as get-out-the-vote drives. The Federal Election Commission (FEC), an agency created in 1974, began allowing this practice in 1978, and within a decade fund-raisers in both parties began to realize its usefulness as a way around existing contribution limits. Under then-existing law, "hard money" contributions (funds contributed directly to the campaigns of particular candidates) were limited to $1,000 per person for each candidate; the assumption was that no candidate can be "bought" for a mere $1,000. But unlimited soft money allowed wealthy donors and interest groups to contribute huge sums to the parties at dinners, coffees and other such gatherings—thus subtly (or not-so-subtly) reminding them of who was buttering their bread. Another concern of those who supported the new law was what they saw as the misuse of "issue advocacy" during campaigns. Interest groups had been able to get around the legal limits on contributions by pouring millions of unregulated dollars into "attack" ads that did not explicitly ask people to vote for or against a candidate. Instead, they said something like "Call Senator Smith and tell him to stop supporting polluters."

The new law sought to plug these loopholes and to bring the existing system of federal campaign finance regulation up-to-date. Among its major provisions are the following:

- A ban on soft money contributions to the national political parties.
- An increase in hard money contribution limits. For example, limits to individual candidates were increased from $1,000 to $2,000 per candidate per election. The increase was meant to take inflation into account.
- Restrictions on the ability of corporations, labor unions, and other interest groups to run "issue ads" featuring the names or likenesses of candidates within 60 days of a general election and 30 days of a primary election.

Even though the new law was not to go into effect until after the 2002 elections, opponents wasted no time in challenging it. Despite President Bush's signature on it, the Republican National Committee sued in federal court, as did both parties in California, the AFL-CIO, and dozens of others. Objections to the law included charges that its restrictions on "issue ads" violated free speech rights, that it interfered with the operation of state and local parties, and that it unconstitutionally favored incumbents and wealthy candidates.

In an earlier debate on the bill that later became the law, Paul D. Wellstone argued that it represented a major first step toward leveling the electoral playing field by preventing rich, powerful interest groups from dominating the process. His argument is presented in the following selection, followed by the argument of John Samples, who contends that the new law will actually reduce electoral competition by suppressing free speech and making it more difficult for challengers to win against incumbents.

 **YES**

Floor Statement of Senator Paul D. Wellstone

Mr. President, let me thank my colleagues. I thank Senator Levin for his remarks. I thank him for his unbelievable dedication in trying to push through reform legislation. He has been at this a long time. This is the time to do it; I agree with my colleague. We have an opportunity. We have a bill that was passed on the House side. It is a bipartisan measure. We have a public that is calling for the change. And I agree with you, I say to the Senator; now is the time to pass this legislation.

I also thank my colleagues, Senator McCain, Republican from Arizona, and Senator Feingold, Democrat from Wisconsin. I have a special kind of affection for both of my colleagues. I think Senator McCain is principled; he speaks out for what he believes in; he is a courageous legislator. I think Senator Feingold has emerged here in the U.S. Senate as a leading reformer. He is my neighbor. I am a Senator from Minnesota, and I tell you, people from Minnesota who follow Russ Feingold's work have a tremendous amount of respect for him. I am honored to be an original cosponsor of this legislation.

I do not know exactly where to get started. It is interesting. Senator Barry Goldwater told it like it is. I went to Senator Goldwater's service in Arizona, not because I was necessarily in agreement with him on all the issues. As a matter of fact, some of my good friends, Republican colleagues, who were on the plane with me kept giving me Barry Goldwater's book "Conscience of a Conservative" and kept telling me if I had read that book when I was 15 I would be going down the right path. I told them I did read the book when I was 15. I just reached different conclusions.

Senator Goldwater about a decade ago said:

> The fact that liberty depended on honest elections was of the utmost importance to the patriots who founded our nation and wrote the Constitution. They knew that corruption destroyed the prime requisite of constitutional liberty, an independent legislature free from any influence other than that of the people. Applying these principles to modern times, we can make the following conclusions. To be successful, representative government assumes that elections will be controlled by the citizenry at large, not by those who

From Paul D. Wellstone, Remarks on the Need for Campaign Finance Reform, U.S. Senate (September 9, 1998).

give the most money. Electors must believe their vote counts. Elected officials must owe their allegiance to the people, not to their own wealth or to the wealth of interest groups who speak only for the selfish fringes of the whole community.

Let me just start out with some examples. I was involved in a debate here on the floor of the Senate last week which was emotional. It was kind of heart rending. You had a small group of people who were sitting where some of our citizens are sitting today. And they were from Sierra Blanca. They were disproportionately poor. They were Hispanic. And you know what? They were saying, "How come when it comes to the question of where a nuclear waste dump site goes, it's put in our community?" How come it always seems to be the case that when we figure out what to do with these incinerators or where to put these power lines or where to dump this waste, it almost always goes to the communities where people don't make the big contributions? They are not the heavy hitters. They are disproportionately poor, disproportionately communities of color; thus, the question of environmental justice.

This was a debate where you had the interests of big money, big contributors, corporate utilities, versus low-income minority communities. I would argue different colleagues voted for different reasons, and some voted because it was not their State and they felt a certain kind of, if you will, deference to Senators from other States. I understand that. But my point is a little different.

I tell you that all too often the conclusion is sort of predetermined. Those who have the clout and those who make the big contributions are the ones who have the influence, and those are the ones we listen to. All too often, a whole lot of citizens—in this particular case, the people from Sierra Blanca—are not listened to at all. Big money prevails, special interests prevail, for the same reason that the people in Sierra Blanca cannot get a fair shake in Texas. That is to say, they do not give the big contributions, they do not have the political clout. For the same reason, they could not get a fair shake here in the U.S. Senate.

In about 20 minutes I am going to be at a meeting with some colleagues from the Midwest. We have an economic convulsion in agriculture. Let me wear my political scientist hat. I really believe that when people look back to 1998, 1999, going into the next century, and raise questions about our economy—because I fear that we are going to be faced with some very difficult times—they are going to be looking at this crisis in agriculture as a sort of precursor.

What has happened in agriculture is record low prices. Not everybody who is watching the debate comes from a State where agriculture is as important as it is in the State of Minnesota, the State I come from. But let me say to people who are listening to the debate, if you are a corn grower and you are getting $1.40 for a bushel of corn, you can be the best manager in the world, you can work from 5 in the morning until midnight, but you and your family will never make it. You will never make it. Record low prices. People are having to give up. They are just leaving. The farm is not only where they work, it is where they live.

It is interesting that we had a farm bill, the 1996 farm bill. It was called the Freedom to Farm bill. I called it then the "freedom to fail" bill. It was a great bill—I am not saying anything on the floor of the Senate that I have not said a million times over in the last 2 years. It was a great bill for the grain companies because what this piece of legislation essentially said to family farmers is, "We're no longer going to give you a loan rate. We're going to cap the loan rate at such a low level that you won't have the bargaining power."

This sounds a little technocratic, but to make a long story short, you have family farmers faced with a monopoly when it comes to whom they sell their grain to. If they do not have some kind of loan rate that the Government guarantees that brings the price to a certain level, they have no bargaining power in the marketplace.

Not surprisingly, the prices have plummeted. There is no safety net whatsoever. And now we see in our part of the country, in the Midwest, a family farm structure of agriculture which is in real peril. We see an economic convulsion. We see many family farmers who are going to be driven off the land.

We are going to be coming to the floor of the Senate—you better believe we are going to be coming to the floor of the Senate—and we are going to be saying to our colleagues, "Look, you could have been for the 'freedom to fail' bill or not, but there's going to have to be a modification. You are going to have to cap off the loan rate, and we're going to have to get the prices up for family farmers."

I would argue that in 1996—and I hope this will not be the debate again—what was going on here was a farm bill that was written by and for big corporate agribusiness interests. That is what it was. It was a great bill for the grain companies, but it was a disaster for family farmers. So we are going to revisit this debate. And once again, is it going to be the grain companies and the big food processors and the big chemical companies and the transportation companies, or is it going to be the family farmers? I hope it will be the family farmers. I hope our appeal to fairness and justice will work on the floor of the U.S. Senate.

But I tell you, all too often, as I look at these different issues in these different debates, it is no wonder, as Senator Levin said, that people are so disappointed and disillusioned with both political parties. It is no wonder that people do not register and do not vote. Because you know what? They have reached the conclusion that if you pay, you play, and if you do not pay, you do not play.

They have reached the conclusion that this political process isn't their political process. I mean, my God, what happens in a representative democracy when people reach the conclusion that they are not stakeholders in the system, that when it comes to their concerns about themselves, about their families and their communities, their concerns are of little concern in the corridors of power in Washington? This is really dangerous. What is at stake is nothing less than our very noble, wonderful, 222-year experiment in self-rule and representative democracy.

That is what it is really all about.

Now, let me give some other examples. We went through a debate about whether or not we were going to do anything to provide our children with some protection from being addicted to tobacco. Guess what happened? Tobacco companies, huge contributors, individual contributions to Senators and

Representatives, big soft money, hundreds of thousands of dollars of contributions to the party, and guess what happened? As a special favor to those big tobacco interests, we didn't even provide our children with sensible protection.

I fear as a special favor to the big insurance companies we are not going to eventually provide patients with the kind of protection that they need. I fear that as a special favor to those bottom dwellers of commerce who don't want to raise the minimum wage, we are not even going to raise the minimum wage for hard-pressed working people.

What I see over and over and over again is a political process hijacked by and dominated by big money. I tell you, that is the opposite of the very idea of representative democracy, because the idea of representative democracy is that each person counts as one and no more than one.

What we have instead is something quite different. Let's just think for a moment about what is on the table and what is not on the table, because I think this mix of money and politics, this is the ethical issue of our time. We are not talking about corruption as in the wrongdoing of individual office holders; we are talking about systematic corruption. What systematic corruption is all about is when too few people have the wealth, the power, and the vast majority of people are locked out. Some people march on Washington every day and other people have a voice that is never heard.

Let's just think a little bit about what is on the table and what is not on the table. I think quite often money determines who runs for office. I will talk about who wins, what issues are put on the table, what passes, what doesn't. Let's talk about what is not on the table and maybe should be on the table. What is not on the table is the concentration of power in certain key sectors of our economy which poses such a threat to consumers in America.

Think for a moment about the concentration of power in the telecommunications industry. If there is anything more important than the flow of information in a democracy, I don't know what it is. This is so important to us. Now, we had a telecommunications bill that passed a couple years ago, which, by the way, I think has led to more monopoly. What was interesting is that the anteroom right outside our Chamber was packed wall to wall. You couldn't get in here if you tried to get through that anteroom. Personally, I couldn't find truth, beauty and justice anywhere. There was a group of people representing a billion dollars here, another group of people representing a billion dollars over there. You name it.

What is not on the table is a concentration of power in financial services or a concentration of power in agriculture or all the ways in which conglomerates have muscled their way to the dinner table and are taking over the food industry. What is not on the table is a concentration of power in the health care system, the way in which just a few insurance companies can own and control most of the managed care plans in the United States of America.

Again, I would say that we are moving toward this new century. I hope the brave new world isn't two airline companies. I come from a State where we now have a strike. In Minnesota we don't have a lot of choice. We can't walk from Minnesota to Washington, DC. Northwest Airlines has 85 percent of the flights in and out. What are we going to have—two airlines, two banks, two oil companies, one supermarket, two financial institutions, two health care plans? It is interesting that this isn't even on the table here. Could it be that these powerful economic interests are able to preempt some of the debate and some of the discussion by virtue of the huge contributions they can make with the soft money loophole that can add up to hundreds of thousands of dollars?

What is not on the table is, I argue, a frightening maldistribution of wealth and income in America. The goal of both political parties, the goal of political leaders, ought to be to improve the standard of living of all the people. Since we started collecting social science data, we have the greatest maldistribution of wealth and income we have ever had in our country. You don't hear a word about it. It is important for people, if they work hard, to be able to participate in the life of our country. It is important for people to be able to receive the fruits of their labor.

We have this huge maldistribution of wealth and income. We are not even going to discuss it. Could it be that some of the people who are the most hard-pressed citizens in this country have basically become invisible? They are out of sight; they are out of mind. They don't have lobbyists. They don't make the big contributions. They don't even register to vote because they don't think either political party has much to say to them. They think both parties have been taken over by the same investors. Unfortunately, there is some truth to that. Unfortunately, we have given people entirely too much justification for that point of view.

What is not on the table? What is not on the table is a set of social arrangements that allow children to be the most poverty-stricken group in America. One out of every four children under the age of 3 is growing up poor in America. One out of every two children of color under the age of 3 is growing up poor in America today. That is a national scandal. That is a betrayal of our heritage. Certainly we can do much better.

Now, there are organizations like the Children's Defense Fund. They do great work. But it is a very unequal fight. It comes to whether or not you are going to have hundreds of billions of dollars of what we call tax expenditures —tax loopholes and deductions, corporation welfare, money that goes to all sorts of financial interests, some of the largest financial institutions, some of the largest corporations in America—or whether or not we are going to make a commitment to make sure that every child has the same opportunity to reach his or her full potential. This is the core issue. I am convinced that so many good things that could happen here get "trumped" by the way in which money dominates politics.

Now, the House has passed a good campaign finance reform bill, the Shays-Meehan proposal. It is not everything that some of us would have liked. As a matter of fact, what is interesting is that the original McCain-Feingold bill applied to Senate races. I thought that was one of the most important things. We had voluntary spending caps—you can't mandate it—and at the same time an exchange for media time. That is gone. That was really important. So we are talking about a proposal that is a milder proposal, but it is an enormous step forward. It is an enormous step forward.

There are other things that are going on in the country that I am excited about, that I wish for, that I think eventually we will get to. The clean money, clean election bill that some of us have introduced here on the Senate side is an exciting proposal. We have a lot of energy behind it at the State level. I think New York City will pass it. I think the State of Massachusetts will pass it. The State of Maine already did pass it. The State of Vermont passed it. There are initiatives in other States.

Basically, with the clean money, clean election proposal, we get the big private money out. You say to the citizen, listen, for $5 a year, would you be willing to contribute to a clean money, clean election trust fund? And then those candidates who abide by spending limits and don't raise the private money, this money goes to their campaigns. You have a level playing field, and you own the elections, and you own your State capitol, and you don't have all of this mix of big money in politics. A lot of people in the country really like this proposal. I think the political problem here is we are not ready for it yet because the system is wired. It is wired to people who can raise the big money, and quite often, they are the incumbents.

And a lot of people don't like to vote out a system that benefits them. But the McCain-Feingold bill represents a very important step forward—following on the heels of a really exciting victory in the House of Representatives. It is very important, very similar. It bans the soft money as my colleague, Senator Levin—and there is nobody with more intellectual capital in this area— discussed. Senator Levin knows all of the specifics. I am so impressed with him as a legislator, with his ability. He talked about it. I will just say that this is a huge loophole. It is all very amorphous.

Corporations and unions can make these huge soft money contributions. We all end up calling for this money now because everybody is trapped by the same rotten system. It restricts issue advocacy, these phony issue ads that are disguised as not really election ads. I went through this. I don't mean this in the spirit of whining, but it started in 1996, in the spring in Minnesota, and it went on all summer. There were all of these ads that would come on TV and they bash you for this and bash you for that, but they don't say "vote against" whether you are Democrat or Republican; they just say "call." It is unbelievable. They could be financed by soft money. A huge loophole, huge problem. This bill codifies the Beck Supreme Court decision requiring unions to notify their dues-paying members of their right to disallow political use of their dues. It improves disclosure and FEC [Federal Election Commission] enforcement. This bill would represent a substantial step forward.

Mr. President, there is a wonderful speech that was given by Bill Moyers in December of 1997, the title of which is "The Soul of Democracy." I want to quote from part of Bill Moyers' speech:

> If Carrie Bolton were here tonight, she could speak to this. The Reverend Carrie Bolton from North Carolina. You'd have a hard time seeing her because she is only so high and her head would barely reach the microphone. But you would hear her, of that I'm sure. The state legislature in North Carolina established a commission to look at campaign financing, and Carrie Bolton came to one of the hearings. She listened patiently as one speaker

after another addressed the commissioners. And then it was her time. She spoke softly at first. Then the passion rose, and her words mesmerized her audience. When Carrie Bolton finished, they stood and cheered. This is what she said; listen to what Carrie Bolton said:

> "I was born to a mother and father married to each other, who were sharecroppers, who proceeded to have ten children. I picked cotton, which made some people rich... I pulled tobacco... I shook peanuts... I dug up potatoes and picked cucumbers, and I went to school... with enthusiasm. And with great enthusiasm I memorized the Preamble to the Constitution of the United States, I learned the Pledge of Allegiance to the flag, and I was inspired to believe that somehow those things symbolized hope for me against any odds I might come upon.
>
> "I am a divorcee, a single parent divorcee, and I earn enough money to take care of my two children and myself. And I have managed to get a high school diploma, a bachelor's degree, two master's degrees, and do post doctoral work.
>
> "I am energetic. I'm smart. I'm intelligent.
>
> "But a snowball would stand a better chance surviving in hell than I would running for political office in this country. Because I have no money. My family has no money. My friends do not have money.
>
> "Yet, I have ideas. I'm strong, I am powerful (with her right hand she lifts her left wrist)—people can feel my pulse. People who are working, and working hard, can feel what I feel.
>
> "But I can't tell them because I don't know how to get the spotlight to tell them.
>
> "Because I have no money."

Anyone who believes Carrie Bolton's cry isn't coming from the soul of democracy is living in a fool's paradise—a rich fool's paradise.

That is from Bill Moyers' speech. He is my hero journalist. I think he has done some of the finest work. He concludes his speech by saying this:

> I have three grandchildren—Henry, 5; Thomas, 3; and 10-month-old Nancy Judith. I want them to grow up in a healthy, civil society, one where their political worth is not measured by their net worth.

That is one of the reasons Bill Moyers goes on to argue that this is his passion, this is his work. He is right. This is the core issue.

Now, Mr. President, I don't know that I would have the eloquence of Carrie Bolton, but I conclude this way because I see other colleagues who may want to speak. I can't forget my own experience. It is not quite Carrie Bolton's experience, but I ran for office in 1990, and it was amazing. I mean, you don't come to the floor to brag, but you don't run for office if you don't think you have the character and ideas. Basically, everywhere I went, the argument was made, "you don't have a chance." I was a teacher, so I didn't have much money. My father was an unsuccessful writer. My mother was a cafeteria worker, a food service worker. My family didn't have any money. My wife Sheila worked in the library at the high school. Everywhere I would go—including on the Democrat side, not just the Republican side—people were trying to decide whether or not I was a viable candidate. It had nothing to do with content of character, nothing to do with ideas, nothing to do with leadership potential, and it had nothing to do with positions on issues. People just wanted to know how much money you raised. You were viable or you weren't viable. You were a good candidate or you were a bad one based upon how much money you yourself had— and I didn't have it—or how much money you would raise.

It is unbelievable, absolutely unbelievable. There are so many people who can't run for that reason alone. I was lucky. I come from Minnesota, and I am emotional about how much I owe to them. They were an exception to the rule. We were outspent six or seven to one, and we won. Sometimes it happens —if you have a great green schoolbus to campaign in and a great grassroots organization.

I am the son of a Jewish immigrant who fled persecution from Russia. We have had a 222-year, bold, important experiment in self-rule in democracy, representative democracy. That is what is at jeopardy here. I have talked to people about potentially running for office. They don't want to. A lot of people, good people, don't want to run for office any longer because they can't stand the thought of this money chase. They can't stand doing it. Moreover, if you combine what the money is used for, with communication technology becoming the weapon of electoral conflict, people using the money for poison politics, all the attack stuff on TV, a lot of very good, sane people don't run.

I think what is happening is a lot of good people aren't going to be involved in public affairs. A lot of young people are not going to get involved in public affairs. You get to where people are either millionaires or they have to raise millions of dollars. I think you get into this awful self-select where a whole lot of good men and women aren't going to run at all. I am not going to cite the polls because we have the evidence for this. Everybody knows it. Every Democrat and Republican knows full well that people are disengaged and disillusioned with politics in this country, and this is one of the central reasons.

So, Mr. President, I simply say to my colleagues that we have a piece of legislation on the floor that follows up on an exciting victory in the House of Representatives, and we need to pass this legislation. I also say to my colleagues —Democrats and Republicans alike—frankly, I can't figure out the opposition. People want to see this changed. People just hate the way in which they feel like money dominates politics. Those of us in office, and even those of us who are challenged for office, hate it. We hate raising the money; we hate this system. I would think if we wanted the people we represent to have more confidence and faith in us, more confidence and faith in this political process, more confidence and faith in the U.S. Senate, we would vote for the McCain-Feingold piece of legislation.

So the debate will go on. We will have this vote.

I say to my colleagues on the other side—which doesn't mean just Republicans because there are some Republicans who support this legislation—that I think they are making a big mistake filibustering. From my point of view, this should go on and on for the next however many weeks it takes. I don't think we should drop this one. This is the core issue. This is the core question. It speaks to all the issues that are important to people's lives. It speaks as to whether or not we are going to have a functioning democracy or not.

As a Senator from Minnesota, from a good government State, from a reform State, from a progressive State, there is no more important position that I can take than to be for this reform legislation.

NO ⬅

John Samples

Making the World Safer
for Incumbents

We're told that Americans are spending more and more money on elections. In 2000 candidates, parties, and outside groups spent about $4 billion on all elections. David Broder of the *Washington Post* noted that soft money—funds raised and spent outside the strictures of federal campaign finance law—increased to $410 million in 2000, a 40 percent increase since 1996.

That increase in spending nettles activists seeking new restrictions on campaign fundraising and spending. Senators McCain, Feingold, and Cochran have introduced legislation to prohibit solicitation of soft money for political parties. The bill also bans election advertising by unions and corporations within 60 days of an election. Some observers believe that the legislation may pass and become the first major revision of federal campaign finance law in almost three decades. [The legislation passed Congress and was signed into law by President George W. Bush on March 27, 2002.—Eds.]

McCain-Feingold-Cochran assumes, wrongly, that soft money corrupts American politics. Banning soft money would have consequences for the nation that campaign finance "reformers" themselves would not want. The prohibition of advertising by labor unions and corporations protects incumbents from attacks and unconstitutionally restricts political speech. Instead of introducing new restrictions, Congress should focus on liberating American elections from current restrictions on speech.

The Origins of Soft Money

The term "soft money" denotes essentially all political contributions not given directly to candidates or their campaigns. Soft money is largely unregulated by federal election law. McCain-Feingold-Cochran takes aim initially at soft money raised and spent by the nation's two major political parties. The three senators and their allies argue that soft money constitutes a giant loophole in the campaign finance laws, a nefarious way around good regulations. The regulatory and legal origins of soft money suggest another story.

The Federal Election Campaign Act [FECA] imposed strict limits on money in politics. It imposed ceilings on contributions accepted by candidates from

From John Samples, "Making the World Safer for Incumbents: The Consequences of McCain-Feingold-Cochran," *Policy Analysis No. 393* (March 14, 2001). Copyright © 2001 by The Cato Institute. Reprinted by permission. Notes omitted.

individuals and from political action committees (PACs) and continued existing prohibitions on federal election contributions from corporations and labor unions. The law also put constraints on the sums parties could spend directly supporting candidates. For the first eight years of FECA (1971–79), only "hard money" in national elections was governed by federal law.

State regulation of campaign finance (then and now) is generally less restrictive than FECA. Often states have few, if any, limits on contributions or expenditures. Of course, most people assumed in the 1970s that the ambit of state regulations on campaign finance was severely limited since they applied only to state and local elections. Until the late 1970s, the relative liberality of state rules seemed irrelevant beside the massive reach and strict constraints of FECA.

Congress and the Federal Election Commission [FEC] made state regulations matter. In 1978 the FEC ruled that the Republican State Committee of Kansas could use corporate and union contributions, which were legal under state law, to conduct a voter turnout effort that helped both federal and non-federal candidates. That FEC ruling meant that both national and state party committees could spend and raise money partially under the authority of state law and thus partially outside the limits set by FECA.

In 1979 Congress amended FECA and loosened certain expenditure ceilings on "grassroots" activities. The new amendments allowed party organizations to spend unlimited sums on voter registration, some campaign materials, and voter turnout programs. Inevitably, such spending aided both national and state election campaigns. Congress loosened the limits to permit party-building activities and to get citizens involved in politics. Those two decisions by Congress and the FEC are the legal origins of soft money.

In 1991 the FEC issued new regulations concerning soft money. Those rules both required disclosure of the sources and disbursements of soft money and established complex formulas for allocating those funds between state and national purposes. The new regulations did not impose ceilings on soft money contributions or expenditures.

Contrary to the claims made by Senator McCain and his allies, soft money is not an evil force working to undermine the purity of American politics. It is not a quasi-legal "loophole" in the campaign finance laws. Soft money came into existence because the FEC honored the federal nature of American politics and because Congress tried to encourage state and local political activities. Most Americans would support both goals. . . .

The Question of Corruption

Political corruption is more than just an effective slogan for campaign finance regulators. Corruption or the appearance of corruption is the legal foundation for regulating campaign fundraising. In its landmark decision in *Buckley v. Valeo*, the U.S. Supreme Court recognized that in modern society political speech and money are inherently tied together. Regulating campaign finance thus encroaches on essential First Amendment freedoms. The only legitimate reason to limit such freedoms, the Court said, would be to prevent "corruption or the appearance of corruption." Such corruption, however, is more asserted than proved.

To assess the idea that campaign finance fosters corruption, we might begin by categorizing possible types of corruption. First, there is direct bribery. Public officials are certainly corrupt when they provide political favors in exchange for bribes. This kind of corruption of American national politics is rare if we judge by the relatively few indictments and convictions of sitting members of Congress.

A second type of corruption might be called indirect bribery. Legislators may be deemed corrupt if they cast their votes in Congress to advance the interests of their contributors. Such influence is difficult to prove. After all, most contributors give to candidates whose policy views they share. We can hardly conclude that contributors corrupt a legislator who would have voted the same way on an issue in the absence of the contribution. In any case, political scientists have found that campaign contributions have little effect on legislative votes.

Perhaps Senator McCain believes that soft money leads to the indirect bribery of legislators. Yet soft money accounts for only 15 percent of total national campaign funds raised. Moreover, individual legislators do not depend directly on soft money. Because it goes to the political parties, soft money has at most an indirect influence on legislators.

The idea of indirect bribery is based on the false premise that the need for campaign funds is the most important influence on legislators. In contrast, political scientists assume that officeholders give primacy to being reelected. Being reelected requires a majority of votes, not the greatest success in fundraising. Gaining election is the end to which fundraising is the means. Providing favors to contributors might well threaten the goal of being elected. Accordingly, we should expect that legislators would not sell their votes to contributors if doing so would jeopardize success at the polls.

If corruption is defined as direct or indirect bribery, the case for regulating core First Amendment activities such as making campaign contributions seems weak. Even advocates of new regulations do not contend that much direct bribery exists. We also have little reason to think that indirect bribery is a big problem.

Advocates of new campaign finance regulations equate corruption with what they see as the "undue influence" of contributors. They argue that large contributions "distort" the legislative process and prevent representatives from acting in the true interests of their constituents. Absent money, members of Congress would attend to those interests and probably support "progressive" causes. Let us consider each of those claims.

All political participation, including the making of campaign contributions, tries to influence policy choices. The Constitution does not contain a metric enabling us to distinguish "proper" and "improper" influence. In fact, restricting fundamental freedoms to achieve equality of influence is not permitted by the Constitution. As the Supreme Court noted in *Buckley*, "[T]he concept that government may restrict the speech of some elements of our society in order to enhance the relative voice of others is wholly foreign to the First Amendment."

Assertions of "distortion" assume too much. Saying that contributions distort legislating implies movement away from an ideal or a proper state of being. In this case, advocates seem to assume that money corrupts the judgment of an ideal representative who but for contributions would act on the true interests of her constituents.

The American political tradition does not have one agreed-on concept of representation; in fact, at least three different conceptions inform our politics and political theory. *Pluralists* see American politics as a struggle in which ambitious and self-interested citizens seek influence through effective organizing and vigorous advocacy. Representatives make policy in response to those efforts by individuals and groups. In contrast, *Burkeans* argue that elected officials should act as trustees for their constituents and deliberate impartially about the public good. *Populists* suggest that lawmakers should eschew the views of contributors and vote only on the basis of the preferences of their constituents.

Looked at this way, McCain-Feingold-Cochran attempts to enforce a "better" (perhaps a Burkean or a populist) conception of representation. Yet arguments about which concept of representation is better are the stuff of contemporary political debates. . . .

Consequences of a Soft Money Ban

The history of campaign finance regulation is filled with unintended consequences. Congress enacted contribution limits in FECA to get average Americans involved in politics, but those limits reinforced the power of established groups and encouraged the candidacies of wealthy individuals. Trade unions fought hard to make sure PACs had special status under federal election law only to discover that the PAC strategy worked almost as well for their opponents as it did for them. Low contribution limits aimed at freeing officials from special interests ended up forcing legislators to spend much of their time raising money.

Many advocates of new campaign finance regulations believe American politics should have more competition and participation. Political scientists and activists have long complained about incumbents in Congress: their high reelection rates, their increasing vote shares, and their advantages in fundraising. Others note that turnout on Election Day in the United States is lower than in European democracies. The McCain-Feingold-Cochran ban on soft money would worsen both electoral competition and turnout.

Scholars have estimated that in 1998 a McCain-Feingold-Cochran ban on party soft money would have cost state and local parties $150 million. In the 2000 election, state and local parties would have forgone more than $300 million. The potential costs in the future would no doubt rise since total soft money expenditures by both parties have increased in recent years. What would happen if this money were taken from the parties?

Vitiating the fundraising capacities of parties would make American elections less competitive. Parties direct soft money to close races, thereby making elections more competitive. A recent analysis shows that PACs tend to donate to incumbents while parties concentrate equally on vulnerable incumbents and credible challengers. In close races, banning soft money would make the life of a challenger marginally more difficult than it already is. In general, banning soft money would tip the scales toward incumbents.

Banning party soft money would also reduce turnout on Election Day. Soft money goes to state and local party organizations. By banning soft money, McCain-Feingold-Cochran would seriously reduce party treasuries in many states. Political scientists Stephen Ansolabehere and James Snyder Jr. found that eliminating party soft money would significantly reduce the campaign activities of state and local party organizations. Those authors note that soft money supports numerous activities, including get-out-the-vote drives, broadcast advertising, and day-to-day operations of the organizations. Cutting federal transfers to the state party organizations would likely reduce grassroots campaign activities and produce lower voter turnout as a result. On the basis of their analysis of how state and local parties use soft money, they argue that a regulation like McCain-Feingold-Cochran would force parties to cut direct campaign expenditures by 20 percent. Given that it costs $15–$20 to get every new voter to the polls, Ansolabehere and Snyder conclude that cutting soft money to the parties would reduce turnout by about 2 percent.

The consequences of McCain-Feingold-Cochran are not hard to foresee. We will have fewer competitive elections. Our campaigns will involve fewer people, both in grassroots activities and in voting. Those who urge a soft money ban on the nation do not seek those outcomes, which may contravene their deepest convictions. The absence of malice does not mean that the fruit of McCain-Feingold-Cochran will be any less. . . .

The Ban on Political Speech

Other things being equal, the soft money McCain would deny to state and local parties would probably show up as spending by independent groups. Interest groups and other organizations independent of a candidate for office have every right to raise and spend money to inform the public about their views on various candidates and issues. The traditional analogy of a balloon is helpful: McCain-Feingold-Cochran would squeeze the balloon in one place (party soft money) causing another part (independent expenditures) to expand.

Senators McCain and Feingold are aware of this possibility and try to partially prevent the migration of party soft money. Their bill bans issue advocacy by for-profit corporations and labor unions if an ad mentions a candidate for office within 60 days of an election. Such ads have discomfited incumbent members of Congress over the last two election cycles. For that reason, this prohibition on political speech is perhaps the worst aspect of a bad bill. To understand how bad the prohibition is, we need to begin with some legal distinctions.

In *Buckley* the Supreme Court distinguished "express advocacy" and "issue advocacy" in elections. The former is direct advocacy of the election or defeat of an identified candidate; such advocacy contains phrases like "vote for," "elect," or "vote against" and other so-called magic words. The latter sets forth a position on an issue. Express advocacy may be regulated by the government; issue advocacy may not. Express advocacy is both the rationale for government regulation and a limit on it. Government may regulate only electoral communications that contain the "magic words." McCain-Feingold-Cochran seeks to break through the "magic words" barrier and subject additional speech to government control.

First, McCain-Feingold-Cochran prohibits "electioneering communications" paid for by for-profit corporations and labor unions. The bill defines "electioneering communications" as radio or TV ads that refer to clearly identified candidates for federal office and that appear within 60 days of a general election or 30 days of a primary. McCain's office notes that this prohibition "addresses the explosion of thinly-veiled campaign advertising funded by corporate and union treasuries." The words "thinly-veiled" are revealing. What had previously been constitutionally protected speech will become prohibited if a "clearly identified candidate" appears in an advertisement that is run 60 days before a general election.

This part of the bill seems to respond to recent unpleasant experiences of members of Congress. In 1996, for example, the AFL-CIO carried out a $35 million television advertising campaign that ran in dozens of congressional districts with vulnerable Republican incumbents. The ads attacked the incumbents' voting records on such issues as Social Security, Medicare, and education. The ads did not expressly advocate the election or defeat of any Republican incumbent; instead, they ended by telling viewers to "call your representative to tell him to stop cutting Medicare" or with a policy message. They were thus issue ads not regulated by the federal election laws. Labor unions undertook similar ad campaigns in the election of 2000. Rep. Clay Shaw, a Republican from Florida, was targeted by union issue ads last year. He drew a revealing lesson from his experience: "After you've been a victim of soft money, you realize the magnitude of the problem. I'm determined to address this problem when we come back. It's really ripping at the fabric of our nation's political structure." The McCain-Feingold-Cochran prohibition on corporate and union ads is intended to protect incumbent members of Congress from ad campaigns launched by their political opponents. If McCain-Feingold-Cochran passes, the Clay Shaws on Capitol Hill will never again be "victims of soft money."

We should ask two questions about the proposed ban on the political speech of labor unions and corporations. First, is it constitutional? Second, even if it is constitutional, does it serve the interests of the nation?

On the constitutional question, the Court said in *Buckley*, "As long as persons and groups eschew expenditures that in express terms advocate the election or defeat of a clearly identified candidate, they are free to spend as much as they want to promote the candidate and his views." The Court has also defined "express advocacy" by the so-called magic words mentioned earlier. McCain-Feingold-Cochran bans speech that merely refers to a candidate, rather than speech that expressly advocates his or her election or defeat. The ban on radio and TV ads is unconstitutional on its face.

Will a ban on such advertising be good for the nation? We should pause a moment and let the magnitude of what is being considered sink in. McCain-Feingold-Cochran proposes that the government prohibit political speech by labor unions and corporations if it takes places 60 or fewer days before an election. As we saw earlier, the government can restrict speech only to prevent "corruption or the appearance of corruption." How did the ads run by labor unions in 1996 corrupt Democratic members of Congress? Did any members change their votes to favor unions in return for the ads? In fact, Democratic members of Congress were likely to support union causes whether the ads ran or not. The assumption that corporate or union ads could influence members of Congress remains unproven. Without proof, such a severe measure as banning speech is unlikely to pass constitutional muster.

Even if the ban were to be approved by the Supreme Court, Americans should be skeptical of this prohibition. The real purpose of the ban is to protect incumbents from criticism during campaigns. Some members of Congress thus expect that banning union and corporate ads will make their lives easier and their reelection more likely. However, making the lives of incumbent members of Congress easier is not a good reason to ban political speech. In fact, it is the worst reason to do so. The ban on the political speech of unions and corporations will constrain the vigorous debate essential to a free and democratic society....

The Threat to Political Advocacy

Senator McCain and his allies are aware that their proposed ban on soft money will expand funding for interest group participation in elections. They also know that the Constitution forbids the federal government to regulate express advocacy in elections by groups (other than unions and for-profit corporations) independent of a candidate's campaign. On its face, McCain-Feingold-Cochran does not try to prohibit or limit issue advocacy by those independent groups. Partisans of free speech may feel some relief that the bill does not restrict the rights of other groups. If so, that feeling is misplaced.

McCain-Feingold-Cochran spends several pages elaborately defining "coordinate activities," which are activities not independent of a candidate's campaign and thus subject to federal election law. This convoluted section of the bill aims at expanding the ambit of federal election restrictions and reducing the area of free speech for independent groups. Expenditures that are deemed to be coordinated will be treated as direct contributions for purposes of applying FECA's limitations and prohibitions. The definition of "coordinated activity" in the bill is complex. For that reason, the concrete consequences of the bill's expansive notion of coordination are not self-evident: it's hard to say that the new definition of coordinated activities will muzzle one group and leave another group free of regulation.

However, the intentions of the main sponsor of the legislation are clear. Appearing on *Hardball with Chris Matthews*, Senator McCain cited the independent ad campaign by the NAACP [National Association for the Advancement of Colored People] against President Bush as a problem his legislation would remedy. Clearly, Senator McCain believes that his legislation would treat that independent expenditure by the NAACP as a "coordinated activity" that could be regulated under FECA. McCain-Feingold-Cochran thus aims to go well beyond its stated intention of regulating ads by unions and corporations. Senator McCain hopes to vastly expand the regulatory reach of FECA. If the NAACP's electoral activities were subject to federal restrictions, there would be few limits on FECA's control over independent groups and issue advocacy.

The fact that Senator McCain and his colleagues are going after independent groups exercising their freedom of speech should come as no surprise. The political incentives to do so are overwhelming. Banning party soft money will push those funds toward independent expenditures and issue advocacy by independent groups. The targets of many such ads will be incumbent members of Congress. Being a target is never easy to bear, especially when you might have the power to stop hostile criticism. The broad definition of "coordinated activities" is one of the tools McCain and others have chosen to stop hostile criticism.

Conclusion

Some Washington observers believe that McCain-Feingold-Cochran's campaign finance restrictions stand a good chance of becoming law. All the rhetoric notwithstanding, the three senators have not made the case that soft money corrupts American politics or that political speech should be constrained or even, in some forms, prohibited by new regulations. Other people have shown that the public cares little about new regulations on campaign finance and that spending on elections has little effect on public trust in government. Advocates lack a legitimate rationale for new restrictions on political speech.

Beyond the specifics, the tone of McCain-Feingold-Cochran is disturbing to anyone who thinks a democratic republic should have robust and competitive elections. McCain-Feingold-Cochran is a command-and-control approach to political speech and is deeply antagonistic to political participation in elections. There is talk of testimony under oath and perjury if a person takes part in a campaign in the wrong way. There are paperwork to be filled out and certifications to be obtained if American citizens want to express their political views in an election season. The section on coordinated activity will inevitably lead to investigations of the political associations and activities of individuals; people will be required to swear under oath about the nature of private conversations and meetings.

In sum, McCain-Feingold-Cochran assumes that elections belong to the government, which has the right to decide who participates and on what terms. In the United States, however, elections belong to the people, who elect a government that should be their servant. McCain-Feingold-Cochran is a profound mistake that deeply offends the spirit of the American republic.

POSTSCRIPT

Are the New Limits on Campaign Spending Justified?

Will the new campaign finance reform law make it easier for less afflu-ent candidates to challenge the power of well-funded interests? Or will it have the unintended effect of tipping the field even more toward incumbents and wealthy candidates by making it more difficult for their opponents to be heard? Supporters of the new law concede that it may not go far enough, and some see the need for additional legislation, such as public funding of congressional campaigns. (Some years ago a bill providing for such funding passed the Sen-ate but failed in the House, whose members, facing elections every two years, were not enthusiastic about funding their opponents.) Other suggested reforms include the provision of free air time, bans on political commercials, and pro-visions aimed at limiting not merely contributions but spending. All of these, however—especially the last—might run afoul of the Supreme Court's landmark decision *Buckley v. Valeo* (1976), which held that limits on spending violate the Constitution's First Amendment.

Thomas Gais, in *Improper Influence: Campaign Finance Law, Political Inter-est Groups, and the Problem of Equality* (University of Michigan Press, 1996), provides a scholarly critique of the campaign finance regulations that were modified by the 2002 law. In *Sold to the Highest Bidder: The Presidency From Dwight D. Eisenhower to George W. Bush* (Prometheus Books, 2002), Daniel M. Friedenberg contends that "money controls the actions of both the executive and legislative branches of our government on the federal and state levels." Bradley A. Smith, in *Unfree Speech: The Folly of Campaign Finance Reform* (Prince-ton University Press, 2001), argues that, contrary to the impression created in the media, not that much is spent on American political campaigns; Americans spend more on potato chips and Barbie dolls. Smith maintains that attempts to fix what is not broken will only make everything worse by favoring incum-bents, discouraging grassroots organizing, and turning campaigns into tedious, uninteresting exercises. *Political Money: Deregulating American Politics, Selected Writings on Campaign Finance Reform* ed. by Annelise Anderson (Hoover In-stitution Press, 2000) is a policy primer on campaign finance that features thoughtful essays on the subject by Floyd Abrams, Tom Bethell, Russell Fein-gold, and others. Republican officials predicted that the $33 million gleaned from a black-tie dinner held for President Bush in spring 2002 would set a record in perpetuity because the soft-money ban would make such events im-possible in the future. "This will be the final punctuation mark on the era of soft money," one Republican leader said. In a country that is always setting new records, this seems unlikely.

ISSUE 4

Do the Media Have a Liberal Bias?

YES: Bernard Goldberg, from *Bias: A CBS Insider Exposes How the Media Distort the News* (Regnery, 2002)

NO: Jim Hightower, from *There's Nothing in the Middle of the Road But Yellow Stripes and Dead Armadillos: A Work of Political Subversion* (HarperPerennial, 1997)

ISSUE SUMMARY

YES: Reporter Bernard Goldberg cites studies of journalists' attitudes and recalls some of his own experiences at CBS News to show that the culture of the news media is hostile to conservatism.

NO: Radio talk show host Jim Hightower cites a number of examples indicating that there is in fact a paucity of "actual liberals, much less progressive populists," with access to a national audience to counter the many conservative voices in the media.

As demonstrated in the introduction to this book, it is not easy to define *liberal* and *conservative*. Not only have the meanings changed over the years, but even in our own time we encounter different kinds of liberalism and conservativism. There are *economic* liberals ("New Deal liberals"), whose emphasis is on the need for government action in regulating business and providing social welfare; and there are *social* liberals, who favor the liberalization of American social mores. A social liberal would likely favor the abolition of laws against homosexuality, oppose restrictions on abortion, and believe that there should be a wall of separation between church and state. On the conservative side, the picture reverses itself: economic conservatives (sometimes called "fiscal conservatives") want low taxes and small government, while social conservatives favor restrictions on abortion, oppose same-sex marriage, and want to see a greater public role for religion. There is, of course, considerable overlap between these two ideological sets, and even a kind of mix-and-match quality about them. Many economic liberals are also social liberals, but many are not, and the same can be said of conservatives. A person could be a liberal on abortion, for example, but conservative on taxes and government spending, or vice-versa.

For decades, conservatives of both varieties have been complaining that American journalists put a liberal spin on the news. The complaint reached high decibels during the Nixon administration, when Vice President Spiro Agnew charged that network TV was controlled by "a small group of men" who foist their liberal opinions on viewers. Agnew, other Nixon operatives, and Nixon himself returned to the theme a number of times, using terms like "elite snobs" and "nattering nabobs of negativism" to describe the journalistic community.

The Nixon administration was brought down by the Watergate scandal (Agnew himself was forced to resign in a separate bribery scandal), but the complaint lived on and, if anything, took on new life as the media began covering some of the new, divisive issues of the 1970s and 1980s. The charge of bias continues today, and conservatives are not the only ones who offer it. Some on the left believe that corporate ownership of the media, which is becoming increasingly concentrated, has made news divisions afraid to expose the questionable practices of the far-flung empires that sponsor their programs.

With few exceptions, journalists reject the charge of bias. They insist that they cover the news with professional neutrality and that the impression of bias is simply "in the eye of the beholder." Who is right? A debate can hardly get under way without agreement on what media are being considered: news and opinion media or "hard" news media only? If opinion is included, then mentioning programs such as Rush Limbaugh's three-hour radio talk show, which inject a good deal of conservatism into the mix, cannot be avoided. But Limbaugh and others like him are openly labeled "conservative," so the word *bias* seems to lose its force. What conservative media critics argue is that those who *claim* to be delivering hard news are actually coloring it with their own liberal views. But is this true? Polls suggest that journalists' views on social issues such as abortion, homosexuality, and school prayer are well to the left of those of most Americans, yet their opinions on such issues as the legitimacy of American capitalism are about the same as or slightly more conservative than the views of most other Americans. But the real question is not whether journalists have liberal or conservative biases but whether or not they carry their biases into their reporting. The claim that they are professionals, that they leave their political opinions at the newsroom door, can perhaps be critically examined. Yet most attempts to do so have been conducted by organizations heavily freighted with their own left or right ideologies. Some studies by political scientists with no apparent ax to grind have followed media coverage of a few presidential elections. Their conclusion is that, while the media have sometimes come down hard on one candidate or another, the bias has not been the result of ideology but a variety of other factors, such as the desire to keep the horse race interesting by slowing down the front-runner. But presidential elections are not ideal for studying the issue of ideological bias in the media, since news directors, reporters, and editors know that they are being watched closely and jealously by political partisans on both sides. The question, then, remains unresolved.

In the following selections, Bernard Goldberg gives us his own insider's view of what he considers to be liberal bias in the media, while Jim Hightower argues that there are in fact few liberals in the media to counter the many conservative voices we hear every day.

 **YES**

How About a Media That Reflects America?

In their book *The Media Elite,* Robert and Susan Lichter along with Stanley Rothman ask the fundamental question: "What do journalists' backgrounds have to do with their work? In general, the way we were brought up and the way we live shape our view of the world."

It sounds fairly obvious. News, after all, isn't just a collection of facts. It's also how reporters and editors see those facts, how they interpret them, and most important, what facts they think are newsworthy to begin with.

So if long ago we came to the conclusion that newsrooms with too many white men were a bad idea because all we got was the white male perspective, then why isn't it just as bad to have so many liberals dominating the culture of the newsroom?

Inevitably, they see the world a certain way, from a liberal perspective—a world where money is often seen as a solution to social problems, where anti-abortionists are seen as kooks and weirdos, where groups, not just individuals, have rights—and because that's how they see things, that's also how they report the news.

None of this would matter, of course, if Dan Rather were right when he told Tom Snyder that "most reporters don't know whether they're Republican or Democrat, and vote every which way [and] . . . would fall in the general category of kind of commonsense moderates." Because if this business that says reporters are a bunch of liberals who almost always vote Democratic is a "myth," as Dan put it, and if this "myth" was concocted by a bunch of right-wingers to make journalists look bad, then this whole issue of liberal bias would just be a "canard," to use another of Dan's words.

"This is basically a canard used by politicians, and I understand why," he told a caller on the Snyder show. "Because they want to blame somebody, anybody but themselves, for people's anger and frustration."

There's some truth there. Some right-wing ideologues do blame "the liberal news media" for everything from crime to cancer. But that doesn't detract from another truth: that, by and large, the media elites really are liberal. And Democrats, too. And both affect their news judgment.

From Bernard Goldberg, *Bias: A CBS Insider Exposes How the Media Distort the News* (Regnery, 2002). Copyright © 2002 by Medium Cool, Inc. Reprinted by permission of Regnery Publishing, Inc., Washington, DC.

None of this should be seen as an argument against liberal values, or as an endorsement of conservative values. This is a big country with a lot of people, and there's room for all sorts of views. This is nothing more than an argument for fairness and balance, something liberals ought to care about as much as conservatives, because if by some unimaginable series of events, conservatives wind up in control of not just a cable network here or there, but hundreds of America's newsrooms, then, if history is any guide, they will slant the news to *their* liking. And the Left in this country will scream about how unfair things are—and they will be right. But they ought to realize that that's how reasonable, honest conservatives feel today.

On December 6, 1998, on a *Meet the Press* segment about Bill Clinton and his relationship with the Washington news corps, one of the capital's media stars, the *Washington Post*'s Sally Quinn, felt she needed to state what to her was the obvious.

The Washington press corps, she insisted, was not some "monolith." "We all work for different organizations," she said, "we all think differently."

Not really, Sally.

Two years earlier, in 1996, the Freedom Forum and the Roper Center released the results of a now famous survey of 139 Washington bureau chiefs and congressional correspondents. The results make you wonder what in the world Sally Quinn was talking about.

The Freedom Forum is an independent foundation that examines issues that involve the media. The Roper Center is an opinion research firm, also with a solid reputation. "No way that the data are the fruit of right-wing press bashers," as the journalist Ben Wattenberg put it.

What these two groups found was that Washington journalists are far more liberal and far more Democratic than the typical American voters:

- 89 percent of the journalists said they voted for Bill Clinton in 1992, compared with just 43 percent of the nonjournalist voters.
- 7 percent of the journalists voted for George Bush; 37 percent of the voters did.
- 2 percent of the news people voted for Ross Perot while 19 percent of the electorate did.

Eighty-nine percent voted for Bill Clinton. This is incredible when you think about it. There's hardly a candidate in the entire United States of America who carries his or her district with 89 percent of the vote. This is way beyond mere landslide numbers. The only politicians who get numbers like that are called Fidel Castro or Saddam Hussein. The same journalists that Sally Quinn tells us do not constitute a "monolith" certainly vote like one.

Sally says they "all think differently." About what? Picking the best appetizer at the Ethiopian restaurant in Georgetown?

What party do journalists identify with?

- 50 percent said they were Democrats.
- *4 percent* said they were Republicans.

When they were asked, "How do you characterize your political orientation?" 61 percent said "liberal" or "moderate to liberal." Only 9 percent said they were "conservative" or "moderate to conservative."

In the world of media elites, Democrats outnumber Republicans by twelve to one and liberals outnumber conservatives by seven to one. Yet Dan Rather believes that "most reporters don't know whether they're Republican or Democrat, and vote every which way." In your dreams, Dan.

After the survey came out, the *Washington Post* media writer, Howard Kurtz, said on *Fox News Sunday,* "Clearly anybody looking at those numbers, if they're even close to accurate, would conclude that there is a diversity problem in the news business, and it's not just the kind of diversity we usually talk about, which is not getting enough minorities in the news business, but political diversity, as well. Anybody who doesn't see that is just in denial."

James Glassman put it this way in the *Washington Post:* "The people who report the stories are liberal Democrats. This is the shameful open secret of American journalism. That the press itself . . . chooses to gloss over it is conclusive evidence of how pernicious the bias is."

Tom Rosenstiel, the director of the Project for Excellence in Journalism, says, "Bias is the elephant in the living room. We're in denial about it and don't want to admit it's there. We think it's less of a problem than the public does, and we just don't want to get into it."

Even *Newsweek's* Evan Thomas (the one who thought Ronald Reagan had a "kind of intuitive idiot genius") has said, "There is a liberal bias. It's demonstrable. You look at some statistics. About 85 percent of the reporters who cover the White House vote Democratic; they have for a long time. There is a, particularly at the networks, at the lower levels, among the editors and the so-called infrastructure, there is a liberal bias."

Nonsense!

That's the response from Elaine Povich, who wrote the Freedom Forum report. No way, she said, that the survey confirms any liberal bias in the media.

"One of the things about being a professional," she said, "is that you attempt to leave your personal feelings aside as you do your work," she told the *Washington Times.*

"More people who are of a liberal persuasion go into reporting because they believe in the ethics and the ideals," she continued. "A lot of conservatives go into the private sector, go into Wall Street, go into banking. You find people who are idealistic tending toward the reporting end."

"Right," says Ben Wattenberg in his syndicated column. "These ethical, idealistic journalists left their personal feelings aside to this extent: When queried [in the Freedom Foundation/Roper poll in 1996] whether the 1994 Contract with America was an 'election-year campaign ploy' rather than 'a serious reform proposal,' 59 percent said 'ploy' and only 3 percent said 'serious.' "

It's true that only 139 Washington journalists were polled, but there's no reason to think the results were a fluke. Because this wasn't the first survey that showed how liberal so many journalists are.

A poll back in 1972 showed that of those reporters who voted, 70 percent went for McGovern, the most liberal presidential nominee in recent memory, while 25 percent went for Nixon—the same Richard Nixon who carried every single state in the union except Massachusetts.

In 1985 the *Los Angeles Times* conducted a nationwide survey of about three thousand journalists and the same number of people in the general public to see how each group felt about the major issues of the day:

- 23 percent of the public said they were liberal; 55 percent of the journalists described themselves as liberal.
- 56 percent of the public favored Ronald Reagan; 30 percent of the journalists favored Reagan.
- 49 percent of the public was for a woman's right to have an abortion; 82 percent of the journalists were pro-choice.
- 74 percent of the public was for prayer in public schools; 25 percent of the journalists surveyed were for prayer in the public schools.
- 56 percent of the nonjournalists were for affirmative action; 81 percent of the journalists were for affirmative action.
- 75 percent of the public was for the death penalty in murder cases; 47 percent of the journalists were for the death penalty.
- Half the public was for stricter handgun controls; 78 percent of the journalists were for tougher gun controls.

A more recent study, released in March 2000, also came to the conclusion that journalists are different from most of the people they cover. Peter Brown, an editor at the *Orlando Sentinel* in Florida, did a mini-census of 3,400 journalists and found that they are less likely to get married and have children, less likely to do volunteer community service, less likely to own homes, and less likely to go to church than others who live in the communities where they work.

"How many members of the *Los Angeles Times* and the *St. Louis Post-Dispatch*," he asks, "belong to the American Legion or the Kiwanis or go to prayer breakfasts?"

But it's not just that so many journalists are so different from mainstream America. It's that some are downright hostile to what many Americans hold sacred.

On April 14, 1999, I sat in on a *CBS Weekend News* conference call from a speakerphone in the Miami bureau. It's usually a routine call with CBS News producers all over the country taking part, telling the show producers in New York about the stories coming up in their territories that weekend. Roxanne Russell, a longtime producer out of the Washington bureau, was telling about an event that Gary Bauer would be attending. Bauer was the conservative, family-values activist who seven days later would announce his candidacy for the Republican nomination for president.

Bauer was no favorite of the cultural Left, who saw him as an annoying right-wing moralist. Anna Quindlen, the annoying left-wing moralist and columnist who writes for *Newsweek,* once called him "a man best known for trying to build a bridge to the 19th century."

So maybe I shouldn't have been surprised by what I heard next, but I was. Without a trace of timidity, without any apparent concern for potential consequences, Roxanne Russell, sitting at a desk inside the CBS News Washington bureau, nonchalantly referred to this conservative activist as "Gary Bauer, the little nut from the Christian group."

The little nut from the Christian group!

Those were her exact words, uttered at exactly 12:36 P.M. If any of the CBS News producers on the conference call were shocked, not one of them gave a clue. Roxanne Russell had just called Gary Bauer, the head of a major group of American Christians, "the little nut from the Christian group" and merrily went on with the rest of the her list of events CBS News in Washington would be covering.

What struck me was not the obvious disrespect for Bauer. Journalists, being as terribly witty and sophisticated as we are, are always putting someone down. Religious people are especially juicy targets. In a lot of newsrooms, they're seen as odd and viewed with suspicion because their lives are shaped by faith and devotion to God and an adherence to rigid principles—opposition to abortion, for one—that seem archaic and closed-minded to a lot of journalists who, survey after survey suggests, are not especially religious themselves.

So it wasn't the hostility to Bauer in and of itself that threw me. It was the lack of concern of any kind in showing that disrespect *so openly.* Producers from CBS News bureaus all over the country were on the phone. And who knows who else was listening, just as I was.

So I wondered: would a network news producer ever make such a disparaging remark, so openly, about the head of a Jewish group? Or a gay group? Or a black group?

"Tomorrow we'll be covering that pro-Israel lobby and Sam Schwartz, the little nut from the Jewish group, will be there."

Or how about this: *"We'll be covering that gay parade on Saturday and Billy Smith, the little fag from the gay group, will be leading it."*

Or try this one: *"There's a rally at the Washington Monument this weekend and Jesse Jackson, the big nut from that black group, will be there."*

Anything even resembling that kind of talk would be grounds for instant dismissal. But calling a prominent Christian "the little nut" is no big deal!

Nor was it any big deal, to Ted Turner anyway, when he once said that Christianity was a religion "for losers," a remark he later apologized for. But that didn't stop him on Ash Wednesday 2001 from sharing more of his wit and wisdom about Christians. Turner was at the CNN bureau in Washington when he noticed that several of his news people had ashes on their foreheads, and it apparently left him befuddled.

"I was looking at this woman and I was trying to figure out what was on her forehead," Turner was quoted as saying. "At first I thought you were in the [Seattle] earthquake, but I realized you're just Jesus freaks."

Coming from someone else, who knows, it might have been taken as nothing more than—to use the catch phrase of the day—an "inappropriate" attempt to be funny. But given the religion "for losers" comment a decade earlier, some Catholic groups understandably were not laughing. When the news got out, Turner again apologized, calling his remark "thoughtless."

But if anyone on the CBS News conference call that day thought the shot at Gary Bauer was thoughtless, you wouldn't know it by the silence. Despite its thirst for diversity, despite years of hiring people to reflect the diversity of America, there apparently wasn't a single producer at CBS News who heard Roxanne's shot at "the little nut from the Christian group" who would stand up and say "this is wrong." I sure as hell couldn't complain. I had made waves three long years earlier, and I was still in the doghouse for it.

So what's a news organization to do? CBS can't have producers running around taking nasty little shots at conservatives who head up Christian organizations, can it? And what about that other disturbing little problem, the one about reporters who seem blissfully detached from the very people watching and reading their news reports?

What to do?

How about some good old-fashioned affirmative action?

Since the *Los Angeles Times* survey shows that more than eight out of ten journalists favor affirmative action for women and minorities, maybe they could get behind an affirmative action program for another underrepresented minority: conservatives in the world of journalism.

Too crazy? Newsroom liberals would never accept it? How do we know?

The polls say they love affirmative action. They think people who are against it are Neanderthals at best and downright bigots at worst. Besides, we're not calling for quotas. That would be wrong. Just some goals and timetables to bring more conservatives into America's newsrooms.

An affirmative action plan for conservative journalists might bring some real diversity to the newsroom, not the make-believe kind we have now. And while we would tell these conservatives to leave their political and ideological baggage at the door *(just as I'm sure liberal journalists have been told for years—ya think?)*, we should welcome the different perspective they would bring to the job of reporting the news.

Of course, in an ideal world, we wouldn't need conservatives to balance liberals. In an ideal world, we wouldn't ask, no matter how subtly, if a prospective hire was conservative or liberal. In an ideal world, none of this would matter. But obviously we don't live in an ideal world. That's why we have affirmative action. Right?

News executives are always saying we need our staffs to look more like the real America. How about if those reporters and editors and executives also *thought* just a little more like the real America? And shared just a little more of their values? And brought just a little more of *their* perspective to the job?

Nahhhh! It's definitely too crazy! The journalists who love affirmative action would hate it.

 **NO**

Liberal Media, My Ass

Let us now praise the liberal media: Rush Limbaugh, George Will, William F. Buckley Jr., John McLaughlin, G. Gordon Liddy, Joe Klein, Linda Chavez, Pat Robertson, Bill Kristol, Charles Krauthammer, Robert Novak, Arianna Huffington, Paul Gigot, Cal Thomas, Michael Barone, Bob Grant, William Safire, Lally Weymouth, Fred Barnes, Ken Hamblin, David Gergen, James Glassman, Pat Buchanan, Bay Buchanan, Kenneth Adelman, Armstrong Williams, John Sununu, Ben Wattenberg, Peggy Noonan, Tony Snow, Lynn Cheney, Richard Perle, Joseph Sobran, Robert Samuelson, Bo Gritz, Roger Ailes, Walter Williams, James J. Kilpatrick, Jeanne Kirkpatrick, Mona Charen, Brit Hume, Ollie North, Mary Matalin, John Leo, Thomas Sowell, Bernard Goldberg, John Stossel, Michael Reagan, P. J. O'Rourke, Jerry Falwell . . .

Liberal media? Give me a break. Sure, there are the delicious bon mots of the untamable Molly Ivins, Bob Herbert's pointed and poignant writing every week in the *New York Times,* Barbara Ehrenreich's insightful essays in *Time,* but contrary to popular misconception, there is a deplorable paucity of actual liberals, much less progressive populists, with access to a national, mass-market megaphone of any kind, either in print or on the air (especially few on the air). So the public gets very little day in and day out to counter the cacophony of voices peppering them from the right.

It is a demonstrably goofy notion that America's media machine is a hotbed of Stalinesque liberalism that spews a steady stream of lefty propaganda from every laptop and lavaliere mike in the land, yet this is a hobgoblin that top Republican politicos have been quick to embrace. Newt Gingrich has been especially cranked up on this theme, whining during the 1996 elections that "the bias in the media is so overwhelming that all the voters hear is the liberal background noise." Bob Dole, too, went around grouching that "We've got to stop the liberal bias in this country. Don't read that stuff. Don't watch television," even though he had been endorsed by nearly two-thirds of the nation's newspapers. Winner of the 1996 "Golden Goofy," though, was Little Stevie Forbes. Despite having inherited his own multibillion-dollar media conglomerate and having his own liberal-bashing column in a mass-market magazine that bears his own name, this '96 GOP presidential wannabe still cried a river during the

From Jim Hightower, *There's Nothing in the Middle of the Road But Yellow Stripes and Dead Armadillos: A Work of Political Subversion* (HarperPerennial, 1997). Copyright © 1997 by Jim Hightower. Reprinted by permission of HarperCollins Publishers, Inc.

Republican primary about being mistreated by that old standby, the "liberal media."

Newt tilted even farther over the edge back in the opening days of his speakership, when his star was ascendant and his ego was at full bloat. In March 1995 he urged newspaper owners to clean house, declaring that every newsroom in America was a viper's nest not merely of liberals ... but of outright *socialists.* Socialists at the *Dallas Morning News?* The *Wall Street Journal? USA Today?* The *Peoria Journal Star?* The *Pflugerville Pflag?* The (Insert Your Paper Here)? Name these red devils, Mr. Speaker, name them! Of course, he could not. As Mike Kelley, a reporter with Austin's daily paper (a distant outpost of the far-flung Cox empire), noted: "I don't even like car-pooling."

But the "liberal media" chant makes a good, hot-button campaign schtick, so Newt, Bob, and Little Stevie played it for all it was worth, and then some. Each of them tried to buttress their assertions by thumping various podiums with what they considered a terribly damning survey of Washington reporters, a high percentage of whom identified themselves as—hold on to your hats!— Democrats. None of the GOP complainers whispered a word about the political leanings of the handful of executives who really run America's media show: the general managers, advertising directors, managing editors, publishers, and owners. And while the study on reporters was widely covered, the supposedly liberal media raised no alarms at all about the Tory bias of the bosses.

By trotting out the tried-and-true liberal bugaboo, Newt and the rest divert public attention from those who own and run today's media combines. Ideologically, this establishmentarian clique is inseparable from what it is structurally: Cold, Calculating Corporatist. This group is happy to be either Republican Corporatist or Democratic Corporatist, whatever it takes to perpetuate and extend their domain. At heart, they are devout disciples of the Holy Global Corporate Orthodoxy, distilled to this three-pronged metaphysical essence: Money ... More ... Now. This is a secular theology once expressed to me in folksier terms by a West Texas land baron: "I don't want *all* the land, Hightower—just all that's next to mine."

"Corporate media" no longer suffices as an umbrella term for today's multinational, multimedia constructs. The news is no longer in the hands of news companies, much less in the hands of news people. Check the latest conglomerate framework of television, for example: NBC is a wholly owned subsidiary of General Electric, CNN has been swallowed by Time Warner, CBS is under the thumb of Westinghouse, and ABC is now just another product of Disney Inc.

So what—with cable TV there is plenty of room for broadcast diversity, right? Check again, Little Nellie Sunshine. Between them, the Big Four also own the Financial Network, TBS, TNT, Headline News, CNN International, Cinemax, HBO, Comedy Central, E!, Sega Channel, CNBC, Court TV, Bravo, American Movie Classics, MS/NBC, A&E, History Channel, Disney Channel, ESPN, ESPN 2, Lifetime Network, Touchstone Television, Buena Vista Television, The Nashville Network ... and even the Cartoon Network, among others.

National broadcasting, though, is just one piece of the media industry that GE, Time Warner, Westinghouse, and Disney have in their tentacles. There is a good chance your local TV stations are owned by these conglomerates, too, and they own the licenses of dozens of radio stations. Westinghouse/CBS alone owns eight radio stations in Chicago, seven in New York City, six in L.A., eight in Dallas, and eight in San Francisco—among many others all across the country, giving this one company control of more than a third of the entire U.S. radio audience. Some also own satellite systems, computer networks, and cable TV franchises. They own major newspapers, national magazines, and book publishers (including the Book-of-the-Month Club), making them a power in the print industry as well. Add their extensive holdings in movies, records, theme parks, and sports franchises, and you'll find that a big slice of your information and entertainment dollars is going to just these four.

Liberal media? Bear in mind that broadcasting is not even the main business of the conglomerate holders of our news networks. General Electric, for example, is the country's second largest builder of nuclear power plants and has been a major builder of nuclear bombs. It is also a bank and a major credit card company, the second largest producer of plastic in the United States, one of the biggest weapons makers and arms dealers in the world, a leading stockbroker on Wall Street, a high-ranking Pentagon contractor, a purveyor of insurance and medical services, and a top manufacturer of everything from locomotives to light bulbs. With $70 billion a year in revenues, GE has the *world's fifty-fifth largest economy*—larger than the total economies of such nations as the Philippines, Iran, Ireland, Pakistan, New Zealand, and Egypt.

Whatever else this monolith might be, one thing it damn sure is not is left wing. One chronicler of the company observed it was "so obsessed with conservatism that it was not unlike the John Birch Society." GE, you might remember, is the outfit that sponsored Ronald Reagan as host of the *General Electric Theater* television series in the fifties. In addition, Reagan was directly on GE's payroll as its PR spokesman for eight years, 1954–1962. His "job" was to make radio broadcasts and travel the rubber-chicken banquet circuit, speechifying against commies, unions, corporate taxes, welfare, social security, and all things liberal. It was this sustaining sponsorship that made Reagan the voice and darling of right-wing Republicans, solidifying a core constituency that propelled him into the governor's office in California and ultimately into the White House.

(Lesson number 14,367G(3)ii on How Politics Works, Entitled "Sponsorship Has Its Privileges": Once the Gipper was safely ensconced in the Oval Office, his old pals from GE came calling, and Reagan's Federal Communications Commission soon began loosening its regulatory grip on television licensing, including making a specific change that allowed General Electric to buy NBC. You see, GE is a convicted felon. Not once, but many times it has been convicted of such felonies as bribery, defrauding us taxpayers, and committing gross environmental and financial crimes. If you had such a rap sheet, you would not be deeded fit to hold an FCC license. But on December 10, 1985, the commission relaxed its fitness restrictions, ruling that felonies would count against a conglomerate buyer of media properties *only* if the company's top executive had been found guilty of the wrongdoing. The very next day GE waltzed through this tailor-made loophole and bought RCA, then the parent of NBC, for 6.2 billion.)

In addition to owning NBC, General Electric also sponsors the *McLaughlin Report,* the inside-Washington gang bang on liberals, which airs on both NBC and PBS. GE does not sponsor any liberal or populist counterpart to McLaughlin's weekly diatribes, and it does not allow any remotely leftish news programming on its own channels—NBC, CNBC, and MS/NBC.

Nor does GE look kindly on any of its media subsidiaries probing the deeds of the parent. Larry Grossman, president of NBC News for the first few years of GE's proprietorship, has related that he literally felt the heavy hand of conglomerate ownership—GE boss Jack Welch poked a finger in his chest and fairly shouted at him: "You work for GE!" Grossman, who later was fired because he balked at the executive suite's meddling ways, soon learned that working for GE means sticking to the company line. A few for-instances:

- In the 1987 stock market crash CEO Welch told his news division not to use the phrase "Black Monday" for fear that it might dampen the company's stock prices.
- Bossman Welch also insisted that *Today* show weatherman Willard Scott be allowed to plug GE light bulbs on the air.
- A 1987 NBC documentary on nuclear power was so pro-nuke that it could have been produced by the industry's PR office, complete with a glowing intro by NBC news anchor Tom Brokaw. Neither Brokaw nor the documentary mentioned that GE makes a killing in the business of building these power plants—a conflict of interest so glaring that offended NBC journalists took to calling the network the "Nuclear Broadcasting Company."
- On November 30, 1989, NBC's *Today* show aired an investigative report about bad bolts used by GE and other firms in building airplanes and bridges . . . except that viewers never saw or heard any reference to GE, since all mentions of NBC's parent were surgically removed by network officials.
- For three nights running in June 1990 *NBC Nightly News* broadcast a gushing series about a new machine to detect breast cancer. The network spent fourteen minutes of air-time on it—the equivalent of *War and Peace* in TV time, where major news stories are lucky to get two minutes. In none of those fourteen minutes was it mentioned that GE makes these particular machines.
- In March 1994 NBC's European cable network canceled a human rights series called *Rights & Wrongs* after it injudiciously produced a show featuring poor working conditions in factories in Mexico—factories owned by GE.

Liberal media? Tune in *Crossfire,* CNN's nightly show that celebrates itself as one television venue where left and right can bare their teeth and go at each other with no holds barred—a kind of verbal mud wrestling for news junkies.

This program was built on a cast of heavies from the right: Pat Buchanan, Robert Novak, Fred Barnes, John Sununu. And on the left? Michael Kinsley. Good grief. Michael Kinsley? It was like sending Tweety Bird into a cockfight.

Nice guy. Bright guy. But at best a squishy corporate centrist who makes Bill Clinton look like a standup guy for the working class. Kinsley's idea of class is the class of '72, the year he graduated from Harvard. Isn't Kinsley the writer who opined in *Time* magazine back in '89 that there should be a movement to draft Margaret Thatcher as America's President? He is.

Mercifully, Kinsley resigned the "left's" chair in 1996 to accept a sinecure at Microsoft, putting his faint "liberalism" in the employ of one of America's leading monopolists. At last, though, this meant there was a chance to put someone in that seat who has real teeth to bare. *Crossfire's* producers led progressive activists to believe that they were serious about wanting a contender, a true progressive scrapper to join the show, so names were submitted. A number of us pushed hard for Jeff Cohen, the founder and director of the highly regarded group FAIR—Fairness and Accuracy In Reporting. Jeff is smart, scrappy, knowledgeable, experienced, articulate, and an unabashed progressive, plus he met a key criterion for the job: He was willing to do it, willing to spend a significant portion of his life in televised shouting matches with the likes of Novak and Sununu. Such is the price of show biz.

The show's producers ran Jeff through the hoops, gave him a couple of tryouts, made positive noises about his professionalism, insisted that he was a finalist, and generally built up the boy's hope. Then they discarded him like a used hankie. It seems that all they really wanted, from the get-go, was someone to defend Bill Clinton.

That's it. Bill Clinton is as far left as the corporatized media is willing to allow the televised right-left dialogue to go, even on *Crossfire,* considered the loosest political format on TV. No Jeff Cohen, who would push the show's right-wing gang to the wall on the job-destroying impacts of NAFTA, on welfare for the privileged, on big-money corruption of the two-party system, on the crushing of America's middle class, on the growing health-care gap between those at the top and America's workaday majority, on . . . well, on the broad range of kitchen-table issues affecting the people—issues that no Clinton defender can hammer, since the President either has gone along with Gingrich Republicans on these issues, or has actually led the fight.

One other issue, too, that undoubtedly dashed any hopes Cohen might have had: the conglomerization of America's media. You can just hear the CNN/ *Crossfire* muckety-mucks saying, "Holy Ed Murrow, this guy might take a poke at *us.* Freedom of speech can go too far. Cohen can't be trusted. Next!"

Instead of Cohen (or Christopher Hitchens, Barbara Ehrenreich, or any of several other tried-and-true progressive candidates who would have brought fire, fun, and political integrity to the show), *Crossfire* meekly went with corporate convention, choosing Geraldine Ferraro, another cautious, big-business Democrat. Whatever small spark she might have added was thoroughly dampened by the fact that she was planning from the start to run in the '98 senatorial race for Republican Senator Al D'Amato's seat in New York, meaning she was not about to say anything to take any positions on television that might be offensive to her corporate backers. *Crossfire's* "debate" was perfectly safe in her hands.

OK, her name has some marquee value that Cohen's doesn't, but then *Crossfire* announced it would name a second host to bolster the left's ranks on the show. And the winner was: Bill Press. Hardly a household name, even in his own household, but another safe choice for the powers-that-be. Press was California Democratic Party chairman at the time, totally dedicated to the big-money corporate politics that dominates the party, and, as he wrote to members of the Democratic Finance Council when he was chosen, "thrilled to have the opportunity to defend Bill Clinton and his agenda with my co-host Geraldine Ferraro every night on *Crossfire.*"

In case you are not quite clear on what that agenda might be, Press explained to the *Los Angeles Times* that Clinton represents a new Democratic effort to reposition the party away from a defender of the have-nots and into a party for the haves: "We have to reshape our agenda and stress the issues that appeal to the haves, like welfare reform and maybe some marginal kind of health reform, but no big, global thing," said *Crossfire*'s latest liberal hope.

On February 19, 1995, Ruth Johnson of Caldwell, Texas, sent this letter to the editor of the *Austin American-Statesman.*

LIBERAL MEDIA. YOU'RE KIDDIN'.

This reminds me of the boxer who took on the champ, because of much insistence from his trainer. After the first round, he came back to his corner with a busted lip and his trainer patted him on the back and said, "You're doing great," then shoved him back in when the bell sounded. Following the second round, he staggered back to his corner with a black eye and a busted cheek and his trainer said, "You're doing great, he hasn't laid a hand on you." With this, the boxer replied, "Well, you'd better keep an eye on the referee, 'cause somebody is beatin' the hell out of me."

POSTSCRIPT

Do the Media Have a Liberal Bias?

As the conflicting arguments of Goldberg and Hightower show, identifying what is liberal or conservative depends in part on where one is positioned in the political spectrum. From Hightower's vantage point, figures like Geraldine Ferraro and Bill Clinton would belong somewhere in the middle, maybe a little to the right, and Jeff Cohen, of Fairness and Accuracy in Reporting (FAIR), would be situated somewhere in the broad range of liberal opinion. But from a conservative standpoint, Clinton and Ferarro belong squarely on the left, and Jeff Cohen belongs on the far left. At any rate, as Hightower notes, Cohen is seldom seen in the supposedly liberal media. Ironically, where Cohen shows up regularly is the Fox News Channel, which is considered the most conservative of all the national TV outlets in America.

William McGowan, in *Coloring the News* (Encounter Books, 2001), argues that liberalism in the media has resulted from well-meaning attempts to "diversify" newsrooms with sprinklings of college-educated blacks, Latinos, gays, and women—groups composed disproportionately of liberals. Martin A. Lee and Norman Solomon, in *Unreliable Sources: A Guide to Detecting Bias in News Media* (Carol Publishing Group, 1992), take a position similar to Hightower's, arguing that the media are owned and operated by people whose bias is toward the conservative status quo. James Fallows, in *Breaking the News: How the Media Undermine American Democracy* (Pantheon, 1996), takes a plague-on-both-your-houses approach, arguing that liberal and conservative "attack journalism" has engendered a sense of futility among American voters. Everette E. Dennis, in "Liberal Reporters, Yes; Liberal Slant No!" *The American Editor* (January–February 1997), endorses the "professionalism" argument popular among reporters—yes, we have our personal views, but no, we do not carry them into our reporting.

Some observers have suggested that the popularity of such programs as *The O'Reilly Factor* and other Fox News offerings proves that there is a hunger among segments of the American public for a conservative alternative to regular network news. But, arguably, there is at least as much liberal hunger for undisguisedly liberal perspectives on the news. If so, one can expect a growing demand for radio programs such as the one hosted by Hightower.

U.S. House of Representatives

This page of the U.S. House of Representatives will lead you to information about current and past House members and agendas, the legislative process, and so on. You can learn about events on the House floor as they happen.

http://www.house.gov

The United States Senate

This page of the U.S. Senate will lead you to information about current and past Senate members and agendas, legislative activities, committees, and so on.

http://www.senate.gov

The White House

Visit the White House page for direct access to information about commonly requested federal services, the White House Briefing Room, and the presidents and vice presidents. The Virtual Library allows you to search White House documents, listen to speeches, and view photos.

http://www.whitehouse.gov/index.html

Supreme Court Collection

Open this Legal Information Institute (LII) site for current and historical information about the Supreme Court. The LII archive contains many opinions issued since May 1990 as well as a collection of nearly 600 of the most historic decisions of the Court.

http://supct.law.cornell.edu/supct/index.html

International Information Programs

This wide-ranging page of the U.S. Department of State provides definitions, related documentation, and a discussion of topics of concern to students of American government. It addresses today's hot topics as well as ongoing issues that form the foundation of the field. Many Web links are provided.

http://usinfo.state.gov

PART 2

The Institutions of Government

*T*he Constitution provides for three governing bodies: the president, Congress, and the Supreme Court. Over the years, the American government has generated another organ with a life of its own: the bureaucracy. In this section, we examine issues that concern all the branches of government (executive, legislative, and judicial). Many of these debates are contemporary manifestations of issues that have been argued since the country was founded.

- Is Congress Barred From Regulating Commerce Within a State?

- Should the Electoral College Be Abolished?

- Was *Bush v. Gore* Correctly Decided?

ISSUE 5

Is Congress Barred From Regulating Commerce Within a State?

YES: William H. Rehnquist, from Majority Opinion, *United States v. Lopez*, U.S. Supreme Court (April 26, 1995)

NO: Stephen G. Breyer, from Dissenting Opinion, *United States v. Lopez*, U.S. Supreme Court (April 26, 1995)

ISSUE SUMMARY

YES: Supreme Court chief justice William H. Rehnquist argues that Congress cannot regulate activities within a state that are not economic and do not substantially affect commerce among the states.

NO: Supreme Court justice Stephen G. Breyer upholds the right of Congress to regulate activities within a state if Congress has a rational basis for believing that it affects the exercise of congressional power.

Federalism—the division of power between the national government and the states—is a central principle of American government. It is evident in the country's name, the United States of America.

The 13 founding states, long separated as British colonies and later cherishing their hard-earned independence, found it necessary to join together for economic stability and military security, but they would not surrender all of their powers to an unknown and untested national government. Many expressed fear of centralized tyranny as well as the loss of state sovereignty.

To reduce those fears, the Framers of the Constitution sought to limit the action of the new government to defined powers. Article 1, Section 8, of the Constitution enumerates the powers granted to Congress, implicitly denying any other. The grants of national power were stated in very general terms to enable the new government to act in unforeseen circumstances. Recognizing that they could not anticipate how powers would be exercised, the Framers added that the national government could make all laws that were "necessary and proper" to execute its constitutional powers.

Even after the Constitution was ratified, the surviving fear of the proposed Constitution's critics that a too-powerful national government might undermine the powers of the states led to incorporation of the Tenth Amendment into the Bill of Rights. It states that powers not enumerated in the Constitution as belonging to the national government belong to the states and the people.

In the first important test of federalism, *McCulloch v. Maryland* (1819), Chief Justice John Marshall wrote, "If any one proposition could command the universal assent of mankind, we might expect it to be this—that the government of the Union, though limited in its powers, is supreme within its sphere of action." Forthright as that sounds, precisely what that sphere of action is has never been definitively decided.

For more than two centuries, the constitutional debate between the two levels of government has focused principally on Congress's powers to regulate commerce among the states and to tax and spend for the general welfare. The greatest challenges to states' rights developed when the national government, in the administrations of Presidents Woodrow Wilson and Franklin D. Roosevelt, began to regulate activities once thought to be wholly within the power of the states. The U.S. Supreme Court declared unconstitutional laws that they thought exceeded the bounds of national power.

The Supreme Court did an about-face in 1941 when it unanimously upheld a federal minimum wage law and reduced the Tenth Amendment to "a truism that all is retained which has not been surrendered." For more than 50 years, it appeared that the Supreme Court would sanction no limits on national power except those explicitly stated in the Constitution, as in the Bill of Rights.

In recent years a more conservative Court has reestablished some limits. In the 1990s it ruled that Congress cannot compel the states to enact and enforce legislation carrying out the will of Congress. More far-reaching is the Supreme Court's 1995 decision in *United States v. Lopez.* In 1990 Congress had outlawed the possession of guns in or near a school. In a five-to-four decision, the Supreme Court concluded that Congress cannot regulate within a state without demonstrating the substantial effect of the regulated activities on commerce among the states. In 2000 the same narrow majority declared unconstitutional a federal law that permitted victims of rape, domestic violence, and other crimes "motivated by gender" to seek remedies in federal courts. Chief Justice William H. Rehnquist declared that "the Constitution requires a distinction between what is truly national and what is truly local." In 2002 the same five-member majority again upheld the claims of a state against the federal government. The Eleventh Amendment forbids private parties to sue states in federal court, but the majority has now extended state "sovereign immunity" to cover proceedings before federal regulatory agencies.

In the following selections from *United States v. Lopez,* Chief Justice Rehnquist, in his majority opinion, concludes that the law barring guns within the vicinity of a school was too far removed from Congress's commerce power or any other valid national power. Associate Justice Stephen G. Breyer, dissenting with three other justices, argues that reducing the risk of violence in education is a valid exercise of congressional power.

 **YES**

Majority Opinion

United States *v.* Lopez

Chief Justice Rehnquist delivered the opinion of the Court.

In the Gun-Free School Zones Act of 1990, Congress made it a federal offense "for any individual knowingly to possess a firearm at a place that the individual knows, or has reasonable cause to believe, is a school zone." The Act neither regulates a commercial activity nor contains a requirement that the possession be connected in any way to interstate commerce. We hold that the Act exceeds the authority of Congress "[t]o regulate Commerce... among the several States...." U.S. Const., Art. I, § 8, cl. 3.

On March 10, 1992, respondent, who was then a 12th-grade student, arrived at Edison High School in San Antonio, Texas, carrying a concealed .38-caliber handgun and five bullets. Acting upon an anonymous tip, school authorities confronted respondent, who admitted that he was carrying the weapon. He was arrested and charged under Texas law with firearm possession on school premises. The next day, the state charges were dismissed after federal agents charged respondent by complaint with violating the Gun-Free School Zones Act of 1990. 18 U.S.C. § 922(q)(1)(A) (1988 ed., Supp. V).[1]

A federal grand jury indicted respondent on one count of knowing possession of a firearm at a school zone, in violation of § 922(q). Respondent moved to dismiss his federal indictment on the ground that § 922(q) "is unconstitutional as it is beyond the power of Congress to legislate control over our public schools." The District Court denied the motion, concluding that § 922(q) "is a constitutional exercise of Congress' well-defined power to regulate activities in and affecting commerce, and the 'business' of elementary, middle and high schools... affects interstate commerce." Respondent waived his right to a jury trial. The District Court conducted a bench trial, found him guilty of violating § 922(q), and sentenced him to six months' imprisonment and two years' supervised release.

On appeal, respondent challenged his conviction based on his claim that § 922(q) exceeded Congress' power to legislate under the Commerce Clause. The Court of Appeals for the Fifth Circuit agreed and reversed respondent's conviction. It held that, in light of what it characterized as insufficient congressional

From *United States v. Lopez,* 514 U.S. 549 (1995). Some notes, references, and case citations omitted.

findings and legislative history, "section § 922(q), in the full reach of its terms, is invalid as beyond the power of Congress under the Commerce Clause." Because of the importance of the issue, we granted certiorari, 511 U.S. 1029 (1994), and we now affirm.

We start with first principles. The Constitution creates a Federal Government of enumerated powers. See Art. I, § 8. As James Madison wrote, "The powers delegated by the proposed Constitution to the federal government are few and defined. Those which are to remain in the State governments are numerous and indefinite." The Federalist No. 45....

The Constitution delegates to Congress the power "[t]o regulate Commerce with foreign Nations, and among the several States, and with the Indian Tribes." Art. I, § 8, cl. 3. The Court, through Chief Justice Marshall, first defined the nature of Congress' commerce power in *Gibbons v. Ogden,* 9 Wheat. 1, 189–190 (1824):

> "Commerce, undoubtedly, is traffic, but it is something more: it is intercourse. It describes the commercial intercourse between nations, and parts of nations, in all its branches, and is regulated by prescribing rules for carrying on that intercourse."

The commerce power "is the power to regulate; that is, to prescribe the rule by which commerce is to be governed. This power, like all others vested in Congress, is complete in itself, may be exercised to its utmost extent, and acknowledges no limitations, other than are prescribed in the constitution." *Id.,* at 196. The *Gibbons* Court, however, acknowledged that limitations on the commerce power are inherent in the very language of the Commerce Clause.

> "It is not intended to say that these words comprehend that commerce, which is completely internal, which is carried on between man and man in a State, or between different parts of the same State, and which does not extend to or affect other States. Such a power would be inconvenient, and is certainly unnecessary.
>
> "Comprehensive as the word 'among' is, it may very properly be restricted to that commerce which concerns more States than one.... The enumeration presupposes something not enumerated; and that something, if we regard the language, or the subject of the sentence, must be the exclusively internal commerce of a State." *Id.,* at 194–195.

For nearly a century thereafter, the Court's Commerce Clause decisions dealt but rarely with the extent of Congress' power, and almost entirely with the Commerce Clause as a limit on state legislation that discriminated against interstate commerce. Under this line of precedent, the Court held that certain categories of activity such as "production," "manufacturing," and "mining" were within the province of state governments, and thus were beyond the power of Congress under the Commerce Clause.

In 1887, Congress enacted the Interstate Commerce Act, and in 1890, Congress enacted the Sherman Antitrust Act. These laws ushered in a new era of federal regulation under the commerce power. When cases involving these laws first reached this Court, we imported from our negative Commerce Clause cases the approach that Congress could not regulate activities such as "production," "manufacturing," and "mining." Simultaneously, however, the Court held that, where the interstate and intrastate aspects of commerce were so mingled together that full regulation of interstate commerce required incidental regulation of intrastate commerce, the Commerce Clause authorized such regulation.

In *A. L. A. Schecter Poultry Corp. v. United States*, 295 U.S. 495, 550 (1935), the Court struck down regulations that fixed the hours and wages of individuals employed by an intrastate business because the activity being regulated related to interstate commerce only indirectly. In doing so, the Court characterized the distinction between direct and indirect effects of intrastate transactions upon interstate commerce as "a fundamental one, essential to the maintenance of our constitutional system." Activities that affected interstate commerce directly were within Congress' power; activities that affected interstate commerce indirectly were beyond Congress' reach. The justification for this formal distinction was rooted in the fear that otherwise "there would be virtually no limit to the federal power and for all practical purposes we should have a completely centralized government."

Two years later, in the watershed case of *NLRB v. Jones & Laughlin Steel Corp.*, 301 U.S. 1 (1937), the Court upheld the National Labor Relations Act against a Commerce Clause challenge, and in the process, departed from the distinction between "direct" and "indirect" effects on interstate commerce. The Court held that intrastate activities that "have such a close and substantial relation to interstate commerce that their control is essential or appropriate to protect that commerce from burdens and obstructions" are within Congress' power to regulate.

In *United States v. Darby*, 312 U.S. 100 (1941), the Court upheld the Fair Labor Standards Act, stating:

> "The power of Congress over interstate commerce is not confined to the regulation of commerce among the states. It extends to those activities intrastate which so affect interstate commerce or the exercise of the power of Congress over it as to make regulation of them appropriate means to the attainment of a legitimate end, the exercise of the granted power of Congress to regulate interstate commerce."

In *Wickard v. Filburn*, the Court upheld the application of amendments to the Agricultural Adjustment Act of 1938 to the production and consumption of home-grown wheat. 317 U.S., at 128–129. The *Wickard* Court explicitly rejected earlier distinctions between direct and indirect effects on interstate commerce, stating:

> "[E]ven if appellee's activity be local and though it may not be regarded as commerce, it may still, whatever its nature, be reached by Congress if it exerts a substantial economic effect on interstate commerce, and this irrespective of whether such effect is what might at some earlier time have been defined as 'direct' or 'indirect.' " *Id.*, at 125.

The *Wickard* Court emphasized that although Filburn's own contribution to the demand for wheat may have been trivial by itself, that was not "enough to remove him from the scope of federal regulation where, as here, his contribution, taken together with that of many others similarly situated, is far from trivial."

Jones & Laughlin Steel, Darby, and *Wickard* ushered in an era of Commerce Clause jurisprudence that greatly expanded the previously defined authority of Congress under that Clause. In part, this was a recognition of the great changes that had occurred in the way business was carried on in this country. Enterprises that had once been local or at most regional in nature had become national in scope. But the doctrinal change also reflected a view that earlier Commerce Clause cases artificially had constrained the authority of Congress to regulate interstate commerce.

But even these modern-era precedents which have expanded congressional power under the Commerce Clause confirm that this power is subject to outer limits. In *Jones & Laughlin Steel,* the Court warned that the scope of the interstate commerce power "must be considered in the light of our dual system of government and may not be extended so as to embrace effects upon interstate commerce so indirect and remote that to embrace them, in view of our complex society, would effectually obliterate the distinction between what is national and what is local and create a completely centralized government." Since that time, the Court has heeded that warning and undertaken to decide whether a rational basis existed for concluding that a regulated activity sufficiently affected interstate commerce.

Similarly, in *Maryland v. Wirtz,* 392 U.S. 183 (1968), the Court reaffirmed that "the power to regulate commerce, though broad indeed, has limits" that "[t]he Court has ample power" to enforce. In response to the dissent's warnings that the Court was powerless to enforce the limitations on Congress' commerce powers because "[a]ll activities affecting commerce, even in the minutest degree, may be regulated and controlled by Congress," the *Wirtz* Court replied that the dissent had misread precedent as "[n]either here nor in *Wickard* has the Court declared that Congress may use a relatively trivial impact on commerce as an excuse for broad general regulation of state or private activities." Rather, "[t]he Court has said only that where *a general regulatory statute bears a substantial relation to commerce,* the *de minimis* character of individual instances arising under that statute is of no consequence." (emphasis added).

Consistent with this structure, we have identified three broad categories of activity that Congress may regulate under its commerce power. First, Congress may regulate the use of the channels of interstate commerce. Second, Congress is empowered to regulate and protect the instrumentalities of interstate commerce, or persons or things in interstate commerce, even though the threat may come only from intrastate activities. Finally, Congress' commerce authority includes the power to regulate those activities having a substantial relation to interstate commerce, *Jones & Laughlin Steel,* 301 U.S., at 37 , i.e., those activities that substantially affect interstate commerce.

Within this final category, admittedly, our case law has not been clear whether an activity must "affect" or "substantially affect" interstate commerce in order to be within Congress' power to regulate it under the Commerce Clause. We conclude, consistent with the great weight of our case law, that the proper test requires an analysis of whether the regulated activity "substantially affects" interstate commerce.

We now turn to consider the power of Congress, in the light of this framework, to enact § 922(q). The first two categories of authority may be quickly disposed of: § 922(q) is not a regulation of the use of the channels of interstate commerce, nor is it an attempt to prohibit the interstate transportation of a commodity through the channels of commerce; nor can § 922(q) be justified as a regulation by which Congress has sought to protect an instrumentality of interstate commerce or a thing in interstate commerce. Thus, if § 922(q) is to be sustained, it must be under the third category as a regulation of an activity that substantially affects interstate commerce.

First, we have upheld a wide variety of congressional Acts regulating intrastate economic activity where we have concluded that the activity substantially affected interstate commerce. Examples include the regulation of intrastate coal mining, intrastate extortionate credit transactions, restaurants utilizing substantial interstate supplies, inns and hotels catering to interstate guests, and production and consumption of home-grown wheat. These examples are by no means exhaustive, but the pattern is clear. Where economic activity substantially affects interstate commerce, legislation regulating that activity will be sustained.

Even *Wickard*, which is perhaps the most far reaching example of Commerce Clause authority over intrastate activity, involved economic activity in a way that the possession of a gun in a school zone does not. Roscoe Filburn operated a small farm in Ohio, on which, in the year involved, he raised 23 acres of wheat. It was his practice to sow winter wheat in the fall, and after harvesting it in July to sell a portion of the crop, to feed part of it to poultry and livestock on the farm, to use some in making flour for home consumption, and to keep the remainder for seeding future crops. The Secretary of Agriculture assessed a penalty against him under the Agricultural Adjustment Act of 1938 because he harvested about 12 acres more wheat than his allotment under the Act permitted. The Act was designed to regulate the volume of wheat moving in interstate and foreign commerce in order to avoid surpluses and shortages, and concomitant fluctuation in wheat prices, which had previously obtained....

Section § 922(q) is a criminal statute that by its terms has nothing to do with "commerce" or any sort of economic enterprise, however broadly one might define those terms. Section § 922(q) is not an essential part of a larger regulation of economic activity, in which the regulatory scheme could be undercut unless the intrastate activity were regulated. It cannot, therefore, be sustained under our cases upholding regulations of activities that arise out of or are connected with a commercial transaction, which viewed in the aggregate, substantially affects interstate commerce.

... The Government argues that possession of a firearm in a school zone may result in violent crime and that violent crime can be expected to affect the functioning of the national economy in two ways. First, the costs of violent crime are substantial, and, through the mechanism of insurance, those costs are spread throughout the population. Second, violent crime reduces the willingness of individuals to travel to areas within the country that are perceived to be unsafe. The Government also argues that the presence of guns in schools poses a substantial threat to the educational process by threatening the learning environment. A handicapped educational process, in turn, will result in a less productive citizenry. That, in turn, would have an adverse effect on the Nation's economic well-being. As a result, the Government argues that Congress could rationally have concluded that § 922(q) substantially affects interstate commerce.

We pause to consider the implications of the Government's arguments. The Government admits, under its "costs of crime" reasoning, that Congress could regulate not only all violent crime, but all activities that might lead to violent crime, regardless of how tenuously they relate to interstate commerce. Similarly, under the Government's "national productivity" reasoning, Congress could regulate any activity that it found was related to the economic productivity of individual citizens: family law (including marriage, divorce, and child custody), for example. Under the theories that the Government presents in support of § 922(q), it is difficult to perceive any limitation on federal power, even in areas such as criminal law enforcement or education where States historically have been sovereign. Thus, if we were to accept the Government's arguments, we are hard-pressed to posit any activity by an individual that Congress is without power to regulate.

Although Justice Breyer argues that acceptance of the Government's rationales would not authorize a general federal police power, he is unable to identify any activity that the States may regulate but Congress may not. Justice Breyer posits that there might be some limitations on Congress' commerce power, such as family law or certain aspects of education. These suggested limitations, when viewed in light of the dissent's expansive analysis, are devoid of substance.

Justice Breyer focuses, for the most part, on the threat that firearm possession in and near schools poses to the educational process and the potential economic consequences flowing from that threat. Specifically, the dissent reasons that (1) gun-related violence is a serious problem; (2) that problem, in turn, has an adverse effect on classroom learning; and (3) that adverse effect on classroom learning, in turn, represents a substantial threat to trade and commerce. This analysis would be equally applicable, if not more so, to subjects such as family law and direct regulation of education.

For instance, if Congress can, pursuant to its Commerce Clause power, regulate activities that adversely affect the learning environment, then, *a fortiori*, it also can regulate the educational process directly. Congress could determine that a school's curriculum has a "significant" effect on the extent of classroom learning. As a result, Congress could mandate a federal curriculum for local elementary and secondary schools because what is taught in local schools has a significant "effect on classroom learning," and that, in turn, has a substantial effect on interstate commerce.

Justice Breyer rejects our reading of precedent and argues that "Congress ... could rationally conclude that schools fall on the commercial side of the line." Justice Breyer's rationale lacks any real limits because, depending on the level of generality, any activity can be looked upon as commercial. Under the dissent's rationale, Congress could just as easily look at child rearing as "fall[ing] on the commercial side of the line" because it provides a "valuable service—namely, to equip [children] with the skills they need to survive in life and, more specifically, in the workplace." ...

The possession of a gun in a local school zone is in no sense an economic activity that might, through repetition elsewhere, substantially affect any sort of interstate commerce. Respondent was a local student at a local school; there is no indication that he had recently moved in interstate commerce, and there is no requirement that his possession of the firearm have any concrete tie to interstate commerce.

To uphold the Government's contentions here, we would have to pile inference upon inference in a manner that would bid fair to convert congressional authority under the Commerce Clause to a general police power of the sort retained by the States. Admittedly, some of our prior cases have taken long steps down that road, giving great deference to congressional action. The broad language in these opinions has suggested the possibility of additional expansion, but we decline here to proceed any further. To do so would require us to conclude that the Constitution's enumeration of powers does not presuppose something not enumerated, and that there never will be a distinction between what is truly national and what is truly local. This we are unwilling to do.

Note

1. The term "school zone" is defined as "in, or on the grounds of, a public, parochial or private school" or "within a distance of 1,000 feet from the grounds of a public, parochial or private school." § 921(a)(25).

NO ←

Stephen G. Breyer

Dissenting Opinion of Stephen G. Breyer

J ustice Breyer, with whom Justice Stevens, Justice Souter, and Justice Ginsburg join, dissenting.

The issue in this case is whether the Commerce Clause authorizes Congress to enact a statute that makes it a crime to possess a gun in, or near, a school. 18 U.S.C. § 922(q)(1)(A) (1988 ed., Supp. V). In my view, the statute falls well within the scope of the commerce power as this Court has understood that power over the last half century.

I

In reaching this conclusion, I apply three basic principles of Commerce Clause interpretation. First, the power to "regulate Commerce... among the several States," U.S. Const., Art. I, § 8, cl. 3, encompasses the power to regulate local activities insofar as they significantly affect interstate commerce. As the majority points out, the Court, in describing how much of an effect the Clause requires, sometimes has used the word "substantial" and sometimes has not.... And, as the majority also recognizes... the question of degree (how *much* effect) requires an estimate of the "size" of the effect that no verbal formulation can capture with precision. I use the word "significant" because the word "substantial" implies a somewhat narrower power than recent precedent suggests. But to speak of "substantial effect" rather than "significant effect" would make no difference in this case.

Second, in determining whether a local activity will likely have a significant effect upon interstate commerce, a court must consider, not the effect of an individual act (a single instance of gun possession), but rather the cumulative effect of all similar instances (*i.e.,* the effect of all guns possessed in or near schools). As this Court put the matter almost 50 years ago:

> "[I]t is enough that the individual activity when multiplied into a general practice... contains a threat to the interstate economy that requires preventative regulation."

From *United States v. Lopez,* 514 U.S. 549 (1995). Some references and case citations omitted.

Third, the Constitution requires us to judge the connection between a regulated activity and interstate commerce, not directly, but at one remove. Courts must give Congress a degree of leeway in determining the existence of a significant factual connection between the regulated activity and interstate commerce—both because the Constitution delegates the commerce power directly to Congress and because the determination requires an empirical judgment of a kind that a legislature is more likely than a court to make with accuracy. The traditional words "rational basis" capture this leeway. Thus, the specific question before us, as the Court recognizes, is not whether the "regulated activity sufficiently affected interstate commerce," but, rather, whether Congress could have had *a rational basis* for so concluding.

I recognize that we must judge this matter independently. "[S]imply because Congress may conclude that a particular activity substantially affects interstate commerce does not necessarily make it so." And, I also recognize that Congress did not write specific "interstate commerce" findings into the law under which Lopez was convicted. Nonetheless, as I have already noted, the matter that we review independently (*i.e.*, whether there is a "rational basis") already has considerable leeway built into it. And, the absence of findings, at most, deprives a statute of the benefit of some *extra* leeway. This extra deference, in principle, might change the result in a close case, though, in practice, it has not made a critical legal difference. It would seem particularly unfortunate to make the validity of the statute at hand turn on the presence or absence of findings. Because Congress did make findings (though not until after Lopez was prosecuted), doing so would appear to elevate form over substance....

II

Applying these principles to the case at hand, we must ask whether Congress could have had a *rational basis* for finding a significant (or substantial) connection between gun-related school violence and interstate commerce. Or, to put the question in the language of the *explicit* finding that Congress made when it amended this law in 1994: Could Congress rationally have found that "violent crime in school zones," through its effect on the "quality of education," significantly (or substantially) affects "interstate" or "foreign commerce"? As long as one views the commerce connection, not as a "technical legal conception," but as "a practical one," the answer to this question must be yes. Numerous reports and studies—generated both inside and outside government—make clear that Congress could reasonably have found the empirical connection that its law, implicitly or explicitly, asserts.

For one thing, reports, hearings, and other readily available literature make clear that the problem of guns in and around schools is widespread and extremely serious. These materials report, for example, that four percent of American high school students (and six percent of inner-city high school students) carry a gun to school at least occasionally; that 12 percent of urban high school students have had guns fired at them; that 20 percent of those students have been threatened with guns; and that, in any 6-month period, several hundred thousand schoolchildren are victims of violent crimes in or near their schools. And, they report that this widespread violence in schools throughout the Nation significantly interferes with the quality of education in those schools. Based on reports such as these, Congress obviously could have thought that guns and learning are mutually exclusive. Congress could therefore have found a substantial educational problem—teachers unable to teach, students unable to learn—and concluded that guns near schools contribute substantially to the size and scope of that problem.

Having found that guns in schools significantly undermine the quality of education in our Nation's classrooms, Congress could also have found, given the effect of education upon interstate and foreign commerce, that gun-related violence in and around schools is a commercial, as well as a human, problem. Education, although far more than a matter of economics, has long been inextricably intertwined with the Nation's economy. When this Nation began, most workers received their education in the workplace, typically (like Benjamin Franklin) as apprentices. As late as the 1920's, many workers still received general education directly from their employers—from large corporations, such as General Electric, Ford, and Goodyear, which created schools within their firms to help both the worker and the firm. As public school enrollment grew in the early 20th century, the need for industry to teach basic educational skills diminished. But, the direct economic link between basic education and industrial productivity remained. Scholars estimate that nearly a quarter of America's economic growth in the early years of this century is traceable directly to increased schooling; that investment in "human capital" (through spending on education) exceeded investment in "physical capital" by a ratio of almost two to one); and that the economic returns to this investment in education exceeded the returns to conventional capital investment.

In recent years the link between secondary education and business has strengthened, becoming both more direct and more important. Scholars on the subject report that technological changes and innovations in management techniques have altered the nature of the workplace so that more jobs now demand greater educational skills....

Increasing global competition also has made primary and secondary education economically more important. The portion of the American economy attributable to international trade nearly tripled between 1950 and 1980, and more than 70 percent of American-made goods now compete with imports. Yet, lagging worker productivity has contributed to negative trade balances and to real hourly compensation that has fallen below wages in 10 other industrialized nations. At least some significant part of this serious productivity problem is attributable to students who emerge from classrooms without the reading or mathematical skills necessary to compete with their European or Asian counterparts....

Finally, there is evidence that, today more than ever, many firms base their location decisions upon the presence, or absence, of a work force with a basic education.... In light of this increased importance of education to individual firms, it is no surprise that half of the Nation's manufacturers have become involved with setting standards and shaping curricula for local schools, that 88 percent think this kind of involvement is important, that more than 20

States have recently passed educational reforms to attract new business, and that business magazines have begun to rank cities according to the quality of their schools.

The economic links I have just sketched seem fairly obvious. Why then is it not equally obvious, in light of those links, that a widespread, serious, and substantial physical threat to teaching and learning *also* substantially threatens the commerce to which that teaching and learning is inextricably tied? That is to say, guns in the hands of six percent of inner-city high school students and gun-related violence throughout a city's schools must threaten the trade and commerce that those schools support. The only question, then, is whether the latter threat is (to use the majority's terminology) "substantial." The evidence of (1) the *extent* of the gun-related violence problem, (2) the *extent* of the resulting negative effect on classroom learning, and (3) the *extent* of the consequent negative commercial effects, when taken together, indicate a threat to trade and commerce that is "substantial." At the very least, Congress could rationally have concluded that the links are "substantial." . . .

To hold this statute constitutional is not to "obliterate" the "distinction between what is national and what is local," nor is it to hold that the Commerce Clause permits the Federal Government to "regulate any activity that it found was related to the economic productivity of individual citizens," to regulate "marriage, divorce, and child custody," or to regulate any and all aspects of education. First, this statute is aimed at curbing a particularly acute threat to the educational process—the possession (and use) of life-threatening firearms in, or near, the classroom. The empirical evidence that I have discussed above unmistakably documents the special way in which guns and education are incompatible. This Court has previously recognized the singularly disruptive potential on interstate commerce that acts of violence may have. Second, the immediacy of the connection between education and the national economic well-being is documented by scholars and accepted by society at large in a way and to a degree that may not hold true for other social institutions. It must surely be the rare case, then, that a statute strikes at conduct that (when considered in the abstract) seems so removed from commerce, but which (practically speaking) has so significant an impact upon commerce.

In sum, a holding that the particular statute before us falls within the commerce power would not expand the scope of that Clause. Rather, it simply would apply pre-existing law to changing economic circumstances. It would recognize that, in today's economic world, gun-related violence near the classroom makes a significant difference to our economic, as well as our social, well-being. In accordance with well-accepted precedent, such a holding would permit Congress "to act in terms of economic . . . realities," would interpret the commerce power as "an affirmative power commensurate with the national needs," and would acknowledge that the "commerce clause does not operate so as to render the nation powerless to defend itself against economic forces that Congress decrees inimical or destructive of the national economy." . . .

IV

In sum, to find this legislation within the scope of the Commerce Clause would permit "Congress... to act in terms of economic... realities." It would interpret the Clause as this Court has traditionally interpreted it, with the exception of one wrong turn subsequently corrected. Upholding this legislation would do no more than simply recognize that Congress had a "rational basis" for finding a significant connection between guns in or near schools and (through their effect on education) the interstate and foreign commerce they threaten. For these reasons, I would reverse the judgment of the Court of Appeals. Respectfully, I dissent.

POSTSCRIPT

Is Congress Barred From Regulating Commerce Within a State?

The difference of views on today's divided Supreme Court may be defined (concededly too simply and neatly) in terms of whether the powers of the states are *reserved*, that is, secure against encroachment or abridgement by Congress or the president, or whether state powers are *residual*, that is, the powers that are left after upholding valid claims of national power.

On the one hand, the historical evidence leaves no doubt that the Constitution was designed to create a national government powerful enough to deal with areas that the states believed required unified action (such as commerce, coinage, and national defense) but not so powerful as to diminish the authority of the states in all other areas. The Constitution's authors went to some pains to define and confine the powers of the new central government.

On the other hand, Chief Justice John Marshall has stated the logic of delegated national power: "Let the end be legitimate, let it be within the scope of the Constitution, and all means which are appropriate, which are plainly adapted to that end, which are not prohibited, but consistent with the letter and spirit of the Constitution, are constitutional." If Congress's exercise of power is valid, no matter how far it extends, the power of the states is reduced by that much.

Congressional hearings have provided a public forum for airing opposing views on the boundaries of national and state power. The U.S. Senate Committee on Governmental Affairs heard testimony on the state of federalism in 1999. In *The Delicate Balance: Federalism, Interstate Commerce and Economic Freedom in the Technological Age* (Heritage Foundation, 1998), Adam D. Thierer seeks to redefine and defend federalism in the modern world. Edward B. McLean and other scholars deplore what they call *Derailing the Constitution: The Undermining of American Federalism* (Doubleday, 1997). In *Disunited States* (Basic Books, 1997), John D. Donahue expresses skepticism of the judicial movement toward reducing the exercise of national power.

Despite the learned constitutional and historical arguments, one may harbor the suspicion that where one stands on the balance of power in American federalism often depends less on abstract theory than on practical considerations of public policy. Perhaps there is a more than a coincidental correspondence between positions on civil rights or national welfare legislation and the defense of either the principle of national supremacy or that of states' rights. As long as political differences exist as to whether we should have "more" or "less" national government, the constitutional debate will continue.

ISSUE 6

Should the Electoral College Be Abolished?

YES: Daniel Lazare, from *The Velvet Coup: The Constitution, the Supreme Court, and the Decline of American Democracy* (Verso, 2001)

NO: Richard A. Posner, from *Breaking the Deadlock: The 2000 Election, the Constitution, and the Courts* (Princeton University Press, 2001)

ISSUE SUMMARY

YES: Freelance writer Daniel Lazare argues that the electoral college is an undemocratic institution that no longer serves to democratically choose a president and that, if it cannot be repealed, it should be by-passed in future elections.

NO: Richard A. Posner, a judge and a legal scholar, sees more difficulties in abolishing the electoral college than in retaining it, and he maintains that the U.S. Supreme Court has the right to ensure that the casting of a state's electoral vote conforms with that state's laws.

Whenever they first learn about it, Americans tend to have difficulty grappling with the fact that the president of the United States is elected not directly by the people but by electors. When voters go to the polls on Election Day—the first Tuesday after the first Monday in November—they choose from among the competing slates of electors from their state and from the District of Columbia. Those elected cast their votes on the first Monday after the second Wednesday in December, but it becomes known who won shortly after the voting booths close on election night. The election of 2000, which was decided 36 days later, is a notable exception.

The Framers of the Constitution imagined that a number of public-spirited citizens—perhaps political elders who had retired from public office—would be chosen in each state to constitute the electoral college. The electoral college is not a college and never meets as a single entity, but it greatly influences the character of the parties, the nominating process, and the outcome of the presidential election. Here is how it works: Each state has a number of electoral votes equal to its membership in the two houses of Congress. Because all states have two senators and at least one representative, the smallest number of electoral votes a state may have is three. There are 50 states (and, therefore, 100 senators), the size of the House of Representatives has been limited to 435 by law, and a constitutional amendment has given the District of Columbia 3 electoral votes, resulting in a total of 538 electoral votes. A majority of 270 is necessary for election. The authors of the Constitution did not anticipate political parties or modern communications, and they believed that many candidates would receive votes in each election. If no candidate received an electoral majority, the president would be chosen by the House of Representatives (with each state casting but one vote) from among the five leading candidates.

The design of the Framers did not function as they had intended for long. Political parties quickly developed, ensuring broad national support for their candidates. The states gradually moved to the popular election of the electors. The composition of the voting population increased with the abolition of property qualifications and the extension of the ballot to African Americans, women, and young adults of 18. Soon all the electors in each state were elected with the understanding that they would cast their votes for the candidates who had received the most votes in that state. (Most electors were bound by party and precedent, not by law, and a small number of so-called faithless electors have ignored the voters' choice.)

The existence of the electoral college usually undermines third parties, which are unlikely to win electoral votes, although some minor parties have sought to win the electoral vote of one or two states in order to prevent a majority and thereby obtain bargaining power in choosing the next president. Also, the electoral vote usually exaggerates the popular strength of the majority party, but in a close election it can result in the election of a candidate who received fewer popular votes than his opponent. That, of course, is what happened for the fourth time in 2000.

Critics argue that the electors are, at best, an anachronism and, at worst, capable of distorting or even altering the result of an election. In defense of the electoral college, its supporters point out that a straight popular election would encourage minor party candidates, making the election of a plurality president, possibly even one with a relatively small percentage of the vote, likely. These arguments are developed in the selections that follow. In them, both Daniel Lazare and Richard A. Posner examine the electoral college from the perspective of the 2000 presidential election, but they reach different conclusions. Lazare examines a hypothetical rematch of the two 2000 presidential candidates four years later, for which he proposes striking changes, including the disregarding of the electoral college. Lazare admits that his scenario is unlikely, but it does raise important questions regarding whether or not the rules can be changed when it is found that they fall short of America's democratic objectives. Posner acknowledges the shortcomings of the electoral college, but he disagrees as to which groups and states benefit from it. Posner also foresees costly and divisive consequences in a close popular election.

Daniel Lazare

 **YES**

The Velvet Coup

Predictably, the year 2000 election mess led to calls to repeal the Electoral College. One came from Hillary Clinton, who declared a few days after her election victory in New York: "I have always thought we had outlived the need for an Electoral College, and now that I am going to the Senate, I am going to try to do what I can to make clear that the popular vote, the will of the people, should be followed." Another came from New York University law professor Ronald Dworkin, who wrote in the *New York Review of Books*:

> We now have the best chance ever to junk [this] anachronistic and danger-ous eighteenth-century system. The public should demand that Congress begin a process of constitutional amendment that would eliminate that system, root and branch, and substitute for it the direct election of the president and vice presidency by a plurality of the national popular vote.

Yet a bit of simple arithmetic shows why any such constitutional amend-ment is out of the question. Not only does the Electoral College triple the political clout of voters in the seven least populous states that elect just one member of the House, it doubles the clout of those in six other states that elect two members of the House and augments by roughly two-thirds the clout of those in four others that elect just three. This is a good deal more than the bare minimum of just thirteen states that the two-thirds/three-fourths rule in Arti-cle V allows to veto any and all efforts at constitutional reform. Barring some miraculous change of heart, consequently, small states that are overwhelmingly rural and white can be counted on to block any change that would place their citizens on an equal footing with those in large states that are urban and mul-tiracial. Although the Supreme Court has repeatedly declared since *Baker v. Carr* in 1962 that one person-one vote must prevail at the state and local level, the Constitution effectively bars it at the federal. Just as "we the people" were pow-erless to do anything about slavery prior to the Civil War, "we the people" are now powerless to do away with an arrangement as patiently unfair as the Electoral College. Rather than guaranteeing democratic liberties, the Ancient Constitution denies them.

　　The dimensions of the Republican victory only gradually became appar-ent in the weeks following the Supreme Court's decision in *Bush v. Gore*. For the

From Daniel Lazare, *The Velvet Coup: The Constitution, the Supreme Court, and the Decline of Ameri-can Democracy* (Verso, 2001). Copyright © 2001 by Daniel Lazare. Reprinted by permission of Verso, the imprint of New Left Books, Ltd. Notes omitted.

first time in postwar history, the GOP had made a clean sweep, gaining control not just of the executive and legislative branches, but of the judiciary, too. Chief Justice William Rehnquist, seventy-six years old at the time of the December 12 ruling, could retire secure in the knowledge that his successor would be someone he would find ideologically congenial. While hardly the first conservative to occupy the Oval Office, George W. Bush was the first Southern conservative since before the Civil War, an important distinction in terms of America's highly charged geopolitics. Meanwhile, Al Gore left Washington to teach journalism, Bill Clinton huddled in disgrace in suburban New York amid a growing furor over a series of his last-minute presidential pardons, while Hillary Clinton, widely considered a possible presidential contender in 2004 or 2008, was similarly neutralized. As the liberal economist Robert Kuttner put it in a magazine column the following January: "It's like a country after a bloodless coup d'état. Daily life goes on. The tame media makes soothing noises. Rituals of democracy endure. The out-party simulates opposition, toothlessly." Yet the substance of democracy had been lost. . . .

Is There a Way Out?

It is August 2004. After nearly four years of hard-right policies under George W. Bush, Democrats are thirsting for revenge. They want nothing more than a rematch with the Republican team that they believe stole the 2000 presidential election. Accordingly, the party once again makes Al Gore the standard-bearer. Looking trim and only a littler grayer, the former vice president bounds onto the stage at the Democratic National Convention as his wife Tipper is winding up her remarks. Jubilantly, he gives her another of those long smackers that have become a personal trademark. Then he launches into his speech.

Coolly, he runs through the Bush administration's record over the previous four years, its tax cuts for the rich, its budget cuts for everyone else, and its scuttling of the Kyoto Accords on global warming. His manner is passionate, yet controlled. Instead of moving forward, he says, Americans have had to stand by while Republicans turned back the clock. Instead of seeing their country advance, they have see it regress to the days of Ronald Reagan and the elder George Bush. This is all quite galling. But what is even more galling, Gore continues, is that these are not the policies that Americans voted for. A clear majority who voted in 2000 for either the Democrats or the Greens voted in favor of environmental protection, stepped-up spending for healthcare and the poor, and a woman's right to choose. Yet even though the Democrats alone won by more than half a million votes, they wound up with a Republican who has waged war on all three.

The candidate pauses. Ten or fifteen seconds tick by as the delegates think back to the events of four years earlier—the butterfly ballots, the goon squads, the police roadblocks scaring away black voters. "With all due respect to my opponent," Gore resumes finally, "this must never happen again. Never again must the will of the people be flouted. Never again must votes be ignored. Never again should the outcome in a single state be allowed to offset the popular vote nationwide. As great as our Founding Fathers were, they were uncertain as to whether they wanted America to be a democracy or an indirectly elected republic. For a long time, Americans themselves were not sure either. But now, after more than two centuries, we have made up our minds. We want a democracy. We want a democracy based on the will of the people. We want a democracy that counts every vote. We want a democracy dedicated to the proposition that all Americans, male or female, black or white, rich or poor, are created equal." Then peering out across a sea of white, black, and brown faces: "We want a democracy that does not give some states greater clout in presidential elections and other states—big states that are multiracial and urban—less clout merely because something called the Electoral College says that's the way it ought to be. Democracy means one person-one vote regardless of the color of your skin, your gender or sexual orientation, or whether you live in California or Wyoming."

This is the red meat the audience has been waiting for. After a full minute of wild cheering, the nominee holds up his hand for silence. "Now, as we all know, it is effectively impossible to change the Electoral College by amending the Constitution. Some seven hundred proposed amendments have been introduced in Congress over the last two centuries in an effort to reform or abolish this system. That's a little more than one every four months. Yet all have failed. Hillary Clinton, our esteemed senator from New York, was the latest to try, and she has failed also. Over the years, the states that benefit disproportionately from the Electoral College have made it plain that they will never consent to the slightest alteration in the status quo, and unfortunately there are too many small states that feel that way to ever allow such an amendment to pass. Therefore, the Electoral College is destined to remain on the books for a long as anyone can foresee.

"But that's not the end of the story," Gore continues. "Even if we can't change the Constitution, there is a way that we can render the Electoral College a dead letter. All we have to do is enter into a simple agreement. I propose that my opponent and I both make a pledge. Regardless of the outcome in the Electoral College, I propose that we both promise to abide by the popular vote and only by the popular vote. As soon as the vote totals are known, I propose that the loser issue a statement conceding defeat and releasing his electors to vote for the other side. While the electors will not have to switch their vote, I am sure that most will follow their candidate's advice and obey the democratic will. Assuming that is the case, a very important precedent will have been set. The Electoral College will continue to meet every four years. But henceforth it will become nothing more than a formality, a body whose purpose is to ratify the results of a free election and acknowledge that the people have spoken. Without changing so much as a comma in the Constitution, we can insure that power will once again reside with the people, from whom it should never have left. America is a democracy, and in a democracy 'we the people' rule."

More cheering erupts.

"I hereby take that pledge. I challenge my opponent to do the same. . . ."

In an essay published a few years ago, a University of Texas law professor named Sanford Levinson posed an intriguing question: Is a constitutional amendment adopted in accordance with the provisions in Article V really an amendment? This may sound like a typical academic jawbreaker, yet it is in fact highly relevant in terms of the current American predicament. In one sense, of course, an amendment approved by two-thirds of each house plus three-fourths of the states does represent change in that it tacks on additional words that modify to some degree the preceding text. When Congress and the states approved an amendment prohibiting "manufacture, sale, or transportation of intoxicating liquors" shortly after World War I, the result was not only to ban alcoholic beverages, but to alter the structure of federal–state relations. Where previously the Constitution had allowed Congress to regulate interstate commerce only, the Eighteenth Amendment allowed it to extend its reach so as to cover at least one aspect of intrastate commerce as well. Ironically, a neo-Jeffersonian campaign wound up contributing to the growth of big government, the Jeffersonian *bête noire*.

In another sense, though, the amendment changed nothing. Indeed, by virtue of its ratification in accordance with the complicated provisions set forth in Article V, the Eighteenth Amendment confirmed that rules dating from the late eighteenth century were as binding as ever. Rather than a departure from past practice, Prohibition therefore represented a continuation. It was an admission, in effect, that the Founders were still paramount and that their rules still prevailed. The amendment served a dual purpose—to ban alcohol and to confirm that Americans must submit to pre-existing constitutional principles —which is one reason why the political atmosphere in 1920s America was so stiflingly conservative.

Change that takes place in accordance with Article V is licensed change, whereas real change means a departure from any such arrangement. The beauty of the foregoing Al Gore scenario is that it entails a genuine rejection of Madisonian dictates. Not only would its goal be to render inoperative an important governing institution, one central to the Founders' concept of checks and balances and separation of powers, but it would introduce an entirely new principle, the notion that the people have a right to reshape political institutions not in their capacity as citizens of the separate states, but as citizens of a single nation. "Electoral despotism" of this sort would have Jefferson spinning in his grave, but that is precisely the point. It would be the first step toward knocking the Founders off their pedestal and hence a step toward the Constitution's de-sanctification. Rather than a sacred mystery, the goal is to enable Americans to see their governing institutions as something created not by a race of giants, but by a group of decidedly flawed individuals.

If Al Gore was to take such a step, what would be the consequence? For starters, we can assume that there would be no shortage of eminent constitutional authorities telling him that such a step would be illegal. If the Constitution says that only the Electoral College College can choose a president, then that's what the Constitution says. Yet the experts would be wrong. The law cannot prevent a candidate from voluntarily withdrawing from the race, nor can it prevent individual electors from changing their votes once he has given them permission to change sides. If Gore stuck to his guns, such protests would soon die away.

We can also assume that the legal professoriat would not be the only ones to react adversely, but that George W. Bush would, too. He would undoubtedly reject any such offer out of hand, not because it would mean surrendering a crucial political advantage, needless to say, but because he believes in God, the Constitution, and standing by the laws that made America great. Dubya's response would be all too predictable: "The Electoral College is how the Founding Fathers wanted us to choose the president, and I would no more disobey the Founding Fathers than I would disobey the word of God." The secret joy that would surge through Republican hearts would be all too predictable also. What more could the GOP ask for than a Democrat campaigning against the Constitution? Chortling that Gore had handed them his head on a silver platter, they would immediately fan out across the country, confident that the people would no more vote against the Founders than the flag.

But if Gore stuck to his guns in this regard also, the results could be dramatic. In essence, it would mean transforming the presidential election into a constitutional referendum. Instead of merely Bush versus Gore, the question before voters would now be that of the Electoral College versus the popular vote. Instead of concentrating on a handful of swing states as they did in 2000, the logic of the Democrats' position would compel them to concentrated. Formerly, it had not mattered whether turnout in such states was fifty, sixty, or seventy percent as long as they remained firmly in the Democratic camp. Once the outcome was secure, each additional vote was superfluous, which is why campaign workers saved their energy for those states where the electoral votes were still up for grabs. But now that the Democrats had pledged to disregard the Electoral College, such considerations would no longer apply. With every last vote suddenly mattering a great deal, Democratic campaign workers in California, New York, and so on would have an incentive to ring every doorbell, canvass every ghetto street, and scour every union hall and homeless shelter in search of Gore supporters who had not yet made it to the polls.

By pledging to abide by the popular vote, Gore would transform how the election was argued and fought. In mobilizing the people against the Electoral College, he would be mobilizing them against a system that favors small over large states, whites over blacks and Hispanics, and farmers and ranchers over subway riders and commuters in crowded urban and suburban districts. Whether he liked it or not, he would be stirring up class passions against a ticket headed by a pair of Texas oilmen and backed by some eighty-six percent of major corporate CEOs. Instead of a struggle for control of the White House, the race would now be a struggle for control of the political system itself, a struggle framed from the start by the issues of race and class.

Given the immense demographic disparities among the fifty states—ten states as of the year 2000 account for fifty-four percent of the US population, while ten others account for under three percent—such a contest would render more likely rather than less the sort of split decision in which one candidate wins the popular vote and the other wins the electoral. This is what happened in 2000, yet in one respect the results a second time around would be very different. Rather than surprised by the outcome, voters on both sides would be prepared. All eyes would be on Bush to see what he did. Would he try to take the White House despite once again losing the popular vote? After specifically voting against the Electoral College, would the majority let him? Depending on his response, the situation could be nothing less than revolutionary. Even if by some fluke, moreover, Bush won both the popular and electoral vote, the cat would still be out of the bag. Eventually, the question would be sure to come up again, and when it did, the outcome would likely be very different. The days in which the US Constitution could carry on in blithe defiance of modern democratic norms would be numbered.

⋘◉⋙

Of course, there is a good deal that makes this scenario implausible as well. As we have seen, such a step would be a radical departure in terms of America's hidebound politics, and someone given to quoting a thirteenth-century legal authority like Henry de Bracton is not generally one for radical departures. Indeed, everything that Al Gore had learned in the course of his long political career would tell him not to embark on such a wild and risky course. Every adviser, every pundit, every academic hoping for a White House job would tell him that the safest thing would be to mount a campaign very much like the one he mounted in 2000 in the hope of gaining the extra sliver of voters needed to put him over the top. Rather than paying less attention to swing states, they would counsel him to pay more. Instead of attacking the Electoral College, they would advise that he wrap himself up in the Constitution all the more completely. All indications are that Gore would do as he was told, just as he did in December 2000. Rather than stirring the people up, he would lull them back to sleep.

Moreover, the real danger from a Democratic point of view is not that a radical departure of this sort would fizzle, but that it would succeed all too well, igniting passions that they would prefer to remain dormant. Although leftists such as the late Michael Harrington argued that the Democrats were a working-class party along the lines of Labour in Britain or the European social democrats, nothing could be farther from the truth. Rather than heightening or even acknowledging class differences, the Democratic Party exists to obscure them under a thick layer of patriotism, nostalgia, and American exceptionalism. While a politician like Al Gore is not above stirring up low-grade populist resentment against some of the GOP's more egregious abuses, a totalizing concept like class is alien to his makeup. Rather than encouraging conflict between labor and capital, Gore, a former senator from a right-to-work state, would do everything in his power to discourage it. Comity, not conflict, is his patriotic ideal.

Challenging the Constitution even obliquely is also alien to his makeup. In calling on voters to render the Electoral College a dead letter, Gore could not avoid encouraging them to grapple with some of the Constitutions's other less palatable features. A Senate organized on the principle of equal state representation regardless of population—shouldn't the people figure out some way of sidelining this pre-modern relic as well? Shouldn't they see to it that the Supreme Court never hands down a judicial atrocity like the one in December 2000? Aren't federal–state relations also due for an overhaul?

The answer is that they are. Indeed, it is hard to imagine an aspect of America's Ancient Constitution that is not in need of being rethought. Yet as someone steeped from childhood in America's superannuated eighteenth-century politics, Gore would likely see democratic change of this sort essentially the same way that the Founders would have seen it, i.e. as something irrational and anarchic. Since he can't imagine an alternative to the *ancien régime,* any attempt to replace it would strike him as purely destructive. His only choice is to somehow make the existing system work. As far as he would be concerned, there is simply no alternative to the House, Senate, and presidency revolving around an immovable Constitution, just as there is no alternative to the sun and planets continuing to resolve around an immovable earth—or is it the other way around?

On the other hand, stranger things have happened. Respectable politicians who open the door to structural reform and then get more than they bargained for are not unknown. Neither are ultra-establishmentarians who none the less recognize that society has reached a dead end and that radical change is unavoidable. Al Gore could usher in democracy, or democracy could usher itself in without him. Regardless of what happens, the United States cannot avoid the problem of what to do with an ossified, eighteenth-century Constitution forever.

NO ⤶

Richard A. Posner

Electoral College Reform

There are two quite different kinds of criticism of the Electoral College. The first is that it is undemocratic, and that this is bad. The second (which the Florida experience has made salient) is that it is an unreliable device for selecting the President.

It is undemocratic in two ways. The first and obvious one is that it is malapportioned, because each state gets two electoral votes, regardless of the state's population, in addition to votes equal to the state's delegation in the House of Representatives. Malapportionment is a common feature of democratic governments, the U.S. Senate being the most conspicuous surviving example in the United States now that the Supreme Court has required that state senators be elected from districts of equal population. But the undemocratic character of malapportionment is masked when each malapportioned district elects a different official. No one bothers to add up the number of votes that all the Republican and all the Democratic senatorial candidates receive in an election and compare the totals; and if the votes were aggregated, the interpretation would be difficult, since the sum of the votes for each party would not be the votes received by a single candidate. Nor are votes in the Senate translated into the number of voters who voted for those Senators who prevailed in the Senate vote, because those voters did not vote for particular bills. The mask is stripped off malapportionment when the popular vote is for electors pledged to a particular candidate, whose name, indeed, appears on the ballot, so that the aggregate popular vote for each candidate is immediately computed and reported. The malapportionment of the Electoral College is thus transparent—one has only to compare a candidate's percentage of the electoral vote with his percentage of the popular vote—especially in elections in which the popular vote winner loses in the Electoral College.

Despite the closeness of the 2000 election, there is no doubt that Gore really did win the popular vote, in the sense that, had the entire nationwide vote been recounted by an infallible counter using the best criteria for determining whether a ballot should be counted as a vote, Bush would not have overcome Gore's lead. Nationwide about 2 percent of all the ballots cast were not counted as votes for one reason or another. Suppose, very optimistically,

From Richard A. Posner, *Breaking the Deadlock: The 2000 Election, the Constitution, and the Courts* (Princeton University Press, 2001). Copyright © 2001 by Princeton University Press. Reprinted by permission of Princeton University Press. Notes omitted.

that the infallible counter would have recovered half of these as votes. Suppose further, rather pessimistically, that 1 percent of the 100 million votes that were recorded for one Presidential candidate or another were not counted carefully. On these assumptions, 2 million votes cast in the 2000 election would be in play. To overcome Gore's lead of 540,000 votes, Bush would have to be awarded 1,270,001 of the 2 million votes, which is almost two-thirds—an unrealistic expectation given the election outcome and the absence of any theory that would point to Bush as the wildly disproportionate favorite of the voters whose votes got botched. Florida's experience suggests that Democratic voters are more likely than Republican ones to spoil their ballots.

The fact that the Electoral College is undemocratic is not decisive against it any more than the fact that the Senate is malapportioned, or that federal judges are not elected at all, need be thought a flaw in our system of government. Ours is not a pure democracy, and we know . . . that pure democracy is as undesirable as it is unattainable. But it is not all that easy to come up with a convincing justification for the Electoral College. From a 1787 political standpoint it was an ingenious—but not necessarily a principled or, had it not been for political imperatives, even a sensible—device for achieving two purposes important to the framers. These were (1) preserving the balance among the states that had been struck in the design of the Congress (2) without confiding the election of the President to the Congress, a method of achieving objective (1) that would have weakened the Presidency unduly.

The invention of the Electoral College also reflected concerns about the administrability of a nationwide popular election that have no current validity; equally anachronistic concerns, rooted in a preference for deferential democracy, that the President's status and dignity would be seriously compromised were he directly elected by *hoi polloi* who should in any event entrust their "betters" with momentous political choices such as the choice of the President; and also expectations, which have proved unfounded, that the contingent election procedure ordained by the Constitution—election of the President by the House of Representatives (the most democratic component of the governmental structure created at Philadelphia in 1787) if no candidate received a majority of the electoral votes—would be used as or more frequently than the normal method. The framers did not foresee political parties, let alone a two-party system, which would make it rare for one of the Presidential candidates to fail to obtain a majority of the Electoral College. The two-party system doomed any hope that the Electoral College would choose the "best" person to be President, since the choice would be limited to the candidates picked by the parties. (The electors could pick the better, but not the best.) Another way to put this is that a party system is already a system of indirect election, making indirect election via the Electoral College otiose. And when there are only two major candidates, both will pitch their appeal to the median voter and so are likely to be much alike, leaving the Electoral College with little scope for choice quite apart from the limited number of choices.

Even in the absence of parties, the type of indirect election envisaged by the creators of the Electoral College did not make a lot of sense. The implicit theory was that the public at large is more competent to pick individuals who can pick a President well than to pick the President directly. But if this is so, then the people will not be exercising a political judgment at all. It is unclear whether they are any better at picking a good President-picker than at picking a good President. But even if they are, they are likely to want to exercise a political judgment rather than be content with picking other people to exercise such a judgment; and then electors will compete by pledging themselves to a particular candidate—which means that instead of electors being the people most competent to pick the President, they will be the people most loyal to the candidate and therefore *least* likely to exercise an independent judgment. . . .

Were Presidents elected by popular vote, a nationwide recount might have been unavoidable in 2000 (and in a number of previous Presidential elections as well, such as those of 1876, 1880, 1884, 1888, 1960, 1968, and 1976, in all of which the popular vote was very close) because Gore's popular vote margin was so slight. He received 51 million votes and Bush 50.5 million, a difference of 0.5 percent. If a plurality of the popular vote were what elected a President, a margin this small would have incited calls for a national recount on the same grounds that Gore argued for a Florida recount. Even though under a post–Electoral College, pure-popular-vote regime the Presidential election would presumably still be administered by the states, no state could refuse the demand for a recount on the ground that the election in that state had not been close. The state would no longer be a relevant entity for purposes of determining the winner of the election. Each candidate would be trolling for votes everywhere in the country.

Suppose Gore had won the popular election by one vote, but in New York his margin was a million votes. Nevertheless, if Bush could in a recount pick up one net vote in New York, he would erase Gore's lead, so it would be worthwhile for Bush to seek a recount there. The example is extreme, but the reality is stark enough. Gore's margin in the nationwide popular vote averaged fewer than eight votes per precinct. There is little doubt that if Bush's people nosed around heavily Democratic precincts throughout the nation they would come up with colorable arguments about voter and tabulation errors—not to mention outright fraud, which remains common, especially with regard to absentee ballots—that might have made the difference (though it would have been a long shot, given Gore's popular-vote margin), while Gore might have been eager to shore up his lead by also hunting for votes all over the country. A national recount would be an expensive nightmare. The risk of protracting the period of deadlock and precipitating a rancorous battle in Congress in January would be greater than under the present system, which localizes the deadlock to one or conceivably a few states.

So there is a case for retaining the Electoral College after all—though not a case the framers of the Constitution would have recognized. I have yet to mention the most undemocratic feature of the Electoral College, however, and this will take us directly to a consideration of the second class of criticisms, that the Electoral College is an unreliable device for determining the winner of a Presidential election. Its most undemocratic feature is that the Constitution requires neither that Presidential electors be elected by popular vote, nor, if the state chooses that method of picking electors, that they cast their electoral votes in conformity with the wishes of the voters who elected them. The Constitution leaves the manner of selecting the electors to each state's legislature, as we know; and it places no limitations on the electors' choice among candidates.

It is true that all states now select their Presidential electors by popular vote, and as no state is about to abandon that approach it would be pedantic to complain that the Constitution does not require it and that Congress could not by statute require it (more on that shortly). The practical concern, rather, is that electors are not bound to cast their votes for the candidate to whom they are pledged. In an election as close as that of 2000, the defection of a tiny handful —in 2000 of only 3—of the 538 electors could swing the election. Bush's margin in the electoral vote was 271 to 266 rather than 267 because one of Gore's electors decided to abstain in protest against the District of Columbia's not having statehood. Had three of Bush's electors voted for Gore, the vote would have been 269 to 268 in Gore's favor. Gore would have had a plurality, but not a majority, of the appointed electors, so the House of Representatives would have chosen the President.

No defection by electors has yet swung an election (out of more than 21,000 electoral votes cast since the first Presidential election, only 10 have violated explicit pledges, which is no surprise, since electors are handpicked by the candidate for their loyalty). The likelihood of its ever happening is even less than the statistics imply. That Gore elector who defected would not have done so if it would have cost Gore the election! But the possibility that runway electors might swing an election cannot be excluded. The 2000 election has sensitized us all to the possibility that small probabilities can become frightening actualities.

Many states have passed laws requiring electors to honor their pledge to the candidate who selected them, but even if these laws are constitutional, the refusal of an elector to comply with the law would have the same effect on the electoral vote as it would if he were legally free to vote his pleasure (unless Congress decided not to count his vote). And it is doubtful that the laws *are* constitutional. The only authority the Constitution grants the states with regard to Presidential electors is authority for the state legislature to determine the manner in which the electors are appointed, not the manner in which they vote. A law that makes the elector a mere rubber stamp of the popular vote is contrary to the notion of indirect election that is at the heart of the Electoral College; the voter *becomes* the elector under such a law. It would likewise be unconstitutional, I believe, for Congress to pass a law requiring that electoral votes be cast in conformity with the state's popular vote. Nothing in the Constitution authorizes Congress to eliminate the system of indirect election that the Electoral College creates.

I do not say that the Supreme Court would hold laws that require electors to stand by their pledges unconstitutional. The fact that such laws have been in force for many years without being questioned, and their utility in averting potential election disasters, are practical arguments for brushing aside merely "logical" objections to their constitutionality; and *Ray v. Blair*, though distinguishable, provides some support. But most states do not have such laws, and those that do cannot actually prevent an elector from violating his pledge even if they could lawfully punish him for doing so. In any case the freedom of electors to defy the popular vote is only one of the concerns with the Electoral College's reliability as a method of determining the choice of President without precipitating the kind of chaos that the Supreme Court may have averted in *Bush v. Gore*. Another concern, of course, is the failure of the Constitution to prescribe a method for resolving disputes over electors.

The fact that the electoral votes are counted in the presence of both houses of Congress implies . . . that Congress is authorized to resolve, with or without judicial review, . . . disputes over whose votes should be counted. Congress took a crack at this in Title III, with very imperfect results, as we have seen. The law could be improved, but the problem is organic rather than accidental. The short time between the election and the inauguration, the necessity under the conditions of modern U.S. government for a transition period before inauguration in order to enable the President-elect to organize the new administration and so hit the ground running on Inauguration Day, the fact that the "old" Congress takes a Christmas recess and the new one is not sworn in until after the first of the year, and the structure of Congress with its two houses and hundreds of members and poor reputation for statesmanship—all these things taken together make a credible, expeditious resolution of a dispute over electors unlikely. Title III did not accomplish much; and anyway there is nothing to prevent the two houses of Congress, when they meet together in January to count the electoral votes, for ignoring Title III, especially given its dubious constitutionality.

We need a constitutional amendment. For it to have any chance of adoption, it should focus on resolving disputes over electors and preventing "runaway" electors, rather than on abolition of the Electoral College. Runaway electors have historically been rare, as I have noted. But they could wreak havoc in a close election, and it is time to shut them down—a more urgent and feasible goal of constitutional reform than abolishing the Electoral College in the name of democracy. Not that abolition is an entirely quixotic long-term goal, despite the assumption that the small states—more plausibly the big ones—will oppose it and the fact that a constitutional amendment requires ratification by three-fourths of the states and so can be blocked by one more than one quarter of them. There was a serious push in 1969 to 1970 to abolish the Electoral College in favor of a nationwide popular vote with a runoff if no candidate received at least 40 percent of the vote. The proposal passed the House by the requisite two-thirds vote but failed in the Senate. The objection to abolition has less to do with considerations of feasibility than with the fact that, as we have seen, a convincing case for abolition has not yet been made.

Of particular pertinence . . . is the fact that the democratizing and dispute resolution goals of Electoral College reform are in conflict, so that doing away with the Electoral College (and even some lesser reforms of the Electoral College) would exacerbate the problem of disputed Presidential elections. Consider the superficially attractive reform of requiring that each state's electoral vote be divided among the Presidential candidates in proportion to their share of the popular vote. This would reduce the likelihood that the popular vote winner would lose in the Electoral College, as well as eliminate the big-state advantage that the winner-take-all system confers. But it would increase the likelihood of deadlocks. Under the winner-take-all system, the only possible deadlock is a 50-50 split in the popular vote in the state. Under a proportional system, every vote combination on which the allocation of an electoral vote turned would be a candidate for deadlock and recount. Suppose a state has 10 electoral votes. Under the proportional system, if a candidate got 10 percent of the votes, he would get one elector; 20 percent, two; and so on. It might be uncertain whether he had gotten just 10 percent, uncertain whether he had gotten just 20 percent, and so on. There would be 10 potential vote combinations rather than one on which a recount would be necessary in order to determine which candidate had obtained an electoral vote.

What may be both feasible and helpful would be a constitutional amendment that did just two things. The first would be to require that each state's electoral votes be cast for the winner of the popular vote for President in their state. With the electors thus bound, there would be no need for electors at all—a welcome simplification of the Presidential selection process that would eliminate, for example, such problems as what to do when electors die or become disabled after the election but before the Electoral College vote. There would still be electoral votes under the proposed reform, but they would be computed automatically from the popular vote in each state and the state's determination of how to allocate electoral votes among candidates (whether winner take all or proportionately). Second, the amendment would require . . . that the winner of the popular vote in each state be determined in the manner directed by the state's legislature by statute passed *before* the election (implicit I think in Article II, but good to make explicit), subject to obligatory, rather than discretionary, review by the U.S. Supreme Court to determine the conformity of the state's determination of the winner with the legislature's directions. Contesting the result of the popular vote election in a state would still be possible, but there would be a streamlined, disciplined, and unquestionably constitutional method of resolution. The only difference so far as the resolution of the 2000 election deadlock is concerned, had the suggested amendment been in effect, would be that Bush, having lost the contest proceeding in the Florida supreme court, would have had a right to insist that the U.S. Supreme Court review the Florida court's decision for conformity to the Florida election law. The Supreme Court would not have had discretion to refuse to hear the appeal; and it would have been obliged to determine whether the Florida court was applying or revising the election statute, as well as to consider any other constitutional challenges to that court's resolution of the contest. This would lay to rest the curious notion that the Florida supreme court was a more appropriate body to rule on issues that might determine the outcome of a Presidential election than the Supreme Court of the United States. But this particular reform would doubtless be blocked by Democratic opposition to any measure that would tend to legitimize the Supreme Court's intervention in the 2000 election.

POSTSCRIPT

Should the Electoral College Be Abolished?

Although there is no serious political movement to abolish the electoral college, the theoretical question has long engaged students and teachers of American government. Is it democratic? How does it affect the conduct of presidential campaigns and of presidents in office? What would be the consequences of using alternative methods to elect a president? There are no easy answers to these questions. Lazare and Posner even disagree on which states and interests gain or lose the most from the electoral college.

The political figures and scholars who defend the electoral college in Gary L. Gregg II, ed., *Securing Democracy: Why We Have an Electoral College* (Intercollegiate Studies Institute, 2001) agree that the institution has done far more good than harm and that the alternatives are less desirable. In the decision of *Bush v. Gore* (2000), the Supreme Court declared that "the individual citizen has no federal constitutional right to vote for electors for President of the United States unless and until the state legislature chooses a statewide election as the means to implement its power to appoint members of the Electoral College." A variety of alternatives to the electoral college are examined in Paul D. Schumaker and Burdett A. Loomis, eds., *Choosing a President: The Electoral College and Beyond* (Chatham House, 2002).

If the electoral college were replaced by direct election, minority candidacies would be encouraged and a president might be elected with a small plurality. If a direct election with a run-off were instituted, there might be even more minor parties because they could not be accused of being spoilers, and the number of voters turning out for the second vote would almost surely be much less than for the first. This would be a dismal prospect in a country in which a 50 percent turnout is barely achieved in one presidential race. If the electoral vote were retained but the electors were elected in districts, a minority candidate could still win. In fact, Richard Nixon would have defeated John F. Kennedy in 1960 under such a scheme. Furthermore, if there had been proportional distribution, minority candidates would have been elected in at least four other elections. Clearly, then, historically pivotal outcomes may result from different methods of choosing a president. Take, for example, Abraham Lincoln's election in 1860. Under popular election with a run-off between the top two candidates in the absence of a majority or of even 40 percent, the two southern candidates would have thrown their support to Democrat Stephen Douglas, defeating Lincoln. Under a parliamentary system, with either single-member districts or proportional representation, Lincoln's Republican Party would have been the single largest party, but the Democrats and Constitutional Unionists could have formed a majority coalition.

ISSUE 7

Was *Bush v. Gore* Correctly Decided?

YES: Robert H. Bork, from "Sanctimony Serving Politics: The Florida Fiasco," *The New Criterion* (March 2001)

NO: Cass R. Sunstein, from "Order Without Law," in Cass R. Sunstein and Richard A. Epstein, eds., *The Vote: Bush, Gore, and the Supreme Court* (University of Chicago Press, 2001)

ISSUE SUMMARY

YES: Former judge Robert H. Bork contends that, in denying the effort of the Florida Supreme Court to rewrite the Florida election law, the U.S. Supreme Court correctly prevented Al Gore from overturning George W. Bush's narrow victory in the 2000 presidential election.

NO: Professor of jurisprudence Cass R. Sunstein concludes that the intervention of the U.S. Supreme Court to halt the vote recount in contested Florida districts lacked precedent, was unprincipled, and raised questions regarding the denial of equal protection, which the Court was unwilling to confront.

Although there had been at least three prior presidential elections in which the winning candidate received fewer popular votes than his opponents, the American people were unprepared for the election of 2000. With the counting and re-counting of votes and challenges in state and federal courts, this election took 36 days to decide. Although Vice President Al Gore had a national plurality of over a half million votes before Florida's 25 electoral votes were decided, he fell 4 electoral votes short of the 270 necessary to be elected president. If Texas governor George W. Bush's slim lead in Florida of fewer than 1,000 votes held, he would be elected.

Florida's county election boards use different methods for collecting votes; some use paper ballots while others use voting machines, for example. Punch card ballots are counted by machine, but a vote might not register if the card were incorrectly or incompletely punched. The so-called butterfly ballot used in Palm Beach County in the 2000 election placed the names of the candidates in two columns with the punch holes running between the columns.

Many voters who supported Gore, whose name was the second one down in the first column on this ballot, punched the second hole (whereas they should have punched the third), thereby mistakenly casting their votes for Reform Party candidate Patrick Buchanan.

Because of this confusion, the Democrats demanded a vote recount in several Florida counties. The opposing parties marshaled a host of arguments to support their views on the fairness or unfairness of voting and vote counting in Florida. Republicans stated that the deadline for reporting the vote was Tuesday, November 14, one week after Election Day; Democrats responded that state law provided for a manual recount but that it could not be completed that quickly. Republicans asserted that prompt counting and reporting of the vote would be necessary to avoid doubt as to the outcome; Democrats responded that many states have later dates for reporting the results and that the electoral college was not scheduled to meet until December 18. The arguments flew back and forth like mortar rounds. Republicans argued that manual counting is unlawful; Democrats, that hand counting is the oldest and most common form of ballot counting. Republicans contended that machine counting is more accurate; Democrats, that punch card ballots can be assessed more accurately by manual examination. The two sides also quarreled over the butterfly ballot, which Democrats argued cost them many votes. Republicans pointed out that the ballot was devised by a Democratic official. Democrats replied that it did not matter who adopted it if it violated common sense, fairness, and Florida law. And there were other quarrels—quarrels over standards for counting, quarrels over the counties that were selected for recounts, and the inevitable quarrel over who started the quarrelling.

The election was finally decided when a 5–4 majority of the U.S. Supreme Court decided in *Bush v. Gore* that equal protection had been denied as long as different ballots were counted in different ways, that the criterion of "the clear intent of the voter" is not a clear standard, and that the vote count must stop because Florida was running out of time to meets its self-imposed deadline of December 12 to choose unchallenged electors. This meant that Bush won Florida's 25 electoral votes and the election. The four dissenters rejected all of these arguments in their strongly worded opinions. Justice John Paul Stevens wrote, "Although we may never know with complete certainty the identity of the winner of this year's presidential election, the identity of the loser is perfectly clear. It is the nation's confidence in the judge as an impartial guardian of the rule of law."

In the following selections, Robert H. Bork asserts that the U.S. Supreme Court correctly called a halt to a selective vote recount in Florida, ending the threat that the Florida Supreme Court would rewrite the state's election law and that the Gore forces would steal the election. Cass R. Sunstein contends that the Court's "unjustifiably aggressive" opinion has no basis in precedent or history and that it constituted an unwarranted intervention in an electoral controversy.

Robert H. Bork

 **YES**

Sanctimony Serving Politics: The Florida Fiasco

Few events illustrate so starkly the debased state of America's political and legal culture as did Vice President Gore's frenzied attempts to overturn Governor Bush's narrow victory in the Florida presidential election. Almost no one and no institution emerged unscathed from the toxic mixture of unrestrained personal ambition and liberal ideology that forced the contest to ultimate resolution in the United States Supreme Court. Yet the lessons of that unseemly brawl have been obscured by the welter of recriminations, celebrations, and invincibly ignorant punditry that have followed.

The battle for Florida's twenty-five electoral votes, and hence for the presidency, involved so many lawsuits on different theories in both state and federal courts, as well as the possibilities of action by the Florida legislature and Congress, that it was impossible for a time to calculate all the possible outcomes of the chaos. Only in retrospect did the story line become clear.

As the entire world now knows, the disputed Florida votes were cast by punching out a chad opposite the preferred candidate's name. The votes, cast on November 7 and counted by machine, gave Bush the victory and, it seemed, the presidency. The closeness of the contest automatically triggered a machine recount, which confirmed the outcome, albeit by a narrower margin. Gore then sought a manual recount of all "undervotes" (ballots on which the machines had detected no vote for president) in four heavily Democratic counties. Florida's secretary of state, to whom the returns were to be made, refused to waive the November 14 statutory deadline, however, which left too little time for the recount and the inevitable challenges in court. But the Florida Supreme Court, composed of six Democrats and one independent, acting on its own motion, enjoined the certification of the vote. Citing the necessity of determining the "will of the people" (a phrase with ominous associations) and the need not to be deterred by a "hypertechnical reliance upon statutory provisions," the unanimous court ordered that the recount proceed to find the "intent" of the unknown persons who had not fully dislodged the chads on their ballots. Purporting to exercise its "equitable powers," the court extended the deadline to November 26, a date unrelated to any statute and apparently chosen simply to help Gore.

From Robert H. Bork, "Sanctimony Serving Politics: The Florida Fiasco," *The New Criterion*, vol. 19, no. 7 (March 2001). Copyright © 2001 by Robert H. Bork. Reprinted by permission of the author.

⋅⊶⊙⊷⋅

The U.S. Supreme Court, to the surprise of almost all court-watchers, took the case, unanimously stayed the recount, and remanded the case to the Florida court for clarification of the basis for its decision. Now divided four to three, the Florida court reinstated the November 26 deadline and held that all Florida counties must be recounted. Yet the court also said that votes counted after November 26 could be included, thus, in defiance of Florida law and its own opinion, creating a flexible "deadline" to give Gore the maximum opportunity to win. The shamelessness of this performance practically forced the U.S. Supreme Court to accept Bush's appeal. In an opinion issued on December 12, the court fractured. Five justices held that the deadline was that same day, that the Equal Protection Clause of the Fourteenth Amendment was violated by the disparate standards used by the recounters to determine the "intent" underlying each ballot, found the time (which amounted to a few hours) too short to conduct a proper recount, and ordered the process stopped. Two justices agreed to the equal protection ruling but thought the deadline was December 18, when the electors were to meet, and would have allowed the state the extra six days to attempt the surely impossible task of adopting adequate standards, completing a recount in all counties, and deciding all court challenges. Two justices would simply have affirmed the Florida court. Though the decision appears to be five to four, seven justices agreed that a violation of equal protection was in progress and, since a valid recount could not have been completed even by December 18, Bush had, in practical effect, won seven to two.

The conclusion that the Equal Protection Clause had been violated raises serious difficulties, however. At first glance, it seems hard to deny that an essentially standardless process by which some votes are valid and other, identical, votes are not raises equal protection problems. Some recounters considered only partially detached chads a vote while others settled for a dent or a crease, and these differences occurred not only from county to county but also within counties and between recounters. But these and similar disparities have always existed within states under our semi-chaotic election processes. By raising that to the level of a constitutional violation, the court federalized state election laws. The opportunities for uncertainty, litigation, and delay in close elections seem endless, which is probably why federal courts have never entered this particular briar patch before. Once the Equal Protection Clause is unleashed, it will apply to every federal, state, and local election in the country. Ironically, several justices known for their concern about the independence of states struck a blow against federalism.

Three justices—Rehnquist, Scalia, and Thomas—offered a better rationale in their concurring opinion. They relied on Article II, Section 1, Clause 2 of the Constitution, which provides that "Each State shall appoint, in such manner as the Legislature thereof may direct, a Number of Electors" and on Section 5 of Title 3 of the United States Code which requires that the laws governing an election must be made beforehand. The Florida court violated these requirements by changing after the election both the final date for certification and the responsibilities of the various state agencies as the legislature had defined them. Counsel for Gore was put in the untenable position at oral argument of contending that the Florida court could make post-election changes in the law that the legislature could not. Had two of the other four justices who relied upon equal protection gone along with this analysis, the decision would have been sounder and much future difficulty avoided. Article II and Section 5 of Title 3 speak only to presidential elections and do not rule out every difference in election procedures within a state. But that rationale did not command a majority, perhaps because the other four justices found the familiar rhetoric of equal protection more comfortable.

So fraught with complications and dangers is the court's equal protection rationale that some commentators have expressed the hope that it will prove to be like a railroad ticket good for this day and train only. If so, that would merely reveal the inadequacy of the original ruling, and, in any event, courts are not supposed to issue decisions that cannot be shown to be aspects of more general principles. But the hope of inconsistency is probably forlorn anyway. If the Supreme Court intends to back away from equal protection in future election cases, that fact will not be known in advance to lower court judges who may proceed to federalize state election laws as the seven justices in *Bush v. Gore* suggest they should. In order to stop that trend, the court may have to shift to the different ground offered in the concurring opinion. That said, it must be remembered, in extenuation, that the justices were working under tremendous pressure of time and public scrutiny. It is no easy thing to hammer out a legal brief in one or two days, and the task is made almost impossible if several law firms are involved. The justices, each with four clerks, operate as nine separate law firms. Herding cats isn't even in it.

❧

Though the majority has been criticized for setting the cutoff date on the twelfth rather than the eighteenth of December, that seems a minor sin given the fact that neither date could realistically have been met. We are entitled to speculate that, with good reason, the majority so distrusted the recount process in Florida and the state's courts that it seemed better to end the matter on the twelfth rather than put the country and the court through six more days of legal chicanery and useless turmoil.

Cruder commentators, with which the print and electronic media and law school faculties are amply supplied, put the decision down to raw political partisanship. But the idea that each of the seven justices who found a constitutional violation and the five who voted to end the recounts immediately were voting for a Bush presidency is a bit too crass to be credited, particularly if you know the people involved.

The more likely explanation is that the justices saw an election being stolen in Florida and that the Supreme Court of Florida was not only complicit but also willing to defy the U.S. Supreme Court. Yet the court majority could not agree on a valid constitutional doctrine to remedy an incipient constitutional crisis. The justices could hardly admit that they shared Justice Stevens's version of the Bush position:

> What must underlie the petitioners' entire federal assault on the Florida election procedures is an unstated lack of confidence in the impartiality and capacity of the state judges who would make the critical decisions if the vote were to proceed.

Stevens was arguing that the court had no right to entertain such misgivings. But there were excellent reasons to do just that. One might add that there was a justified lack of confidence in those who would do the actual recounting. Canvassing boards regularly split two to one along party lines in finding valid votes for Gore. Once the boards decided that a dimple or a crease on a chad could indicate a voter's intent, an impossibly subjective element was introduced. (A crease may be created, of course, by the thumbnail of the recounter.) Scalia noted, moreover, that it was "generally agreed that each manual recount produces a degradation of the ballots, which renders a subsequent recount inaccurate."

The court's choice was between an inadequate majority opinion and permitting the stealing of a presidential election. It does not help a great deal to say, as some have, that the court's performance was statesmanlike. That is an excellent quality in other branches of government but it is not a primary aspect of judicial virtue. Adherence to law is. It is just as well, therefore, that there is a valid rationale for what the majority did even if only three justices subscribed to it. The defiance shown by the Florida Supreme Court coupled with the obvious purpose of the repeated recounts of selected counties to produce a victory for Al Gore cried out for someone or some institution to save the integrity of the electoral process. That the U.S. Supreme Court did.

❧

The majority opinion raises a further question: whether a desirable result can ever be an adequate reason for law-bending. That seems to depend on one's political sympathy. The question lay at the heart of the court's ruling in *United States v. Nixon* requiring the president to comply with the special prosecutor's subpoena of White House tapes. Strictly speaking, the case was not justiciable, for it involved a dispute between the head of the executive branch and a subordinate officer. Such disputes can be resolved definitively by an order from the president to the subordinate, which means that there is not the "case" or "controversy" that Article III of the Constitution requires for the exercise of judicial power. James St. Clair, Mr. Nixon's attorney, tried to make that argument to the Supreme Court but Justice Potter Stewart responded that in the ordinary case that would be true, but here the president, through the acting attorney general, me, had given the prosecutor a charter that guaranteed his right to go to court. That was not, of course, a complete answer. The case would not have been different if a president gave a charter to the secretary of defense promising not to interfere in military decisions and then sued to make a reluctant secretary order the invasion of Grenada. No court, in the ordinary course, would have entertained that suit since, charter or no, the president has the constitutional power as commander in chief to control the military. The issue would be as nonjusticiable a question as can be imagined. St. Clair, however, did not respond to the charter argument, and the court relied upon it in deciding the case against Nixon.

The court was, however, under enormous "hydraulic pressure." The Watergate scandal had reached the highest pitch of public emotion, and it was unthinkable to the public that the court would refuse to decide; the general outrage that there seemed to be no way to get the (expected) incriminating evidence from the White House, that the Watergate controversy was unresolvable, was more than the court could be expected to bear. So it was with the ongoing subversion of the presidential election in the seemingly endless demand for selective recounts in Florida. With a difference: when, jurisdiction or no jurisdiction, the tapes case went against Nixon, there was no suggestion by liberals, and little enough by anybody else, that the decision was illegitimate. Instead, there was general satisfaction. But when a decision that may be criticized goes against a Democrat, as this one did against Gore, there is widespread denunciation of the court as having behaved politically.

It is possible to be at once critical of the majority's legal performance in *Bush v. Gore* and yet recognize that such performances are inevitable, or at least almost irresistible, when the pressure is high enough. Very few people today are critical of the court's 1803 decision in *Marbury v. Madison*, though this first broad assertion of the power of judicial review came in a case over which the Supreme Court had no jurisdiction and which required the wilful misconstruction of a congressional statute in order to gin up a bogus constitutional issue. John Marshall was combating the centrifugal force of the Jeffersonians, who held the presidency and a congressional majority and who sought to weaken the national government so that the United States would once more resemble a confederacy rather than a unified nation. That may not be an adequate justification, but the case is now regarded as sacred writ.

Some of the fiercest attacks upon the *Bush v. Gore* majority came from within the court. Justice Stevens announced that the "loser" is "the nation's confidence" in the judiciary "as an impartial guardian of the rule of law." The judiciary, and in particular the court upon which Stevens sits, has not been an impartial guardian of, or even particularly interested in, the rule of law. Stevens is himself a leader of the most political wing of the court, regularly finding policies in the Constitution that are really only items on the liberal agenda for the nation.

Public comments on the case, some of them thoughtful, more of them intemperate, virtually all missed the point that there was a solid rationale for the decision even though only three Justices articulated it. Stuart Taylor, Jr., one of the more thoughtful commentators, said in *National Journal* on December 16 that

> the U.S. and Florida Supreme Courts have done very little to make the law respectable. If this cloud has a silver lining, it comes as a reminder to a court-

worshipping nation that judges are as fallible (and sometimes as political) as politicians.

Aside from the fact that the nation is very likely to go on worshipping courts, what, exactly, could the nation do if it got over its worshipping ways? The courts might modify their adventurism somewhat if public opinion turned decisively against them, but that is unlikely. Too many influential groups—law school and university faculties, print and electronic journalists, Hollywood, all of our faux intelligentsia—support and encourage the court's political role because it usually results in the political results they like.

Taylor also holds out a hope that seems to me forlorn:

> [F]orceful criticism of unstatesmanlike decisions such as this one—and of the Florida court's hubristic, judicial imperialism—is a vital antidote to the tendency of judges of all political stripes to aggrandize their own power. Indeed, if judges cannot be persuaded to restrain themselves, they risk a dangerous and destabilizing popular backlash.

It is unclear what would be dangerous and destabilizing about a popular backlash against judges who undertake to rule without a warrant. The questions to be asked are whether the courts are not now themselves a dangerous and destabilizing force in our polity and whether a popular backlash could produce a result worse than the continuing displacement of popular self-government by judges. Indeed, it is not at all clear what a backlash could accomplish. We are hardly likely to deprive courts of their power of judicial review. Perhaps for that reason, repeated warnings of an effective backlash have never been borne out.

❦

During the era of the Warren Court, the contempt for law and the desire to make major policy were so blatant that even the court's supporters repeatedly warned that results reached with so little respect for craftsmanship and candor made the court vulnerable. We have learned that those failings, however egregious, have not lessened the power of the court to do want it wants. There is, unfortunately, no particular reason to believe that will change. Indeed, Earl Warren, the exemplar of lawless judges, is now celebrated as a great and humane jurist.

The New York Times reporter Linda Greenhouse, who has covered the court for years, cautions that the need for the court to explain its actions in terms the public can understand and accept "is arguably greater than ever when the court can be perceived as stepping over the fine but nonetheless still distinct line that separates law and politics." "Beyond debate" she said, "is the fact that the court has now placed itself in the midst of a political thicket where it has always most doubted its institutional competence and where as a personal matter the justices have always appeared least comfortable." That would be a remarkably obtuse observation for any observer of the court's adventures. But it is a particularly astounding admonition coming from a woman who marched in pro-abortion demonstrations to the Supreme Court to support abortion and

Roe v. Wade. She should have no illusions about the political thicket the court long ago entered, with her enthusiastic approval.

The most strident attacks on the court's performance, however, came from Jeffrey Rosen of *The New Republic* and the lawyer-novelist Scott Turow. In an article with the title "Disgrace: The Supreme Court commits suicide," Rosen wrote that the five justices in the majority have "made it impossible for citizens of the United States to sustain any kind of faith in the rule of law as something larger than the self-interested political preferences" of the five. "We've had," Mr. Rosen informs us, "quite enough of judicial saviors." He thinks "The appropriate response [to *Bush v. Gore*] is to appoint genuinely restrained judges, in the model of Ginsburg and Breyer, who will use their power cautiously, if at all, and will dismantle the federal judiciary's imperious usurpation of American democracy." That sentence produces intellectual whiplash. Ginsburg? Breyer? Those are two of the four activist liberal judges on the court. They regularly ignore the Constitution as those who wrote and ratified it understood its principles, substituting instead their own extremely liberal social and cultural preferences. Justice Ginsburg wrote *U.S. v. Virginia et al.*, suddenly finding that after a century and a quarter of peaceful coexistence, the Fourteenth Amendment and the maintenance of the Virginia Military Institute as all-male were in irreconcilable conflict. Justice Breyer, as the junior member of the court, has been assigned few major opinions but has joined, with Justice Ginsburg, in cases such as VMI, Romer v. Evans—creating special voting rights for homosexuals—*Stenberg v. Carhart*—striking down a ban on partial birth abortions—and *Santa Fe School District v. Doe*—holding unconstitutional student elections permitting speech that might be used for prayer prior to high school football games. Sadly for Mr. Rosen's panegyric to the judicial left, the only justices who in any way resemble, though in different degrees, a restrained judiciary are the very justices he denounces as lawless.

Turow wrote in *The Washington Post* that the court' s decision "to stay the hand count of undervote ballots was the most overtly politicized action by a court that I have seen in 22 years of practicing law. It was an act of judicial lawlessness that effectively terminated Gore's chance to win the presidency." The prize for sanctimony in the service of politics, however, must be awarded jointly to the 554 law professors whose full-page ad in *The New York Times*, paid for by the left-wing People for the American Way Foundation, declared that

> By stopping the vote count in Florida, the U.S. Supreme Court used its power to act as political partisans, not judges of a court of law.... By taking power from the voters, the Supreme Court has tarnished its own legitimacy. As teachers whose lives have been dedicated to the rule of law, we protest.

The insufferable smugness of this statement is difficult to top. It is to be doubted, given the notorious politicization of the nation's law schools, that there are anything close to five-hundred professors whose lives are dedicated to the rule of law. There are many times that number, including many who signed the ad, whose professional careers have been devoted to seeing that the rule of law does not hamper judicial advancement of the liberal agenda.

Even more extreme and shrill was Alan Dershowitz's labelling the Florida Secretary of State Katherine Harris a "crook" aiding and abetting the Bush campaign. Character assassination is merely part of the ultra-liberal repertoire. More dangerous was Jesse Jackson's and the congressional Black Caucus's claims that Bush's victory had been won by fraud, intimidation of black voters, a partisan Republican Supreme Court, and that racism infected the whole process. This added racial tension to an already emotionally charged controversy and could only intensify the damaging sense of perpetual victimization that such leaders rely upon for their continuing power.

⋅✿⋅

Such hypocrisy did not, fortunately, go entirely unmasked. Fred Barbash, a *Washington Post* columnist, wrote,

> The shock expressed by partisan critics, their portrayal of a once-pristine court now forever sullied, drips with irony. Liberals counted on, and exploited, ideologically predictable court voting patterns for decades.

Randy E. Barnett, a professor at Boston University School of Law, also put paid to the liberal commentators' nonsense. Writing in *The Wall Street* Journal, he noted that

> we are urged that conservative judges must exercise the restraint they say they believe in. It is a convenient argument indeed. A kind of intellectual jujitsu that tries to turn an opponent's own thrusts against him. Activist judges are acting true to their principles when they escape the bounds of the law, while conservative justices are hypocrites if they abandon their principles of 'restraint' to bring wayward courts back to earth. Heads, activist justices win; tails, conservative justices lose.

The reaction and ferocity of the liberal assaults upon the court majority were stunning. Conservatives in the modern era have never mounted anything comparable. It is clear that liberals do not view conservatives as legitimate adversaries but rather as vermin—sexist, racist, hysterical about homosexuality—in short, primitives who are not entitled to govern, who win elections solely because large portions of the American public are equally corrupt. It follows that conservatism has no legitimate role in our politics or law, and, since civilization is at stake, any weapon may be used.

Liberal viciousness and mendacity in its current virulence may be traced to the election of Ronald Reagan in 1980. Since several prominent leftish Democratic senators went down to defeat along with Jimmy Carter, some of us made the mistake of thinking that the election represented a decisive shift in American culture. We could not have been more mistaken. That was the point at which the liberals became vicious, and their fury seems only to have intensified since. The Eighties was the time when the 1960s generation became active in national politics, and they brought their intransigence, intolerance, and irrationality (including a disregard for facts) with them from the campuses to politics and to a swarm of activist organizations. Hatred and intolerance migrated from the campuses to the national scene.

Republicans and conservatives (overlapping but by no means identical categories) behaved as the university faculties and administrations had before them: they went on the defensive and made concessions in futile attempts at appeasement. When they resist, they do so apologetically, rarely with the vigor and relentlessness necessary to meet the liberal attack. As Richard Brookhiser wittily if wistfully said of Republicans, "In their hearts they know they're wrong."

The attacks on Katherine Harris and others demonstrated that the politics of personal destruction, an invention of the Democratic Party, is alive and flourishing. I know something of that technique as do Clarence Thomas, Kenneth Starr, Henry Hyde and the House managers in the Clinton impeachment proceedings, and now John Ashcroft. It is by no means confined to politicians but is the common tactic of much of the media, of academics, and of the luminaries, so to speak, of the entertainment world. America is engaged in a religious war: a contest about culture and the proper ways to live. Judges, though this court-worshipping nation does not realize it, are combatants and extremely powerful ones. The activists, however, know what the public does not. Courts today are, more often than not, the heavy artillery of liberalism, engaged, for example, in creating and expanding a right to abortion, normalizing homosexuality, and driving religion from our public life. . . .

Viewing the win-at-any-cost temper of the Gore forces in Florida, I and others quoted [American jurist] Learned Hand's familiar passage:

> This much I think I do know—that a society so riven that the spirit of moderation is gone, no court can save; that a society where that spirit flourishes, no court need save; that in a society which evades its responsibility by thrusting upon the courts the nurture of that spirit, that spirit in the end will perish.

True enough, but those words do not quite fit our situation today. Too often overlooked is Hand's immediately following observation. Speaking of the temper of moderation and faith in the sacredness of the individual, he said:

> If you ask me how such a temper and such a faith are bred and fostered, I cannot answer. They are the last flowers of civilization, delicate and easily overrun by the weeds of our sinful human nature; we may even now be witnessing their uprooting and disappearance until in the progress of the ages their seeds can once more find some friendly soil.

Hand was prescient in suggesting that even in his day America might be witnessing the suffocation of the last flowers of civilization by the weeds of our nature. What we see, then, is not courts powerless to enforce moderation but courts too often actively destroying that indispensable virtue. *Bush v. Gore* was a valiant effort, legitimate in law, to rein in runaway political passions and a lawless state court those passions had captured.

NO ↩

Cass R. Sunstein

Order Without Law

U nder the leadership of Chief Justice William Rehnquist, the Supreme Court of the United States has generally been minimalist, in the sense that it has attempted to say no more than is necessary to decide the case at hand, without venturing anything large or ambitious. To some extent, the Court's minimalism appears to have been a product of some of the justices' conception of the appropriately limited role of the judiciary in American political life. To some extent, the tendency toward minimalism has been a product of the simple need to assemble a majority vote. If five or more votes are sought, the opinion might well tend in the direction of minimalism, reflecting judgments and commitments that can command agreement from diverse people.

To be sure, the Court has been willing, on occasion, to be extremely aggressive. In a number of cases, the Court has asserted its own, highly contestable vision of the Constitution against the democratic process. This aggressive strand has been most evident in a set of decisions involving federalism; it can be found elsewhere as well. But generally these decisions have been minimalist too. Notwithstanding their aggressiveness, they tend to decide the case at hand, without making many commitments for the future. Sometimes those decisions have even been "subminimalist," in the sense that they have said less than is required to justify the particular outcome.

In the Court's two decisions involving the 2000 presidential election, minimalism was on full display. The Court's unanimous decision in *Bush v Palm Beach County Canvassing Board* was firmly in the minimalist camp. Here the Court refused to resolve the most fundamental issues and merely remanded to the Florida Supreme Court for clarification. The Court's 5–4 decision in *Bush v Gore* was also minimalist in its own way, for it purported to resolve the case without doing anything for the future. But here the Court effectively ended the presidential election. It did so with rulings, on the merits and (especially) on the question of remedy, that combined hubris with minimalism.

The Court's decision in *Bush v Gore* did have two fundamental virtues. First, it produced a prompt and decisive conclusion to the chaotic post-election period of 2000. Indeed, it probably did so in a way that carried more simplicity and authority than anything that might have been expected from the United States Congress. The Court might even have avoided a genuine constitutional

From Cass R. Sunstein, "Order Without Law," in Cass R. Sunstein and Richard A. Epstein, eds., *The Vote: Bush, Gore, and the Supreme Court* (University of Chicago Press, 2001). Copyright © 2001 by University of Chicago Press. Reprinted by permission. Notes omitted.

crisis. Second, the Court's equal protection holding carries considerable appeal. On its face, that holding has the potential to create the most expansive, and perhaps sensible, protection for voting rights since the court's one-person, one-vote decisions of mid-century. In the fullness of time, that promise might conceivably be realized within the federal courts, policing various inequalities with respect to voting and voting technology. But it is far more likely that the Court's decision, alongside the evident problems in the Florida presidential vote, will help to spur corrective action from Congress and state legislatures.

The Court's decision also had two large vices. First, the Court effectively resolved the presidential election not unanimously, but by a 5–4 vote, with the majority consisting entirely of the Court's most conservative justices. Second, the Court's rationale was not only exceedingly ambitious but also embarrassingly weak. However appealing, its equal protection holding had no basis in precedent or in history. It also raises a host of puzzles for the future, which the Court appeared to try to resolve with its minimalist cry of "here, but nowhere else." Far more problematic, as a matter of law, was the majority's subminimalist decision on the issue of remedy. By terminating the manual recount in Florida, the Court resolved what it acknowledged to be a question of Florida law, without giving the Florida courts the chance to offer an interpretation of their own state's law.

In a case of this degree of political salience, the Court should assure the nation, through its actions and its words, that it is speaking for the law, and not for anything resembling partisan or parochial interests. A unanimous or near-unanimous decision can go a long way toward providing that assurance, because agreement between diverse people suggests that the Court is really speaking for the law. So too for an opinion that is based on reasoning that, whether or not unassailable, is so logical and clear as to dispel any doubt about the legitimacy of the outcome. The Court offered no such opinion.

From the standpoint of constitutional order, the Court might well have done the nation a service. From the standpoint of legal reasoning, the Court's decision was very bad. In short, the Court's decision produced order without law.

Preliminaries

Bush v Gore was actually the fourth intervention, by the United States Supreme Court, in the litigation over the outcome of the presidential election in Florida. In sequence, the Court's interventions consisted of the surprising grant of certiorari on November 24, 2000; the unanimous, minimalist remand on December 4, 2000; the grant of a stay, and certiorari, on December 9, 2000; and the decisive opinion in *Bush v Gore* on December 12, 2000.

The Unanimous, Minimalist Remand

On November 13, Florida Secretary of State Katherine Harris announced that the statutory deadline of November 14, 2000, was final, and that she would not exercise her discretion so as to allow extensions. On November 21, the Florida

Supreme Court interpreted state law to require the Secretary of State to extend the statutory deadline for a manual recount. This was a highly controversial interpretation of Florida law, and it might well have been wrong. At the time, however, any errors seemed to raise issues of state rather than federal law.

In seeking certiorari, Bush raised three federal challenges to the decision of the Florida Supreme Court. First, he argued that by changing state law, the Florida Court had violated Article II of the United States Constitution, which provides that states shall appoint electors "in such Manner as the Legislature," and not any court, may direct. Second, Bush invoked a federal law saying that a state's appointment of electors is "conclusive" if a state provides for the appointment of electors "by laws enacted prior to the day fixed" for the election. According to Bush, the Florida court did not follow, but instead changed, the law "enacted prior" to Election Day, and in his view this change amounted to a violation of federal law. Third, Bush argued that the manual recount would violate the Due Process and Equal Protection Clauses, because no clear standards had been established to ensure that similarly situated people would be treated similarly.

At the time, most observers thought it exceedingly unlikely that the Court would agree to hear the case. Even if the Florida Supreme Court had effectively "changed" state law, it appeared improbable that the United States Supreme Court could be convinced to say so. Whatever the merits, the Court seemed unlikely to intervene into a continuing controversy over the presidential vote in Florida. This was not technically a "political question," but it did not seem to be the kind of question that would warrant Supreme Court involvement, certainly not at this preliminary stage. To the general surprise of most observers, the Court agreed to grant certiorari, limited to the first two questions raised by Bush.

Bush asked the United States Supreme Court to hold that because the Florida Supreme Court had violated the federal Constitution and federal law, Florida's Secretary of State had the authority to certify the vote as of November 14. For his part, Gore wanted the Court to affirm the Florida Supreme Court on the ground that that court had merely interpreted the law. The United States Supreme Court refused these invitations and took an exceptionally small step, asking the state supreme court to clarify the basis for its decision. Did the state court use the Florida Constitution to override the will of the Florida legislature? In the Court's view, that would be a serious problem, because the United States Constitution requires state legislatures, not state constitutions, to determine the manner of appointing electors. The Supreme Court also asked the state court to address the federal law requiring electors to be appointed under state law enacted "prior to" Election Day. In its own opinion, the Florida Supreme Court had said nothing about that law.

This was judicial minimalism in action. Why did the Court proceed in this way? It seems possible that some of the justices refused to settle the merits on principle, thinking that the federal judiciary should insert itself as little as possible into the continuing electoral struggle. But the most likely explanation is that the Court sought unanimity and found, as groups often do, that unanimity is possible only if as little as possible is decided.

The Astonishing Stay

On December 8, the Florida Supreme Court ruled, by a vote of 4 to 3, that a manual recount was required by state law, and it thus accepted Gore's contest. This decision threw the presidential election into apparent disarray. With the manual recount beginning, it became quite unclear whether Bush or Gore would emerge as the winner.

On December 9, the Supreme Court issued a stay of the decision of the Florida Supreme Court. This was the first genuinely extraordinary action taken by the United States Supreme Court. It was not only extraordinary but also a departure from conventional practice, and one that is difficult to defend on conventional legal grounds—not because Bush lacked a substantial probability of success, but because he had shown no irreparable harm.

To be sure, some harm would come to Bush from the continuation of the manual recount. It is entirely possible that the recount would have narrowed the gap between Bush and Gore. This would have been an unquestionable harm to Bush, in the nontrivial sense that it would have raised some questions about the legitimacy of his ensuing presidency, if it had subsequently been determined that the manual recount was unlawful. But the question remains: How serious and irreparable would this "harm" have been? If the manual recount was soon to be deemed unlawful, would the Bush presidency really have been "irreparably" harmed? This is extremely doubtful.

At the same time, the stay of the manual recount would seem to have worked an irreparable harm to Gore. For Gore, time was very much of the essence, and if the counting was stopped, the difficulty of completing it in the requisite period would become all the more serious. By itself, the Supreme Court's stay of the manual recount did not hand the election to Bush. But it came very close to doing precisely that.

In these circumstances, can anything be said on behalf of the stay? A reasonable argument is available, at least in retrospect. Suppose that a majority of the Court was entirely convinced that the manual recount was unlawful, perhaps because in the absence of uniform standards, similarly situated voters would not be treated similarly. If the judgment on the merits was clear, why should the voting be allowed to continue, in light of the fact that it would undoubtedly have to be stopped soon in any case, and its continuation in the interim would work some harm to the legitimacy of the next president? The question suggests that if the ultimate judgment on the merits was clear, the stay would not be so hard to defend. If the likelihood of success is overwhelming, the plaintiff should not be required to make the ordinary showing of irreparable harm. The problem, then, was less the stay than the Court's ambitious, poorly reasoned judgment on the merits.

Order and Law

Merits: What the Court Said

On the merits, there are two especially striking features to the Court's decision. The first is that six justices were unwilling to accept Bush's major submission, to the effect that the Florida Supreme Court had produced an unacceptable change in Florida law. The second is that five members of the Court accepted the adventurous equal protection argument.

The equal protection claim does have considerable appeal, at least as a matter of common sense. If a vote is not counted in one area when it would be counted in another, something certainly seems to be amiss. Suppose, for example, that in one county, a vote will not count unless the stylus goes all the way through, whereas in another county, a vote counts merely because it contains a highly visible "dimple." If this is the situation, some voters can legitimately object that they are being treated unequally for no good reason.

In its per curiam opinion, the Court spelled out the equal protection rationale in some detail. "In some cases a piece of the card—a chad—is hanging, say by two corners. In other cases there is no separation at all, just an indentation." The disparate treatment of these markings in different counties was unnecessary, because the "search for intent can be confined by specific rules designed to ensure uniform treatment." In Florida, that search was not so confined, for the record suggested that in Miami-Dade County, different standards had been applied in defining legal votes; and Palm Beach County appeared to go so far as to change its standards during the process of counting. To this, the Court added "further concerns." These included an absence of specification of "who would recount the ballots," leading to a situation in which untrained members of "ad hoc teams" would be involved in the process. And "while others were permitted to observe, they were prohibited from objecting during the recount." Thus the Court concluded that the recount process "is inconsistent with the minimum procedures necessary to protect the fundamental right of each voter in the special instance of a statewide recount under the authority of a single state judicial officer."

The Court was well aware that its equal protection holding could have explosive implications for the future, throwing much of state election law into constitutional doubt. Thus the Court emphasized the limited nature of its ruling: "The question before the Court is not whether local entities, in the exercise of their expertise, may develop different systems for implementing elections. Instead, we are presented with a situation where a state court with the power to assure uniformity has ordered a statewide recount with minimal procedural safeguards.

Merits: Three Problems

There are three problems with this reasoning. First, the Court's decision lacked any basis in precedent. Second, the Court's effort to cabin the reach of its decision seemed ad hoc and unprincipled—a common risk with minimalism. And third, the system that the Court let stand seemed at least as problematic, from the standpoint of equal protection, as the system that the Court held invalid.

Precedent.   Nothing in the Court's previous decisions suggested that constitutional questions would be raised by this kind of inequality. The cases that the Court invoked on behalf of the equal protection holding—mostly involving one-person, one-vote and the poll tax—were entirely far afield. To be sure, the absence of precedential support is not decisive; perhaps the problem had simply never arisen. But manual recounts are far from uncommon, and no one had ever thought that the Constitution requires that they be administered under clear and specific standards.

To make the problem more vivid, suppose that in 1998, a candidate for statewide office—say, the position of attorney general—lost after a manual recount, and brought a constitutional challenge on equal protection grounds, claiming that county standards for counting votes were unjustifiably variable. Is there any chance that the disappointed candidate would succeed in federal court? In all likelihood the constitutional objection would fail; in most courts, it would not even be taken seriously. The rationale would be predictable, going roughly like this: "No previous decision of any court supports the view that the Constitution requires uniformity in methods for ascertaining the will of the voter. There is no violation here of the principle of one-person, one-vote. Nor is there any sign of discrimination against poor people or members of any identifiable group. There is no demonstration of fraud or favoritism or self-dealing. In the absence of such evidence, varying local standards, chosen reasonably and in good faith by local officials, do not give rise to a violation of the federal Constitution. In addition, a finding of an equal protection violation would entangle federal courts in what has, for many decades, been seen as a matter for state and local government."

Of course it is possible to think that this equal protection holding would be wrong. Whether the federal Constitution should be read to cabin local discretion in this way is a difficult question. The problem is that in a case of such great public visibility, the Court embraced the principle with no support in precedent, with little consideration of implications, and as a kind of bolt from the blue.

Reach.   It is not at all clear how the rationale of *Bush v Gore* can be cabined in the way that the Court sought to do. What is missing from the opinion is an explanation of why the situation in the case is distinctive, and hence to be treated differently from countless apparently similar situations involving equal protection problems. The effort to cabin the outcome, without a sense of the principle to justify the cabining, gives the opinion an unprincipled cast.

Suppose, for example, that a particular area in a state has an old technology, one that misses an unusually high percentage of intended votes. Suppose that many areas in that state have new technology, capable of detecting a far higher percentage of votes. Suppose that voters in that area urge that the Equal Protection Clause is violated by the absence of uniformity in technology. Why doesn't *Bush v Gore* make that claim quite plausible? Perhaps it can be urged that budgetary considerations, combined with unobjectionable and longstanding rules of local autonomy, make such disparities legitimate. In the context of a statewide recount administered by a single judge—the situation in *Bush v Gore*—these considerations appear less relevant. But it is easy to imagine cases in which those considerations do not seem weighty. I will return to these questions below.

Arbitrariness on all sides.   The system that the recount was designed to correct might well have been as arbitrary as the manual recount that the Court struck down—and hence the Court's decision might well have created an even more severe problem of inequality. Consider the multiple inequalities in the certified vote. Under that vote, some machines counted votes that were left uncounted by other machines, simply because of different technology. Where optical scan ballots were used, for example, voters were far more likely to have their votes counted than where punchcard ballots were used. In Florida, fifteen of every one thousand punchcard ballots showed no presidential vote, whereas only three of every optically scanned ballot showed no such vote. These disparities might have been reduced with a manual recount. If the broad principle of *Bush v Gore* is correct, manual recounts might even seem constitutionally compelled. But the Court's decision, forbidding manual recounts, ensured that the relevant inequalities would not be corrected.

Nor were the machine recounts free from inequality. Some counties merely checked the arithmetic; others put ballots through a tabulating machine. The result is a significant difference in the effect of the machine recount. If the constitutional problem consists of the different treatment of the similarly situated, then it seems entirely possible that the manual recount, under the admittedly vague "intent of the voter" standard, would have made things better rather than worse—and the decision of the United States Supreme Court aggravated the problem of unjustified inequality.

Overall evaluation.   On the merits, then, the most reasonable conclusion is not that the Court's decision was senseless—it was not—but that it lacked support in precedent or history, that it raised many unaddressed issues with respect to scope, and that it might well have authorized equality problems as serious as those that it prevented. In these ways, the majority's opinion has some of the most severe vices of judicial minimalism. In fact this was a subminimalist opinion, giving the appearance of having been built for the specific occasion.

Remedy

Now turn to the Court's decision on the issue of remedy. If the manual recount would be unconstitutional without clear standards, what is the appropriate federal response? Should the manual recount be terminated, or should it be continued with clear standards? At first glance, that would appear to be a question of Florida law. If the Florida legislature would want manual recounts to continue, at the expense of losing the federal safe harbor, then manual recounts should continue. If the Florida legislature would want manual recounts to stop, in order to preserve the safe harbor, then manual recounts should stop.

Why did the Supreme Court nonetheless halt the manual recount? The simple answer is that the Court thought it clear that the Florida Supreme Court would interpret Florida law so as to halt the process. As the Court wrote,

> The Supreme Court of Florida has said that the legislature intended the State's electors to "participat[e] fully in the federal electoral process" .... Because it is evident that any recount seeking to meet the December 12 date will be unconstitutional for the reasons we have discussed, we reverse the judgment of the Supreme Court of Florida ordering a recount to proceed.

Thus the Court concluded that as a matter of Florida law, a continuation of the manual recount "could not be part of an 'appropriate' order authorized by" Florida law.

This was a blunder. It is true that the Florida Supreme Court had emphasized the importance, for the Florida legislature, of the safe harbor provision. But the Florida courts had never been asked to say whether they would interpret Florida law to require a cessation in the counting of votes, if the consequence of the counting would be to extend the choice of electors past December 12. In fact the Florida Court's pervasive emphasis on the need to ensure the inclusion of lawful votes would seem to indicate that if a choice must be made between the safe harbor and the inclusion of votes, the latter might have priority. It is not easy to explain the United States Supreme Court's failure to allow the Florida Supreme Court to consider this issue of Florida law.

Here, then, is the part of the United Sates Supreme Court's opinion that is most difficult to defend on conventional legal grounds....

A Large New Right?

For the future, the most important question involves the scope of the right recognized in *Bush v Gore*. Notwithstanding the Court's efforts, that right is not at all easy to cabin, at least as a matter of basic principle. On its face, the Court appears to have created the most expansive voting right in many decades.

A Minimalist Reading

At its narrowest, the Court has held that in the context of a statewide recount proceeding overseen by a single judge, the standard for counting votes must be (a) uniform and (b) concrete enough to ensure that similarly situated people will be treated similarly. This holding extends well beyond the context of presidential elections; it applies to statewide offices, not just federal offices.

By itself this is a substantial renovation of current law, since over thirty states fail to specify concrete standards for manual recounts. This does not mean that state legislatures must set down clear standards in advance; a decision by state judges should suffice. But the inevitable effect of the opinion will be to increase the pressure for legislative reform at the state and possibly even the national level. Any state legislature would be well advised to specify the standard by which votes will be counted in the context of a manual recount. All this should count, by itself, as a gain for sense and rationality in the recount process.

Equality in Voting

It is hard to understand why the principle of *Bush v Gore* does not extend much further than the case itself, at least in the context of voting. Consider the following easily imaginable cases.

1. Poor counties have old machinery that successfully counts 97 percent of votes; wealthy counties have newer machinery that successfully counts 99 percent of votes. Those in poor counties mount a constitutional challenge, claiming that the difference in rejection rates is a violation of the Equal Protection Clause.
2. Same as the immediately preceding case, except the division does not involve poor and rich counties. It is simply the case that some areas use machines that have a near-perfect counting rate, and others do not. The distribution of machines seems quite random.
3. Ballots differ from county to county. Some counties use a version of the controversial "butterfly ballot"; most do not. It is clear that where the butterfly ballot is used, an unusual number of voters are confused, and do not successfully vote for the candidate of their choice. Does this violate the Equal Protection Clause?
4. It is a national election. Citizens in Alabama use different machinery from that used by citizens in New York. The consequence is that citizens in Alabama are far more likely to have their votes uncounted than citizens in New York. Do they have a valid equal protection claim? What if the statistical disparity is very large?

The *Bush* Court's suggestion that ordinary voting raises "many complexities" is correct; but how do those complexities justify unequal treatment in the cases just given? The best answer would point to two practical points: budgetary considerations and the tradition of local control. In light of these points, it might be difficult for some areas to have the same technology as others. Wealthy counties might prefer to purchase more expensive machinery, whereas poorer communities might devote their limited resources to other problems. Perhaps judicial caution in the cases just given can be justified in this way. But even if this is so, *Bush v Gore* plainly suggests the legitimacy of both state and national action designed to combat disparities of this kind. It is for this reason that the Court's decision, however, narrowly intended, set out a rationale that might well create an extremely important (and appealing) innovation in the law of voting rights. Perhaps legislatures will respond to the invitation if courts refuse to do so.

A General Requirement of Rules?

In fact the Court's rationale might extend more broadly still. Outside of the context of voting, governments do not impose the most severe imaginable constraints on official discretion. Because discretion exists, the similarly situated

are treated differently. Perhaps the most obvious example is the "beyond a reasonable doubt" standard for criminal conviction, a standard that different juries
will inevitably interpret in different ways. Is this unacceptable?

In the abstract, the question might seem fanciful; but analogous constitutional challenges are hardly unfamiliar. In the 1960s and 1970s, there was
an effort to use the Due Process and Equal Protection Clauses to try to ensure
more rule-bound decisions, in such contexts as licensing and admission to public housing. Plaintiffs argued that without clear criteria to discipline the exercise
of discretion, there was a risk that the similarly situated would not be treated
similarly, and that this risk was constitutionally unacceptable. But outside of
the most egregious settings, these efforts failed, apparently on the theory that
rule-bound decisions produce arbitrariness of their own, and courts are in a
poor position to know whether rules are better than discretionary judgments.
Does *Bush v Gore* require courts to extend the limited precedents here?

Perhaps it could be responded that because the choice between rule-
bound and more discretionary judgments is difficult in many cases, judicial
deference is generally appropriate—but not when fundamental rights, such as
the right to vote, are at risk. If so, *Bush v Gore* has a limited scope. But does this
mean that methods must be in place to ensure against differential treatment of
those subject to capital punishment? To life imprisonment? I cannot explore
these questions here. But for better or for worse, the rationale in *Bush v Gore*
appears to make it necessary to consider these issues anew.

Conclusion

If the Supreme Court is asked to intervene in an electoral controversy, especially a presidential election, it should try to avoid even the slightest appearance
that the justices are speaking for something other than the law. Unanimity, or
near-unanimity, can go a long way toward providing the necessary assurance.
Whether or not this is possible, the Court's opinion should be well-reasoned
and rooted firmly in the existing legal materials.

In *Bush v. Gore,* the Court did not succeed on these counts. The 5–4 division was unfortunate enough; it was still worse that the five-member majority
consisted of the most conservative justices. Regrettably, the Court's opinion
had no basis in precedent or history. To be sure, the equal protection argument
had a certain appeal in common sense. But even if it were correct, the natural
remedy would have been to remand to the Florida Supreme Court, to ask that
court to say whether Florida law would favor the manual recount over the safe
harbor provision, or vice-versa. This remedy seems especially sensible in light
of the fact that the inequalities that the Court condemned might well have been
less serious than the inequalities that the recount would have corrected.

Nonetheless, there are two things to be said on behalf of the Court's ruling. First, the Court brought a chaotic situation to an abrupt end. From the
standpoint of constitutional order, it is reasonable to speculate that any other
conclusion would have been far worse. In all likelihood, the outcome would
have been resolved in Congress, and here political partisanship might well have

spiraled out of control. Second, the principle behind the equal protection ruling has considerable appeal. In a statewide recount, it is not easy to explain
why votes should count in one area when they would not count elsewhere.
In fact the principle has even more appeal if understood broadly, so as to for-
bid similarly situated voters from being treated differently because their votes
are being counted through different technologies. Understood in that broader
way, the principle of *Bush v Gore* should bring a range of questionable practices
under fresh constitutional scrutiny.

Bush v Gore is likely to intensify public concern about unjustifiably aggressive decisions from the Supreme Court, and perhaps that concern will give the
Court an incentive to be more cautious about unsupportable intrusions into
the democratic arena. Far more important, *Bush v Gore* might come to stand for
a principle, in legislatures if not courts, that greatly outruns the Court's subminimalist holding—a principle that calls for an end to the many unjustified
disparities in treatment in voting and perhaps beyond. It would be a nice irony
if the Court's weak and unprecedented opinion, properly condemned on democratic grounds, led to significant social improvements from the democratic
point of view.

POSTSCRIPT

Was *Bush v. Gore* Correctly Decided?

The 2000 election produced more books by far than any other presidential contest, and they are largely focused on the legal questions of whether a Florida manual recount was desirable or necessary, why the Florida Supreme Court intervened, whether its decisions were justified or whether they represented an unconstitutional rewriting of the state's election laws, whether or not the U.S. Supreme Court had a right or responsibility to take the case on appeal, and how the Court finally resolved the case.

The unanswered questions will likely arise again. Should there be better methods of casting and counting votes? Should each state have a single criterion for vote counting? Is an unelected court the correct institution to resolve sharp disagreements regarding an election's outcome? If not the courts, then who? These and other questions are considered in a number of provocative studies of that election. Day-by-day, case-by-case, and virtually blow-by-blow accounts of this extraordinary post-election crisis have been compiled by correspondents of the *New York Times,* in *Thirty-Six Days: The Complete Chronicle of the 2000 Presidential Election Crisis* (Times Books, 2001), and of the *Washington Post,* in *Deadlock: The Story of America's Closest Election* (Public Affairs, 2001). More partisan are Dana Milbank, *Smashmouth: Two Years in the Gutter With Al Gore and George W. Bush* (Basic Books, 2001); John Tapper, *Down and Dirty: The Plot to Steal the Presidency* (Little, Brown, 2001); and Jeffrey Toobin, *Too Close to Call: The 36-Day Battle to Decide the 2000 Election* (Random House, 2001).

Although most book-length studies of the 2000 election are critical of the U.S. Supreme Court, Judge Richard Posner, in *Breaking the Deadlock: The 2000 Election, the Constitution, and the Courts* (Princeton University Press, 2001), offers a moderate defense, arguing that the Court's legal conclusions were "tenuous" and "a stretch," but a stretch justified by reasonable concern about the consequences of doing nothing. In contrast, Howard Gilman, in *The Votes That Counted* (University of Chicago Press, 2001), concludes that the Court should have done nothing. The results, he says, are "irrelevant to the key question of the Court's institutional obligation.... The election was a perfect tie. It wasn't the Court's responsibility to make the right call." Two collections of essays offer varied perspectives. Cass R. Sunstein and Richard A. Epstein, eds., *The Vote: Bush, Gore, and the Supreme Court* (University of Chicago Press, 2001), from which Sunstein's selection was taken, also contains Epstein's vigorous defense of the decision, " 'In Such Manner as the Legislature Thereof May Direct': The Outcome in *Bush v. Gore* Defended." Second, Larry J. Sabato, ed., *Overtime! The Election 2000 Thriller* (Longman, 2002) is a collection of essays reflecting different and often opposing viewpoints.

On the Internet ...

New American Studies Web

This eclectic site provides links to a wealth of Internet resources for research in American studies, including agriculture and rural development, government, and race and ethnicity.

http://www.georgetown.edu/crossroads/asw/

Public Agenda Online

Public Agenda, a nonpartisan, nonprofit public opinion research and citizen education organization, provides links to policy options for issues ranging from abortion to Social Security.

http://www.publicagenda.org

NCPA Idea House

Through this site of the National Center for Policy Analysis, access discussions on an array of topics that are of major interest in the study of American government, from regulatory policy and privatization to economy and income.

http://www.ncpa.org/iss/

RAND

RAND is a nonprofit institution that works to improve public policy through research and analysis. Links offered on this home page provide for keyword searches of certain topics and descriptions of RAND activities and major research areas.

http://www.rand.org

Policy Library

This site provides a collection of documents on social and policy issues submitted by different research organizations all over the world.

http://www.policylibrary.com/US/index.html

PART 3

Social Change and Public Policy

*F*ew topics are more emotional and divisive than those that involve so-cial morality. Whatever consensus once existed on such issues as capital punishment, abortion, and equality of opportunity, that consensus has been shattered in recent years as Americans have lined up very clearly on opposing sides—and what is more important, they have taken those competing views into Congress, state legislatures, and the courts.

The issues in this section generate intense emotions because they ask us to clarify our values on a number of very personal concerns.

- Is Capital Punishment Justified?

- Do We Need Tougher Gun Control Laws?

- Does Affirmative Action Advance Racial Equality?

- Should Hate Speech Be Punished?

- Should Abortion Be Restricted?

- Are Americans Taxed Too Much?

- Is Socioeconomic Inequality Increasing in America?

ISSUE 8

Is Capital Punishment Justified?

YES: Robert W. Lee, from "Deserving to Die," *The New American* (August 13, 1990)

NO: Eric M. Freedman, from "The Case Against the Death Penalty," *USA Today Magazine* (March 1997)

ISSUE SUMMARY

YES: Essayist Robert W. Lee argues that capital punishment is the only fair way for society to respond to certain heinous crimes.

NO: Law professor Eric M. Freedman contends that the death penalty does not reduce crime but does reduce public safety and carries the risk of innocent people being executed.

From 1995 through 1999, 373 inmates were executed in the United States, and at the beginning of 2000, 3,652 more were on death row. The numbers are small relative to the murder rate during those years, but the issue of capital punishment remains bitterly divisive.

Polls have shown that somewhat more than half of all Americans approve of capital punishment. If a shift in opinion is taking place, it is in response to the concern that innocent people may be executed in error. In 2000 Illinois governor George Ryan, who supports the death penalty, announced a moratorium on executions because he believed that the state's criminal justice system, in which 13 death row inmates had been exonerated since 1987, was "fraught with error." In Texas, where one-third of the executions in America have taken place in recent years (127 from 1995 through 1999), Governor George W. Bush expressed confidence that every person executed in that state was guilty.

Capital punishment is an ancient penalty, but both the definition of a capital crime and the methods used to put convicted persons to death have changed dramatically. In eighteenth-century Massachusetts, for example, capital crimes included blasphemy and the worship of false gods. Slave states often imposed the death penalty upon blacks for crimes that were punished by only two or three years' imprisonment when committed by whites. It has been estimated that in the twentieth century approximately 10 percent of all legal executions have been for the crime of rape, 1 percent for all other crimes except murder (robbery, burglary, attempted murder, etc.), and nearly 90 percent for the commission of murder.

Long before the Supreme Court severely limited the use of the death penalty, executions in the United States were becoming increasingly rare. In the 1930s there were 1,667; the total for the 1950s was 717. In the 1960s the numbers fell even more dramatically. For example, seven persons were executed in 1965, one in 1966, and two in 1967.

Then came the Supreme Court case *Furman v. Georgia* (1972), which many thought—mistakenly—"abolished" capital punishment in America. Actually, only two members of the *Furman* majority thought that capital punishment *per se* violates the Eighth Amendment's injunction against "cruel and unusual punishment." The other three members of the majority took the view that capital punishment is unconstitutional only when applied in an arbitrary or racially discriminatory manner, as they believed it was in this case. The four dissenters in the *Furman* case were prepared to uphold capital punishment both in general and in this particular instance. Not surprisingly, then, with a slight change of Court personnel—and with a different case before the Court—a few years later, the majority vote went the other way.

In the latter case, *Gregg v. Georgia* (1976), the majority upheld capital punishment under certain circumstances. In his majority opinion in the case, Justice Potter Stewart noted that the law in question (a new Georgia capital punishment statute) went to some lengths to avoid arbitrary procedures in capital cases. For example, Georgia courts were not given complete discretion in handing out death sentences to convicted murderers but had to consult a series of guidelines spelling out "aggravating circumstances," such as if the murder had been committed by someone already convicted of murder, if the murder endangered the lives of bystanders, and if the murder was committed in the course of a major felony. These guidelines, Stewart said, together with other safeguards against arbitrariness included in the new statute, preserved it against Eighth Amendment challenges.

Although the Court has upheld the constitutionality of the death penalty, it can always be abolished by state legislatures. However, that seems unlikely to happen in many states. If anything, the opposite is occurring. Almost immediately after the *Furman* decision of 1972, state legislatures began enacting new death penalty statutes designed to meet the objections raised in the case. By the time of the *Gregg* decision, 35 new death penalty statutes had been enacted.

In response to the public mood, Congress has put its own death penalty provisions into federal legislation. In 1988 Congress sanctioned the death penalty for drug kingpins convicted of intentionally killing or ordering anyone's death. More recently, in the 1994 crime bill, Congress authorized the death penalty for dozens of existing or new federal crimes, such as treason or the murder of a federal law enforcement agent.

In the following selections, Robert W. Lee argues that capital punishment is an appropriate form of retribution for certain types of heinous offenses, while Eric M. Freedman asserts that the practice of capital punishment fails every practical and moral test that may be applied to it.

Robert W. Lee

 **YES**

Deserving to Die

Akey issue in the debate over capital punishment is whether or not it is an effective deterrent to violent crime. In at least one important respect, it unquestionably is: It simply cannot be contested that a killer, once executed, is forever deterred from killing again. The deterrent effect on others, however, depends largely on how swiftly and surely the penalty is applied. Since capital punishment has not been used with any consistency over the years, it is virtually impossible to evaluate its deterrent effect accurately. Abolitionists claim that a lack of significant difference between the murder rates for states with and without capital punishment proves that the death penalty does not deter. But the states with the death penalty on their books have used it so little over the years as to preclude any meaningful comparison between states. Through July 18, 1990 there had been 134 executions since 1976. Only 14 states (less than 40 percent of those that authorize the death penalty) were involved. Any punishment, including death, will cease to be an effective deterrent if it is recognized as mostly bluff. Due to costly delays and endless appeals, the death penalty has been largely turned into a paper tiger by the same crowd that calls for its abolition on the grounds that it is not an effective deterrent!

To allege that capital punishment, if imposed consistently and without undue delay, would not be a deterrent to crime is, in essence, to say that people are not afraid of dying. If so, as columnist Jenkin Lloyd Jones once observed, then warning signs reading "Slow Down," "Bridge Out," and "Danger—40,000 Volts" are futile relics of an age gone by when men feared death. To be sure, the death penalty could never become a 100-percent deterrent to heinous crime, because the fear of death varies among individuals. Some race automobiles, climb mountains, parachute jump, walk circus high-wires, ride Brahma bulls in rodeos, and otherwise engage in endeavors that are more than normally hazardous. But, as author Bernard Cohen notes in his book *Law and Order,* "there are even more people who refrain from participating in these activities mainly because risking their lives is not to their taste."

From Robert W. Lee, "Deserving to Die," *The New American* (August 13, 1990). Copyright © 1990 by *The New American.* Reprinted by permission.

Merit System

On occasion, circumstances *have* led to meaningful statistical evaluations of the death penalty's deterrent effect. In Utah, for instance, there have been three executions since the Supreme Court's 1976 ruling:

- Gary Gilmore faced a firing squad at the Utah State Prison on January 17, 1977. There had been 55 murders in the Beehive State during 1976 (4.5 per 100,000 population). During 1977, in the wake of the Gilmore execution, there were 44 murders (3.5 per 100,000), a 20 percent decrease.

- More than a decade later, on August 28, 1987, Pierre Dale Selby (one of the two infamous "hi-fi killers" who in 1974 forced five persons in an Ogden hi-fi shop to drink liquid drain cleaner, kicked a ballpoint pen into the ear of one, then killed three) was executed. During all of 1987, there were 54 murders (3.2 per 100,000). The count for January through August was 38 (a monthly average of 4.75). For September–December (in the aftermath of the Selby execution) there were 16 (4.0 per month, a nearly 16 percent decrease). For July and August there were six and seven murders, respectively. In September (the first month following Selby's demise) there were three.

- Arthur Gary Bishop, who sodomized and killed a number of young boys, was executed on June 10, 1988. For all of 1988 there were 47 murders (2.7 per 100,000, the fewest since 1977). During January–June, there were 26; for July–December (after the Bishop execution) the tally was 21 (a 19 percent difference).

In the wake of all three Utah executions, there have been notable decreases in both the number and the rate of murders within the state. To be sure, there are other variables that could have influenced the results, but the figures are there and abolitionists to date have tended simply to ignore them.

Deterrence should never be considered the *primary* reason for administering the death penalty. It would be both immoral and unjust to punish one man merely as an example to others. The basic consideration should be: Is the punishment deserved? If not, it should not be administered regardless of what its deterrent impact might be. After all, once deterrence supersedes justice as the basis for a criminal sanction, the guilt or innocence of the accused becomes largely irrelevant. Deterrence can be achieved as effectively by executing an innocent person as a guilty one (something that communists and other totalitarians discovered long ago). If a punishment administered to one person deters someone else from committing a crime, fine. But that result should be viewed as a bonus of justice properly applied, not as a reason for the punishment. The decisive consideration should be: Has the accused *earned* the penalty?

The Cost of Execution

The exorbitant financial expense of death penalty cases is regularly cited by abolitionists as a reason for abolishing capital punishment altogether. They prefer to ignore, however, the extent to which they themselves are responsible for the interminable legal maneuvers that run up the costs....

As presently pursued, death-penalty prosecutions *are* outrageously expensive. But, again, the cost is primarily due to redundant appeals, time-consuming delays, bizarre court rulings, and legal histrionics by defense attorneys:

Willie Darden, who had already survived three death warrants, was scheduled to die in Florida's electric chair on September 4, 1985 for a murder he had committed in 1973. Darden's lawyer made a last-minute emergency appeal to the Supreme Court, which voted against postponing the execution until a formal appeal could be filed. So the attorney (in what he later described as "last-minute ingenuity") then requested that the emergency appeal be technically transformed into a formal appeal. Four Justices agreed (enough to force the full court to review the appeal) and the execution was stayed. After additional years of delay and expense, Darden was eventually put out of our misery on March 15, 1988.

Ronald Gene Simmons killed 14 members of his family during Christmas week in 1987. He was sentenced to death, said he was willing to die, and refused to appeal. But his scheduled March 16, 1989 execution was delayed when a fellow inmate, also on death row, persuaded the Supreme Court to block it (while Simmons was having what he expected to be his last meal) on the grounds that the execution could have repercussions for other death-row inmates. It took the Court until April 24th of [1990] to reject that challenge. Simmons was executed on June 25th.

Robert Alton Harris was convicted in California of the 1978 murders of two San Diego teenagers whose car he wanted for a bank robbery. Following a seemingly interminable series of appeals, he was at last sentenced to die on April 3rd of [1990]. Four days earlier, a 9th U.S. Circuit Court of Appeals judge stayed the execution, largely on the claim that Harris was brain-damaged and therefore may possibly have been unable to "premeditate" the murders (as required under California law for the death penalty). On April 10th, the *Washington Times* reported that the series of tests used to evaluate Harris's condition had been described by some experts as inaccurate and "a hoax."

The psychiatric game is being played for all it is worth. On May 14th, Harris's attorneys argued before the 9th Circuit Court that he should be spared the death penalty because he received "inadequate" psychiatric advice during his original trial. In 1985, the Supreme Court had ruled that a defendant has a constitutional right to "a competent psychiatrist who will conduct an appropriate examination." Harris had access to a licensed psychiatrist, but now argues that—since the recent (highly questionable) evaluations indicated brain damage and other alleged disorders that the original psychiatrist failed to detect (and which may have influenced the jury not to impose the death sentence)—a new trial (or at least a re-sentencing) is in order. If the courts buy this argument, hundreds (perhaps thousands) of cases could be reopened for psychiatric challenge.

On April 2, 1974 William Neal Moore shot and killed a man in Georgia. Following his arrest, he pleaded guilty to armed robbery and murder and was convicted and sentenced to death. On July 20, 1975 the Georgia Supreme Court denied his petition for review. On July 16, 1976 the U.S. Supreme Court denied his petition for review. On May 13, 1977 the Jefferson County Superior Court turned down a petition for a new sentencing hearing (the state Supreme Court affirmed the denial, and the U.S. Supreme Court again denied a review). On March 30, 1978 a Tattnall County Superior Court judge held a hearing on a petition alleging sundry grounds for a writ of *habeas corpus,* but declined on July 13, 1978 to issue a writ. On October 17, 1978 the state Supreme Court declined to review that ruling. Moore petitioned the U.S. District Court for Southern Georgia. After a delay of more than two years, a U.S. District Court judge granted the writ on April 29, 1981. After another two-year delay, the 11th U.S. Circuit Court of Appeals upheld the writ on June 23, 1983. On September 30, 1983 the Circuit Court reversed itself and ruled that the writ should be denied. On March 5, 1984 the Supreme Court rejected the case for the third time.

Moore's execution was set for May 24, 1984. On May 11, 1984 his attorneys filed a petition in Butts County Superior Court, but a writ was denied. The same petition was filed in the U.S. District Court for Georgia's Southern District on May 18th, but both a writ and a stay of execution were denied. Then, on May 23rd (the day before the scheduled execution) the 11th Circuit Court of Appeals granted a stay. On June 4, 1984 a three-judge panel of the Circuit Court voted to deny a writ. After another delay of more than three years, the Circuit Court voted 7 to 4 to override its three-judge panel and rule in Moore's favor. On April 18, 1988, the Supreme Court accepted the case. On April 17, 1989 it sent the case back to the 11th Circuit Court for review in light of new restrictions that the High Court had placed on *habeas corpus.* On September 28, 1989 the Circuit Court ruled 6 to 5 that Moore had abused the writ process. On December 18, 1989 Moore's attorneys again appealed to the Supreme Court.

Moore's case was described in detail in *Insight* magazine for February 12, 1990. By the end of [1989] his case had gone through 20 separate court reviews, involving some 118 state and federal judges. It had been to the Supreme Court and back four times. There had been a substantial turnover of his attorneys, creating an excuse for one team of lawyers to file a petition claiming that all of the prior attorneys had given ineffective representation. No wonder capital cases cost so much!

Meanwhile, the American Bar Association proposes to make matters even worse by requiring states (as summarized by *Insight*) "to appoint two lawyers for every stage of the proceeding, require them to have past death penalty experience and pay them at 'reasonable' rates to be set by the court."

During an address to the American Law Institute on May 16, 1990, Chief Justice Rehnquist asserted that the "system at present verges on the chaotic" and "cries out for reform." The time expended between sentencing and execution, he declared, "is consumed not by structured review ... but in fits of frantic action followed by periods of inaction." He urged that death row inmates be given one chance to challenge their sentences in state courts, and one challenge in federal courts, period.

Lifetime to Escape

Is life imprisonment an adequate substitute for the death penalty? Presently, according to the polls, approximately three-fourths of the American people favor capital punishment. But abolitionists try to discount that figure by claiming that support for the death penalty weakens when life imprisonment without the possibility of parole is offered as an alternative. (At other times, abolitionists argue that parole is imperative to give "lifers" some hope for the future and deter their violent acts in prison.)

Life imprisonment is a flawed alternative to the death penalty, if for no other reason than that so many "lifers" escape. Many innocent persons have died at the hands of men previously convicted and imprisoned for murder, supposedly for "life." The ways in which flaws in our justice system, combined with criminal ingenuity, have worked to allow "lifers" to escape include these recent examples:

- On June 10, 1977, James Earl Ray, who was serving a 99-year term for killing Dr. Martin Luther King Jr., escaped with six other inmates from the Brushy Mountain State Prison in Tennessee (he was captured three days later).
- Brothers Linwood and James Briley were executed in Virginia on October 12, 1984 and April 18, 1985, respectively. Linwood had murdered a disc jockey in 1979 during a crime spree. During the same spree, James raped and killed a woman (who was eight months pregnant) and killed her five-year-old son. On May 31, 1984, the Briley brothers organized and led an escape of five death-row inmates (the largest death-row breakout in U.S. history). They were at large for 19 days.

- On August 1, 1984 convicted murderers Wesley Allen Tuttle and Walter Wood, along with another inmate, escaped from the Utah State Prison. All were eventually apprehended. Wood subsequently sued the state for $2 million for violating his rights by allowing him to escape. In his complaint, he charged that, by allowing him to escape, prison officials had subjected him to several life-threatening situations: "Because of extreme fear of being shot to death, I was forced to swim several irrigation canals, attempt to swim a 'raging' Jordan River and expose myself to innumerable bites by many insects. At one point I heard a volley of shotgun blasts and this completed my anxiety."
- On April 3, 1988 three murderers serving life sentences without the chance of parole escaped from the maximum-security West Virginia Penitentiary. One, Bobby Stacy, had killed a Huntington police officer in 1981. At the time, he had been free on bail after having been arrested for shooting an Ohio patrolman.
- On November 21, 1988 Gonzalo Marrero, who had been convicted of two murders and sentenced to two life terms, escaped from New Jersey's Trenton state prison by burrowing through a three-foot-thick cell wall, then scaling a 20-foot outer wall with a makeshift ladder.
- In August 1989 Arthur Carroll, a self-proclaimed enforcer for an East Oakland street gang, was convicted of murdering a man. On September 28th, he was sentenced to serve 27-years-to-life in prison. On October 10th he was transferred to San Quentin prison. On October 25th he was set free after a paperwork snafu led officials to believe that he had served enough time. An all-points bulletin was promptly issued.
- On February 11, 1990 six convicts, including three murderers, escaped from their segregation cells in the maximum security Joliet Correctional Center in Illinois by cutting through bars on their cells, breaking a window, and crossing a fence. In what may be the understatement of the year, a prison spokesman told reporters: "Obviously, this is a breach of security."

Clearly, life sentences do not adequately protect society, whereas the death penalty properly applied does so with certainty.

Equal Opportunity Execution

Abolitionists often cite statistics indicating that capital punishment has been administered in a discriminatory manner, so that the poor, the black, the friendless, etc., have suffered a disproportionate share of executions. Even if true, such discrimination would not be a valid reason for abandoning the death penalty unless it could be shown that it was responsible for the execution of *innocent* persons (which it has not been, to date). Most attempts to pin the "discrimination" label on capital convictions are similar to one conducted at Stanford University a few years ago, which found that murderers of white people (whether white or black) are more likely to be punished with death than are killers of black people (whether white or black). But the study also concluded that blacks who murdered whites were somewhat *less* likely to receive death sentences than were whites who killed whites.

Using such data, the ACLU attempted to halt the execution of Chester Lee Wicker in Texas on August 26, 1986. Wicker, who was white, had killed a white person. The ACLU contended that Texas unfairly imposes the death penalty because a white is more likely than a black to be sentenced to death for killing a white. The Supreme Court rejected the argument. On the other hand, the execution of Willie Darden in Florida attracted worldwide pleas for amnesty from sundry abolitionists who, ignoring the Stanford study, claimed that Darden had been "railroaded" because he was black and his victim was white.

All criminal laws—in all countries, throughout all human history—have tended to be administered in an imperfect and uneven manner. As a result, some elements in society have been able to evade justice more consistently than others. But why should the imperfect administration of justice persuade us to abandon any attempt to attain it?

The most flagrant example of discrimination in the administration of the death penalty does not involve race, income, or social status, but gender. Women commit around 13 percent of the murders in America, yet, from 1930 to June 30, 1990, only 33 of the 3991 executions (less than 1 percent) involved women. Only one of the 134 persons executed since 1976 (through July 18th [1990]) has been a woman (Velma Barfield in North Carolina on November 2, 1984). One state governor commuted the death sentence of a woman because "humanity does not apply to women the inexorable law that it does to men."

According to L. Kay Gillespie, professor of sociology at Weber State College in Utah, evidence indicates that women who cried during their trials had a better chance of getting away with murder and avoiding the death penalty. Perhaps the National Organization for Women can do something about this glaring example of sexist "inequality" and "injustice." In the meantime, we shall continue to support the death penalty despite the disproportionate number of men who have been required to pay a just penalty for their heinous crimes.

Forgive and Forget?

Another aspect of the death penalty debate is the extent to which justice should be tempered by mercy in the case of killers. After all, abolitionists argue, is it not the duty of Christians to forgive those who trespass against them? In Biblical terms, the most responsible sources to extend mercy and forgiveness are (1) God and (2) the victim of the injustice. In the case of murder, so far as *this* world is concerned, the victim is no longer here to extend mercy and forgiveness. Does the state or any other earthly party have the right or authority to intervene and tender mercy on behalf of a murder victim? In the anthology *Essays on the Death Penalty,* the Reverend E. L. H. Taylor clarifies the answer this way: "Now it is quite natural and proper for a man to forgive something you do to *him.* Thus if somebody cheats me out of $20.00 it is quite possible and reasonable for me to say, 'Well, I forgive him, we will say no more about it.' But what would you say if somebody had done you out of $20.00 and I said, 'That's all right. I forgive him on your behalf'?"

The point is simply that there is no way, in *this* life, for a murderer to be reconciled to his victim, and secure the victim's forgiveness. This leaves the civil authority with no other responsible alternative but to adopt *justice* as the standard for assigning punishment in such cases.

Author Bernard Cohen raises an interesting point: " ... if it is allowable to deprive a would-be murderer of his life, in order to forestall his attack, why is it wrong to take away his life after he has successfully carried out his dastardly business?" Does anyone question the right of an individual to kill an assailant should it be necessary to preserve his or her life or that of a loved one?

Happily, however, both scripture and our legal system uphold the morality and legality of taking the life of an assailant, if necessary, *before* he kills us. How, then, can it be deemed immoral for civil authority to take his life *after* he kills us?

Intolerant Victims?

Sometimes those who defend the death penalty are portrayed as being "intolerant." But isn't one of our real problems today that Americans are *too tolerant* of evil? Are we not accepting acts of violence, cruelty, lying, and immorality with all too little righteous indignation? Such indignation is not, as some would have us believe, a form of "hatred." In *Reflections on the Psalms,* C. S. Lewis discussed the supposed spirit of "hatred" that some critics claimed to see in parts of the Psalms: "Such hatreds are the kind of thing that cruelty and injustice, by a sort of natural law, produce.... Not to perceive it at all—not even to be tempted to resentment—to accept it as the most ordinary thing in the world—argues a terrifying insensibility. Thus the absence of anger, especially that sort of anger which we call indignation, can, in my opinion, be a most alarming symptom."

When mass murderer Ted Bundy was executed in Florida on January 24, 1989, a crowd of some 2000 spectators gathered across from the prison to cheer and celebrate. Many liberal commentators were appalled. Some contended that it was a spectacle on a par with Bundy's own callous disrespect for human life. One headline read: "Exhibition witnessed outside prison was more revolting than execution." What nonsense! As C. S. Lewis observed in his commentary on the Psalms: "If the Jews cursed more bitterly than the Pagans this was, I think, at least in part because they took right and wrong more seriously." It is long past time for us all to being taking right and wrong more seriously....

Seeds of Anarchy

As we have seen, most discussions of the death penalty tend to focus on whether it should exist for murder or be abolished altogether. The issue should be reframed so that the question instead becomes whether or not it should be imposed for certain terrible crimes in addition to murder (such as habitual law-breaking, clearly proven cases of rape, and monstrous child abuse).

In 1953 the renowned British jurist Lord Denning asserted: "Punishment is the way in which society expresses its denunciation of wrongdoing; and in order to maintain respect for law, it is essential that the punishment for grave crimes shall adequately reflect the revulsion felt by a great majority of citizens for them." Nineteen years later, U.S. Supreme Court Justice Potter Stewart noted (while nevertheless concurring in the Court's 1972 opinion that temporarily banned capital punishment) that the "instinct for retribution is part of the nature of man and channeling that instinct in the administration of criminal justice serves an important purpose in promoting the stability of a society governed by law. When people begin to believe that organized society is unwilling or unable to impose upon criminal offenders the punishment they 'deserve,' then there are sown the seeds of anarchy—of self-help, vigilante justice, and lynch law."

To protect the innocent and transfer the fear and burden of crime to the criminal element where it belongs, we must demand that capital punishment be imposed when justified and expanded to cover terrible crimes in addition to murder.

NO ↙

Eric M. Freedman

The Case Against the Death Penalty

On Sept. 1, 1995, New York rejoined the ranks of states imposing capital punishment. Although the first death sentence has yet to be imposed, an overwhelming factual record from around the country makes the consequence of this action easily predictable: New Yorkers will get less crime control than they had before.

Anyone whose public policy goals are to provide a criminal justice system that delivers swift, accurate, and evenhanded results—and to reduce the number of crimes that actually threaten most people in their daily lives—should be a death penalty opponent. The reason is simple: The death penalty not only is useless in itself, but counterproductive to achieving those goals. It wastes enormous resources—fiscal and moral—on a tiny handful of cases, to the detriment of measures that might have a significant impact in improving public safety.

Those who believe the death penalty somehow is an emotionally satisfying response to horrific crimes should ask themselves whether they wish to adhere to that initial reaction in light of the well-documented facts:

Fact: The death penalty does not reduce crime.

Capital punishment proponents sometimes assert that it simply is logical to think that the death penalty is a deterrent. Whether or not the idea is logical, it is not true, an example of the reality that many intuitively obvious propositions—*e.g.*, that a heavy ball will fall faster if dropped from the Leaning Tower of Pisa than a light one—are factually false.

People who commit capital murders generally do not engage in probability analysis concerning the likelihood of getting the death penalty if they are caught. They may be severely mentally disturbed people like Ted Bundy, who chose Florida for his final crimes *because* it had a death penalty.

Whether one chooses to obtain data from scholarly studies, the evidence of long-term experience, or accounts of knowledgeable individuals, he or she

From Eric M. Freedman, "The Case Against the Death Penalty," *USA Today Magazine* (March 1997). Copyright © 1997 by The Society for the Advancement of Education. Reprinted by permission.

will search in vain for empirical support for the proposition that imposing the death penalty cuts the crime rate. Instead, that person will find:

- The question of the supposed deterrent effect of capital punishment is perhaps the single most studied issue in the social sciences. The results are as unanimous as scholarly studies can be in finding the death penalty not to be a deterrent.
- Eighteen of the 20 states with the highest murder rates have and use the death penalty. Of the nation's 20 big cities with the highest murder rates, 17 are in death penalty jurisdictions. Between 1975 and 1985, almost twice as many law enforcement officers were killed in death penalty states as in non-death penalty states. Over nearly two decades, the neighboring states of Michigan, with no death penalty, and Indiana, which regularly imposes death sentences and carries out executions, have had virtually indistinguishable homicide rates.
- Myron Love, the presiding judge in Harris County, Tex. (which includes Houston), the county responsible for 10% of all executions in the entire country since 1976, admits that "We are not getting what I think we should be wanting and that is to deter crime.... In fact, the result is the opposite. We're having more violence, more crime."

Fact: The death penalty is extraordinarily expensive.

Contrary to popular intuition, a system with a death penalty is vastly more expensive than one where the maximum penalty is keeping murderers in prison for life. A 1982 New York study estimated the death penalty cost conservatively at three times that of life imprisonment, the ratio that Texas (with a system that is on the brink of collapse due to underfunding) has experienced. In Florida, each execution runs the state $3,200,000—six times the expense of life imprisonment. California has succeeded in executing just two defendants (one a volunteer) since 1976, but could save about $90,000,000 *per year* by abolishing the death penalty and re-sentencing all of its Death Row inmates to life.

In response, it often is proposed to reduce the costs by eliminating "all those endless appeals in death penalty cases." This is not a new idea. In recent years, numerous efforts have been made on the state and Federal levels to do precisely that. Their failure reflects some simple truths:

- Most of the extra costs of the death penalty are incurred prior to and at trial, not in postconviction proceedings. Trials are far more likely under a death penalty system (since there is so little incentive to plea-bargain). They have two separate phases (unlike other trials) and typically are preceded by special motions and extra jury selection questioning—steps that, if not taken before trial, most likely will result in the eventual reversal of the conviction.

- Much more investigation usually is done in capital cases, particularly by the prosecution. In New York, for instance, the office of the State Attorney General (which generally does not participate in local criminal prosecutions) is creating a new multi-lawyer unit to provide support to county district attorneys in capital cases.

- These expenses are incurred even though the outcome of most such trials is a sentence other than death and even though up to 50% of the death verdicts that are returned are reversed on the constitutionally required first appeal. Thus, the taxpayers foot the bill for all the extra costs of capital pretrial and trial proceedings and then must pay either for incarcerating the prisoner for life or the expenses of a retrial, which itself often leads to a life sentence. In short, even if all post-conviction proceedings following the first appeal were abolished, the death penalty system still would be more expensive than the alternative.

In fact, the concept of making such an extreme change in the justice system enjoys virtually no support in any political quarter. The writ of *habeas corpus* to protect against illegal imprisonment is available to every defendant in any criminal case, whether he or she is charged with being a petty thief or looting an S&L. It justly is considered a cornerstone of the American system of civil liberties. To eliminate all those "endless appeals" either would require weakening the system for everyone or differentially with respect to death penalty cases.

Giving less due process in capital cases is the opposite of what common sense and elementary justice call for and eventually could lead to innocent people being executed. Since the rate of constitutional violations is far greater in capital cases than in others—capital defendants seeking Federal *habeas corpus* relief succeed some 40% of the time, compared to a success rate of less than five percent for non-capital defendants—the idea of providing less searching review in death penalty cases is perverse.

Considering that the vast majority of post-conviction death penalty appeals arise from the inadequacies of appointed trial counsel, the most cost-effective and just way of decreasing the number of years devoted to capital proceedings, other than the best way—not enacting the death penalty—would be to provide adequate funding to the defense at the beginning of the process. Such a system, although more expensive than one without capital punishment, at least would result in some predictability. The innocent would be acquitted speedily; the less culpable would be sentenced promptly to lesser punishments; and the results of the trials of those defendants convicted and sentenced to death ordinarily would be final.

Instead, as matters now stand, there is roughly a 70% chance that a defendant sentenced to death eventually will succeed in getting the outcome set aside. The fault for this situation—which is unacceptable to the defense and prosecution bars alike—lies squarely with the states. It is they that have created the endless appeals by attempting to avoid the ineluctable monetary costs of death penalty systems and to run them on the cheap by refusing to provide adequate funding for defense counsel.

Fact: The death penalty actually reduces public safety.

The costs of the death penalty go far beyond the tens of millions of dollars wasted in the pursuit of a chimera. The reality is that, in a time of fixed or declining budgets, those dollars are taken away from a range of programs that would be beneficial. For example:

- New York State, due to financial constraints, can not provide bullet-proof vests for every peace officer—a project that, unlike the death penalty, certainly would save law enforcement lives.
- According to FBI statistics, the rate at which murders are solved has dropped to an all-time low. Yet, empirical studies consistently demonstrate that, as with other crimes, the murder rate decreases as the probability of detection increases. Putting money into investigative resources, rather than wasting it on the death penalty, could have a significant effect on crime.
- Despite the large percentage of ordinary street crimes that are narcotics-related, the states lack the funding to permit drug treatment on demand. The result is that people who are motivated to cure their own addictions are relegated to supporting themselves through crime, while the money that could fund treatment programs is poured down the death penalty drain.

Fact: The death penalty is arbitrary in operation.

Any reasonably conscientious supporter of the death penalty surely would agree with the proposition that, before someone is executed by the state, he or she first should receive the benefits of a judicial process that is as fair as humanly possible.

However, the one thing that is clear about the death penalty system that actually exists—as opposed to the idealized one some capital punishment proponents assume to exist—is that it does not provide a level of fairness which comes even close to equaling the gravity of the irreversible sanction being imposed. This failure of the system to function even reasonably well when it should be performing excellently breeds public cynicism as to how satisfactorily the system runs in ordinary, non-capital cases.

That reaction, although destructive, is understandable, because the factors that are significant in determining whether or not a particular defendant receives a death sentence have nothing at all to do with the seriousness of his or her crime. The key variables, rather, are:

- Racial discrimination in death-sentencing, which has been documented repeatedly. For instance, in the five-year period following their re-institution of the death penalty, the sentencing patterns in Georgia and Florida were as follows: when black kills white—Georgia, 20.1% (32 of 159 cases) and Florida, 13.7% (34 of 249); white kills white—Georgia, 5.7% (35 of 614) and Florida, 5.2% (80 of 1,547); white kills black—

Georgia, 2.9% (one of 34) and Florida, 4.3% (three of 69); black kills black—Georgia, 0.8% (11 of 1,310) and Florida, 0.7% (three of 69).

A fair objection may be that these statistics are too stark because they fail to take into account other neutral variables—*e.g.*, the brutality of the crime and the number and age of the victims. Nevertheless, many subsequent studies, whose validity has been confirmed in a major analysis for Congress by the General Accounting Office, have addressed these issues. They uniformly have found that, even when all other factors are held constant, the races of the victim and defendant are critical variables in determining who is sentenced to death.

Thus, black citizens are the victim of double discrimination. From initial charging decisions to plea bargaining to jury sentencing, they are treated more harshly when they are defendants, but their lives are given less value when they are victims. Moreover, all-white or virtually all-white juries still are commonplace in many places.

One common reaction to this evidence is not to deny it, but to attempt to evade the facts by taking refuge in the assertion that any effective system for guarding against racial discrimination would mean the end of the death penalty. Such a statement is a powerful admission that governments are incapable of running racially neutral capital punishment systems. The response of any fair-minded person should be that, if such is the case, governments should not be running capital punishment systems.

- Income discrimination. Most capital defendants can not afford an attorney, so the court must appoint counsel. Every major study of this issue, including those of the Powell Commission appointed by Chief Justice William Rehnquist, the American Bar Association, the Association of the Bar of the City of New York, and innumerable scholarly journals, has found that the quality of defense representation in capital murder trials generally is far lower than in felony cases.

  The field is a highly specialized one, and since the states have failed to pay the amounts necessary to attract competent counsel, there is an overwhelming record of poor people being subjected to convictions and death sentences that equally or more culpable—but more affluent—defendants would not have suffered.

- Mental disability. Jurors are more likely to sentence to death people who seem different from themselves than individuals who seem similar to themselves. That is the reality underlying the stark fact that those with mental disabilities are sentenced to death at a rate far higher than can be justified by any neutral explanation. This reflects prejudice, pure and simple.

Fact: Capital punishment inevitably will be inflicted on the innocent.

It is ironic that, just as New York was reinstating the death penalty, it was in the midst of a convulsive scandal involving the widespread fabrication of evidence by the New York State Police that had led to scores of people—

including some innocent ones—being convicted and sentenced to prison terms. Miscarriages of justice unquestionably will occur in any human system, but the death penalty presents two special problems in this regard:

- The arbitrary factors discussed above have an enormous negative impact on accuracy. In combination with the emotional atmosphere generally surrounding capital cases, they lead to a situation where the truth-finding process in capital cases is *less* reliable than in others. Indeed, a 1993 House of Representatives subcommittee report found 48 instances over the previous two decades in which innocent people had been sentenced to death.
- The stark reality is that death is final. A mistake can not be corrected if the defendant has been executed.

How often innocent people have been executed is difficult to quantify; once a defendant has been executed, few resources generally are devoted to the continued investigation of the case. Nonetheless, within the past few years, independent investigations by major news organizations have uncovered three cases, two in Florida and one in Mississippi, where people were put to death for crimes they did not commit. Over time, others doubtless will come to light (while still others will remain undiscovered), but it will be too late.

The fact that the system sometimes works—for those who are lucky enough to obtain somehow the legal and investigative resources or media attention necessary to vindicate their claims of innocence—does not mean that most innocent people on Death Row are equally fortunate. Moreover, many Death Row inmates who have been exonerated would have been executed if the legal system had moved more quickly, as would occur if, as those now in power in Congress have proposed, Federal *habeas corpus* is eviscerated.

The death penalty is not just useless—it is positively harmful and diverts resources from genuine crime control measures. Arbitrarily selecting out for execution not the worst criminals, but a racially determined handful of the poorest, most badly represented, least mentally healthy, and unluckiest defendants—some of whom are innocent—breeds cynicism about the entire criminal justice system.

Thus, the Criminal Justice Section of the New York State Bar Association—which includes prosecutors, judges, and defense attorneys—opposed reinstitution of the death penalty because of "the enormous cost associated with such a measure, and the serious negative impact on the delivery of prosecution and defense services throughout the state that will result." Meanwhile, Chief Justice Dixon of the Louisiana Supreme Court put it starkly: "Capital punishment is destroying the system."

POSTSCRIPT

Is Capital Punishment Justified?

In their arguments, Lee and Freedman cite some of the same facts and figures but draw opposite conclusions. Both, for example, note how expensive it is to keep prisoners on death row for so many years while appeals continue. Lee, however, draws from this the conclusion that appeals should be limited, while Freedman uses it to show that it costs taxpayers less to keep a felon in prison for life than to try to kill him.

Note that Lee does not rest his case for capital punishment on deterrence. He calls deterrence a "bonus" but not a primary justification. What really counts, he says, is whether or not the accused has "earned" the death penalty. For a similar argument developed at greater length, see Walter Berns, *For Capital Punishment: Crime and the Morality of the Death Penalty* (Basic Books, 1979). Directly opposed to the contention that capital punishment is moral is the view of the late judge Lois G. Forer: "Killing human beings when carried out by government as a matter of policy is, I believe, no less abhorrent than any other homicide." Forer's case against capital punishment is presented in her book *A Rage to Punish: The Unintended Consequences of Mandatory Sentencing* (W. W. Norton, 1994). For a moving account of how one condemned man was put into the electric chair *twice* (the first time the jolt was not enough to kill him) after losing a Supreme Court appeal based on "double jeopardy" and "cruel and unusual punishment," see chapter 10 of Fred W. Friendly and Martha Elliott, *The Constitution: That Delicate Balance* (Random House, 1984). *Dead Man Walking: An Eyewitness Account of the Death Penalty in the United States* by Helen Prejean (Vintage Books, 1994) is an impassioned account by a Catholic nun of her friendship with two death row inmates and her pleas for the abolition of capital punishment. Prejean makes all the expected arguments against capital punishment, but the book's power lies in her account of executions. (This story has been made into a motion picture of the same name.)

How often are innocent people convicted of crimes punishable by death? How often are these innocent people executed? In *In Spite of Innocence: Erroneous Convictions in Capital Cases* (Northeastern University Press, 1992), Michael L. Radelet, Hugo Adam Bedau, and Constance E. Putnam describe more than 400 incidents in which they contend that wrongful convictions in capital cases occurred as a result of confused eyewitness testimony, perjury, coerced confessions, or police conspiracy.

Finally, in *The Death Penalty: An American History* (Harvard University Press, 2002), Stuart Banner provides an overview of American attitudes toward capital punishment from the seventeenth century to the present.

ISSUE 9

Do We Need Tougher Gun Control Laws?

YES: Carl T. Bogus, from "The Strong Case for Gun Control," *The American Prospect* (Summer 1992)

NO: John R. Lott, Jr., from *More Guns, Less Crime: Understanding Crime and Gun-Control Laws* (University of Chicago Press, 1998)

ISSUE SUMMARY

YES: Writer Carl T. Bogus argues that even local gun control laws will reduce the number of gun-related crimes.

NO: Social analyst John R. Lott, Jr., argues that giving law-abiding citizens the right to carry concealed handguns deters street crime.

Aslow but significant decline in the murder rate and violent crime in the United States generally began in 1992. By 1998 the murder rate had declined to its lowest level in three decades. But the country was in for a shocking series of gun murders by young people directed primarily at other young people in schools.

In 1998 alone, two boys, aged 11 and 13, shot at classmates and teachers from the woods in Arkansas, killing 4 students and 1 teacher and wounding 10 others during a false fire alarm; a 14-year-old boy killed a teacher and wounded 2 students at a dance at a Pennsylvania middle school; an 18-year-old killed his ex-girlfriend's new boyfriend in the parking lot of a Tennessee high school; and 15-year-old Kip Kinkel killed 2 students and wounded 22 others in an Oregon high school cafeteria. A day before the shooting, Kinkel had been arrested and released to his parents after it was discovered that he had a gun at school. His parents were later found dead in their home. The nation's deadliest school shooting took place the following year at a Colorado high school, when two students, aged 17 and 18, killed 12 students and a teacher and wounded 23 before they killed themselves.

These tragic events brought to public attention the shocking fact that in a single year more than 4,000 children are killed by guns in the United States. In May 2000 the Million Mom March brought several hundred thousand mothers and others to the Washington Mall to advocate more gun control. The demonstrators urged licensing, safety checks, and limiting purchases to one handgun per month.

What has been done? What can be done? Can gun control make a difference, or are the causes of gun violence and its reduction to be found elsewhere?

In November 1993, after seven years of wrangling, Congress finally passed the Brady Bill. For several years, James Brady, a press secretary to President Ronald Reagan who was partially paralyzed by a bullet intended for Reagan in 1981, had been heading a campaign to regulate handguns. The National Rifle Association (NRA) and other opponents of gun control had fought hard against any such legislation, and Republican presidents had largely agreed with the NRA position that the best way to curb gun violence is not to ban guns but to stiffen penalties against those who use them illegally. But President Bill Clinton threw his support behind the Brady Bill, and it was enacted by Congress.

The Brady Act, requiring a background check on potential gun purchasers, has resulted in the rejection of 100,000 prospective gun buyers, but criminals can buy weapons on the black market or abroad, obtain them in informal transactions, and steal them.

The year following passage of the Brady Act, Congress confirmed the fears of those who argued that it would be the opening wedge for more gun control. The 1994 crime act included a ban on assault weapons. An assault weapon has a magazine capable of holding many rounds that can be fired each time the trigger is pulled. The 1994 law placed a 10-year ban on the manufacture and sale of 19 types of assault weapons as well as copycat models and certain other guns with features similar to assault weapons.

Is it too late to curb gun possession in the United States? There are at least 200 million guns in private hands in the United States, and approximately one-half of all American households contain at least one gun. This has not changed much over the past 40 years, which means that most people who buy guns already own guns. In some rural areas, it is unusual for a household not to have a gun.

Advocates and opponents differ in their assessments of the consequences of gun control laws. Those supporting gun control point to Great Britain and Japan, which have very tough firearm laws and very low murder rates. Opponents respond that low murder rates in these countries result from their cultures. They point to countries like Switzerland, New Zealand, and Israel, where firearms are prevalent and murder rates are very low. Opponents also echo the National Rifle Association's argument that "guns do not kill people; people do." Supporters of gun control point out that it is harder to kill (especially large numbers of) people without guns.

In the following selections, Carl T. Bogus and John R. Lott, Jr., focus on the consequences of gun control and reach opposed conclusions. Bogus presents evidence suggesting that, even with other demographic factors held nearly constant, there is less gun-related crime in areas that have gun control. Lott's research indicates that depriving law-abiding citizens of the right to own and carry handguns takes away a powerful deterrent to crime.

Carl T. Bogus  **YES**

The Strong Case for Gun Control

While abhorring violence, Americans generally believe that gun control cannot do much to reduce it. A majority of Americans questioned in a 1992 CBS-*New York Times* poll responded that banning handguns would only keep them away from law-abiding citizens rather than reduce the amount of violent crime. Many serious scholars have accepted the argument that the huge number of guns already in circulation would make any gun control laws ineffective. Until recently, it has been difficult to answer these objections. But in the past few years, new research has demonstrated that some gun control laws do work, dramatically reducing murder rates.

Gun violence is a plague of such major proportions that its destructive power is rivaled only by wars and epidemics. During the Vietnam War, more than twice as many Americans were shot to death in the United States as died in combat in Vietnam. Besides the 34,000 Americans killed by guns each year, more than 60,000 are injured—many seriously—and about a quarter of a million Americans are held up at gunpoint.

Measures that demonstrably reduce gun violence would gain wide public support. But that has been exactly the problem: A public that approves of gun control by wide margins also is skeptical about its effectiveness and even its constitutionality. Both of these sources of doubt can now be put to rest.

A Tale of Two Cities

Perhaps the most dramatic findings about the efficacy of gun control laws come from a study comparing two cities that have followed different policies for regulating handguns: Seattle, Washington and Vancouver, British Columbia.[1] Only 140 miles apart, the two cities are remarkably alike despite being located on opposite sides of an international border. They have populations nearly identical in size and, during the study period (1980–86), had similar socio-economic profiles. Seattle, for example, had a 5.8 percent unemployment rate while Vancouver's was 6.0 percent. The median household income in Seattle was $16,254; in Vancouver, adjusted in U.S. dollars, it was $16,681. In racial and ethnic makeup, the two cities are also similar. Whites represent 79 percent of

From Carl T. Bogus, "The Strong Case for Gun Control," *The American Prospect* (Summer 1992). Copyright © 1992 by New Prospect, Inc. Reprinted by permission.

Figure 1

Aggravated Assaults per 100,000 People, 1980–1983, by Weapon

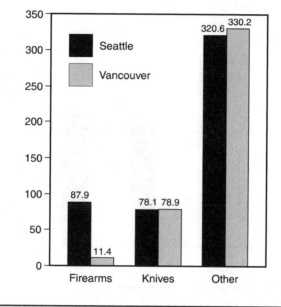

Source: John Henry Sloan, et al., "Handgun Regulations, Crime, Assaults, and Homicide," *The New England Journal of Medicine,* Nov. 10, 1988, pp. 1256–62. Reprinted by permission.

Seattle's inhabitants and 76 percent of Vancouver's. The principal racial difference is that Asians make up a larger share of Vancouver's population (22 percent versus 7 percent). The two cities share not only a common frontier history but a current culture as well. Most of the top ten television shows in one city, for example, also rank among the top ten in the other.

As one might expect from twin cities, burglary rates in Seattle and Vancouver were nearly identical. The aggravated assault rate was, however, slightly higher in Seattle. On examining the data more closely, the Sloan study found "a striking pattern." There were almost identical rates of assaults with knives, clubs and fists, but there was a far greater rate of assault with firearms in Seattle. Indeed, the firearm assault rate in Seattle was nearly eight times higher than in Vancouver [see Figure 1].

The homicide rate was also markedly different in the two cities. During the seven years of the study, there were 204 homicides in Vancouver and 388 in Seattle—an enormous difference for two cities with comparable populations. Further analysis led to a startling finding: the entire difference was due to gun-related homicides. The murder rates with knives—and all other weapons excluding firearms—were virtually identical, but the rate of murders involving

Figure 2

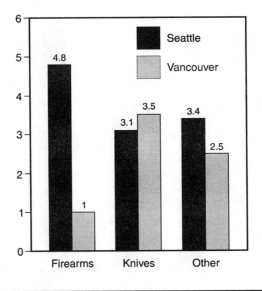

Murders per 100,000 People, 1980–1986, by Weapon

Source: John Henry Sloan, et al., "Handgun Regulations, Crime, Assaults, and Homicide," *The New England Journal of Medicine*, Nov. 10, 1988, pp. 1256–62. Reprinted by permission.

guns was five times greater in Seattle [see Figure 2]. That alone accounted for Seattle having nearly twice as many homicides as Vancouver.

People in Seattle may purchase a handgun for any reason after a five-day waiting period; 41 percent of all households have handguns. Vancouver on the other hand, requires a permit for handgun purchases and issues them only to applicants who have a lawful reason to own a handgun and who, after a careful investigation, are found to have no criminal record and to be sane. Self-defense is not a valid reason to own a handgun, and recreational uses of handguns are strictly regulated. The penalty for illegal possession is severe—two years' imprisonment. Handguns are present in only 12 percent of Vancouver's homes.

The Seattle-Vancouver study provides strong evidence for the efficacy of gun control. Sloan and his colleagues concluded that the wider proliferation of handguns in Seattle was the sole cause of the higher rate of murders and assaults. The study answered other important questions as well.

- *Do handguns deter crime?* If handguns deter burglary, the burglary rate in Seattle—where so many more homes have handguns—should have been lower than the burglary rate in Vancouver. But it was not.
- *How often are handguns used for self-defense?* Less than 4 percent of the homicides in both cities resulted from acts of self-defense.

- Perhaps most important: *If handguns are unavailable, will people merely use other weapons instead?* The answer must be "no." Otherwise, the cities would have had similar total murder rates and Vancouver would have had higher rates of homicide with other weapons.

                             ✦

A more recent study measured gun control legislation more directly.[2] In 1976 the District of Columbia enacted a new gun control law. Residents who lawfully owned firearms had sixty days to reregister them. After the sixty-day period, newly acquired handguns became illegal. Residents could continue to register rifles and shotguns, provided they purchased them from licensed dealers and complied with other regulations.

The researchers compared gun-related violence in the nine years prior to the law's enactment with the following nine years. They also compared the experience within the District with that of the immediately surrounding metropolitan area. The law was, of course, only in force within the boundaries of the District itself and not in contiguous areas of Maryland and Virginia that belong to the same metropolitan area, as the Census Bureau defines it.

The results of the study were surprising even to the most ardent gun control advocates. Within the District, gun-related homicides fell by more than 25 percent and gun-related suicides declined by 23 percent. Meanwhile, there was no statistically significant change in either gun-related homicides or suicides in the adjacent areas. Here again the data demonstrated that people did not switch to other weapons: within the District there was no statistically significant change in either homicides or suicides with other weapons.

Perhaps most surprising of all was the suddenness of the change. Any decline in murders and suicides was expected to be gradual, as the number of weapons in the district slowly shrank. Yet homicides and suicides abruptly declined when the law went into effect. The D.C. law, therefore, had a significant and virtually immediate benefit.

The D.C. study demonstrates that gun control can work in the United States. Despite the similarities between Seattle and Vancouver, some critics of the Sloan study have suggested that Canada and the United States are sufficiently different to make extrapolations questionable. The D.C. study shows that even local gun control laws can be effective in the U.S. Previously, the prevailing opinion was that only national legislation could be effective. Critics said that if local laws blocked handgun purchases, buyers would simply import one from a nearby area. Many people probably do just that, and there is little doubt that national legislation would be far more effective.

Washington D.C.'s gun control law has not transformed the city into a utopia. It has remained a violent city and—along with many other large cities—its murder rate rose sharply in the last few years of the study (1986–88), when the use of "crack" cocaine was increasing. Yet the fact remains that for the full nine-year period after the gun control law was enacted, the mean D.C. murder rate was more than 25 percent lower and its mean suicide rate was 23 percent lower than in the preceding nine years. The effect of the law was not only immediate but sustained as well.

Why Gun Control Works

The gun lobby is fond of saying, "If guns are outlawed, only outlaws will have guns." What's wrong with this picture?

The National Rifle Association (NRA) slogan leads us to envision two groups—solid citizens and hardened criminals—but the real world cannot be neatly divided into good guys and bad guys. Many people are law-abiding citizens until they become inflamed in a domestic dispute, a drunken argument in a bar, even a fender-bender on the highway. Murder is usually an act of rage; it is more often impulsive than premeditated. In fact, 80 percent of all murders occur during altercations and 71 percent involve acquaintances, including lovers, family members, and neighbors. Only 29 percent of those arrested for murder are previously convicted felons.

Rage can pass quickly, but if there is a gun available, even a few seconds may not be soon enough. Of course, enraged lovers and brawlers use other weapons, but it is better to be attacked with anything other than a gun. Guns are, by far, the most lethal weapons. The second deadliest is the knife, but knife attacks result in death only one-fifth as often as those with guns.

For the same reason that it is better to face a knife than a gun in a lover's quarrel, it is better to be robbed at knife point rather than gunpoint. There are good reasons to believe that reducing the number of guns in the general population will reduce them in the hands of muggers and robbers. Prison inmates report that they acquired one-third of their guns by stealing them, typically in home burglaries. There are also people at the margin—not yet career criminals but drifting in that direction—who are more inclined to have guns if they are cheap and readily available. And since handguns are lawful almost everywhere, these people do not even have to cross a psychological Rubicon to get a gun.

❧❦❧

Many of the people at the margin are youngsters. Nearly 70 percent of all serious crimes are committed by boys and young men, ages fourteen to twenty-four. Many of them are not yet career criminals. They are the children of despair, kids from dysfunctional families and impoverished communities who thirst for a feeling of importance. They are angry, immature, and unstable. In the 1950s, they carried switchblades, but since the early 1960s they have increasingly been carrying handguns. Packing a gun makes them feel like men, and it just takes a little alcohol or drugs, a buddy's dare, or a moment of bravado to propel them into their first mugging or holdup of a convenience store. Many juvenile robbers say that they did not intend to commit a robbery when they went out. The nation will be a less dangerous place if these kids go out without guns.

There is a frightening increase in the number of youngsters carrying guns. The National Adolescent Student Health Survey discovered that by 1987, nearly 2 percent of all eighth and tenth graders across the nation said that they carried a gun to school within the past year. A third of those said they took a gun to school with them every day, which translates into more than 100,000 students packing a pistol all the time. In just the first two months of 1992, more than a hundred firearms were confiscated in New York City schools.

And kids are not just carrying guns, they are using them. New York City was shaken earlier this year when, moments before Mayor David Dinkins was to give a speech to the students at Brooklyn's Thomas Jefferson High School, a fifteen-year-old pulled out a Smith & Wesson .38 and killed two other students. Had it not been for the mayor's presence at the school, the shootings might not have been front-page news.

It is somewhat disingenuous to be shocked about youths with handguns. Kids emulate adults. They live in a society that has not attached a sense of gravity to owning handguns. In half of the fifty states, handguns are completely unregulated; anyone may walk into a gun shop and buy a handgun just as easily as a quart of milk at a grocery. Most of the other states have only modest handgun regulations; four states, for example, have forty-eight hour waiting periods. Except in a very few locales, automobiles are regulated far more rigorously than handguns.

There are 35 million handguns in the United States; a quarter of all homes have at least one handgun in them. We can tell a teenage boy that he is really safer if he does not pack a gun. But why should he believe adults who keep handguns in their nightstand drawers, even though they have been told that a gun in the home is six times more likely to be used to shoot a family member than an intruder?

For more than a decade some observers, such as Charles Silberman, have noted a rising tide of savagery. Today, for example, my morning newspaper carries a report about a robbery at a local McDonald's restaurant. A man with a pistol demanded the restaurant's cash, which the manager immediately gave him. The robber then told the manager and two other employees to lie down, and proceeded to shoot two to death while one of the three ran away. Not long ago it would have been extraordinarily rare for a robber—with the money in his hand—to kill his victims gratuitously; now it seems commonplace. We may wonder what impels someone to top off a robbery with a double murder, but whatever the motive, the handgun makes that act possible.

꘎◉꘎

We are also witnessing a bewildering escalation in suicides. In 1960 there were about 19,000 suicides in the United States; now there are more than 30,000 each year. (This represents a rise in the suicide rate from 10.6 per 100,000 in 1960 to 12.4 per 100,000 in 1988.) Nearly two-thirds of all suicides in the United States are committed with firearms, more than 80 percent of those with handguns. The rising number of suicides is due almost completely to firearm suicides. While the number of suicides with other weapons has remained relatively stable (even slightly declining over the past two decades), the number of firearm suicides has more than doubled since 1960.

Why should that be so? If someone really wants to kill himself, is he not going to find a way to do so regardless of whether a handgun is available? This is something of a trick question. The rabbit in the hat is the phrase "really wants to kill himself" because suicide, like murder, is often an impulsive act, particularly among the 2,000 to 3,000 American teenagers who commit suicide each year. If an individual contemplating suicide can get through the moment of dark despair, he may reconsider. And if a gun is not available, many potential suicides will resort to a less lethal method, survive, and never attempt suicide again. Nothing is as quick and certain as a gun. The desire to die need only last as long as it takes to pull a trigger, and the decision is irrevocable.

In the Seattle-Vancouver study, the researchers found a 40-percent higher suicide rate among the fifteen- to twenty-five-year-olds in Seattle, a difference they discovered was due to a firearm suicide rate that is ten times higher among Seattle adolescents. Other research reveals that a potentially suicidal adolescent is *seventy-five times* as likely to kill himself when there is a gun in the house.[3]

This is the one area, however, where the type of gun may not matter. While more than 80 percent of all gun-related suicides are with handguns, research suggests that when handguns are not available, people attempting suicide may just as readily use long guns. But many homes only have a handgun, and reducing the number of homes with handguns will therefore reduce the number of suicides.

What Kind of Gun Control Works?

No one suggests that gun control legislation will be a panacea. Nevertheless, the strong evidence is that the right kind of gun control legislation can reduce murders, suicides, and accidents substantially in the United States.

First and foremost, gun control means controlling handguns. Handguns account for only about one-third of all firearms in general circulation, but they are used in more than 75 percent of all gun-related homicides and more than 80 percent of all gun-related robberies. No other weapon is used nearly so often to murder: While handguns are used in half of all murders in America, knives are used in 18 percent, shotguns in 6 percent, rifles in 4 percent.

Two basic approaches are available to regulate handguns. One is to allow anyone to have a handgun, except for individuals in certain prohibited categories such as convicted felons, the mentally ill, drunkards, and the like. This approach is fatally flawed. The vast majority of people who end up abusing handguns do not have records that place them in a high-risk category. Whenever someone commits a murder, we can in retrospect always say that the murderer was mentally unstable, but it is not easy to check potential handgun purchasers for signs of instability or smoldering rage. There is no test to give. Many mentally unstable individuals have no record of psychiatric treatment and, even if they do, their records are confidential. Because we want to encourage people who need psychological help to seek treatment, legislation that would open psychiatric records to the government or place them in some national data bank would be counterproductive. Moreover, even someone who clearly falls into a prohibited category, such as a convicted felon, can easily circumvent this system by sending a surrogate to purchase a handgun for him.

&

The second approach, known as a need-based or a restrictive permitting system, allows only people who fall within certain categories to own handguns. Handgun permits are, of course, issued to law enforcement personnel, but among the general population someone who wants a handgun permit must demonstrate a special need. Simply wanting a handgun for self-defense is not enough, but someone who can provide a sufficiently concrete reason to fear attack would be granted a handgun permit. Sportsmen can obtain special permits, but their handguns must be kept under lock and key at a gun club. It may inconvenience them, but when public safety is balanced against recreation, public safety must win out.

Many states have similar systems for permits to carry a concealed weapon in public, but in the United States only New Jersey and a few cities have true need-base permitting systems for handgun possession. Canada adopted this system nationally in 1978. . . .

Handgun registration should be part of a restrictive permitting system. Owners should be required to register their handguns, and a permanent identification number should be engraved on every handgun. All transfers should be recorded. Everyone who has a driver's license or owns a car understands such a system, and even 78 percent of gun owners in America favor the registration of handguns, according to a 1991 Gallup poll.

&

With one exception, long guns do not present the same kind of threat to public safety as handguns. The exception, of course, is assault weapons. We remember how Patrick Purdy fired his AK-47 into a schoolyard in Stockton, California. In less than two minutes, he fired 106 rounds at children and teachers, killing five and wounding twenty-nine.

The NRA argues that it is impossible to differentiate an assault weapon from a standard hunting rifle—and to some extent it is right. Both hunting rifles and the assault weapons that are sold to the general public are semi-automatic. With a semi-automatic, firing repeat rounds requires pulling the trigger back for each one; with an automatic weapon, one must only pull the trigger back once and keep it depressed. This, however, is an inconsequential difference. A thirty-round magazine can be emptied in two seconds with a fully automatic weapon and in five seconds with a semi-automatic.

The way to regulate long guns, therefore, is to limit the size of magazines. Civilians should not be permitted to have magazines that hold more than five rounds. This simply means that after firing five rounds one must stop, remove the empty magazine and either reload it or insert another full magazine. No hunter worth his salt blasts away at a deer as if he were storming the beach at Guadalcanal, and therefore this is no real inconvenience for hunters. But as Patrick Purdy demonstrated with his seventy-five-round magazine in Stockton, large-capacity magazines pose an unreasonable danger to public safety and should not be available to civilians.

The gun lobby urges that instead of regulating handguns (or assault weapons), severe and mandatory penalties should be imposed on persons who violate firearm laws. The weight of the evidence, however, suggests that these laws are not as effective. In 1987, for example, Detroit enacted an ordinance that imposed mandatory jail sentences on persons convicted of unlawfully concealing a handgun or carrying a firearm within the city. The strategy was to allow the general population to keep guns in their homes and offices but to reduce the number of people carrying guns on the streets. After evaluating the law, researchers concluded that, at best, "the ordinance had a relatively small preventive effect on the incidence of homicides in Detroit."[4] The researchers were, in fact, dubious that there was any effect. An analysis of the case histories of more than a thousand persons charged under the ordinance revealed that only 3 percent spent time in prison. With overcrowded jails, judges choose instead to incarcerate people convicted of more serious crimes. This is consistent with other studies of mandatory sentencing laws.[5] . . .

◦◦◉◦◦

Blame for the failure of gun control is generally laid at the feet of the NRA, but the problem is not so much a zealous minority as it is a quiescent majority. There has not been a sufficiently clear understanding of why the majority of Americans want gun control but do not want it enough to make it a priority in the voting booth. Much effort has been wasted describing the magnitude and horror of gun violence in America. The gun lobby has taken one broadside after another—from television network specials and newsweekly cover stories—all to no avail.

In talking about the horror of gun violence, however, the news media are preaching to the converted. Americans are aware of the level of gun violence, and they detest it. But news specials decrying gun violence may unwittingly have the same effect as the entertainment media's glorification of gun violence. They only reinforce a sense of hopelessness. If things could be different, Americans think, they would be. Otherwise, the carnage would not be tolerated. The media portrayals may also have a numbing effect. Research shows that if people are frightened but believe there is no way to escape or to improve conditions, the fear becomes debilitating.

Majority passivity is rooted in the belief that the status quo is immutable. It is this attitude that gun control advocates must try to change, by communicating the evidence that gun control laws do work. Americans know how bad gun violence is; they must now hear the evidence that reducing the violence is possible.

Notes

1. John Henry Sloan, et al., "Handgun Regulations, Crime, Assaults, and Homicide," *The New England Journal of Medicine,* Nov. 10, 1988, pp. 1256–62.

2. Colin Liftin, et al., "Effects of Restrictive Licensing of Handguns on Homicide and Suicide in the District of Columbia," *The New England Journal of Medicine,* Dec. 5, 1991, pp. 1615–1649.

3. David A. Brent, et al., "The Presence and Accessibility of Firearms in the Homes of Adolescent Suicides," *Journal of the American Medical Association,* Dec. 4, 1991, pp. 2989–93.

4. Patrick W. O'Carroll, "Preventing Homicide: An Evaluation of the Efficacy of a Detroit Gun Ordinance," *American Journal of Public Health,* May 1991, pp. 576–81.

5. Alan Lizotte and Marjorie A. Zatz, "The Use and Abuse of Sentence Enhancement for Firearms Offenses in California," *Law and Contemporary Problems* (1986), pp. 199–221.

John R. Lott, Jr.

More Guns, Less Crime

American culture is a gun culture—not merely in the sense that 75 to 86 million people own a total of about 200 to 240 million guns, but in the broader sense that guns pervade our debates on crime and are constantly present in movies and the news. How many times have we read about shootings, or how many times have we heard about tragic accidental gun deaths—bad guys shooting innocent victims, bad guys shooting each other in drug wars, shots fired in self-defense, police shootings of criminals, let alone shooting in wars? We are inundated by images through the television and the press. Our kids are fascinated by computer war games and toy guns.

So we're obsessed with guns. But the big question is: What do we really know? How many times have most of us actually used a gun or seen a gun being used? How many of us have ever seen somebody in real life threatening somebody else with a gun, witnessed a shooting, or seen people defend themselves by displaying or firing guns?

The truth is that most of us have very little firsthand experience with using guns as weapons. Even the vast majority of police officers have never exchanged shots with a suspect. Most of us receive our images of guns and their use through television, film, and newspapers.

Unfortunately, the images from the screen and the newspapers are often unrepresentative or biased because of the sensationalism and exaggeration typically employed to sell news and entertainment. A couple of instances of news reporting are especially instructive in illustrating this bias. In a highly publicized incident, a Dallas man recently became the first Texas resident charged with using a permitted concealed weapon in a fatal shooting. Only long after the initial wave of publicity did the press report that the person had been savagely beaten and in fear for his life before firing the gun. In another case a Japanese student was shot on his way to a Halloween party in Louisiana in 1992. It made international headlines and showed how defensive gun use can go tragically wrong. However, this incident was a rare event: in the entire United States during a year, only about 30 people are accidentally killed by private citizens who mistakenly believe the victim to be an intruder. By comparison, police accidentally kill as many as 330 innocent individuals annually. In neither the Louisiana case nor the Texas case did the courts find the shooting to be criminal.

From John R. Lott, Jr., *More Guns, Less Crime: Understanding Crime and Gun-Control Laws* (University of Chicago Press, 1998). Copyright © 1998 by John R. Lott, Jr. Reprinted by permission of University of Chicago Press and the author. Notes omitted.

While news stories sometimes chronicle the defensive uses of guns, such discussions are rare compared to those depicting violent crime committed with guns. Since in many defensive cases a handgun is simply brandished, and no one is harmed, many defensive uses are never even reported to the police. I believe that this underreporting of defensive gun use is large, and this belief has been confirmed by the many stories I received from people across the country after the publicity broke on my original study. On the roughly one hundred radio talk shows on which I discussed that study, many people called in to say that they believed having a gun to defend themselves with had saved their lives. For instance, on a Philadelphia radio station, a New Jersey woman told how two men simultaneously had tried to open both front doors of the car she was in. When she brandished her gun and yelled, the men backed away and fled. Given the stringent gun-control laws in New Jersey, the woman said she never thought seriously of reporting the attempted attack to the police. . . .

Criminals are motivated by self-preservation, and handguns can therefore be a deterrent. The potential defensive nature of guns is further evidenced by the different rates of so-called "hot burglaries," where a resident is at home when a criminal strikes. In Canada and Britain, both with tough gun-control laws, almost half of all burglaries are "hot burglaries." In contrast, the United States, with fewer restrictions, has a "hot burglary" rate of only 13 percent. Criminals are not just behaving differently by accident. Convicted American felons reveal in surveys that they are much more worried about armed victims than about running into the police. The fear of potentially armed victims causes American burglars to spend more time than their foreign counterparts "casing" a house to ensure that nobody is home. Felons frequently comment in these interviews that they avoid late-night burglaries because "that's the way to get shot."

To an economist such as myself, the notion of deterrence—which causes criminals to avoid cab drivers, "dope boys," or homes where the residents are in—is not too surprising. We see the same basic relationships in all other areas of life: when the price of apples rises relative to that of oranges, people buy fewer apples and more oranges. To the non-economist, it may appear cold to make this comparison, but just as grocery shoppers switch to cheaper types of produce, criminals switch to attacking more vulnerable prey. Economists call this, appropriately enough, "the substitution effect."

Deterrence matters not only to those who actively take defensive actions. People who defend themselves may indirectly benefit other citizens. . . . [C]ab drivers and drug dealers who carry guns produce a benefit for cab drivers and drug dealers without guns. In . . . "hot burglaries," homeowners who defend themselves make burglars generally wary of breaking into homes. These spillover effects are frequently referred to as "third-party effects" or "external benefits." In both cases criminals cannot know in advance who is armed.

The case for allowing concealed handguns—as opposed to openly carried handguns—relies on this argument. When guns are concealed, criminals are unable to tell whether the victim is armed before striking, which raises the risk to criminals of committing many types of crimes. On the other hand, with "open-carry" handgun laws, a potential victim's defensive ability is readily identified, which makes it easier for criminals to choose the more vulnerable prey. In interviews with felony prisoners in ten state correctional systems, 56 percent claimed that they would not attack a potential victim who was known to be armed. Indeed, the criminals in states with high civilian gun ownership were the most worried about encountering armed victims....

The Numbers Debate and Crime

Unfortunately, the debate over crime involves many commonly accepted "facts" that simply are not true. For example, take the claim that individuals are frequently killed by people they know.... According to the FBI's *Uniform Crime Reports,* 58 percent of the country's murders were committed either by family members (18 percent) or by those who "knew" the victims (40 percent). Although the victim's relationship to their attackers could not be determined in 30 percent of the cases, 13 percent of all murders were committed by complete strangers.

Surely the impression created by these numbers has been that most victims are murdered by close acquaintances. Yet this is far from the truth. In interpreting the numbers, one must understand how these classifications are made. In this case, "murderers who know their victims" is a very broad category. A huge but not clearly determined portion of this category includes rival gang members who know each other. In larger urban areas, where most murders occur, the majority of murders are due to gang-related turf wars over drugs.

The Chicago Police Department, which keeps unusually detailed numbers on these crimes, finds that just 5 percent of all murders in the city from 1990 to 1995 were committed by nonfamily friends, neighbors, or roommates. This is clearly important in understanding crime. The list of nonfriend acquaintance murderers is filled with cases in which the relationships would not be regarded by most people as particularly close: for example, relationships between drug pushers and buyers, gang members, prostitutes and their clients, bar customers, gamblers, and cabdrivers killed by their customers.

While I do not wish to downplay domestic violence, most people do not envision gang members or drug buyers and pushers killing each other when they hear that 58 percent of murder victims were either relatives or acquaintances of their murderers. If family members are included, 17 percent of all murders in Chicago for 1990–95 involved family members, friends, neighbors, or roommates. While the total number of murders in Chicago grew from 395 in 1965 to 814 in 1995, the number involving family members, friends, neighbors, or roommates remained virtually unchanged. What has grown is the number of murders by nonfriend acquaintances, strangers, identified gangs, and persons unknown....

The news media also play an important role in shaping what we perceive as the greatest threats to our safety. Because we live in such a national news market, we learn very quickly about tragedies in other parts of the country. As a result, some events appear to be much more common than they actually are. For instance, children are much less likely to be accidentally killed by guns (particularly handguns) than most people think. Consider the following numbers:

in 1995 there were a total of 1,400 accidental firearm deaths in the entire country. A relatively small portion of these involved children: 30 deaths involved children up to four years of age and 170 more deaths involved five- to fourteen-year-olds. In comparison, 2,900 children died in motor-vehicle crashes, 950 children lost their lives from drowning, and over 1,000 children were killed by fire and burns. More children die in bicycle accidents each year than die from all types of firearm accidents.

Of course, any child's death is tragic, and it offers little consolation to point out that common fixtures in life from pools to heaters result in even more deaths. Yet the very rules that seek to save lives can result in more deaths. For example, banning swimming pools would help prevent drowning, and banning bicycles would eliminate bicycling accidents, but if fewer people exercise, life spans will be shortened. Heaters may start fires, but they also keep people from getting sick and from freezing to death. So whether we want to allow pools or space heaters depends not only on whether some people may be harmed by them, but also on whether more people are helped than hurt.

Similar trade-offs exist for gun-control issues, such as gun locks. As President [Bill] Clinton has argued many times, "We protect aspirin bottles in this country better than we protect guns from accidents by children." Yet gun locks require that guns be unloaded, and a locked, unloaded gun does not offer ready protection from intruders. The debate is not simply over whether one wants to save lives or not; it involves the question of how many of these two hundred accidental gun deaths would have been avoided under different rules versus the extent to which such rules would reduce people's ability to defend themselves....

The survey evidence of defensive gun use weighs importantly in this debate. At the lowest end of these estimates, ... according to Philip Cook, the U.S. Department of Justice's National Crime Victimization Survey reports that each year there are "only" 80,000 to 82,000 defensive uses of guns during assaults, robberies, and household burglaries. Other national polls weight regions by population and thus have the advantage, unlike the National Crime Victimization Survey, of not replying too heavily on data from urban areas. These national polls should also produce more honest answers, since a law-enforcement agency is not asking the questions. They imply much higher defensive use rates. Fifteen national polls, including those by organizations such as the *Los Angeles Times,* Gallup, and Peter Hart Research Associates, imply that there are 760,000 to 3.6 million defensive uses of guns per years. Yet even if these estimates are wrong by a very large factor, they still suggest that defensive gun use is extremely common.

Some evidence on whether concealed-handgun laws will lead to increased crimes is readily available. Between October 1, 1987, when Florida's "concealed-carry" law took effect, and the end of 1996, over 380,000 licenses had been issued, and only 72 had been revoked because of crimes committed by license holders (most of which did not involve the permitted gun). A statewide breakdown on the nature of those crimes is not available, but Dade County records indicate that for crimes involving a permitted handgun took place there between September 1987 and August 1992, and none of those cases resulted in injury. Similarly, Multnomah County, Oregon, issued 11,140 permits over the period from January 1990 to October 1994; only five permit holders were involved in shootings, three of which were considered justified by grand juries. Of the other two cases, one involved a shooting in a domestic dispute, and the other involved an accident that occurred while a gun was being unloaded; neither resulted in a fatality....

During state legislative hearings on concealed-handgun laws, the most commonly raised concerns involved fears that armed citizens would attack each other in the heat of the moment following car accidents or accidentally shoot a police officer. The evidence shows that such fears are unfounded: although thirty-one states have so-called nondiscretionary concealed-handgun laws, some of them decades old, there exists only one recorded incident of a permitted, concealed handgun being used in a shooting following a traffic accident, and that involved self-defense. No permit holder has ever shot a police officer, and there have been cases where permit holders have used their guns to save officers' lives.

Let us return to the fundamental issue of self-protection. For many people, the ultimate concern boils down to protection from violence. Unfortunately, our legal system cannot provide people with all the protection that they desire, and yet individuals are often prevented from defending themselves. A particularly tragic event occurred recently in Baltimore:

> Less than a year ago, James Edward Scott shot and wounded an intruder in the back yard of his West Baltimore home, and according to neighbors, authorities took away his gun.
>
> Tuesday night, someone apparently broke into his three-story row house again. But this time the 83-year-old Scott didn't have his .22-caliber rifle, and police said he was strangled when he confronted the burglar.
>
> "If he would have had the gun, he would be OK," said one neighbor who declined to give his name, fearing retribution from the attacker, who had not been arrested as of yesterday....
>
> Neighbors said burglars repeatedly broke into Scott's home. Ruses [a neighbor] said Scott often talked about "the people who would harass him because he worked out back by himself."

Others find themselves in a position in which either they no longer report attacks to the police when they have used a gun to defend themselves, or they no longer carry guns for self-defense. Josie Cash learned this lesson the hard way, though charges against her were ultimately dropped. "The Rockford [Illinois] woman used her gun to scare off muggers who tried to take her pizza delivery money. But when she reported the incident to police, they filed felony charges against her for carrying a concealed weapon."

A well-known story involved Alan Berg, a liberal Denver talk-show host who took great delight in provoking and insulting those with whom he disagreed. Berg attempted to obtain a permit after receiving death threats from white supremacists, but the police first attempted to talk him out of applying and then ultimately rejected his request. Shortly after he was denied, Berg was murdered by members of the Aryan Nations....

Overall, my conclusion is that criminals as a group tend to behave rationally—when crime becomes more difficult, less crime is committed. Higher arrest and conviction rates dramatically reduce crime. Criminals also move out of jurisdictions in which criminal deterrence increases. Yet criminals respond to more than just the actions taken by the police and the courts. Citizens can take private actions that also deter crime. Allowing citizens to carry concealed handguns reduces violent crimes, and the reductions coincide very closely with the number of concealed-handgun permits issued. Mass shootings in public places are reduced when law-abiding citizens are allowed to carry concealed handguns.

Not all crime categories showed reductions, however. Allowing concealed handguns might cause small increases in larceny and auto theft. When potential victims are able to arm themselves, some criminals turn away from crimes like robbery that require direct attacks and turn instead to such crimes as auto theft, where the probability of direct contact with victims is small.

There were other surprises as well. While the support for the strictest gun-control laws is usually strongest in large cities, the largest drops in violent crime from legalized concealed handguns occurred in the most urban counties with the greatest populations and the highest crime rates. Given the limited resources available to law enforcement and our desire to spend those resources wisely to reduce crime, the results of my studies have implications for where police should concentrate their efforts. For example, I found that increasing arrest rates in the most crime-prone areas led to the greatest reductions in crime. Comparisons can also be made across different methods of fighting crime. Of all the methods studied so far by economists, the carrying of concealed handguns appears to be the most cost-effective method for reducing crime. Accident and suicide rates were unaltered by the presence of concealed handguns.

Guns also appear to be the great equalizer among the sexes. Murder rates decline when either more women or more men carry concealed handguns, but the effect is especially pronounced for women. One additional woman carrying a concealed handgun reduces the murder rate for women by about 3–4 times more than one additional man carrying a concealed handgun reduces the murder rate for men. This occurs because allowing a woman to defend herself with a concealed handgun produces a much larger change in her ability to defend herself than the change created by providing a man with a handgun.

While some evidence indicates that increased penalties for using a gun in the commission of a crime reduce crime, the effect is small. Furthermore, I find no crime-reduction benefits from state-mandated waiting periods and background checks before people are allowed to purchase guns. At the federal level, the Brady law [the violence prevention act named for former White House press secretary James Brady, who was wounded in a 1981 assassination attempt on President Ronald Reagan] has proven to be no more effective. Surprisingly, there is also little benefit from training requirements or age restrictions for concealed-handgun permits....

Many factors influence crime, with arrest and conviction rates being the most important. However, nondiscretionary concealed-handgun laws are also important, and they are the most cost-effective means of reducing crime. The cost of hiring more police in order to change arrest and conviction rates is much higher, and the net benefits per dollar spent are only at most a quarter as large as the benefits from concealed-handgun laws. Even private, medium-security prisons cost state governments about $34 a day per prisoner ($12,267 per year). For concealed handguns, the permit fees are usually the largest costs borne by private citizens. The durability of guns allows owners to recoup their investments over many years. Using my yearly cost estimate of $43 per concealed handgun for Pennsylvanians, concealed handguns pay for themselves if they have only 1/285 of the deterrent impact of an additional year in prison. This calculation even ignores the other costs of the legal system, such as prosecution and defense costs—criminals will expend greater effort to fight longer prison sentences in court. No other government policy appears to have anywhere near the same cost-benefit ratio as concealed-handgun laws.

Allowing citizens without criminal records or histories of significant mental illness to carry concealed handguns deters violent crimes and appears to produce an extremely small and statistically insignificant change in accidental deaths. If the rest of the country had adopted right-to-carry concealed-handgun provisions in 1992, about 1,500 murders and 4,000 rapes would have been avoided. On the other hand, consistent with the notion that criminals respond to incentives, county-level data provide some evidence that concealed-handgun laws are associated with increases in property crimes involving stealth and in crimes that involve minimal probability of contact between the criminal and the victim. Even though both the state-level data and the estimates that attempt to explain why the law and the arrest rates change indicate that crime in all the categories declines, the deterrent effect of nondiscretionary handgun laws is largest for violent crimes. Counties with the largest populations, where the deterrence of violent crimes is the greatest, are also the counties where the substitution of property crimes for violent crimes by criminals is the highest. The estimated annual gain in 1992 from allowing concealed handguns was over $5.74 billion.

Many commonly accepted notions are challenged by these findings. Urban areas tend to have the most restrictive gun-control rules and have fought the hardest against nondiscretionary concealed-handgun laws, yet they are the very places that benefit the most from nondiscretionary concealed-handgun laws. Not only do urban areas tend to gain in their fight against crime, but reductions in crime rates are greatest precisely in those urban areas that have the highest crime rates, largest and most dense populations, and greatest concentrations of minorities. To some this might not be too surprising. After all, law-abiding citizens in these areas must depend on themselves to a great extent for protection. Even if self-protection were accepted, concerns would still arise over whether these law-abiding citizens would use guns properly. This study provides a very strong answer: a few people do and will use permitted concealed handguns improperly, but the gains completely overwhelm these concerns.

Another surprise involves women and blacks. Both tend to be the strongest supporters of gun control, yet both obtain the largest benefits from nondiscretionary concealed-handgun laws in terms of reduced rates of murder and other crimes. Concealed handguns also appear to be the great equalizer among the sexes. Murder rates decline when either more women or more men carry concealed handguns, but the effect is especially pronounced for women. An additional woman carrying a concealed handgun reduces the murder rate for women by about three to four times more than an additional man carrying a concealed handgun reduces the murder rate for men. Providing a woman with a concealed handgun represents a much larger change in her ability to defend herself than it does for a man.

The benefits of concealed handguns are not limited to those who use them in self-defense. Because the guns may be concealed, criminals are unable to tell whether potential victims are carrying guns until they attack, thus making it less attractive for criminals to commit crimes that involve direct contact with victims. Citizens who have no intention of ever carrying concealed handguns in a sense get a "free ride" from the crime-fighting efforts of their fellow citizens. However, the "halo" effect created by these laws is apparently not limited to people who share the characteristics of those who carry the guns. The most obvious example is the drop in murders of children following the adopting of nondescretionary laws. Arming older people not only may provide direct protection to these children, but also causes criminals to leave the area.

Nor is the "halo" effect limited to those who live in areas where people are allowed to carry guns. The violent-crime reduction from one's own state's adopting the law is in fact greatest when neighboring states also allow law-abiding citizens to carry concealed handguns. The evidence also indicates that the states with the most guns have the lowest crime rates. Urban areas may experience the most violent crime, but they also have the smallest number of guns. Blacks may be the racial group most vulnerable to violent crime, but they are also much less likely than whites to own guns. . . .

Preventing law-abiding citizens from carrying handguns does not end violence; it merely makes victims more vulnerable to attack. While people have strong views on either side of this debate, and one study is unlikely to end this discussion, the size and strength of my deterrence results and the lack of evidence that holders of permits for concealed handguns commit crimes should at least give pause to those who oppose concealed handguns. In the final analysis, one concern unites us all: Will allowing law-abiding citizens to carry concealed handguns save lives? The answer is yes, it will.

POSTSCRIPT

Do We Need Tougher Gun Control Laws?

What does the Second Amendment mean? In its entirety it reads, "A well regulated Militia, being necessary to the security of a free State, the right of the people to keep and bear Arms, shall not be infringed." Does this confer an unqualified right to bear arms? Or is it a right conditioned by the clause preceding the statement of right? Does the militia refer to the people generally, or does it specifically relate to the organized ("well regulated") military bodies of state and national guards and the armed forces?

Wayne LaPierre, chief executive officer and spokesman for the National Rifle Association (NRA), has written *Guns, Crime, and Freedom* (Regnery, 1994), which may be the most authoritative defense of the NRA's unqualified opposition to gun control. Gary Wills, in "To Keep and Bear Arms," *New York Review of Books* (September 21, 1995), argues that the constitutional right to bear arms is limited to its military usage.

As far back as 1976, Barry Bruce-Briggs anticipated some of the arguments made by Lott. See "The Great American Gun War," *The Public Interest* (Fall 1976). For a similar view, see Don B. Kates, Jr., *Restricting Handguns: The Liberal Skeptics Speak Out* (North River Press, 1979). Neal Bernards, *Gun Control* (Lucent Books, 1991) and David E. Newton, *Gun Control: An Issue for the Nineties* (Enslow, 1992) are both attempts to summarize fairly the chief arguments for and against gun control. To put the issue of guns in a larger historical perspective, readers may wish to examine the impact of the American frontier, with its gun-slinging heroes and villains, on modern American culture. Richard Slotkin's *Gunfighter Nation* (Atheneum, 1992) is an illuminating study of this enduring American myth.

In the second edition of *More Guns, Less Crime: Understanding Crime and Gun Control Laws* (University of Chicago Press, 2000), Lott rebuts some criticisms of his thesis and provides up-to-date statistics to support it. A related defense of gun ownership is examined in the editorial "Gun Availability and Violent Death," *American Journal of Public Health* (June 1997). In a 1993 survey gun owners indicated that in an incident during the previous year, someone "almost certainly would have" died if a gun had not been used for protection. In contrast, 38,000 people died in that year because of injuries due to firearms. The result would appear to be that guns took far fewer lives than they saved. But how exaggerated are the estimates of certain death? How many of the deaths by firearms might have taken place by other means if guns had not been available? The public debate continues.

ISSUE 10

Does Affirmative Action Advance Racial Equality?

YES: Mary Frances Berry, from "Affirmative Action: Why We Need It, Why It Is Under Attack," in George E. Curry, ed., *The Affirmative Action Debate* (Perseus, 1996)

NO: Linda Chavez, from "Promoting Racial Harmony," in George E. Curry, ed., *The Affirmative Action Debate* (Perseus, 1996)

ISSUE SUMMARY

YES: Mary Frances Berry, chair of the U.S. Civil Rights Commission, contends that affirmative action is needed because minorities have suffered so much negative action throughout American history.

NO: Columnist Linda Chavez argues that racial preferences create a surface appearance of progress while destroying the substance of minority achievement.

We didn't land on Plymouth Rock, my brothers and sisters—Plymouth Rock landed on *us!*" Malcolm X's observation is borne out by the facts of American history. Snatched from their native land, transported thousands of miles —in a nightmare of disease and death—and sold into slavery, blacks were reduced to the legal status of farm animals. Even after emancipation, blacks were segregated from whites—in some states by law, and by social practice almost everywhere. American apartheid continued for another century.

In 1954 the Supreme Court declared state-compelled segregation in schools unconstitutional, and it followed up that decision with others that struck down many forms of official segregation. Still, discrimination survived, and in most southern states blacks were either discouraged or prohibited from exercising their right to vote. Not until the 1960s was compulsory segregation finally and effectively challenged. Between 1964 and 1968 Congress passed the most sweeping civil rights legislation since the end of the Civil War. It banned discrimination in employment, public accommodations (hotels, motels, restaurants, etc.), and housing; it also guaranteed voting rights for blacks and even authorized federal officials to take over the job of voter registration in areas suspected of disenfranchising blacks. Today, several agencies in the federal government exercise sweeping powers to enforce these civil rights measures.

But is that enough? Equality of condition between blacks and whites seems as elusive as ever. The black unemployment rate is double that of whites, and the percentage of black families living in poverty is nearly four times that of whites. Only a small percentage of blacks ever make it into medical school or law school.

Advocates of affirmative action have focused upon these *de facto* differences to bolster their argument that it is no longer enough just to stop discrimination. The damage done by three centuries of racism now has to be remedied, they argue, and effective remediation requires a policy of "affirmative action." At the heart of affirmative action is the use of "numerical goals." Opponents call them "racial quotas." Whatever the name, what they imply is the setting aside of a certain number of jobs or positions for blacks or other historically oppressed groups. Opponents charge that affirmative action penalizes innocent people simply because they are white, that it often results in unqualified appointments, and that it ends up harming instead of helping blacks.

Affirmative action has had an uneven history in U.S. federal courts. In *Regents of the University of California v. Allan Bakke* (1978), which marked the first time the Supreme Court directly dealt with the merits of affirmative action, a 5–4 majority ruled that a white applicant to a medical school had been wrongly excluded due to the school's affirmative action policy; yet the majority also agreed that "race-conscious" policies may be used in admitting candidates —as long as they do not amount to fixed quotas. Since *Bakke,* Supreme Court decisions have gone one way or the other depending on the precise circumstances of the case. In recent years, however, most of the Court's decisions seem to have run against affirmative action programs. For example, the Court has ruled against federal "set-aside" programs, which offer fixed percentages of federal contracts to minority-owned firms, although in the past it has permitted them. A more direct legal challenge to affirmative action was handed down by a federal appeals court in 1996 when it struck down the affirmative action policy of the University of Texas law school on grounds that it discriminated against whites, Asians, and other groups. The university appealed the case, but the Supreme Court declined to review it.

The most radical popular challenge to affirmative action was the ballot initiative endorsed by California voters in 1996. Proposition 209 banned any state program based upon racial or gender "preferences." Among the effects of this ban was a sharp decline in the numbers of non-Asian minorities admitted to the elite campuses of the state's university system, especially Berkeley and UCLA. (Asian admissions to the elite campuses either stayed the same or increased, and non-Asian minority admissions to some of the less-prestigious branches increased.)

In the following selections, Mary Frances Berry contends that affirmative action is needed because minorities have suffered so much negative action throughout American history, while Linda Chavez argues that racial preferences create only the appearance of progress, all the while destroying the substance of minority achievement.

181

Mary Frances Berry

 **YES**

Affirmative Action: Why We Need It, Why It Is Under Attack

T hose now calling for an end to affirmative action—including Republican leaders on Capitol Hill and some black conservatives—ignore one fundamental fact: the reason we need affirmative action is because we minorities have suffered so much negative action throughout American history. Those negative actions began with slavery and have continued, with African-Americans being treated at best as second-class citizens for more than two centuries.

Contrary to the recent headlines, the battle over affirmative action is not new. For its entire history, affirmative action has been subject to attack. Political opponents such as Senator Jesse Helms, former attorney general Edwin Meese, and former assistant attorney general William Bradford Reynolds repeatedly tried to overturn it in the past fifteen years. Their efforts have drawn support from African-American writers such as Shelby Steele, Stephen Carter, and Thomas Sowell. Each time they have been defeated by civil rights groups, rank-and-file Americans, business leaders, and Republicans and Democrats both in Congress and across the nation....

The History Behind Today's Affirmative Action

Since the end of slavery, African-Americans have struggled for economic justice, an equal opportunity to enter the workplace and to have access to higher education. Generations of African-Americans swept the floors in factories while being denied the opportunity to become higher-paid operatives on the machines. In grocery and department stores, clerks were white and janitors and elevator operators were black. College-educated African-Americans worked as bellboys, porters, and domestics if they could not get the scarce teaching positions in local all-black schools, which were usually the only alternative to preaching or perhaps working in the post office. Some progress in job opportunities for African-Americans was made during the labor shortages of World War II and beyond, but it was limited. By the 1960s African-Americans were still segregated for the most part in low-wage jobs.

From Mary Frances Berry, "Affirmative Action: Why We Need It, Why It Is Under Attack," in George E. Curry, ed., *The Affirmative Action Debate* (Perseus Books, 1996). Copyright © 1996 by George E. Curry.

The pre–affirmative action racial reality also included thousands of towns and cities in which police and fire departments remained entirely white and male. Women and African-Americans were even forbidden to apply. There were no merit standards for employing the white men who occupied the best jobs, because merit would have required accepting applications from all corners and picking the best people. Men with the benefit of white skin, whether their granddaddies ever owned slaves or not, whether they themselves or their remote ancestors were immigrants, had the good-job pie all to themselves.

In higher education, most African-Americans attended predominantly black colleges, many established by states as segregated institutions. Most concentrated on teacher training, to the exclusion of professional education. A few African-Americans went to largely white institutions; in 1954, that figure was about 1% of entering freshmen.

The history of corrective measures dates to the 1930s, when federal labor legislation required employers to use affirmative action to remedy unfair labor practices. In the civil rights context, affirmative action derives from presidential executive orders to end discrimination in employment. In 1941, President Franklin Roosevelt issued an order in response to a threat by A. Philip Randolph, the president of the Brotherhood of Sleeping Car Porters, to march on Washington to protest racial discrimination by defense contractors. Roosevelt's order established the first Fair Employment Practices Committee. But little progress resulted for African-Americans. The federal compliance programs were routinely understaffed and underfunded, and they lacked enforcement authority.

The ten million workers on the payrolls of the one hundred largest defense contractors included few blacks in 1960. The $7.5 billion in federal grants-in-aid to the states and cities for highway, airport, and school construction went almost exclusively to white businesses. The number of skilled black workers on public housing and slum clearance projects was minuscule. The U.S. Employment Service, which provided funds for state-operated employment bureaus, encouraged skilled blacks to register for unskilled jobs, accepted requests from lily-white employers, and made no effort to get employers to hire African-American workers. Black businesses had expanded and diversified since the days of slavery, but they were still excluded from competing on contracts offered by state and local governments. Essentially, using taxes paid in part by African-Americans, the government was directly subsidizing discrimination.

As a result of the civil rights movement, President John F. Kennedy's executive order on contract compliance created the Committee on Equal Employment Opportunity. In 1965 President Lyndon Johnson issued Executive Order 11246, which required federal contractors to take affirmative action to ensure equality of employment opportunity. It said, in part, "the contractor will, in all solicitations or advertisements for employees placed by or on behalf of the contractor, state that all qualified applicants will receive consideration for employment without regard to race, creed, color or national origin...."

Under the prodding of the U.S. Civil Rights Commission and Arthur Fletcher, a black Republican assistant secretary of labor, the Nixon administration issued specific requirements for enforcing contract compliance which established the general outlines of the program as it exists today. The employer self-analyzes the employment of minorities and women in all job categories; assesses the level of utilization compared with those in the workforce; and develops goals and timetables for each job group in which minorities and women are underrepresented. Compliance officers are supposed to review the results. The goals are not inflexible targets; all that is required is a good-faith effort, and no employer is required to hire unqualified applicants.

Title VII of the Civil Rights Act of 1964 and its amendments were enacted to end discrimination by large private employers, whether or not they had government contracts. The Equal Employment Opportunity Commission, which was established by the act, was to resolve complaints. The act aims to compensate employees for illegal discrimination and to encourage employers to end discrimination. It calls for voluntary action. A valid affirmative action plan includes a systematic, comprehensive, and reviewable effort to dismantle discrimination processes. Measures that implicitly take race, sex, national origin, or religion into account may also be implemented apart from an affirmative action plan. Affirmative action may involve simply remaining aware of the need to broaden the search for qualified people unlike those already in the workforce. The 1971 Supreme Court decision in *Griggs v. Duke Power* further reinforced the policy, directing that employment qualifications must be related to the job in question and not designed simply to perpetuate racial exclusion.

Affirmative action has also been important in alleviating discrimination in higher education for women as well as African-Americans and other people of color. After the enactment of Title VI of the Civil Rights Act of 1964 and Title IX of the educational amendments of 1972 and through voluntary affirmative action efforts, women and racial minorities have taken advantage of increased opportunities in higher education. The enrollment of women in higher education has risen steadily. Women now make up more than 50% of undergraduate students and 50% or more of the students in law and medicine and other graduate and professional schools. Through the availability of student aid programs and aggressive recruitment and retention programs, the college-going rate for blacks and whites who graduated from high school was about equal by 1977....

The Backlash Is Based on Distortions

In [the] latest assault on affirmative action, opponents have armed themselves with old and new arguments. Opponents of affirmative action distort the meaning of the principle, rewrite history, and ignore present realities in their eagerness to prevail. They claim that the test of whether affirmative action is needed is whether it alleviates poverty. Affirmative action was never intended to substitute for jobs, nutritional aid for poor families, and other social programs. But it has lifted many out of poverty by providing enhanced job and entrepreneurial opportunities, and their success sends out a ray of hope to the poor that if they make the effort, they will be able to better themselves.

Opponents also argue that affirmative action requires a lowering of standards, pointing to standardized test scores as the measure of who is worthy for a job or seat in a college or professional school. Of course, they cannot be serious, because neither African-Americans nor non-Jewish whites are the leaders in test score performance. If opportunity were awarded only on the basis of test scores, Asian- and Jewish Americans would hold the best jobs everywhere and almost entirely fill the best colleges and universities, since they uniformly make the highest scores on standardized tests. In any case, experts agree that using standardized test scores alone is probably the worst way to determine admissions or who is hired for a job.

To be sure, our economic system creates certain dilemmas. When there is not enough economic opportunity for everyone, keeping blacks out of jobs or seats in our universities allows whites to continue to dominate both the workplace and our educational system. If the rationale for excluding African-Americans can be based on lack of qualifications or inability to perform, then so much the better. We African-Americans may even believe that we *should* be excluded and confined to the lowest ranks. The conundrum is that when we have been included, we have usually performed.

Critics also ask why we do not replace affirmative action based on race and sex with affirmative action based entirely on poverty or economic disadvantage. The answer is that race and sex discrimination are one thing and poverty is another. There is no reason not to support targeted efforts to relieve poverty, but that does not preclude relieving discrimination based on race or sex, which may or may not be accompanied by poverty. For example, affirmative action can help middle-class African-American employees to break through the glass ceiling when they seek promotions in the workplace.

Opponents also argue that targeting remedies by race or gender is contrary to the American belief in individualism. However, an African-American is discriminated against not because his name is James or John but because he is an African-American. A woman is discriminated against not because her name is Nancy or Jane but because she is a woman. Those who want to eradicate group remedies should first eradicate group discrimination.

Enemies of affirmative action cloak their views with rhetoric about the ideal of color blindness, which requires the removal of the affirmative action blot from our understanding of the Constitution. We must never forget that as appealing as the idea may appear on the surface, our society has never been color-blind. From the beginning the Constitution permitted discrimination on the basis of color and sex. Congress knowingly perpetuated slavery and the subjugation of African-Americans, as reflected in its pro-slavery compromises. American society remained color conscious despite the Civil War, Emancipation, and the enactment of the Thirteenth, Fourteenth, and Fifteenth Amendments.

Societal and constitutional color consciousness made race-conscious remedies necessary. The brief submitted by the NAACP Legal Defense and Educational Fund in the 1978 *Bakke* case describes how color-conscious remedies were enacted by the same Congress that wrote the Fourteenth Amendment. That Congress enacted a series of social welfare laws expressly delineating the racial groups entitled to participate in or benefit from each program. It did so over the objections of critics who opposed targeting particular groups.

The Fourteenth Amendment appeared to provide legal equality for all Americans. However, while corporations used it successfully for protection against state regulation, both federal and state governments helped to maintain the subordination of African-Americans. Indeed, in the 1896 *Plessy v. Ferguson* decision the Court majority affirmed racial discrimination, which is why Justice Harlan had to *dissent* in order to insist that the Constitution is color-blind. Not until *Brown v. Board of Education* in 1954 did the Court reverse "separate but equal" as legal doctrine. Nevertheless, race-conscious discrimination continues to plague African-Americans today and requires race-conscious remedies.

In a report several years ago, the Federal Reserve Board, drawing on the records of more than nine thousand lending institutions, found that not only were African-Americans more likely to experience discrimination, but the rejection rate for blacks in the highest income bracket was identical to the denial rates of the poorest whites. Housing and Urban Development secretary Henry Cisneros concluded that the report "tells us that discrimination is still alive and well in America." Hugh Price, president of the National Urban League, observed in a speech to the Commonwealth Club in San Francisco, "It is not yet time for impatient whites and successful blacks to hoist the gangplank behind them." African-Americans who object to affirmative action apparently have a different view. Some, perhaps, do not understand how they got where they are. Some may be in denial or refuse to believe the policy is needed. Some may really believe African-Americans are inferior or that there is something called pure "merit" and that white people have more of it, which is just about as rational as believing their ice is colder.

Affirmative Action Remains Constitutional

The courts, aware of the perpetuation of invidious discrimination, have routinely upheld race- and gender-conscious affirmative action. Unlike opponents of affirmative action, who keep speaking of discrimination as something that used to happen, they are aware that discrimination exists here and now. The Supreme Court has upheld ordering unions to hire numerically to make up for excluding nonwhites from membership. In the 1987 case *United States v. Paradise,* the Court also upheld a remedial order requiring one black promotion for every white one for state troopers in the Alabama Department of Public Safety. The department had refused to promote African-Americans after it finally began permitting them to become troopers, though by the 1980s blacks made up about 25% of the force. The Court ordered one-to-one promotions until the share of officers was about the same as in the ranks. The order was temporary and could be waived. No one who did not meet the requirements had to be promoted.

Even in the 1989 case *Richmond v. J. A. Croson Co.,* in which the Court invalidated a set-aside program for African-American businesses, the justices did not rule out race-conscious relief. The Court upheld the rule that race-conscious relief is permitted, but specified that it must be narrowly tailored. However, those who challenged the set-aside achieved their objective, to reduce the possibility that blacks, who had received less than 1% of municipal contracts before the set-aside program, could gain a larger share of Richmond's construction business.

The Supreme Court has also ruled in favor of voluntary affirmative action plans. In *United Steelworkers of America v. Brian Weber* (1979), the Court upheld a voluntary plan reserving half of the places in a training program for blacks as remedial and not unnecessarily trammeling the rights of white men. The plan was designed to eliminate conspicuous racial imbalance in Kaiser Steel's almost exclusively white craft workforce by reserving for black employees half of the openings in plant training programs, until the number of black craftworkers was commensurate with the size of the workforce. At the time, only 1.8% of skilled workers at Kaiser were black. The Court held that the law did not intend to constrain management, and that Kaiser could lawfully break down patterns of racial segregation and hierarchy.

In *Johnson v. Transportation Agency* (1987), the Court upheld a voluntary affirmative action plan under which a government agency alleviated the under-representation of women in certain job categories by using sex as one factor in evaluating otherwise qualified candidates. There had never been a female road dispatcher in the agency. The plan was challenged by a man who was passed over for promotion to a position in favor of a qualified white woman. The Court determined that it was not unreasonable to take sex into account as one factor under the circumstances.

In the education arena, the 1978 *Bakke* case is still the major precedent. The case grew out of the reservation of sixteen out of one hundred available places in the University of California Medical School at Davis for qualified minorities. The Supreme Court essentially decided that, in the absence of proof of past discrimination, setting aside a specific number of places was illegal but that minority status could be used in admissions as a factor in an applicant's favor. The desire to obtain a "diverse" student body was a permissible goal.

In 1995 the Supreme Court decided a major case that tested its support of the principle of affirmative action. In the *Adarand Constructors, Inc. v. Pena*, the Court considered whether to further restrict the use of set-asides for minority contractors. A white contractor who submitted the low bid for a government-funded highway project claimed that a Hispanic company received the contract because race was used as a plus factor. The Court in a five-to-four decision decided that the *Croson* standards apply to federal government minority contracting programs. It remains to be seen how many federal contractors are able to meet the standards.

The Ongoing Battle for Advantage

The irony is that even though whites still receive the lion's share of contracts, scholarships, or well-paying jobs, many white Americans will make any argument and go to any lengths to fight to withdraw any portion that might be awarded to African-Americans. President Clinton has finally come down on the side of "mending" but not ending affirmative action. However, his voice is only one among many in the contention for state and national political advantage.

Although the social conditions that occasioned affirmative action have improved for some African-Americans, victory is far from won. For more than a generation, American law has prohibited race, national origin, and gender discrimination. However, government reports as well as television documentaries show that African-Americans, whether middle-class, upper-class, or no class, suffer discrimination in obtaining jobs or promotions, borrowing money to buy houses or start businesses, renting apartments, or getting served in restaurants. You can be a government official, Oprah Winfrey, or Johnnie or Susie No-Name—it sometimes makes no difference.

This brings to mind a story told by one vigorous opponent of affirmative action in the 1980s, Clarence Pendleton, Jr., then chairman of the U.S. Commission on Civil Rights. He was pleased to be invited to a major White House dinner soon after his first media forays on behalf of the Reagan administration's policy and was enjoying himself enormously. As he walked from his table to greet some acquaintances on the other side of the room, one of the white guests collared him to say that his table needed more wine. Pendleton recalled, "It was obvious the bastard thought I was a waiter." . . .

When civil rights concerns were in vogue, the African-American protest tradition at its most vibrant, and enforcement likely, affirmative action worked to increase opportunity for blacks. That evidence means we need more affirmative action, however we label it—promoting "diversity" or "banana" or something else. African-Americans are only slowly mobilizing to repel a very real threat, which is part of the across-the-board war on the poor in general and African-Americans in particular.

When I despair, my mother always says, "God is my president and also the Speaker of my House." But the Lord helps those who help themselves. If we do not see to our own interests and consolidate our allies, the Congress and the states are likely to repeal affirmative action, along with anything else characterized as benefiting African-Americans. The political signaling that has already had a chilling effect in the workplace in recent years will further constrain the opportunities of qualified African-Americans. The anger and alienation of young African-Americans, many of whom are separatists or black nationalists and have already written off the system, are likely to increase. . . . The problem of the twenty-first century, like that of the twentieth, will remain what W. E. B. Du Bois called the problem of the color line.

NO ⬅

Linda Chavez

Promoting Racial Harmony

Senator Hubert Humphrey took the floor of the Senate in 1964 to defend the landmark Civil Rights Act. Humphrey, the bill's chief sponsor, had to respond to conservatives who said that the bill would violate individual rights. He declared that the Civil Rights Act would make it a crime to classify human beings into racial groups and give preference to some groups but not others. He denied assertions that the bill would force employers to hire less qualified people because of their race. The goal, he said, was to ensure race-neutral treatment for all individuals. "Title VII [of the bill]," he noted, "does not require an employer to achieve any sort of racial balance in his work force by giving preferential treatment to any individual or group." Sure of his principles, Humphrey promised to eat the pages of the Civil Rights Act if it ever came to require racial preferences.

Today, of course, the Civil Rights Act of 1964 is interpreted by many civil rights advocates as requiring all sorts of racial preference programs. Assistant attorney general for civil rights Deval Patrick cited that law in court to defend race-based layoffs being used in a New Jersey school district to maintain racial balance. A law that was intended to replace racial rights with individual rights is being used to install a new system of racial rights.

The very words "affirmative action" have also been bent to new purposes. Originally, that phrase referred only to outreach and training programs to help minorities compete equally with whites. Today it designates programs that exclude whites from participation altogether (such as minority scholarships and government contract "set-asides") or enforce artificially low standards for minorities.

Playing the Game by the Rules

My recent exchange with William Raspberry shows the difference. At a National Press Club panel discussion and in his syndicated *Washington Post* column, Mr. Raspberry drew an analogy he thought would put the issue in focus. Suppose, he said, that during halftime at a basketball game it is discovered that the referees cheated during the first half of the game. The crooked referees allowed one team to rack up sixteen undeserved points. The referees are expelled from the game, but that doesn't fix the score. What to do?

From Linda Chavez, "Promoting Racial Harmony," in George E. Curry, ed., *The Affirmative Action Debate* (Perseus Books, 1996). Copyright © 1996 by George E. Curry. Reprinted by permission of the author.

My response to Mr. Raspberry was simple: Compensate the victims of discrimination. Give sixteen points to the team that was discriminated against. Wherever we can, in basketball or in society, we should apply specific remedies to specific victims of discrimination. The antidiscrimination laws of this country already allow us to do just that. Courts are empowered to force employers to hire or promote victims of discrimination and award the back pay and seniority those employees would have had. Similar tools are available to redress discrimination in housing, schools, and contracting. It's not even necessary for every person who is discriminated against to file a complaint; courts routinely provide relief to whole groups of people when they find that an individual or company has discriminated against more than one person.

Let's return to the basketball analogy. If a particular team in a particular game has been unfairly deprived of sixteen points, it would certainly be foolish and unfair to award sixteen extra points to that team in every game it plays from that time forward. It would be even more perverse to extend this preferential treatment to the children of the players on that team, awarding them extra points in their playground games because their parents suffered. Yet government-sponsored racial preference programs, which disregard individual cases of discrimination, are considered by some to be the only reasonable solution to discrimination.

Now, the analogy between a basketball game and American society may not be perfect, but it certainly is instructive. In sports, all participants are treated in a race-neutral manner. Team colors, not skin colors, are the basis of group affiliation. It may be true that the rules are often broken, but specific remedies and punishments for specific violations are available when this happens. Everybody is expected to play by the same rules—in fact, fans are never angrier than when they think the referees favor one team. Isn't that the model we should strive toward in our society?

The alternative to that model is to continue classifying our citizens by race, attaching an official government label "black," "white," "Asian," "Hispanic," and so on to each individual. Then the all-wise federal bureaucracy can decide how much special privilege each group deserves and spoon out benefits based on the labels: five portions to this group, three to that one, seven and a half to the next.

The Race Box Problem

Any attempt to systematically classify human beings according to race will fail, because race is an arbitrary concept. There will always be people—lots of them —who disagree with the way the labels are dispensed. An ugly power struggle among racial groups competing to establish their claims to victimhood is the inevitable result.

Native Hawaiians, for example, are currently classified as Native Americans. But many of them want their own racial classification.... The National Congress of American Indians, however, insists that Native Hawaiians are really just Native Americans. The classification of 250,000 Native Hawaiians is at stake, and being able to claim a quarter-million people in your racial group makes a big difference when it's time to dole out federal benefits.

Other groups make similar claims. Many Americans of eastern European ancestry complain about being lumped into the "white" box. Five different Asian groups have petitioned for sub-boxes. The U.S. Department of Housing and Urban Development has gone so far as to establish preference for "Hasidic Jewish Americans." Before he changed his mind about racial preferences, California governor Pete Wilson approved a law that gives special protections to Portuguese-Americans.

For years, the government of Puerto Rico has forbidden the Census Bureau from asking any question about race on forms distributed on the island, so vexing is the issue among Puerto Ricans. Now the national council of La Raza demands that "Hispanics," currently an ethnic group, be declared a separate race. When the Census Bureau created a special racial category for Mexicans in the 1930 census, the government of Mexico lodged an official protest that the move was racist. The bureau quickly abandoned the practice. My, how times change.

Black leaders who demand "race-conscious" remedies are discovering that race consciousness cuts both ways. A proposal to add a "multiracial" box to census forms brought outrage from those leaders. The most recent study, done in 1980, found that 70% of multiracial Americans check "black" on the census— meaning that a multiracial box would reduce the number of people defined as black, and hence the power base of black leaders, because a significant number of people who now check "black" would check "multiracial" instead. Roderick Harrison, head of the Census Bureau's Racial Statistics division, estimated that a multiracial box would reduce the "black" population by 10%.

Aware of this possibility, Billy Tidwell of the National Urban League complained in a hearing before the House Census Subcommittee in June 1993 that a multiracial box would "turn the clock back on the well-being" of African-Americans because it would be divisive, splitting light-skinned blacks from dark-skinned ones. Perhaps it has not occurred to him that any kind of racial classification is arbitrarily divisive in the same way—splitting light-skinned Americans from dark-skinned ones and, to the extent that they are treated differently, turning them against each other. Is it divisive for the government to group black people and treat them differently on the basis of their skin color, but acceptable—even necessary—for it to group other Americans and treat them differently on the basis of skin color?

Racial categories are never permanent anyway. Earlier this century, "whites" were not considered a single race. Nativists like Madison Grant, writing in his book *The Passing of the Great Race,* worried about the dilution of "Nordic" bloodlines by immigrants from eastern and southern Europe. Alarmists cried out that within fifty years "Nordic" Americans, a false category if there ever was one, would sink into the minority. By the time that actually occurred, nobody noticed. Nobody cared about the purity of "Nordic" blood anymore. The definition of race had changed.

Today, alarmists cry out that within fifty years whites will be in the minority in the United States. But today's young people, raised in a society where racism is no longer acceptable, marry between races at record rates. Half of all Mexican-Americans in California now marry non-Hispanic spouses. Half of Japanese-Americans now marry non-Japanese spouses, and similarly high rates prevail among other Asian groups. More and more children defy racial classification. In fifty years, our racial categories will no longer exist as such. Should we write those categories into our laws today, and count on the government to update them constantly to reflect the changing population? Better we should acknowledge the simple fact that categorizing people by race is not just divisive and degrading. It is impossible.

Who Really Needs Help?

Just as it's impossible to classify people by race, it's impossible to say that one race or ethnic group is clearly lagging behind whites socially and economically. Minorities are not clearly lagging behind anybody.

Hispanics, as I have said for years, are doing quite well. The category of "Hispanics" seems to trail others because it includes a large number of immigrants—nearly half of the adult Hispanic population is foreign-born. These immigrants often come to this country with practically nothing and therefore skew the economic numbers downward. Unfortunately, most statistics do not distinguish between native-born and foreign-born Hispanics. Those that do, however, indicate that native-born Hispanics earn wages commensurate to their educational level. Mexican-American men with thirteen years of education, for example, earn 93% of the earnings of non-Hispanic whites with comparable education. Other statistics indicate that even immigrants do just find if they work hard and learn English. Despite all this, people who claim to represent the interests of Hispanics continue to deny their record of success, painting them as a failed underclass in order to persuade government bureaucrats to give them special treatment. Rather than treat them as a downtrodden minority, we should see Hispanics for what they are—an upwardly mobile immigrant group.

Asian-Americans are also doing well. By many measures, they are doing better than whites. In fact, they are doing so well that racial preference programs sometimes discriminate against them in order to make room for other races. For years, the University of California has, as a matter of official policy, denied bright young Asian-American students admission to college, law school, medical school, and the rest of the university system because they are Asian-American. They have "too many" qualified Asian-American applicants, so discrimination against them is necessary to uphold the system of racial rights.

According to Michael Lynch of the Pacific Research Institute, Asian-American applicants to the University of California [UC] qualify for admission based on merit at more than six times the rate of blacks and Hispanics, and more than two and a half times the rate of whites. "These inconvenient facts create problems for UC administrators seeking ethnic proportionality," says Lynch. "Without bending the rules for some groups, there is no hope of achieving proportionality." According to a report released by the UC, Asian-American admissions would increase by 15 to 25% if the university based its decisions on academics and socioeconomic status but not race. That means countless Asian-Americans have been shut out of UC by racial preferences.

In a very recent case, two grade-schoolers in Montgomery County, Maryland, were initially denied permission to transfer to a new school in order to participate in a French language immersion program. The two girls are half Asian-American, and country bureaucrats decided that their departure would disrupt the delicate racial balance of the school they are currently attending. The school system denied these students an extraordinary educational opportunity solely because they are of the wrong race. If they were white, county policy would have favored them. The *Washington Post,* hardly a right-wing newspaper, denounced this discrimination in an editorial titled "Asians Need Not Apply." Under public pressure, the girls were allowed to transfer.

Blacks, too, are moving up in society. There is a healthy, thriving black middle class in America. There are blacks at the top levels of society. A recent *New York Times* story, for example, reported that 18% of working, non-Hispanic blacks in New York City between the ages of twenty-five and sixty-five held managerial or professional jobs, and that another 28% held technical, sales, and administrative support positions. Furthermore, 30% were living in households with incomes of $50,000 or more. Statistics that seem to show lingering effects of racism often hide other explanations. For example, household income among blacks is lower than household income among whites, but to a large extent this is caused by the fact that black households are much more likely than white households to include only one adult, usually a single woman, and therefore only one income.

I am the first to say that some minorities are wrestling with enormous problems, racial discrimination among them. Significant groups of minorities, especially blacks, are living in poverty. The condition of our inner cities is a disgrace, and that is a special problem that deserves special attention. But we have to ask: Do all minorities face these problems?

Clearly, the answer to the first part of that question is no. People from ethnic minorities have been successful in climbing into the middle class. If we are going to help minorities who are still struggling, we have to find programs that target those minorities and not the broad spectrum of blacks, Hispanics, and other minorities in the middle class. But racial preferences are irrelevant to minorities who are truly in need. Richard Rodriguez writes in the *Baltimore Sun:* "I was talking to a roomful of black teen-agers, most of them street kids or kids from the projects. Only one of them in a room of 13 had ever heard of anything called affirmative action." Racial preferences, he says, don't reach the people who need help because they depend on a trickle-down effect that never actually occurs. "Many leftists today have [a] domino theory," he writes. "They insist that by creating a female or a non-white leadership class at Harvard or Citibank, people at the bottom will be changed."

The time is past when every member of a racial minority is truly "disadvantaged." It is illogical, even cynical, to cite statistics about minority inner-city poverty in defense of preferences for minority bankers, CEOs, contractors, and investors, but this is what happens all the time. The federal government has nineteen separate regulations giving preferential treatment to rich, but "economically disadvantaged," bank owners. It has innumerable "minority set-asides" for its public contracts, which go to corporations owned by minorities who are rich enough to own corporations. It allows rich minorities to buy broadcasting licenses and facilities far below market values—in one famous case, the then mayor of Charlotte, North Carolina, Harvey Gantt, who is black, and his partners made $3 million by buying a TV station under minority-preference rules and then selling it to whites four months later at full price. This didn't advance the status of blacks in society, but it did boost Gantt's bank account. Ironically, anyone who is already in a position to benefit from racial preference programs in these fields does not need special help in the first place.

The same can be said of racial preference policies at universities. Contrary to what many big universities say, racial preference programs in university admissions generally help people who don't really need the help. The vast majority of minority applicants to top universities come from comfortable, middle-class homes. Some of them come from affluent families. The University of California at Berkeley says that the average Hispanic student admitted through its racial preference program comes from a middle-class family; many, if not most, attended integrated schools, often in the suburbs. In fact, 17% of Hispanic entering freshmen in 1989, along with 14% of black freshmen, were truly well off, coming from families with incomes over $75,000. That's about twice the median family income in the United States. Yet these comfortable middle- and upper middle-class students were admitted under reduced standards because of their race. Why should a university lower its expectations of affluent students who are minorities?

Racial Preferences Don't Help Minorities

The answer to the further question of whether racial preferences are effective in solving the problems some minorities face is also no. Not only do racial preference programs generally help people who don't need help, but more important, racial preferences create a surface appearance of progress while destroying the substance of minority achievement. Holding people to lower standards or giving them special help will make them look as if they are succeeding, but it can't make them succeed. B students who are admitted to top universities because of their race are still B students.

The Pacific Research Institute's Michael Lynch cites graduation rates at UCLA of 50% for blacks and 62% for Hispanics. By comparison, whites and Asians graduate at rates of 80% and 77%, respectively. UCLA admits blacks and Hispanics based on drastically lower standards. Forty-one percent of Hispanic students and over half of black students at UCLA gained admission on a special "minority track," where the standards are significantly lower than they are for other students. These students could have gone to any of California's less competitive colleges and received their degrees, but instead they were placed in California's most rigorous colleges by racial preference programs.

Companies that aren't efficient enough to survive in the marketplace but which get government contracts anyway because they are owned by minorities are still inefficient businesses. "The prospect of getting government contracts as a result of belonging to a protected group is sometimes a false inducement for people to go into business without being adequately prepared," wrote successful black businessman and University of California regent Ward Connerly in *Policy Review.* "They often are undercapitalized and lack the business acumen to remain in business without government contracts." Ultimately, success depends on ability. No preference program can protect minorities from that fact forever. In the meantime, the beneficiaries of such programs *are* protected from having to learn the skills and habits they need to become truly successful.

Furthermore, racial preferences rob minorities of the credit they deserve. How many times have people assumed that a particular member of a minority got a job, a promotion, a college admission, a scholarship, or any other achievement because of racial preference? The hard work of minority executives, employees, and students can easily be brushed off if there is even a small chance that their honors and accolades were awarded because of their skin color. "It is time for America to acknowledge that affirmative action doesn't work," writes black businessman Daniel Colimon, head of a litigation support firm with over two hundred clients, in *Policy Review.* "Affirmative-action programs have established an extremely damaging stereotype that places African-Americans and other racial minorities in a very precarious position. We are now perceived as a group of people who regardless of how hard we work, how educated we become, or what we achieve, would not be where we are without the preferential treatment afforded by affirmative-action programs."

Remember Rutgers president Francis Lawrence? A strong supporter of racial preferences throughout his career, he let the cat out of the bag [recently] when he told a faculty group that minorities need admissions preferences because they are a "disadvantaged population that doesn't have the genetic hereditary background" to do as well as whites on the SAT. Racial preferences encourage that kind of belief, and they will continue to do so as long as they exist.

Along with that is the racial antagonism caused by racial preferences. More and more whites are getting angry and resentful about perceived reverse discrimination. No doubt many whites exaggerate the extent to which they have been discriminated against, but that's beside the point. Any time groups are treated differently because of their race, the group that is treated worse has a legitimate complaint. This makes it all the more difficult to get whites to feel sympathy across racial lines. "If anything, the white 'backlash' to affirmative action has perpetuated the polarization of America's various ethnic groups," writes Colimon. When whites complain about racial preference programs, many minority supporters of these programs become all the more antagonistic toward whites. It's a vicious circle that can't be broken as long as racial preference programs are in force.

Racial preferences may not cause whites to hate minorities when they would not otherwise do so, but they undeniably stir up negative feelings. Paul Sniderman, a political science professor at Stanford University, and Thomas Piazza, a survey researcher at the University of California at Berkeley, authors of the 1993 book *The Scar of Race,* found that "merely asking whites to respond to the issue of affirmative action increases significantly the likelihood that they will perceive blacks as irresponsible and lazy." In a poll, they asked one group of whites to evaluate certain images of black people in general. They asked another group of whites the same questions, but this group was first asked to give an opinion on a racial preference program in a nearby state. Forty-three percent of whites who were first asked about racial preferences said that blacks in general were "irresponsible," compared with 26% of whites who were not asked about racial preferences. "No effort was made to whip up feelings about affirmative action," wrote the authors. But one neutral question about racial preferences "was sufficient to excite a statistically significant response, demonstrating that dislike of particular racial policies can provoke dislike of blacks, as well as the other way around."

That is why racial preferences cannot be justified by the desire for "diversity." Some say employers and college administrators should seek to promote diversity by hiring more minorities than they otherwise would. But racial harmony and integration are much more important goals than diversity—the purpose of seeking diversity is to promote racial harmony and the integration of different races into one society. Racial preferences produce a diversity of skin colors but a division of sentiments. They put people of many different races together in a way that makes each racial group see other racial groups as competitors for arbitrary advantage. That's not the way to produce an integrated, harmonious society.

Racial preferences have divided us for too long. We are all for equal opportunity. We all agree that antidiscrimination laws should be vigorously enforced. We have the legal tools and the consensus we need to go after people who discriminate against minorities. We should be getting on with that job instead of arguing over how much privilege the government should dispense to which racial groups. Nobody should be entitled to something just for being born with a certain color of skin.

POSTSCRIPT

Does Affirmative Action Advance Racial Equality?

Much of the argument between Berry and Chavez turns on the question of "color blindness." To what extent should our laws be color-blind? During the 1950s and early 1960s, civil rights leaders were virtually unanimous on this point. Martin Luther King, Jr., in a speech given at a civil rights march on Washington, said, "I have a dream that my four little children will one day live in a nation where they will not be judged by the color of their skin but by the content of their character." This was the consensus view in 1963, but today it may need to be qualified: In order to *bring about* color blindness, it may be necessary to become temporarily color-conscious. But for how long? And is there a danger that this temporary color consciousness may become a permanent policy?

Chavez recounts the evolution of her own thinking on matters of race relations in *An Unlikely Conservative: The Transformation of a Renegade Democrat* (HarperCollins, 2001). Girardeau A. Spann's *The Law of Affirmative Action: Twenty-Five Years of Supreme Court Decisions on Race and Remedies* (New York University Press, 2000) is a comprehensive chronicle of the Supreme Court's involvement with the affirmative action issue from *DeFunis v. Odegaard* in 1974 through the cases decided in the Court's 1998–1999 term. Clint Bolick, in *The Affirmative Action Fraud: Can We Restore the Civil Rights Vision?* (Cato Institute, 1996), argues that racial and gender preferences deepen racial hostilities and undermine individual freedom without doing minorities much good. Columnist Jim Sleeper's *Liberal Racism* (Viking, 1997) is critical of affirmative action and other race-based programs, as is a book by *ABC News* reporter Bob Zelnick, *Backfire: A Reporter's Look at Affirmative Action* (Regnery, 1996). Barbara Bergmann supports affirmative action in *In Defense of Affirmative Action* (Basic Books, 1996), while Stephan Thernstrom and Abigail Thernstrom, in their comprehensive survey of racial progress in America entitled *America in Black and White: One Nation, Indivisible* (Simon & Schuster, 1997), argue that it is counterproductive. In *Collision Course: The Strange Convergence of Affirmative Action and Immigration Policy in America* (Oxford University Press, 2002), Hugh David Graham maintains that affirmative action is now at loggerheads with America's expanded immigration policies, in that employers use affirmative action to hire new immigrants at the expense of American blacks.

Affirmative action is one of those issues, like abortion, in which the opposing sides seem utterly intransigent. But there may be a large middle sector of opinion that is simply weary of the whole controversy and may be willing to support any expedient solution worked out by pragmatists in the executive and legislative branches of the government.

ISSUE 11

Should Hate Speech Be Punished?

YES: Charles R. Lawrence III, from "Crossburning and the Sound of Silence: Antisubordination Theory and the First Amendment," *Villanova Law Review* (vol. 37, no. 4, 1992)

NO: Jonathan Rauch, from "In Defense of Prejudice: Why Incendiary Speech Must Be Protected," *Harper's Magazine* (May 1995)

ISSUE SUMMARY

YES: Law professor Charles R. Lawrence III asserts that speech should be impermissible when, going beyond insult, it inflicts injury on its victims.

NO: Author Jonathan Rauch maintains that there can be no genuine freedom of expression unless it includes the freedom to offend those who oppose the expressed opinion.

In 1942, on a busy public street in Rochester, New Hampshire, a man named Walter Chaplinsky was passing out literature promoting the Jehovah's Witnesses, which would have been all right except that the literature denounced all other religions as "rackets." As might be expected, Chaplinsky's activities caused a stir. The city marshal warned Chaplinsky that he was on the verge of creating a riot and told him that he ought to leave, whereupon Chaplinsky answered him in these words: "You are a Goddamned racketeer ... a damned Fascist, and the whole government of Rochester are Fascists or agents of Fascists." Chaplinsky was arrested for disturbing the peace, and he appealed on the grounds that his First Amendment right to free speech had been violated. The Supreme Court of the United States ruled unanimously against him. In *Chaplinsky v. New Hampshire* (1942) the Court said that his words were "fighting words," not deserving of First Amendment protection because they were "likely to provoke the average person to retaliation."

In 1984 a Texan named Gregory Lee Johnson stood in front of Dallas City Hall, doused an American flag in kerosene, and set it on fire while chanting, "Red, white, and blue, we spit on you." When he was arrested for flag desecration, he appealed to the Supreme Court on grounds of free speech—and won. In *Texas v. Johnson* (1989) the Court ruled that flag burning was a form of "symbolic speech" protected by the First Amendment.

So Chaplinsky used his mouth and was punished for it, and Johnson burned a flag and was not. How do we square these decisions, or should we? If a state can punish a person for calling someone a "Goddamned racketeer," can it also punish someone for shouting racial epithets?

Some municipalities have enacted laws that punish "hate speech" directed at women and minorities. The intention of these codes and laws is to ensure at least a minimum of civility in places where people of very diverse backgrounds must live and work together. But do they infringe upon essential freedoms?

In 1992 the Supreme Court confronted this issue in a case testing the constitutionality of a St. Paul, Minnesota, statute punishing anyone who displays symbols attacking people because of their "race, color, creed, religion, or gender." A group of St. Paul teenagers had burned a cross in the yard of a black family. Prosecutors used this newly enacted law, which raised the essential issues in the case: Did the statute violate freedoms guaranteed by the First Amendment? If so, why? In its decision of *R. A. V. v. St. Paul* (1992), the Court gave a unanimous answer to the first question. All nine justices agreed that the statute was indeed a violation of the First Amendment. But on the second question—*why* was it a violation?—the Court was deeply divided. Four members thought that it was unconstitutional because it was "overbroad," that is, worded in such general language that it would reach beyond the narrow bounds of speech activities that the Court has deemed punishable. But the majority, in an opinion by Justice Antonin Scalia, struck down the statute for a very different reason: because it contained "content discrimination." By punishing speech that attacks people because of their "race, color, creed, religion, or gender," it was prohibiting speech "solely on the basis of the subjects the speech addresses." A statute punishing speech may not single out specific categories like race or creed for protection, for to do so is to involve the state in deciding which sorts of people deserve protection against "hate speech."

In response to increasing incidents of highly derogatory racial, religious, and sexual remarks and writing on college campuses, a number of colleges adopted speech codes that went beyond what the Supreme Court had characterized as "fighting words" in *Chaplinsky*. These restrictions prompted outcries that "political correctness" was stifling the expression of unpopular ideas. Lower federal courts voided antidiscrimination codes at the Universities of Michigan and Wisconsin as overbroad and vague, calling into question similar codes at other public and private institutions.

However, the Supreme Court in *Wisconsin v. Mitchell* (1993) unanimously upheld a hate crimes law. This case was distinguished from hate speech cases in that the speech per se was not punished, but the determination that hatred inspired the commission of a crime could be the basis for increasing the penalty for that crime.

In the following selections, Charles R. Lawrence III argues that speech has the power to inflict injury and curtail the freedom of the victims of hate. Jonathan Rauch defends incendiary speech on the ground that the rights of all are better protected by pluralism than purism.

Charles R. Lawrence III  **YES**

Crossburning and the Sound of Silence: Antisubordination Theory and the First Amendment

In the early morning hours of June 21, 1990, long after they had put their five children to bed, Russ and Laura Jones were awakened by voices outside their house. Russ got up, went to his bedroom window and peered into the dark. "I saw a glow," he recalled. There, in the middle of his yard, was a burning cross. The Joneses are black. In the spring of 1990 they had moved into their four-bedroom, three-bathroom dream house on 290 Earl Street in St. Paul, Minnesota. They were the only black family on the block. Two weeks after they had settled into their predominantly white neighborhood, the tires on both their cars were slashed. A few weeks later, one of their cars' windows was shattered, and a group of teenagers had walked past their house and shouted "nigger" at their nine-year-old son. And now this burning cross. Russ Jones did not have to guess at the meaning of this symbol of racial hatred. There is not a black person in America who has not been taught the significance of this instrument of persecution and intimidation, who has not had emblazoned on his mind the image of black men's scorched bodies hanging from trees, and who does not know the story of Emmett Till.[1] One can only imagine the terror which Russell Jones must have felt as he watched the flames and thought of the vulnerability of his family and of the hateful, cowardly viciousness of those who would attack him and those he loved under cover of darkness.

This assault on Russ Jones and his family begins the story of *R.A.V. v. City of St. Paul,* the "hate speech" case recently decided by the United States Supreme Court. The Joneses, however, are not the subject of the Court's opinion. The constitutional injury addressed in *R.A.V.* was not this black family's right to live where they pleased, or their right to associate with their neighbors. The Court was not concerned with how this attack might impede the exercise of the Joneses' constitutional right to be full and valued participants in the political community, for it did not view *R.A.V.* as a case about the Joneses' injury. Instead, the Court was concerned primarily with the alleged constitutional injury to those who assaulted the Joneses, that is, the First Amendment rights of the crossburners.

From Charles R. Lawrence III, "Crossburning and the Sound of Silence: Antisubordination Theory and the First Amendment," *Villanova Law Review,* vol. 37, no. 4 (1992), pp. 787–804. Copyright © 1992 by Villanova University. Reprinted by permission. Some notes omitted.

There is much that is deeply troubling about Justice Scalia's majority opinion in *R.A.V.* But it is the utter disregard for the silenced voice of the victims that is most frightening. Nowhere in the opinion is any mention made of the Jones family or of their constitutional rights. Nowhere are we told of the history of the Ku Klux Klan or of its use of the burning cross as a tool for the suppression of speech. Justice Scalia turns the First Amendment on its head, transforming an act intended to silence through terror and intimidation into an invitation to join a public discussion. In so doing, he clothes the crossburner's terroristic act in the legitimacy of protected political speech and invites him to burn again.

"Let there be no mistake about our belief that burning a cross in someone's front yard is reprehensible," writes Justice Scalia at the close of his opinion. I am skeptical about his concern for the victims. These words seem little more than an obligatory genuflection to decency. For even in this attempt to assure the reader of his good intentions, Justice Scalia's words betray his inability to see the Joneses or hear their voices. "Burning a cross in *someone's* front yard is *reprehensible*," he says. It is reprehensible but not injurious, or immoral, or violative of the Joneses' rights. For Justice Scalia, the identity of the "someone" is irrelevant. As is the fact that it is a *cross* that is burned.

When I first read Justice Scalia's opinion it felt as if another cross had just been set ablaze. This cross was burning on the pages of U.S. Reports. It was a cross like the cross that Justice Taney had burned in 1857,[2] and that which Justice Brown had burned in 1896.[3] Its message: "You have no rights which a white man is bound to respect (or protect).[4] If you are injured by this assaultive act, the injury is a figment of your imagination that is not constitutionally cognizable."[5]

For the past couple of years I have been struggling to find a way to talk to my friends in the civil liberties community about the injures which are ignored in the *R.A.V.* case. I have tried to articulate the ways in which hate speech harms its victims and the ways in which it harms us all by undermining core values in our Constitution.

The first of these values is full and equal citizenship expressed in the Fourteenth Amendment's Equal Protection Clause. When hate speech is employed with the purpose and effect of maintaining established systems of caste and subordination, it violates that core value. Hate speech often prevents its victims from exercising legal rights guaranteed by the Constitution and civil rights statutes. The second constitutional value threatened by hate speech is the value of free expression itself. Hate speech frequently silences its victims, who, more often than not, are those who are already heard from least. An understanding of both of these injuries is aided by the methodologies of feminism and critical race theory that give special attention to the structures of subordination and the voices of the subordinated.

My own understanding of the need to inform the First Amendment discourse with the insights of an antisubordination theory began in the context of the debate over the regulation of hate speech on campus. As I lectured at universities throughout the United States, I learned of serious racist and anti-Semitic hate incidents. Students who had been victimized told me of swastikas appearing on Jewish holy days. Stories of cross burnings, racist slurs and vicious verbal assaults made me cringe even as I heard them secondhand. Universities, long the home of institutional and euphemistic racism, were witnessing the worst forms of gutter racism. In 1990, the Chronicle of Higher Education reported that approximately 250 colleges and universities had experienced serious racist incidents since 1986, and the National Institute Against Prejudice and Violence estimated that 25% of all minority students are victimized at least once during an academic year.

I urged my colleagues to hear these students' voices and argued that *Brown v. Board of Education* and its antidiscrimination principle identified an injury of constitutional dimension done to these students that must be recognized and remedied. We do not normally think of *Brown* as being a case about speech. Most narrowly read, it is a case about the rights of black children to equal educational opportunity. But *Brown* teaches us another very important lesson: that the harm of segregation is achieved by the meaning of the message it conveys. The Court's opinion in *Brown* stated that racial segregation is unconstitutional not because the "physical separation of black and white children is bad or because resources were distributed unequally among black and white schools. *Brown* held that segregated schools were unconstitutional primarily because of the message segregation conveys—the message that black children are an untouchable caste, unfit to be educated with white children." Segregation stamps a badge of inferiority upon blacks. This badge communicates a message to others that signals their exclusion from the community of citizens.

The "Whites Only" signs on the lunch counter, swimming pool and drinking fountain convey the same message. The antidiscrimination principle articulated in *Brown* presumptively entitles every individual to be treated by the organized society as a respected, responsible and participating member. This is the principle upon which all our civil rights laws rest. It is the guiding principle of the Equal Protection Clause's requirement of nondiscriminatory government action. In addition, it has been applied in regulating private discrimination.

The words "Women Need Not Apply" in a job announcement, the racially exclusionary clause in a restrictive covenant and the racial epithet scrawled on the locker of the new black employee at a previously all-white job site all convey a political message. But we treat these messages as "discriminatory practices" and outlaw them under federal and state civil rights legislation because they are more than speech. In the context of social inequality, these verbal and symbolic acts form integral links in historically ingrained systems of social discrimination. They work to keep traditionally victimized groups in socially isolated, stigmatized and disadvantaged positions through the promotion of fear, intolerance, degradation and violence. The Equal Protection Clause of the Fourteenth Amendment requires the disestablishment of these practices and systems. Likewise, the First Amendment does *not* prohibit our accomplishment of this compelling constitutional interest simply because those discriminatory practices are achieved through the use of words and symbols.

The primary intent of the cross burner in *R.A.V.* was not to enter into a dialogue with the Joneses, or even with the larger community, as it arguably was in *Brandenburg v. Ohio*. His purpose was to intimidate—to cast fear in the hearts of his victims, to drive them out of the community, to enforce the practice of residential segregation, and to encourage others to join him in the enforcement of that practice. The discriminatory impact of this speech is of even more importance than the speaker's intent. In protecting victims of discrimination, it is the presence of this discriminatory impact, which is a compelling government interest unrelated to the suppression of the speaker's political message, that requires a balancing of interests rather than a presumption against constitutionality. This is especially true when the interests that compete with speech are also interests of constitutional dimension.

One such interest is in enforcing the antidiscrimination principle. Those opposed to the regulation of hate speech often view the interest involved as the maintenance of civility, the protection of sensibilities from offense, or the prohibition of group defamation. But this analysis misconstrues the nature of the injury. "Defamation—injury to group reputation—is not the same as discrimination—injury to group status and treatment." The former "is more ideational and less material" than the latter, "which recognizes the harm of second-class citizenship and inferior social standing with the attendant deprivation of access to resources, voice, and power."

The Title VII paradigm of "hostile environment" discrimination best describes the injury to which victims of racist, sexist and homophobic hate speech are subjected. When plaintiffs in employment discrimination suits have been subjected to racist or sexist verbal harassment in the workplace, courts have recognized that such assaultive speech denies the targeted individual equal access to employment. These verbal assaults most often occur in settings where the relatively recent and token integration of the workplace makes the victim particularly vulnerable and where the privately voiced message of denigration and exclusion echoes the whites-only and males-only practices that were all-too-recently official policy.

Robinson v. Jacksonville Shipyards, Inc., a Title VII case that appears to be headed for review in the Supreme Court, presents a clear example of the tension between the law's commitment to free speech and its commitment to equality. Lois Robinson, a welder, was one of a very small number of female skilled craftworkers employed by Jacksonville Shipyards. She brought suit under Title VII of the Civil Rights Act of 1964, alleging that her employer had created and encouraged a sexually hostile, intimidating work environment. A U.S. District Court ruled in her favor, finding that the presence in the workplace of pictures of women in various stages of undress and in sexually suggestive or submissive poses, as well as remarks made by male employees and supervisors which demeaned women, constituted a violation of Title VII "through the maintenance of a sexually hostile work environment." Much of District Court Judge Howell Melton's opinion is a recounting of the indignities that Ms. Robinson and five other women experienced almost daily while working with 850 men over the course of ten years. In addition to the omnipresent display of sexually explicit drawings, graffiti, calendars, centerfold-style pictures, magazines and cartoons, the trial record contains a number of incidents in which sexually suggestive pictures and comments were directed at Robinson. Male employees admitted that the shipyard was "a boys' club" and "more or less a man's world."

The local chapter of the American Civil Liberties Union (ACLU) appealed the District Court's decision, arguing that "even sexists have a right to free speech." However, anyone who has read the trial record cannot help but wonder about these civil libertarians' lack of concern for Lois Robinson's right to do her work without being subjected to assault.

The trial record makes clear that Lois Robinson's male colleagues had little concern for advancing the cause of erotic speech when they made her the target of pornographic comments and graffiti. They wanted to put the usurper of their previously all-male domain in her place, to remind her of her sexual vulnerability and to send her back home where she belonged. This speech, like the burning cross in *R.A.V.*, does more than communicate an idea. It interferes with the victim's right to work at a job where she is free from degradation because of her gender.

But it is not sufficient to describe the injury occasioned by hate speech only in terms of the countervailing value of equality. There is also an injury to the First Amendment. When Russ Jones looked out his window and saw that burning cross, he heard a message that said, *"Shut up, black man, or risk harm to you and your family."* It may be that Russ Jones is especially brave, or especially foolhardy, and that he may speak even more loudly in the face of this threat. But it is more likely that he will be silenced, and that *we* will lose the benefit of his voice.

Professor Laurence H. Tribe has identified two values protected by the First Amendment. The first is the intrinsic value of speech, which is the value of individual self expression. Speech is intrinsically valuable as a manifestation of our humanity and our individuality. The second is the instrumental value of speech. The First Amendment protects dissent to maximize public discourse, and to achieve the great flowering of debate and ideas that we need to make our democracy work. Both of these values are implicated in the silencing of Russ Jones by his nocturnal attacker.

For African-Americans, the intrinsic value of speech as self-expression and self-definition has been particularly important. The absence of a "black voice" was central to the ideology of European-American racism, an ideology that denied Africans their humanity and thereby justified their enslavement. African-American slaves were prevented from learning to read and write, and they were prohibited from engaging in forms of self-expression that might instill in them a sense of self-worth and pride. Their silence and submission was then interpreted as evidence of their subhuman status. The use of the burning cross as a method of disempowerment originates, in part, in the perpetrators' understanding of how, in the context of their ideology, their victims are rendered subhuman when they are silenced. When, in the face of threat and intimidation, the oppressors' victims are afraid to give full expression to their individuality, the oppressors achieve their purpose of denying the victims the liberty guaranteed to them by the Constitution.

When the Joneses moved to Earl Street in St. Paul, they were expressing their individuality. When they chose their house and their neighbors, they were saying, "This is who we are. We are a proud black family and we want to live here." This self-expression and self-definition is the intrinsic value of speech.

The instrumental value of speech is likewise threatened by this terrorist attack on the Joneses. Russ and Laura Jones also brought new voices to the political discourse in this St. Paul community. Ideally, they will vote and talk politics with their neighbors. They will bring new experiences and new perspectives to their neighborhood. A burning cross not only silences people like the Joneses, it impoverishes the democratic process and renders our collective conversation less informed.

First Amendment doctrine and theory have no words for the injuries of silence imposed by private actors. There is no language for the damage that is done to the First Amendment when the hateful speech of the crossburner or the sexual harasser silences its victims. In antidiscrimination law, we recognize the necessity of regulating private behavior that threatens the values of equal citizenship. Fair housing laws, public accommodations provisions and employment discrimination laws all regulate the behavior of private actors. We recognize that much of the discrimination in our society occurs without the active participation of the state. We know that we could not hope to realize the constitutional ideal of equal citizenship if we pretended that the government was the only discriminator.

But there is no recognition in First Amendment law of the systematic private suppression of speech. Courts and scholars have worried about the heckler's veto, and, where there is limited access to speech fora, we have given attention to questions of equal time and the right to reply. But for the most part, we act as if the government is the only regulator of speech, the only censor. We treat the marketplace of ideas as if all voices are equal, as if there are no silencing voices or voices that are silenced. In the discourse of the First Amendment, there is no way to talk about how those who are silenced are always less powerful than those who do the silencing. First Amendment law ignores the ways in which patriarchy silences women, and racism silences people of color. When a woman's husband threatens to beat her the next time she contradicts him, a First Amendment injury has occurred. "Gay-bashing" keeps gays and lesbians "in the closet." It silences them. They are denied the humanizing experience of self-expression. We *all* are denied the insight and beauty of their voices.

Professor Mari Matsuda has spoken compellingly of this problem in a telling personal story about the publication of her own thoughtful and controversial *Michigan Law Review* article on hate speech, "Public Response to Racist Speech: Considering the Victim's Story." When she began working on the article, a mentor at Harvard Law School warned her not to use this topic for her tenure piece. "It's a lightning rod," he told her. She followed his advice, publishing the article years later, only after receiving her university tenure and when visiting offers from prestigious schools were in hand.

"What is the sound of a paper unpublished?" writes Professor Matsuda. "What don't we hear when some young scholar chooses tenure over controversial speech? Every fall, students return from summer jobs and tell me of the times they didn't speak out against racist or anti-Semitic comments, in protest over unfairness or ethical dilemmas. They tell of the times they were invited to discriminatory clubs and went along in silence. What is the sound of all those silenced because they need a job? These silences, these things that go unsaid, aren't seen as First Amendment issues. The absences are characterized as private and voluntary, beyond collective cure."

In the rush to protect the "speech" of crossburners, would-be champions of the First Amendment must not forget the voices of their victims. If First Amendment doctrine and theory is to truly serve First Amendment ideals, it must recognize the injury done by the private suppression of speech; it must take into account the historical reality that some members of our community are less powerful than others and that those persons continue to be systematically silenced by those who are more powerful. If we are truly committed to free speech, First Amendment doctrine and theory must be guided by the principle of antisubordination. There can be no free speech where there are still masters and slaves.

Notes

1. Emmett Till, a 14-year-old boy from Chicago, was killed while visiting relatives in Mississippi in 1955. His alleged "wolf whistle" at a white woman provoked his murderer. CONRAD LYNN, THERE IS A FOUNTAIN: THE AUTOBIOGRAPHY OF A CIVIL RIGHTS LAWYER 155 (1979); *see also* STEPHEN J. WHITFIELD, A DEATH IN THE DELTA: THE STORY OF EMMETT TILL (1988) (recounting story of black teenager murdered for allegedly whistling at white woman).

2. Dred Scott v. Sanford, 60 U.S. (19 How.) 393 (1856).

3. Plessy v. Ferguson, 163 U.S. 537 (1896).

4. Justice Taney, in holding that African Americans were not included and were not intended to be included under the word "citizen" in the Constitution, and could therefore claim none of the rights and privileges which that instrument provides for and secures opined, "[the colored race] had for more than a century before been regarded as being of an inferior order, and altogether unfit to associate with the white race, either in social or political relations; and so far inferior, that they had no rights which the white man was bound to respect." *Dred Scott,* 60 U.S. at 407.

5. In rejecting plaintiff's argument in *Plessy v. Ferguson* that enforced separation of the races constituted a badge of inferiority Judge Brown stated, "[i]f this be so, it is not by reason of anything found in the act, but solely because the colored race chooses to put that construction upon it." *Plessy,* 163 U.S. at 551....

NO ↵

Jonathan Rauch

In Defense of Prejudice: Why Incendiary Speech Must Be Protected

The war on prejudice is now, in all likelihood, the most uncontroversial social movement in America. Opposition to "hate speech," formerly identified with the liberal left, has become a bipartisan piety. In the past year, groups and factions that agree on nothing else have agreed that the public expression of any and all prejudices must be forbidden. On the left, protesters and editorialists have insisted that Francis L. Lawrence resign as president of Rutgers University for describing blacks as "a disadvantaged population that doesn't have that genetic, hereditary background to have a higher average." On the other side of the ideological divide, Ralph Reed, the executive director of the Christian Coalition, responded to criticism of the religious right by calling a press conference to denounce a supposed outbreak of "name-calling, scapegoating, and religious bigotry." Craig Rogers, an evangelical Christian student at California State University, recently filed a $2.5 million sexual-harassment suit against a lesbian professor of psychology, claiming that anti-male bias in one of her lectures violated campus rules and left him feeling "raped and trapped."

In universities and on Capitol Hill, in workplaces and newsrooms, authorities are declaring that there is no place for racism, sexism, homophobia, Christian-bashing, and other forms of prejudice in public debate or even in private thought. "Only when racism and other forms of prejudice are expunged," say the crusaders for sweetness and light, "can minorities be safe and society be fair." So sweet, this dream of a world without prejudice. But the very last thing society should do is seek to utterly eradicate racism and other forms of prejudice....

Indeed, "eradicating prejudice" is so vague a proposition as to be meaningless. Distinguishing prejudice reliably and nonpolitically from non-prejudice, or even defining it crisply, is quite hopeless. We all feel we know prejudice when we see it. But do we? At the University of Michigan, a student said in a classroom discussion that he considered homosexuality a disease treatable with therapy. He was summoned to a formal disciplinary hearing for violating the school's policy against speech that "victimizes" people based on

From Jonathan Rauch, "In Defense of Prejudice: Why Incendiary Speech Must Be Protected," *Harper's Magazine* (May 1995). Copyright © 1995 by *Harper's Magazine*. Reprinted by permission. All rights reserved.

"sexual orientation." Now, the evidence is abundant that this particular hypothesis is wrong, and any American homosexual can attest to the harm that the student's hypothesis has inflicted on many real people. But was it a statement of prejudice or of misguided belief? Hate speech or hypothesis? Many Americans who do not regard themselves as bigots or haters believe that homosexuality is a treatable disease. They may be wrong, but are they all bigots? I am unwilling to say so, and if you are willing, beware. The line between a prejudiced belief and a merely controversial one is elusive, and the harder you look the more elusive it becomes. "God hates homosexuals" is a statement of fact, not of bias, to those who believe it; "American criminals are disproportionately black" is a statement of bias, not of fact, to those who disbelieve it. . . .

Pluralism is the principle that protects and makes a place in human company for that loneliest and most vulnerable of all minorities, the minority who is hounded and despised among blacks and whites, gays and straights, who is suspect or criminal among every tribe and in every nation of the world, and yet on whom progress depends: the dissident. I am not saying that dissent is always or even usually enlightened. Most of the time it is foolish and self-serving. No dissident has the right to be taken seriously, and the fact that Aryan Nation racists or Nation of Islam anti-Semites are unorthodox does not entitle them to respect. But what goes around comes around. As a supporter of gay marriage, for example, I reject the majority's view of family, and as a Jew I reject its view of God. I try to be civil, but the fact is that most Americans regard my views on marriage as a reckless assault on the most fundamental of all institutions, and many people are more than a little discomfited by the statement "Jesus Christ was no more divine than anybody else" (which is why so few people ever say it). Trap the racists and anti-Semites, and you lay a trap for me too. Hunt for them with eradication in your mind, and you have brought dissent itself within your sights.

The new crusade against prejudice waves aside such warnings. Like earlier crusades against antisocial ideas, the mission is fueled by good (if cocksure) intentions and a genuine sense of urgency. Some kinds of error are held to be intolerable, like pollutants that even in small traces poison the water for a whole town. Some errors are so pernicious as to damage real people's lives, so wrongheaded that no person of right mind or goodwill could support them. Like their forebears of other stripe—the Church in its campaigns against heretics, the McCarthyites in their campaigns against Communists—the modern anti-racist and anti-sexist and anti-homophobic campaigners are totalists, demanding not that misguided ideas and ugly expressions be corrected or criticized but that they be eradicated. They make war not on errors but on error, and like other totalists they act in the name of public safety—the safety, especially, of minorities.

⚬❦⚬

The sweeping implications of this challenge to pluralism are not, I think, well enough understood by the public at large. Indeed, the new brand of totalism has yet even to be properly named. "Multiculturalism," for instance, is much too broad. "Political correctness" comes closer but is too trendy and snide. For lack of anything else, I will call the new anti-pluralism "purism," since its major tenet is that society cannot be just until the last traces of invidious prejudice have been scrubbed away. Whatever you call it, the purists' way of seeing things has spread through American intellectual life with remarkable speed, so much so that many people will blink at you uncomprehendingly or even call you a racist (or sexist or homophobe, etc.) if you suggest that expressions of racism should be tolerated or that prejudice has its part to play....

❧

What is especially dismaying is that the purists pursue prejudice in the name of protecting minorities. In order to protect people like me (homosexual), they must pursue people like me (dissident). In order to bolster minority self-esteem, they suppress minority opinion. There are, of course, all kinds of practical and legal problems with the purists' campaign: the incursions against the First Amendment; the inevitable abuses by prosecutors and activists who define as "hateful" or "violent" whatever speech they dislike or can score points off of; the lack of any evidence that repressing prejudice eliminates rather than inflames it. But minorities, of all people, ought to remember that by definition we cannot prevail by numbers, and we generally cannot prevail by force. Against the power of ignorant mass opinion and group prejudice and superstition, we have only our voices. If you doubt that minorities' voices are powerful weapons, think of the lengths to which Southern officials went to silence the Reverend Martin Luther King Jr. (recall that the city commissioner of Montgomery, Alabama, won a $500,000 libel suit, later overturned in *New York Times v. Sullivan* [1964], regarding an advertisement in the *Times* placed by civil-rights leaders who denounced the Montgomery police). Think of how much gay people have improved their lot over twenty-five years simply by refusing to remain silent. Recall the Michigan student who was prosecuted for saying that homosexuality is a treatable disease, and notice that he was black. Under that Michigan speech code, more than twenty blacks were charged with racist speech, while no instance of racist speech by whites was punished. In Florida, the hate-speech law was invoked against a black man who called a policeman a "white cracker"; not so surprisingly, in the first hate-crimes case to reach the Supreme Court, the victim was white and the defendant black.

In the escalating war against "prejudice," the right is already learning to play by the rules that were pioneered by the purist activists of the left. Last year leading Democrats, including the President, criticized the Republican Party for being increasingly in the thrall of the Christian right. Some of the rhetoric was harsh ("fire-breathing Christian radical right"), but it wasn't vicious or even clearly wrong. Never mind: when Democratic Representative Vic Fazio said Republicans were "being forced to the fringes by the aggressive political tactics of the religious right," the chairman of the Republican National Committee, Haley Barbour, said, "Christian-bashing" was the "left's preferred form of religious bigotry." Bigotry! Prejudice! "Christians active in politics are now on the receiving end of an extraordinary campaign of bias and prejudice," said the conservative leader William J. Bennett. One discerns, here, where the new purism leads. Eventually, any criticism of any group will be "prejudice."

Here is the ultimate irony of the new purism: words, which pluralists hope can be substituted for violence, are redefined by purists *as* violence. "The experience of being called 'nigger,' 'spic,' 'Jap,' or 'kike' is like receiving a slap in the face," Charles Lawrence wrote in 1990. "Psychic injury is no less an injury than being struck in the face, and it often is far more severe." This kind of talk is commonplace today. Epithets, insults, often even polite expressions of what's taken to be prejudice are called by purists "assaultive speech," "words that wound," "verbal violence." "To me, racial epithets are not speech," one University of Michigan law professor said. "They are bullets." In her speech accepting the 1993 Nobel Prize for Literature in Stockholm, Sweden, the author Toni Morrison said this: "Oppressive language does more than represent violence; it is violence."

It is not violence. I am thinking back to a moment on the subway in Washington, a little thing. I was riding home late one night and a squad of noisy kids, maybe seventeen or eighteen years old, noisily piled into the car. They yelled across the car and a girl said, "Where do we get off?"

A boy said, "Farragut North."

The girl: "*Faggot* North!"

The boy: "Yeah! Faggot North!"

General hilarity.

First, before the intellect resumes control, there is a moment of fear, an animal moment. Who are they? How many of them? How dangerous? Where is the way out? All of these things are noted preverbally and assessed by the gut. Then the brain begins an assessment: they are sober, this is probably too public a place for them to do it, there are more girls than boys, they were just talking, it is probably nothing.

They didn't notice me and there was no incident. The teenage babble flowed on, leaving me to think. I became interested in my own reaction: the jump of fear out of nowhere like an alert animal, the sense for a brief time that one is naked and alone and should hide or run away. For a time, one ceases to be a human being and becomes instead a faggot.

⚜

The fear engendered by these words is real. The remedy is as clear and as imperfect as ever: protect citizens against violence. This, I grant, is something that American society has never done very well and now does quite poorly. It is no solution to define words as violence or prejudice as oppression, and then by cracking down on words or thoughts pretend that we are doing something about violence and oppression. No doubt it is easier to pass a speech code or hate-crimes law and proclaim the streets safer than actually to make the streets safer, but the one must never be confused with the other. Every cop or prosecutor chasing words is one fewer chasing criminals. In a world rife with real violence and oppression, full of Rwandas and Bosnias and eleven-year-olds spraying bullets at children in Chicago and in turn being executed by gang lords, it is odious of Toni Morrison to say that words are violence.

Indeed, equating "verbal violence" with physical violence is a treacherous, mischievous business. Not long ago a writer was charged with viciously and gratuitously wounding the feelings and dignity of millions of people. He was charged, in effect, with exhibiting flagrant prejudice against Muslims and outrageously slandering their beliefs. "What is freedom of expression?" mused Salman Rushdie a year after the ayatollahs sentenced him to death and put a price on his head. "Without the freedom to offend, it ceases to exist." I can think of nothing sadder than that minority activists, in their haste to make the world better, should be the ones to forget the lesson of Rushdie's plight: for minorities, pluralism, not purism, is the answer. The campaigns to eradicate prejudice—all of them, the speech codes and workplace restrictions and mandatory therapy for accused bigots and all the rest—should stop, now. The whole objective of eradicating prejudice, as opposed to correcting and criticizing it, should be repudiated as a fool's errand. Salman Rushdie is right, Toni Morrison wrong, and minorities belong at his side, not hers.

POSTSCRIPT

Should Hate Speech Be Punished?

Many forms of hate speech are punished in countries other than the United States, but other democracies do not have the American tradition of freedom of opinion and expression. At the same time, the United States has more races, religions, and nationalities than other countries, giving rise to suspicion, prejudice, and hostility.

On one hand, this diversity has given rise to sharp political disagreement on issues relating to race, religion, women, homosexuals, and others. On the other hand, this diversity has stimulated greater sensitivity to the claims of these groups for equal treatment and social justice. Free speech on controversial issues risks giving offense. At what point, if any, does giving offense curtail the liberty of the offended group? Should such speech be punished?

Nowhere have these questions provoked greater controversy than on college campuses. Do college codes inhibiting or punishing racist, sexist, or other biased speech protect the liberty of the victims of these insults or injuries? Or do they prevent the examination of disapproved beliefs and threaten the suppression of other unpopular ideas?

Steven H. Shiffrin, in *Dissent, Injustice, and the Meanings of America* (Princeton University Press, 1999), argues that Americans should not just tolerate controversial speech, they should encourage it. Timothy C. Shiell, in *Campus Hate Speech on Trial* (University Press of Kansas, 1998), provides background for some of the recent court cases involving hate speech. Edward J. Cleary's *Beyond the Burning Cross: The First Amendment and the Landmark R. A. V. Case* (Random House, 1994) is an account of the attorney who represented the accused youth in *R. A. V. v. St. Paul.* Robert J. Kelly, ed., *Bias Crime: American Law Enforcement and Legal Responses,* rev. ed. (Office of International Criminal Justice, 1993) includes essays on a variety of issues, including religious and gay bias, bias on college campuses, and the Rodney King case, in which four white Los Angeles police officers were filmed beating a black suspect.

Arguing for absolute freedom of expression is Nat Hentoff, *Free Speech for Me—But Not for Thee: How the American Left and Right Relentlessly Censor Each Other* (HarperCollins, 1992). Less absolutist in defending all speech is Cass R. Sunstein, in *Democracy and the Problem of Free Speech* (Free Press, 1993), who attempts to define a distinction between protected and unprotected speech. A case for suppressing speech based on what the authors call "critical race theory" can be found in the essays in Mari J. Matsuda et al., *Words That Wound: Critical Race Theory, Assaultive Speech, and the First Amendment* (Westview Press, 1993).

A somewhat similar argument is developed by Richard Delgado and Jean Stefancic in *Must We Defend Nazis? Hate Speech, Pornography, and the First Amendment* (New York University Press, 1996). The authors insist that free speech must always be weighed against the sometimes-competing values of human dignity and equality. Judith Butler, in *Excitable Speech: A Politics of the Performance* (Routledge, 1997), examines the linguistics of hate and reflects on the implications of speech as a form of conduct. Milton Heumann et al., eds., *Hate Speech on Campus: Cases, Case Studies, and Commentary* (Northeastern University Press, 1997) reprints some classic Supreme Court opinions on free speech as well as excerpts from essays by John Stuart Mill, Herbert Marcuse, and others who have struggled with the question of whether or not freedom should be allowed for "words that wound." Finally, in *Destructive Messages: How Hate Speech Paves the Way for Harmful Social Movements* (New York University Press, 2002), Alexander Tsesis argues that hate speech should not be measured only by its immediate threat but also for its long-term effects—making hatred of minorities an acceptable part of civic debate.

ISSUE 12

Should Abortion Be Restricted?

YES: Robert P. George, from *The Clash of Orthodoxies: Law, Religion, and Morality in Crisis* (ISI Books, 2001)

NO: Mary Gordon, from "A Moral Choice," *The Atlantic Monthly* (March 1990)

ISSUE SUMMARY

YES: Legal philosopher Robert P. George asserts that, since each of us was a human being from conception, abortion is a form of homicide and should be banned.

NO: Writer Mary Gordon maintains that having an abortion is a moral choice that women are capable of making for themselves, that aborting a fetus is not killing a person, and that antiabortionists fail to understand female sexuality.

Until 1973 the laws governing abortion were set by the states, most of which barred legal abortion except where pregnancy imperiled the life of the pregnant woman. In that year, the U.S. Supreme Court decided the controversial case *Roe v. Wade.* The *Roe* decision acknowledged both a woman's "fundamental right" to terminate a pregnancy before fetal viability and the state's legitimate interest in protecting both the woman's health and the "potential life" of the fetus. It prohibited states from banning abortion to protect the fetus before the third trimester of a pregnancy, and it ruled that even during that final trimester, a woman could obtain an abortion if she could prove that her life or health would be endangered by carrying to term. (In a companion case to *Roe*, decided on the same day, the Court defined *health* broadly enough to include "all factors—physical, emotional, psychological, familial, and the woman's age —relevant to the well-being of the patient.") These holdings, together with the requirement that state regulation of abortion had to survive "strict scrutiny" and demonstrate a "compelling state interest," resulted in later decisions striking down mandatory 24-hour waiting periods, requirements that abortions be performed in hospitals, and so-called informed consent laws.

The Supreme Court did uphold state laws requiring parental notification and consent for minors (though it provided that minors could seek permission from a judge if they feared notifying their parents). And federal courts have affirmed the right of Congress not to pay for abortions. Proabortion groups, proclaiming the "right to choose," have charged that this and similar action at the state level discriminates against poor women because it does not inhibit the ability of women who are able to pay for abortions to obtain them. Efforts to adopt a constitutional amendment or federal law barring abortion have failed, but antiabortion forces have influenced legislation in many states.

Can legislatures and courts establish the existence of a scientific fact? Opponents of abortion believe that it is a fact that life begins at conception and that the law must therefore uphold and enforce this concept. They argue that the human fetus is a live human being, and they note all the familiar signs of life displayed by the fetus: a beating heart, brain waves, thumb sucking, and so on. Those who defend abortion maintain that human life does not begin before the development of specifically human characteristics and possibly not until the birth of a child. As Justice Harry A. Blackmun put it in 1973, "There has always been strong support for the view that life does not begin until live birth."

Antiabortion forces sought a court case that might lead to the overturning of *Roe v. Wade*. Proabortion forces rallied to oppose new state laws limiting or prohibiting abortion. In *Webster v. Reproductive Health Services* (1989), with four new justices, the Supreme Court pulled back from its proabortion stance. In a 5–4 decision, the Court upheld a Missouri law that banned abortions in public hospitals and abortions that were performed by public employees (except to save a woman's life). The law also required that tests be performed on any fetus more than 20 weeks old to determine its viability—that is, its ability to survive outside the womb.

In the later decision of *Planned Parenthood v. Casey* (1992), however, the Court affirmed what it called the "essence" of the constitutional right to abortion while permitting some state restrictions, such as a 24-hour waiting period and parental notification in the case of minors.

During the Clinton presidency, opponents of abortion focused on what they identified as "partial-birth" abortions; that is, where a fetus is destroyed during the process of birth. President Clinton twice vetoed partial-birth bans that allowed such abortions to save a woman's life but not her health. By early 1998, 22 states adopted such bans, but in 11 of these states challenges to the law's constitutionality were upheld in federal or state courts. In 1998, in the first of these cases to reach the U.S. Supreme Court, the Court let stand without a written opinion (but with three dissenters) a federal court of appeals decision declaring Ohio's law unconstitutional. The Supreme Court did not confront the question of how it would decide a law that narrowly defined the procedure and provided a maternal health exception.

In the following selections, Robert P. George contends that, since each of us was a human being from conception, abortion is a form of homicide and should be banned. Mary Gordon asserts that the fetus removed in most abortions may not be considered a person and that women must retain the right to make decisions regarding their sexual lives.

Robert P. George

 **YES**

God's Reasons

In his contributions to the February 1996 issue of *First Things* magazine—contributions in which what he has to say (particularly in his critique of liberalism) is far more often right than wrong—Stanley Fish of Duke University cites the dispute over abortion as an example of a case in which "incompatible first assumptions [or] articles of opposing faiths"—make the resolution of the dispute (other than by sheer political power) impossible. Here is how Fish presented the pro-life and pro-choice positions and the shape of the dispute between their respective defenders:

> A pro-life advocate sees abortion as a sin against God who infuses life at the moment of conception; a pro-choice advocate sees abortion as a decision to be made in accordance with the best scientific opinion as to when the beginning of life, as we know it, occurs. No conversation between them can ever get started because each of them starts from a different place and they could never agree as to what they were conversing *about*. A pro-lifer starts from a belief in the direct agency of a personal God, and this belief, this religious conviction, is not incidental to his position; it is his position, and determines its features in all their detail. The "content of a belief" is a *function* of its source, and the critiques of one will always be the critique of the other.

It is certainly true that the overwhelming majority of pro-life Americans are religious believers and that a great many pro-choice Americans are either unbelievers or less observant or less traditional in their beliefs and practice than their fellow citizens. Indeed, although most Americans believe in God, polling data consistently show that Protestants, Catholics, and Jews who do not regularly attend church or synagogue are less likely than their more observant co-religionists to oppose abortion. And religion is plainly salient politically when it comes to the issue of abortion. The more secularized a community, the more likely that community is to elect pro-choice politicians to legislative and executive offices.

Still, I don't think that Fish's presentation of the pro-life and pro-choice positions, or of the shape of the dispute over abortion, is accurate. True, inasmuch as most pro-life advocates are traditional religious believers who, as such,

From Robert P. George, *The Clash of Orthodoxies: Law, Religion, and Morality in Crisis* (ISI Books, 2001). Copyright © 2001 by Robert P. George. Reprinted by permission of ISI Books, an imprint of The Intercollegiate Studies Institute. Notes omitted.

see gravely unjust or otherwise immoral acts as sins—and understand sins precisely as offenses against God—"a pro-life advocate sees abortion as a sin against God." But most pro-life advocates see abortion as a sin against God *precisely because it is the unjust taking of innocent human life.* That is their reason for opposing abortion; and that is God's reason, as they see it, for opposing abortion and requiring that human communities protect their unborn members against it. And, they believe, as I do, that this reason can be identified and acted on even independently of God's revealing it. Indeed, they typically believe, as I do, that the precise content of what God reveals on the subject ("in they mother's womb I formed thee") cannot be known without the application of human intelligence, by way of philosophical and scientific inquiry, to the question.

Fish is mistaken, then, in *contrasting* the pro-life advocate with the pro-choice advocate by depicting (only) the latter as viewing abortion as "a decision to be made in accordance with the best scientific opinion as to when the beginning of life ... occurs." First of all, supporters of the pro-choice position are increasingly willing to sanction the practice of abortion even where they concede that it constitutes the taking of innocent human life. Pro-choice writers from Naomi Wolfe to Judith Jarvis Thomson have advanced theories of abortion as "justifiable homicide." But, more to the point, people on the pro-life side *insist* that the central issue in the debate is the question "as to when the beginning of life occurs." And they insist with equal vigor that this question is not a "religious" or even "metaphysical" one: it is rather, as Fish says, "scientific." In response to this insistence, it is pro-choice advocates who typically want to transform the question into a "metaphysical" or "religious" one. It was Justice Harry Blackmun who claimed in his opinion for the Court legalizing abortion in *Roe v. Wade* (1973) that "at this point in man's knowledge" the scientific evidence was inconclusive and therefore could not determine the outcome of the case. And twenty years later, the influential pro-choice writer Ronald Dworkin went on record claiming that the question of abortion is inherently "religious." It is pro-choice advocates, such as Dworkin, who want to distinguish between when a human being comes into existence "in the biological sense and when a human being comes into existence "in the moral sense. It is they who want to distinguish a class of human beings "with rights" from pre- (or post-) conscious human beings who "don't have rights." And the reason for this, I submit, is that, short of defending abortion as "justifiable homicide," the pro-choice position collapses if the issue is to be settled purely on the basis of scientific inquiry into the question of when a new member of Homo sapiens comes into existence as a self-integrating organism whose unity, distinctiveness, and identity remain intact as it develops without substantial change from the point of its beginning through the various stages of its development and into adulthood.

All this was, I believe, made wonderfully clear at a debate at the 1997 meeting of the American Political Science Association between Jeffrey Reiman of American University, defending the pro-choice position, and John Finnis of Oxford and Notre Dame, defending the pro-life view. That debate was remarkable for the skill, intellectual honesty, and candor of the interlocutors. What is most relevant to our deliberations, however, is the fact that it truly was a debate Reiman and Finnis did not talk past each other. They did not proceed from "incompatible first assumptions." They *did* manage to agree as to what they were talking *about*—and it was not about whether or when life was infused by God. It was precisely about the *rational* (i.e., scientific and philosophical) grounds, if any, available for distinguishing a class of human beings "in the moral sense" (with rights) from a class of human beings "in the (merely) biological sense" (without rights). Finnis did not claim any special revelation to the effect that no such grounds existed. Nor did Reiman claim that Finnis's arguments against his view appealed implicitly (and illicitly) to some such putative revelation. Although Finnis is a Christian and, as such, believes that the new human life that begins at conception is in each and every case created by God in His image and likeness, his argument never invoked, much less did it "start from a belief in the direct agency of a personal God." It proceeded, rather, by way of point-by-point philosophical challenge to Reiman's philosophical arguments. Finnis marshaled the scientific facts of embryogenesis and intrauterine human development and defied Reiman to identify grounds, compatible with those facts, for denying a right to life to human beings in the embryonic and fetal stages of development.

Interestingly, Reiman began his remarks with a statement that would seem to support what Fish said in *First Things*. While allowing that debates over abortion were useful in clarifying people's thinking about the issue, Reiman remarked that they "never actually cause people to change their minds." It is true, I suppose, that people who are deeply committed emotionally to one side or the other are unlikely to have a road-to-Damascus type conversion after listening to a formal philosophical debate. Still, any open-minded person who sincerely wishes to settle his mind on the question of abortion—and there continue to be many such people, I believe—would find debates such as the one between Reiman and Finnis to be extremely helpful toward that end. Anyone willing to consider the *reasons* for and against abortion and its legal prohibition or permission would benefit from reading or hearing the accounts of these reasons proposed by capable and honest thinkers on both sides. Of course, when it comes to an issue like abortion, people can have powerful motives for clinging to a particular position even if they are presented with conclusive reasons for changing their minds. But that doesn't mean that such reasons do not exist.

I believe that the pro-life position is superior to the pro-choice position precisely because the scientific evidence, considered honestly and dispassionately, fully supports it. A human being is conceived when a human sperm containing twenty-three chromosomes fuses with a human egg also containing twenty-three chromosomes (albeit of a different kind) producing a single-cell human zygote containing, in the normal case, forty-six chromosomes that are mixed differently from the forty-six chromosomes as found in the mother or father. Unlike the gametes (that is, the sperm and egg), the zygote is genetically unique and distinct from its parents. Biologically, it is a separate organism. It produces, as the gametes do not, specifically human enzymes and proteins. It possesses, as they do not, the active capacity or potency to develop itself into a human embryo, fetus, infant, child, adolescent, and adult.

Assuming that it is not conceived *in vitro*, the zygote is, of course, in a state of dependence on its mother. But independence should not be confused with distinctness. From the beginning, the newly conceived human being, not its mother, directs its integral organic functioning. It takes in nourishment and converts it to energy. Given a hospitable environment, it will, as Dianne Nutwell Irving says, "develop continuously without any biological interruptions, or gaps, throughout the embryonic, fetal, neo-natal, childhood and adulthood stages—until the death of the organism."

≈◈≈

Some claim to find the logical implication of these facts—that is, that life begins at conception—to be "virtually unintelligible." A leading exponent of that point of view in the legal academy is Jed Rubenfeld of Yale Law School, author of an influential article entitled "On the Legal Status of the Proposition that 'Life Begins at Conception.'" Rubenfeld argues that, like the zygote, *every* cell in the human body is "genetically complete"; yet nobody supposes that every human cell is a distinct human being with a right to life. However, Rubenfeld misses the point that there comes into being at conception, not a mere clump of human cells, but a distinct, unified, self-integrating organism, which develops itself, truly himself or herself, in accord with its own genetic "blueprint." The significance of genetic completeness for the status of newly conceived human beings is that no outside genetic material is required to enable the zygote to mature into an embryo, the embryo into a fetus, the fetus into an infant, the infant into a child, the child into an adolescent, the adolescent into an adult. What the zygote needs to function as a distinct self-integrating human organism, a human being, it already possesses.

At no point in embryogenesis, therefore, does the distinct organism that came into being when it conceived undergo what is technically called "substantial change" (or a change of natures). It is human and will remain human. This is the point of Justice Byron White's remark in his dissenting opinion in *Thornburgh v. American College of Obstetricians & Gynecologists* that "there is no non-arbitrary line separating a fetus from a child." Rubenfeld attacks White's point, which he calls "[t]he argument based on the gradualness of gestation," by pointing out that, "[n]o non-arbitrary line separates the hues of green and red. Shall we conclude that green is red?"

White's point, however, was *not* that fetal development is "gradual," but that it is *continuous* and is the (continuous) development of a single lasting (fully human) being. The human zygote that actively develops itself is, as I have pointed out, a genetically complete organism directing its own integral organic functioning. As it matures, *in utero* and *ex utero,* it does not "become" a human being, for it is a human being *already,* albeit an immature human being, just as a newborn infant is an immature human being who will undergo quite dramatic growth and development over time.

These considerations undermine the familiar argument, recited by Rubenfeld, that "the potential" of an *unfertilized* ovum to develop into a whole human being does not make it into "a person." The fact is, though, that an ovum is not a whole human being. It is, rather, a part of another human being (the woman whose ovum it is) with merely the potential to give rise to, in interaction with a part of yet another human being (a man's sperm cell), a new and whole human being. Unlike the zygote, it lacks both genetic distinctness and completeness, as well as the active capacity to develop itself into an adult member of the human species. It is living human cellular material, but, left to itself, it will never become a human being, however hospitable its environment may be. It will "die" as a human ovum, just as countless skin cells "die" daily as nothing more than skin cells. If successfully fertilized by a human sperm, which, like the ovum (but dramatically unlike the zygote), lacks the active potential to develop into an adult member of the human species, then *substantial* change (that is, a change of *natures*) will occur. There will no longer be merely an egg, which was part of the mother, sharing her genetic composition, and a sperm, which was part of the father, sharing his genetic composition; instead, there will be a genetically complete, distinct, unified, self-integrating human organism, whose nature differs from that of the gametes—not mere human material, but a human being.

These considerations also make clear that it is incorrect to argue (as some pro-choice advocates have argued) that, just as "I" was never a week-old sperm or ovum, "I" was likewise never a week-old embryo. It truly makes no sense to say that "I" was once a sperm (or an unfertilized egg) that matured into an adult. Conception was the occasion of substantial change (that is, change from one complete individual entity to another) that brought into being a distinct self-integrating organism with a specifically human nature. By contrast, it makes every bit as much sense to say that I was once a week-old embryo as to say that I was once a week-old infant or a ten-year-old child. It was the new organism created at conception that, without itself undergoing any change of substance, matured into a week-old embryo, a fetus, an infant, a child, an adolescent, and, finally, an adult.

But Rubenfeld has another argument: "Cloning processes give to non-zygotic cells the potential for development into distinct, self-integrating human beings; thus to recognize the zygote as a human being is to recognize all human cells as human beings, which is absurd."

It is true that a distinct, self-integrating human organism that came into being by a process of cloning would be, like a human organism that comes into being as a monozygotic twin, a human being. That being, no less than human beings conceived by the union of sperm and egg, would possess a human nature and the active potential to mature as a human being. However, even assuming the possibility of cloning human beings from non-zygotic human cells, the non-zygotic cell must be activated by a process that effects substantial change and not mere development or maturation. Left to itself, apart from an activation process capable of effecting a change of substance or natures, the cell will mature and die as a human cell, not as a human being.

⋗⦿⋖

The scientific evidence establishes the fact that each of us was, from conception, a human being. Science, not religion, vindicates this crucial premise of the pro-life claim. From it, there is no avoiding the conclusion that deliberate feticide is a form of homicide. The only real questions remaining are moral and political, not scientific: Although I will not go into the matter here, I do not see how direct abortion can even be considered a matter of "justified homicide." It is important to recognize, however, as traditional moralists always have recognized, that not all procedures that foreseeably result in fetal death are, properly speaking, abortions. Although any procedure whose precise objective is the destruction of fetal life is certainly an abortion, and cannot be justified, some procedures result in fetal death as an unintended, albeit foreseen and accepted, side effect. Where procedures of the latter sort are done for very grave reasons, they may be justifiable. For example, traditional morality recognizes that a surgical operation to remove a life-threateningly cancerous uterus, even in a woman whose pregnancy is not far enough along to enable the child to be removed from her womb and sustained by a life support system, is ordinarily morally permissible. Of course, there are in this area of moral reflection, as in others, "borderline" cases that are difficult to classify and evaluate. Mercifully, modern medical technology has made such cases exceptionally rare in real life. Only in the most extraordinary circumstances today do women and their families and physicians find it necessary to consider a procedure that will result in fetal death as the only way of preserving maternal life. In any event, the political debate about abortion is not, in reality, about cases of this sort; it is about "elective" or "social indication" abortions, viz., the deliberate destruction of unborn human life for non-therapeutic reasons.

A final point: In my own experience, conversion from the pro-choice to the pro-life cause is often (though certainly not always) a partial cause of religious conversion rather than an effect. Frequently, people who are not religious, or who are only weakly so, begin to have doubts about the moral defensibility of deliberate feticide. Although most of their friends are pro-choice, they find that position increasingly difficult to defend or live with. They perceive practical inconsistencies in their, and their friends', attitudes toward the unborn depending on whether the child is "wanted" or not. Perhaps they find themselves arrested by sonographic (or other even more sophisticated) images of the child's life in the womb. So the doubts begin creeping in. For the first time, they are really prepared to listen to the pro-life argument (often despite their negative attitude toward people—or "the kind of people"—who are pro-life); and somehow, it sounds more compelling than it did before. Gradually, as they become firmly pro-life, they find themselves questioning the whole philosophy of life—in a word, the secularism—associated with their former view. They begin to understand the reasons that led them out of the pro-choice and into the pro-life camp as God's reasons, too.

Mary Gordon

← **NO**

A Moral Choice

Iam having lunch with six women. What is unusual is that four of them are in their seventies, two of them widowed, the other two living with husbands beside whom they've lived for decades. All of them have had children. Had they been men, they would have published books and hung their paintings on the walls of important galleries. But they are women of a certain generation, and their lives were shaped around their families and personal relations. They are women you go to for help and support. We begin talking about the latest legislative act that makes abortion more difficult for poor women to obtain. An extraordinary thing happens. Each of them talks about the illegal abortions she had during her young womanhood. Not one of them was spared the experience. Any of them could have died on the table of whatever person (not a doctor in any case) she was forced to approach, in secrecy and in terror, to end a pregnancy that she felt would blight her life.

I mention this incident for two reasons: first as a reminder that all kinds of women have always had abortions; second because it is essential that we remember that an abortion is performed on a living woman who has a life in which a terminated pregnancy is only a small part. Morally speaking, the decision to have an abortion doesn't take place in a vacuum. It is connected to other choices that a woman makes in the course of an adult life.

Anti-choice propagandists paint pictures of women who choose to have abortions as types of moral callousness, selfishness, or irresponsibility. The woman choosing to abort is the dressed-for-success yuppie who gets rid of her baby so that she won't miss her Caribbean vacation or her chance for promotion. Or she is the feckless, promiscuous ghetto teenager who couldn't bring herself to just say no to sex. A third, purportedly kinder, gentler picture has recently begun to be drawn. The woman in the abortion clinic is there because she is misinformed about the nature of the world. She is having an abortion because society does not provide for mothers and their children, and she mistakenly thinks that another mouth to feed will be the ruin of her family, not understanding that the temporary truth of family unhappiness doesn't stack up beside the eternal verity that abortion is murder. Or she is the dupe of her husband or boyfriend, who talks her into having an abortion because a child will be a drag on his life-style. None of these pictures created by the anti-choice

From Mary Gordon, "A Moral Choice," *The Atlantic Monthly* (March 1990). Copyright © 1990 by Mary Gordon. Reprinted by permission of Sterling Lord Literistic, Inc.

movement assumes that the decision to have an abortion is made responsibly, in the context of a morally lived life, by a free and responsible moral agent.

The Ontology of the Fetus

How would a woman who habitually makes choices in moral terms come to the decision to have an abortion? The moral discussion of abortion centers on the issue of whether or not abortion is an act of murder. At first glance it would seem that the answer should follow directly upon two questions: Is the fetus human? and Is it alive? It would be absurd to deny that a fetus is alive or that it is human. What would our other options be—to say that it is inanimate or belongs to another species? But we habitually use the terms "human" and "live" to refer to parts of our body—"human hair," for example, or "live red-blood cells"—and we are clear in our understanding that the nature of these objects does not rank equally with an entire personal existence. It then seems important to consider whether the fetus, this alive human thing, is a *person*, to whom the term "murder" could sensibly be applied. How would anyone come to a decision about something so impalpable as personhood? Philosophers have struggled with the issue of personhood, but in language that is so abstract that it is unhelpful to ordinary people making decisions in the course of their lives. It might be more productive to begin thinking about the status of the fetus by examining the language and customs that surround it. This approach will encourage us to focus on the choosing, acting woman, rather than the act of abortion—as if the act were performed by abstract forces without bodies, histories, attachments.

This focus on the acting woman is useful because a pregnant woman has an identifiable, consistent ontology, and a fetus takes on different ontological identities over time. But common sense, experience, and linguistic usage point clearly to the fact that we habitually consider, for example, a seven-week-old fetus to be different from a seven-month-old one. We can tell this by the way we respond to the involuntary loss of one as against the other. We have different language for the experience of the involuntary expulsion of the fetus from the womb depending upon the point of gestation at which the experience occurs. If it occurs early in the pregnancy, we call it a miscarriage; if late, we call it a stillbirth.

We would have an extreme reaction to the reversal of those terms. If a woman referred to a miscarriage at seven weeks as a stillbirth, we would be alarmed. It would shock our sense of propriety; it would make us uneasy; we would find it disturbing, misplaced—as we do when a bag lady sits down in a restaurant and starts shouting, or an octogenarian arrives at our door in a sailor suit. In short, we would suspect that the speaker was mad. Similarly, if a doctor or a nurse referred to the loss of a seven-month-old fetus as a miscarriage, we would be shocked by that person's insensitivity: could she or he not understand that a fetus that age is not what it was months before?

Our ritual and religious practices underscore the fact that we make distinctions among fetuses. If a woman took the bloody matter—indistinguishable from a heavy period—of an early miscarriage and insisted upon putting it in a tiny coffin and marking its grave, we would have serious concerns about her mental health. By the same token, we would feel squeamish about flushing a seven-month-old fetus down the toilet—something we would quite normally do with an early miscarriage. There are no prayers for the matter of a miscarriage, nor do we feel there should be. Even a Catholic priest would not baptize the issue of an early miscarriage.

The difficulties stem, of course, from the odd situation of a fetus's ontology: a complicated, differentiated, and nuanced response is required when we are dealing with an entity that changes over time. Yet we are in the habit of making distinctions like this. At one point we know that a child is no longer a child but an adult. That this question is vexed and problematic is clear from our difficulty in determining who is a juvenile offender and who is an adult criminal and at what age sexual intercourse ceases to be known as statutory rape. So at what point, if any, do we on the pro-choice side say that the developing fetus is a person, with rights equal to its mother's?

The anti-choice people have one advantage over us; their monolithic position gives them unity on this question. For myself, I am made uneasy by third-trimester abortions, which take place when the fetus could live outside the mother's body, but I also know that these are extremely rare and often performed on very young girls who have had difficulty comprehending the realities of pregnancy. It seems to me that the question of late abortions should be decided case by case, and that fixation on this issue is a deflection from what is most important: keeping early abortions, which are in the majority by far, safe and legal. I am also politically realistic enough to suspect that bills restricting late abortions are not good-faith attempts to make distinctions about the nature of fetal life. They are, rather, the cynical embodiments of the hope among anti-choice partisans that technology will be on their side and that medical science's ability to create situations in which younger fetuses are viable outside their mothers' bodies will increase dramatically in the next few years. Ironically, medical science will probably make the issue of abortion a minor one in the near future. The RU-486 pill, which can induce abortion early on, exists, and whether or not it is legally available (it is not on the market here, because of pressure from anti-choice groups), women will begin to obtain it. If abortion can occur through chemical rather than physical means, in the privacy of one's home, most people not directly involved will lose interest in it. As abortion is transformed from a public into a private issue, it will cease to be perceived as political; it will be called personal instead.

An Equivocal Good

But because abortion will always deal with what it is to create and sustain life, it will always be a moral issue. And whether we like it or not, our moral thinking about abortion is rooted in the shifting soil of perception. In an age in which much of our perception is manipulated by media that specialize in the sound bite and the photo op, the anti-choice partisans have a twofold advantage over us on the pro-choice side. The pro-choice moral position is more complex, and the experience we defend is physically repellent to contemplate. None of us in the pro-choice movement would suggest that abortion is not a regrettable occurrence. Anti-choice proponents can offer pastel photographs of babies in buntings, their eyes peaceful in the camera's gaze. In answer, we can't offer the material of an early abortion, bloody, amorphous in a paper cup, to prove that what has just been removed from the woman's body is not a child, not in the same category of being as the adorable bundle in an adoptive mother's arms. It is not a pleasure to look at the physical evidence of abortion, and most of us don't get the opportunity to do so.

The theologian Daniel Maguire, uncomfortable with the fact that most theological arguments about the nature of abortion are made by men who have never been anywhere near an actual abortion, decided to visit a clinic and observe abortions being performed. He didn't find the experience easy, but he knew that before he could in good conscience make a moral judgment on abortion, he needed to experience through his senses what an aborted fetus is like: he needed to look at and touch the controversial entity. He held in his hand the bloody fetal stuff; the eight-week-old fetus fit in the palm of his hand, and it certainly bore no resemblance to either of his two children when he had held them moments after their birth. He knew at that point what women who have experienced early abortions and miscarriages know: that some event occurred, possibly even a dramatic one, but it was not the death of a child.

Because issues of pregnancy and birth are both physical and metaphorical, we must constantly step back and forth between ways of perceiving the world. When we speak of gestation, we are often talking in terms of potential, about events and objects to which we attach our hopes, fears, dreams, and ideals. A mother can speak to the fetus in her uterus and name it; she and her mate may decorate a nursery according to their vision of the good life; they may choose for an embryo a college, a profession, a dwelling. But those of us who are trying to think morally about pregnancy and birth must remember that these feelings are our own projections onto what is in reality an inappropriate object. However charmed we may be by an expectant father's buying a little football for something inside his wife's belly, we shouldn't make public policy based on such actions, nor should we force others to live their lives conforming to our fantasies.

As a society, we are making decisions that pit the complicated future of a complex adult against the fate of a mass of cells lacking cortical development. The moral pressure should be on distinguishing the true from the false, the real suffering of living persons from our individual and often idiosyncratic dreams and fears. We must make decisions on abortion based on an understanding of how people really do live. We must be able to say that poverty is worse than not being poor, that having dignified and meaningful work is better than working in conditions of degradation, that raising a child one loves and has desired is better than raising a child in resentment and rage, that it is better for a twelve-year-old not to endure the trauma of having a child when she is herself a child.

When we put these ideas against the ideas of "child" or "baby," we seem to be making a horrifying choice of life-style over life. But in fact we are telling the truth of what it means to bear a child, and what the experience of abortion really is. This is extremely difficult, for the object of the discussion is hidden, changing, potential. We make our decisions on the basis of approximate and inadequate language, often on the basis of fantasies and fears. It will always be crucial to try to separate genuine moral concern from phobia, punitiveness, superstition, anxiety, a desperate search for certainty in an uncertain world.

One of the certainties that is removed if we accept the consequences of the pro-choice position is the belief that the birth of a child is an unequivocal good. In real life we act knowing that the birth of a child is not always a good thing: people are sometimes depressed, angry, rejecting, at the birth of a child. But this is a difficult truth to tell; we don't like to say it, and one of the fears preyed on by anti-choice proponents is that if we cannot look at the birth of a child as an unequivocal good, then there is nothing to look toward. The desire for security of the imagination, for typological fixity, particularly in the area of "the good," is an understandable desire. It must seem to some anti-choice people that we on the pro-choice side are not only murdering innocent children but also murdering hope. Those of us who have experienced the birth of a desired child and felt the joy of that moment can be tempted into believing that it was the physical experience of the birth itself that was the joy. But it is crucial to remember that the birth of a child itself is a neutral occurrence emotionally: the charge it takes on is invested in it by the people experiencing or observing it.

The Fear of Sexual Autonomy

These uncertainties can lead to another set of fears, not only about abortion but about its implications. Many anti-choice people fear that to support abortion is to cast one's lot with the cold and technological rather than with the warm and natural, to head down the slippery slope toward a brave new world where handicapped children are left on mountains to starve and the old are put out in the snow. But if we look at the history of abortion, we don't see the embodiment of what the anti-choice proponents fear. On the contrary, excepting the grotesque counterexample of the People's Republic of China (which practices forced abortion), there seems to be a real link between repressive anti-abortion stances and repressive governments. Abortion was banned in Fascist Italy and Nazi Germany; it is illegal in South Africa and in Chile. It is paid for by the governments of Denmark, England, and the Netherlands, which have national health and welfare systems that foster the health and well-being of mothers, children, the old, and the handicapped.

Advocates of outlawing abortion often refer to women seeking abortion as self-indulgent and materialistic. In fact these accusations mask a discomfort with female sexuality, sexual pleasure, and sexual autonomy. It is possible for a woman to have a sexual life unriddled by fear only if she can be confident that she need not pay for a failure of technology or judgment (and who among us has never once been swept away in the heat of a sexual moment?) by taking upon herself the crushing burden of unchosen motherhood.

It is no accident, therefore, that the increased appeal of measures to restrict maternal conduct during pregnancy—and a new focus on the physical autonomy of the pregnant woman—have come into public discourse at precisely the time when women are achieving unprecedented levels of economic and political autonomy. What has surprised me is that some of this new anti-autonomy talk comes to us from the left. An example of this new discourse is an article by Christopher Hitchens that appeared in *The Nation* last April, in which the author asserts his discomfort with abortion. Hitchens's tone is impeccably British: arch, light, we're men of the left.

> Anyone who has ever seen a sonogram or has spent even an hour with a textbook on embryology knows that the emotions are not the deciding factor. In order to terminate a pregnancy, you have to still a heartbeat, switch off a developing brain, and whatever the method, break some bones and rupture some organs. As to whether this involves pain on the "Silent Scream" scale, I have no idea. The "right to life" leadership, again, has cheapened everything it touches. ["Silent Scream" refers to Dr. Bernard Nathanson's widely debated antiabortion film *The Silent Scream,* in which an abortion on a 12-week-old fetus is shown from inside the uterus.—Eds.]

"It is a pity," Hitchens goes on to say, "that... the majority of feminists and their allies have stuck to the dead ground of 'Me Decade' possessive individualism, an ideology that has more in common than it admits with the prehistoric right, which it claims to oppose but has in fact encouraged." Hitchens proposes, as an alternative, a program of social reform that would make contraception free and support a national adoption service. In his opinion, it would seem, women have abortions for only two reasons: because they are selfish or because they are poor. If the state will take care of the economic problems and the bureaucratic messiness around adoption, it remains only for the possessive individualists to get their act together and walk with their babies into the communal utopia of the future. Hitchens would allow victims of rape or incest to have free abortions, on the grounds that since they didn't choose to have sex, the women should not be forced to have the babies. This would seem to put the issue of volition in a wrong and telling place. To Hitchens's mind, it would appear, if a woman chooses to have sex, she can't choose whether or not to have a baby. The implications of this are clear. If a woman is consciously and volitionally sexual, she should be prepared to take her medicine. And what medicine must the consciously sexual male take? Does Hitchens really believe, or want us to believe, that every male who has unintentionally impregnated a woman will be involved in the lifelong responsibility for the upbringing of the engendered child? Can he honestly say that he has observed this behavior—or, indeed, would want to see it observed—in the world in which he lives?

Real Choices

It is essential for a moral decision about abortion to be made in an atmosphere of open, critical thinking. We on the pro-choice side must accept that there are indeed anti-choice activists who take their position in good faith. I believe, however, that they are people for whom childbirth is an emotionally overladen topic, people who are susceptible to unclear thinking because of their unrealistic hopes and fears. It is important for us in the pro-choice movement to be open in discussing those areas involving abortion which are nebulous and unclear. But we must not forget that there are some things that we know to be undeniably true. There are some undeniable bad consequences of a woman's being forced to bear a child against her will. First is the trauma of going through a pregnancy and giving birth to a child who is not desired, a trauma more long-lasting than that experienced by some (only some) women who experience an early abortion. The grief of giving up a child at its birth—and at nine months it is a child whom one has felt move inside one's body—is underestimated both by anti-choice partisans and by those for whom access to adoptable children is important. This grief should not be forced on any woman—or, indeed, encouraged by public policy.

We must be realistic about the impact on society of millions of unwanted children in an overpopulated world. Most of the time, human beings have sex not because they want to make babies. Yet throughout history sex has resulted in unwanted pregnancies. And women have always aborted. One thing that is not hidden, mysterious, or debatable is that making abortion illegal will result in the deaths of women, as it has always done. Is our historical memory so short that none of us remember aunts, sisters, friends, or mothers who were killed or rendered sterile by septic abortions? Does no one in the anti-choice movement remember stories or actual experiences of midnight drives to filthy rooms from which aborted women were sent out, bleeding, to their fate? Can anyone genuinely say that it would be a moral good for us as a society to return to those conditions?

Thinking about abortion, then, forces us to take moral positions as adults who understand the complexities of the world and the realities of human suffering, to make decisions based on how people actually live and choose, and not on our fears, prejudices, and anxieties about sex and society, life and death.

POSTSCRIPT

Should Abortion Be Restricted?

The real issue dividing George and Gordon is whether or not the fetus is fully human, in the sense of being entitled to the treatment that civilized society gives to human beings. Their respective arguments use different methods of proof. George reasons from the biological premise that sperm and egg, each with 23 chromosomes, produce a fertilized human organism with the human's full 46 chromosomes; what occurs after that is simply human growth, which no one has the right to interrupt. Gordon reasons from the appearance of the fetus and how people normally react to it. Since even pro-lifers do not conduct funeral services and memorials for the "bloody matter" resulting from an early miscarriage, Gordon reasons, the Supreme Court was right to exclude early fetuses from legal protection. Such reactions, in George's view, proceed from emotion rather than reason.

Dozens of books have dealt with these questions since the Supreme Court's decision in *Roe v. Wade* in 1973. A comprehensive selection can be found in J. Douglas Butler and David F. Walbert, eds., *Abortion, Medicine, and the Law,* 3rd ed. (Facts on File, 1986). More briefly, most of the legal, ethical, and medical issues are considered in Hyman Rodman, Betty Sarvis, and Joy Walker Bonar, *The Abortion Question* (Columbia University Press, 1987). In *Real Choices* (Multnomah Press, 1994), Frederica Mathewes-Green argues the case against abortion from the standpoint of the harm (physical and psychological) that it inflicts on women. A similar approach is taken by David C. Reardon in *Making Abortion Rare* (Acorn Books, 1996) and in *Victims and Victors* (Acorn Books, 2000), coauthored with Julie Makimaa and Amy Sobie.

Robert M. Baird and Stuart E. Rosenbaum, eds., *The Ethics of Abortion: Pro-Life vs. Pro-Choice,* rev. ed. (Prometheus Books, 1993), contains a wide variety of views. An unbiased history of abortion as an American political issue can be found in Barbara Hinkson Craig and David M. O'Brien, *Abortion and American Politics* (Chatham House, 1993). In the world arena, Andrzej Kulczycki's *The Abortion Debate in the World Arena* (Routledge, 1999) examines how cultural history, feminist movements, the Catholic Church, and international influences have shaped abortion policies in Kenya, Mexico, and Poland.

If, as Gordon argues, the best way to determine the humanity of the fetus is by its appearance, what of late-term abortions? By the sixth month of pregnancy, the fetus begins to look very much like a baby. Should it then be protected by law? Although she confesses to be "uneasy" about third-trimester abortions, Gordon suspects that those who advocate bans on late-term abortions are not doing so in good faith. The suspicion between the warring parties to the abortion debate will likely continue.

ISSUE 13

Are Americans Taxed Too Much?

YES: Amity Shlaes, from *The Greedy Hand: How Taxes Drive Americans Crazy and What to Do About It* (Random House, 1999)

NO: Liam Murphy and Thomas Nagel, from *The Myth of Ownership: Taxes and Justice* (Oxford University Press, 2002)

ISSUE SUMMARY

YES: *Wall Street Journal* editorial writer Amity Shlaes maintains that the federal income tax is too high, too complex, unfair in withholding income from wage earners, and biased against high-income earners.

NO: Philosophy professors Liam Murphy and Thomas Nagel contend that the issue of tax fairness is misunderstood because, contrary to what most people believe, taxes do not take one's property but, in fact, help to establish property rights.

Benjamin Franklin is credited with having first said, "In this world nothing is certain but death and taxes." That does not mean that we have to look forward to either one. When the colonists confronted the collection of taxes by Great Britain, they proclaimed "No taxation without representation" and moved toward revolution and the creation of the United States.

In 1912 the Sixteenth Amendment to the Constitution was adopted, enabling the federal government to levy taxes directly on income. The following year Congress adopted a graduated income tax, ranging from a 1 percent tax on individuals and businesses earning over $4,000 (most Americans did not earn that much) up to 6 percent on incomes over $500,000. Since then, tax rates have gone up and down, but some measure of progressivity—higher rates for higher incomes—has been retained. However, every change in the tax code has produced new deductions, concessions, and loopholes that benefit some groups to the disadvantage of others, lengthen and complicate the law, and stimulate a major tax-filing occupation for accountants and tax lawyers.

No one likes taxes, but upon reflection most Americans are likely to agree with Supreme Court Justice Oliver Wendell Holmes, Jr., that "taxes are what we pay for civilized society." No other way has been devised to pay for such essential services as public education, police and fire protection, roads and public transport, and the military defense of the nation. So the question is not whether or not Americans should be taxed but how and how much.

By the standards of other nations, American taxes are low. In fact, every other industrial nation has higher rates of taxation, except Japan, whose tax rate is about the same as that of the United States. Nevertheless, Americans appear to respond more favorably than citizens of other countries to proposals to lower taxes. When presidential candidate George Bush in 1988 said, "Read my lips: No new taxes," he enhanced his prospects for election. But when then–president Bush ran for reelection in 1992, his broken promise contributed to his defeat.

When George W. Bush entered the presidency in 2001, he secured enactment of legislation that substantially reduced income and other taxes. He argued that money belongs to the people who earn it and that reducing taxes would result in more investment and greater prosperity. One of the controversial provisions in the new tax law involved the gradual abolition of the estate tax, which that year began at a taxable inheritance of $1,350,000 for a married couple. Advocates of ending the tax argued that it taxed for a second time money that had been taxed when it was initially earned. Moreover, they stated that the tax harms the owners of small businesses and family farms. Defenders of the estate tax maintain that its abolition would deprive the federal government of hundreds of billions of dollars within two decades. Less than 1 percent of families are subject to this tax because the superrich create foundations, trusts, and other devices to reduce or avoid paying estate taxes. Warren Buffet, probably the second wealthiest person in America (Bill Gates, of Microsoft, is the first), criticized those who would abolish the estate tax: "All those people who think that food stamps are debilitating and lead to a cycle of poverty are the same ones who want to leave a ton of money to their kids."

Almost all critics of federal taxation (apart from anarchists and extreme libertarians) acknowledge that the government has a role in national security, creating trade policy, and continuing social welfare programs, such as Social Security and Medicare. However, their feelings on how taxes should be collected vary. Proposals for improving the system include a cap on federal taxes, a flat single rate of taxation on all income, and a consumption tax. Liberal critics believe that the system should be more progressive—that higher incomes should be taxed at higher rates, possibly yielding a somewhat less unequal distribution of net income.

In the following selection, Amity Shlaes argues that the American tax system is ill-advised with regard to a withholding tax that takes earnings before wage-earners receive them, a tax code that is too complex, a tax rate that is too high, and a tax burden that reduces the productivity and the ultimate tax payments of the rich. In the second selection, Liam Murphy and Thomas Nagel offer an unconventional approach to tax policy, arguing that without government there is no private property and that without taxation there is no government. Consequently, real property is what citizens retain after taxation, and the justification of a particular tax policy must be seen in a broader social context.

 **YES**

The Greedy Hand

The father of the modern American state was a pipe-puffing executive at R. H. Macy & Co. named Beardsley Ruml. Ruml, the department store's treasurer, also served as chairman of the board of directors of the Federal Reserve Bank of New York and advisor to President Franklin Roosevelt during World War II. In those years Washington was busy marshaling the forces of the American economy to halt Japan and Germany. In 1942, not long after Pearl Harbor, lawmakers raised income taxes radically, with rates that aimed to capture twice as much revenue as in the previous year. They also imposed the income tax on tens of millions of Americans who had never been acquainted with the levy before. The change was so dramatic that the chroniclers of that period have coined a phrase to describe it. They say that the "class tax" became a "mass tax."

The new rates were law. But Americans were ill-prepared to face a new and giant tax bill. A Gallup poll from the period showed that only some 5 million of the 34 million people who were subject to the tax for the first time were saving to make their payment. In those days, March 15, not April 15, was the nation's annual tax deadline.

The Treasury nervously launched a huge public relations campaign to remind Americans of their new duties. A Treasury Department poster exhorted citizens: "You are one of 50,000,000 Americans who must fill out an income tax form by March 15. DO IT NOW!" For wartime theatergoers, Disney had prepared an animated short film featuring citizen Donald Duck laboring over his tax return beside a bottle of aspirin. Donald claimed exemptions and dependent credits for Huey, Dewey, and Louie.

As March 15, 1943 neared, though, it became clear that many citizens still were not filing returns. Henry Morgenthau, the Treasury secretary, confronted colleagues about the nightmarish prospect of mass tax evasion: "Suppose we have to go out and try to arrest five million people?"

The Macy's Model

Enter Ruml, man of ideas. At Macy's, he had observed that customers didn't like big bills. They preferred making payments bit by bit, in the installment plan, even if they had to pay for the pleasure with interest. So Ruml devised a plan,

From Amity Shlaes, *The Greedy Hand: How Taxes Drive Americans Crazy and What to Do About It* (Random House, 1999). Copyright © 1998 by Amity Shlaes. Reprinted by permission of Random House, Inc.

which he unfolded to his colleagues at the Federal Reserve and to anyone in Washington who would listen. The government would get business to do its work, collecting taxes for it. Employers would retain a percentage of taxes from workers every week—say, 20 percent—and forward it directly to Washington's war chest. This would hide the size of the new taxes from the worker. No longer would the worker ever have to look his tax bill square in the eye. Workers need never even see the money they were forgoing. Withholding as we know it today was born.

This was more than change, it was transformation. Government would put its hand into the taxpayer's pocket and grab its share of tax—without asking.

Ruml hadn't invented withholding. His genius was to make its introduction palatable by adding a powerful sweetener: the federal government would offer a tax amnesty for the previous year, allowing confused and indebted citizens to start on new footing. It was the most ambitious bait-and-switch plan in America's history.

Ruml advertised his project as a humane effort to smooth life in the disruption of the war. He noted it was a way to help taxpayers out of the habit of carrying income tax debt, debt that he characterized as "a pernicious fungus permeating the structure of things." The move was also patriotic. At Macy's, executives had found that a "young man in the comptroller's office who was making $75 or $100 [a week was] called into the navy at a salary of $2,600 and we had to get together and take care of his income tax for him." The young man, Ruml saw, would face a tax bill for a higher income at a time when he was earning less money in the service of his country. This Ruml deemed "an impossible situation."

Ruml had several reasons for wagering that his project would work. One was that Americans, smarting from the Japanese assault, were now willing to sacrifice more than at any other point in memory. The second was that the federal government would be able to administer withholding—six successful years of Social Security showed that the government, for the first time ever, was able to handle such a mass program of revenue collection. The third was packaging. He called his program not "collection at source" or "withholding," two technical terms for what he was doing. Instead he chose a zippier name: "pay as you go." And most important of all, there was the lure of the tax amnesty.

The policy thinkers of the day embraced the Ruml arrangement. This was an era in which John Maynard Keynes dominated the world of economics. The Keynesians placed enormous faith in government. The only thing they liked about the war was that it demonstrated to the world all the miracles that Big Government could work. The Ruml plan would give them the wherewithal to have their projects even, they sensed, after the war ended. Keynesianism also said high taxes were crucial to controlling inflation. The Keynesians saw withholding as the right tool for getting those necessary high taxes.

Conservatives played their part in the drama. Among withholding's backers was the man who was later to become the world's leading free-market economist, Milton Friedman. Decades after the war, Friedman called for the abolition of the withholding system. In his memoirs he wrote that "we concentrated single-mindedly on promoting the war effort. We gave next to no consideration to any longer-run consequences. It never occurred to me at the time that I was helping to develop machinery that would make possible a government that I would come to criticize severely as too large, too intrusive, too destructive of freedom. Yet, that was precisely what I was doing." With an almost audible sigh, Friedman added: "There is an important lesson here. It is far easier to introduce a government program than to get rid of it."

Such questions, though, had no place in the mind of a nation under attack. At the moment what seemed most important was that voters accepted the Ruml plan. Randolph Paul, a Treasury Department official and Ruml critic, wrote resignedly that "his plan had political appeal. Though he conceived the plan as getting people out of debt to the government, the public thought that Ruml had found a very white rabbit"—a magic trick—"which would somehow lighten their tax load."

✦

... Adam Smith described the "invisible hand," the hand of free commerce that brings magic order and harmony to our lives. Thomas Paine wrote of another hand, all too visible and intrusive: "the greedy hand of government, thrusting itself into every corner and crevice of industry." Today the invisible hand is a very busy one. Markets are wider and freer than ever, and we profit from that by living better than before. But the "greedy hand of government" is also at work. Indeed, in relative terms, the greedy hand has grown faster than the invisible hand. In the late 1990s, economists noted with astonishment that federal taxes made up one-fifth of the economy, a rate higher than at any time in American history outside of war. We can not assign the blame for changes of such magnitude to Beardsley Ruml, who was, after all, not much more than a New Deal package man. The real force here is not even withholding, whatever its power. Behind Ruml's withholding lurks Paine's greedy hand.

... Today, more than half of the budget goes to social transfers mandated by expensive programs whose value many Americans question. Working citizens sense that someone is getting something, but that someone is often not they.

The avid tax haters who pop up occasionally in the news are the expression of this national unease. Their froth-mouthed manifestos strike us as extreme—how many of us truly want to "kill the IRS"?—but they reflect something that all Americans feel to some degree. Even the most moderate of us often feel a tick of sympathy when we hear the shouts of the tax haters. We think of our forefathers who felt compelled to rebel against the Crown for "imposing Taxes on us without our consent." We know we live in a democracy, and so must have chosen this arrangement. Yet nowadays we too find ourselves feeling that taxes are imposed on us "without our consent."

Washington doesn't necessarily recognize the totality of this tax frustration. The purview of the House Ways and Means Committee is limited to federal taxes, and so the committee writes tax law as if the federal income tax were the only tax in the country. The commissions that monitor Social Security concern themselves only with the solvency of Social Security, and so ignore the consequences of raising payroll taxes, or taxing pensions, at a time when income taxes are already high. Old programs with outdated aims stay in place. Newer ones, added piecemeal, often conflict with the old.

"Rube Goldberg machine," "unstoppable contraption"—none of the stock phrases adequately captures the complication that is our tax structure. As William E. Simon, a former Treasury secretary, once said, "The nation should have a tax system which looks like someone designed it on purpose." . . .

⊷⊙⊶

Americans today are more prosperous than we have ever been. As a nation, we have come very far, so far that even our past is beginning to look different. In the 1960s, 1970s, and even the 1980s, we took Big Government America, the America of the postwar period, to be the only America, an America that permanently supplanted something antiquated. This conviction strengthened when we considered the enormous troubles that plagued us in those decades. Who else but government could end the underclass, right the wrongs of Vietnam, combat inflation?

We can see now that in those years we had a foreshortened view of history. From the heights of our new achievement, we recognize that the Great Society, for all its ideals, was something of an aberration. It is clear now that the self-doubt and gray misgivings of the Vietnam period were, in their way, just a momentary interruption. The inflation of the 1970s was an acute and terrible problem but a short-lived one. Our famous deficit agony—which so many commentators and foreigners alleged would bring us down—has, at least for the moment, receded. Today we are in many ways more like the America of Andrew Jackson or even Thomas Jefferson than we are like the America of Jimmy Carter.

This change was the result of enormous and serious work. We developed microchips and computers that secured our global economic dominance. We started the welfare state and then, when we saw it wasn't working, successfully ended it. We grew a stock market that will provide pensions for the baby boom and beyond. Serious challenges loom ahead. Unpredictable rogue states threaten our national security; the economy will not always live up to its 1990s boom. But we understand now that the key to sustaining our prosperity is recognizing that we are our own best providers. Thinkers from left, center, and right agree: we don't need a nanny state.

This American confidence is not new. It is simply a homecoming to older ideals, ideals that we held through most of our history. Self-reliance is the ultimate American tradition. Even through a good part of the Depression "no handouts" was Americans' self-imposed rule. We are coming to a new appreciation of what Tocqueville admiringly called "self-interest, rightly understood."

Yet we are still saddled with our tax structure, the unwieldy artifact of an irrelevant era.

Unburdening ourselves is not easy, but it is something we have in our power to do. Our impasse, in fact, contains the outline of its own solution, if only we allow ourselves to look at it clearly. What, exactly, does our long struggle with Paine's greedy hand tell us?

Taxes have to be visible.   Beardsley Ruml's trap worked because it made taxes invisible. No one today willingly gives a third or a half of his income into a strange hand; we only pay our taxes now because the trap locked shut long ago. We never see our tax bill in its entirety except during the madness of filing season.

When we rewrite our arrangement with government, we need to write into it a tax structure that is clear and comprehensible, whose outlines we can see and consider whenever we choose.

Taxes have to be simple.   The tax code is a monster of complexity, but it doesn't have to be. When rules are added to rules, the change may benefit certain classes, but they hurt the rest of us. The best thing is to settle on one system, even if someone shouts that it's not "fair" to everyone.

Taxes are for revenue.   For fifty years we have used taxes to steer behavior. Indeed, politicians often used the argument that they were promoting social good through the tax code as window dressing for their real aim: getting at the revenue. None of us likes the result. We are responsible for our own fate; let government take what we choose to give it and then retreat.

Taxes have to be lower.   We have managed to achieve prosperity notwithstanding high taxes. But that prosperity would have been greater without those taxes. The microchip, in its way, has allowed us to postpone our date with tax reform.

But epochal transformations like the computer revolution, or the Industrial Revolution for that matter, cannot be counted on to come every decade. Taxes will slow our economy if we don't bring them down to rates that allow us to sustain desirable growth.

We don't have to load extra taxes on the rich.   We've learned that a tax system that punishes the rich also punishes the rest of us. Those who have money should pay taxes like everyone else. In fact the rich already carry more of the tax burden than any other income group. Yet history—the history of the 1980s in particular—has shown an amazing thing—that lower rates on the rich produce more revenue from them.

Progressivity has had its day. Let us move on to a tax system that is more worthy of us, one that makes sense for the country.

It's time to privatize Social Security.   Many of the core tax problems we face today are in reality Social Security problems. Markets have taught us that they can do a better job than government in providing public pensions. We should privatize a portion of Social Security—at least three of the percentage points that individuals carry.

The only thing to guard against is a privatization that is not a true privatization. When government enters the stock market on behalf of citizens, as many advocates of Social Security privatization would like, that is not privatization. That is expanding the public sector at the cost of the private sector. An office in government that invests on behalf of citizens, as many are proposing, is an office open to enormous moral hazard. To understand this you need only to consider what would happen if the chairman of the Securities and Exchange Commission directly controlled a few hundred million shares of blue-chip stocks.

Individuals need to control their own accounts, just as they control the rest of their money. Government guarantees of returns are also guarantees of disaster. One need only look to our recent history with savings and loans to see that. Raising the ceiling on federal insurance of S & L accounts led to that disaster by giving S & L directors license without accountability. The cost ran into the hundreds of billions, but it was far lower than the cost a government guarantee on privatized Social Security would be.

Local is good.   The enduring lesson of our schools crisis is that centralizing school finance to the state and federal level has not given us the equity or the academic performance we hoped for. These results have ramifications far beyond schools. The federal government cannot solve everything. Many problems —from school to health care to welfare—are better handled lower down. A wise tax reform is a tax reform that leaves much of the nation's work to the people and the officials they know. Trying to write a federal tax law that addresses all our national problems is a recipe for a repeat of the current trouble.

We must lock in change.   In the 1980s, through tremendous political and social exertion, the nation joined together to lower tax rates and prune out many of the code's absurdities. Within a few years, Washington had destroyed its own child. This time we must fix our change so the fiddlers can't get at it....

Most Americans are not fire-breathing radicals or Ruby Ridge survivalists. They don't want to "kill the IRS." They just want a common-sense change in the system. And that is what they are telling lawmakers. When Steve LaTourette, a Republican congressman from Ohio, surveyed his constituents, he found that just about half wanted the IRS abolished. But a full three quarters wanted to see the tax code itself abolished. They saw that the code, not the bureaucrats, was the problem.

The second part of the program is to make the change truly permanent through a constitutional amendment. Our nation's last experience of trying to pass a significant-seeming constitutional amendment—the Equal Rights Amendment—was a bitter one. It soured Washington on amendments in general. Hesitation over amendments goes a long way toward explaining the current Republican foundering.

A constitutional amendment that calls for limiting federal taxes, including Social Security, to 25 percent of our income, or even a lower share, would be an important first step out of the logjam. For one thing, states would have to ratify the change, and that would allow us to have a much needed national discussion about taxes. Citizens would have to consider what lawmakers were proposing. This would give voters a chance to get around the lobbies and politicians who have kept the tax debate to themselves. It would get us all back into the discussion.

The third step is to realize that as a people we want to pay taxes. Roosevelt called taxes "the dues we pay for organized society." We still feel that way.

But people want a tax system that doesn't intrude on our private lives while it collects those dues; and we want those dues to be spent in a reasonable, limited way. We want a tax code that, to quote former Treasury secretary William Simon again, looks as if somebody designed it on purpose. Not a giant machine that collects our money merely to feed the monster.

NO

Liam Murphy and Thomas Nagel

The Myth of Ownership

Our main message [is] that societal fairness, rather than tax fairness, should be the value that guides tax policy, and that property rights are conventional: they are to a large extent the product of tax policies that have to be evaluated by standards of social justice; so they cannot be used to determine what taxes are just....

Where our approach departs greatly from the standard mentality of day-to-day politics is in our insistence on the conventionality of property, and our denial that property rights are morally fundamental. Resistance to traditional concepts of tax fairness and their political analogues requires rejection of the idea that people's pretax income and wealth are theirs in any morally meaningful sense. We have to think of property as what is created by the tax system, rather than what is disturbed or encroached on by the tax system. Property rights are the rights people have in the resources they are entitled to control after taxes, not before.

This doesn't mean we can't speak of taking money by taxation from the rich to give to the poor, for example. But what that means is not that we are taking from some people what is already theirs, but rather that the tax system is assigning to them less that counts as theirs than they would have under a less redistributive system that left the rich with more money under their private control, that is, with more that is theirs....

The state does not own its citizens, nor do they own each other collectively. But individual citizens don't own anything except through laws that are enacted and enforced by the state. Therefore, the issues of taxation are not about how the state should appropriate and distribute what its citizens already own, but about how it should allow ownership to be determined.

We recognize that it is a lot to hope that this philosophical point should become psychologically real to most people. Pretax economic transactions are so salient in our lives that the governmental framework that determines their consequences and gives them their real meaning recedes into the background of consciousness. What is left is the robust and compelling fantasy that we earn our income and the government takes some of it away from us, or in some cases supplements it with what it has taken from others. This results in widespread hostility to taxes, and a political advantage to those who campaign against them

From Liam Murphy and Thomas Nagel, *The Myth of Ownership: Taxes and Justice* (Oxford University Press, 2002). Copyright © 2002 by Oxford University Press, Inc. Reprinted by permission of Oxford University Press. Notes omitted.

and attack the IRS as a tyrannical bureaucracy, trying to get its hands on our hard-earned money.

If political debate were not over how much of what is mine the government should take in taxes, but over how the laws, including the tax system, should determine what is to count as mine, it would not end disagreements over the merits of redistribution and public provision, but it would change their form. The question would become what values we want to uphold and reflect in our collectively enacted system of property rights—how much weight should be given to the alleviation of poverty and the provision of equal chances; how much to ensuring that people reap the rewards and penalties for their efforts or lack thereof; how much to leaving people free of interference in their voluntary interactions. It is not ruled out that the preferred system would be one that denied the state substantial responsibility for combating economic inequality; but that position could not rely on the support of pretax property rights....

⚜

We believe that the main problem of socioeconomic justice is this. A capitalist market economy is the best method we have for creating employment, generating wealth, allocating capital to production, and distributing goods and services. But it also inevitably generates large economic and social inequalities, often hereditary, that leave a significant segment of society not only relatively but also absolutely deprived, unless special measures are taken to combat those effects. Our view is that while every government has the fundamental duty to guarantee security against coercion and violence, both foreign and domestic, and to provide the legal order that makes prosperity possible, it is almost as important to find ways of limiting the damage to the inevitable losers in market competition without undermining the productive power of the system.

It isn't possible to ensure that everyone will have exactly the same chances in life. The most realistic aim is to try to ensure that everyone in the society should have at least a minimally decent quality of life—that none should start out with two strikes against them because of low-earning capacity, poor education, a severely deprived childhood and home environment, inadequate food, shelter, and medical care; and that even people who fail to take advantage of reasonably favorable initial opportunities should not be left to fall into destitution. Preventing or compensating for those harms is overwhelmingly more important than attacking inequalities at the upper end of the distribution. It is the fundamental positive responsibility we have toward our fellow citizens.

Any view more laissez-faire than this depends on the moral belief that the only positive obligations of government are: (a) to provide institutions that make a market economy possible, (b) to protect people from violence and coercion, and (c) to supply certain public goods that serve everyone's interests but cannot be provided privately.... [W]e reject the everyday libertarianism that lies behind such a view. Without that support it seems arbitrarily restrictive: Why just those positive obligations and not also the obligation to ensure a minimally decent standard of living for all citizens? The idea that it is the function of government merely to provide the conditions for peaceful economic cooperation and competition, without any concern for the equity of the results, is just too minimal. On the other hand, while we are sympathetic to more robust egalitarian views that take social responsibility substantially beyond the level of minimal decency, their political prospects seem dim, at least in the short run.

It goes without saying that exemption from tax for a minimum basic income would be one element in the institutional scheme that ensures a decent social minimum; but the most effective way of improving the condition of people below the average would be not only to exempt them from tax but also to substantially increase their disposable income. The difficulty is to come up with methods of doing this that really work and don't have seriously objectionable effects of other kinds. The perennial debate about rises in the minimum wage provides an example; it seems likely that this is a measure that could achieve only modest improvement in the income of those with the least marketable skills, because large increases would be too damaging economically.

We believe that direct cash transfers are a better method, and that the hard question is how they could be designed so as not to deter recipients from paid work. The importance of this issue cannot be exaggerated. Remunerated and productive work, by at least someone in the family, is a vital condition of self-respect, stability, independence, and a sense of social membership. Cash transfers that provide disincentives to work are socially destructive.

On the other hand, transfers to those who cannot work or who have passed the age when they are expected to work do not have the same disadvantage. That is why Social Security benefits are unproblematic. They protect everyone in the society from falling through a certain floor in old age, and while they provide some disincentive to go on working forever in this age of no compulsory retirement, they do not discourage work by anyone whom the society should want to keep in employment. While the fact is somewhat disguised by the Social Security taxes that all workers pay, and the benefits that are a function of contribution, the program is clearly redistributive: low earners get back more than they put in, and high earners less.

But a program of cash transfers to those of working age, even if it is targeted partly at the support of children too young to work, ought to take a form that encourages work and doesn't lower the gains from employment or lead to the breakup of households, in the way that some welfare programs can. Tax-supported wage supplements channeled through employers would be one way to do this; we will not try to evaluate that method here. In Europe, direct grants in the form of family allowances are common, providing some support to every family with children. Clearly, there are political advantages to such a universal program, and if it could be financed in a redistributive way, it would do a lot to correct the current skewing of entitlement programs toward the old, through Social Security and Medicare.

But a more targeted, need-based form of income supplement has been tried with some success in the United States: the Earned Income Tax Credit, while is worth 40% of income up to $8,890 per year for a family with two children. This kind of direct benefit to the working poor—those who lose out in a competitive labor market, whose intrinsic inequalities are now widely recognized—seems to have gained mainstream political acceptance. It has appeal both for enemies of inequality and for those champions of individual responsibility who recognize that low-earning power need not be the victim's fault.

It is hard to know how much more extensive, either in amount or in range of recipients, such programs of direct income supplement could realistically hope to become. Our guess is that a targeted program of cash transfers could lose all political viability if it went above the bottom quarter of the income distribution, and that a serious effort to guarantee a decent social minimum would probably have to take the alternative form of universal benefits, funded in a redistributive way. A family allowance is something that may take hold in the United States eventually. If so, the currently dim prospects for general acceptance of demogrants might even improve.

More specific programs like universal health insurance and adequate funding for public education in all communities are also necessary parts of any fully adequate social safety net. If some such measures were added to Social Security, Medicare, and the existing public support for educational opportunity, it would be a significant move toward social justice as we understand it. But we recognize that there is much more resistance to direct public provision of social benefits—"big government"—here than in other rich countries, so it seems particularly desirable to expand the redistribution of disposable cash through the tax system, which does not involve the creation of government-run programs....

Two of the practical issues of tax policy—progressivity and inheritance taxes—are connected with another question of justice. That is the question of whether large inequalities toward the top of the economic distribution are objectionable, independently of the value of lifting the standard of living and opportunities of those toward the bottom. The political and moral climate in the United States is not currently hostile to huge salaries and huge accumulations of wealth, as such, and there is not even much concern over the intergenerational transmission of these fortunes. Public opinion seems to take the view that capitalism at its most successful will inevitably generate large upward inequalities, and that, in themselves, they don't do much harm. In any event, the tolerance for vast private wealth is a natural response to the sense of its inevitability.

We are uncertain about this question. There is something palpably unfair about a society in which a small minority are vastly richer than their compatriots, and in which successive generations are born into these positions of wealth, even if no one in the society is very badly off in absolute terms. Clearly, a significant part of this good fortune is undeserved. But we don't know how much this matters—whether it is bad, in particular, for the less-privileged members of the society to live in such an unequal situation. Probably comparing yourself with people slightly above you is more painful than contemplating those in the economic stratosphere. In any case, fantastic good luck that is undeserved is in itself nothing to object to. And bringing down the top, unless it is a means of bringing up the rest, is not a policy that can be easily defended by politically attractive arguments.

But we also firmly reject the opposite view that economic winners morally deserve to keep their big gains and to pass them on to their children. Something like this view seems to underlie the hostility to estate and gift taxes, even for the very rich, that is increasingly common in our society. The broad support for abolition of all taxes on estates cannot express merely the self-interest of those in the top economic tier, since under the present combined estate and gift tax only a small minority of bequests are subject to tax at all.

Taxation of large family fortunes at death should certainly be regarded as a legitimate source of revenue for redistribution and other purposes, and it should be politically possible to make the case that this is not a violation of a moral entitlement or natural property right based on justice.... [T]he strongest case can be made for including bequests in the taxable income of the recipient. But even if the only politically viable option is to continue to tax bequests to the donor in a separate estate and gift tax, eliminating this source of revenue would be a clear step toward greater injustice.

Finally, any policy proposals that reduce the after-tax disposable resources of the wealthy have to contend with the importance of money in American politics. People will spend money, where they can, to gain or retain still more money. If political contributions are not limited, we can expect the pursuit of socioeconomic justice to be handicapped by the disproportionate influence of those who have the most to lose from it financially. Fortunately, this is now widely appreciated, and there is a serious movement for campaign finance reform. The same forces that make such reform necessary will make it difficult to enact. But if limits on campaign spending become law and are judged constitutional, one significant injustice resulting from large concentrations of wealth will have been eliminated....

❧✦❧

Nothing could be more mundane than taxes, but they provide a perfect setting for constant moral argument and possible moral progress. Process in moral thinking is slow, and effective progress cannot come exclusively from theoreticians, as it can in mathematics, for example. In mathematics, everyone else is content to trust the experts, but when it comes to justice, a new conception or argument will not acquire authority until many people take it into their own thinking and come to be motivated by it in their judgments of what to do and what to favor or oppose.

We see how long moral changes can take by looking back on the abolition of slavery, the growth of democracy, and the public recognition of full sexual and racial equality. What is obvious to us was once far from obvious to many people—though there have always been individuals morally in advance of their time (as well, of course, as people who remain behind).

The development of a conception of justice compatible with capitalism and realizable under democracy is a formidable intellectual task. It would require more than simply letting the demands of justice yield to pressure from the other two. But the spread of such a conception so that it becomes part of the habit of thought of most of those who live in the capitalist liberal democracies is a problem of a different kind. The moral ideas that do the work of legitimation have to be graspable and intuitively appealing, not just correct.

In the aftermath of the century during which the Marxist conception of equality played itself out, at enormous cost, the question is whether a different kind of egalitarian social ideal, one not intrinsically incompatible with capitalist economic institutions, can take hold in the Western democracies that are now firmly committed both to democracy and to capitalism, with its inevitably unequal distribution of income and wealth. This would have to be a replacement for the old capitalist conception of responsibility for human welfare in terms of charity, understood as a morally motivated personal gift from the fortunate to the unfortunate—replacement by an understanding that legal institutions define who owns what and that those institutions must satisfy independent standards of distributive justice.

We believe that there is hope in this direction from the increasingly widespread understanding of how capitalism works—the gradual increase of popular economic literacy in democratic societies. The ways in which people can be both the beneficiaries and the victims of the market, and the respects in which it does and does not provide opportunities for individuals to enrich themselves through contributions to investment and production, are increasingly understood by the general public.

The egalitarian attitude that has a chance of taking hold against this background is the idea that in a pure labor market poverty may be nobody's fault, and that if wages are set at what the market will bear, significant numbers of people will not earn enough to maintain a decent standard of living. These inequalities, generated by a system that benefits most people substantially and some people spectacularly, should come to be seen as unacceptable properties of the system, requiring rectification by some form of publicly financed social minimum—either in cash or in public provision. This is close to the moderate social democratic ideal that is a significant element of opinion in contemporary Europe, and there is no reason why it should not become part of the everyday moral consensus of Western politics. If so, more robust egalitarian views could begin to be treated as falling within the range of reasonable political opinion, even in the United States.

The older equalities had to be won against ancient traditions of exclusion —by heredity rank, by religion, by race, or by sex. Those victories are embodied in recognized rights that confer a common legal and political status on all members of the society. Nothing so simple will do for the expression of an egalitarian socioeconomic ideal in the context of capitalism. But the acceptance of socioeconomic inequality as inevitable can coexist with an insistence that those who do worst out of our common system should not fare too badly, and that those who do well out of it have no cause for complaint if the universal guarantee of a decent social minimum leaves them with less than they would have if low earners were left in poverty.

We may hope that in spite of the decisive failure of public ownership of the means of production in the twentieth century, most people are coming to believe that even under capitalism the organization of the economy, and the allocation of its product between public and private control, is a legitimate object of continual collective choice, and that this choice must be made on grounds that justify it not only economically but morally, and by a democratic procedure that legitimizes it. There will always be room for disagreement over the values that should determine that choice. But at least such an outlook provides a clear place for the application of standards of justice to tax policy and a role for the philosophical pursuit of disagreements among them.

POSTSCRIPT

Are Americans Taxed Too Much?

There is an obvious conflict between wanting to keep (and perhaps extend) most of the services and benefits that government provides and simultaneously wanting to lower taxes. There is no free lunch in the space program, or the National Institutes of Health, or old-age survivors' insurance (Social Security), or a thousand other federal activities. At the same time, Americans are increasingly skeptical about the uses to which their tax money is put. They do not understand how taxes are imposed, and they suspect that somebody else is getting a tax cut at their expense.

The significant tax reductions that were adopted in 2001 appear to have at least contributed to the disappearance of an anticipated surplus in federal revenues. The consequences will likely be debated for many years. Do these tax cuts increase incentives for investment and spending, thus bolstering the economy and increasing tax revenues in the long run? Or do they unfairly reward upper-income earners, re-create federal deficits, and make it more difficult for Congress to adopt costly reforms that would benefit lower- and middle-income citizens?

Critics of progressive income tax rates have supported Representative Dick Armey (R-Texas), author of *The Flat Tax: A Citizen's Guide to the Facts on What It Will Do for You, Your Country, and Your Pocketbook* (Fawcett Columbine, 1996), in his advocacy of a tax that is flat (same rate for all) and simple (the tax return fits on a postcard). Armey maintains that a flat tax will be fairer and will stimulate economic growth. In sharp disagreement, Charles Lewis and Bill Allison, in *The Cheating of America: How Tax Avoidance and Evasion by the Super Rich Are Costing the Country Billions and What You Can Do About It* (William Morrow, 2001), argue that the problem is not that Americans are taxed too much but that too many get away with paying too little.

A critical approach to many so-called reforms of tax policy is taken by Joel Slemrod and Jon Bakija in *Taxing Ourselves: A Citizen's Guide to the Great Debate Over Tax Reform* (MIT Press, 1998). The authors examine the difficulties inherent in various tax reform proposals and conclude that a national sales tax would be difficult to enforce; a broad-based, value-added tax would be highly regressive; a flat tax would also be regressive; and a consumption tax would be more complicated than the present income tax.

A broad and thoughtful perspective on the relationship of taxation to public policy can be found in *The Government We Deserve: Responsive Democracy and Changing Expectations* by C. Eugene Steuerle, Edward M. Gramlich, Hugh Heclo, and Demetra Smith Nightingale (Urban Institute Press, 1998). In it, the authors argue that without restoring citizen-owned government, confidence in public policy and its tax burdens will continue to decline.

ISSUE 14

Is Socioeconomic Inequality Increasing in America?

YES: Paul Krugman, from "The Spiral of Inequality," *Mother Jones* (November/December 1996)

NO: Christopher C. DeMuth, from "The New Wealth of Nations," *Commentary* (October 1997)

ISSUE SUMMARY

YES: Economist Paul Krugman maintains that corporate greed, the decline of organized labor, and changes in production have contributed to a sharp increase in social and economic inequality in America.

NO: Christopher C. DeMuth, president of the American Enterprise Institute, asserts that Americans have achieved an impressive level of wealth and equality and that a changing economy ensures even more opportunities.

There has always been a wide range in real income in the United States. In the first three decades after the end of World War II, family incomes doubled, income inequality narrowed slightly, and poverty rates declined. Prosperity declined in the mid-1970s, when back-to-back recessions produced falling average incomes, greater inequality, and higher poverty levels. Between the mid-1980s and the late 1990s, sustained economic recovery resulted in a modest average growth in income, but high poverty rates continued.

Defenders of the social system maintain that, over the long run, poverty has declined. Many improvements in social conditions benefit virtually all people and, thus, make us more equal. The increase in longevity (attributable in large measure to advances in medicine, nutrition, and sanitation) affects all social classes. In a significant sense, the U.S. economy is far fairer now than at any time in the past. In the preindustrial era, when land was the primary measure of wealth, those without land had no way to improve their circumstances. In the industrial era, when people of modest means needed physical strength and stamina to engage in difficult and hazardous labor in mines, mills, and factories, those who were too weak, handicapped, or too old stood little chance of gaining or keeping reasonable jobs.

In the postindustrial era, many of the manufactured goods that were once "Made in U.S.A.," ranging from clothing to electronics, are now made by cheaper foreign labor. Despite this loss, America achieved virtually full employment in the 1990s, largely because of the enormous growth of the information and service industries. Intelligence, ambition, and hard work—qualities that cut across social classes—are likely to be the determinants of success.

In the view of the defenders of the American economic system, the sharp increase in the nation's gross domestic product has resulted in greater prosperity for most Americans. Although the number of superrich has grown, so has the number of prosperous small business owners, middle-level executives, engineers, computer programmers, lawyers, doctors, entertainers, sports stars, and others who have gained greatly from the longest sustained economic growth in American history. For example, successful young pioneers in the new technology and the entrepreneurs whose capital supported their ventures have prospered, and so have the technicians and other workers whom they hired. Any change that mandated more nearly equal income would greatly diminish the incentives for invention, discovery, and risk-taking enterprises. As a result, the standard of living would be much lower and rise much more slowly, and individual freedom would be curtailed by the degree of state interference in people's private lives.

None of these objections satisfies those who deplore what they characterize as an increasing disparity in the distribution of income and wealth. In 2002 the U.S. Census Bureau concluded that the relative prosperity of the 1990s left poverty virtually unchanged, with 8 percent of American families earning less than $17,600, the income level below which a family of four is considered to be living in poverty. One in five households was broke, with nothing to tide them over when confronted with unemployment or a health crisis—not to mention being unable to save for college or retirement. Contrary to the popular cliché, a rising tide does not lift all boats; it does not lift the leaky boats or those who have no boat. *Business Week* reported that the pay gap between top executives and production workers in the 362 largest U.S. companies soared from a ratio of 42 to 1 to 475 to 1 in 1989. The financial wealth of the top 1 percent of households now exceeds the combined household financial wealth of the bottom 98 percent.

Advocates of more nearly equal income argue that a reduced pay gap would lead to less social conflict, less crime, more economic security, and better and more universal social services. Also, more nearly egalitarian societies (Scandinavia and Western Europe, for example) offer more nearly equal access to education, medical treatment, and legal defense. What happens to democracy, some ask, when more money means better access to those who write and administer the laws and to the very offices of political power themselves?

This sharp contrast can be seen in the following selections, in which Paul Krugman examines factors that sustain and increase inequality and Christopher C. DeMuth outlines a number of forces that have reduced inequality.

The Spiral of Inequality

Ever since the election of Ronald Reagan, right-wing radicals have insisted that they started a revolution in America. They are half right. If by a revolution we mean a change in politics, economics, and society that is so large as to transform the character of the nation, then there is indeed a revolution in progress. The radical right did not make this revolution, although it has done its best to help it along. If anything, we might say that the revolution created the new right. But whatever the cause, it has become urgent that we appreciate the depth and significance of this new American revolution—and try to stop it before it becomes irreversible.

The consequences of the revolution are obvious in cities across the nation. Since I know the area well, let me take you on a walk down University Avenue in Palo Alto, California.

Palo Alto is the de facto village green of Silicon Valley, a tree-lined refuge from the valley's freeways and shopping malls. People want to live here despite the cost—rumor has it that a modest three-bedroom house sold recently for $1.6 million—and walking along University you can see why. Attractive, casually dressed people stroll past trendy boutiques and restaurants; you can see a cooking class in progress at the fancy new kitchenware store. It's a cheerful scene, even if you have to detour around the people sleeping in doorways and have to avoid eye contact with the beggars. (The town council plans to crack down on street people, so they probably won't be here next year, anyway.)

If you tire of the shopping district and want to wander further afield, you might continue down University Avenue, past the houses with their well-tended lawns and flower beds—usually there are a couple of pickup trucks full of Hispanic gardeners in sight. But don't wander too far. When University crosses Highway 101, it enters the grim environs of East Palo Alto. Though it has progressed in the past few years, as recently as 1992 East Palo Alto was the murder capital of the nation and had an unemployment rate hovering around 40 percent. Luckily, near the boundary, where there is a cluster of liquor stores and check-cashing outlets, you can find two or three police cruisers keeping an eye on the scene—and, not incidentally, serving as a thin blue line protecting the nice neighborhood behind them.

From Paul Krugman, "The Spiral of Inequality," *Mother Jones* (November/December 1996). Copyright © 1996 by The Foundation for National Progress. Reprinted by permission. Notes omitted.

Nor do you want to head down 101 to the south, to "Dilbert Country" with its ranks of low-rise apartments, the tenements of the modern proletariat —the places from which hordes of lower-level white-collar workers drive to sit in their cubicles by day and to which they return to watch their VCRs by night.

No. Better to head up into the hills. The "estates" brochure at Coldwell Banker real estate describes the mid-Peninsula as "an area of intense equestrian character," and when you ascend to Woodside-Atherton, which the *New York Times* has recently called one of "America's born-again Newports," there are indeed plenty of horses, as well as some pretty imposing houses. If you look hard enough, you might catch a glimpse of one of the new $10 million-plus mansions that are going up in growing numbers.

What few people realize is that this vast gap between the affluent few and the bulk of ordinary Americans is a relatively new fixture on our social landscape. People believe these scenes are nothing new, even that it is utopian to imagine it could be otherwise.

But it has not always been thus—at least not to the same extent. I didn't see Palo Alto in 1970, but longtime residents report that it was a mixed town in which not only executives and speculators but schoolteachers, mailmen, and sheet-metal workers could afford to live. At the time, I lived on Long Island, not far from the old *Great Gatsby* area on the North Shore. Few of the great mansions were still private homes then (who could afford the servants?); they had been converted into junior colleges and nursing homes, or deeded to the state as historic monuments. Like Palo Alto, the towns contained a mix of occupations and education levels—no surprise, given that skilled blue-collar workers often made as much as, or more than, white-collar middle managers.

Now, of course, Gatsby is back. New mansions, grander than the old, are rising by the score; keeping servants, it seems, is no longer a problem. A couple of years ago I had dinner with a group of New York investment bankers. After the business was concluded, the talk turned to their weekend homes in the Hamptons. Naively, I asked whether that wasn't a long drive; after a moment of confused silence, the answer came back: "But the helicopter only takes half an hour."

You can confirm what your eyes see, in Palo Alto or in any American community, with dozens of statistics. The most straightforward are those on income shares supplied by the Bureau of the Census, whose statistics are among the most rigorously apolitical. In 1970, according to the bureau, the bottom 20 percent of U.S. families received only 5.4 percent of the income, while the top 5 percent received 15.6 percent. By 1994, the bottom fifth had only 4.2 percent, while the top 5 percent had increased its share to 20.1 percent. That means that in 1994, the average income among the top 5 percent of families was more than 19 times that of the bottom 20 percent of families. In 1970, it had been only about 11.5 times as much. (Incidentally, while the change in distribution is most visible at the top and bottom, families in the middle have also lost: The income share of the middle 20 percent of families has fallen from 17.6 to 15.7 percent.) These are not abstract numbers. They are the statistical signature of a seismic shift in the character of our society.

The American notion of what constitutes the middle class has always been a bit strange, because both people who are quite poor and those who are objectively way up the scale tend to think of themselves as being in the middle. But if calling America a middle-class nation means anything, it means that we are a society in which most people live more or less the same kind of life.

In 1970 we were that kind of society. Today we are not, and we become less like one with each passing year. As politicians compete over who really stands for middle-class values, what the public should be asking them is, *What* middle class? How can we have common "middle-class" values if whole segments of society live in vastly different economic universes?

If this election was really about what the candidates claim, it would be devoted to two questions: Why has America ceased to be a middle-class nation? And, more important, what can be done to make it a middle-class nation again?

The Sources of Inequality

Most economists who study wages and income in the United States agree about the radical increase in inequality—only the hired guns of the right still try to claim it is a statistical illusion. But not all agree about why it has happened.

Imports from low-wage countries—a popular villain—are part of the story, but only a fraction of it. The numbers just aren't big enough. We invest billions in low-wage countries—but we invest trillions at home. What we spend on manufactured goods from the Third World represents just 2 percent of our income. Even if we shut out imports from low-wage countries (cutting off the only source of hope for the people who work in those factories), most estimates suggest it would raise the wages of low-skill workers here by only 1 or 2 percent.

Information technology is a more plausible villain. Technological advance doesn't always favor elite workers, but since 1970 there has been clear evidence of a general "skill bias" toward technological change. Companies began to replace low-skill workers with smaller numbers of high-skills ones, and they continue to do so even though low-skill workers have gotten cheaper and high-skill workers more expensive.

These forces, while easily measurable, don't fully explain the disparity between the haves and the have-nots. Globalization and technology may explain why a college degree makes more difference now than it did 20 years ago. But schoolteachers and corporate CEOs typically have about the same amount of formal education. Why, then, have teachers' salaries remained flat while those of CEOs have increased fivefold? The impact of technology and of foreign trade do not answer why it is harder today for most people to make a living but easier for a few to make a killing. Something else is going on.

Values, Power, and Wages

In 1970 the CEO of a typical Fortune 500 corporation earned about 35 times as much as the average manufacturing employee. It would have been unthinkable to pay him 150 times the average, as is now common, and downright outrageous to do so while announcing mass layoffs and cutting the real earnings of many of the company's workers, especially those who were paid the least to start with. So how did the unthinkable become first thinkable, then doable, and finally—if we believe the CEOs—unavoidable?

The answer is that values changed—not the middle-class values politicians keep talking about, but the kind of values that helped to sustain the middle-class society we have lost.

Twenty-five years ago, prosperous companies could have paid their janitors minimum wage and still could have found people to do the work. They didn't, because it would have been bad for company morale. Then, as now, CEOs were in a position to arrange for very high salaries for themselves, whatever their performance, but corporate boards restrained such excesses, knowing that too great a disparity between the top man and the ordinary worker would cause problems. In short, though America was a society with large disparities between economic classes, it had an egalitarian ethic that limited those disparities. That ethic is gone.

One reason for the change is a sort of herd behavior: When most companies hesitated to pay huge salaries at the top and minimum wage at the bottom, any company that did so would have stood out as an example of greed; when everyone does it, the stigma disappears.

There is also the matter of power. In 1970 a company that appeared too greedy risked real trouble with other powerful forces in society. It would have had problems with its union if it had one, or faced the threat of union organizers if it didn't. And its actions would have created difficulties with the government in a way that is now unthinkable. (Can anyone imagine a current president confronting a major industry over price increases, the way John F. Kennedy did the steel industry?)

Those restraining forces have largely disappeared. The union movement is a shadow of its former self, lucky to hold its ground in a defensive battle now and then. The idea that a company would be punished by the government for paying its CEO too much and its workers too little is laughable today: since the election of Ronald Reagan the CEO would more likely be invited to a White House dinner.

In brief, much of the polarization of American society can be explained in terms of power and politics. But why has the tide run so strongly in favor of the rich that it continues regardless of who is in the White House and who controls the Congress?

The Decline of Labor

The decline of the labor movement in the United States is both a major cause of growing inequality and an illustration of the larger process under way in our society. Unions now represent less than 12 percent of the private workforce, and their power has declined dramatically. In 1970 some 2.5 million workers participated in some form of labor stoppage; in 1993, fewer than 200,000 did. Because unions are rarely able or willing to strike, being a union member no longer carries much of a payoff in higher wages.

There are a number of reasons for the decline of organized labor: the shift from manufacturing to services and from blue-collar to white-collar work, growing international competition, and deregulation. But these factors can't explain the extent or the suddenness of labor's decline.

The best explanation seems to be that the union movement fell below critical mass. Unions are good for unions: In a nation with a powerful labor movement, workers have a sense of solidarity, one union can support another during a strike, and politicians take union interests seriously. America's union movement just got too small, and it imploded.

We should not idealize the unions. When they played a powerful role in America, they often did so to bad effect. Occasionally they were corrupt, often they extracted higher wages at the consumer's expense, sometimes they opposed new technologies and enforced inefficient practices. But unions helped keep us a middle-class society—not only because they forced greater equality within companies, but because they provided a counterweight to the power of wealthy individuals and corporations. The loss of that counterweight is clearly bad for society.

The point is that a major force that kept America a more or less unified society went into a tailspin. Our whole society is now well into a similar downward spiral, in which growing inequality creates the political and economic conditions that lead to even more inequality.

The Polarizing Spiral

Textbook political science predicts that in a two-party democracy like the United States, the parties will compete to serve the interests of the median voter—the voter in the middle, richer than half the voters but poorer than the other half. And since ordinary workers are more likely to lose their jobs than strike it rich, the interests of the median voter should include protecting the poor. You might expect, then, the public to demand that government work against the growing divide by taxing the rich more heavily and by increasing benefits for lower-paid workers and the unemployed.

In fact, we have done just the opposite. Tax rates on the wealthy—even with Clinton's modest increase of 1993—are far lower now than in the 1960s. We have allowed public schools and other services that are crucial for middle-income families to deteriorate. Despite the recent increase, the minimum wage has fallen steadily compared with both average wages and the cost of living. And programs for the poor have been savaged: Even before the recent bipartisan gutting of welfare, AFDC payments for a typical family had fallen by a third in real terms since the 1960s.

The reason why government policy has reinforced rather than opposed this growing inequality is obvious: Well-off people have disproportionate political weight. They are more likely to vote—the median voter has a much higher income than the median family—and far more likely to provide the campaign contributions that are so essential in a TV age.

The political center of gravity in this country is therefore not at the median family, with its annual income of $40,000, but way up the scale. With decreasing voter participation and with the decline both of unions and of traditional political machines, the focus of political attention is further up the income ladder than it has been for generations. So never mind what politicians say; political parties are competing to serve the interests of families near the 90th percentile or higher, families that mostly earn $100,000 or more per year.

Because the poles of our society have become so much more unequal, the interests of this political elite diverge increasingly from those of the typical family. A family at the 95th percentile pays a lot more in taxes than a family at the 50th, but it does not receive a correspondingly higher benefit from public services, such as education. The greater the income gap, the greater the disparity in interests. This translates, because of the clout of the elite, into a constant pressure for lower taxes and reduced public services.

Consider the issue of school vouchers. Many conservatives and even a few liberals are in favor of issuing educational vouchers and allowing parents to choose among competing schools. Let's leave aside the question of what this might do to education and ask what its political implications might be.

Initially, we might imagine, the government would prohibit parents from "topping up" vouchers to buy higher-priced education. But once the program was established, conservatives would insist such a restriction is unfair, maybe even unconstitutional, arguing that parents should have the freedom to spend their money as they wish. Thus, a voucher would become a ticket you could supplement freely. Upper-income families would realize that a reduction in the voucher is to their benefit: They will save more in lowered taxes than they will lose in a decreased education subsidy. So they will press to reduce public spending on education, leading to ever-deteriorating quality for those who cannot afford to spend extra. In the end, the quintessential American tradition of public education for all could collapse.

School vouchers hold another potential that, doubtless, makes them attractive to the conservative elite: They offer a way to break the power of the American union movement in its last remaining stronghold, the public sector. Not by accident did Bob Dole, in his acceptance speech at the Republican National Convention, pause in his evocation of Norman Rockwell values to take a swipe at teachers' unions. The leaders of the radical right want privatization of schools, of public sanitation—of anything else they can think of—because they know such privatization undermines what remaining opposition exists to their program.

If public schools and other services are left to deteriorate, so will the skills and prospects of those who depend on them, reinforcing the growing inequality of incomes and creating an even greater disparity between the interests of the elite and those of the majority.

Does this sound like America in the '90s? Of course it does. And it doesn't take much imagination to envision what our society will be like if this process continues for another 15 or 20 years. We know all about it from TV, movies, and best-selling novels. While politicians speak of recapturing the virtues of small-town America (which never really existed), the public—extrapolating from the trends it already sees—imagines a *Blade Runner*-style dystopia, in which a few people live in luxury while the majority grovel in Third World living standards.

Strategies for the Future

There is no purely economic reason why we cannot reduce inequality in America. If we were willing to spend even a few percent of national income on an enlarged version of the Earned Income Tax Credit, which supplements the earnings of low-wage workers, we could make a dramatic impact on both incomes and job opportunities for the poor and near-poor—bringing a greater number of Americans into the middle class. Nor is the money for such policies lacking: America is by far the least heavily taxed of Western nations and could easily find the resources to pay for a major expansion of programs aimed at limiting inequality.

But of course neither party advanced such proposals during the electoral campaign. The Democrats sounded like Republicans, knowing that in a society with few counterweights to the power of money, any program that even hints at redistribution is political poison. It's no surprise that Bill Clinton's repudiation of his own tax increase took place in front of an audience of wealthy campaign contributors. In this political environment, what politician would talk of taxing the well-off to help the low-wage worker?

And so, while the agenda of the GOP would surely accelerate the polarizing trend, even Democratic programs now amount only to a delaying action. To get back to the kind of society we had, we need to rebuild the institutions and values that made a middle-class nation possible.

The relatively decent society we had a generation ago was largely the creation of a brief, crucial period in American history: the presidency of Franklin Roosevelt, during the New Deal and especially during the war. That created what economic historian Claudia Goldin called the Great Compression—an era in which a powerful government, reinforced by and in turn reinforcing a newly powerful labor movement, drastically narrowed the gap in income levels through taxes, benefits, minimum wages, and collective bargaining. In effect, Roosevelt created a new, middle-class America, which lasted for more than a generation. We have lost that America, and it will take another Roosevelt, and perhaps the moral equivalent of another war, to get it back.

Until then, however, we can try to reverse some of the damage. To do so requires more than just supporting certain causes. It means thinking strategically—asking whether a policy is not only good in itself but how it will affect the political balance in the future. If a policy change promises to raise average income by a tenth of a percentage point, but will widen the wedge between the interests of the elite and those of the rest, it should be opposed. If a law reduces average income a bit but enhances the power of ordinary workers, it should be supported.

In particular, we also need to apply strategic thinking to the union movement. Union leaders and liberal intellectuals often don't like each other very much, and union victories are often of dubious value to the economy. Nonetheless, if you are worried about the cycle of polarization in this country, you should support policies that make unions stronger, and vociferously oppose those that weaken them. There are some stirrings of life in the union movement —a new, younger leadership with its roots in the service sector has replaced the manufacturing-based old guard, and has won a few political victories. They must be supported, almost regardless of the merits of their particular case. Unions are one of the few *political* counterweights to the power of wealth.

Of course, even to talk about such things causes the right to accuse us of fomenting "class warfare." They want us to believe we are all members of a broad, more or less homogeneous, middle class. But the notion of a middle-class nation was always a stretch. Unless we are prepared to fight the trend toward inequality, it will become a grim joke.

Christopher C. DeMuth

 **NO**

The New Wealth of Nations

The Nations of North America, Western Europe, Australia, and Japan are wealthier today than they have ever been, wealthier than any others on the planet, wealthier by far than any societies in human history. Yet their governments appear to be impoverished—saddled with large accumulated debts and facing annual deficits that will grow explosively over the coming decades. As a result, government spending programs, especially the big social-insurance programs like Social Security and Medicare in the United States, are facing drastic cuts in order to avert looming insolvency (and, in France and some other European nations, in order to meet the Maastricht treaty's criteria of fiscal rectitude). American politics has been dominated for several years now by contentious negotiations over deficit reduction between the Clinton administration and the Republican Congress. This past June, first at the European Community summit in Amsterdam and then at the Group of Eight meeting in Denver, most of the talk was of hardship and constraint and the need for governmental austerity ("Economic Unease Looms Over Talks at Denver Summit," read the *New York Times* headline).

These bloodless problems of governmental accounting are said, moreover, to reflect real social ills: growing economic inequality in the United States; high unemployment in Europe; an aging, burdensome, and medically needy population everywhere; and the globalization of commerce, which is destroying jobs and national autonomy and forcing bitter measures to keep up with the bruising demands of international competitiveness.

How can it be that societies so surpassingly wealthy have governments whose core domestic-welfare programs are on the verge of bankruptcy? The answer is as paradoxical as the question. We have become not only the richest but also the freest and most egalitarian societies that have ever existed, and it is our very wealth, freedom, and equality that are causing the welfare state to unravel.

⁕

That we have become very rich is clear enough in the aggregate. That we have become very equal in the enjoyment of our riches is an idea strongly resisted

From Christopher C. DeMuth, "The New Wealth of Nations," *Commentary* (October 1997). Copyright © 1997 by The American Jewish Committee. Reprinted by permission. Notes omitted.

by many. Certainly there has been a profusion of reports in the media and political speeches about increasing income inequality: the rich, it is said, are getting richer, the poor are getting poorer, and the middle and working classes are under the relentless pressure of disappearing jobs in manufacturing and middle management.

Although these claims have been greatly exaggerated, and some have been disproved by events, it is true that, by some measures, there has been a recent increase in income inequality in the United States. But it is a very small tick in the massive and unprecedented leveling of material circumstances that has been proceeding now for almost three centuries and in this century has accelerated dramatically. In fact, the much-noticed increase in measured-income inequality is in part a result of the increase in real social equality. Here are a few pieces of this important but neglected story.

• First, progress in agriculture, construction, manufacturing, and other key sectors of economic production has made the material necessities of life—food, shelter, and clothing—available to essentially everyone. To be sure, many people, including the seriously handicapped and the mentally incompetent, remain dependent on the public purse for their necessities. And many people continue to live in terrible squalor. But the problem of poverty, defined as material scarcity, has been solved. If poverty today remains a serious problem, it is a problem of individual behavior, social organization, and public policy. This was not so 50 years ago, or ever before.

• Second, progress in public health, in nutrition, and in the biological sciences and medical arts has produced dramatic improvements in longevity, health, and physical well-being. Many of these improvements—resulting, for example, from better public sanitation and water supplies, the conquest of dread diseases, and the abundance of nutritious food—have affected entire populations, producing an equalization of real personal welfare more powerful than any government redistribution of income.

The Nobel prize-winning economist Robert Fogel has focused on our improved mastery of the biological environment—leading over the past 300 years to a doubling of the average human life span and to large gains in physical stature, strength, and energy—as the key to what he calls "the egalitarian revolution of the 20th century." He considers this so profound an advance as to constitute a distinct new level of human evolution. Gains in stature, health, and longevity are continuing today and even accelerating. Their outward effects may be observed, in evolutionary fast-forward, in the booming nations of Asia (where, for example, the physical difference between older and younger South Koreans is strikingly evident on the streets of Seoul).

• Third, the critical *source* of social wealth has shifted over the last few hundred years from land (at the end of the 18th century) to physical capital (at the end of the 19th) to, today, human capital—education and cognitive ability. This development is not an unmixed gain from the standpoint of economic equality. The ability to acquire and deploy human capital is a function of intelligence, and intelligence is not only unequally distributed but also, to a significant degree, heritable. As Charles Murray and the late Richard J. Herrnstein argue in *The Bell Curve,* an economy that rewards sheer brainpower replaces one old source of inequality, socioeconomic advantage, with a new one, cognitive advantage.

⋅❦⋅

But an economy that rewards human capital also tears down far more artificial barriers than it erects. For most people who inhabit the vast middle range of the bell curve, intelligence is much more equally distributed than land or physical capital ever was. Most people, that is, possess ample intelligence to pursue all but a handful of specialized callings. If in the past many were held back by lack of education and closed social institutions, the opportunities to use one's human capital have blossomed with the advent of universal education and the erosion of social barriers.

Furthermore, the material benefits of the knowledge-based economy are by no means limited to those whom Murray and Herrnstein call the cognitive elite. Many of the newest industries, from fast food to finance to communications, have succeeded in part by opening up employment opportunities for those of modest ability and training—occupations much less arduous and physically much less risky than those they have replaced. And these new industries have created enormous, widely shared economic benefits in consumption; I will return to this subject below.

• Fourth, recent decades have seen a dramatic reduction in one of the greatest historical sources of inequality: the social and economic inequality of the sexes. Today, younger cohorts of working men and women with comparable education and job tenure earn essentially the same incomes. The popular view would have it that the entry of women into the workforce has been driven by falling male earnings and the need "to make ends meet" in middle-class families. But the popular view is largely mistaken. Among married women (as the economist Chinhui Juhn has demonstrated), it is wives of men with high incomes who have been responsible for most of the recent growth in employment.

• Fifth, in the wealthy Western democracies, material needs and desires have been so thoroughly fulfilled for so many people that, for the first time in history, we are seeing large-scale voluntary reductions in the amount of time spent at paid employment. This development manifests itself in different forms: longer periods of education and training for the young; earlier retirement despite longer life spans; and, in between, many more hours devoted to leisure, recreation, entertainment, family, community and religious activities, charitable and other nonremunerative pursuits, and so forth. The dramatic growth of the sports, entertainment, and travel industries captures only a small slice of what has happened. In Fogel's estimation, the time devoted to nonwork activities by the average male head of household has grown from 10.5 hours per week in 1880 to 40 hours today, while time per week at work has fallen from 61.6 hours to 33.6 hours. Among women, the reduction in work (including not only outside employment but also household work, food preparation, childbearing and attendant health problems, and child rearing) and the growth in nonwork have been still greater.

There is a tendency to overlook these momentous developments because of the often frenetic pace of modern life. But our busy-ness actually demonstrates the point: time, and not material things, has become the scarce and valued commodity in modern society.

⋅⟨◉⟩⋅

One implication of these trends is that in very wealthy societies, income has become a less useful gauge of economic welfare and hence of economic equality. When income becomes to some degree discretionary, and when many peoples' incomes change from year to year for reasons unrelated to their life circumstances, *consumption* becomes a better measure of material welfare. And by this measure, welfare appears much more evenly distributed: people of higher income spend progressively smaller shares on consumption, while in the bottom ranges, annual consumption often exceeds income. (In fact, government statistics suggest that in the bottom 20 percent of the income scale, average annual consumption is about twice annual income—probably a reflection of a substantial underreporting of earnings in this group.) According to the economist Daniel Slesnick, the distribution of consumption, unlike the distribution of reported income, has become measurably *more* equal in recent decades.

If we include leisure-time pursuits as a form of consumption, the distribution of material welfare appears flatter still. Many such activities, being informal by definition, are difficult to track, but Dora Costa of MIT has recently studied one measurable aspect—expenditures on recreation—and found that these have become strikingly more equal as people of lower income have increased the amount of time and money they devote to entertainment, reading, sports, and related enjoyments.

Television, videocassettes, CD's, and home computers have brought musical, theatrical, and other entertainments (both high and low) to everyone, and have enormously narrowed the differences in cultural opportunities between wealthy urban centers and everywhere else. Formerly upper-crust sports like golf, tennis, skiing, and boating have become mass pursuits (boosted by increased public spending on parks and other recreational facilities as well as on environmental quality), and health clubs and full-line book stores have become as plentiful as gas stations. As some of the best things in life become free or nearly so, the price of pursuing them becomes, to that extent, the "opportunity cost" of time itself.

The substitution of leisure activities for income-producing work even appears to have become significant enough to be contributing to the recently much-lamented increase in inequality in measured income. In a new AEI study, Robert Haveman finds that most of the increase in earnings inequality among U.S. males since the mid-1970's can be attributed not to changing labor-market opportunities but to voluntary choice—to the free pursuit of nonwork activities at the expense of income-producing work.

Most of us can see this trend in our own families and communities. A major factor in income inequality in a wealthy knowledge economy is age—many people whose earnings put them at the top of the income curve in their late fifties were well down the curve in their twenties, when they were just get-ting out of school and beginning their working careers. Fogel again: today the average household in the top 10 percent might consist of a professor or accoun-tant married to a nurse or secretary, both in their peak years of earning. As for the stratospheric top 1 percent, it includes not only very rich people like Bill Cosby but also people like Cosby's fictional Huxtable family: an obstetrician married to a corporate lawyer. All these individuals would have appeared well down the income distribution as young singles, and that is where their young counterparts appear today.

That more young people are spending more time in college or graduate school, taking time off for travel and "finding themselves," and pursuing inter-esting but low- or non-paying jobs or apprenticeships before knuckling down to lifelong careers is a significant factor in "income inequality" measured in the aggregate. But this form of economic inequality is in fact the social equality of the modern age. It is progress, not regress, to be cherished and celebrated, not feared and fretted over.

❧❦❧

Which brings me back to my contention that it is our very wealth and equality that are the undoing of the welfare state. Western government today largely consists of two functions. One is income transfers from the wages of those who are working to those who are not working: mainly social-security payments to older people who have chosen to retire rather than go on working and education subsidies for younger people who have chosen to extend their schooling before beginning work. The other is direct and indirect expenditures on medical care, also financed by levies on the wages of those who are working. It is precisely these aspects of life—nonwork and expenditures on medical care and physical well-being—that are the booming sectors of modern, wealthy, technologically advanced society.

When the Social Security program began in America in the 1930's, re-tirement was still a novel idea: most men worked until they dropped, and they dropped much earlier than they do today. Even in the face of our approaching demographic crunch, produced by the baby boom followed by the baby bust, we could solve the financial problems of the Social Security program in a flash by returning to the days when people worked longer and died younger. Similarly, a world without elaborate diagnostic techniques, replaceable body parts, and po-tent pharmaceutical and other means of curing or ameliorating disease—a world where medical care consisted largely of bed rest and hand-holding—would present scant fiscal challenge to government as a provider of health insurance.

Our big government-entitlement programs truly are, as conservatives like to call them, obsolete. They are obsolete not because they were terrible ideas to begin with, though some of them were, but because of the astounding growth in social wealth and equality and because of the technological and economic developments which have propelled that growth. When Social Security was in-troduced, not only was retirement a tiny part of most people's lives but people of modest means had limited ability to save and invest for the future. Today, anyone can mail off a few hundred dollars to a good mutual fund and hire the best investment management American finance has to offer.

In these circumstances it is preposterous to argue, as President Clinton has done, that privatizing Social Security (replacing the current system of income transfers from workers to retirees with one of individually invested retirement savings) would be good for Warren Buffett but bad for the little guy. Private savings—through pension plans, mutual funds, and personal investments in housing and other durables—are *already* a larger source of retirement income than Social Security transfers. Moreover, although there is much talk nowadays about the riskiness of tying retirement income to the performance of financial markets, the social developments I have described suggest that the greater risk lies in the opposite direction. The current Social Security program ties retirement income to the growth of wage earners' payrolls; that growth is bound to be less than the growth of the economy as a whole, as reflected in the financial markets.

Similarly, Medicare is today a backwater of old-fashioned fee-for-service medicine, hopelessly distorted by a profusion of inefficient and self-defeating price-and-service controls. Over the past dozen years, a revolution has been carried out in the private financing and organization of medical care. The changes have not been unmixed blessings; nor could they be, so long as the tax code encourages people to overinsure for routine medical care. Yet substantial improvements in cost control and quality of service are now evident throughout the health-care sector—except under Medicare. These innovations have not been greeted by riots or strikes at the thousands of private organizations that have introduced them. Nor will there be riots in the streets if, in place of the lame-brained proposals for Medicare "spending cuts" and still more ineffective price controls currently in fashion in Washington, similar market-based innovations are introduced to Medicare.

* * *

In sum, George Bush's famous statement in his inaugural address that "we have more will than wallet" was exactly backward. Our wallets are bulging; the problems we face are increasingly problems not of necessity, but of will. The political class in Washington is still marching to the tune of economic redistribution and, to a degree, "class warfare." But Washington is a lagging indicator of social change. In time, the progress of technology and the growth of private markets and private wealth will generate the political will to transform radically the redistributive welfare state we have inherited from an earlier and more socially balkanized age.

There are signs, indeed, that the Progressive-era and New Deal programs of social insurance, economic regulation, and subsidies and protections for farming, banking, labor organization, and other activities are already crumbling, with salutary effects along every point of the economic spectrum. Anyone who has been a business traveler since the late 1970's, for example, has seen firsthand how deregulation has democratized air travel. Low fares and mass marketing have brought such luxuries as foreign travel, weekend getaways to remote locales, and reunions of far-flung families—just twenty years ago, pursuits of the wealthy—to people of relatively modest means. Coming reforms, including the privatization of Social Security and, most of all, the dismantling of the public-school monopoly in elementary and secondary education, will similarly benefit the less well-off disproportionately, providing them with opportunities enjoyed today primarily by those with high incomes.

I venture a prediction: just as airline deregulation was championed by Edward Kennedy and Jimmy Carter before Ronald Reagan finished the job, so the coming reforms will be a bipartisan enterprise. When the political class catches on (as Prime Minister Tony Blair has already done in England), the Left will compete vigorously and often successfully with the Right for the allegiance of the vast new privileged middle class. This may sound implausible at a moment when the Clinton administration has become an energetic agent of traditional unionism and has secured the enactment of several new redistributive tax provisions and spending programs. But the watershed event of the Clinton years will almost certainly be seen to be not any of these things but rather the defeat of the President's national health-insurance plan in the face of widespread popular opposition.

The lesson of that episode is that Americans no longer wish to have the things they care about socialized. What has traditionally attracted voters to government as a provider of insurance and other services is not that government does the job better or more efficiently or at a lower cost than private markets; it is the prospect of securing those services through taxes paid by others. That is why today's advocates of expanding the welfare state are still trying to convince voters to think of themselves as members of distinct groups that are net beneficiaries of government: students, teachers, women, racial minorities, union members, struggling young families, retirees, and so forth. But as the material circumstances of the majority become more equal, and as the proficiency and social reach of private markets increasingly outstrip what government can provide, the possibilities for effective redistribution diminish. The members of an egalitarian, middle-class electorate cannot improve their lot by subsidizing one another, and they know it.

With the prospects dimming for further, broad-based socialization along the lines of the Clinton health-care plan, the private supply of important social services will continue to exist and, in general, to flourish alongside government programs. Defenders of the welfare state will thus likely be reduced to asserting that private markets and personal choice may be fine for the well-off, but government services are more appropriate for those of modest means. This is the essence of President Clinton's objection to privatizing Social Security and of the arguments against school choice for parents of students in public elementary and high schools. But "capitalism for the rich, socialism for the poor" is a highly unpromising banner for liberals to be marching under in an era in which capitalism has itself become a profound egalitarian force.

⋅◈⋅

Where, then, will the battlegrounds be for the political allegiance of the new middle class? Increasingly, that allegiance will turn on policies involving little or no redistributive cachet but rather society-wide benefits in the form of personal amenity, autonomy, and safety: environmental quality and parks, medical and other scientific research, transportation and communications infrastructure, defense against terrorism, and the like. The old welfare-state debates between Left and Right will be transformed into debates over piecemeal incursions into private markets that compete with or replace government services. Should private insurers be required to cover annual mammograms for women in their forties? Should retirement accounts be permitted to invest in tobacco companies? Should parents be permitted to use vouchers to send their children to religious schools? Thus transformed, these debates, too, will tend to turn on considerations of general social advantage rather than on the considerations of social justice and economic desert that animated the growth of the welfare state.

Political allegiance will also turn increasingly on issues that are entirely nonmaterial. I recently bumped into a colleague, a noted political analyst, just after I had read the morning papers, and asked him to confirm my impression that at least half the major political stories of the past few years had something to do with sex. He smiled and replied, "Peace and prosperity."

What my colleague may have had in mind is that grave crises make all other issues secondary: President Roosevelt's private life received less scrutiny than has President Clinton's, and General Eisenhower's private life received less scrutiny than did that of General Ralston (whose nomination to become chairman of the Joint Chiefs of Staff was torpedoed by allegations of an extramarital affair). There is, however, another, deeper truth in his observation. The stupendous wealth, technological mastery, and autonomy of modern life have freed man not just for worthy, admirable, and self-improving pursuits but also for idleness and unworthy and self-destructive pursuits that are no less a part of his nature.

And so we live in an age of astounding rates of divorce and family breakup, of illegitimacy, of single teenage motherhood, of drug use and crime, of violent and degrading popular entertainments, and of the "culture of narcissism" —and also in an age of vibrant religiosity, of elite universities where madrigal singing and ballroom dancing are all the rage and rampant student careerism is a major faculty concern, and of the Promise Keepers, over a million men of all incomes and races who have packed sports stadiums around the United States to declare their determination to be better husbands, fathers, citizens, and Christians. Ours is an age in which obesity has become a serious public-health problem—and in which dieting, fitness, environmentalism, and self-improvement have become major industries.

It is true, of course, that the heartening developments are in part responses to the disheartening ones. But it is also true that *both* are the results of the economic trends I have described here. In a society as rich and therefore as free as ours has become, the big question, in our personal lives and also in our politics, is: what is our freedom for?

POSTSCRIPT

Is Socioeconomic Inequality Increasing in America?

Almost from the day of its publication, *The Bell Curve: Intelligence and Class Structure in American Life* by Richard J. Herrnstein and Charles Murray (Free Press, 1994) became the basic text against equality in America. Murray insists that the book is about intelligence; his critics say that it is about race. It is about both, but above all it is about equality, why it does not exist (people are very unequal intellectually), why it cannot exist (intelligence is largely a product of inheritance), and why we should reconcile ourselves to its absence (because income differences and intermarriage among intelligent people will widen the gap).

The enormous publicity and sales generated by *The Bell Curve* led to the publication of books and essays rejecting its thesis. A large number of critical essays (by biologist Stephen Jay Gould, philosopher Alan Ryan, educator Howard Gardner, psychologist Leon J. Kamin, and others) purporting to refute what the authors call the unwarranted premises, shaky statistics, and pseudoscience of *The Bell Curve* have been gathered together in Russell Jacoby and Naomi Glauberman, eds., *The Bell Curve Debate: History, Documents, Opinions* (Times Books, 1995).

The issue of inherited intelligence and other capacities is not new. It is relevant to any consideration of whether or not America can or should be more egalitarian. What kind of equality—education, right to vote, before the law, economic opportunity, income—and what degree of equality is necessary for democracy to exist and thrive? According to Christopher Lasch, in *The Revolt of the Elites: And the Betrayal of Democracy* (W. W. Norton, 1996), the widening gulf between the haves and the have-nots has led to the creation of professional and managerial elites that abandon the middle class and betray the idea of democracy for all Americans.

Scholarly studies tend to support the conclusion that the distance between the wealthiest Americans and the rest is increasing. Lisa Keister, in *Wealth in America: Trends in Wealth Inequality* (Cambridge University Press, 2000), provides an account of how wealth is acquired (she does not find a high correlation between income and wealth) and how it declines and increases over decades. In *Wealth and Democracy: How Great Fortunes and Government Created America's Aristocracy* (Broadway Books, 2002), Kevin Phillips argues that "laissez-faire is a pretense" because the rich consciously and successfully use government to increase their wealth and political power.

The differences in income, wealth, and social circumstances between whites and blacks are explored in Dalton Conley, *Being Black, Living in the Red:*

Race, Wealth, and Social Policy in America (University of California Press, 1999). Conley concludes that the inheritance of property and net worth results in better schools, preferable residences, higher wages, and more opportunities for whites, further increasing the gap. Conley suggest an affirmative action policy that is based on social class as defined by family wealth levels rather than on race.

U.S. State Department

View this site for understanding into the workings of a major U.S. executive branch department. Links explain exactly what the department does, what services it provides, and what it says about U.S. interests around the world, as well as provide other information.

http://www.state.gov

Marketplace of Political Ideas/University of Houston Libraries

Here is a valuable collection of links to campaign, conservative/liberal perspectives, and political party sites. There are general political sites, Democratic sites, Republican sites, third-party sites, and much more.

http://info.lib.uh.edu/politics/markind.htm

United States Senate Committee on Foreign Relations

This site is an excellent up-to-date resource for information about the United States' reaction to events regarding foreign policy.

http://www.senate.gov/~foreign/

Voice of the Shuttle: Politics and Government

This site, created and maintained by Alan Liu of the University of California, Santa Barbara, offers numerous links to political resources on the Internet. In addition to general political resources, categories include general international politics, political theory and philosophy, and political commentary.

http://vos.ucsb.edu/browse.asp?id=2726

American Diplomacy

American Diplomacy is an online journal of commentary, analysis, and research on U.S. foreign policy and its results around the world.

http://www.unc.edu/depts/diplomat/

Foreign Affairs

This page of the well-respected foreign policy journal *Foreign Affairs* is a valuable research tool. It allows users to search the journal's archives and provides indexed access to the field's leading publications, documents, online resources, and so on. Link to dozens of other related Web sites from here too.

http://www.foreignaffairs.org

PART 4

America and the World

*W*hat is the role of the United States in world affairs? From what premise—realism or idealism—should American foreign policy proceed? What place in the world does America now occupy, and in what direction is it heading? American government does not operate in isolation from the world community, and the issues in this section are crucial ones indeed.

- Does China Threaten World Peace and Security?

- Should America Restrict Immigration?

- Is America's War on Terrorism Justified?

- Is Free Trade Fair Trade?

- Must America Exercise World Leadership?

- Should Terrorist Suspects Be Tried by Military Tribunals?

ISSUE 15

Does China Threaten World Peace and Security?

YES: Lucian W. Pye, from "After the Collapse of Communism: The Challenge of Chinese Nationalism and Pragmatism," in Eberhard Sandschneider, ed., *The Study of Modern China* (St. Martin's Press, 1999)

NO: David M. Lampton, from "Think Again: China," *Foreign Policy* (Spring 1998)

ISSUE SUMMARY

YES: Political science professor Lucian W. Pye warns that China is not to be trusted in its economic and political dealings with the United States and other nations.

NO: Chinese studies professor David M. Lampton maintains that popular assumptions about China's military, political, and economic objectives are wrong and should be corrected.

With over 1 billion people, China is the most populous nation in the world. Ancient China was the most advanced and powerful. By the nineteenth century, however, it was victimized and forced to pay tribute to invading European powers. In the twentieth century it was long governed by a dictatorship that was America's ally in World War II. After the war a communist revolution took place that inaugurated an era of ruthless repression at home and military expansion abroad. Beginning with President Richard Nixon's 1972 visit to the communist leaders in Beijing in 1972, a profound change has taken place, transforming China from a communist nation that was closed off from the industrial world to its fastest-growing economic power.

By 2000 China had become the world's third largest producer of information technology (after the United States and Japan). Almost one-third of all foreign investment in developing countries is in China, accounting for almost half of its exports in 2000. For its part, China does not buy many consumer goods abroad; more than half of its imports are machinery, equipment, and parts for joint-venture factories—in other words, items used to produce goods that can be sold abroad. One consequence of this purchasing pattern is that the U.S. trade debt with China reached an estimated $84.4 billion in 2001. The European Union and Japan, like the United States, have growing deficits in their trade with China, and emerging markets in Asia and Mexico have already suffered declines.

In December 2001, after 15 years of negotiation, China joined the World Trade Organization (WTO). The U.S. trade representative Charlene Barshefsky, who led U.S. negotiations with China, said that China's WTO commitments to reduce import quotas and to allow foreign investments in new economic sectors "will open the world's largest nation to our goods, farm products, and services in a way we have not seen in the modern era." Critics deride this prediction because China has already become the preferred location for American firms that make labor-intensive goods because they find it cheaper to open factories and train workers (who earn as little as 13 cents an hour) in China and then to sell their products in the United States for the same prices as American-manufactured goods.

Presidents Bill Clinton and George W. Bush both favored normalization of trade relations with China, arguing that not only would this contribute to American prosperity but it would also create the economic climate in which political liberty could grow in China. Supporters of this new policy point out that economic growth helped bring democracy to South Korea, Taiwan, and Mexico. The adoption of Permanent Normal Trade Relations (PNTR) has meant that Congress no longer needs to engage in an annual review of whether or not to impose trade sanctions in response to declines in China's human rights record. That power had never been invoked and was unlikely to be used anyway.

Critics of normal Sino-American trade relations argue that China remains the ruthless dictatorship whose tanks and machine guns crushed peaceful pro-democracy demonstrations by students in Beijing's Tiananmen Square in 1989. They also maintain that China's human rights record has worsened. Hundreds of millions of dollars of China's new wealth go to its rulers to finance the imprisonment and murder of democratic activists, minorities (including Buddhists in Tibet, Muslims in Xinjiang, and ethnic minorities in other frontier zones), religious practitioners, and labor organizers. A *Washington Post* editorial called PNTR "a vote for greed in which the nightmare of lost sales mattered more than the crushing of rights and lives in a country far away." On the eve of Secretary of State Colin Powell's visit to Beijing in July 2001, two imprisoned scholars with American ties were convicted of spying and deported, but this had no impact on the thousands of other political prisoners in Chinese jails. Powell was promised an uncensored interview on Beijing television, but his remarks were edited so that references to human rights and the sovereignty of Taiwan were omitted.

In the following selections, Lucian W. Pye is harshly critical of China's political motives and behavior and concludes that it must change in fundamental ways in order to improve relations with America. Believing that our understanding of China has been distorted by popular misconceptions of what China wants and does, David M. Lampton takes up each of the indictments of China and rebuts them.

Lucian W. Pye

After the Collapse of Communism

Bilateral relations between the United States and China are among the most complex and difficult in world politics. It is a relationship stacked with irritants and attractions, clashes but also convergences of interests. Success in managing the relationship is indeed a matter of considerable importance because it is a truism that relations between the one remaining superpower and the largest country in the world will be central for maintaining peace and stability in the Asia-Pacific region. At present, however, Washington and Beijing increasingly confront each other in a state of frustration and barely suppressed aggression, but the craving for better relations is so strong that a single meeting of high officials is enough to raise a chorus of congratulations.

Washington has been torn over what to do about China's pirating of intellectual property rights, its continued flagrant disregard of human rights, its sabre-rattling in the Taiwan Straits, its covert nuclear and missile aid to Pakistan and Iran, and even the smuggling of automatic weapons into America itself. Solutions proposed, such as trade sanctions, would probably hurt American interests more than Chinese, and thus seem foolish, like 'picking up a boulder to drop it on one's own toes'—as the Chinese saying goes. To make matters worse, different agencies of the U.S. government have focused on different issues, and thus there has been little coordination or sense of priorities. Instead of any authoritative guidance for U.S. policy, it is usually the mass media which determine what issues will command attention at any moment. All this means that in Americans' ambivalent love-hate feelings about China, the tilt is ever more towards the latter, to the point that some 65% now have negative views of China.

China, for its part, has been convinced off and on that the United States is a superpower in decline, and thus jealously driven to wanting to 'contain' China, a superpower on the rise. Both reformers and hardliners have been united in the conviction that they must appear firm and bold if they are to make a smooth transition into the post-Deng era. Leading international relations specialists in Beijing were struck with the fact that at the time of the Nixon opening, Washington thought that there was a 'China card' to be played against the Soviet Union. They, of course, knew that China was at the time helpless, indeed truly impotent, because of the chaos of the Cultural Revolution. They

From Lucian W. Pye, "After the Collapse of Communism: The Challenge of Chinese Nationalism and Pragmatism," in Eberhard Sandschneider, ed., *The Study of Modern China* (St. Martin's Press, 1999). Copyright © 1999 by Eberhard Sandschneider. Reprinted by permission of Palgrave, Global Publishing at St. Martin's Press.

could only conclude that the United States must in fact be in serious trouble if it needed China to help balance the Soviet Union. In the years that followed, Chinese analysts have read and believed the literature produced in the United States by the American declinists who argued that America's day was over and that having overreached itself militarily, it was on the downgrade, similar to what happened to Rome and Britain. The Gulf War helped correct this picture of a failed America to some degree, but then the Chinese were quick to pick up on the idea that China is destined in a few years to have the world's largest economy, and thus become truly a world power. Consequently Beijing has become headily self-confident and even boastful—generally ignoring the fact that it has a host of daunting domestic problems. In a spirit of blended glee and indignation, the Chinese rebut every American charge, and point instead to American sins, such as 'dumping its garbage' in China.

In contrast, Washington has remained markedly ambivalent, vacillating between engaging and ignoring China. Its actions have not matched its words, and its words have not reflected careful thought or strong conviction. Statements about China have been made to satisfy various domestic constituencies and have not been backed by actions towards China. Teams of American officials who visit Beijing seem to alternate between beating the drum for greater trade or threatening trade sanctions. In the end though, the one guiding principle seems to be the dream of making money in China's supposedly lucrative market.

The fact that relations with China are troubled should not be surprising, for the relationship has rarely been as close as ritual diplomatic toasts about 'old friendships' would suggest. Except for the brief period of near alliance to fend off the common enemy of Soviet expansionism, there have been just too many fundamental obstacles to make the political relationship as warm as right-thinking people would want it to be. This is particularly disturbing to those Americans who in their private and non-political relations are strongly attracted to the charms they find in Chinese culture and to the outstanding qualities of the wonderful Chinese people. The problems in Sino-American relations are clearly the most acute in the political and diplomatic realms. Even in economics they are not so severe as to prevent American companies from elbowing each other to get advantages [in] trade and investment in China.

It is tempting to suggest that the troubles can be explained by the manifest differences in political culture, history, ideology, and levels of development. Yet, whereas at one time those differences were far greater and therefore misunderstandings more natural, now, despite the economic successes of Deng Xiaoping's reforms which have led to a significant degree of convergence, there have also been greater tensions and frustrations.

One might have hoped that their remarkable accomplishments in economic growth and the manifest improvements in living conditions would have made the Chinese more self-confident and at ease with the outside world, less touchy about slights to their sovereignty or perceived meddling in their internal affairs. However, Chinese successes seem to have only generated greater distrust and frustration. Taking seriously the forecast that in the foreseeable future they will have the world's largest economy, the Chinese feel that they deserve recognition and respect as a superpower-in-waiting. It is not enough that they are already a permanent member of the United Nations Security Council and one of the five nuclear powers, for somehow all their accomplishments of the last two decades have not produced as great a change in their international status as they had expected. Therefore they suspect that there has been a conscious effort to thwart their rise in prestige, and they are sure that the United States must be the black hand behind such a devious plot.

... [T]he central theme of modern Chinese history has been precisely the country's unsuccessful quest for a set of national values and principles which might satisfy the need for a modern national identity. In fact, what led Mao's generation of leaders to go down the dead-end road of Marxism-Leninism was their belief that in that ideology they would find satisfaction for this fundamental need. As a result of that commitment, the Chinese people have been exposed to nearly half a century of unrelenting propaganda attacks against all the ideas, values and symbols associated with China's great historic civilization. Confucianism and Taoism have been steadily denounced as abominable 'feudal remnants' which must be totally purged from the collective memory of the Chinese people. All that was once seen as great in Chinese history has been decried as a part of a curse which had held the Chinese people back in their now all-important race to modernity.

A nationalism without ideals can only generate mindless anti-foreign sentiments....

With Chinese nationalism consisting of little more than ethnicity and xenophobia, the Chinese people tend to vacillate between indiscriminately adoring, indeed almost fawning over, what is foreign, and sudden outbursts of anti-foreign passions. In the main cities there is a frantic striving to be a part of the modern world and to absorb all that foreign popular cultures have to offer. Yet, at the same time, one of the hottest selling books in 1996 was *China Can Say No*, an angry tirade by five journalists who proclaim that the United States is engaged in all manner of devious plots against China, and who in their rage over American complaints about intellectual property rights came up with the bizarre demand that America should be paying 'royalties' for using China's 'great inventions' of paper and gunpowder.[1] ...

The record of Chinese governments, from the warlords right through to the disastrous years of Mao's reign with its Great Leap, which produced the worst famine in all of human history, and the subhuman brutalities of the Cultural Revolution, is unquestionably one of the worst in all history. Therefore it is not surprising that the Chinese must try to blame others in order to put their own failings out of mind. Moreover the current leadership has to block the search for more solid foundations for a modern sense of Chinese nationalism because it cannot afford to allow the Chinese public to reflect on the regime's history of failures. Above all, there cannot be any thought of a 'reversal of the verdict' on Tiananmen, and thus any discussion of a democratic option for China is forbidden....

The same rules of pragmatism which guide their behaviour in their domestic politics will also operate in foreign affairs. This is because the unstructured near-anarchy of post-Cold War international politics resembles to a remarkable degree the world of Chinese Communist factional politics. The Chinese leaders all learned well the Leninist doctrine that the highest right is to support 'truth' with falsehood, and they still cling to that code even as their faith in the ultimate truth of Marxism has come into question. Above all, the Chinese leaders' compelling need to cling to power and to rule without the benefits of a strong set of legitimizing myths, or a believable ideology, will give a strongly opportunistic cast to their behaviour....

This is not the place for a full review of the rules of Chinese pragmatism, but a few of its outstanding features which are most likely to complicate relations between Beijing and Washington need to be noted....

It pays to be firm, even threatening.   The first cardinal rule of Chinese pragmatism is: never hesitate to seek the advantage that can come from causing worry and fear in others. Real authority knows the value of intimidation. The traditional wording of imperial decrees ended with, 'Now read this, and with fear and trembling, obey'. True obedience demands fear. In all hierarchical relationships it is essential to make subordinates worry about being criticized and punished. The vocabulary of punishment should be used freely to remind people that they are in danger if they displease their superiors. One also proves that one is superior by freely using threatening language. Moreover, it can be expected that in bilateral relations the Chinese will routinely dictate the aggressively declare what the other party should and should not do.

Although the Confucian ideal of leadership stressed benevolence, the Chinese leaders today are more inclined to the Leninist principle of treating opponents as enemies. Moreover, they believe that a reputation for intimidation establishes the idea that one is fearless, indeed possibly even reckless, which they believe will make others cautious in any future dealings....

Openly play favourites.   Just as the Chinese father feels no need to treat all his children equally but freely plays favorites, so Chinese officials will openly acknowledge who at any time is the favourite among their subordinates. In international relations the Chinese willingness to reveal which states are rising in their favour and which are losing favour is matched only by their practice of making finely calibrated judgments as to which state's power is on the rise and which is in decline. There has been of course, a long tradition in Chinese state-craft of 'playing off one barbarian against another'....

To make an enemy is also to make new friends.   In the highly fluid political environment that Chinese leaders operate in, there can be much easy talk about 'old friends', but in the actual play of politics the line between friend and enemy is easily crossed. More particularly, leaders do not hesitate in piling demands on friends for they see little risk in turning a friend into an enemy because they believe that with every new enemy there will usually come one or more new friends. In the factional struggles of elite politics there can be quick realignments as a once friendly relationship is broken and everyone involved has to readjust their ties and seek new allies. The Chinese have found that the same rule applies in foreign relations. Conflict with the United States in the 1950s strengthened ties with the Soviet Union; the break with Moscow was quickly followed by the opening to Washington; tensions with Japan help strengthen relations with ASEAN [Association of Southeast Asian Nations]; trade and human rights problems with Washington open the way to better relations with Moscow and Europe, to say nothing of the rest of Asia. Problems with any particular foreign company will only motivate other competing companies to seek favour with China. If there are problems with Jeep there are always the eager Japanese car-makers; difficulties with General Electric can easily lead to better relations with Westinghouse; indeed candidates for joint ventures seem limitless as entrepreneurs from a host of countries seek greedily to profit from China's economic growth. The Chinese also expect that by merely proclaiming a new friendship they can make an old friend jealous and thereby anxious to improve relations with them. Thus, faced with problems with Washington the Chinese have played up symbols of friendship with Moscow.

In both domestic and foreign policy the rule applies that authority should never fear to challenge a friend or ally for not being truly 'faithful' or fully 'reliable'. Suggesting doubt will make the 'friend' work harder to prove the charge false; and if not, there is still psychic satisfaction to be derived from knowing that one's judgment about reliability was right in the first place. Hence, never fear pushing your 'friends' to do more. A good example of this tactic was the way the Chinese treated James McGregor, head of the American Chamber of Commerce in Beijing and the China representative of Dow Jones & Co., who earlier, as a reporter had established a record of faithfully explaining Chinese positions. While in Washington lobbying hard on China's behalf for the continuation of MFN ["Most Favored Nation" status], the Chinese authorities chose that moment to announce tough regulations to exercise control over foreign news services which were particularly damaging to Dow Jones. For Americans the timing of the Chinese action seemed stupid, indeed self-destructive, but according to the Chinese way of thinking the timing was perfect because if Mr. McGregor had slackened in his enthusiasm for selling China on Capitol Hill it would have shown that he was only motivated by material self-interest. So, the Chinese reasoned he would have to carry on his lobbying and try to rationalize what had happened; and they were correct, for this is exactly what happened.

According to this same timing principle, the right moment to arrest a dissident is just before or after a 'friendly' visit by a high US official seeking better relations with China. Just as Secretary of State Warren Christopher was arriving in Beijing to discuss among other things China's human rights record, the Chinese arrested a leading dissident. The Secretary, following the American rule that all trips abroad have to yield 'progress', put the best face he could on his trip, but that was his last visit to China. Within a few years the American press, surreptitiously encouraged by Chinese feeds, began castigating Christopher for visiting Beijing only once while making 24 trips to Damascus to meet with the certifiable tyrant Hafez al-Assad. Score: one up for the Chinese, and a faulted American Secretary of State.

In a similar timing ploy, Beijing arrested Yao Zhenxiang a few days after the U.N. Commission on Human Rights had voted not to criticize China's human rights record. For those who had voted in China's favour to complain would only make them look foolish for having initially supported China. The effect was to consolidate the champions of 'Asian values' and to isolate further the United States and European governments who were said to be trying to 'impose their values on others'....

Symbols are important, but words are cheap and logical consistency is a hobgoblin of the small mind.   In Chinese politics it is often quite enough just to manipulate symbols without necessarily changing substantive reality....

Not infrequently, Chinese officials will promise something with the full expectation that the other party should be satisfied with just the symbolic act of the promise, and not expect the promise to be actually kept....

Also, in contrast to American politicians, who will go to extraordinary lengths to uphold the pretence of consistency and to insist that they have always held to the same opinions, Chinese leaders are quite comfortable with changing their positions. They place little value on consistency because they assume that when circumstances change all intelligent people should adjust their positions. These views also mean that it is possible to have dramatic changes and even total reversals of policies in Chinese politics with little stress or consternation. Political right and wrong can suddenly be turned on their heads and nobody seems surprised. It was the Western world and not the Chinese public that was astonished when Chinese politics changed overnight from the ideological politics of the Mao Zedong era to the pragmatic reforms of Deng Xiaoping. Passionate believers in Communism could in less than a year's time become avid capitalists with no more psychic stress than comes with changing from winter to summer clothes....

Secrecy is invaluable, but discount what is said in private.   Secrecy envelops the entire workings of the Chinese political process, and it is taken for granted that true power always operates behind the scenes and not in public. Aside from a few ritualistic and essentially theatrical appearances, important leaders strive to be invisible....

Above all, the task of framing a successful China-policy requires an American leadership capable of articulating a compelling vision of what America wants in its relations with both China and Asia in general. Then there needs to be continuous high level engagement with China so as to bring China even more into the international system and thereby encourage Beijing to abandon its more troublesome propensities and to adhere more to standard international practices. Engagement, however, means that Washington must recognize the games and ploys that the Chinese are employing and not be either manipulated or unduly irritated by them. It requires that Washington have a clear and consistent view as to exactly what it wants the relationship to be.

If relations are to become smoother and more stable, China, however, will also have to change, but in a much more fundamental way. The imperative need is for the Chinese as a people to finally succeed in their long quest to find a modern national identity so that they can face the world armed with an appropriate version of nationalism and not be consumed just with xenophobic passions. However, until China is politically opened up enough for the Chinese people as a whole to freely participate in a collective process of articulating a more coherent sense of national identity, other countries will have to deal with a prickly Chinese government and a people who can easily swing between xenophilia and xenophobia. As long as the attempt to define a new nationalism is monopolized by China's autocratic leaders, the result will either be a continuation of Leninist stagnation or some version of national socialism or fascism.

Note

1. The Chinese seem impervious to embarrassment about using quirky arguments in support of their national interest. Most recently they have believed that they could advance their claims to disputed islands in the South China Seas by insisting that the wreckage of a Song dynasty ship with its cargo of shattered pottery justifies China's rights of ownership.

NO

David M. Lampton

Think Again: China

China is a giant screen upon which outsiders project their hopes and fears. Expectations of economic gain coexist with worries about financial crisis; shrill alarms about Chinese power with dire forecasts of collapse; visions of democratic change with caricatures of current reality. It is time to step back and look at where China is today, where it might be going, and what consequences that direction will hold for the rest of the world.

China Is a Rogue State With Hegemonic Ambitions

Not true. Strident voices in the West assert that the People's Republic of China (PRC) sees little to be gained from being a good international citizen. This view has three defects: 1) The record of the last two decades does not support it; 2) it is not in Beijing's interest to be perceived and treated as a rogue state; and 3) if other nations begin to regard it in that light, they will help bring about the very Chinese behavior they seek to avert.

Consider China's actions as a permanent member of the UN Security Council. Surely, "the next 'rogue' superpower"—to quote one recent characterization of China in the U.S. press—would not have hesitated to throw its weight around over the years. Yet, since 1972, while China has abstained on some Security Council resolutions, it has cast only two vetoes in open session. Although deeply apprehensive of resolutions condoning sanctions or interventions, the PRC has not sought to stop UN missions in the former Yugoslavia, Haiti, Somalia, or Iraq during the Gulf War and thereafter. As Foreign Minister Qian Qichen said in late 1997 about Beijing's position on sanctions against Iraq: "Despite the fact that we have not supported these [UN] resolutions, they must be respected."

This generally constructive stance extends to the growing number of international organizations that China has joined since former leader Deng Xiaoping's opening to the outside world almost two decades ago. In 1977, China belonged to 21 international governmental organizations and 71 international nongovernmental organizations. By 1994, the respective numbers were

From David M. Lampton, "Think Again: China," *Foreign Policy* (Spring 1998). Copyright © 1998 by The Carnegie Endowment for International Peace. Reprinted in entirety by permission of *Foreign Policy*.

50 and 955. In institutions such as the Asian Development Bank, the International Monetary Fund (IMF), and the World Bank, China has been a model citizen. Beijing has also acted responsibly in Asia's recent economic crisis, contributing U.S.$1 billion to the IMF stabilization package for Thailand, clearly conveying its intention to defend the Hong Kong dollar, and (so far) resisting the temptation to devalue its own currency.

Closer to home, the record is mixed. But Beijing's missile exercises in the Taiwan Strait in 1995–96 and its occupation of several reefs in the Spratly Islands must be set next to its concerted and successful efforts during the last decade to improve relations with every country in the neighborhood. In Cambodia, China played an essential role in the settlement leading to UN-sponsored elections. Looking north and west, the PRC has resolved disputes with Kazakstan, Kyrgyzstan, Russia, and Tadjikistan through negotiated agreement. To the south, Beijing has improved relations with Hanoi and New Delhi and joined the Association of South East Asian Nations' regional forum on security.

Beijing's adherence to various international institutions, treaties, and regimes has been best where it has been engaged in writing the rules it is asked to observe and where the international community has made available tangible resources to assist implementation. Indeed, for all the controversy surrounding China's behavior in the field of nonproliferation, it has generally complied with the international nonproliferation regimes to which it has been a full party, including the Treaty on the Non-Proliferation of Nuclear Weapons, the Comprehensive Test Ban Treaty, and the Chemical Weapons Convention. China's relations with Pakistan and Iran have been worrisome. Nonetheless, Beijing addressed these issues during President Jiang Zemin's October 1997 state visit to the United States and reassured the Clinton administration in writing about China's future nuclear cooperation with Iran.

Beijing's compliance has been less praiseworthy in areas where it has not been a member of the rule-writing club, where compliance would conflict with its perceived strategic interests, or where it lacks the necessary resources and enforcement mechanisms. In the case of some missile-related and nuclear technology transfers to Pakistan—long a Chinese strategic ally—Beijing has sought to use its compliance with agreements, or lack thereof, as leverage to obtain stricter adherence in Washington to the Joint Communiqué on Weapons Sales to Taiwan of 1982. Then again, the transfer of ring magnets to Pakistan probably owes less to government directives than to Beijing's inability to exercise effective supervision and control over industries and companies—a problem that bedevils the United States, Great Britain, and other countries with a strong stake in nonproliferation.

China Is Undertaking a Huge Military Buildup

Wrong. There is little uncertainty about China's modest military capabilities, much speculation about what those capabilities may be 20 years hence, and considerable debate about current and future Chinese intentions.

China's defense budget presents a daunting challenge for analysts, not least because much military spending occurs outside the regular defense budget. Those who wish to point to a Chinese threat often use figures from China's defense budget that show a dramatic rise in official spending from 1988 to 1996. However, a 1997 RAND study of China's official defense budget, which adjusts these figures for inflation, suggests that the increase in official defense spending is much less significant.

The Institute for International Strategic Studies and the Stockholm International Peace Research Institute assert that total spending by the People's Liberation Army (PLA) is four to five times the amount officially reported (which Chinese military officers hotly dispute). If true, this would put actual 1996 PLA spending at U.S.$35.5 to 44.4 billion. The Heritage Foundation puts the upper range estimate at U.S.$40 billion. Japan, in 1996, with the American nuclear umbrella and the U.S.-Japan Security Treaty, spent about U.S.$45 billion. China has a long coastline, land borders with 14 states, many of which have presented, and might again present, security problems, and no protective alliance; the PLA also has domestic control responsibilities (as we saw tragically in 1989). And not only do many of China's neighbors have more modern weapons, but as a report recently issued by the Pacific Council on International Policy and RAND noted, "China's military expenditures as a percentage of total defense expenditures by all Asian countries have been decreasing steadily since the mid-1970s."

What about China's development and purchase of advanced technologies? A 1996 report by the U.S. Department of Defense covering 17 families of technologies with military applications shows that, with a few important exceptions (nuclear and chemical technologies among them), China lagged well behind first- and second-tier countries such as France, Israel, Japan, Russia, the United Kingdom, and the United States. True, current estimates of Chinese purchases of advanced technology from Russia during 1990–96 ranged from U.S.$1 to 2 billion annually. By way of comparison, however, the U.S. military spent U.S.$11.99 billion with one American prime defense contractor, Lockheed Martin, in FY 1996 alone.

While it would be foolish to dismiss China's increasing ability to project force beyond its borders and to affect U.S. and other interests, it would be even more foolish to allow exaggerated perceptions of Chinese strength to shape U.S. policy—a development that would stoke nationalist resentment in Beijing and likely fuel support for the very buildup that some U.S. commentators regularly decry.

A Peaceful Resolution of Taiwan's Status Is Only a Matter of Time

Maybe not. The conventional wisdom is that the Taiwan Strait missile crisis from mid-1995 to March 1996 had a sobering effect on Beijing, Taipei, and Washington. In Beijing, there had been those who thought that Washington

Figure 1

China's Defense Budget in Billions of Renminbi (RMB), Official Figures, and Official Figures Adjusted for Inflation

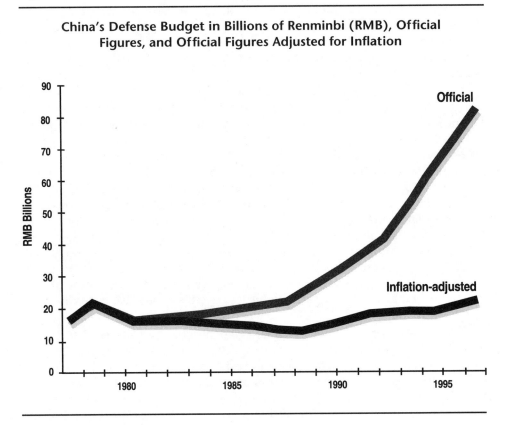

Source: James Mulvenon, the Rand Corporation.

lacked the will to uphold its commitment to a "peaceful resolution" of the Taiwan issue and to stability in East Asia. The March 1996 dispatch of two aircraft carrier groups was a credible assertion of American interest. In Taipei, President Lee Teng-hui and others seemed to have concluded that Beijing could not, or would not, do much about Taiwan's search for a more dignified international role. Beijing's missiles and the resultant dislocations of markets and capital flight were an abrupt comeuppance. And after the PRC missile exercises (particularly those in the spring of 1996), many in the U.S. Congress professed a new appreciation for Beijing's sensitivity to the Taiwan issue. In short, there is now a happy assumption that everyone has become more cautious. One can hope so, but there are other forces at work.

First, something fundamental drives Taipei's search for a greater role in the international community—a changing sense of identity among its population. In recent years, there has been a progressive decline in the percentage of people on Taiwan who consider themselves "Chinese" and a corresponding rise in the percentage identifying themselves as "Taiwanese." Taiwan's ever

Figure 2

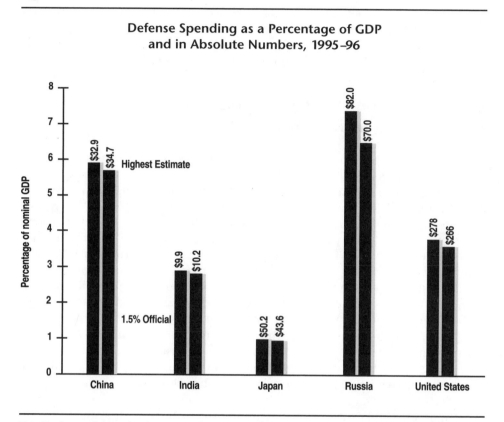

**Defense Spending as a Percentage of GDP
and in Absolute Numbers, 1995–96**

Note: The figures above each column report defense expenditures, according to NATO definitions and are converted to billions of U.S. dollars.

Source: The Military Balance: 1997/98 (London: International Institute for Strategic Studies, 1997).

more competitive political system has given voice to this new, distinct identity. In the Taiwan presidential election of the year 2000, a president may well be elected from the Democratic Progressive Party (DPP), which historically has stood for the island's independence.

Beijing has said it will employ force to prevent independence or outside intervention. How Beijing would actually react to the DPP's assumption of power, how the DPP would lead Taiwan, and how the Taiwanese will respond in an indefinite future are all imponderables. And yet, the answers to these questions will influence whether peace and stability can be maintained in the Taiwan Strait in the years ahead.

There is another part to the equation: How long will Beijing remain "patient?" As Beijing's attention shifts from the return of Hong Kong and Macao (in 1999), it will focus increasingly on "reunification with Taiwan." Not only do PRO leaders worry about trends on Taiwan, they believe that, were the island to achieve de jure independence, their own right to role would be forfeited. Moreover, they fear that areas from Mongolia to Xinjiang to Tibet would use Taiwan's moves to justify their own efforts to break away. Beijing sees everything at stake in the Taiwan issue and is unsure that time works in its favor, despite the ties that about U.S.$35 billion in investment by Taiwan on the mainland create.

In short, continued stability depends on restraint by Beijing, Taipei, and Washington, none of which has an unblemished record of self-control.

China Will Be the Next Asian Economic Domino to Fall

Not necessarily.   The financial crash in Northeast and Southeast Asia since mid-1997 is already taking a toll on the PRC. China now faces the prospects of declining regional demand for its exports and stiffening competition from regional economies in other export markets. Its still robust 1997 GDP growth of 8.8 percent was below earlier government forecasts, there are signs that growth will slow further (perhaps to 6 percent), and some Chinese and foreign analysts believe that the PRC may devalue its currency to maintain its export competitiveness. Beijing asserts that it will vigorously resist such a move. Yet, if unemployment rises, growth slows, and domestic exporters apply political pressure, policy could change. Declining asset values in East and Southeast Asia will probably also reduce capital flow to China from the region.

Many of the considerations that have undermined confidence in other Asian financial systems apply to China: a lack of transparency; financial cronyism; banks with huge portfolios of nonperforming loans; poor regulatory systems; property bubbles; heavy borrowing abroad; and new, volatile equity markets.

And yet, China's economy has important differences that may provide a breathing spell. In a forthcoming book, economist Nicholas Lardy lays them out clearly: 1) China's currency is not freely convertible, thereby reducing speculative pressures; 2) Beijing reports hard currency reserves of about U.S.$140 billion, not including the separate resources of Hong Kong; 3) a large proportion of foreign investment in China has come in the form of direct investment in factories and other assets, not hot money put into more volatile stock markets; 4) although Chinese entities have large foreign debts, most are long-term, unlike elsewhere in Asia; and 5) although foreign direct investment has been important for growth over the last 15 years, the high domestic savings rate has been the principal fuel—growth can continue if savings can be more productively utilized.

The key to avoiding a meltdown will be whether Beijing moves to accelerate reform of the banking and state enterprise sectors—an apparent commitment of the current leadership. But deciding and doing are two different things: Will Beijing recapitalize its banks and operate them on sound financial principles? Simply training the personnel to accomplish this is a gargantuan task. And will China tackle the problem of state enterprises (at least 40 percent of which lose money), whose bad debts to the banks are a principal cause of the financial system's current woes? The restructuring of state enterprises and the bankruptcy

Figure 3

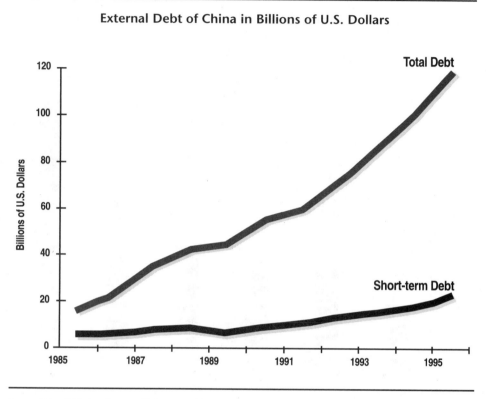

External Debt of China in Billions of U.S. Dollars

Source: *China 2020: Development Challenges in the New Century* (Washington, DC: World Bank, 1997).

of many others could put millions more workers onto the streets, just as growth slows. Can China meet these challenges and avoid serious political dislocation? Nobody can be sure.

China's Large, Fast-Growing Exports Come Principally at the Expense of Jobs in the West

Wrong. Chinese exports to the United States and Europe have grown rapidly and often dominate in labor-intensive sectors such as toys, footwear, apparel, and textiles. But PRC exports in these areas generally surged after domestic jobs in these industries had already migrated to Indonesia, South Korea, and Taiwan, and elsewhere in East Asia and Latin America. In garment manufacturing, for example, World Bank data suggests that, especially for the European Union, employment had already fallen sharply before Chinese exports achieved even the relatively low penetration rate of 2 percent. And economist Marcus Noland

Figure 4

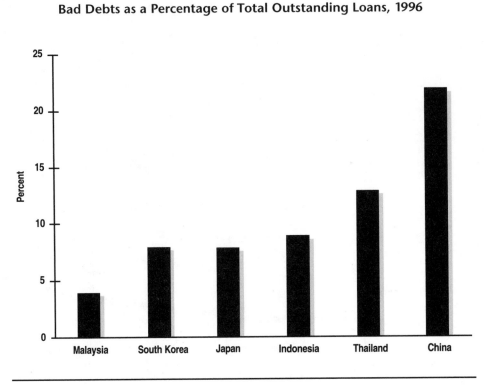

Bad Debts as a Percentage of Total Outstanding Loans, 1996

Source: Nicholas Lardy, the Brookings Institution. Calculations were made in billions of U.S. dollars.

calculated that from 1988 to 1994, almost 90 percent of the increase in the Chinese share of U.S. consumption had merely displaced imports from other countries. The real fear of Chinese export competition ought to be found in low-cost producing economies, not Main Street, U.S.A. or Europe.

China Has Been a Bust for U.S. Firms

Not really. According to U.S. Commerce Department figures for 1990–96, China was the fastest-growing major U.S. export market. During that period, American exports grew at a compound rate of more than 19 percent, if one includes U.S. exports initially exported to Hong Kong but then reexported to China. The PRC is now America's ninth largest export market. By way of comparison, U.S. exports to Japan grew at 6 percent, and those to Brazil by 15 percent, annually. American-invested joint ventures and wholly owned U.S. subsidiaries in China also increasingly sell goods there; although some of the profit is repatriated to the United States, much is reinvested in China, where it can generate future returns.

However, it is also true that the United States has a mounting trade deficit with China—U.S. government estimates peg it at about U.S.$50 billion for 1997 —a figure that many economists believe overstates the problem. The reality of these rising exports to China and the simultaneously mounting trade deficit suggest that Washington—quite appropriately—is proceeding to secure more market access.

Those who assert that the Chinese market has been a bust have a deeper, more erroneous point. Their implicit assumption is that the United States and other industrialized economies do not have a lot riding on economic relations with China. Wrong. Everyone has a great deal at stake in whether or not China can sustain (and how it sustains) growth as other economies deflate.

China Is the World's Biggest Intellectual Thief

Wrong, for now.   Stealing copyrighted music, software, and movies—the "piracy" of intellectual property rights (IPR)—is a serious and legitimate concern. One 1996 study estimated that "of the 523 million new business software applications used globally during 1996, 225 million units—nearly one in every two— were pirated." China does its share of wrongdoing in this regard. But the sorry fact is that developed nations and Americans themselves inflict the biggest dollar losses on U.S. industry, though the highest piracy rates (the percentage of protected items in use that have been illegally appropriated) are to be found in low-income economies with weak to nonexistent legal structures.

Looking at dollar losses through software piracy in 1996 (and the industry's methodology is subject to criticism for inflating losses), Eastern Europe, Japan, Western Europe, and the United States itself all inflicted greater losses on U.S. industry than China (with 22 percent of the world's population). However, if one looks at the "piracy rate" in 1996, China was surpassed only by Vietnam and Indonesia. Russia and the rest of the Commonwealth of Independent States were close behind.

In short, owners of intellectual property confront a global circumstance in which losses to developed countries (with high rates of personal computer ownership) exceed losses to poorer countries (with fewer PCs, weaker legal and regulatory structures, and more extensive official corruption).

The music recording industry faces similar problems. The Recording Industry Association of America reported in 1996 that lost revenue through CD piracy in Japan came to U.S.$500 million annually—"more than the U.S.$300 million the American record industry says it is losing annually from the far more well-known piracy in China."

China is trying to build an IPR enforcement regime. In addition to constructing a (yet imperfect) framework of domestic law in the late 1980s and 1990s, Beijing signed two agreements with Washington (in 1992 and 1995) and from May 1996 to March 1997 closed 37 factories illegally copying CDs—58 CD and CD-ROM production lines by January 1998. As China develops its own innovators and artists with commercially salable products, demands for stricter IPR protection will grow.

China Is a Totalitarian State

Simplistic. To reject this characterization is not to assert that the PRC is a democracy—it is not. But words should have meaning. Totalitarian refers to a state that has the intention and capability to control nearly all aspects of human behavior, thought, and communication. Totalitarian described the ambitions and, to a considerable extent, the system during much of Mao Zedong's reign, when a trip to Albania was considered broadening and children were expected to inform on parents.

Ironically, many of China's domestic problems and irresponsible behavior abroad—from piracy to proliferation—stem from a lack of central control. Most significantly, between 30 and 200 million people slosh around China in search of temporary employment, encamping in and around cities and creating a potentially volatile pool of poor and discontented citizens.

In fact, for all its imperfections and injustices, China today is freer than it has been at any time in the last five decades. About 40,000 Chinese students are now enrolled in tertiary U.S. educational institutions; during the Soviet Union's entire 70-year history, it never sent that many students to the United States. In 1965, there were 12 television and 93 radio stations in China; today, PLA receiving dishes are sold illegally to citizens who pull in satellite TV. The Internet is growing by leaps and bounds. Newspapers and magazines have become not just more numerous but far more diverse and autonomous. In 1978, the state controlled more than 90 percent of GNP; in 1996, that number was about 45 percent and falling. The state now employs only 18 percent of the work force, compared with more than 90 percent in 1978 (including peasants in communes at that time). In September 1997, at the Fifteenth Party Congress, the concept of "public" ownership was morphed from Marx's concept into "public" in the sense of "initial public offering" of stock. While under Mao the concept of the individual suing the state for damages was inconceivable, it now happens increasingly often.

China Is Wrecking Hong Kong

No. The broadcast networks that spent large sums covering the July 1, 1997, handover to the PRC left disappointed, not at the absence of disaster but at the absence of a "story." The days since then have been notable for both what Beijing has and has not done.

Beijing has not militarized the city, as some feared. There are fewer army troops there under Chinese rule than there were generally in Hong Kong under British governors—reinforcements are, of course, only a few miles away in China proper. Beijing has not stopped political demonstrations, which have continued on an almost daily basis since the night of June 30–July 1, 1997, when Martin Lee, the leader of democratic forces in Hong Kong, spoke to a crowd from the balcony of the Legislative Council. Although it is hard to measure press self-censorship—and there is some, as evidenced by the reluctance of Hong Kong Chinese to show three controversial movies dealing with sensitive subjects—Hong Kong still has one of the most freewheeling journalism communities in Asia. In terms of governance, it appears that the new chief executive, C.H. Tung, has great latitude in leading Hong Kong.

U.S. naval ships have been permitted to continue to make port calls—as of January 1998, 34 naval vessels, including two aircraft carrier battle groups and two nuclear submarines. When equity and property markets throughout the region, including Hong Kong, precipitously declined in the latter half of 1997 and early 1998, Beijing let markets work (even though many PRC interests lost heavily). Chinese leaders also quietly let it be known that China's large hard-currency reserves could be brought to the defense of the Hong Kong–U.S. dollar peg.

Less reassuring has been Beijing's determination, expressed well before the takeover, to reverse British governor Christopher Patten's October 1992 speedup in the agreed-upon process of broadening the popular franchise. Instead, immediately after the handover, a provisional legislative council was installed to sit during the interim period before new elections. The elections that Tung has announced for May 1998 will be widely criticized for narrowing functional constituencies and employing proportional representation in ways that can be expected to weaken the power of Martin Lee's Democratic Party.

On balance, however, Beijing has played a responsible role. This pattern of PRC behavior probably will persist, depending on the fate of China's own reforms, regional economic stability, and whether Hong Kong's own people stay out of the business of promoting political change in the PRC.

China Is an Effective, Major Player in the Washington Lobbying Game

Wrong. No misconception is further from reality. Until May 1995, when Lee Teng-hui was given a visa to visit Cornell University as a result of congressional pressure (by a House vote of 396–0), Beijing paid little heed to Capitol Hill. PRC leaders rested secure in the mistaken belief that when U.S. presidents wish to prevail over Congress, they do.

This inattention to Congress is reflected in a number of ways. Beijing has one law firm under retention in Washington—Taipei is reported to have 14. The PRC has (off and on) one public relations firm in the United States— Taipei has many. Even if one adds to the PRC's legal lobbying expenditures the alleged U.S.$100,000 in illegal campaign contributions that the FBI says may have occurred (although the Thompson committee failed to demonstrate this), China does not rank even among the top 10 nations (or territories) in terms of lobbying efforts. Even Haiti (no. 7) and Angola (no. 9) outspend Beijing!

The PRC recently augmented efforts to bring members of the U.S. Congress to China. Beijing knows that there has been high congressional turnover since 1992, that most members have not traveled much, and that seeing China's dynamism leaves few views unchanged. But the PRC efforts lag well behind Taipei's. In 1996, members of Congress took 58 all-expense paid trips to China—still a distant second to the 139 trips they took to Taiwan. When the numbers for 1997 are in, Beijing probably will be seen to have narrowed the gap considerably.

POSTSCRIPT

Does China Threaten World Peace and Security?

$\mathbf{C}$an China reconcile communism and capitalism? How will it be changed by the movement toward the production of more goods for export and the investment of foreign capital? Will the dictatorship be moved to release its control over the lives of its people? Will China's increasing involvement in the marketplace of goods make the Chinese government and people more receptive to the marketplace of ideas?

All these questions imply that, for better or worse, China will likely play an increasingly important role in world affairs. Yet there is the possibility that hopes and fears of China's rise to international influence are premature. Industrialization in China has increased the misery of millions of poor people. Unemployment is high, and the gap between the new rich and the poor has been increasing. Many natural resources are lacking, and the cities are overcrowded and polluted. Despite these obstacles, most students of China believe that China must be seriously reckoned with as a nation, economy, and ideology because of its emergence into the modern economy, its desire to play a role in world affairs, its aggressiveness in dealing with neighbors, and the raw determination of its people.

David Zweig, who teaches at the Hong Kong University of Science and Technology, contends that advocates of economic liberalization mistakenly believe that this must inevitably lead to political democratization. In "Undemocratic Capitalism: China and the Limits of Economism," *The National Interest* (Summer 1999), Zweig favors cautious American engagement while the United States observes whether or not China moves in another direction.

China today may not be a first-rate military power, but Aaron L. Friedberg, in "Arming China Against Ourselves," *Commentary* (July–August 1999), argues that China continues to increase its armed forces and has shown great interest in American thermonuclear devices (and may have employed spies to acquire their designs). Given China's threats to Taiwan, says Friedberg, the risk of military action involving the United States cannot be discounted, if the United States is true to its pledge to protect Taiwan's independence.

A standard short history of American-Chinese relations can be found in the fourth edition of Warren I. Cohen, *America's Response to China: A History of Sino-American Relations* (Columbia University Press, 2000). Nicholas R. Lardy, *Integrating China Into the Global Economy* (Brookings Institution Press, 2002) offers a comprehensive examination of alternative prospects regarding China's relationship with the rest of the world.

ISSUE 16

Should America Restrict Immigration?

YES: Patrick J. Buchanan, from *The Death of the West: How Dying Populations and Immigrant Invasions Imperil Our Country and Civilization* (Thomas Dunne Books, 2002)

NO: Daniel T. Griswold, from "Immigrants Have Enriched American Culture and Enhanced Our Influence in the World," *Insight on the News* (March 11, 2002)

ISSUE SUMMARY

YES: Political commentator Patrick J. Buchanan argues that large-scale, uncontrolled immigration has increased America's social and economic problems and deprived it of the shared values and common language that define a united people.

NO: Daniel T. Griswold, associate director of the Cato Institute's Center for Trade Policy Studies, while acknowledging the need to protect the United States against terrorists, contends that immigration gives America an economic edge, does not drain government finances, and is not remarkably high compared with past eras.

In 1949 a delegation of Native Americans went to Washington to tell lawmakers about the plight of America's original occupants. After meeting with Vice President Alben Barkley, one old Sioux chief delivered a parting word to the vice president. "Young fellow," he said, "let me give you a little advice. Be careful with your immigration laws. We were careless with ours."

As America prospered and offered the hope of opportunity and freedom, increasing numbers of immigrants came to the United States. In the last two decades of the nineteenth century, Congress barred further immigration by convicts, paupers, idiots, and Chinese. That, however, did not stem the tide.

Between 1870 and 1920, more than 26 million people came to live in the United States. The National Origins Act was adopted in 1924 to restrict the number of new immigrants, ban east Asian immigration, and establish a European quota based on the population of the United States in 1890, when there had been far fewer new arrivals from eastern and southern Europe. In 1965 the national origins formula was abandoned, but strict limits on the number of immigrants were retained. The end of quotas spurred a dramatic increase of immigrants from Central and South America and Asia. Between 1965 and 1995, nearly one-half of all immigrants came from Mexico, the Caribbean, and the rest of Latin America, and nearly one-third arrived from Asia.

The number of illegal arrivals from Latin America prompted passage of the Immigration Reform and Control Act of 1987, requiring that employers confirm the legal status of their employees. At the same time, undocumented workers who had entered the United States before 1982 were granted amnesty.

Why do so many people want to come to the United States? They come to flee tyranny and terrorism, to escape the ravages of war, and to join relatives already here. Above all, they come because America offers economic opportunity, in stark contrast to the poverty they endure in their native countries.

Do immigrants endanger or improve the American standard of living? Critics fear that the new immigrants, who are generally willing to work longer hours at lower pay, will take jobs away from American workers. Supporters of immigration believe that the new immigrants fill jobs that most Americans do not want and that they stimulate economic growth.

Do immigrants undermine or enrich American culture? New immigrant groups have enriched the culture with new ideas, new customs, and new artistic expression, but critics argue that the cultural coherence and political unity of the United States are now being threatened. They maintain that the new immigrants are less educated, more isolated, less motivated to join the mainstream, and more likely to become an economic burden to society.

Two-thirds of America's population growth in the 1990s was due to immigration, and two-thirds of those immigrants were Hispanic. Hispanics, defined as both whites and blacks who identify themselves as being of Hispanic origin, are now as numerous in the United States as blacks. Based on present population trends, it is estimated that by 2050, Hispanics will constitute 25 percent of the American population; blacks, 13 percent; Asians, 8 percent; American Indians, less than 1 percent; and whites, slightly more than 50 percent.

Earlier immigrants who came to America speaking a variety of languages quickly assimilated, learned English, and adopted American cultural patterns. Conversely, it is likely that modern Spanish-speaking immigrants, particularly illegal immigrants, find it easier to live within a closed culture that largely excludes adoption of the morals, manners, and language of the larger society. The effects of this change in population and culture can be seen most dramatically in California, the nation's most populous state, which has the greatest influx of illegal immigrants. For example, California's effort to deny welfare and public education to the children of illegal immigrants has been opposed in the courts. Some people have argued that children born to illegal immigrants in the United States should be denied citizenship. Others have sought better border defenses between the United States and Mexico to curb illegal entry in the first place.

Many of the criticisms of the new immigration are voiced in the following selection by Patrick J. Buchanan, who sees a decline in American traditions and values as a result of immigration. In the second selection, Daniel T. Griswold rejects criticisms of immigration as unfounded, citing the economic and cultural contributions that immigrants make to American society.

Patrick J. Buchanan  **YES**

La Reconquista

Our old image is of Mexican folks as docile, conservative, friendly, Catholic people of traditional beliefs and values. There are still millions of these hard-working, family-oriented, patriotic Americans of Mexican heritage, who have been among the first to answer America's call to arms. And any man, woman, or child, from any country or continent, can be a good American. We know that from our history.

But the demographic sea change, especially in California, where a fourth of the people are foreign-born and almost a third are Latino, has spawned a new ethnic chauvinism. When the U.S. soccer team played Mexico in the Los Angeles Coliseum a few years back, the "Star-Spangled Banner" was hooted and jeered, an American flag was torn down, and the American team and its few fans were showered with water bombs, beer bottles, and garbage.

Two years ago, the south Texas town of El Cenizo declared Spanish its official language and ordered that all official documents be written in Spanish and all town business conducted in Spanish. Any cooperation with U.S. immigration authorities was made a firing offense. El Cenizo has, de facto, seceded from the United States.

In the New Mexico legislature in 2001, a resolution was introduced to rename the state "Nuevo Mexico," the name it carried before it became a part of the American Union. When the bill was defeated, the sponsor, Rep. Miguel Garcia, suggested to reporters that "covert racism" may have been the cause—the same racism, he said, that was behind naming the state New Mexico in the first place.

A spirit of separatism, nationalism, and irredentism has come alive in the barrio. The Latino student organization MEChA [Movement Estudiantil Chicano de Aztlan] demands return of the Southwest to Mexico. Charles Truxillo, a professor of Chicano Studies at the University of New Mexico, says a new "Aztlan" [the mythical place of origin of the Aztec peoples] with its capital in Los Angeles is inevitable, and Mexicans should seek it by any means necessary.

"We're recolonizing America, so they're afraid of us. It's time to take back what is ours," rants Ricky Sierra of the Chicano National Guard. One demonstration leader in Westwood exulted, "We are here ... to show white Protestant Los Angeles that we're the majority ... and we claim this land as ours. It's always

From Patrick J. Buchanan, *The Death of the West: How Dying Populations and Immigrant Invasions Imperil Our Country and Civilization* (Thomas Dunne Books, 2002). Copyright © 2002 by Patrick J. Buchanan. Reprinted by permission of St. Martin's Press, LLC. Notes omitted.

been ours and we're still here . . . if anybody is going to be deported it's going to be you."

José Angel Gutierrez, a political science professor at the University of Texas at Arlington and director of the UTA Mexican-American Study Center, told a university crowd: "We have an aging white America. They are not making babies. They are dying. The explosion is in our population. They are shitting in their pants in fear! I love it."

Now, this may be Corona talk in the cantina, but more authoritative voices are sounding the same notes, and they resonate in the barrio. The Mexican consul general José Pescador Osuna remarked in 1998, "Even though I am saying this part serious, part joking, I think we are practicing La Reconquista in California." California legislator Art Torres called Proposition 187, to cut off welfare to illegal aliens, "the last gasp of white America."

"California is going to be a Mexican State. We are going to control all the institutions. If people don't like it, they should leave," exults Mario Obledo, president of the League of United Latin American Citizens and recipient of the Medal of Freedom from President Clinton. Mexican president Ernesto Zedillo told Mexican-Americans in Dallas: "You are Mexicans, Mexicans who live north of the border."

Why should Mexican immigrants not have greater loyalty to their homeland than to a country they broke into simply to find work? Why should nationalistic and patriotic Mexicans not dream of *reconquista?* . . .

⋅◦❀◦⋅

Meanwhile, the invasion rolls on. America's once-sleepy two-thousand-mile Mexican border is now the scene of daily confrontations. Ranches in Arizona have become nightly bivouac areas for thousands of aliens, who cut fences and leave poisoned cattle and trails of debris in the trek north. Even the Mexican army is showing its contempt. The State Department reported fifty-five military incursions in the five years before the incident in 2000, when truckloads of Mexican soldiers barreled through a barbed wire fence, fired shots, and pursued two mounted officers and a U.S. Border Patrol vehicle. Border Patrol agents believe some Mexican army units collaborate with the drug cartels.

America has become a spillway for an exploding population that Mexico is unable to employ. With Mexico's population growing by ten million every decade, there will be no end to the long march north before the American Southwest is fully Hispanicized. Mexican senator Adolfo Zinser conceded that Mexico's "economic policy is dependent on unlimited emigration to the United States." The Yanqui-baiting academic and "onetime Communist supporter" Jorge Casteñada warned in *Atlantic Monthly,* six years ago, that any American effort to cut back immigration "will make social peace in . . . Mexico untenable. . . . Some Americans dislike immigration, but there is very little they can do about it." These opinions take on weight, with Senator Zinser now President Fox's national security adviser and Jorge Casteñada his foreign minister. . . .

America is no longer the biracial society of 1960 that struggled to erase divisions and close gaps in a nation 90 percent white. Today we juggle the rancorous and rival claims of a multiracial, multiethnic, and multicultural country. Vice President Gore captured the new America in his famous howler, when he translated our national slogan, "E Pluribus Unum," backward, as "Out of one, many."

Today there are 28.4 million foreign-born in the United States. Half are from Latin America and the Caribbean, a fourth from Asia. The rest are from Africa, the Middle East, and Europe. One in every five New Yorkers and Floridians is foreign-born, as is one of every four Californians. With 8.4 million foreign-born, and not one new power plant built in a decade, small wonder California faces power shortages and power outages. With endless immigration, America is going to need an endless expansion of its power sources—hydroelectric power, fossil fuels (oil, coal, gas), and nuclear power. The only alternative is blackouts, brownouts, and endless lines at the pump.

In the 1990s, immigrants and their children were responsible for 100 percent of the population growth of California, New York, New Jersey, Illinois, and Massachusetts, and over half the population growth of Florida, Texas, Michigan, and Maryland. As the United States allots most of its immigrant visas to relatives of new arrivals, it is difficult for Europeans to come, while entire villages from El Salvador are now here.

The results of the Third World bias in immigration can be seen in our social statistics. The median age of Euro-Americans is 36; for Hispanics, it is 26. The median age of all foreign-born, 33, is far below that of the older American ethnic groups, such as English, 40, and Scots-Irish, 43. These social statistics raise a question: Is the U.S. government, by deporting scarcely 1 percent of an estimated eleven million illegal aliens each year, failing in its constitutional duty to protect the rights of American citizens? Consider:

- A third of the legal immigrants who come to the United States have not finished high school. Some 22 percent do not even have a ninth-grade education, compared to less than 5 percent of our native born.
- Over 36 percent of all immigrants, and 57 percent of those from Central America, do not earn twenty thousand dollars a year. Of the immigrants who have come since 1980, 60 percent still do not earn twenty thousand dollars a year.
- Of immigrant households in the United States, 29 percent are below the poverty line, twice the 14 percent of native born.
- Immigrant use of food stamps, Supplemental Social Security, and school lunch programs runs from 50 percent to 100 percent higher than use by native born.
- Mr. Clinton's Department of Labor estimated that 50 percent of the real-wage losses sustained by low-income Americans is due to immigration.
- By 1991, foreign nationals accounted for 24 percent of all arrests in Los Angeles and 36 percent of all arrests in Miami.

- In 1980, federal and state prisons housed nine thousand criminal aliens. By 1995, this had soared to fifty-nine thousand criminal aliens, a figure that does not include aliens who became citizens or the criminals sent over by Castro in the Mariel boat lift.
- Between 1988 and 1994, the number of illegal aliens in California's prisons more than tripled from fifty-five hundred to eighteen thousand.

None of the above statistics, however, holds for emigrants from Europe. And some of the statistics, on low education, for example, do not apply to emigrants from Asia.

Nevertheless, mass emigration from poor Third World countries is "good for business," especially businesses that employ large numbers at low wages. In the spring of 2001, the Business Industry Political Action Committee, BIPAC, issued "marching orders for grass-roots mobilization." The *Wall Street Journal* said that the 400 blue-chip companies and 150 trade associations "will call for continued normalization of trade with China . . . and easing immigration restrictions to meet labor needs. . . ." But what is good for corporate America is not necessarily good for Middle America. When it comes to open borders, the corporate interest and the national interest do not coincide, they collide. Should America suffer a sustained recession, we will find out if the melting pot is still working.

But mass immigration raises more critical issues than jobs or wages, for immigration is ultimately about America herself.

What Is a Nation?

Most of the people who leave their homelands to come to America, whether from Mexico or Mauritania, are good people, decent people. They seek the same better life our ancestors sought when they came. They come to work; they obey our laws; they cherish our freedoms; they relish the opportunities the greatest nation on earth has to offer; most love America; may wish to become part of the American family. One may encounter these newcomers everywhere. But the record number of foreign-born coming from cultures with little in common with Americans raises a different question: What is a nation?

Some define as one people of common ancestry, language, literature, history, heritage, heroes, traditions, customs, mores, and faith who have lived together over time on the same land under the same rulers. This is the blood-and-soil idea of a nation. Among those who pressed this definition were Secretary of State John Quincy Adams, who laid down these conditions on immigrants: "They must cast off the European skin, never to resume it. They must look forward to their posterity rather than backward to their ancestors." Theodore Roosevelt, who thundered against "hyphenated-Americanism," seemed to share Adam's view. Woodrow Wilson, speaking to newly naturalized Americans in 1915 in Philadelphia, echoed T.R.: "A man who thinks of himself as belonging to a particular national group in America has yet to become an

American." This idea, of Americans as a separate and unique people, was first given expression by John Jay in *Federalist 2*:

> Providence has been pleased to give this one connected country to one united people—a people descended from the same ancestors, speaking the same language, professing the same religion, attached to the same principles of government, very similar in their manners and customs, and who, by their joint counsels, arms, and efforts, fighting side by side throughout a long and bloody war, have nobly established their general liberty and independence.

But can anyone say today that we Americans are "one united people"?

We are not descended from the same ancestors. We no longer speak the same language. We do not profess the same religion. We are no longer simply Protestant, Catholic, and Jewish, as sociologist Will Herberg described us in his *Essay in American Religious Sociology* in 1955. We are now Protestant, Catholic, Jewish, Mormon, Muslim, Hindu, Buddhist, Taoist, Shintoist, Santeria, New Age, voodoo, agnostic, atheist, humanist, Rastafarian, and Wiccan. Even the mention of Jesus' name at the Inauguration by the preachers Mr. Bush selected to give the invocations evoked fury and cries of "insensitive," "divisive," and "exclusionary." A *New Republic* editorial lashed out at these "crushing Christological thuds" from the Inaugural stand. We no longer agree on whether God exists, when life begins, and what is moral and immoral. We are not "similar in our manners and customs." We never fought "side by side throughout a long and bloody war." The Greatest Generation did, but it is passing away. If the rest of us recall a "long and bloody war," it was Vietnam, and, no, we were not side by side.

We remain "attached to the same principles of government." But common principles of government are not enough to hold us together. The South was "attached to the same principles of government" as the North. But that did not stop Southerners from fighting four years of bloody war to be free of their Northern brethren.

In his Inaugural, President Bush rejected Jay's vision: "America has never been united by blood or birth or soil. We are bound by ideals that move us beyond our background, lift us above our interests, and teach us what it means to be a citizen." In his *The Disuniting of America,* Arthur Schlesinger subscribes to the Bush idea of a nation, united by shared belief in an American Creed to be found in our history and greatest documents: the Declaration of Independence, the Constitution, and the Gettysburg Address. Writes Schlesinger:

> The American Creed envisages a nation composed of individuals making their own choices and accountable to themselves, not a nation based on inviolable ethnic communities. For our values are not matters or whim and happenstance. History has given them to us. They are anchored in our national experience, in our great national documents, in our national heroes, in our folkways, our traditions, and standards. [Our values] work for us; and, for that reason, we live and die by them.

But Americans no longer agree on values, history, or heroes. What one-half of America sees as a glorious past the other views as shameful and wicked. Columbus, Washington, Jefferson, Jackson, Lincoln, and Lee—all of them heroes of the old America—are all under attack. Those most American of words, equality and freedom, today hold different meanings for different Americans. As for our "great national documents," the Supreme Court decisions that interpret our Constitution have not united us; for forty years they have divided us, bitterly, over prayer in school, integration, busing, flag burning, abortion, pornography, and the Ten Commandments.

Nor is a belief in democracy sufficient to hold us together. Half of the nation did not even bother to vote in the presidential election of 2000; three out of five do not vote in off-year elections. Millions cannot name their congressman, senators, or the Supreme Court justices. They do not care.

Whether one holds to the blood-and-soil idea of a nation, or to the creedal idea, or both, neither nation is what it was in the 1940s, 1950s, or 1960s. We live in the same country, we are governed by the same leaders, but can we truly say we are still one nation and one people?

It is hard to say yes, harder to believe that over a million immigrants every year, from every country on earth, a third of them breaking in, will reforge the bonds of our disuniting nation. John Stuart Mill warned that "free institutions are next to impossible in a country made up of different nationalities. Among a people without fellow-feeling, especially if they read and speak different languages, the united public opinion necessary to the working of representative government cannot exist."

We are about to find out if Mill was right.

Daniel T. Griswold

 **NO**

Immigrants Have Enriched American Culture and Enhanced Our Influence in the World

Immigration always has been controversial in the United States. More than two centuries ago, Benjamin Franklin worried that too many German immigrants would swamp America's predominantly British culture. In the mid-1800s, Irish immigrants were scorned as lazy drunks, not to mention Roman Catholics. At the turn of the century a wave of "new immigrants"—Poles, Italians, Russian Jews—were believed to be too different ever to assimilate into American life. Today the same fears are raised about immigrants from Latin America and Asia, but current critics of immigration are as wrong as their counterparts were in previous eras.

Immigration is not undermining the American experiment; it is an integral part of it. We are a nation of immigrants. Successive waves of immigrants have kept our country demographically young, enriched our culture and added to our productive capacity as a nation, enhancing our influence in the world.

Immigration gives the United States an economic edge in the world economy. Immigrants bring innovative ideas and entrepreneurial spirit to the U.S. economy. They provide business contacts to other markets, enhancing America's ability to trade and invest profitably in the global economy. They keep our economy flexible, allowing U.S. producers to keep prices down and to respond to changing consumer demands. An authoritative 1997 study by the National Academy of Sciences (NAS) concluded that immigration delivered a "significant positive gain" to the U.S. economy. In testimony before Congress [in 2001], Federal Reserve Board Chairman Alan Greenspan said, "I've always argued that this country has benefited immensely from the fact that we draw people from all over the world."

Contrary to popular myth, immigrants do not push Americans out of jobs. Immigrants tend to fill jobs that Americans cannot or will not fill, mostly at the high and low ends of the skill spectrum. Immigrants are disproportionately represented in such high-skilled fields as medicine, physics and computer science, but also in lower-skilled sectors such as hotels and restaurants, domestic service, construction and light manufacturing.

From Daniel T. Griswold, "Immigrants Have Enriched American Culture and Enhanced Our Influence in the World," *Insight on the News* (March 11, 2002). Copyright © 2002 by News World Communications, Inc. Reprinted by permission of *Insight on the News*.

Immigrants also raise demand for goods as well as the supply. During the long boom of the 1990s, and especially in the second half of the decade, the national unemployment rate fell below 4 percent and real wages rose up and down the income scale during a time of relatively high immigration.

Nowhere is the contribution of immigrants more apparent than in the high-technology and other knowledge-based sectors. Silicon Valley and other high-tech sectors would cease to function if we foolishly were to close our borders to skilled and educated immigrants. These immigrants represent human capital that can make our entire economy more productive. Immigrants have developed new products, such as the Java computer language, that have created employment opportunities for millions of Americans.

Immigrants are not a drain on government finances. The NAS study found that the typical immigrant and his or her offspring will pay a net $80,000 more in taxes during their lifetimes than they collect in government services. For immigrants with college degrees, the net fiscal return is $198,000. It is true that low-skilled immigrants and refugees tend to use welfare more than the typical "native" household, but the 1996 Welfare Reform Act made it much more difficult for newcomers to collect welfare. As a result, immigrant use of welfare has declined in recent years along with overall welfare rolls.

Despite the claims of immigration opponents, today's flow is not out of proportion to historical levels. Immigration in the last decade has averaged about 1 million per year, high in absolute numbers, but the rate of 4 immigrants per year per 1,000 U.S. residents is less than half the rate during the Great Migration of 1890–1914. Today, about 10 percent of U.S. residents are foreign-born, an increase from 4.7 percent in 1970, but still far short of the 14.7 percent who were foreign-born in 1910. Nor can immigrants fairly be blamed for causing "overpopulation." America's annual population growth of 1 percent is below our average growth rate of the last century. In fact, without immigration our labor force would begin to shrink within two decades. According to the 2000 Census, 22 percent of U.S. counties lost population between 1990 and 2000. Immigrants could help revitalize demographically declining areas of the country, just as they helped revitalize New York City and other previously declining urban centers.

Drastically reducing the number of foreigners who enter the United States each year only would compound the economic damage of Sept. 11 while doing nothing to enhance our security. The tourist industry, already reeling, would lose millions of foreign visitors, and American universities would lose hundreds of thousands of foreign students if our borders were closed.

Obviously the U.S. government should "control its borders" to keep out anyone who intends to commit terrorist acts. The problem is not that we are letting too many people into the United States but that the government has failed to keep the wrong people out. We can stop terrorists from entering the United States without closing our borders or reducing the number of hardworking, peaceful immigrants who settle here.

We must do whatever is necessary to stop potentially dangerous people at the border. Law-enforcement and intelligence agencies must work closely with the State Department, the Immigration and Naturalization Service (INS) and

U.S. Customs to share real-time information about potential terrorists. Computer systems must be upgraded and new technologies adopted to screen out the bad guys without causing intolerable delays at the border. More agents need to be posted at ports of entry to more thoroughly screen for high-risk travelers. We must bolster cooperation with our neighbors, Canada and Mexico, to ensure that terrorists cannot slip across our long land borders.

In the wake of Sept. 11, longtime critics of immigration have tried to exploit legitimate concerns about security to argue for drastic cuts in immigration. But border security and immigration are two separate matters. Immigrants are only a small subset of the total number of foreigners who enter the United States every year. Only about one of every 25 foreign nationals who enter the United States come here to immigrate. The rest are tourists, business travelers, students and Mexican and Canadians who cross the border for a weekend to shop or visit family and then return home with no intention of settling permanently in the United States.

The 19 terrorists who attacked the United States on Sept. 11 did not apply to the INS to immigrate or to become U.S. citizens. Like most aliens who enter the United States, they were here on temporary tourist and student visas. We could reduce the number of immigrants to zero and still not stop terrorists from slipping into the country on nonimmigrant visas.

To defend ourselves better against terrorism, our border-control system requires a reorientation of mission. For the last two decades, U.S. immigration policy has been obsessed with nabbing mostly Mexican-born workers whose only "crime" is their desire to earn an honest day's pay. Those workers pose no threat to national security.

Our land border with Mexico is half as long as our border with Canada, yet before Sept. 11 it was patrolled by 10 times as many border agents. On average we were posting an agent every five miles along our 3,987-mile border with Canada and every quarter-mile on the 2,000-mile border with Mexico. On the Northern border there were 120,000 entries per year per agent compared with 40,000 entries on the Southwestern border. This is out of proportion to any legitimate fears about national security. In fact terrorists seem to prefer the northern border. Let's remember that it was at a border-crossing station in Washington state in December 1999 that a terrorist was apprehended with explosives that were to be used to blow up Los Angeles International Airport during the millennium celebrations.

At a February 2000 hearing, former Sen. Slade Gorton (R-Wash.) warned that "understaffing at our northern border is jeopardizing the security of our nation, not to mention border personnel, while in at least some sections of the southern border, there are so many agents that there is not enough work to keep them all busy."

We should stop wasting scarce resources in a self-destructive quest to hunt down Mexican construction workers and raid restaurants and chicken-processing plants, and redirect those resources to track potential terrorists and smash their cells before they can blow up more buildings and kill more Americans.

For all these reasons, President George W. Bush's initiative to legalize and regularize the movement of workers across the U.S.-Mexican border makes sense in terms of national security as well as economics. It also is politically smart.

In his latest book, *The Death of the West,* Pat Buchanan argues that opposing immigration will be a winning formula for conservative Republicans. His own political decline and fall undermine his claim. Like former liberal Republican Gov. Pete Wilson in California, Buchanan has tried to win votes by blaming immigration for America's problems. But voters wisely rejected Buchanan's thesis. Despite $12 million in taxpayer campaign funds, and an assist from the Florida butterfly ballot [a ballot with candidates' names on both sides of a column of punch holes, which caused some voters to mistakenly vote for Buchanan instead of Gore], Buchanan won less than 0.5 percent of the presidential vote in 2000. In contrast Bush, by affirming immigration, raised the GOP's share of the Hispanic vote to 35 percent from the 21 percent carried by Bob Dole in 1996. If conservatives adopt the anti-immigrant message, they risk following Buchanan and Wilson into political irrelevancy.

It would be a national shame if, in the name of security, we closed the door to immigrants who come here to work, save and build a better life for themselves and their families. Immigrants come here to live the American Dream; terrorists come to destroy it. We should not allow America's tradition of welcoming immigrants to become yet another casualty of Sept. 11.

POSTSCRIPT

Should America Restrict Immigration?

There is no accurate census of illegal immigrants, but the best estimate is that 5 million people have entered the United States illegally within the past 10 years. What are the consequences for American society? The issue of immigration encompasses both legal and illegal immigrants. Immigration policy should begin by examining who comes and the consequences for the nation. Who are they, and what impact do they have? What do they cost, and what do they contribute?

Until the early years of the new republic, immigrants were predominantly white, English-speaking, Protestant Europeans and African slaves who were forcibly brought to the New World. This soon changed, and for a half-century —until the adoption of laws restricting immigration in the 1920s—Catholics and Jews, southern and eastern Europeans, most of them non-English speakers, came to the United States. Since World War II, Asian and Hispanic immigrants have come in ever-increasing numbers. George Henderson and Thompson Olasiji's *Migrants, Immigrants, and Slaves: Racial and Ethnic Groups in America* (University Press of America, 1995) is a useful introduction to the patterns of immigration into the United States.

Georgie Anne Geyer's *Americans No More* (Atlantic Monthly Press, 1996) is a lament on the decline of civic life in America as a result of both legal and illegal immigration. Geyer does not deplore illegal immigration but the recent tendency of legal immigrants to resist assimilation. Peter Brimelow, in *Alien Nation: Common Sense About America's Immigration Disaster* (Random House, 1995), catalogs what he perceives to be the consequences of what he calls America's "immigration disaster." Brimelow argues that no multicultural society has lasted.

In opposition to Brimelow's view, Sanford J. Ungar, in *Fresh Blood: The New American Immigrants* (Simon & Schuster, 1995), argues, "To be American means being part of an ever more heterogeneous people and participating in the constant redefinition of a complex, evolving cultural fabric." Somewhere in between multiculturalists like Ungar and assimilationists like Brimelow and Geyer is Peter D. Salins. In *Assimilation, American Style* (Basic Books, 1997), Salins argues that the naturalization process is the best means for absorbing the flood of immigrants who arrive in America each year.

Often forgotten in these debates are the experiences of the immigrants themselves. Newer immigrants to America have recounted some of these experiences in recent books by and about them. In *Becoming American: Personal Essays by First Generation Immigrant Women* (Hyperion, 2000), Ghanaian American writer Meri Nana-Ama Danquah brings together the personal recollections and reflections by immigrant women from Europe, Latin America, Africa, Asia, and the Caribbean. In *American by Choice: The Remarkable Fulfillment of an Immigrant's Dreams* (Thomas Nelson, 1998), Sam Moore describes his rise in America from a poor Lebanese immigrant to president and CEO of Thomas Nelson Publishers, a major religious publishing house. A more troubling account of the immigrant experience is that of Mary C. Waters, in *Black Identities: West Indian Immigrant Dreams and American Realities* (Harvard University Press, 2000). Waters finds that when West Indian immigrants first arrive, their skills, knowledge of English, and general optimism carry them forward, but later on, a variety of influences, from racial discrimination to low wages and poor working conditions, tend to erode their self-confidence.

Attitudes toward immigration change with time and circumstances. September 11, 2001, was one of those times. The terrorist attacks on the World Trade Center have increased the fear that many Americans have of all foreigners. Tamar Jacoby examines the changing circumstances in "Too Many Immigrants?" *Commentary* (April 2002).

The literature on immigration seems to grow as rapidly as immigration itself. Christopher Jencks has assessed this literature in two long essays entitled "Who Should Get In?" *New York Review of Books* (November 29 and December 20, 2001). Among the controversial issues that he examines is whether or not permanent status can be granted to illegal immigrants who are presently residing in the United States without encouraging the influx of many more and, if so, how.

Americans confront a choice. On the one hand, there are the ethical and political consequences of restricting immigration into a country whose attraction to poor or persecuted people is as great as its borders are vast. On the other hand, there are the problems of absorbing new, generally non-English-speaking populations into an economy that may have to provide increasing public support and into a society whose traditions and values may clash with those of the newcomers.

ISSUE 17

Is America's War on Terrorism Justified?

YES: Norman Podhoretz, from "How to Win World War IV," *Commentary* (February 2002)

NO: Thomas Harrison, from "Only a Democratic Foreign Policy Can Combat Terrorism," *New Politics* (Winter 2002)

ISSUE SUMMARY

YES: Editor Norman Podhoretz maintains that America must not only eliminate the Al Qaeda network terrorists but also overthrow state regimes that sponsor terrorism.

NO: Editor Thomas Harrison argues that America's war on terrorism is simply an attempt to preserve an oppressive status quo and that the only way to eliminate terrorism is to form a third party that seeks a more democratic and egalitarian world.

O n the morning of September 11, 2001, foreign terrorists attacked the American homeland, killing thousands of people and causing billions of dollars in damage. After the shock of the attacks came the realization that Americans had to begin thinking anew about their nation: about what it should be doing in the world and how it should be protecting its people at home. In somewhat the same way that the Japanese attack on Pearl Harbor in 1941 awoke Americans from the illusion that America could remain isolated from the rest of the world, September 11 ended what columnist Charles Krauthammer called a decade-long "holiday from history," when the American news media were preoccupied with stories about O. J. Simpson, Monica Lewinsky, and Gary Condit. Now there was something more serious on the television screen: the flaming, doomed towers; the gaping hole in the Pentagon; and the mass murder of Americans.

America had faced mortal danger before, most recently from Soviet nuclear weapons, but the Soviets were considered rational enemies. Quiet understandings had been established between the two superpowers; there were usually clear signals on how far one could go before inviting a nuclear response. No such reasoning seemed to be possible with the terrorists of September 11: they appeared simply to be madmen, bent upon killing American "infidels" and recognizing no distinction, even in theory, between combatants and noncombatants. Osama bin Laden, head of the Al Qaeda network responsible for what he called "the blessed attacks" of September 11, announced that his campaign was against "any American who pays taxes." With the overwhelming support of both Congress and the American public, President George W. Bush responded by declaring war against him and his network of terrorists.

But there were obvious differences between this war and past wars. In the cold war and in other wars, America's enemies occupied finite pieces of geography, and the United States won those wars when the countries either surrendered or collapsed. But in the war against terror the enemy is a secret organization spread throughout the globe, with cells operating even inside our own country. How do we rout this elusive enemy? How will we know when we have gotten it all? When will the war end? Is it appropriate to call it a "war" at all?

Some of these questions have been answered, at least provisionally, by the Bush administration. In his address to a special joint session of Congress on September 20, 2001, President Bush made it clear that there were indeed some finite pieces of geography in the war against terrorism; he announced that the United States considered its enemies not only to be the ever-shifting terrorist cells but also any state that harbored them. By that time the United States had already begun its incursion into Afghanistan, assisting the so-called Northern Alliance and other forces fighting the ruling Taliban regime. In a surprisingly short time this produced the overthrow of the regime, the capture or death of many of its fighters, and a new, friendlier regime in Afghanistan. That was the easy part. The hard part, aside from preventing the overthrow of the new government or its drift into anarchy, is deciding what to do next.

Some decisions have apparently been made. An American Special Forces unit has been sent to the Philippines to help train local army units fighting terrorist forces. But the rest is still unresolved. Should the United States try to overthrow Saddam Hussein in Iraq? Earlier reports of a meeting between one of the September 11 hijackers and an Iraqi intelligence agent have now been discounted by American officials, but in 2002 CIA director George Tenet insisted that Iraq has had contact with Al Qaeda officials, and a report in the March 25 edition of *The New Yorker* magazine seemed to lend credence to his claim. Saddam's continued refusal to allow UN inspectors into his country to see whether or not he is building weapons of mass destruction might be the last straw, provoking some form of U.S. intervention. But should such an operation be undertaken? Indeed, should the war against terrorism be conducted primarily as a military operation? Or should the United States take greater account of political and social inequities in the Middle East, including some by our very "allies" in the region? These are among the questions considered in the following selections by Norman Podhoretz and Thomas Harrison. Podhoretz maintains that America must not only eliminate the Al Qaeda network terrorists but also overthrow state regimes that sponsor terror, while Harrison argues that America's present war on terrorism is simply an attempt to preserve an oppressive status quo and that the only way to eliminate terrorism is to work toward establishing a more democratic and egalitarian world.

Norman Podhoretz  **YES**

How to Win World War IV

Ever since the very beginning of the war into which the United States was violently hurled on September 11, efforts have been made to define its nature. The Bush administration, from the President on down, kept telling us that this would be a war unlike any other, but the very nearly self-evident truth of that proposition did not prevent an energetic search for analogies. On the contrary: when we first went into Afghanistan, and progress seemed slow, the ghost of conflicts past immediately materialized, each one croaking in menacing tones, "Remember me."

In a piece in the *Weekly Standard,* for example, I summoned up the Gulf war fought by the President's father ten years ago. At that time, I said, the broad coalition assembled by the United States, together with the imprimatur we had sought and acquired from the United Nations, resulted not in the consummation of a decisive victory but in an act of military and political coitus interruptus. Having driven Saddam Hussein out of Kuwait—which was all we had a "mandate" to do from our allies and the UN—we did not then push on to drive him out of Baghdad. Nor, in the event, did we even render him incapable of building the weapons of mass destruction he now possesses.

My worry was that the same kind of thing might happen now—and for much the same reason. I never doubted that, just as we had succeeded in the limited aim of rolling back Saddam Hussein's invasion of Kuwait, we would unseat the Taliban regime in Afghanistan and deprive the al Qaeda terrorists of their main sanctuary. What I feared was that then, succumbing again to the pressures of the coalition and the timorous counsels of Colin Powell (chairman of the Joint Chiefs of Staff under Bush I and Secretary of State under Bush II), we would declare victory and go home.

Others were not so confident that we would accomplish even that rather narrow objective. R.W. Apple of the *New York Times,* among others, was haunted by—what else?—Vietnam. To these observers, it seemed that we were once more falling victim to the illusion that we could rely on an incompetent local force to do the fighting on the ground while we supplied advice and air support, and that the inevitable failure of this strategy would suck us into the same "quagmire" into which we had been dragged in Vietnam. After all, the Soviet Union had suffered its own "Vietnam" in Afghanistan—and it had not been hampered, as

From Norman Podhoretz, "How to Win World War IV," *Commentary,* vol. 113, no. 2 (February 2002). Copyright © 2002 by Norman Podhoretz. Reprinted by permission of *Commentary* and the author.

we were, by the logistical problems of projecting power over a great distance. How could we expect to do better?

When, however, the B-52's and the 15,000-pound "Daisy Cutter" bombs[1] were unleashed (which many, including me, interpreted as a victory of Secretary of Defense Donald Rumsfeld over the incorrigibly cautious Colin Powell), the ghost of Vietnam was exorcised. Along with it went the skepticism about what air power could do, especially in a country that was supposedly too primitive to offer juicy targets.

But the Daisy Cutters were only the half of it. As we were to discover, our "smart-bomb" technology had advanced way beyond the stage it had reached in 1991, when it was first introduced. In Afghanistan, such bombs, guided by "spotters" on the ground using radios, laptops, and lasers, and unmanned satellite drones and other systems in the air, were both incredibly precise in avoiding civilian casualties and absolutely lethal in destroying military personnel. It was this "new kind of American power," the *New York Times* reported, that "enabled a ragtag opposition [i.e., the Northern Alliance] to rout the Taliban army."

As for the 15,000-pound Daisy Cutters, far from being good for nothing but "pounding the rubble," as critics of air power had derisively charged, they exerted a "terrifying psychological impact as they explode[d] just above ground, wiping out everything for hundreds of yards."

All this shook loose the "battle-hardened troops" of the Taliban regime in less than three months, and at the cost of only a handful of American casualties. Like the allegedly crack units of Saddam Hussein's Revolutionary Guard, which (against similar predictions to the contrary) we had sent fleeing with relative ease a decade earlier, the reputedly fearsome Taliban fighters, and Osama bin Laden's al Qaeda terrorists alongside them, emerged as the paper tiger that they had imagined us to have become.

❦

But it is important to recognize that bin Laden and his followers had good reason to arrive at this contemptuous assessment of our present condition. For a very long time, both before and after the Gulf war, the United States had been the target of terrorist attacks in the name of Islam or the Palestinian cause. (Sometimes, as with Hizbullah and Hamas, the two overlapped. But the religious card was often played even by the Palestine Liberation Organization—or PLO—and some of its constituent groups like the Popular Front for the Liberation of Palestine—or PFLP—that were more deeply rooted in Marx than in Muhammad.) Yet we had done virtually nothing in response to those attacks—or anyway nothing that might induce second thoughts or hesitations in those who were planning to undertake more such atrocities.

Thus, from 1970 to 1975, during the administrations of Richard Nixon and Gerald Ford, several American diplomats were murdered in Sudan and Lebanon while others were kidnapped. The perpetrators were all agents of one or another faction of the PLO. In Israel, too, many American citizens were killed by the PLO, though except for the rockets fired at our embassy and other American facilities in Beirut by the PFLP, these attacks were not directly aimed at the United States. In any case, there were no American military reprisals.

Our diplomats, then, were for some years already being murdered with impunity by Muslim terrorists when, in 1979, with Jimmy Carter now in the White House, Iranian students—with either the advance or subsequent blessing of the country's clerical ruler, Ayatollah Khomeini—broke into the American embassy in Tehran and seized 52 Americans as hostages. For a full five months, Carter dithered. At last, steeling himself, he authorized a military rescue operation that had to be aborted after a series of mishaps that would have fit well into a Marx Brothers movie like *Duck Soup* if they had not been more humiliating than comic. After 444 days, and just hours after Ronald Reagan's inauguration in January 1981, the hostages were finally released by the Iranians, evidently because they feared that the hawkish new President might actually launch a military strike against them.

Yet if they had foreseen what was coming under Reagan, they would not have been so fearful. In April 1983, Hizbullah—an Islamic terrorist organization nourished by Iran and Syria—sent a suicide bomber to explode his truck in front of the American embassy in Beirut, Lebanon. Sixty-three employees, among them the Middle East CIA director, were killed and another 120 wounded. But Reagan sat still.

Six months later, in October 1983, another Hizbullah suicide bomber blew up an American barracks in the Beirut airport, killing 241 U.S. marines in their sleep and wounding another 81. This time Reagan signed off on plans for a retaliatory blow, but he then allowed his Secretary of Defense, Caspar Weinberger, to cancel it (because it might damage our relations with the Arab world, of which Weinberger was always tenderly solicitous). Shortly thereafter, the President pulled the marines out of Lebanon.

Having cut and run in Lebanon in October, Reagan again remained passive in December, when the American embassy in Kuwait was bombed. Nor did he hit back when, hard upon the withdrawal of the American marines from Beirut, the CIA station chief there, William Buckley, was kidnapped by Hizbullah and then murdered. Buckley was the fourth American to be kidnapped in Beirut, and many more suffered the same fate between 1982 and 1992 (though not all died or were killed in captivity).

These kidnappings were apparently what led Reagan, who had sworn that he would never negotiate with terrorists, to make an unacknowledged deal with Iran, involving the trading of arms for hostages, which triggered the Iran-*contra* crisis. But whereas the Iranians were paid off handsomely in the coin of nearly 1,500 antitank missiles (some of them sent at our request through Israel), all we got in exchange was three American hostages.

In September 1984, six months after the murder of Buckley, the U.S. embassy annex near Beirut was hit by yet another truck bomb (also traced to Hizbullah). Again Reagan sat still. Or rather, after giving the green light to covert proxy retaliations by Lebanese intelligence agents, he put a stop to them when one such operation, directed against the cleric thought to be the head of Hizbullah, failed to get its main target while unintentionally killing 80 other people.

It took only another two months for Hizbullah to strike once more. In December 1984, a Kuwaiti airliner was hijacked and two American passengers employed by the U.S. Agency for International Development were murdered. The Iranians, who had stormed the plane after it landed in Tehran, promised to try the hijackers themselves, but instead allowed them to leave the country. At this point, all the Reagan administration could come up with was the offer of a $250,000 reward for information that might lead to the arrest of the hijackers. There were no takers.

The following June, Hizbullah operatives hijacked still another airliner, an American one (TWA flight 847), and then forced it to fly to Beirut, where it was held for more than two weeks. During those weeks, an American naval officer aboard the plane was shot, his body ignominiously hurled onto the tarmac, after which the demands of the hijackers for the freeing of hundreds of terrorists held by Israel began to be met in exchange for the release of the other passengers. Both the United States and Israel denied that they were violating their own policy of never bargaining with terrorists, but as with the arms-for-hostages deal, no one believed them, and it was almost universally assumed that Israel had acted under pressure from Washington. Later, four of the hijackers were caught, but only one wound up being tried and jailed (by Germany, not the United States).

The sickening beat went on. In October 1985, the *Achille Lauro*, an Italian cruise ship, was hijacked by a group under the leadership of the PLO's Abu Abbas, working with the support of Libya. One of the hijackers threw an elderly wheelchair-bound American passenger, Leon Klinghoffer, overboard. When the hijackers attempted to escape in a plane, the United States sent Navy fighters to intercept and force it down. Klinghoffer's murderer was eventually apprehended and sent to prison in Italy, but the Italian authorities let Abu Abbas himself go. Washington—evidently having exhausted its repertoire of military reprisals—now confined itself to protesting the release of Abu Abbas. To no avail.

Libya's involvement in the *Achille Lauro* hijacking was, though, the last free pass that country's dictator, Muammar Qaddafi, was destined to get from the United States under Reagan. In December 1985, five Americans were among the twenty people killed when the Rome and Vienna airports were bombed, and then in April 1986 another bomb exploded in a discotheque in West Berlin that was a hang-out for American servicemen. U.S. intelligence tied Libya to both of these bombings, and the eventual outcome was an American air attack in which one of the residences of Qaddafi was hit.

In retaliation, the Palestinian terrorist Abu Nidal executed three U.S. citizens who worked at the American University in Beirut. But Qaddafi himself—no doubt surprised and shaken by the American reprisal—seems to have gone into a brief period of retirement as a sponsor of terrorism. So far as we know, it took nearly three years (until December 1988) before he could pull himself together to the point of undertaking another operation: the bombing of Pan Am flight 103 over Lockerbie, Scotland, in which a total of 270 people lost their lives. Of the two Libyan intelligence agents who were tried for planting the bomb, one was convicted (though not until the year 2001) and the other acquitted. Qaddafi himself suffered no further punishment from American warplanes.

✦❦✦

In January 1989, Reagan was succeeded by the first George Bush, who, in handling the fallout from the destruction of Pan Am 103, copied and intensified the law-enforcement approach to terrorism. During Bush's four-year period in the White House, there were several attacks on Americans in Turkey by Islamic terrorist organizations, and there were others in Egypt, Saudi Arabia, and Lebanon. None of these was as bloody as previous incidents, and none provoked any military response from the United States.

In January 1993 Bill Clinton became President. Over the span of his two terms in office, American citizens continued to be injured or killed in Israel and other countries by terrorists who were not aiming specifically at the United States. But several spectacular terrorist operations occurred on Clinton's watch of which the U.S. was most emphatically the target.

The first, on February 26, 1993, only 38 days after his inauguration, was the explosion of a truck bomb in the parking garage of the World Trade Center. As compared with what would happen on September 11, 2001, this was a minor incident in which "only" six people were killed and over a thousand injured. The six Muslim terrorists responsible were caught, tried, convicted, and sent to prison for long terms.

But in treating the attack as a common crime, or the work of a rogue group acting on its own, the Clinton administration willfully turned a deaf ear to outside experts like Steven Emerson and even the director of the CIA, R. James Woolsey, who strongly suspected that behind the individual culprits was a terrorist Islamic network with (at that time) its headquarters in Sudan. This network, then scarcely known to the general public, was called al Qaeda, and its leader was a former Saudi national who had fought on our side against the Soviets in Afghanistan but had since turned against us as fiercely as he had been against the Russians. His name was Osama bin Laden.[2]

The next major episode was not long in trailing the bombing of the World Trade Center. In April 1993, less than two months after that attack, former President Bush visited Kuwait, where an attempt was made to assassinate him by—as our own investigators were able to determine—Iraqi intelligence agents. The Clinton administration spent two more months seeking approval from the UN and the "international community" to retaliate for this egregious assault on the United States. In the end, a few cruise missiles were fired into the Iraqi capital of Baghdad, where they fell harmlessly onto empty buildings in the middle of the night.

In the years immediately ahead, many Islamic terrorist operations in which Americans were murdered or kidnapped or injured continued in Turkey, Pakistan, Saudi Arabia, Lebanon, Yemen, and Israel, but these were not specifically aimed at the United States. In March 1995, however, a van belonging to the U.S. consulate in Karachi, Pakistan, was hit by gunfire, killing two American diplomats and injuring a third. In November of the same year, five Americans died when a car bomb was exploded in Riyadh, Saudi Arabia, near a building in which a U.S. military advisory group lived.

ᴥᐧᰀᐤᰀᐧᴥ

All this was trumped in June 1996, when another building in which American military personnel lived—the Khobar Towers in Dhahran, Saudi Arabia—was blasted by a truck bomb. Nineteen of our airmen were killed, and 240 other Americans on the premises were wounded.

In 1993, Clinton had been so intent on treating the World Trade Center as a matter for law enforcement that he refused even to meet with his own CIA director, James Woolsey. Perhaps he anticipated that he would be told things about terrorist networks and the states sponsoring them that he did not wish to hear because he had no intention of embarking on the military action that such knowledge might force upon him. Now, in the wake of the bombing of the Khobar Towers, Clinton again handed the matter over to law enforcement, but the man in charge, his FBI director, Louis Freeh, who had intimations of an Iranian connection, could no more get through to him than Woolsey had before. There were a few arrests, and the action then moved into the courts.

In June 1998, grenades were unsuccessfully hurled at the U.S. embassy in Beirut. A little later, our embassies in the capitals of Kenya (Nairobi) and Tanzania (Dar es Salaam) were not so lucky. On the very same day—August 7, 1998—car bombs went off in both places, leaving more than 200 people dead, of whom twelve were Americans. Credit for this coordinated operation was claimed by al Qaeda. In what was widely interpreted, especially abroad, as a move to distract attention from his legal troubles over the Monica Lewinsky affair, Clinton fired cruise missiles at an al Qaeda training camp in Afghanistan, where bin Laden was supposed to be at that moment, and at a building in Sudan, where al Qaeda also had a base. But bin Laden escaped harm, while it remains uncertain to this day whether the building in Sudan was actually manufacturing chemical weapons or was just a harmless pharmaceutical factory.

This fiasco—so we have learned from former members of his administration—discouraged any further such action by Clinton against bin Laden, though a lengthy two-part series by Barton Gellman in the *Washington Post* discloses that there were covert counterterrorist operations and a number of diplomatic initiatives that led to arrests in foreign countries. Woolsey (who after a brief tenure resigned from the CIA out of sheer frustration) does not dispute this. But as Dick Morris, then Clinton's political adviser, writes in the *New York Post*:

> The weekly strategy meetings at the White House throughout 1995 and 1996 featured an escalating drumbeat of advice to President Clinton to take decisive steps to crack down on terrorism. The polls gave these ideas a green light. But Clinton hesitated and failed to act, always finding a reason why some other concern was more important.

Gellman's articles cover a later period when more was going on behind the scenes, but most of it remained in the realm of talk or planning that went nowhere. All in all, in an interview with Byron York in *National Review*, Woolsey's retrospective description of Clinton's overall approach to terrorism is devastating: "Do something to show you're concerned. Launch a few missiles in the desert, bop them on the head, arrest a few people. But just keep kicking the ball down field."

Bin Laden, picking up that ball on October 12, 2000, when the *USS Cole* docked for refueling in Yemen, dispatched a team of suicide bombers. The bombers did not succeed in sinking the ship, but seventeen American sailors died and another 39 were wounded.

Judith Miller in the *New York Times* cites both "intelligence analysts" and the director of counterterrorism in the White House as having no doubt that the culprit was al Qaeda. But the heads neither of the CIA nor of the FBI thought the case was "conclusive." Hence the United States did not so much as lift a military finger against bin Laden or the Taliban regime in Afghanistan where he was now holed up and being protected. As for Clinton, so obsessively was he then wrapped up in a futile attempt to broker a deal between the Israelis and the Palestinians that all he could see in this attack on an American warship was an effort "to deter us from our mission of promoting peace and security in the Middle East." The terrorists, he resoundingly vowed, would "fail utterly" in this objective.

Never mind that not the slightest indication existed that bin Laden was in the least concerned over Clinton's negotiations with the Israelis and the Palestinians at Camp David, or even that the Palestinian issue was of great importance to him. In any event, it was Clinton who failed, not bin Laden. The Palestinians under Yasir Arafat, spurning an unprecedentedly generous offer that had been made by the Israeli prime minister Ehud Barak with Clinton's enthusiastic endorsement, unleashed a new round of terrorism. But bin Laden succeeded all too well in his actual intention of striking another brazen blow at the United States.[3]

The sheer audacity of what bin Laden went on to do on September 11 was unquestionably a product of his contempt for American power. Our persistent refusal for so long to use that power against him and his terrorist brethren—or to do so effectively whenever we tried—reinforced his conviction that we were a nation on the way down, destined to be defeated by the resurgence of the same Islamic militancy that had once conquered and converted large parts of the world by the sword.

As bin Laden saw it, thousands or even millions of his followers and sympathizers all over the Muslim world were willing, and even eager, to die a martyr's death in the jihad, the holy war, against the "Great Satan," as the Ayatollah Khomeini had called us. But we in the West, and especially in America, were all so afraid to die that we lacked the will even to stand up for ourselves and defend our degenerate way of life.

Bin Laden was never reticent or coy in laying out this assessment of the United States. In an interview on CNN in 1997, he declared that "the myth of the superpower was destroyed not only in my mind but also in the minds of all Muslims" when the Soviet Union had been defeated in Afghanistan. That American-supplied arms had made this outcome possible did not seem to enter into his calculations. Indeed, in an interview a year earlier, he had belittled the United States as compared with the Soviet Union. "The Russian soldier is more courageous and patient than the U.S. soldier," he said. Hence, "Our battle with the United States is easy compared with the battles in which we engaged in Afghanistan."

Becoming still more explicit, he wrote off the Americans as cowards. Had Reagan not taken to his heels in Lebanon after the bombing of the marine barracks in 1983? And had not Clinton done the same a decade later when only a few American Rangers were killed in Somalia, where they had been sent to participate in a "peace-keeping" mission? Bin Laden did not boast of this as one of his victories, but a State Department dossier charged that al Qaeda had trained the terrorists who ambushed the American servicemen.

Bin Laden summed it all up in a third interview, this one with John J. Miller, that was published in *Esquire* in 1998:

> After leaving Afghanistan the Muslim fighters headed for Somalia and pre- pared for a long battle thinking that the Americans were like the Russians. The youth were surprised at the low morale of the American soldiers and realized, more than before, that the American soldier was a paper tiger and after a few blows ran in defeat.

In short: just as Khomeini had been emboldened by the decline of Amer- ican power in the 1970's, so perfectly personified by Jimmy Carter, to seize and hold American hostages; and just as all the hysterical talk here in 1990 about the tens of thousands of "body bags" that would be flown home if we went to war with Iraq had encouraged Saddam Hussein to believe that we would acquiesce in his bid to seize control of the oil fields of the Middle East—so the ineffec- tual policy toward terrorism adopted by a long string of American Presidents (including, for his first eight months in office, George W. Bush) persuaded bin Laden that he could strike us massively on our own soil and get away with it.

Conversely, however, just as Saddam Hussein underestimated American military might and overestimated the dedication of his own troops (even the much vaunted Revolutionary Guard went scampering toward home rather than dig in and fight when the heat was on), Osama bin Laden misread how the Americans would react to being hit where, literally, they lived. He probably ex- pected a collapse into despair and demoralization; what he elicited instead was an outpouring of rage and an upsurge of patriotic sentiment such as younger Americans had never witnessed except in the movies, let alone experienced in their own souls and on their own flesh. The sleeping American giant was awak- ened and, stretching his mighty arms to a distance of seven thousand miles, swatted the putatively indomitable terrorists like so many bothersome flies.

In that sense, bin Laden did for this country what the Ayatollah Khomeini had done before him. By this I mean that the humiliation Khomeini inflicted on us by the seizure of the hostages in 1979 bred a resistance to Carter's view that American decline was inevitable and that we should acknowledge, accept, and adjust to this inexorable historical development. The entire episode thereby became one of the forces behind the already burgeoning determination to re- build American power that culminated in the election of Ronald Reagan, who campaigned on the promise to do just that. For all the shortcomings of his own handling of terrorism, Reagan did in fact keep this promise to rebuild American power, which was what set the stage for victory in our long struggle with the Soviet Union.

⋅⟨❦⟩⋅

The horrors of September 11 followed rather than preceded a presidential election. Yet with all due respect to Karl Rove's claim that his boss George W. Bush is no different from what he always was, what happened on that most fateful day obviously effected a transformation in the new President. One hears that Bush, who entered the White House without a clear sense of what he wanted to do there, now feels that there was a purpose behind his election all along: as a born-again Christian, it is said, he believes he was chosen by God to eradicate the evil of terrorism from the world. I think it is a plausible rumor, and I would even guess that in his heart of hearts, Bush identifies more in this respect with Ronald Reagan—the President who rid the world of the "evil empire"—than with his own father, who never finished the job he started in taking on Saddam Hussein.

But what would finishing the job in the war against terrorism mean? The President himself defined it from the start in very broad terms. Our aim was not merely to capture or kill Osama bin Laden and wipe out the al Qaeda terrorists under his direct leadership in Afghanistan. Bush vowed that we would also uproot and destroy the entire network of interconnected terrorist organizations and cells "with global reach" that existed in as many as 50 or 60 countries. No longer would we treat the members of these groups as criminals to be arrested by the police, read their Miranda rights, and brought to trial. From now on, they were to be regarded as the irregular troops of a military alliance at war with the United States, and indeed the civilized world as a whole.

Furthermore, the governments that gave terrorists help of any kind— sanctuary, money, arms, diplomatic and logistical support, training facilities —would either join us in getting rid of them or would also be regarded as in a state of war with the United States. Bush was unequivocal. These governments, he repeated over and over again, were either with us in the war against terrorism, or they were against us: there was to be no middle or neutral ground.

In defining the war and the enemy in such terms, the President, seconded by both major parties and a vast majority of the American people, was acknowledging the rightness of those who had been stubbornly insisting against the skeptical and the craven alike that terrorism posed a serious threat and that it could not be fought by the police and the courts. Perhaps most important of all was the corollary of such an analysis: that, with rare exceptions, terrorists were not individual psychotics acting on their own but agents of organizations that depended on the sponsorship of various governments.

Not that this analysis of terrorism had exactly been a secret. The State Department itself had a list of seven state sponsors of terrorism (all but two of which, Cuba and North Korea, were predominantly Muslim[4]) and it regularly issued reports on terrorist incidents throughout the world. But aside from the previously mentioned token lobbing of a cruise missile or two, the application of diplomatic and/or economic sanctions that were themselves inconsistently and even perfunctorily enforced, and a number of covert operations, the law-enforcement approach still prevailed.

September 11 changed much—if not yet all—of that. While atavistic phrases like "bringing the terrorists to justice" kept being used, no one could any longer dream that the American answer to what had been done to us in New York and Washington would begin with an FBI investigation and end with a series of ordinary criminal trials. War had been declared on the United States, and to war we were going to go.

But against whom? Almost immediately it became certain that Osama bin Laden had masterminded September 11, and since he and the top leadership of al Qaeda were in Afghanistan, the first target, so to speak, chose itself. Here, however, a complication arose.

⋯◈⋯

I have speculated that, with respect to the war against terrorism, Bush probably came to identify more with Reagan than with his father. And yet in the days just after September 11, his administration went through what looked like a knee-jerk imitation of the method by which the elder Bush had maneuvered his way into a military engagement with Iraq.

Like his father, George W. Bush set about forming a coalition, even though he was in an entirely different position. The elder Bush had enjoyed the support of only half the country during the run-up to Desert Storm, and thus needed a coalition, and the permission of the United Nations, for political cover and even legitimation in the eyes of the Democrats. But the younger Bush, with about 90 percent of the people and a nearly unanimous Congress behind him for a war against terrorism, had more than enough political support to act on his own, without permission from anyone.

Nevertheless, before going into Afghanistan, the President (acting for the most part through Colin Powell) went around courting and wooing countries throughout the Middle East, some of which were on the State Department's own list of state sponsors of terrorism, or had given houseroom to terrorists without for some reason making it onto this roll of dishonor. Under the doctrine the President himself had promulgated in describing his war aims, these countries should have been seen not as potential allies but as enemies. The absurdity of, in effect, asking them to join with us in a war against themselves was well captured by Richard Lowry, the editor of *National Review*, who remarked that it was silly to expect the leaders of the states sponsoring terrorism to bone up on the United Nations Charter and then change their ways.

To add to the absurdity, none of these countries could or would provide us with assistance of any great value. (Such had not been the case in the Gulf war, when some of them not only allowed us to use their territory as bases but even sent troops into combat.) Nor, for that matter, were our great friends, the "moderate" Middle Eastern governments like Saudi Arabia and Egypt, willing to give us much, if any, help. The claim was that they were providing us with valuable intelligence, but if so, it was not valuable enough to result in the capture of Osama bin Laden. In fact, the *New York Times* reported: "Even in the post-September 11 meetings, one senior Bush administration official said, the Saudis 'dribble out a morsel of insignificant information one day at a time.'"

Worse yet—and even leaving aside the awkward detail that fifteen of the nineteen hijackers on September 11 carried Saudi passports—we had the greatest difficulty getting the Saudi rulers to freeze the assets being sent by private "charities" in their own country to al Qaeda, or to make available the passenger lists of flights coming from there to the United States so that they might be screened in advance by our customs officials. Even Kuwait, the country we had liberated from Saddam Hussein a decade earlier, refused our request for such lists, thus setting a new world record for chutzpah.

Then there was Egypt, whose official government newspapers continued spewing out viciously anti-American diatribes, while its president, Hosni Mubarak, not lacking in chutzpah himself, pretended that there was nothing he could do about this. As he shamelessly and with a straight face told several American interviewers, the press enjoyed the same freedom in his country as it did in ours.

Like Saudi Arabia, Pakistan, too, had a population sympathetic to Osama bin Laden, and (while it was not on our State Department's list of state sponsors of terrorism) its security services maintained close connections with al Qaeda and with the Taliban regime. Yet there was a huge difference between Pakistan and the other Islamic countries in the region.

Most of these other countries clucked their tongues sympathetically over what had been done to us on September 11, and declared themselves members of our coalition. But then—after we had begun bombing Afghanistan in earnest—their contribution to our war effort consisted of urging us to prevent the Israelis from *retaliating* against terrorist attacks by Palestinians, and to suspend our own military operations during the Muslim holy month of Ramadan (something none of them had ever done while at war either with one another or with Israel). By contrast, Pakistan, by permitting us to launch air operations from its territory, actually made our eventual victory over the Taliban regime in land-locked Afghanistan far easier than it would have been if we had depended on distant bases and aircraft carriers alone.

These military considerations supplied a justification for the alliance with Pakistan that was lacking where other Islamic members of the coalition were concerned. But even here there was a downside, since some indeterminate number of al Qaeda fighters escaped from Afghanistan into Pakistan when defeat became inevitable, and were able to blend in with a still sympathetic population. Whether they would pose a threat to us again in the future remained to be seen, as did the extent to which President Musharaff of Pakistan would remain willing and/or able to cooperate with us against them.

But if the coalition was unnecessary both from a political and from a military point of view, and if the inclusion within it of states harboring terrorists undermined and obfuscated the moral clarity of the war we were determined to wage, why did the administration devote so much energy to assembling it?

The explanation is that getting a minimal endorsement from as many predominantly Muslim states as possible helped create the impression that our war was not against Islam but against terrorism. Bin Laden might claim to be fighting in the name of Islam against the Christian "Crusaders" of today, but with the backing of several Islamic countries, Bush could charge the terrorists with having "hijacked" a religion that—as he persisted in saying and perhaps even believed—in reality stood for peace and love. (Actually, the word "Islam" means not "peace" but "submission.")

⋯⊙⋯

As I write in late December, the campaign in Afghanistan is winding down. The Taliban regime has been routed, many or most of the al Qaeda forces it had been harboring have either been killed or captured, and a new government is being installed that, whatever else it may do, will not offer hospitality to terrorists. No one yet knows where Osama bin Laden is, or whether he is even still alive, and the hunt is on for him or for clues to his whereabouts, and also for intelligence concerning any future plans, in the caves of Tora Bora.

But with Afghanistan gradually fading from attention, the focus is now on phase two of the war, and the main issue is whether or not Iraq should be next. Some commentators are convinced that Saddam Hussein had a hand in September 11, as well as in the bombing of the World Trade Center in 1993, and that Iraq was the original source of the anthrax sent through the mails to several congressional leaders. Others are equally persuaded that Saddam had nothing to do with any of these. But no one seems ready to absolve Saddam Hussein of the responsibility for attempting to assassinate the elder Bush after he left office.

Anyway, it is by now no longer necessary to prove that Saddam is a sponsor of terrorism in order to consider Iraq a target of the war against it, since the President has already established a rationale in stating that, "If you develop weapons of mass destruction [with which] you want to terrorize the world, you'll be held accountable." There is no doubt that Saddam already possesses large stores of chemical and biological weapons, and may (according to Khidhir Hamza, a defector who was once his chief nuclear adviser) be "on the precipice of nuclear power."

Both within the administration and in the country at large, a sharp debate is now raging over this issue (though all the members of the coalition, including even the British under Tony Blair, who were our staunchest supporters in phase one, not to mention the lukewarm Muslim states, are—or say in public that they are—against going after Saddam Hussein). Some urge that we defer confronting Iraq, and instead concentrate on easier targets first. Others contend that the longer we wait, the more dangerous Saddam will grow.

Yet whether or not Iraq becomes the second front in the war against terrorism, one thing is certain: there can be no victory in this war if it ends with

Saddam Hussein still in power. As Eliot A. Cohen, one of our leading students of military strategy, has written in the *Wall Street Journal:*

> War with Iraq will have its perils. Some are likely to be illusory: the Arab "street," for example, which never quite rises as promised. Others may be quite real, to include the use of chemical and biological weapons. Should the U.S. fail to take the challenge, sooner or later it is sure to find Iraqi terror on its doorstep. It may have already. Should the U.S. rise to the occasion, however, it may begin a transformation of the Middle East that could provide many benefits to the populations of an unfree region. That will, in the end, make us infinitely more secure at home.

ᴄᴏʀᴏᴠ

In my opinion, by raising the possibility of a transformation of the Middle East, Cohen cuts to the heart of the matter. All wars have consequences that those who enter into them cannot always foresee or may not desire. But big wars do much more than that: they invariably end by reshaping the world. The war of September 11 will be just such a big one—if, as I hope, President Bush is serious about pursuing it to the end, and can hold onto the necessary political support at home for doing so.

In a different piece in the *Wall Street Journal,* Eliot Cohen has also proposed that we look upon this as World War IV, the immediate successor to the cold war, which he rightly characterizes as World War III and to which he sees many similarities in the struggle we are now conducting:

> The cold war was World War III, which reminds us that not all global conflicts entail the movement of multi-million-man armies, or conventional front lines on a map. The analogy with the cold war does, however, suggest some key features of that conflict: that it is, in fact, global; that it will involve a mixture of violent and nonviolent efforts; that it will require mobilization of skill, expertise and resources, if not of vast numbers of soldiers; that it may go on for a long time; and that it has ideological roots.

The last point—around which "Americans still tiptoe"—again cuts to the heart of the matter. The real enemy in this war, Cohen argues—as Daniel Pipes has also so persistently and authoritatively done at greater length—is not the generalized abstraction "terrorism," but rather "militant Islam."[5]

Militant Islam today represents a revival of the expansionism by the sword that carried the new religion from its birthplace in Arabia in the 7th century C.E. through North Africa, the Balkans, Spain, and as far West as the gates of Vienna in the 1680's. In the East, it swept through, among other countries, India, Iran, Afghanistan, and Indonesia, and also penetrated southward into the African lands that became Nigeria and Sudan.

Never in any of those places did Islam undergo anything resembling the various forms of modernization and reform that took place within Christianity and Judaism. The lone exception was Turkey after World War I, under the secularist Kemal Ataturk. But the expectation that Turkey would set a model for the future was not fulfilled. It is true that there are rival traditions—Sunni, Shi'a,

Wahabbi—in the many other predominantly Muslim states, but all these sects are equally orthodox.

Certainly not all Muslims are terrorists. Like any other collection of human beings, they can as individuals be good or evil, kind or cruel, intelligent or stupid, sweet or sour. But it would be dishonest to ignore the plain truth that Islam has become an especially fertile breeding-ground of terrorism in our time. This can only mean that there is something in the religion itself that legitimizes the likes of Osama bin Laden, and indeed there is: the obligation imposed by the Koran to wage holy war, or jihad, against the "infidels."

Two months before September 11, a talk show on the Arabic TV network al-Jazeera broadcast a debate on the topic "Bin Laden—The Arab Despair and American Fear." At the conclusion of the program, the host said to the guest who had been attacking bin Laden as a terrorist: "I am looking at the viewers' reactions for one that would support your positions—but... I can't find any." He then cited "an opinion poll in a Kuwaiti paper which showed that 69 percent of Kuwaitis, Egyptians, Syrians, Lebanese, and Palestinians think bin Laden is an Arab hero and an Islamic jihad warrior." He also cited a poll on the station's Internet site in which

> 82.7 percent saw bin Laden as a jihad fighter, 8.8 percent as a terrorist, and 8.4 percent didn't know.... There is an Arab consensus from the Gulf to the [Atlantic] Ocean.... The people who use the Internet are the educated class—and if this is the situation with them, you can only imagine what it is among the poor, the persecuted, and those who have been stripped [of their rights]. Maybe even 99.99 percent.[6]

⋯⊙⋯

If these numbers are even remotely accurate, what hope is there for winning the war we are fighting against militant Islam and the terrorism it uses as its main weapon against us?

One answer is that the defeat of bin Laden will diminish his support dramatically. As he himself once stated, "When people see a strong horse and a weak horse, by nature they will like the strong horse." But I would suggest that a better answer to this enormously difficult question lies in the outburst of relief and happiness that became so vivid among the people of Kabul after we had driven out their Taliban oppressors. Surely what we saw in Kabul provides evidence that Muslims no more like being pushed around and repressed and beaten and killed by thugs—even thugs in clerical garb or quoting from the Qur'an—than does anyone else. Surely they do not enjoy being poor and hungry and ill-housed. Surely they would welcome the comforts and conveniences that are taken for granted in the developed world (remember the poignant run on videocassettes in liberated Kabul?).

In this connection, Bernard Lewis, the greatest contemporary scholar of the Islamic world, makes a very striking observation:

> Generally speaking, popular good will toward the United States is in inverse proportion to the policies of [Islamic] governments. In countries like Saudi Arabia and Egypt, with governments seen as American allies, the popular

mood is violently anti-American, and it is surely significant that the majority of known hijackers and terrorists come from these countries. In Iran
and Iraq, with governments seen as anti-American, public opinion is pro-
American. The joy displayed by the Afghan people at the ending of Taliban
rule could be repeated, on a larger scale, in both these countries.

It does not follow that capitalist democracies can be established overnight
throughout the "house of Islam" simply by the force of American arms or the
American example. No such inverse instant conversion by the sword is at all
likely. But it is not so outlandish to expect huge changes in that realm—or at
least large parts of it—that will bring about the long-delayed reform and modernization of Islam. This, in turn, would finally give adherents of Islam a chance
to set their feet on the path to greater freedom and greater prosperity—and, not
so incidentally, to make their peace with the existence of Israel.

Big wars, to say it again, usually end with the world being reshaped in
forms unanticipated when they begin. The Middle East is itself a case in point.
For the Middle East we know today was not created by a mandate from heaven,
and the miserable despotisms there did not evolve through some unstoppable
natural or historical process. As it happens, most of the states in question were
conjured into existence less than a hundred years ago out of the ruins of the
defeated Ottoman empire in World War I. Their boundaries were drawn by
the victorious British and French with the stroke of an often arbitrary pen,
and their hapless peoples were handed over in due course to one tyrant after
another. There is thus no warrant to assume that these states will last forever in
their present forms, or that the only alternatives to them are necessarily worse.

In a long article in *Newsweek*, Fareed Zakaria has contended that the way
"to save the Arab world" is for the United States to get over this "fear of the
worse alternative" that has prevented us from pressuring for political and economic reforms:

> We do not seek democracy in the Middle East—at least not yet. We seek
> first what might be called the preconditions for democracy... the rule of
> law, individual rights, private property, independent courts, the separation
> of church and state.... We should not assume that what took hundreds of
> years in the West can happen overnight in the Middle East.

Well, yes—and fulfilling Zakaria's agenda would be a tremendous leap forward. But I have to take issue with the idea that democracy and capitalism can
grow only in a soil that has been cultivated for centuries. After all, in the aftermath of World War II, the United States managed in a few short years to
transform both Nazi Germany and imperial Japan into capitalist democracies.
And thanks to our victory in World War III, something similar seems to be
happening on its own steam in Central and Eastern Europe, and even in the
old heartland of the evil empire itself. Why should the Islamic world eternally
remain an exception?

Consider: the campaign against al Qaeda required us to topple the Taliban
regime, and we may willy-nilly find ourselves forced by the same political and
military logic to topple five or six or seven more tyrannies in the Islamic world
(including that other sponsor of terrorism, Yasir Arafat's Palestinian Authority).

I can even go along with David Pryce-Jones in imagining the turmoil of this war leading to some new species of an imperial mission for America, whose purpose would be to oversee the emergence of successor governments in the region more amenable to reform and modernization than the despotisms now in place. Like Pryce-Jones, I can also envisage the establishment of some kind of American protectorate over the oil fields of Saudi Arabia, as we more and more come to wonder why 7,000 princes should go on being permitted to exert so much leverage over us and everyone else.

I fully realize that we are judged both by others, and by ourselves, as lacking the stomach and the skills to play even so limited an imperial role as we did in occupying Germany and Japan after World War II. I confess that I myself am sometimes prey to such doubts about our capabilities, or to other doubts stemming from our nature as a nation. Moreover, thinking about our long record of inattention and passivity toward terrorism, I fear a relapse into appeasement, diplomatic evasion, and ineffectual damage control.[7]

⋖⊙⋗

Yet, given the transfiguring impact of major wars on the victors no less than on the vanquished, who can tell what we may wind up doing and becoming as we fight our way through World War IV? Whatever the exact contours may turn out to be, the Islamic countries in particular, and the world in general, will look very different by the time this war is over. Very different, and very much better for the vast majority of people everywhere. Unless, that is, the United States is held back by its coalition from moving all the way forward, or the President breaks the promise he made, in his magnificent speech to Congress on September 20, not to waver or falter or tire or lose patience until victory is achieved—a victory that would leave us not with "an age of terror" but with "an age of liberty here and across the world."

Notes

1. We are instructed by *Aviation Week & Space Technology* that the proper name for these bombs is BLU-82, nicknamed "Big Blue," and that a daisy cutter is not a bomb at all but a type of fuse. Even so, the latter term, inaccurately applied to the bomb itself, has stuck, whereas the nickname never managed to enter popular discourse.

2. By now, according to the *New York Times*, the suspicions of Emerson and Woolsey have been accepted by the intelligence officials who had originally rejected them in favor of the rogue-group theory. Not so, however, with Laurie Mylroie's (to me) plausible case implicating Saddam Hussein as well.

3. For a much fuller and more detailed account of terrorist attacks originating in the Middle East since 1970, see the chronology compiled by Caroline Tail-landier for the *Middle East Review of International Affairs* (MERIA), December 2001(meria.idc.ac.il). I have relied on this document in my own sketchier summary, as well as on "Terrorist Attacks on Americans," a "timeline" put together by the PBS *Frontline* series in conjunction with one of its post-September 11 broadcasts (www.pbs.org/wgbh/pages/frontline/shows/target/etc/cron.html).

    Another listing, going back further than either of these, was recently compiled by the U.S. State Department (www.state.gov/r/pa/ho/pubs/fs/index.cfm).

Entitled "Significant Terrorist Incidents, 1961–2001," this compilation is not re-stricted to attacks emanating from the Middle East or directed at the United States; but neither does it contain any information about responses by the targets of such attacks. And it inexplicably omits some major terrorist incidents, such as "Black September" in Jordan in 1970 and a series of PFLP attacks in the late 1960's.

4. The other five were Iran, Iraq, Libya, Sudan, and Syria.

5. See, most recently, Pipes's "Who Is the Enemy?" in the January [2002] COMMEN-TARY. Cohen and Pipes do not go into the question of the relation between Saddam Hussein and militant Islam. But David Pryce-Jones, whose *The Closed Circle* (1989, recently reissued in paperback by Ivan Dee with a new post-September 11 intro-duction) is one of our best books on the Arabs, has put it this way: "To Saddam, bin Laden is a religious fanatic of the kind he usually hangs on the gallows. To bin Laden, Saddam is secular, an apostate. [But] what they share is hatred for the United States . . . and they seek its destruction." To this I would add that, like the PLO, Saddam plays the Islamic card whenever it suits him.

6. Many more excerpts from this debate, from which I have quoted only a tiny por-tion, are accessible on the website of the Middle East Media and Research Institute, or MEMRI (www.memri.org/sd/SP31901.html).

7. This record is richly documented by Gabriel Schoenfeld in "Could September 11 Have Been Averted?" (COMMENTARY, December 2001). Then there is the statement of Michael A. Sheehan, Clinton's last assistant secretary of state for counterter-rorism, that is quoted by Gellman in his two-part series in the *Washington Post:* "[I]t was the collective judgment of the American people, not just the Clinton administration, that the impact of terrorism was at a level that was acceptable."

NO ↰

Thomas Harrison

Only a Democratic Foreign Policy
Can Combat Terrorism

A Crime Against Humanity

Writing three months after September 11, I can only recall the horror and incomprehension I felt, like millions of others, at the colossal and utterly sickening cruelty of the attack on the World Trade Center. Familiarity with history's countless barbarities doesn't help one understand how human beings can do such things. As a New Yorker, a Manhattanite, who once had a fine view of the Twin Towers from my apartment window, I struggle now to recall exactly where they were on the skyline. They were hardly beautiful, but they *were* impressive. Impossible to fully grasp, even after having seen "ground zero," that they are now nothing but smoking graveyards.

Whatever bin Laden's expectations, it might so easily have been far worse. Nearly three thousand dead is bad enough. But for all the hijackers and their masters knew, most of the 50,000 people who normally worked in the World Trade Center might have been at their jobs that morning, and far fewer might have managed to escape. The Twin Towers might have toppled over, rather than collapsing vertically, crushing a great many nearby buildings.

The September 11 terrorists must have carefully selected the targets for their symbolic significance. But the goal of Osama bin Laden and Al Qaeda, with, one must assume, the hearty approval of their Taliban hosts, was also to kill Americans—"infidels" or Muslims, it didn't matter—as many as possible and in the most spectacular way imaginable, not to force the U.S. government to accede to some set of demands. Military deterrence is America's ultimate weapon against all foreign foes, actual and potential. There was no way to deter the terrorists by threats of retaliation, however—nor could they be "appeased." Suicidal holy warriors are not put off by the promise of deadly response, and it is hard to imagine any sort of concessions by the United States that would have stopped these possessed zealots. Their mental universe is a supernatural, not a political, one—not, that is, a world defined by human-scale means and ends. But they live in the real world, and in that world U.S. foreign policy,

From Thomas Harrison, "Only a Democratic Foreign Policy Can Combat Terrorism," *New Politics*, vol. 8, no. 4 (Winter 2002). Copyright © 2002 by *New Politics*. Reprinted by permission.

especially toward the Muslim countries, could have made and can still make a big difference.

"War Is the Health of the State"

Americans have lost their "invulnerability," it is said. As inhabitants of the world's chief superpower, Americans have long been shielded from some of the harsher realities faced by our fellow human beings, and they have gotten used to a feeling of privileged isolation. September 11 has seriously challenged this smug fortress mentality. At the same time, however, it has only strengthened Americans' belief that their country is entitled to lord it over the rest of the world. This belief is not unshakeable, as we know from past history, but at the moment it is probably flourishing as never before since the 1950s.

There was nothing admirable about Americans' belief that they led some sort of charmed existence. It was always part of this country's monumental imperialist conceit, and it encouraged ignorance and indifference to the fate of other peoples. Nevertheless, there is no justification for sanctimony or speaking of chickens coming home to roost. Neither Americans nor any other people, it should go without saying, "deserve" the sort of thing that occurred on September 11, no matter what crimes their government has committed.

But the fact remains that the American government, the American military and American corporations preside over a world-system that is catastrophically irrational and deeply inhumane. And now, for the time being, that dominance is more secure than it has been in a long time, which is very bad news for the rest of the world—and for us. Abroad, billions will continue to toil and die in the most abysmal squalor, thanks in large part to the tyranny of American-backed rulers, the policies of American-dominated international financial institutions and the needs of the global capitalist order. A vast portion of the world's population, perhaps as much as one third, is unemployed. These billions could be put to work building, educating, producing the things that people so desperately need. But under the present system this can never happen.

At home, the trend for the past decade and more has been for the Democrats to close ranks with the Republicans over foreign and military policy. But now, in the aftermath of September 11, almost no one in Congress or the media will have the courage to suggest that the U.S. should not continue to guard its global preeminence at all costs, that it is madness to maintain a bloated military establishment, bristling with ever-more horrifying weapons, sucking up vital resources that could be used to support decent lives for millions both here and abroad. There will be very little talk of eliminating or even scaling down the country's massive nuclear arsenal, which poses a world-wide security threat that makes Osama bin Laden look like a juvenile delinquent.

Meanwhile, no one seems to know where the war is going—perhaps including the war makers themselves. Even among many of those who support the war, there is a sense of dread as Congress rubber-stamps the administration's demands for extraordinary war powers, arrangements are made for secret military tribunals, and talk of fifth columnists and traitors proliferates. As for the President, his glaring personal inadequacies and his political illegitimacy—the stolen election of 2000—have been all but forgotten. Now this grotesque windup-doll, absurd and evil at the same time, this utter cipher gets to strut across the national and world stage, a servile press hanging on his every inane word, issuing peremptory edicts and attempting to sound stern and menacing....

The Attack on Afghanistan Is No Just War

The Prussian military theorist Karl von Clausewitz famously described war as the continuation of politics by other—military—means. The politics of this war have nothing to do with stopping terrorism per se—American leaders know full well that they cannot do this. The real politics are about something else— extending U.S. hegemony over Afghanistan and, more importantly, reasserting American predominance as the world's leading superpower and chief cop of the global capitalist order. Even the war's open-endedness, the administration's refusal to clearly define goals, has a definite political meaning: the assertion of an unlimited "right" to attack any country the United States chooses.

Strengthening ties to the Saudi royal family, winning the discreet concordance of the Iranian mullahs, and forging links with the Central Asian republics have served to further shore up American domination of the Persian Gulf region and its hinterland. A new U.S. military presence has already been established in Pakistan, Uzbekistan, and Tajikistan, as well as Afghanistan itself. As I write, it is not yet clear if the war will be carried to Iraq, Yemen, Lebanon and Somalia: here too, striking at a vicious dictator in Baghdad or at terrorist nests in the other countries would have the effect primarily of advancing American power, with all the malign consequences that would flow from that—and not promoting democracy and "civilized values."

The war's brevity (assuming it ends with the final elimination of the Taliban and Al Qaeda), and relatively limited civilian casualties do not obviate its essential immorality. One has to be cautious about describing civilian deaths as "limited," of course, because the press has no reliable estimates at this point. The Pentagon probably has a pretty good idea how many civilians have perished under the bombardments, but for obvious reasons it is keeping this information secret. The number of civilian casualties is in all likelihood well above the toll in the World Trade Center attack. U.S. policy of relying on the Northern Alliance and anti-Taliban Pashtun militias as ground forces (there has been very little sustained combat on the ground), while conducting heavy aerial bombardment guarantees the deaths of thousands of innocent Afghans. But no matter how many or few have died and will die, there can be no justification for killing Afghan peasants and other noncombatants to extract vengeance for September 11 or to further the interests of American power. There is no reason to doubt the word of [President George W.] Bush and [Secretary of Defense Donald] Rumsfeld that they don't *want* innocent people to perish, but they obviously know that numerous civilian casualties are inevitable and, frankly, it's hard to imagine them losing much sleep over it....

Varieties of Terrorism

The claim that the American government is waging a war against "terrorism" is absolutely Orwellian. To be sure, the incident that began the current conflict was an act of terrorism in the fullest sense and of the most horrific kind. By plunging those planes into the World Trade Center and the Pentagon, Al Qaeda declared war on the entire American people, not just on the U.S. government. Its object was to frighten and demoralize the whole population, to make it so that no American can feel safe. But terrorism comes in many forms.

Terrorism—instilling fear for political ends—originally meant state terrorism, used against domestic opponents of a government as during the French Revolution. Later it came to be applied almost exclusively to anti-state actions, what anarchists called the "propaganda of the deed." In the 1970s "international terrorism" emerged—bombings, hostage seizures, plane hijackings—often supported by "rogue states." Since World War II, however, terrorism perpetrated by the world's most powerful (non-"rogue") states against foreign countries has devastated great swaths of the globe and taken far more victims than any band of hijackers or suicide bombers.

The chief culprit in this sort of terrorism has been none other than the United States. Through direct military intervention and the sponsorship of foreign proxies, the U.S. government has terrorized vast populations as a means of crushing popular insurgencies and keeping pro-American elites in power. Instead of hijacking and hostage-taking, the U.S. has trained torturers and death squads, provided weaponry and intelligence, and, when necessary, itself bombed civilians from the air to secure its aims. This state terrorism in defense of the status quo has simply dwarfed the other kind (which, of course, does not justify terrorism by less powerful states or by non-state forces).

The anti-terrorist credentials of America's current allies simply cannot be taken seriously. Pakistan and Saudi Arabia, along with the United States, helped create the very networks that gave birth to the Taliban and Al Qaeda. In the 1980s, Pakistan's military dictator, general Zia-ul-Haq, the recipient of billions of dollars in U.S. and Saudi aid, set up hundreds of fundamentalist madrasas, religious schools, to train young men to be terrorist fanatics. Pakistan continues to sponsor terrorist attacks on India. Within Saudi Arabia, the fantastically corrupt autocracy, increasingly cut off from its subjects, has in its panic and desperation poured millions into violent fundamentalist groups as protection money—even though these groups are dedicated to its overthrow. Russia wages a war of terror against Chechen civilians. China's totalitarian regime, with its secret police, vast gulag of prisons and thousands of executions, is a terror state par excellence. Actually, none of the big powers currently supporting the anti-terrorist crusade have any objection to terrorism as such, just to terrorism directed against them. As the wildly overrated Colin Powell put it, with truly breathtaking cynicism: "One man's terrorist is another man's freedom fighter."

"Why Do They Hate Us?"

Bin Laden, the Taliban and the Islamists *depend* on the crimes of American foreign policy. Without these crimes, their political appeal would be much weaker. The answer to the question so often asked in the aftermath of September 11 —"Why do they hate us?"—is that it's our country's actions, our government's foreign policy above all, rather than our "values"—what we *do*, not what we supposedly stand for—that fuels popular anger in the Muslim world. Like people in all poor, tradition-bound societies, the consciousness of the broad majority is fairly conservative and patriarchal. This is especially true where a mass-based secularist, democratic left has either been crushed or hasn't yet developed— which is the case throughout the Muslim world. Plus, of course, the teachings of mainstream Islam—like those of most religions—tend to have a conservatizing impact on popular consciousness. But if many Muslims respond to the appeals of political Islamism it is not—apart from a hard core—because they want to obliterate "Western civilization" and establish a global theocracy. Political sympathy for Islamism is fundamentally *reactive*—to the policies of the U.S. and other Western countries, and to the authoritarian rule of Western client regimes.

When American leaders proclaim their commitment to democracy and human rights, most citizens of Muslim countries know that this is a lie, that the U.S. has been a determined and very effective enemy of every attempt to empower the mass of Muslim people. For decades now, the American government has supported every dictator and corrupt royal family that has agreed to play along with it. Our vaunted "way of life" is a privilege we jealously reserve for ourselves, Western Europe and a few other rich nations. Muslims regard the U.S. as an arrogant, hypocritical, and totally self-interested bully, a global thug, a genuine rogue state that does exactly as it pleases. And to top it all off, in their eyes the U.S. is a cowardly thug that wages risk-free wars, firing missiles at its enemies from hundreds of miles away and dropping bombs from 15,000 feet in the air.

There can be little doubt that this is how our country is perceived by the mass of Muslims from Morocco to Indonesia—even Iranian young people chafing under the mullahs and longing for Western-style freedoms, or Afghans temporarily elated by the fall of the Taliban and grateful to their "liberators." Actual *political* support for the U.S.—that is, support for its global role as the dominant superpower—is limited to a small minority among the privileged elite. Among ordinary people, only those who have actually experienced life under Islamist regimes—as in Iran and Afghanistan—will gravitate toward the U.S., but even then only temporarily. In the last analysis, the American government can have little appeal to the masses in the Muslim world because it does not trust or respect them, and because it fears their democratic power like poison....

The Appeal of Islamism

Symbiosis—a relationship of mutual support between two quite different organisms—describes the relationship between American foreign policy and Islamic fundamentalism—and the war has reinforced it. Western fear of totalitarian Islamism has long served to mute domestic criticism of U.S. policy toward the Muslim world. And now the attack on the World Trade Center has herded even more critics into the war camp and provided new justification for the use of military force in the Middle East and Central Asia. On the other side, the pervasive Muslim resentment of the United States, the anger at American policy in the Middle East, Iraq, the Arabian Peninsula and elsewhere, has long been exploited by bin Laden and the Islamists. In the face of an increasingly monolithic American public opinion, Muslims, especially young men, are attracted to ever more desperate forms of anti- Americanism.

The cause of Al Qaeda and other apocalyptic and ultra-violent elements among the Islamists is not democracy, Palestinian rights, social justice for the poor—not at all. Their goal is a grim regime of total oppression, a Taliban-like state for every Muslim nation, virtual imprisonment for every Muslim girl and woman, extermination or expulsion for the Jews of Israel. They would not abandon their bloody schemes even if the U.S. pursued entirely different policies. Behind them are the Muslims who make up the rank and file of the much larger and less apocalyptic (though still generally reactionary and anti-democratic) Islamist parties and underground movements. These groups flourish in the absence of a secular, anti-imperialist left, most of which has been destroyed or discredited (for example in Afghanistan by its association with the Soviet occupation).

With no democratic left-wing alternative, millions of the poor and aggrieved are attracted to political Islamism, while millions more reject theocracy but are still strongly anti-American, many even admiring bin Laden. Most detest the Taliban and Al Qaeda, and many explicitly repudiate the terrorist attacks on Americans—while at the same time opposing the war against Afghanistan and wishing defeat and disgrace to the United States. The Turkish novelist Orhan Pamuk (*New York Review of Books,* Nov. 15, 2001) described one of his neighbors in Istanbul, an old man, not religious at all, who barely makes a living doing minor repair work. On hearing of the World Trade Center attacks, he told Pamuk: "Sir, have you seen? They have bombed America," and added, "They did the right thing." Pamuk notes that this old man later regretted his comment, but of course it is the initial response that is so telling and, there is every reason to believe, so typical. That fewer innocent Afghans than expected have been killed does not fundamentally alter the perception that America has bombed a ruined nation and a helpless population in order to satisfy it's craving for revenge and power. . . .

Not Containment but Liberation

The anti-war movement has so far concentrated on getting the bombing stopped and the starving fed in Afghanistan and on defending Muslims against racist attacks in this country. These are important goals, of course, but they don't by themselves address Americans' legitimate security concerns, nor do they get at the root of the reactionary global dynamic, fueled by U.S. foreign policy, that drives people in Muslim countries toward terrorist fundamentalism.

Opposition to the war and to current U.S. foreign policy must be accompanied by opposition to totalitarian Islamism, indeed to all regimes and political movements that trample on human rights in the name of religion or any other ideology. And not just opposition either, but proposals for a political offensive against Islamism and terrorism as well—including *all* terrorism, notably that of our own government. This is a cause that the peace movement should champion. It must not be left to the American Establishment to exploit the real problem of terrorism for its own purposes.

The Bush administration, as well as the rest of the Establishment, knows that it cannot eliminate the sort of terrorism with which it is now at war. They accept the permanent existence of conditions throughout the Muslim world that nurture Islamic fundamentalism and terrorism. Their real policy is containment, not elimination. Apart from what containment might mean in terms of further bombing attacks on Muslim countries and certainly will mean in terms of the perpetuation of a monstrously unjust global status quo, it projects a bleak future for us in the West. Networks like Al Qaeda may be wiped out, but the kind of terrorism they practice never will be. Christopher Hitchens dismisses such predictions as "witless and fatalistic" (The Nation, Dec. 3, 2001). If new bin Ladens rise up, he assures us, "tens of thousands of people would also rise up to rid the world of bin Ladens all over again." So, for Hitchens too, containment—and, evidently, perpetual war—is the only realistic perspective.

Now *this* is fatalism, and the American left and the anti-war movement must not succumb to it. A slogan seen on posters at peace demonstrations is "Justice Not Bombs." This begins to suggest a *positive political* program to counter terrorism. But the anti-war movement needs to advocate justice just as strongly as peace. Progressives in general need to start talking about what American foreign policy—a *new* foreign policy—can actually do to promote justice in the Muslim world. Our alternative to imperial intervention should be not "hands off" Afghanistan or wherever, but political engagement, a kind of "intervention from below"—identifying and linking up with groups that are fighting for democracy, secularism, women's rights. With Iraq looking like the next target of American military intervention, it is crucial to make connections with democratic Iraqi oppositionists. Political solidarity and concrete acts of assistance from the American left would also help counter any attempts by our government to suck opposition groups into its orbit.

Making these links would be one step in the development of a clear alternative to the militaristic containment policy of the American Establishment. The left needs to propose a new deal for the Muslim world: democracy and economic development. It needs to say: our position is not the acceptance of a "contained" terrorism, while leaving the Muslim world to fester in its misery. We want to do all we can—and to use the immense political and material resources of the United States—to help the peoples of the Muslim world liberate themselves. Self-emancipation, not control and manipulation, should be the guiding principle of American policy. We want to see the people of Iran, Iraq, and the Arabian Peninsula take possession of their oil resources and use the wealth to raise their standard of living, not to enrich parasitical elites. Freedom and prosperity will reduce terrorism to insignificance in all those countries where millions, in their poverty and desperation, now celebrate bin Laden as a hero and lend apocalyptic Islamism a sympathetic ear.

A Democratic Foreign Policy: Deeds, Not Just Words

Stanley Hoffman writes that the fight against terrorism "needs to begin with an adequate understanding of our adversaries' grievances, if only to allow us to shape a perceptive policy." Terror feeds "on experiences of despair and humiliation, and these can be understood and to some degree addressed." Also writing in the *New York Review* (Nov. 15, 2001), Tony Judt is even more forthright: "The U.S. needs thoroughly to reassess its relationship to the rest of the world"—a promising suggestion! "Our efforts to eradicate terrorism will go for nothing if we keep uncritical company for tactical ends with rulers who practice at home the very crimes we claim to abhor." But in the end Hoffman and Judt propose only words, not deeds. Judt wants Washington to "distance itself" from repressive governments and to "take its political case" to Muslim public opinion—presumably as Tony Blair did on the Al Jazeera satellite network. The problem is, without deeds—that is, without actually pulling the American props out from under these governments—there *is* no political case, at least not one that is likely to make much of an impression on Muslim public opinion.

But if centrists like Hoffman and Judt have little to offer, not much more can be said of the left. A *Nation* editorial complains, "we wish Secretary of State Powell had shown more urgency" in calling on Israel to halt settlements in the Occupied Territories. The same editorial calls for a new Marshall Plan for the Islamic world, insisting that it is "not utopian" to hope this government might sponsor such a scheme. Unfortunately it is thoroughly utopian. What *this* government wants in the Muslim nations is oil and "stability"—meaning authoritarian regimes that keep the masses at bay—not democracy and economic development. Whether Republicans or Democrats are in charge, it is by its very nature incapable of fostering anything else, and one misleads people by suggesting otherwise.

There's nothing wrong with calling on the government to do the right thing in its foreign policy, of course. Indeed, it is essential to demand that it provide things like famine relief, economic aid, sanctions on South Africa, lifting the arms embargo on Bosnia, etc. We certainly must insist that *this* government put pressure on Sharon to withdraw from the Occupied Territories, that it lift the cruel sanctions on Iraq, that it stop supporting repressive regimes wherever they are, and so on. But if that's *it*, if your strategy is *mainly directed* at urging those in power to be more democratic and you've based everything on this perspective, then you're facing a dead end. The only strategy that has a hope of transforming U.S. foreign policy is one that focuses on building a movement to throw both the Republicans and the Democrats out of power. As part of *that* effort, it makes sense to demand of the powers that be that they pursue a democratic foreign policy—while openly stating that you know they cannot do it. A serious third party that campaigned for a new foreign policy might even extract important foreign policy concessions—just as the anti-apartheid movement did in the 1980s—but it would not be able to change the basic orientation of U.S. foreign policy until it won political power. The leopard will never change its spots.

A systematically democratic foreign policy, championed by an independent progressive political party, would take Americans' fears for their security seriously by arguing that real security is only possible in a democratic and egalitarian world. To start bringing this new world into being, it would propose, first of all, withdrawal of all support for dictators, kings and emirs. To counter those who insist that only by keeping these unsavory rulers in power can Americans be assured of oil supplies, the proponents of a new foreign policy would respond that democratic governments are much more reliable trading partners —but also that a rational energy policy must emphasize the development of alternative fuels.

By promoting democracy and development, this new foreign policy would drive a wedge between the fundamentalists and the Muslim people. Its goal would not be to appease people like Osama bin Laden but to defeat him and all that he represents politically. U.S. troops would be withdrawn from Saudi Arabia not because their presence is something bin Laden and his ilk particularly object to, but because they have no legitimate business being there in the first place.

Economic sanctions against Iraq would be ended, not because we want "peace" with Saddam Hussein; on the contrary, we should actively support all democratic forces aiming for his overthrow, even to the point of supplying them with arms. An absolutely central part of any democratic foreign policy toward the Muslim world, an indispensable proof of this country's seriousness, would be to stop all military aid to Israel and finally put serious pressure on it to withdraw completely from the Occupied Territories. The United States must give full political support to an independent, democratic Palestinian state in the West Bank and Gaza; at least as much foreign aid as that now lavished on Israel should be given to the Palestinians, who for so long have been the victims of U.S.-backed Israeli aggression.

All military aid to the crooks and torturers who rule Egypt would be terminated forthwith. Similar action would be taken against the Turkish government, along with demands that it fully recognize the right of the Kurdish people to self-determination. Real pressure would be exerted on Russia to pull out of Chechnya. The list could go on.

This would be a program of deeds, not just words. If it were implemented, how could the Islamists capitalize on the crimes of American foreign policy to peddle their reactionary remedies? Nothing would be left but their naked ideology—and in a democratizing Muslim world, this would have less and less appeal.

Organizing and building support for a new party and winning elections won't happen tomorrow or the next day—but, equally obviously, it will never happen unless we start now. However, even the act of forming a significant third party that advocates a democratic foreign policy would have an enormous effect. It would encourage democratic movements throughout the world by letting them know that there is "another America"—and that it is determined to wrest control of this country from the corporations and their political lackeys and military enforcers.

POSTSCRIPT

Is America's War on Terrorism Justified?

$\mathbf{P}$odhoretz thinks the United States is a benign force in the world, while Harrison considers it the leader of "a world-system that is catastrophically irrational and deeply inhumane." And yet, in a curious way, they agree on a number of points. They agree that Al Qaeda is indeed composed of irrational Muslim fanatics, that most of America's Arab allies in the region are enemies of freedom and democracy, and that America's chief enemy, Saddam Hussein, should be removed from power.

William J. Bennett, in *Why We Fight: Moral Clarity and the War on Terrorism* (Doubleday, 2002), no doubt has in mind critics like Harrison when he complains about those who reacted to the events of September 11 by "America-bashing." He worries that such criticism, if repeated too often, may make Americans lose their resolve in the fight against terrorism. Allan J. Cigler has edited a slim but useful book, *Perspectives on Terrorism* (Houghton Mifflin, 2002), containing short essays by authorities in various areas affected by the events of September 11. In *What Went Wrong? Western Impact and Middle Eastern Response* (Oxford University Press, 2001), Bernard Lewis, one of the most respected authorities on the Near East, shows how Islamic civilization fell from its premier position in the Middle Ages to its present condition as "poor, weak, and ignorant." Samuel P. Huntington goes over some of the same ground, but with an emphasis on the militant aspects of Islam today, in *The Clash of Civilizations and the Remaking of World Order* (Touchstone Books, 1998). As'ad AbuKhalil, in *Bin Laden, Islam, and America's New "War on Terrorism"* (Seven Stories Press, 2002), examines long-standing historical tensions between America and the Islamic world, which may have contributed to the events of September 11. Robert Baer, *See No Evil: The True Story of a Ground Soldier in the CIA's War on Terrorism* (Crown Publishers, 2002) is an account of the author's 21-year career as a CIA agent and an indictment of the agency's increasingly out-of-touch and corrupt bureaucratic structure.

It is difficult to imagine what course the war on terror will take in the future or how long it will last. By the middle of 2002 it seemed clear that there were two different factions within the Bush administration: one, represented by Secretary of State Colin Powell, emphasized coalition building and diplomatic initiatives, and the other, led by Secretary of Defense Donald Rumsfeld, pressed for military intervention in Iraq to bring about a "regime change" (a polite expression for overthrowing the government of Saddam Hussein). Powell's position was closer to that of most Europeans, but polls in America showed considerable support for the harder line of Rumsfeld.

ISSUE 18

Is Free Trade Fair Trade?

YES: Douglas A. Irwin, from *Free Trade Under Fire* (Princeton University Press, 2002)

NO: David Morris, from "Free Trade: The Great Destroyer," in Jerry Mander and Edward Goldsmith, eds., *The Case Against the Global Economy: And for a Return to the Local* (Sierra Club Books, 1996)

ISSUE SUMMARY

YES: Professor of economics Douglas A. Irwin asserts that all countries benefit from free trade because it promotes efficiency, spurs production, and forces the least productive companies to reduce their output or shut down, resulting in better goods at lower prices.

NO: David Morris, vice president of the Institute for Local Self-Reliance, argues that free trade is unnecessary because gains in efficiency do not require large-scale multinational enterprises and undesirable because it widens the standard-of-living gap between rich and poor nations.

An economic and cultural revolution like none before it has taken place over the past two decades. In centuries marked by Western imperialism, weak nations were ruled by powerful nations, and their raw and natural resources were expropriated for manufacture by the imperial powers. Now the owners are multinational corporations that know no national boundaries (although their principal owners are usually citizens of the industrial nations), and the manufacturing of the most highly sophisticated technological products takes place in the poorer nations, which achieve higher rates of employment, albeit for much lower wages than workers in the richer nations had earned.

This is globalization—a profound change in the ways in which large-scale business is conducted. It also reflects the computer and the Internet, through which new ideas are communicated without respect to physical boundaries. Globalization is supported by technological breakthroughs, the new markets and profits that powerful corporations now pursue, and governments that subscribe to the changes it brings. For the underdeveloped nations, the advantages include training and employment for poor people and economic development support from international agencies. For the economically advanced nations, the advantages include cheaper manufactured goods and the profits that accrue to stockholders.

In the sense that the world has become more economically interdependent, globalization seems inescapable. Perhaps the most important and controversial characteristic of this change has been a movement toward free markets, or the removal of trade barriers and other constraints on doing business. Free trade is advocated because it fosters openness to new ideas and innovation, with a minimum degree of regulation, and, in the view of its supporters, it encourages the spread of democracy in societies that have not enjoyed political freedom.

Globalization and free trade are opposed by those who believe that the principal and perhaps only beneficiaries are the multinational corporations that sharply reduce their labor costs and even more sharply increase their profits. Opponents acknowledge that investors gain added value, but they maintain that highly skilled and well-paid workers in America and other advanced nations lose good jobs and that poorly paid workers in the underdeveloped countries are exploited. Furthermore, because the owners and most of the customers of industry do not live in the countries where the electronics, clothing, and other manufactured goods are produced, they have little or no concern for the consequences of their investments for those countries.

Thus, the critics charge, free trade is not fair trade. This protest comes from members of labor unions, who witness declining membership as their jobs are taken by workers in poor countries who will accept a fraction of the pay; environmentalists, who deplore deforestation, the pollution of rivers and the air by toxic chemicals, and other health hazards that accompany unregulated industry; and human rights groups, which oppose low wages that perpetuate poverty and exploitation. These groups organized the demonstrations at the 1999 World Trade Organization (WTO) ministerial meeting in Seattle, Washington, which have been repeated at subsequent meetings of the WTO and the World Bank.

The WTO denies that it advocates free trade at any cost. The organization maintains that countries must decide for themselves when, how, and how much to protect domestic producers from dumped or subsidized imports. However, agreements such as the North American Free Trade Agreement (NAFTA) permit foreign investors to sue a national government if their company's property assets, including the intangible property of expected profits, are damaged by that nation's laws, even if those laws were designed to protect the environment or public safety and health. Some advocates of free trade oppose NAFTA and other regional agreements on the grounds that they are preferential arrangements that compromise true free trade.

In the following selection, Douglas A. Irwin concludes that free trade is beneficial because countries that adopt it improve their productivity and increase their per capita income. According to trade studies, says Irwin, the complete elimination of global barriers to trade brings gains to all nations. In the second selection, David Morris discusses the environmental harm and devastating effects in local communities that result from free trade.

337

Douglas A. Irwin

 **YES**

The Case for Free Trade:
Old Theories, New Evidence

For more than two centuries, economists have pointed out the benefits of free trade and the costs of trade restrictions. As Adam Smith argued more than two centuries ago, "All commerce that is carried on betwixt any two countries must necessarily be advantageous to both," and therefore "all duties, customs, and excise [on imports] should be abolished, and free commerce and liberty of exchange should be allowed with all nations." The economic case for free trade, however, is not based on outdated theories in musty old books. The classic insights into the nature of economic exchange between countries have been refined and updated over the years to retain their relevance to today's circumstances. More importantly, over the past decade economists have gathered extensive empirical evidence that contributes appreciably to our understanding of the free trade. This [selection] reviews the classic theories and examines the new evidence, noting as well the qualifications to the case for free trade.

Specialization and Trade

The traditional case for free trade is based on the gains from specialization and exchange. These gains are easily understood at the level of the individual. Most people do not produce for themselves even a fraction of the goods they consume. Rather, we earn an income by specializing in certain activities and then using our earnings to purchase various goods and services—food, clothing, shelter, health care—produced by others. In essence, we "export" the goods and services that we produce with our own labor and "import" the goods and services produced by others that we wish to consume. This division of labor enables us to increase our consumption beyond that which would be possible if we tried to be self-sufficient and produce everything for ourselves. Specialization allows us access to a greater variety and better quality of goods and services.

Trade between nations is simply the international extension of this division of labor. For example, the United States has specialized in the production of aircraft, industrial machinery, and agricultural commodities (particularly corn,

From Douglas A. Irwin, *Free Trade Under Fire* (Princeton University Press, 2002). Copyright © 2002 by Princeton University Press. Reprinted by permission of Princeton University Press. Notes omitted.

soybeans, and wheat). In exchange for exports of these products, the United States purchases, among other things, imports of crude oil, clothing, and iron and steel mill products. Like individuals, countries benefit immensely from this division of labor and enjoy a higher real income than countries that forgo such trade. Just as there seems no obvious reason to limit the free exchange of goods within a country without a specific justification, there is no obvious reason why trade between countries should be limited in the absence of a compelling reason for doing so. . . .

Adam Smith, whose magnificent work *The Wealth of Nations* was first published in 1776, set out [the] case for free trade with a persuasive flair that still resonates today. Smith advocated the "obvious and simple system of natural liberty" in which individuals would be free to pursue their own interests, while the government provided the legal framework within which commerce would take place. With the government enforcing a system of justice and providing certain public goods (such as roads, in Smith's view), the private interests of individuals could be turned toward productive activities, namely, meeting the demands of the public as expressed in the marketplace. Smith envisioned a system that would give people the incentive to better themselves through economic activities, where they would create wealth by serving others through market exchange, rather than through political activities, where they might seek to redistribute existing wealth through, for example, legal restraints on competition. Under such a system, the powerful motivating force of self-interest could be channeled toward socially beneficial activities that would serve the general interest rather than socially unproductive activities that might advance the interests of a select few but would come at the expense of society as a whole.

Free trade is an important component of this system of economic liberty. Under a system of natural liberty in which domestic commerce is largely free from restraints on competition, though not necessarily free from government regulation, commerce would also be permitted to operate freely between countries. According to Smith, free trade would increase competition in the home market and curtail the power of domestic firms by checking their ability to exploit consumers through high prices and poor service. Moreover, the country would gain by exchanging exports of goods that are dear on the world market for imports of goods that are cheap on the world market. . . .

Comparative Advantage

In 1799, a successful London stockbroker named David Ricardo came across a copy of *The Wealth of Nations* while on vacation and quickly became engrossed in the book. Ricardo admired Smith's great achievement, but thought that many of the topics deserved further investigation. For example, Smith believed that a country would export goods that it produces most efficiently and import goods that other countries produce most efficiently. In this way, trade is a mutually beneficial way of increasing total world output and thus the consumption of every country. But, Ricardo asked, what if one country was the most efficient at producing everything? Would that country still benefit from trade? Would disadvantaged countries find themselves unable to export anything?

To overcome this problem, Ricardo arrived at a brilliant deduction that became known as the theory of comparative advantage. Comparative advantage implies that a country could find it advantageous to import some goods even if it could produce those same goods more efficiently than other countries. Conversely, a country would be able to export some goods even if other countries could produce them more efficiently. In either case, countries would be able to benefit from trade. Ricardo's conclusions about the benefits of trade were similar to Smith's, but his approach contains a deeper insight.

At first, the principle of comparative advantage seems counterintuitive. Why would a country ever import a good that it could produce more efficiently than another country? Yet comparative advantage is the key to understanding the pattern of international trade. For example, imagine a consulting firm hired to examine the factors explaining international trade in textiles. The consultants would probably start by examining the efficiency of textile production in various countries. If one country was found to be more efficient than another in producing textiles, the firm might conclude that this country would export textiles and other countries would import them. Yet because this single comparison is insufficient for determining the pattern of trade, this conclusion might well be wrong.

According to Ricardo and the other classical economists of the early nineteenth century, international trade is not driven by the *absolute* costs of production, but by the *opportunity* costs of production. The country most efficient at producing textiles might be even more efficient than other countries at producing other goods, such as shoes. In that case, the country would be best served by directing its labor to producing shoes, in which its margin of productive advantage is even greater than in textiles. As a result, despite its productivity advantage in textiles, the country would export shoes in exchange for imports of textiles. In the absence of other information, the absolute efficiency of one country's textile producers in comparison to another country's is insufficient to determine whether the country produces all of the textiles it consumes or imports some of them....

The Gains From Trade

While the idea that all countries can benefit from international trade goes back to Smith and Ricardo, subsequent research has described the gains from trade in much greater detail. In the *Principles of Political Economy* (1848), John Stuart Mill, one of the leading economists of the nineteenth century, pointed to three principal gains from trade. First, there are what Mill called the "direct economical advantages of foreign trade." Second, there are "indirect effects" of trade, "which must be counted as benefits of a high order." Finally, Mill argued that the economical benefits of commerce are surpassed in importance by those of its effects which are intellectual and moral." What, specifically, are these three advantages of trade?

The "direct economical advantages" of trade are the standard gains that arise from specialization, as described by Smith and Ricardo. By exporting some of its domestically produced goods in exchange for imports, a country engages in mutually advantageous trade that enables it to use its limited productive resources (such as land, labor, and capital) more efficiently and therefore achieve a higher real national income than it could in the absence of trade. A higher real income translates into an ability to afford more of all goods and services than would be possible without trade.

These static gains from specialization are sizable. The classic illustration of the direct gains from trade comes from Japan's opening to the world economy. In 1858, as a result of American pressure, Japan opened its ports to international trade after decades of autarky (economic isolation). The gains from trade can be summarized by examining the prices of goods in Japan before and after the opening of trade. For example, the price of silk and tea was much higher on world markets than in Japan prior to the opening of trade, while the price of cotton and woolen goods was much lower on world markets. Japan therefore exported silk and tea in exchange for imports of clothing and other goods. With the introduction of trade, prices of those goods in Japan converged to the prices on the world market. Japan's terms of trade—the prices of the goods it exported relative to the prices of the goods it imported—improved by a factor of more than three and increased Japan's real income by as much as 65 percent.

Unlike nineteenth-century Japan, most countries have been open to some international trade for centuries, making it difficult to measure the overall gain from free trade. However, economists can estimate the gains from increased trade as a result of the reduction in trade barriers. Computable general equilibrium models, which are complex computational models used to simulate the impact of various trade policies on specific industries and the overall economy, calculate the gains that arise from shifting resources between various sectors of the economy. Specifically, these models examine the shift of labor and capital away from industries that compete against imports toward those in which the country has a comparative advantage as a result of changes in trade policy.

For example, one study showed that the agreements to reduce trade barriers reached under the Uruguay Round of multilateral trade negotiations in 1994 would result in an annual gain of $13 billion for the United States, about 0.2 percent of its GDP [gross domestic product], and about $96 billion in gains for the world, roughly 0.4 percent of world GDP. Another recent study suggests that the gains from further global liberalization are even larger. If a new trade round reduced the world's tariffs on agricultural and industrial goods and barriers on services trade by one third, the welfare gain for the United States would be $177 billion, or 1.95 percent of GDP. Most of this gain comes from liberalizing trade in services. The gain for the world amounts to $613 billion, or about 2 percent of world GDP.

As these examples indicate, the calculated welfare gains that emerge from these simulations are sometimes small as a percentage of GDP. Even some economists have interpreted these calculations to mean that trade liberalization is not especially valuable. But the small numbers arise partly because these agreements usually lead to modest policy changes for the United States. For example, what the United States undertook in signing the Uruguay Round or the North American Free Trade Agreement [NAFTA], essentially making already low import tariffs somewhat lower, cannot be compared to Japan's move from autarky to free trade. The numbers do not reflect the entire gains from trade, just the marginal gains from an additional increase in trade as a consequence of a partial reduction in trade barriers. A complete elimination of global barriers to trade in goods and services would bring much larger gains. According to the last study mentioned in the previous paragraph, removing all such barriers would generate $537 billion in gains for the United States (5.9 percent of GDP) and $1,857 billion in gains for the world (6.2 percent of world GDP).

More importantly, the reallocation of resources across industries as calculated in the simulation models does not take into account the other channels by which trade can improve economic performance. What are these other channels? One view is that greater openness to trade allows firms to sell in a potential larger market, and that firms are able to reduce their average costs of production by expanding the size of their output. The lower production costs resulting from these economies of scale are passed on to consumers and thereby generate additional gains from trade. In evaluating the impact of NAFTA through general equilibrium simulations, for example, moving from the assumption of constant returns to scale to increasing returns to scale boosted the calculated U.S. welfare gain from 1.67 percent of 2.55 percent of its GDP, Canadian welfare gain from 4.87 percent to 6.75 percent of its GDP, and Mexican welfare gain from 2.28 percent to 3.29 of its GDP, according to one study.

These numbers are more impressive, but there are also reasons to be skeptical. Evidence from both developed and developing economies suggests that economies of scale at the plant level for most manufacturing firms tend to be small relative to the size of the market. As a result, most plants have attained their minimum efficient scale. Average costs seem to be relatively unaffected by changes in output, so that a big increase in a firm's output does not lead to lower costs, and a big reduction in output does not lead to higher costs. For example, many firms are forced to reduce output as a result of competition from imports, but these firms' production costs rarely rise significantly. This suggests that the importance of scale economies may be overstated, and yet the simulation models sometimes include them.

There is much better, indeed overwhelming, evidence that free trade improves economic performance by increasing competition in the domestic market. This competition diminishes the market power of domestic firms and leads to a more efficient economic outcome. This benefit does not arise because foreign competition changes a domestic firm's costs through changes in the scale of output, as just noted. Rather, it comes through a change in the pricing behavior of imperfectly competitive domestic firms. Firms with market power tend to restrict output and raise prices, thereby harming consumers while increasing their own profits. With international competition, firms cannot get away with such conduct and are forced to behave more competitively. After Turkey's trade liberalization in the mid-1980s, for example, price-cost margins fell for most industries, consistent with a more competitive outcome. Numerous studies confirm this finding in other countries, providing powerful evidence that trade disciplines domestic firms with market power. Yet the beneficial effects of increasing competition are not always taken into account in simulation models because they frequently assume that perfect competition already exists....

Productivity Gains

Trade improves economic performance not only by allocating a country's resources to their most efficient use, but by making those resources more productive in what they are doing. This is the second of John Stuart Mill's three gains from trade, the one he called "indirect effects." These indirect effects include "the tendency of every extension of the market to improve the processes of production. A country which produces for a larger market than its own can introduce a more extended division of labour, can make greater use of machinery, and is more likely to make inventions and improvements in the processes of production."

In other words, trade promotes productivity growth. The higher is an economy's productivity level, the higher is that country's standard of living. International trade contributes to productivity growth in at least two ways: it serves as a conduit for the transfer of foreign technologies that enhance productivity, and it increases competition in a way that stimulates industries to become more efficient and improve their productivity, often by forcing less productive firms out of business and allowing more productive firms to expand. After neglecting them for many decades, economists are finally beginning to study these productivity gains from trade more systematically.

The first channel, trade as a conduit for the transfer of foreign technologies, operates in several ways. One is through the importation of capital goods. Imported capital goods that embody technological advances can greatly enhance an economy's productivity. For example, the South Carolina textile magnate Roger Milliken (an active financier of anti-free-trade political groups) has bought textile machinery from Switzerland and Germany because domestically produced equipment is more costly and less sophisticated. This imported machinery has enabled his firms to increase productivity significantly. Between a quarter and half of growth in U.S. total factor productivity may be attributed to new technology embodied in capital equipment. To the extent that trade barriers raise the price of imported capital goods, countries are hindering their ability to benefit from technologies that could raise productivity. In fact, one study finds that about a quarter of the differences in productivity across countries can be attributed to differences in the price of capital equipment.

Advances in productivity are usually the result of investment in research and development, and the importation of foreign ideas can be a spur to productivity. Sometimes foreign research can be imported directly. For example, China has long been struggling against a devastating disease known as rice blast, which in the past destroyed millions of tons of rice a year, costing farmers billions of dollars. Recently, under the direction of an international team of scientists, farmers in China's Yunnan province started planting a mixture of two different types of rice in the same paddy. By this simple technique of biodiversity, farmers nearly eliminated rice blast and doubled their yield. Foreign R&D [research and development] enabled the Chinese farmers to increase yields of a staple commodity and to abandon the chemical fungicides they had previously used to fight the disease.

At other times, the benefits of foreign R&D are secured by importing goods that embody it. Countries more open to trade gain more from foreign R&D expenditures because trade in goods serves as a conduit for the spillovers of productive knowledge generated by that R&D. Several studies have found that a country's total factor productivity depends not only on its own R&D, but also on how much R&D is conducted in the countries that it trades with. Imports of specialized intermediate goods that embody new technologies, as well as reverse-engineering of such goods, are sources of R&D spillovers. Thus, developing countries, which do not conduct much R&D themselves, can benefit from R&D done elsewhere because trade makes the acquisition of new technology less costly. These examples illustrate Mill's observation that "whatever causes a greater quantity of anything to be produced in the same place, tends to the general increase of the productive powers of the world."

The second channel by which trade contributes to productivity is by forcing domestic industries to become more efficient. We have already seen that trade increases competition in the domestic market, diminishing the market power of any firm and forcing them to behave more competitively. Competition also stimulates firms to improve their efficiency; otherwise they risk going out of business. Over the past decade, study after study has documented this phenomenon. After the Côte d'Ivoire reformed its trade policies in 1985, overall productivity growth tripled, growing four times more rapidly in industries that became less sheltered from foreign competition. Industry productivity in Mexico increased significantly after its trade liberalization in 1985, especially in traded-goods sectors. Detailed studies of India's trade liberalization in 1991 and Korea's in the 1980s reached essentially the same conclusion: trade not only disciplines domestic firms and forces them to behave more like a competitive industry, but helps increase their productivity.

Competition can force individual firms to adopt more efficient production techniques. But international competition also affects the entry and exit decisions of firms in a way that helps raise the aggregate productivity of an industry. In any given industry, productivity is quite heterogeneous among firms: not all firms are equally efficient. Trade acts to promote high-productivity firms and demote low-productivity firms. On the export side, exposure to trade allows more productive firms to become experts and thereby expand their output. In the United States, plants with higher labor productivity within an industry tend to be the plants that export; in other words, more efficient firms are the ones that become exporters. The opportunity to trade, therefore, allows more efficient firms to grow.

On the import side, competition forces the least productive firms to reduce their output or shut down. For example, when Chile began opening up its economy to the world market in the 1970s, exiting plants were, on average, 8 percent less productive than plants that continued to produce. The productivity of plants in industries competing against imports grew 3 to 10 percent more than in non-traded-goods sectors. Protection had insulated less productive firms from foreign competition and allowed them to drag down overall productivity within an industry, whereas open trade weeded out inefficient firms and allowed more efficient firms to expand. Thus, trade brings about certain firm-level adjustments that increase average industry productivity in both export-oriented and import-competing industries.

The impact of the U.S.-Canada Free Trade Agreement on Canadian manufacturing is also suggestive. Tariff reductions helped boost labor productivity by a compounded rate of 0.6 percent per year in manufacturing as a whole and by 2.1 percent per year in the most affected (i.e., high tariff) industries. These are astoundingly large effects. This amounts to a 17 percent increase in productivity in the post-FTA period in the highly affected sectors, and a 5 percent increase for manufacturing overall. These productivity effects were not achieved through scale effects or capital investment, but rather due to a mix of plant turnover and rising technical efficiency within plants. By raising productivity, the FTA also helped increase the annual earnings of production workers, particularly in the most protected industries.

To sum up, traditional calculations of the gains from trade stress the benefits of shifting resources from protected industries to those with an international comparative advantage. But new evidence shows that, because large productivity differences exist between plants within any given industry, shifting resources between firms within an industry may be even more important. Trade may affect the allocation of resources among firms within an industry as much as, if not more than, it affects the allocation of resources among different industries. In doing so, trade helps improve productivity.

While difficult to quantify, these productivity effects of trade may be an order of magnitude more important than the standard gains. Countries that have embarked upon the course of trade liberalization over the past few decades, such as Chile, New Zealand, and Spain, have experienced more rapid grown in productivity than previously. Free trade contributes to a process by which a country can adopt better technology and exposes domestic industries to new competition that forces them to improve their productivity. As a consequence, trade helps raise per capita income and economic well-being more generally.

David Morris

Free Trade: The Great Destroyer

Free trade is the religion of our age. With its heaven as the global economy, free trade comes complete with comprehensive analytical and philosophical underpinnings. Higher mathematics are used in stating its theorems. But in the final analysis, free trade is less an economic strategy than a moral doctrine. Although it pretends to be value-free, it is fundamentally value-driven. It assumes that the highest good is to shop. It assumes that mobility and change are synonymous with progress. The transport of capital, materials, goods, and people takes precedence over the autonomy, the sovereignty, and, indeed, the culture of local communities. Rather than promoting and sustaining the social relationships that create a vibrant community, the free trade theology relies on a narrow definition of efficiency to guide our conduct.

The Postulates of Free Trade

For most of us, after a generation of brain washing about its supposed benefits, the tenets of free trade appear almost self-evident:

- Competition spurs innovation, raises productivity, and lowers prices.
- The division of labor allows specialization, which raises productivity and lowers prices.
- The larger the production unit, the greater the division of labor and specialization, and thus the greater the benefits.

The adoration of bigness permeates all political persuasions. The Treasury Department proposes creating five to ten giant U.S. banks. "If we are going to be competitive in a globalized financial services world, we are going to have to change our views on the size of American institutions," it declares. The vice chair of Citicorp warns us against "preserving the heartwarming idea that 14,000 banks are wonderful for our country." The liberal *Harper's* magazine agrees: "True, farms have gotten bigger, as has nearly every other type of economic enterprise. They have done so in order to take advantage of the economies of scale offered by modern production techniques." Democratic

From David Morris, "Free Trade: The Great Destroyer," in Jerry Mander and Edward Goldsmith, eds., *The Case Against the Global Economy: And for a Return to the Local* (Sierra Club Books, 1996). Copyright © 1996 by Jerry Mander and Edward Goldsmith. Reprinted by permission of Sierra Club Books.

presidential adviser Lester Thurow criticizes antitrust laws as an "old Democratic conception [that] is simply out of date." He argues that even IBM, with $50 billion in sales, is not big enough for the global marketplace. "Big companies do sometimes crush small companies," Thurow concedes, "but far better that small American companies be crushed by big American companies than that they be crushed by foreign companies." The magazine *In These Times*, which once called itself an independent socialist weekly, concluded, "Japanese steel companies have been able to outcompete American steel companies partly by building larger plants."

The infatuation with large-scale systems leads logically to the next postulate of free trade: the need for global markets. Anything that sets up barriers to ever-wider markets reduces the possibility of specialization and thus raises costs, making us less competitive.

The last pillar of free trade is the law of comparative advantage, which comes in two forms: absolute and relative. Absolute comparative advantage is easier to understand: Differences in climate and natural resources suggest that Guatemala should raise bananas and Minnesota should raise walleyed pike. Thus, by specializing in what they grow best, each region enjoys comparative advantage in that particular crop. Relative comparative advantage is a less intuitive, but ultimately more powerful concept. As the nineteenth-century British economist David Ricardo, the architect of free trade economics, explained: "Two men can both make shoes and hats and one is superior to the other in both employments; but in making hats he can only exceed his competitor by one-fifth or 20 percent, and in making shoes he can exceed him by one-third or 33 percent. Will it not be for the interest of both that the superior man should employ himself exclusively in making shoes and the inferior man in making hats?"

Thus, even if one community can make every product more efficiently than another, it should specialize only in those items it produces most efficiently, in relative terms, and trade for others. Each community, and ultimately each nation, should specialize in what it does best.

What are the implications of these tenets of free trade? That communities and nations abandon self-reliance and embrace dependence. That we abandon our capacity to produce many items and concentrate only on a few. That we import what we need and export what we produce.

Bigger is better. Competition is superior to cooperation. Material self-interest drives humanity. Dependence is better than independence. These are the pillars of free trade. In sum, we make a trade. We give up sovereignty over our affairs in return for a promise of more jobs, more goods, and a higher standard of living.

⋯⟨●⟩⋯

The economic arguments in favor of free trade are powerful. Yet for most of us it is not the soundness of its theory but the widely promoted idea that free trade is an inevitable development of our market system that makes us believers. We believe that economies, like natural organisms, evolve from the simple to the complex.

From the Dark Ages, to city-states, to nation-states, to the planetary economy, and, soon, to space manufacturing, history has systematically unfolded. Free trade supporters believe that trying to hold back economic evolution is like trying to hold back natural evolution. The suggestion that we choose another developmental path is viewed, at best, as an attempt to reverse history and, at worst, as an unnatural and even sinful act.

This kind of historical determinism has corollaries. We not only move from simple to complex economies. We move from integrated economies to segregated ones, separating the producer from the consumer, the farmer from the kitchen, the power plant from the appliance, the dump site from the garbage can, the banker from the depositor, and, inevitably, the government from the citizenry. In the process of development we separate authority and responsibility—those who make the decisions are not those who are affected by the decisions.

Just as *Homo sapiens* is nature's highest achievement, so the multinational and supranational corporation becomes our most highly evolved economic animal. The planetary economy demands planetary institutions. The nation-state itself begins to disappear, both as an object of our affection and identification and as a major actor in world affairs.

The planetary economy merges and submerges nations. Yoshitaka Sajima, vice president of Mitsui and Company, USA, asserts, "The U.S. and Japan are not just trading with each other anymore—they've become a part of each other." Lamar Alexander, former Republican Governor of Tennessee, agreed with Sajima's statement when he declared that the goal of his economic development strategy was "to get the Tennessee economy integrated with the Japanese economy."

In Europe, the Common Market has grown from six countries in the 1950s to ten in the 1970s to sixteen today, and barriers between these nations are rapidly being abolished. Increasingly, there are neither Italian nor French nor German companies, only European supracorporations. The U.S., Canadian, and Mexican governments formed NAFTA [North American Free Trade Agreement] to merge the countries of the North American continent economically.

Promotion of exports is now widely accepted as the foundation for a successful economic development program. Whether for a tiny country such as Singapore or a huge country such as the United States, exports are seen as essential to a nation's economic health.

Globalism commands our attention and our resources. Our principal task, we are told, is to nurture, extend, and manage emerging global systems. Trade talks are on the top of everybody's agenda, from Yeltsin to Clinton. Political leaders strive to devise stable systems for global financial markets and exchange rates. The best and the brightest of this generation use their ingenuity to establish the global financial and regulatory rules that will enable the greatest possible uninterrupted flow of resources among nations.

This emphasis on globalism rearranges our loyalties and loosens our neighborly ties. "The new order eschews loyalty to workers, products, corporate structure, businesses, factories, communities, even the nation," the *New York Times* announces. Martin S. Davis, chair of Gulf and Western, declares, "All such allegiances are viewed as expendable under the new rules. You cannot be emotionally bound to any particular asset."

We are now all assets.

Jettisoning loyalties isn't easy, but that is the price we believe we must pay to receive the benefits of the global village. Every community must achieve the lowest possible production cost, even when that means breaking whatever remains of its social contract and long-standing traditions.

The revised version of the American Dream is articulated by Stanley J. Mihelick, executive vice president for production at Goodyear: "Until we get real wage levels down much closer to those of the Brazils and Koreas, we cannot pass along productivity gains to wages and still be competitive."

Wage raises, environmental protection, national health insurance, and liability lawsuits—anything that raises the cost of production and makes a corporation less competitive—threatens our economy. We must abandon the good life to sustain the economy. We are in a global struggle for survival. We are hooked on free trade.

The Doctrine Falters

At this very moment in history, when the doctrines of free trade and globalism are so dominant, the absurdities of globalism are becoming more evident. Consider the case of the toothpick and the chopstick.

A few years ago I was eating at a Saint Paul, Minnesota, restaurant. After lunch, I picked up a toothpick wrapped in plastic. On the plastic was printed the word *Japan.* Japan has little wood and no oil; nevertheless, it has become efficient enough in our global economy to bring little pieces of wood and barrels of oil to Japan, wrap the one in the other and send the manufactured product to Minnesota. This toothpick may have traveled 50,000 miles. But never fear, we are now retaliating in kind. A Hibbing, Minnesota, factory now produces one billion disposable chopsticks a year for sale in Japan. In my mind's eye, I see two ships passing one another in the northern Pacific. One carries little pieces of Minnesota wood bound for Japan; the other carries little pieces of Japanese wood bound for Minnesota. Such is the logic of free trade.

Nowhere is the absurdity of free trade more evident than in the grim plight of the Third World. Developing nations were encouraged to borrow money to build an economic infrastructure in order to specialize in what they do best, (comparative advantage, once again) and thereby expand their export capacity. To repay the debts, Third World countries must increase their exports.

One result of these arrangements has been a dramatic shift in food production from internal consumption to export. Take the case of Brazil. Brazilian per capita production of basic foodstuffs (rice, black beans, manioc, and potatoes) fell 13 percent from 1977 to 1984. Per capita output of exportable foodstuffs (soybeans, oranges, cotton, peanuts, and tobacco) jumped 15 percent. Today, although some 50 percent of Brazil suffers malnutrition, one leading

Brazilian agronomist still calls export promotion "a matter of national survival." In the global village, a nation survives by starving its people.

✥

What about the purported benefits of free trade, such as higher standards of living?

It depends on whose standards of living are being considered. Inequality between and, in most cases, within countries has increased. Two centuries of trade has exacerbated disparaties in world living standards. According to economist Paul Bairoch, per capita GNP in 1750 was approximately the same in the developed countries as in the underdeveloped ones. In 1930, the ratio was about 4 to 1 in favor of the developed nations. Today it is 8 to 1.

Inequality is both a cause and an effect of globalism. Inequality within one country exacerbates globalism because it reduces the number of people with sufficient purchasing power; consequently, a producer must sell to wealthy people in many countries to achieve the scale of production necessary to produce goods at a relatively low cost. Inequality is an effect of globalism because export industries employ few workers, who earn disproportionately higher wages than their compatriots, and because developed countries tend to take out more capital from Third World countries than they invest in them.

Free trade was supposed to improve our standard of living. Yet even in the United States, the most developed of all nations, we find that living standards have been declining since 1980. More dramatically, according to several surveys, in 1988 U.S. workers worked almost half a day longer for lower real wages than they did in 1970. We who work in the United States have less leisure time in the 1990s than we had in the 1970s.

A New Way of Thinking

It is time to re-examine the validity of the doctrine of free trade and its creation, the planetary economy. To do so, we must begin by speaking of values. Human beings may be acquisitive and competitive, but we are also loving and cooperative. Several studies have found that the voluntary, unpaid economy may be as large and as productive as the paid economy. There is no question that we have converted more and more human relationships into commercial transactions, but there is a great deal of question as to whether this was a necessary or beneficial development.

We should not confuse change with progress. Bertrand Russell once described change as inevitable and progress as problematic. Change is scientific. Progress is ethical. We must decide which values we hold most dear and then design an economic system that reinforces those values.

Reassessing Free Trade's Assumptions

If price is to guide our buying, selling, and investing, then price should tell us something about efficiency. We might measure efficiency in terms of natural resources used in making products and the lack of waste produced in converting raw material into a consumer or industrial product. Traditionally, we have measured efficiency in human terms; that is, by measuring the amount of labor-hours spent in making a product.

But price is actually no measure of real efficiency. In fact, price is no reliable measure of anything. In the planetary economy, the prices of raw materials, labor, capital, transportation, and waste disposal are all heavily subsidized. For example, wage-rate inequities among comparably skilled workforces can be as disparate as 30 to 1. This disparity overwhelms even the most productive worker. An American worker might produce twice as much per hour as a Mexican worker but is paid ten times as much.

In Taiwan, for example, strikes are illegal. In South Korea, unions cannot be organized without government permission. Many developing nations have no minimum wage, maximum hours, or environmental legislation. As economist Howard Wachtel notes, "Differences in product cost that are due to totalitarian political institutions or restrictions on economic rights reflect no natural or entrepreneurial advantage. Free trade has nothing to do with incomparable political economic institutions that protect individual rights in one country and deny them in another."

The price of goods in developed countries is also highly dependent on subsidies. For example, we in the United States decided early on that government should build the transportation systems of the country. The public, directly or indirectly, built our railroads, canals, ports, highways and airports.

Heavy trucks do not pay taxes sufficient to cover the damage they do to roads. California farmers buy water at as little as 5 percent of the going market rate; the other 95 percent is funded by huge direct subsidies to corporate farmers. In the United States, society as a whole picks up the costs of agricultural pollution. Having intervened in the production process in all these ways, we then discover it is cheaper to raise produce near the point of sale.

Prices don't provide accurate signals within nations; they are not the same as cost. *Price* is what an individual pays; cost is what the community as a whole pays. Most economic programs in the industrial world result in an enormous disparity between the price of a product or service to an individual and the cost of that same product or service to the society as a whole.

When a U.S. utility company wanted to send electricity across someone's property, and that individual declined the honor, the private utility received governmental authority to seize the land needed. This is exactly what happened in western Minnesota in the late 1970s. Since larger power plants produced electricity more cheaply than smaller ones, it was therefore in the "public interest" to erect these power lines. If landowners' refusal to sell had been respected, the price of electricity would be higher today, but it would reflect the cost of that power more accurately.

Because the benefit of unrestricted air transportation takes precedence over any damage to public health and sanity, communities no longer have the authority to regulate flights and noise. As a consequence, airplanes awaken us or our children in the middle of the night. By one survey, some four million people in the United States suffer physical damage due to airport noise. If communities were given the authority to control noise levels by planes, as they already control noise levels from radios and motorcycles, the price of a plane ticket would increase significantly. Its price would be more aligned with its actual cost to society.

It is often hard to quantify social costs, but this doesn't mean they are insignificant. Remember urban renewal? In the 1950s and 1960s inner-city neighborhoods were leveled to assemble sufficient land area to rebuild our downtowns. Skyscrapers and shopping malls arose; the property tax base expanded; and we considered it a job well done. Later, sociologists, economists, and planners discovered that the seedy areas we destroyed were not fragmented, violence-prone slums but more often cohesive ethnic communities where generations had grown up and worked and where children went to school and played. If we were to put a dollar figure on the destruction of homes, the pain of broken lives, and the expense of relocation and re-creation of community life, we might find that the city as a whole actually lost money in the urban renewal process. If we had used a full-cost accounting system, we might never have undertaken urban renewal.

Our refusal to understand and count the social costs of certain kinds of development has caused suffering in rural and urban areas alike. In 1944, Walter Goldschmidt, working under contract with the Department of Agriculture [USDA], compared the economic and social characteristics of two rural California communities that were alike in all respects, except one. Dinuba was surrounded by family farms; Arvin by corporate farms. Goldschmidt found that Dinuba was more stable, had a higher standard of living, more small businesses, higher retail sales, better schools and other community facilities, and a higher degree of citizen participation in local affairs. The USDA invoked a clause in Goldschmidt's contract forbidding him to discuss his finding. The study was not made public for almost thirty years. Meanwhile, the USDA continued to promote research that rapidly transformed the Dinubas of our country into Arvins. The farm crisis we now suffer is a consequence of this process.

How should we deal with the price-versus-cost dilemma as a society? Ways do exist by which we can protect our life-style from encroachment by the global economy, achieve important social and economic goals, and pay about the same price for our goods and services. In some cases we might have to pay more, but we should remember that higher prices may be offset by the decline in overall costs. Consider the proposed Save the Family Farm legislation drafted by farmers and introduced in Congress several years ago by Iowa Senator Tom Harkin. It proposed that farmers limit production of farm goods nationwide at the same time as the nation establishes a minimum price for farm goods that is sufficient to cover operating and capital costs and provides farm families with an adequate living. The law's sponsors estimate that such a program would increase the retail cost of agricultural products by 3 to 5 percent, but the increase would be more than offset by dramatically reduced public tax expenditures spent on farm subsidies. And this doesn't take into consideration the cost benefits of a stable rural America: fewer people leaving farms that have been in their families for generations; less influx of jobless rural immigrants into already economically depressed urban areas; and fewer expenditures for medical bills, food stamps, and welfare.

Economists like to talk about externalities. The costs of job dislocation, rising family violence, community breakdown, environmental damage, and cultural collapse are all considered "external." External to what, one might ask?

The theory of comparative advantage itself is fast losing its credibility. Time was when technology spread slowly. Three hundred years ago in northern Italy, stealing or disclosing the secrets of silk-spinning machinery was a crime punishable by death. At the beginning of the Industrial Revolution, Britain protected its supremacy in textile manufacturing by banning both the export of machines and the emigration of men who knew how to build and run them. A young British apprentice, Samuel Slater, brought the Industrial Revolution to the United States by memorizing the design of the spinning frame and migrating here in 1789.

Today, technology transfer is simple. According to Dataquest, a market research firm, it takes only three weeks after a new U.S.-made product is introduced before it is copied, manufactured, and shipped back to the U.S. from Asia. So much for comparative advantage.

The Efficiencies of Small Scale

This brings us to the issue of scale. There is no question that when I move production out of my basement and into a factory, the cost per item produced declines dramatically. But when the factory increases its output a hundredfold, production costs no longer decline proportionately. The vast majority of the cost decreases are captured at fairly modest production levels.

In agriculture, for example, the USDA studied the efficiency of farms and concluded, "Above about $40–50,000 in gross sales—the size that is at the bottom of the end of medium sized sales category—there are no greater efficiencies of scale." Another USDA report agreed: "Medium sized family farms are as efficient as the large farms."

Harvard Professor Joseph Bain's pioneering investigations in the 1950s found that plants far smaller than originally believed can be economically competitive. Further, it was found that the factory could be significantly reduced in size without requiring major price increases for its products. In other words, we might be able to produce shoes for a region rather than for a nation at about the same price per shoe. If we withdrew government subsidies to the transportation system, then locally produced and marketed shoes might actually be less expensive than those brought in from abroad.

Modern technology makes smaller production plants possible. For instance, traditional float glass plants produce 550 to 600 tons of glass daily, at an annual cost of $100 million. With only a $40 to 50 million investment, new miniplants can produce about 250 tons per day for a regional market at the same cost per ton as the large plants.

The advent of programmable machine tools may accelerate this tendency. In 1980, industrial engineers developed machine tools that could be programmed to reproduce a variety of shapes so that now a typical Japanese machine tool can make almost one hundred different parts from an individual block of material. What does this mean? Erich Bloch, director of the National Science Foundation, believes manufacturing "will be so flexible that it will be able to make the first copy of a product for little more than the cost of the thousandth." "So the ideal location for the factory of the future," says Patrick A. Toole, vice president for manufacturing at IBM, "is in the market where the products are consumed."

Conclusion

When we abandon our ability to produce for ourselves, when we separate authority from responsibility, when those affected by our decisions are not those who make the decisions, when the cost and the benefit of production or development processes are not part of the same equation, when price and cost are no longer in harmony, we jeopardize our security and our future.

You may argue that free trade is not the sole cause of all our ills. Agreed. But free trade as it is preached today nurtures and reinforces many of our worst problems. It is an ideological package that promotes ruinous policies. And, most tragically, as we move further down the road to giantism, globalism, and dependence, we make it harder and harder to back up and take another path. If we lose our skills, our productive base, our culture, our traditions, our natural resources; if we erode the bonds of personal and familial responsibility, it becomes ever more difficult to re-create community. It is very, very hard to put Humpty Dumpty back together again.

Which means we must act now. The unimpeded mobility of capital, labor, goods, and raw materials is not the highest social good. We need to challenge the postulates of free trade head on, to propose a different philosophy, to embrace a different strategy. There is another way. To make it the dominant way, we must change the rules; indeed, we must challenge our own behavior. And to do that requires not only that we challenge the emptiness of free trade but that we promote a new idea: economics as if community matters.

POSTSCRIPT

Is Free Trade Fair Trade?

In 2002, in order to overcome congressional objections based on the possible negative economic impact of foreign goods on particular districts, President George W. Bush imposed tariff barriers on steel imports to protect domestic manufacturers against cheaper or better imported steel. This is old-fashioned protectionism, the economic opposite of free trade. The president calculated that he could not get the trade power he sought without disarming some anti–free trade sentiment, so he made his concession to business owners, workers, and communities in which the steel industry is located. Underdeveloped nations, calling such concessions hypocritical, contend that they have more reasons to protect their weaker businesses but, unlike the United States, they are subject to the pressures of the international agencies that lend them investment capital as well as of the multinational enterprises whose investment they want to get, keep, and enlarge.

Laissez-faire economics holds that if Asian countries can produce electronic products better and less expensively than other nations, then those products will be sold throughout the world. Similarly, if the United States can produce movies that are more entertaining than those made elsewhere, then they will be seen throughout the world. According to Brink Lindsay, in *Against the Dead Hand: The Uncertain Struggle for Global Capitalism* (John Wiley, 2002), if these results have not yet followed in every economic area, it is because the economy has not yet gotten rid of state ownership, price controls, trade barriers, and other remnants of an earlier age. Protectionism has been discredited but it has not yet been banished, says Jagdish N. Bhagwati in *Free Trade Today* (Princeton University Press, 2002). Critics of free trade maintain that the agencies providing economic support to the poorer countries sponsor a kind of capitalism that may not be congenial to other cultures. In *Open Society: Reforming Global Capitalism* (Public Affairs, 2000), George Soros, one of the foremost capitalist investors, advocates for spending more money on global public goods and foreign aid.

Edward S. Herman, in "Free Trade: The Sophistry of Imperialism," *Z Magazine* (March 2002), argues that free trade diminishes the ability of less developed countries to shape their economic policies, provide public services, and protect the environment. In addition, he contends that free trade agreements protect investor rights against taxes, business rules, labor practices, and other policies by which a sovereign state can protect its interests. This and other anti–free trade views are amplified in the essays in Jerry Mander and Edward Goldsmith, eds., *The Case Against the Global Economy: And for a Return to the Local* (Sierra Club Books, 1996).

Must America Exercise World Leadership?

YES: William Kristol and Robert Kagan, from "Introduction: National Interest and Global Responsibility," in William Kristol and Robert Kagan, eds., *Present Dangers: Crisis and Opportunity in American Foreign and Defense Policy* (Encounter Books, 2000)

NO: Benjamin Schwarz and Christopher Layne, from "A New Grand Strategy," *The Atlantic Monthly* (January 2002)

ISSUE SUMMARY

YES: William Kristol, editor of *The Weekly Standard,* and Robert Kagan, a senior associate at the Carnegie Endowment for International Peace, maintain that, as the only superpower, America must exercise a role of world preeminence to shape the international environment in order to protect American economic interests and national security.

NO: Benjamin Schwarz, a correspondent for *The Atlantic Monthly,* and Christopher Layne, a MacArthur Fellow in Peace and International Security Studies, conclude that the United States must encourage other nations to become partners in power because it is burdensome, risky, and ultimately futile for America to attempt to preserve its status as the only great power.

T he United States retains the unique status of being the world's only superpower since the end of the cold war. This is not a function of its extraordinary military power or its industrial and technological resources alone. It is also a recognition of the ubiquity and influence of American movies, music, invention, and language. This is not to say that the whole world approves. On the contrary, American power and culture are viewed with suspicion by many allies and with hostility by many nations that cooperate with the United States only to further their own interests or that do not cooperate at all.

Since the failure of American intervention in Vietnam, the United States has shown reluctance to go it alone in potentially dangerous foreign policy commitments. It has needed to be persuaded that its national interest was involved before committing itself to war or peacekeeping in foreign lands. As a result, the United States did not overtly intervene in the decade-long war between Iran and Iraq but did so when its oil supply was endangered by Iran's invasion of Kuwait and threat to Saudi Arabia. Also, only reluctantly and after several years did the United States and its allies enter into the Balkan conflict. And it wasn't until the September 11 attacks that the United States was moved to wage war against the Taliban government of Afghanistan, which harbored the terrorists of Al Qaeda.

Although it is reluctant to act unilaterally to commit its power abroad, the United States does not hesitate to refrain or withdraw from international commitments. For example, although President Bill Clinton signed a treaty establishing an international criminal court designed to prosecute individuals for genocide, crimes against humanity, and other war crimes, the Senate did not ratify the treaty, and President George W. Bush abrogated it. President Bush has also rejected the Kyoto Treaty to reduce gases that contribute to global warming, the Antiballistic Missile Treaty, and biological weapons inspections to enforce the international treaty banning such weapons.

As far as international leadership goes, the United States is strongest in the area of economic leadership because of the important role it plays in the World Bank and the International Monetary Fund. Both reflect dominant American thinking, both receive the support of most of the business community, and both arouse the opposition of and demonstrations by labor unions and environmental groups. But even here America's commitment is compromised by domestic economic and political interests, as was demonstrated when President Bush provided tariff protection for the American steel industry.

Bolder American world leadership could take several forms. The most obvious is the provision of much greater sums in foreign aid to provide medical care and other basic aid to the poorest nations and to ensure the political and economic survival of weak friendly nations. Another possibility would be the provision of positive support for nation-building. It is difficult to imagine such a blanket commitment by the United States, but it is even more difficult to envision its success in either the UN Security Council, where any effective policy would be subject to vetoes by other nations, or the UN General Assembly, where every country (including the United States) has the same single vote.

An alternative view to world leadership is the conviction that the United States does not possess the infinite resources to support failed economies, the political will to place American military forces in dangerous distant conflicts, or the moral hubris to impose its will on states that may choose other political and economic systems.

The case for American primacy is elaborated in the following selection by William Kristol and Robert Kagan, who urge the United States to take the initiative in defending its interests, rather than simply responding to dangerous challenges. In the second selection, Benjamin Schwarz and Christopher Layne argue that the United States will be more secure and the world more stable if America rejects hegemony (dominant influence over other nations) and seeks coexistence and cooperation with other powerful nations.

William Kristol and Robert Kagan    **YES**

National Interest and Global Responsibility

Alittle over twenty years ago, a group of concerned Americans formed the Committee on the Present Danger. The danger they feared, and sought to rally Americans to confront, was the Soviet Union.

It is easy to forget these days how controversial was the suggestion in the mid- to late 1970s that the Soviet Union was really a danger, much less one that should be challenged by the United States. This was hardly the dominant view of the American foreign policy establishment. Quite the contrary: prevailing wisdom from the Nixon through the Carter administrations held that the United States should do its utmost to coexist peaceably with the USSR, and that the American people in any case were not capable of sustaining a serious challenge to the Soviet system. To engage in an arms race would either bankrupt the United States or lead to Armageddon. To challenge communist ideology at its core, to declare it evil and illegitimate, would be at best quixotic and at worst perilous. When the members of the Committee on the Present Danger challenged this comfortable consensus, when they criticized détente and arms control and called for a military buildup and a broad ideological and strategic assault on Soviet communism, their recommendations were generally dismissed as either naive or reckless. It would take a revolution in American foreign policy, the fall of the Berlin Wall, and the disintegration of the Soviet empire to prove just how right they were.

Does this Cold War tale have any relevance today as Americans grapple with the uncertainties of the post–Cold War era? The Soviet Union has long since crumbled. No global strategic challenger has emerged to take its place; none appears visible on the horizon; and the international scene at present seems fairly benign to most observers. Many of our strategists tell us that we will not face another major threat for twenty years or more, and that we may as a consequence enjoy a "strategic pause." According to opinion polls, the American public is less interested in foreign policy than at any time since before World War II. Intermittent fears of terrorist attack, worries about the proliferation of weapons of mass destruction, distant concerns about the possible outbreak of war in the Taiwan Strait or in the Balkans—all attract attention, but

From William Kristol and Robert Kagan, "Introduction: National Interest and Global Responsibility," in William Kristol and Robert Kagan, eds., *Present Dangers: Crisis and Opportunity in American Foreign and Defense Policy* (Encounter Books, 2000). Copyright © 2000 by William Kristol and Robert Kagan. Reprinted by permission of Encounter Books, San Francisco, CA. Notes omitted.

only fleetingly. The United States, both at the level of elite opinion and popular sentiment, appears to have become the Alfred E. Newman of superpowers, with its national motto being, "What, me worry?"

But there *is* today a "present danger." It has no name. It is not to be found in any single strategic adversary. It does not fit nearly under the heading of "international terrorism" or "rogue states" or "ethnic hatred." In fact, the ubiquitous post–Cold War question—where is the threat?—is misconceived. Rather, the present danger is that the United States, the world's dominant power on whom the maintenance of international peace and the support of liberal democratic principles depends, will shrink its responsibilities and—in a fit of absentmindedness, or parsimony, or indifference—allow the international order that it created and sustains to collapse. Our present danger is one of declining military strength, flagging will and confusion about our role in the world. It is a danger, to be sure, of our own devising. Yet, if neglected, it is likely to yield very real external dangers, as threatening in their way as the Soviet Union was a quarter century ago.

⁘

In fact, beneath the surface calm of world affairs today, there has already been an erosion of the mostly stable, peaceful and democratic international order that emerged briefly at the end of the Cold War. Americans and their political leaders have spent the years since 1991 lavishing the gifts of an illusory "peace dividend" upon themselves, and frittering away the opportunity to strengthen and extend an international order uniquely favorable to the United States.

It is worth reviewing the record of the past ten years, if only to show how great is the opportunity we have wasted and the dangers that may await us in the future as a result.

The 1990s, for all their peace and prosperity, were a squandered decade. The decade began with America's triumph in the Cold War and its smashing victory over Iraq in Desert Storm. In the wake of those twin triumphs, the United States had assumed an unprecedented position of power and influence in the world. By the traditional measures of national power, the United States held a position unmatched since Rome dominated the Mediterranean world. American military power dwarfed that of any other nation, both in its war-fighting capabilities and in its ability to intervene in conflicts anywhere in the world on short notice. There was a common acceptance, even by potential adversaries, that America's position as the sole global superpower might not be challenged for decades to come. Meanwhile, the American economic precepts of liberal capitalism and free trade had become almost universally accepted as the best model for creating wealth, and the United States itself stood at the center of that international economic order. The American political precepts of liberal democracy had spread across continents and cultures as other peoples cast off or modified autocratic methods of governance and adopted, or at least paid lip-service to, the American credo of individual rights and freedoms. American culture, for better or for worse, had become the dominant global culture. To a degree scarcely imaginable at mid-century, or even as late as the 1970s, the world had indeed been transformed in America's image.

Our country, in other words, was—or could have been—present at another creation similar to the one Dean Acheson saw emerge after World War II. For the first time in its history, the United States had the chance to shape the international system in ways that would enhance its security and advance its principles without opposition from a powerful, determined adversary. A prostrate and democratizing Russia had neither the ability nor the inclination to challenge the American-led international democratic order. Though it turned toward harsh repression at home in 1989, China had barely begun to increase its military capabilities, and rather than thinking about launching a challenge to American dominance in East Asia, China's military leaders stood in awe of the military prowess and technological superiority America had exhibited in the Gulf War. The world's strongest economies in Europe and Japan, meanwhile, were American allies and participants in the international economic and political system, with the United States at its center. The newly liberated nations of Eastern and Central Europe yearned for membership in the American-led North Atlantic alliance. In the Middle East, the defeat of Saddam's armies, the liberation of Kuwait, and the waning of Soviet and then Russian influence seemed to open a new era of American influence.

⋅⟨◉⟩⋅

The task for America at the start of the 1990s ought to have been obvious. It was to prolong this extraordinary moment and to guard the international system from any threats that might challenge it. This meant, above all, preserving and reinforcing America's benevolent global hegemony, which undergirded what President George Bush rightly called a "new world order." The goal of American foreign policy should have been to turn what Charles Krauthammer called a "unipolar moment" into a unipolar era.

The great promise of the post–Cold War era, however, began to dim almost immediately—and even before Bill Clinton was elected. The United States, which had mustered the world's most awesome military force to expel Saddam Hussein from Kuwait, failed to see that mission through to its proper conclusion: the removal of Saddam from power in Baghdad. Instead, vastly superior U.S. forces stood by in March 1991 as Shi'ite and Kurdish uprisings against Saddam were brutally crushed and the Iraqi tyrant, so recently in fear of his life, began to re-establish his control over the country. Three months later, Yugoslav President Slobodan Milosevic launched an offensive against the breakaway province of Slovenia, following up with a much larger attack on Croatia. In the spring of 1992, Serb forces began their bloody siege of Sarajevo and a war of ethnic cleansing that would cost the lives of 200,000 Bosnian Muslims over the next three years. In the second half of 1992, meanwhile, American intelligence learned that North Korea had begun surreptitiously producing materials for nuclear weapons.

Saddam Hussein, Slobodan Milosevic, and the totalitarian regime of North Korea, each in their own way, would be the source of one crisis after another throughout the remainder of the decade. Each of these dangerous dictatorships appears certain to survive the end of the twentieth century and go on to present continuing risks to the United States and its allies in the new millennium. And their very survival throughout the 1990s has established a disturbing principle in the post–Cold War world: that dictators can challenge the peace, slaughter innocents in their own or in neighboring states, threaten their neighbors with missile attacks—and still hang on to power. This constitutes a great failure in American foreign policy, one that will surely come back to haunt us.

But these were not the only failures that made the 1990s a decade of squandered opportunity for American foreign policy. The past decade also saw the rise of an increasingly hostile and belligerent China, which had drawn its own conclusions about U.S. behavior after the Gulf War. While every other great power in the world cut its defense budget throughout the 1990s, China alone embarked on a huge military buildup, augmenting both its conventional and its nuclear arsenal in an effort to project power beyond its shores and deter the United States from defending its friends and allies. China used this power to seize contested islands in the South China Sea, to intimidate its neighbors in East Asia, and, in the most alarming display of military might, to frighten the people of Taiwan by launching ballistic missiles off their shores. Throughout the 1990s, moreover, the Chinese government continued and intensified the repression of domestic dissent, both political and religious, that began with the massacre in Tiananmen Square. The American response to China's aggressive behavior at home and abroad has, with but a few exceptions, been one of appeasement.

In the face of the moral and strategic challenges confronting it, the United States engaged in a gradual but steady moral and strategic disarmament. Rather than seeking to unseat the dangerous dictatorships in Baghdad and Belgrade, the Clinton administration combined empty threats and ineffectual military operations with diplomatic accommodation. Rather than press hard for changes of regime in Pyongyang and Beijing, the Clinton administration—and in the case of China, the Bush administration before it—tried to purchase better behavior through "engagement." Rather than squarely facing our world responsibilities, American political leaders chose drift and evasion.

In the meantime, the United States allowed its military strength to deteriorate to the point where its ability to defend its interests and deter future challenges is now in doubt. From 1989 to 1999, the defense budget and the size of the armed forces were cut by a third; the share of America's GNP [gross national product] devoted to defense spending was halved, from nearly 6 to around 3 percent; and the amount of money spent on weapons procurement and research and development declined about 50 percent. There was indeed a "peace dividend," and as a result, by the end of the decade the U.S. military was inadequately equipped and stretched to the point of exhaustion. And while defense experts spent the 1990s debating whether it was more important to maintain current readiness or to sacrifice present capabilities in order to prepare for future challenges, the United States, under the strain of excessive budget cuts, did neither.

Yet ten years from now, and perhaps a good deal sooner, we likely will be living in a world in which Iraq, Iran, North Korea and China all possess the ability to strike the continental United States with nuclear weapons. Within the next decade we may have to decide whether to defend Taiwan against a Chinese attack. We could face another attempt by a rearmed Saddam Hussein to seize Kuwait's oil fields. An authoritarian regime in Russia could move to reclaim some of what it lost in 1991.

Other, still greater challenges can be glimpsed on the horizon, involving a host of unanswerable questions. What will China be in ten years: a modernizing economy peacefully integrating itself into the international system, an economic basket case ruled by a desperate dictatorship and a hypernationalistic military, or something in between? What will Russia be: a struggling democracy shedding its old imperial skin, or a corrupt autocracy striving to take back some of what it lost in 1989 and 1991? And there are other imponderables that derive from these. If Japan feels increasingly threatened by North Korean missiles and growing Chinese power, will it decide to rearm and perhaps build its own nuclear arsenal? What would Germany do if faced by an increasingly disaffected, revanchist, and bellicose Russia?

These threats and challenges do not exhaust the possibilities, for if history is any guide we are likely to face dangers, even within the next decade, that we cannot even imagine today. Much can happen in ten years. In 1788 for instance, while Louis XVI sat comfortably on his French throne, French philosophers preached the dawning of a new age of peace based on commerce, and no one had ever heard of Napoleon Bonaparte. Ten years later, a French king had lost his head and Napoleon was rampaging across Europe. In 1910, Norman Angell won international acclaim for a book, *The Great Illusion,* in which he declared that the growth of trade between capitalist countries had made war between the great powers obsolete. By 1920, the world had suffered through the costliest war in human history, fought among the world's great capitalist trading powers, and had seen a communist takeover in Russia, a development that was literally unimaginable a decade earlier. In 1928, the American economy was soaring, Weimar Germany was ruled by a moderate democrat, and Europe was at peace. Ten years later, the United States was struggling to emerge from the Great Depression, and Neville Chamberlain was handing Czechoslovakia over to Adolf Hitler.

While none of this argues that the world *must* become a vastly more dangerous place, the point is that the world *can* grow perilous with astonishing speed. Should this happen once more, it would be terrible to have to look back on the current era as a great though fleeting opportunity that was recklessly wasted. Everything depends on what we do now.

No "Return to Normalcy"

Contrary to prevailing wisdom, the missed opportunities of the 1990s cannot be made up for merely by tinkering around the edges of America's current foreign and defense policies. The middle path many of our political leaders would prefer, with token increases in the defense budget and a more "humble" view of America's role in the world, will not suffice. What is needed today is not better management of the status quo, but a fundamental change in the way our leaders and the public think about America's role in the world.

Serious thinking about the role should begin by recalling those tenets that guided American policy through the more successful phases of the Cold War. Many writers treat America's Cold War strategy as an aberration in the history of American foreign policy. Jeane Kirkpatrick expressed the common view of both liberal and conservative foreign policy thinkers when she wrote at the decade's start that, while the United States had "performed heroically in a time when heroism was required," the day had passed when Americans ought to bear such "unusual burdens." With a return to "normal" times, the United States could "again become a normal nation." In the absence of a rival on the scale of the Soviet Union, the United States should conduct itself like any other great power on the international scene, looking to secure only its immediate, tangible interests, and abjuring the broader responsibilities it had once assumed as leader of the Free World.

What is striking about this point of view is how at odds it is with the assumptions embraced by the leaders who established the guiding principles of American foreign policy at the end of World War II. We often forget that the plans for world order devised by American policy-makers in the early 1940s were not aimed at containing the Soviet Union, which many of them still viewed as a potential partner. Rather, those policy-makers were looking backward to the circumstances that had led to the catastrophe of global war. Their purpose was to construct a more stable international order than the one that had imploded in 1939; an economic system that furthered the aim of international stability by promoting growth and free trade; and a framework for international security that, although it placed too much faith in the ability of the great powers to work together, rested ultimately on the fact that American power had become the keystone in the arch of world order.

American leaders in the early to mid-1940s believed, in fact, that the "return to normalcy" that President Harding had endorsed in 1920 was the fatal error that led to the irresponsible isolationism of the 1930s. Franklin Roosevelt said in 1941 that "We will not accept a world, like the postwar world of the 1920s, in which the seeds of Hitlerism can again be planted and allowed to grow." Men like James Forrestal and Dean Acheson believed the United States had supplanted Great Britain as the world's leader and that, as Forrestal put it in 1941, "America must be the dominant power of the twentieth century."

Henry Luce spoke for most influential Americans inside and outside the Roosevelt administration when he insisted that it had fallen to the United States not only to win the war against Germany and Japan, but to create both "a vital international economy" and "an international moral order" that would together spread American political and economic principles—and in the process avoid the catastrophe of a third world war. Such thinking was reflected in Roosevelt's Atlantic Charter and, more concretely, in the creation of the international financial system at Bretton Woods in 1944 and of the United Nations a year later.

Thus, before the Soviet Union had emerged as the great challenge to American security and American principles, American leaders had arrived at the conclusion that it would be necessary for the United States (together, they hoped, with the other great powers), to deter aggression globally, whoever the aggressor might be. In fact, during the war years they were at least as worried about the possible re-emergence of Germany and Japan as about the Soviets. John Lewis Gaddis has summarized American thinking in the years between 1941 and 1946 thus:

> The American President and his key advisers were determined to secure the United States against whatever dangers might confront it after victory, but they lacked a clear sense of what those might be or where they might arise. Their thinking about post-war security was, as a consequence, more general than specific.

Few influential government officials, moreover, were under the illusion that "collective security" and the United Nations could be counted on to keep the peace. In 1945 Harry Truman declared that the United States had become "one of the most powerful forces for good on earth," and the task now was to "keep it so" and to "lead the world to peace and prosperity." The United States had "achieved a world leadership which does not depend solely upon our military and naval might," Truman asserted. But it was his intention, despite demobilization, to ensure that the United States would remain "the greatest naval power on earth" and would maintain "one of the most powerful air forces in the world." Americans, Truman declared, would use "our military strength solely to preserve the peace of the world. For we now know that this is the only sure way to make our own freedom secure."

The unwillingness to sustain the level of military spending and preparedness required to fulfill this expansive vision was a failure of American foreign policy in the immediate aftermath of the war. It took the Iron Curtain and the outbreak of war in Korea to fully awaken Americans to the need for an assertive and forward-leaning foreign policy. But while the United States promptly rose to meet these challenges, a certain intellectual clarity was lost in the transition from the immediate postwar years to the beginning of the Cold War era. The original postwar goal of promoting and defending a decent world order became conflated with the goal of meeting the challenge of Soviet power. The policies that the United States should have pursued even in the absence of a Soviet challenge—seeking a stable and prosperous international economic order; playing a large role in Europe, Asia and the Middle East; upholding rules of international behavior that benefited Americans; promoting democratic reform where possible and advancing American principles abroad—all these became associated with the strategy of containing the Soviet Union. In fact, America was pursuing two goals at once during the Cold War: first, the promotion of a world order conducive to American interests and principles; and second, a defense against the most immediate and menacing obstacle to achieving that order. The stakes surrounding the outcome of that latter effort became so high, in fact, that when the Cold War ended, many Americans had forgotten about the former.

Leadership

But the collapse of the Soviet empire has not altered the fundamental purposes of American foreign policy. Just as sensible Americans after World War II did not imagine that the United States should retreat from global involvement and await the rise of the next equivalent to Nazi Germany, so American statesmen today ought to recognize that their charge is not to await the arrival of the next great threat, but rather to shape the international environment to prevent such a threat from arising in the first place. To put it another way: the overarching goal of American foreign policy—to preserve and extend an international order that is in accord with both our interests and our principles—endures.

Certainly, the dramatic shift in international strategic circumstances occasioned by the Soviet collapse requires a shift in the manner in which this goal is pursued. But it is not a shift to "normalcy." In the post–Cold War era, the maintenance of a decent and hospitable international order requires continued American leadership in resisting, and where possible undermining, rising dictators and hostile ideologies; in supporting American interests and liberal democratic principles; and in providing assistance to those struggling against the more extreme manifestations of human evil. If America refrains from shaping this order, we can be sure that others will shape it in ways that reflect neither our interests nor our values.

This does not mean that the United States must root out evil wherever and whenever it rears its head. Nor does it suggest that the United States must embark on a crusade against every dictatorship. No doctrine of foreign policy can do away with the need for judgment and prudence, for weighing competing moral considerations. No foreign policy doctrine can provide precise and unvarying answers to the question of where, when and how the United States ought to intervene abroad. It is easy to say that the United States must have criteria for choosing when to intervene. But it is a good deal harder to formulate those criteria than simply to say they must exist. Henry Kissinger writes in *Diplomacy* that what is most needed in American foreign policy are "criteria for selectivity." But he does not venture to suggest exactly what those criteria might be. Yet if one admits that closely linked matters of prestige, principle and morality play a role in shaping foreign policy, then rigid criteria for intervention quickly prove illusory. As Kissinger well knows, the complicated workings of foreign policy and the exceptional position of the United States should guard us against believing that the national interest can be measured in a quasi-scientific fashion, or that areas of "vital" national interest can be located, and other areas excluded, by purely geopolitical determinations. Determining what is in America's national interest is an art, not a science. It requires not only the measurement of power but also an appreciation of beliefs, principles and perceptions, which cannot be quantified. That is why we choose statesmen, not mathematicians, to conduct foreign policy. That is why we will occasionally have to intervene abroad even when we cannot prove that a narrowly construed "vital interest" of the United States is at stake.

It is worth pointing out, though, that a foreign policy premised on American hegemony, and on the blending of principle with material interest, may in fact mean fewer, not more, overseas interventions than under the "vital interest" standard. Had the Bush administration, for example, realized early on that there was no clear distinction between American moral concerns in Bosnia and America's national interest there, the United States, with the enormous credibility earned in the Gulf War, might have been able to put a stop to Milosevic's ambitions with a well-timed threat of punishing military action. But because the Bush team placed Bosnia outside the sphere of "vital" American interests, the resulting crisis eventually required the deployment of thousands of troops on the ground.

The same could be said of American interventions in Panama and the Gulf. A passive worldview encouraged American leaders to ignore troubling developments which eventually metastasized into full-blown threats to American security. Manuel Noriega and Saddam Hussein were given reason to believe that the United States did not consider its interests threatened by their behavior; only to discover that they had been misled. In each case, a broader and more forward-leaning conception of the national interest might have made the later, large and potentially costly interventions unnecessary.

The question, then, is not whether the United States should intervene everywhere or nowhere. The decision Americans need to make is whether the United States should generally lean forward, as it were, or sit back. A strategy aimed at preserving American hegemony should embrace the former stance, being more rather than less inclined to weigh in when crises erupt, and preferably before they erupt. This is the standard of a global superpower that intends to shape the international environment to its own advantage. By contrast, the vital interest standard is that of a "normal" power that awaits a dramatic challenge before it rouses itself into action.

Tools and Tactics

Is the task of maintaining American primacy and making a consistent effort to shape the international environment beyond the capacity of Americans? Not if American leaders have the understanding and the political will to do what is necessary. Moreover, what is required is not particularly forbidding. For much of the task ahead consists of building on already existing real strengths.

Despite its degradation in the last decade, for example, the United States still wields the strongest military force in the world. It has demonstrated its prowess in war on several occasions since the end of the Cold War—in Panama in 1989, in the Persian Gulf in 1991, and most recently in the air war over Kosovo. Those victories owed their success to a force built in the Reagan years. This is a legacy the United States has lived off for over a decade, an account it has drawn too far down. Today the United States spends too little on its military capabilities, in terms of both present readiness and investment in future weapons technologies. The gap between America's strategic ends and the means available to accomplish those ends is growing, a fact that becomes more evident each time the United States deploys forces abroad.

To repair these deficiencies and to create a force that can shape the international environment today, tomorrow, and twenty years from now will probably require spending some $60 billion to $100 billion per year above current defense budgets. This price tag may seem daunting, but in historical terms it represents only a modest commitment of America's wealth to defense. And in a time of large budget surpluses, spending a tiny fraction on defense ought to be politically feasible. For the United States to have the military capability to shape the international environment now and for the foreseeable future would require spending about 3.5 percent of GDP [gross domestic product] on defense, still low by the standards of the past fifty years, and throughout history. Is the aim of maintaining American primacy not worth a hike in defense spending from 3 to 3.5 percent of GDP?

The United States also inherited from the Cold War a legacy of strong alliances in Europe and Asia, and with Israel in the Middle East. Those alliances are a bulwark of American power and, more important still, they constitute the heart of the liberal democratic civilization that the United States seeks to preserve and extend. Critics of a strategy of American pre-eminence sometimes claim that it is a call for unilateralism. It is not. The notion that the United States could somehow "go it alone" and maintain its pre-eminence without its allies is strategically misguided. It is also morally bankrupt. What would "American leadership" mean in the absence of its democratic allies? What kind of nation would the United States be if it allowed Great Britain, Germany, Japan, Israel, Poland and other democratic nations to fend for themselves against the myriad challenges they will face?

In fact, a strategy aimed at preserving American pre-eminence would require an even greater U.S. commitment to its allies. The United States would not be merely an "offshore balancer," a savior of last resort, as many recommend. It would not be a "reluctant sheriff," rousing itself to action only when the threatened townsfolk turn to it in desperation. American pre-eminence cannot be maintained from a distance, by means of some post–Cold War version of the Nixon doctrine, whereby the United States hangs back and keeps its powder dry. The United States would instead conceive of itself as at once a European power, an Asian power, a Middle Eastern power and, of course, a Western Hemispheric power. It would act as if threats to the interest of our allies are threats to us, which indeed they are. It would act as if instability in important regions of the world, and the flouting of civilized rules of conduct in those regions, are threats that affect us with almost the same immediacy as if they were occurring on our doorstep. To act otherwise would make the United States appear a most unreliable partner in world affairs, which would erode both American pre-eminence and the international order, and gradually undermine the very alliances on which U.S. security depends. Eventually, the crises *would* appear at our doorstep.

This is what it means to be a global superpower with global responsibilities. The costs of assuming these responsibilities are more than made up by the benefits to American long-term interests. It is short-sighted to imagine that a policy of "keeping our powder dry" is either safer or less expensive than a policy that aims to preclude and deter the emergence of new threats, that has the United States arriving quickly at the scene of potential trouble before it has fully erupted, that addresses threats to the national interest before they have developed into full-blown crises. Senator Kay Bailey Hutchison expressed a common but mistaken view last year when she wrote that "a superpower is more credible and effective when it maintains a measured distance from all regional conflicts." In fact, this is precisely the way for a superpower to cease being a superpower.

A strong America capable of projecting force quickly and with devastating effect to important regions of the world would make it less likely that challengers to regional stability would attempt to alter the status quo in their favor. It might even deter such challengers from undertaking expensive efforts to arm themselves in the first place. An America whose willingness to project force is in doubt, on the other hand, can only encourage such challenges. In Europe, in Asia and in the Middle East, the message we should be sending to potential foes is: "Don't even think about it." That kind of deterrence offers the best recipe for lasting peace; it is much cheaper than fighting the wars that would follow should we fail to build such a deterrent capacity.

This ability to project force overseas, however, will increasingly be jeopardized over the coming years as smaller powers acquire weapons of mass destruction and the missiles to launch them at American forces, at our allies and at the American homeland. The *sine qua non* for a strategy of American global pre-eminence, therefore, is a missile defense system that can protect all three of these targets. Only a well-protected America will be capable of deterring— and when necessary moving against—"rogue" regimes when they rise to challenge regional stability. Only a United States reasonably well shielded from the blackmail of nuclear, biological or chemical weapons will be able to shape the international environment to suit its interests and principles.

With the necessary military strength, strong and well-led alliances, and adequate missile defense, the United States can set about making trouble for hostile and potentially hostile nations, rather than waiting for them to make trouble for us. Just as the most successful strategy in the Cold War combined containment of the Soviet Union with an effort to undermine the moral legitimacy of the Moscow regime, so in the post–Cold War era a principal aim of American foreign policy should be to bring about a change of regime in hostile nations—in Baghdad and Belgrade, in Pyongyang and Beijing, and wherever tyrannical governments acquire the military power to threaten their neighbors, our allies and the United States itself.

NO ↵

**Benjamin Schwarz and
Christopher Layne**

A New Grand Strategy

Since the end of the Cold War, U.S. grand strategy has revolved around maintaining this country's overwhelming military, economic, and political preponderance. Until now most Americans have acquiesced in that strategy, because the costs seemed to be tolerably low. But the September 11 attacks have proved otherwise. Those assaults were neither random nor irrational. Those who undertook them acted with cool calculation to force the United States to alter specific policies—policies that largely flow from the global role America has chosen. The attacks were also a violent reaction to the very fact of America's pre-eminence.

Several tasks confront us. The most immediate is the one that rightly preoccupies the nation now: tracking down the al Qaeda terrorists and destroying their networks and their infrastructure, and waging war on the Taliban movement that harbors them. The larger task will take time, because it amounts to inventing a new American stance toward the world for the century ahead. We need to come to grips with an ironic possibility: that the very preponderance of American power may now make us not more secure but less secure. By the same token, it may actually be possible to achieve more of our ultimate foreign-policy goals by means of a diminished global presence.

Great powers have two basic strategic options: they can pursue geopolitical dominance (a "unipolar" strategy), or they can seek to maintain a rough balance of power among the strongest states in a region or around the world (a "multipolar" strategy). Since the late 1940s the United States has chosen the former course. True, even during the Cold War, when the world was essentially divided between the United States and the Soviet Union, a number of astute foreign-policy thinkers—including Walter Lippmann, George Kennan, and J. William Fulbright—argued that it was in America's interest to encourage Western Europe's and Japan's revival as independent great powers to relieve the United States of what Kennan called the "burdens of 'bi-polarity.'" But almost all American policymakers held that the United States had to contain its allies as much as it had to contain Moscow. By providing for the security of Britain, France, and (especially) Germany and Japan—by defending their access to far-flung economic and natural resources, and by enmeshing their foreign and military policies in alliances that America dominated—Washington prevented these former and potential great powers from embarking on independent, and

From Benjamin Schwarz and Christopher Layne, "A New Grand Strategy," *The Atlantic Monthly* (January 2002). Copyright © 2002 by Benjamin Schwarz and Christopher Layne. Reprinted by permission.

(from the U.S. perspective) possibly destabilizing, foreign policies. This "reassurance strategy" (to use a term currently favored by policymakers) allowed for an unprecedented level of political and economic cooperation among the states of Western Europe and East Asia.

As noted, American policy since the end of the Cold War has aimed to ensure that the United States maintains its lofty perch. Every post-Cold War Pentagon assessment of national-security needs has insisted that America maintain its globe-girdling Cold War alliances, along with its Cold War defense-spending levels, even though the threat against which those alliances and budgets were ostensibly erected has disappeared. Some critics argue that this apparent stasis is born of bureaucratic inertia, or of a defense establishment's jealous guarding of its turf (and its trough). But in fact, given the logic behind American grand strategy, this continuity is entirely justifiable. The collapse of the Soviet Union hasn't altered the conviction among many American policymakers that a stable global economic and political order depends on Washington's maintaining preponderance (or, according to the official rhetoric, "leadership") over potential great powers. This means ameliorating their security problems.

The now infamous draft of the Pentagon's Defense Planning Guidance (prepared under the direction of the current undersecretary of defense for policy, Paul Wolfowitz), which was leaked to *The New York Times* in 1992, merely stated in undiplomatic language the logic that has long informed Washington's strategy. The United States, it argued, must continue to dominate the international system and thus to "discourage" the "advanced industrial nations from challenging our leadership or... even aspiring to a larger regional or global role." To accomplish this Washington must do nothing less than "retain the pre-eminent responsibility for addressing... those wrongs which threaten not only our interests, but those of our allies or friends, or which could seriously unsettle international relations." In other words, America must provide its allies with what one of the document's authors (now a special assistant to the President on the National Security Council) termed "adult supervision": the United States must not only impose a military protectorate over Europe and East Asia—regions composed of wealthy and technologically sophisticated states—but also safeguard Europe's and East Asia's worldwide interests, so that they need not develop military forces capable of "global power projection." (As Gabriel Robin, a former French representative to NATO [North Atlantic Treaty Organization], acknowledged, the U.S.-led alliance's "real function... is to serve as the chaperon of Europe." It is, Robin said, "the means to prevent [Europe] from establishing itself as an independent fortress and perhaps one day, a rival.") Those who argue that America's national-security spending is too high, given the end of the Cold War, often fail to appreciate the task Washington has assigned itself. The adult supervision of the world is an enormously expensive and complex undertaking, which perforce means that the United States must spend more on its military than do the next nine countries together—including Russia, Japan, China, France, Britain, and Germany.

An adult-supervision strategy entails a peculiar and recondite calculation of the world situation. For instance, although most Americans might believe that a reunified, democratic Korea would indisputably be in America's interests, the former National Security Advisor Zbigniew Brzezinski, in his 1997 book *The Grand Chessboard* (probably the fullest and frankest public exposition of America's post-Cold War global strategy), repeatedly explains how this development would in fact jeopardize America's unipolar strategy: it would, he argues, reflecting views long and widely held in policymaking circles, obviate the ostensible need for U.S. troops on the peninsula, which could lead to a U.S. pullback from East Asia, which could, in turn, lead to Japan's becoming "militarily more self-sufficient," which would lead to political, military, and economic rivalry among the region's states. Thus the best situation is the status quo in Korea, which allows for U.S. forces to be stationed there indefinitely.

Similar—and more urgent, given the current war on terrorism—is the thinking underlying Washington's policy in the Persian Gulf. Why is the United States so deeply embroiled in this turbulent region? Many people, echoing a comment by Secretary of State James A. Baker during the Persian Gulf War, would probably answer with one word: oil. This answer is—and was—both true and misleading. America derives most of its oil from Alaska, Canada, the continental United States, Mexico, and Venezuela. About 25 percent of U.S. petroleum imports come from the Persian Gulf. If the United States adopted a national energy strategy, it could free itself from dependence on Persian Gulf oil. Nevertheless, Washington assumes responsibility for stabilizing the region because Western Europe and Japan are heavily dependent on its oil, and because soon China, owing to rapid economic growth, will be as well— and America wants to discourage those powers from developing the means to protect that resource for themselves. In an interview on National Public Radio early in October, Walter Russell Mead, a senior foreign-policy analyst at the Council on Foreign Relations, explained the basis of U.S. policy in the terms that NSC staffers, think-tank analysts, and State and Defense Department policy planners have used for years: "We do not get that large a percentage of our oil from the Middle East. Japan gets a lot more.... And one of the reasons that we are sort of assuming this role of policeman of the Middle East, more or less, has more to do with making Japan and some other countries feel that their oil flow is assured ... so that they don't then feel more need to create a great power, armed forces, and security doctrine, and you don't start getting a lot of great powers with conflicting interests sending their militaries all over the world."

◄◉►

Despite its sometimes esoteric logic, America's strategy of preponderance is seductive. In the abstract it makes sense that the United States should seek to amass as much power as possible. In this way the rationale behind U.S. strategy is analogous to that of a firm in an oligopolistic market, which drives its rivals out of business rather than risk its profits in a competitive environment. Theoretically, if a state can establish—and maintain—itself as the only great power in the international system, it will enjoy something very close to absolute security. But as history amply shows, when one state acquires too much power, others invariably fear that it will aggrandize itself at their expense. "Hegemonic empires," Henry Kissinger recently noted, "almost automatically elicit universal resistance, which is why all such claimants have sooner or later exhausted themselves."

More than two hundred years ago Edmund Burke warned his countrymen,

> Among precautions against ambition it may not be amiss to take one precaution against our own.... I dread our being too much dreaded.... We may say that we shall not abuse this astonishing and hitherto unheard-of power. But every nation will think we shall abuse it.... Sooner or later, this state of things must produce a combination against us which may end in our ruin.

Like some optimistic Britons in the late eighteenth century, many American strategists today assert that the United States, the only superpower, is a "benevolent" hegemon, immunized from a backlash against its preponderance by what they call its "soft power"—that is, by the attractiveness of its liberal-democratic ideology and its open, syncretic culture. Washington also believes that others don't fear U.S. geopolitical pre-eminence because they know the United States will use its unprecedented power to promote the good of the international system rather than to advance its own selfish aims.

But states must always be more concerned with a predominant power's capabilities than with its intentions, and in fact well before September 11—indeed, throughout most of the past decade—other states have been profoundly anxious about the *im*balance of power in America's favor. This simmering mistrust of U.S. predominance intensified during the Clinton Administration, as other states responded to American hegemony by concerting their efforts against it. Russia and China, although long estranged, found common ground in a nascent alliance that opposed U.S. "hegemonism" and expressly aimed at re-establishing "a multipolar world." Arguing that the term "superpower" is inadequate to convey the true extent of America's economic and military pre-eminence, the French Foreign Minister Hubert Vedrine called the United States a "hyperpower." Even the Dutch Prime Minister declared that the European Union should make itself "a counterweight to the United States."

American intervention in Kosovo crystallized fears of U.S. hegemony, prompting the emergence of an anti-U.S. constellation of China, Russia, and India. Viewing the Kosovo war as a dangerous precedent establishing Washington's self-declared right to interfere in other countries' internal affairs, and asserting their support for a multipolar world, these three states increased their arms transfers and their sharing of military technology, specifically to counter American power. Also, the Kosovo conflict made apparent the disparity between America's geopolitical power and Europe's, inciting Europe to take its first serious steps toward redressing that disparity by acquiring—through the European Defense and Security Identity [EDSI]—the kinds of military capabilities it would need to act independent of the United States. If the European Union fulfills EDSI's longer-term goals, it will emerge as an unfettered strategic player in world politics. And that emergence will have been driven by the clear objective of investing Europe with the capability to act as a brake on America's aspirations.

Any remaining doubt that American hegemony could trigger a hostile reaction, whether reasonable or not, surely dissipated on September 11. The role the United States has assigned itself in the Persian Gulf has made it—not Japan, not the states of Western Europe, not China—vulnerable to a backlash. Iran, Iraq, and Afghanistan resent America's intrusion into regional affairs. The widespread perception within the region that the Middle East has long been a victim of "Western imperialism" of course exacerbates this animosity. Moreover, aggrieved groups throughout the Middle East contest the legitimacy of the regimes in Saudi Arabia, Kuwait, and the Gulf emirates which the United States is compelled to support, making America even more of a lightning rod for the politically disaffected. In this sense Osama bin Laden's brand of terrorism (which aims to compel the United States to remove its military forces from the Persian Gulf, and to replace America's client, the Saudi monarchy, with a fundamentalist Islamic government) dramatically illustrates U.S. vulnerability to the kind of "asymmetric warfare" of which some defense experts have warned.

꒰◉꒱

The rise of new great powers is inevitable, and America's very primacy accelerates this process. If Washington continues to follow an adult-supervision strategy, which treats its "allies" as irresponsible adolescents and China and Russia as future enemies to be suppressed, its relations with these emerging great powers will be increasingly dangerous, as they coalesce against what they perceive as an American threat. But that is not even the worst conceivable outcome. What if a sullen and resentful China were to align itself with Islamic fundamentalist groups? Such a situation is hardly beyond the realm of possibility; partners form alliances not because they are friends, or because they have common values, but because they fear someone else more than they fear each other.

A strategy of preponderance is burdensome, Sisyphean, and profoundly risky. It is therefore time for U.S. policymakers to adopt a very different grand strategy: one that might be called offshore balancing. Rather than fear multipolarity, this strategy embraces it. It recognizes that instability—caused by the rise and fall of great powers, great-power rivalries, and messy regional conflicts—is a geopolitical fact of life. Offshore balancing accepts that the United States cannot prevent the rise of new great powers, either within the present American sphere (the European Union [EU], Germany, Japan) or outside it (China, a resurgent Russia). Instead of exhausting its resources and drawing criticism or worse by keeping these entities weak, the United States would allow them to develop their militaries to provide for their own national and regional security. Among themselves, then, these states would maintain power balances, check the rise of overly ambitious global and regional powers, and stabilize Europe, East Asia, and the Persian Gulf. It would naturally be in their interests to do so.

It's always safest and cheapest to get others to stabilize the turbulent regions of the globe. Historically, however, this has seldom been an option, because if one lives in a dangerous neighborhood, one must be prepared to protect oneself from troublemakers rather than relying on someone else to do so.

In fact, the only two great powers in modern history that successfully devolved onto others the responsibility for maintaining regional stability are Britain during its great-power heyday (1700–1914) and the United States (until 1945). They were able to do so because they had moats—a narrow one for England, and two very big ones for the United States—that kept predatory Eurasian great powers at bay.

As offshore balancers, Britain and the United States reaped enormous strategic dividends. While they were shielded from threatening states by geography, London and Washington could afford to maintain militaries smaller than those of Continental powers, and concentrate instead on getting rich. Often they could stay out of Europe's turmoil entirely, gaining in strength as other great powers fought debilitating wars. And even in wartime offshore balancers have enjoyed advantages that Continental powers have not. Instead of sending big armies to fight costly Continental wars, Britain, for instance, relied on its navy to blockade those states bidding for mastery of Europe and on its financial power to underwrite coalitions against them, and stuck its allies with the greater part of the blood price of defeating those powers that aspired to dominate the Continent.

The United States, of course, followed a similar strategy during World War II. From 1940 to 1944 it confined its role in the European war to providing economic assistance and munitions to the Soviet Union and Britain and—after entering the war, in December of 1941—to relatively low-cost strategic air bombardment of Germany, and peripheral land campaigns in North Africa and Italy. The United States was more than happy to delay the invasion of Europe until June of 1944. By then the Red Army—which inflicted about 88 percent of the Wehrmacht's casualties throughout the war—had mortally weakened Germany, but at a staggering cost.

Taken together, the experiences of Britain and America highlight the central feature of the offshore balancing strategy: it allows for burden *shifting*, rather than burden sharing. Offshore balancers can afford to be bystanders in the opening stages of conflict. Because the security of others is most immediately at risk, an offshore balancer can be confident that those others will attempt to defend themselves. Often they will do so expeditiously, obviating the offshore balancer's intervention. If, on the other hand, a predominant power seems to be winning, an offshore balancer can intervene decisively to forestall its victory (as Britain did against Philip II, Louis XIV, and Napoleon). And if the offshore balancer must intervene, the state aspiring to dominance will already have been at least somewhat bloodied, and thus not as formidable as it was for those who had the geopolitical misfortune to constitute the first line of defense.

The same dynamics apply—or would, if the United States gave them a chance—in regional conflicts, although not quite as dramatically. Great powers that border restive neighbors, or that are economically dependent on unstable regions, have a much larger interest than does the United States in policing those areas. Most regional power balances (the relative positions of, say, Hungary and Romania, or of one sub-Saharan state and another) need not concern the United States. America must intervene only to prevent a single power from dominating a strategically crucial area—and then only if the efforts of great powers with a larger stake in that region have failed to redress the imbalance. So for an offshore balancing strategy to work, the world must be multipolar—that is, there must be several other great powers, and major regional powers as well, onto which the United States can shift the burden of maintaining stability in various parts of the world.

For America the most important grand-strategic issue is what relations it will have with these new great powers. In fostering a multipolar world—in which the foreign and national-security policies of the emerging great powers will be largely devoted to their rivalries with one another and to quelling and containing regional instability—an offshore balancing strategy is, of course, opportunistic and self-serving. But it also exercises restraint and shows geopolitical respect. By abandoning the "preponderance" strategy's extravagant objectives, the United States can minimize the risks of open confrontation with the new great powers.

Although jockeying for advantage is a fact of life for great powers, coexistence, and even cooperation between and among them, is not unusual. Offshore balancing seeks to promote America's relative power and security, but it also aims to maximize the opportunity for the United States to be on decent terms with the other great powers. In this sense the strategy has much in common with Richard Nixon and Henry Kissinger's vision of détente. That policy was a significant departure from previous Cold War approaches, in that the United States explicitly recognized the Soviet Union as a collaborator in, rather than a challenger to, the effort to maintain the stability of the international system. To understand this dramatic shift, contrast the inaugural address of John F. Kennedy, in which that paragon of Cold War liberalism advanced the stirring but rather dangerous notion that in the struggle with communism the United States would "pay any price, bear any burden," with Nixon's first inaugural address, which promulgated the realistic but conciliatory message that "we cannot expect to make everyone our friend, but we can try to make no one our enemy." This was détente's animating sentiment.

Détente was based on the assumption (hardly contested at the time) that the USSR wouldn't go away. Because the superpower rivalry could not be resolved without destroying humanity, there was, as Kissinger declared, "no alternative to coexistence." Détente, then, was a strategy for managing a permanent relationship. In what Nixon and Kissinger hoped would evolve into a mature relationship, Moscow and Washington would acknowledge each other's legitimate interests and try not to allow disagreements to poison accommodations. Détente was a shift in style with substance—or, rather, a shift in style with substantive consequences. The Soviets and the Chinese were to be approached not as alien ideologues but as intelligent adults with whom the United States should find a substantial area of common interest.

Similarly, an offshore balancing strategy would dictate that in order to coexist with the emerging great powers, or even to enjoy cooperative ties with them (in efforts to combat Islamic terrorism, for instance), the United States must start treating such powers like fellow adults. This would mean both accepting them as peers and acknowledging the legitimacy of their national interests.

In concrete terms, here is how an offshore balancing strategy would apply to particular cases.

- Today, not for the first time in its history, Russia is down and out as a great power. But it has come back before and probably will do so again. Moreover, for the United States, Russia is crucial as a potential ally in three regions: Europe (vis-à-vis a European "superstate," or Germany if the EU project fails), East Asia (vis-à-vis China), and the Persian Gulf and Central Asia. As an offshore balancer, the United States would abandon plans for NATO expansion (which Russia regards as a strategic threat), and if Washington decides to undertake a national missile-defense program, it would follow through on the recent agreement to make deep cuts in its strategic nuclear arsenal to reassure Russia and China that it doesn't seek to gain a first-strike advantage. It would allow Russia to supervise its legitimate sphere of influence—in Chechnya and in Central Asia, where it is combating Islamic fundamentalists, as well as in parts of Eastern Europe and in the states that formerly composed the Soviet Union. America's direct sphere of influence embraces the area from the Canadian Arctic to Tierra del Fuego and from Greenland to Guam. Surely we can tolerate other great powers' enjoying spheres of influence in their own parts of the world.
- With respect to China, the United States would recognize that the Taiwan issue is an internal Chinese matter. Taiwan's unresolved status is a legacy of the civil war that ended on the mainland in 1949. It is worth recalling that before the outbreak of the Korean War, Secretary of State Dean Acheson advised that the United States should extricate itself from the unfinished business of the Chinese civil war and leave Taiwan to its fate. A half century later it is time for the United States finally to do so. Washington would also fundamentally re-examine its notion of what constitutes a "China threat." That China, the largest and potentially most powerful state in East Asia, would seek a more assertive political, economic, and military role in the region—and would even want to end America's current strategic superiority there—hardly meets that threshold (although it is no doubt alarming to China's immediate neighbors). The United States should also mute its criticism of China's human-rights policy. Washington simply can't transform China into a liberal, free-market democracy, and U.S. pressure only exacerbates the friction in Sino-American relations. Generally, an offshore balancing strategy would hold that fatalism should replace idealism in America's attitude toward what used to be called the internal arrangements of other countries. It would also hold that our pragmatic policy choices, born of self-interest, should be embraced as such, and not clothed in altruism or idealism. Seeking to engender changes in other nations' fundamental values so that they resemble America's is an unreasonable goal of foreign policy. An offshore balancing strategy would accept other nations for what they are, or what their history has made them.

- With respect to Europe, the United States would endorse the EU's efforts—which Washington now opposes—to acquire the military capabilities it needs to defend its interests independent of the United States. At the same time, the United States would begin a phased withdrawal from its European security commitments. To be sure, many U.S. policymakers have argued that the Europeans have demonstrated their incapacity (during the Balkan crises, for instance) to act effectively without U.S. "leadership." But these protests are hypocritical—who can blame the Europeans for their inability to assert themselves in security affairs when Washington has for decades repeatedly squelched European initiatives that would have made that assertion possible? An offshore balancing strategy would hold that America's strategic interest in Europe does not demand that Washington insure against every untoward event there. Disorder in the Balkans and other places on Europe's fringes should be a matter for Europeans, who have the wherewithal to combat it, quarantine it, or, if they choose, ignore it. The United States would follow a similar policy with respect to Japan. Washington would announce to Tokyo its intention to terminate the Mutual Cooperation and Security Treaty within a specified time period (say, five years), at the end of which Japan, for more than fifty years a politically stable state, would have developed whatever military means it believes necessary to function as an independent great power. An offshore balancing strategy would turn on a simple truth: other states have at least as much interest as the United States does in secure sea-lanes, access to resources, and regional stability. The less America does, and the less others expect it to do, the more other states will do to help themselves.

Recognizing the legitimacy of other great powers' spheres of influence offers the United States a further strategic advantage. The Persian Gulf and Central Asia show why. Russia and China both are profoundly concerned about the spread of Islamic fundamentalism on their peripheries. In Chechnya, in Central Asia (where Russian troops help to defend the former Soviet republics of Uzbekistan and Tajikistan), and in the Caucasus, Moscow has fought major military campaigns to protect its southern flank against militant Islam. China, too, is combating terrorism fomented by Islamic separatists, in the Xinjiang province. Last June, Beijing and Moscow entered into a security relationship, the Shanghai Cooperation Organization (which also embraces three of the former Soviet republics in Central Asia), to coordinate efforts to combat the common threat to their security posed by these Islamic fundamentalist terrorist groups—groups linked to the Taliban and Osama bin Laden. Similarly, India, a possible future great power, has been battling Islamic terrorists who are waging a proxy war on Pakistan's behalf to wrest the disputed province of Kashmir away from New Delhi. Simply put, for reasons of security and access to oil, Russia, China, India, Western Europe, and Japan have strong reasons—stronger than America's—

to pacify Central Asia and the Persian Gulf. By adopting an offshore balancing strategy, the United States will compel them to do so.

Passing the buck would help the United States out of the impasse that securing Afghanistan promises to be. The political and military challenges the war poses underscore how difficult and costly will be the effort to restore order in the country and the region when the fighting stops. When the United States has achieved its military goals in Afghanistan, it should announce a phased withdrawal from its security commitments in the region, shifting to others the hard job of stabilizing it.

The complexities involved in that job are numerous. Washington's very strategy of primacy, and America's concomitant military presence in the region, are in themselves a source of instability, especially for the regimes on which the United States relies. The regimes in Saudi Arabia and Pakistan, for instance, face doubtful prospects precisely because their close connection to Washington intensifies radical nationalist and Islamic fundamentalist opposition within those countries. For this reason none of the regional regimes in the current coalition can be especially dependable allies. Only with enormous pressure did a few of them even allow American forces to conduct offensive strikes on Afghanistan from bases on their territory. And fearing that popular anger at the U.S. military campaign will trigger domestic political explosions, many of these states pressed Washington to bring an early end to the war.

If America remains in the region indefinitely, it will have to prop up these unpopular or failing regimes. In Saudi Arabia the United States could easily find itself militarily involved if internal upheaval threatens the monarchy's hold on power. To forestall economic collapse in Pakistan, Washington will have to donate billions of dollars in direct and indirect assistance. Finally, if the United States continues to play the role of regional gendarme, it will assume the thankless—and probably hopeless—burden of trying to put Afghanistan together again. Divided along ethnic, linguistic, and clan fault lines, the various factions inside Afghanistan cannot agree on that country's future political organization. (The forces making up the anti-Taliban contingent seem only to agree that they resent U.S. bombing of their country.) That the outside powers have conflicting goals for Afghanistan's future further complicates any sorting out of Afghanistan's political structure. If ever there was a place where America should devolve security responsibilities to others, it is the Persian Gulf and Southwest Asia region. Again, Western Europe, Japan, Russia, China, and India all have greater security and economic interests in the region than does the United States, and if America pulls out, they will police it because they must.

◦◦◦◦

Rather than attempt to impose a Pax Americana on this endemically turbulent area, the United States should devote the resources it currently spends on this costly and dangerous job to rendering the region economically and strategically irrelevant. That is, America should pursue a national energy policy that would develop alternative sources of energy for the United States and, more important, the rest of the industrialized world. This colossal scientific and industrial effort should be our highest national-security priority (see "Mideast Oil Forever?," by Joseph J. Romm and Charles B. Curtis, April, 1996, *Atlantic*). If the United States shifts responsibility for stabilizing the region to the other great powers, the real price of Persian Gulf oil will become extremely high for them. It would then be in their interests to pool resources and expertise with America in what would amount to an international Manhattan Project to obviate the need for that oil—thus dramatically reducing the revenue streams to the regimes in Iran, Iraq, and Saudi Arabia. Doing so is surely a common international interest. If Washington were to spend the approximately $106 billion that—according to Earl Ravenal, a former Pentagon analyst—it is devoting this year to defending the Persian Gulf region, and if Western Europe, Japan, China, and Russia were to kick in what they would otherwise spend on policing the region, it's hard to imagine that this goal couldn't be achieved.

Some will assert, correctly, that if it abjures a strategy of preponderance, America will sacrifice some of the awe with which it is viewed by the world. But less awe and less influence will bring the United States more security. Some will object that the policy we advocate shuns the inspiring role of America as "the indispensable nation." But such a grandiose vision, while pleasing to our image of ourselves, is the antithesis of statecraft, which must be guided by discrimination on the basis of power, interest, and circumstance. Historically, the most imaginative statesmen and policies have hardly been visionary. For centuries, with flexibility and subtlety, British diplomats pursued a grand strategy that aimed at nothing more inspiring than ensuring a balance of power among the states of Western Europe. This was really just tactical fine-tuning on a grand scale, and so aroused the consternation of idealists of every stripe. For their part, America's nineteenth-century statesmen could not have been less idealistic or more pragmatic as they, by adroitly exploiting European great-power rivalries, maneuvered the British, the French, and the Spanish out of North America and established American predominance in the Western Hemisphere—probably the most stunning diplomatic achievement of modern history, and the very model of a successful multipolar strategy.

The policy we advocate is informed by the conviction that history is "just one damned thing after another"; we see no end to power politics. And we hold that the purpose of grand strategy isn't the pursuit of new world orders but simply making the best of bad choices—to use the political philosopher Michael Oakeshott's metaphor, keeping afloat in "a boundless and bottomless sea; there is neither harbor for shelter nor floor for anchorage, neither starting point nor appointed destination." Ours is a grand strategy for the long haul—and so, by the lights of visionaries who see foreign policy as a means of pursuing millennialist goals, not a very grand one. But the grander its foreign-policy vision, the more a state is trapped in the tyranny of its own construct: although recent administrations display an odd compulsion to devise and promulgate such visions of America's role in the world, those visions are in fact incompatible with the push and pull of strategy.

Finally, although some might characterize an offshore balancing strategy as isolationist, it emphatically is not. Rather, its guiding principle is a clear-eyed realism. It is a workaday policy—pragmatic, flexible, and opportunistic. But it will also bring America into a more respectful and natural relationship with the other great powers, as the United States forsakes the temptations of hegemony. "A mature great power will make measured and limited use of its power," Walter Lippmann wrote in 1965.

> It will eschew the theory of a global and universal duty, which not only commits it to unending wars of intervention, but intoxicates its thinking with the illusion that it is a crusader for righteousness.... I am in favor of learning to behave like a great power, of getting rid of the globalism, which would not only entangle us everywhere, but is based on the totally vain notion that if we do not set the world in order, no matter what the price, we cannot live in the world safely.... In the real world, we shall have to learn to live as a great power which defends itself and makes its way among other great powers.

POSTSCRIPT

Must America Exercise World Leadership?

Whether one espouses the world leadership role advocated by Kristol and Kagan or the cooperation with other nations sought by Schwarz and Layne, the task of American foreign policy is to spell out the particular policies that the United States should pursue. Former secretary of state Henry Kissinger, in *Does America Need a Foreign Policy?* (Simon & Schuster, 2001), answers his title question with a resounding yes but suggests that the United States does not have one. Instead of having a long-range strategy, he argues, the United States has for too long responded to international challenges as they have occurred. Kissinger also notes that foreign policy has not been seriously discussed by recent presidential candidates (the reason for this is that, except in times of war, domestic policy issues have far more influence over voters than foreign policy issues).

Opting for American supremacy suggests that the United States will seek to remain the sole superpower, unilaterally choosing its issues and commitments. This could mean that its influence would span the world, including such troubling areas as sub-Saharan Africa, where war, disease, hunger, and high birth rates challenge social stability and provide fertile ground for tyrants and terrorists. It might also imply that it is America's duty to police the world. Something like that could be seen in President Bush's characterizing as "evil" states that employ weapons of mass destruction against their own populations or neighbors or that sponsor or harbor terrorists. When an American president calls another nation "evil," is he suggesting that it is America's duty to eliminate that evil, or is he merely stating a moral platitude?

Electing cooperation with other nations and compliance with international agreements acknowledges that America will not impose its will on other nations and will not act unilaterally to achieve its own international goals when they are challenged by its allies. In *The Paradox of American Power: Why the World's Only Superpower Can't Go It Alone* (Oxford University Press, 2002), former assistant secretary of defense Joseph P. Nye, Jr., states that the United States is not powerful enough to ignore the views and needs of other nations. Nye agrees that nothing can be done in international relations without the United States, but he maintains that there is very little that the United States can achieve alone. Nye makes an interesting distinction between hard power (military and economic strength) and soft power (openness, prosperity, and other values that persuade and attract rather than coerce). He contends that the information revolution and globalization require America to exercise more soft than hard power.

ISSUE 20

Should Terrorist Suspects Be Tried by Military Tribunals?

YES: Pierre-Richard Prosper, from Testimony Before the Committee on the Judiciary, U.S. Senate (December 4, 2001)

NO: Aryeh Neier, from "The Military Tribunals on Trial," *The New York Review of Books* (February 14, 2002)

ISSUE SUMMARY

YES: Ambassador Pierre-Richard Prosper defends military tribunals as consistent with established law and as necessary to protect American jurors and court personnel from an international terror network.

NO: Aryeh Neier, of the American Civil Liberties Union, contends that the proposed military tribunals would deprive defendants of essential rights guaranteed under both American and international law.

On September 20, 2001, nine days after the terrorist attacks on the World Trade Center and the Pentagon, President George W. Bush told a joint session of Congress that "an act of war" had been committed against America by "enemies of freedom." To defeat these enemies, Bush said, "we will direct every resource at our command." He mentioned several resources, including "every instrument of law enforcement," and in November he issued an executive order creating one such instrument: military tribunals, or "commissions," as the administration later called them.

Military tribunals derive their authority not from the judicial branch of the government (Article 3 in the Constitution) but from the president's authority as commander in chief (Article 2). As such, they are not bound by all of the procedures followed in civilian courts. These are special courts, convened to adjudicate extraordinary cases, usually (though not always) involving foreigners during wartime. Such tribunals have a long history in the United States. Americans used them during the Revolutionary War to try suspected spies and saboteurs. President Lincoln resorted to them during the Civil War. And President Franklin D. Roosevelt used military tribunals to convict and execute German saboteurs caught in the United States during World War II.

According to Defense Department guidelines, the present tribunals would apply only to foreign nationals, not American citizens. They would have juries of three to seven military officers. Other provisions in the guidelines include the following:

- A two-thirds vote will be required for conviction and sentencing, not the unanimous vote required in civilian proceedings. (An exception, requiring unanimity in death penalty cases, was later added.)
- In some cases the panels will be able to hear secondhand and hearsay evidence, which is banned in civilian courts.
- Defendants will be provided with military lawyers, though they can hire civilian attorneys at their own expense.
- Defendants will not be allowed to appeal decisions in federal courts, though they will be able to petition a panel of review, which may include civilians as well as military officers. Final review will be in the hands of the president.

Why try terrorist suspects before military tribunals? Why not use civilian courts, as the United States has already done successfully in the case of the Oklahoma City bombing and the 1993 bombing of the World Trade Center? Timothy McVeigh, who was tried and convicted in the Oklahoma City case, was involved with one or two others, but those who carried out the attacks of September 11 were part of an international terrorist network operating in dozens of countries and at war with the United States. Arguably, those involved in the earlier attack on the World Trade Center were also enlisted in that war, but U.S. authorities in 1993 were not as alert to the nature of the threat as they are today. Moreover, the judge in that case is still under 24-hour protection by federal marshals. One of the arguments for military tribunals, then, is that civilian judges and jurors will not be under threats of reprisals by terrorist organizations. The risk of reprisals grows the longer the trial and appeals process continue, and in civilian cases the appeal process alone can stretch out over many years. So another reason given for military tribunals is that they will permit a more expeditious hearing, with rules of evidence more flexible than is possible in ordinary legal proceedings. Still another argument is that military commissions can allow the use of classified information without endangering sources and methods.

For opponents of military tribunals, the very qualities of these tribunals that the defenders praise—secrecy, speed, and relaxed rules of evidence—are worrisome. In their view, dispensing with unanimous jury verdicts, using hearsay evidence, and prohibiting appeals to civilian courts are serious departures from the very standard of justice that America seeks to promote in the world. As Harvard University law professor Ann Marie Slaughter put it, to forsake that standard "is to betray the cause we're fighting for."

In the following selections, Pierre-Richard Prosper defends military tribunals as consistent with established law and as necessary to protect American jurors and court personnel from an international terror network, while Aryeh Neier contends that the proposed military tribunals would deprive defendants of essential rights guaranteed under both American and international law.

 **YES**

Testimony of Pierre-Richard Prosper

Mr. Chairman, members of the committee, I come before you as the Ambassador-at-Large for War Crimes Issues and also as a former prosecutor. Prior to my appointment to this post, I spent ten years in the trenches as a line prosecutor. As a deputy district attorney in Los Angeles, I prosecuted hundreds of cases and tried dozens of murder cases and multiple murder cases as a member of the Hard Core Gang Division. As an Assistant United States Attorney, I prosecuted and investigated sophisticated international drug cartels trafficking tons of cocaine into the streets of Los Angeles. And as a lead prosecutor for the United Nations International Criminal Tribunal for Rwanda, I successfully prosecuted, in a 14-month trial, the first-ever case of genocide before an international tribunal under the 1948 Genocide Convention.

With this experience, I recognize, understand, and truly believe that there are different approaches that can be used to achieve justice. I recognize that different procedures are allowed and that different procedures are appropriate. No one approach is exclusive and the approaches need not be identical for justice to be administered fairly. But in all approaches what is important is that the procedures ensure fundamental fairness. And that is what the President's [November 13 Military Order] calls for. After the tragic events of September 11th, we as a nation were forced to reexamine our traditional notions of security, our conceptions of our attackers, and our approaches to bringing the perpetrators to justice. The conventional view of terrorism as isolated acts of egregious violence did not fit. The atrocities committed by the al Qaida organization at the World Trade Center in New York, at the headquarters of our Department of Defense, and in Pennsylvania were of the kind that defied the imagination and shocked the conscience.

These atrocities are just as premeditated, just as systematic, just as evil as the violations of international humanitarian law that I have seen around the world. As the President's order recognizes, we must call these attacks by their rightful name: war crimes.

President Bush recognized that the threat we currently face is as grave as any we have confronted. While combating these war crimes committed against U.S. citizens, it is important that the President be able to act in the interest of this country to protect the security of our citizens and ensure that justice is

From U.S. Senate. Committee on the Judiciary. *Department of Justice Oversight: Preserving Our Freedoms While Defending Against Terrorism.* Hearing, December 4, 2001. Washington, DC: Government Printing Office, 2001.

achieved. He has repeatedly promised to use all the military, diplomatic, economic and legal options available to ensure the safety of the American people and our democratic way of life. The President should have the full range of options available for addressing these wrongs. The Military Order adds additional arrows to the President's quiver.

Should we be in a position to prosecute Bin Laden, his top henchmen, and other members of al Qaida, this option should be available to protect our civilian justice system against this organization of terror. We should all ask ourselves whether we want to bring into the domestic system dozens of persons who have proved they are willing to murder thousands of Americans at a time and die in the process. We all must think about the safety of the jurors, who may have to be sequestered from their families for up to a year or more while a complex trial unfolds. We all ought to remember the employees in the civilian courts, such as the bailiff, court clerk, and court reporter and ask ourselves whether this was the type of service they signed up for—to be potential victims of terror while justice was pursued. And we all must think also about the injured city of New York and the security implications that would be associated with a trial of the al Qaida organization.

With this security threat in mind, we should consider the option of military commissions from two perspectives. First, the President's Military Order is consistent with the precepts of international law. And second, military commissions are the customary legal option for bringing to justice the perpetrators of war crimes during times of war. The Military Order's conclusion that we are in a state of armed conflict deserves comment. Because military commissions are empowered to try violations of the law of war, their jurisdiction is dependent upon the existence of an armed conflict, which we have.

It is clear that this series of attacks against the United States is more than isolated and sporadic acts of violence, or other acts of a similar nature. Rather, a foreign, private terrorist network, with the essential harboring and other support of the Taliban-led Afghanistan, has issued a declaration of war against the United States. It has organized, campaigned, trained, and over the course of years repeatedly carried out cowardly, indiscriminate attacks, including the largest attack in history against the territory of the United States in terms of number of persons killed and property damage.

Tracing the criminal history of the organization further confirms the state of armed conflict. A decade's worth of hostile statements by Bin Laden over and over and over again state that he is at war against the United States. He has instructed his followers to kill each and every American civilian. We should also consider the intensity of the hostilities and the systematic nature of the assaults. Consider the fact that al Qaida is accused of bombing the World Trade Center in 1993 and attacking U.S. military service personnel serving in Somalia in the same year. Consider that Bin Laden and al Qaida are accused of attacking and bombing our embassies in Nairobi, Kenya and Dar es Salaam, Tanzania.

Remember that al Qaida is accused of perpetrating last year's bombing of the U.S.S. *Cole*. And of course, added to this history are the horrifying and unprovoked air assaults on the twin towers in New York, the Pentagon, and the airplane tragedy in Pennsylvania.

It is clear that the conduct of al Qaida cannot be considered ordinary domestic crimes, and the perpetrators are not common criminals. Indeed, one needs to look no further than the international reaction to understand that September 11 was perceived as an armed attack on the United States. NATO's North Atlantic Council declared that the attack was directed from abroad and "regarded as an action covered by Article V of the Washington Treaty, which states that an armed attack against one or more of the Allies in Europe or North America shall be considered an attack against them all." The Organization of American States, Australia and New Zealand activated parallel provisions in their mutual defense treaties. UN Security Council Resolutions 1368 and 1373 recognized our inherent right to exercise self-defense. And UN Security Council Resolution 1377 added: "acts of international terrorism constitute one of the most serious threats to international peace and security in the twenty-first century."

We can also look at our domestic response, including the joint resolution passed by this Congress authorizing "the use of all necessary and appropriate force" in order to prevent any future acts of international terrorism. Mr. Chairman, members of the committee, we are at war, an unconventional war conducted by unconventional means by an unprecedented aggressor. Under long established legal principles, the right to conduct armed conflict, lawful belligerency, is reserved only to states and recognized armed forces or groups under responsible command. Private persons lacking the basic indicia of organization and the ability or willingness to conduct operations in accordance with the laws of armed conflict have no legal right to wage warfare against a state. In waging war the participants become unlawful combatants.

Because the members of al Qaida do not meet the criteria to be lawful combatants under the law of war, they have no right to engage in armed conflict and are unlawful combatants. And because their intentional targeting and killing of civilians in time of international armed conflict amount to war crimes, military commissions are available for adjudicating their specific violations of the laws of war. As the U.S. Supreme Court unanimously stated in Ex Parte Quirin: "by universal agreement and practice, the law of war draws a distinction between the armed forces and the peaceful populations of belligerent nations, and also between those who are lawful and unlawful combatants. Lawful combatants are subject to capture and detention as prisoners of war by opposing military forces. Unlawful combatants are likewise subject to capture and detention, but, in addition, they are subject to trial and punishment by military tribunals for acts which render their belligerency unlawful."

In this campaign against terrorism, it is important that the President have the full range of available forums for seeking criminal accountability against persons for their individual and command responsibility for violations of the law of war. The military commission provides a traditionally available mechanism to address these unconventional crimes.

Military commissions have been utilized and legally accepted throughout our history to prosecute persons who violate the laws of war. They were used by General Winfield Scott during his operations in Mexico, in the Civil War by President Lincoln, and in 1942 by President Roosevelt. They are an internationally accepted practice with deep historical roots. The international community has utilized military commissions and tribunals to achieve justice, most notably at Nuremberg and in the Far East. The tribunals which tried most of the leading perpetrators of Nazi and Japanese war crimes were military tribunals. These tribunals were followed by thousands of Allied prosecutions of the lower-level perpetrators under the Control Council Law No. 10.

By the end of 1958, the Western Allies had used military tribunals to sentence 5,025 Germans for war crimes. In the Far East, 4,200 Japanese were convicted before military tribunals convened by U.S., Australian, British, Chinese, Dutch, and French forces for their atrocities committed during the war.

Today, the commissions as envisioned by the President in the Military Order, while different from those found in our Article III courts, are in conformity with these historical precedents and the world's current efforts to prosecute war crimes through the United Nations in the International Criminal Tribunals for the Former Yugoslavia and Rwanda. To understand this it may be helpful for me to articulate the commonalities. Like it's predecessors, in the Nuremberg and Far East International Military Tribunals, the Allied Control Council Law No. 10 proceedings, and the International Criminal Tribunals for the former Yugoslavia and Rwanda, the judges sit as both triers of law and of fact. In addition, decisions such as judicial orders, judgments, and sentences are reached by a majority vote and not unanimity. Evidence of a probative value is admitted. And in the United Nations International Criminal Tribunals for the former Yugoslavia and Rwanda, portions of the proceedings have been and are authorized to be closed, just as is contemplated by the President's military order. Mr. Chairman, members of the committee, since September 11th I have been asked about our criticisms of foreign military tribunals. In these cases, we criticized the process and not the forum.

Since September 11th I have also been asked why we do not create an international tribunal? In our view, the international practice should be to support sovereign states seeking justice domestically when it is feasible and would be credible, as we are trying to do in Sierra Leone and Cambodia. International tribunals are not and should not be the courts of first redress, but of last resort. When domestic justice is not possible for egregious war crimes due to a failed state or a dysfunctional judicial system, the international community may, through the Security Council or by consent, step in on an ad hoc basis as in Rwanda and Yugoslavia. That is not the case in the United States.

Our goal should be and this administration's policy is to encourage states to pursue credible justice rather than abdicating the responsibility. Because justice and the administration of justice are a cornerstone of any democracy, pursuing accountability for war crimes while respecting the rule of law by a sovereign state must be encouraged at all times. The President understands our sovereign responsibility and has taken action to fulfill his duty to the American people. In creating an additional option, the nation is now prepared and will have an additional forum to address these wrongs when needed.

Aryeh Neier

The Military Tribunals on Trial

Among the many defects of President Bush's order for military commissions to try suspected al-Qaeda members or supporters is that it lumps together at least four categories of persons who have distinct sets of rights under either domestic or international law. The four categories of persons subject to trial by military commissions under the President's order are: (1) prisoners of war captured in Afghanistan; (2) unlawful combatants arrested in Afghanistan or elsewhere in the world outside the United States; (3) illegal aliens in the United States or aliens who came to the United States legally—as with student or visitor visas—but with the alleged purpose of engaging in terrorism; and (4) legal aliens with permanent resident status who are accused of engaging in terrorist acts.

As written, the order violates, in different ways, the rights of all four categories; it recalls [the French prime minister Georges] Clemenceau's famous comment about the Dreyfus case that "military justice is to justice as military music is to music." Fortunately, public debate over the order has been far more extensive than it has been over the many other violations of rights by the Bush administration since September 11. In consequence, the President's order is being modified by Defense Department regulations and Justice Department practice. These developments demonstrate that even at a time when a commencement speaker at a university is booed off the stage for giving a talk about constitutional rights, and when only one member of the US Senate voted against sweeping federal legislation abridging civil liberties, it is possible for rights advocates—along with some of the officials within the federal bureaucracy itself—to take on an overwhelmingly popular president and force him and his administration to back away from draconian measures.

The first two categories of people subject to trial—prisoners of war and unlawful combatants arrested outside the United States—derive their rights from international law. The essential difference between the two is that prisoners of war engage in open, announced combat in accordance with the customs of war. Unlawful combatants, on the other hand, attempt to conceal their activities. They include those who disguise themselves as civilians as well as spies, saboteurs, and terrorists. Under international law, in particular the Geneva Conventions, both categories may be tried before military tribunals. It is true that

From Aryeh Neier, "The Military Tribunals on Trial," *The New York Review of Books* (February 14, 2002). Copyright © 2002 by NYREV, Inc. Reprinted by permission of *The New York Review of Books*. Notes omitted.

there is no mechanism for international enforcement of the Geneva Conventions other than public pressure. But the conventions set forth clear legal standards that the US has agreed to observe, and failure to do so will be seen as a violation of fundamental international law.

The Third Geneva Convention of August 12, 1949, ratified by the United States Senate on July 6, 1955, defines prisoners of war as:

> (1) Members of the armed forces of a Party to the conflict, as well as members of militias or volunteer corps forming part of such armed forces.
>
> (2) Members of other militias and members of other volunteer corps, including those of organized resistance movements, belonging to a Party to the conflict and operating in or outside their own territory, even if this territory is occupied, provided that such militias or volunteer corps, including such organized resistance movements, fulfill the following conditions:
>
> (a) that of being commanded by a person responsible for his subordinates;
> (b) that of having a fixed distinctive sign recognizable at a distance;
> (c) that of carrying arms openly;
> (d) that of conducting their operations in accordance with the laws and customs of war.

— (Article 4)

In Afghanistan, neither Taliban fighters nor members of the Northern Alliance have worn uniforms. Therefore the requirement of a "fixed distinctive sign" can't be met literally; but since most of these combatants were not attempting to disguise themselves as civilians pretending to be other than what they were, the lack of uniforms should not prevent those captured in combat from being recognized as prisoners of war. Whether they are Afghans, Pakistanis, Arabs, or of some other nationality is immaterial. It is the kind of combat in which they were engaged that determines their rights. . . .

Though the terms of President Bush's order could apply to prisoners of war, it appears that its main purpose is to provide a means of bringing to justice unlawful combatants such as those who conspired to blow up the US embassies in East Africa and to hijack planes and use them as weapons on September 11, 2001. The order gives the President exclusive authority to determine that a person "is or was a member" of al-Qaeda; has "engaged in, aided or abetted, or conspired to commit, acts of international terrorism, or acts in preparation therefor"; or has "knowingly harbored" such persons. This order is dangerously sweeping. For example, an Irish-American immigrant who participates in a fund-raising event for widows and orphans of those killed in the struggle in Northern Ireland could be hauled before a military tribunal for aiding or abetting international terrorism.

No standards for making such determinations are provided in the order, which explicitly prohibits recourse to any court in order to question the President's unilateral decisions. Here again, the order runs afoul of the Third Geneva Convention. Though the convention's purpose is only to protect prisoners of war, it makes the question of whether someone in a doubtful case is entitled to such status subject to determination "by a competent tribunal." Until that has happened, "such persons shall enjoy the protection of the present Convention" (Article 5). That is, a suspected al-Qaeda terrorist captured in combat in Afghanistan must be treated as a prisoner of war until a court says he is not entitled to such status.

Once a court decides that a prisoner is an unlawful combatant, his rights under international law diminish substantially but they do not entirely disappear. The question of those rights is addressed in the 1977 First Additional Protocol to the Geneva Conventions. Though not ratified by the United States, some provisions of the First Additional Protocol are so widely accepted that they are recognized as expressing norms of customary international law which, for the past century, the United States has accepted as binding. Among the provisions with the apparent degree of support that qualifies them as customary international law is Article 75, which deals with the due process rights of "persons who are in the power of a Party to the conflict and who do not benefit from more favorable treatment under the Conventions." The protocol says that, at a minimum, the rights of such persons include trial "by an impartial and regularly constituted court"; "all necessary rights and means of defense"; the right to be "presumed innocent until proved guilty according to law"; the right not to "be compelled to testify against himself"; "the right to examine, or have examined, the witnesses against him and to obtain the attendance and examination of witnesses on his behalf"; and the right to "be advised on conviction of his judicial and other remedies." . . .

⌘

A main source of the controversy over President Bush's order is its application to aliens in the United States. Hostility to aliens during tense periods has a long history in the US. Attorney General A. Mitchell Palmer rounded up thousands in response to terrorist attacks after World War I (including the bombing of Palmer's house), and hundreds of radicals were deported—among them, the anarchist leader Emma Goldman—to Soviet Russia. By drawing a line between citizens and noncitizens in establishing the jurisdiction of the military tribunals, President Bush associates himself with this tradition.

He also pays lip service to the decision by the Supreme Court in the landmark case of *Ex parte Milligan,* which challenged President Abraham Lincoln's suspension of *habeas corpus* during a Civil War trial of a civilian before a military commission. The court ruled that trials before military commissions "can never be applied to *citizens* . . . where the courts are open and their process un-obstructed" (emphasis added). In making such an argument in order to limit the rights of noncitizens, President Bush reverts to the nativist politics that were in vogue in Congress during the period of Newt Gingrich's "Contract with America." He rejects the traditions of American jurisprudence and practice that treat citizens and legal permanent residents of the United States alike except in matters that directly relate to citizenship such as the rights to vote and to run for office. As Justice Harry Blackmun wrote for the Supreme Court in a case involving the denial of welfare benefits to noncitizens, "classifications based on alienage, like those based on nationality or race, are inherently suspect."

That does not mean such classifications are never permissible. It does mean they must be justified by a compelling state interest. A case might be made that such an interest justifies treating differently those who can be shown, through fair procedures, to have come to the United States for the express purpose of engaging in terrorism and who cross our borders illegally, or fraudulently obtain a visa, in order to carry out terrorist acts. But to deny 9.3 million permanent residents the right to trial in civilian courts is surely excessive. Such persons might engage in terrorism, but—as with Timothy McVeigh and Terry Nichols—the same is true of American citizens. What compelling state interest justifies treating them differently? . . .

                              ෂ☺ෂ

Though it appears that a number of the issues respecting the lawfulness of President Bush's order for military commissions are being addressed, there remains the question of whether the commissions are a good idea from the standpoint of international public policy. In at least three respects, plainly they are not. First, there is the question of whether other governments will cooperate with the United States in bringing to trial alleged members of the terrorist network. According to Baltazar Garzon, the Spanish investigative judge who has charged eight men with involvement in the September 11 attacks: "No country in Europe could extradite detainees to the United States if there were any chance they would be put before these military tribunals." He cited the European Convention on Human Rights, a treaty that is binding on the forty-three member states of the Council of Europe.

It is unclear whether the modifications that are being made to President Bush's order by Defense Department regulations will cause Spain and other foreign governments to allow such extraditions. Probably they will not, since it is the issue of military tribunals *per se*, as well as their ability to impose the death penalty, that is likely to be objectionable to European countries. If the US cannot secure custody over such persons, the damage to American interests should be clear. Our government will be denied the opportunity to bring criminal proceedings against people who may be part of the conspiracy to commit terrorist attacks. Even if they are guilty, they could go free because prosecutors in Spain, or elsewhere, may not be able to prove their complicity in crimes committed in the United States. In turn, American prosecutors may be deprived of crucial links in a chain of evidence that could implicate others. And the tribunals will further tarnish the reputation of the United States in Europe, where the United States is increasingly regarded as violating human rights because of its use of the death penalty, as well as the shoddy legal representation provided defendants in capital cases in states such as Texas and the high proportion of our population behind bars—approximately seven times as great as in the fifteen countries of the European Union.

Another defect of military tribunals is that their judgments are unlikely to have much legitimacy in the countries that are the probable breeding grounds for international terrorism. We can hardly expect that those who cheered the attacks of September 11 and who lionized Osama bin Laden are going to pay heed to the judgment of any court. But to the extent possible, it is in America's interest that verdicts against those tried for terrorism should be credible to shopkeepers in Cairo or Jakarta or civil servants in Marrakech, Islamabad, or Dacca. Their opinion should matter to us because Americans are safer in a world in which such people are willing to oppose terrorism. If we want to persuade them that the verdicts are just, military tribunals at Guantánamo are not our best choice.

Military tribunals, moreover, will further erode the effectiveness of the United States as a defender of human rights internationally. Quite aside from the proposed tribunals, the reputation of the US as an advocate of human rights in many parts of the world has in other ways been impaired by some of its post–September 11 policies. Though our intervention in Afghanistan has clearly improved the human rights situation in that country by ending the Taliban's repressive rule, our current alliances with such regimes as Russia, China, Uzbekistan, and Pakistan have sharply limited our capacity to speak out about their abuses. This is especially true when the victims can be linked, however tenuously, to al-Qaeda, whether the Chechens in Russia, the Uighurs in China, and the thousands of Islamists in President Islam Karimov's viciously brutal prisons in Uzbekistan.

By establishing special military tribunals to deal with terrorists, we also undermine our ability to criticize governments such as Peru, Cuba, and Turkey that have made use of such tribunals, bypassing their regular courts in order to deal with alleged threats. On December 25, a Russian military tribunal, meeting behind closed doors, sentenced the Soviet journalist Grigory Pasko to four years in prison for disclosing information on environmental abuses by the Russian Pacific Fleet to Japanese journalists. If the US were to resort to closed military tribunals, any complaints it makes about such procedures elsewhere would ring hollow.

In effect, parts of the President's order make the implicit claim that terrorists don't deserve protections of due process. As President Bush has put it, "We must not let foreign enemies use the forums of liberty to destroy liberty itself." But the President ignores the fact that one of the purposes of due process is to ensure that the right persons are convicted. Scores of death sentences are being overturned because DNA evidence has established that convictions were mistaken even after defendants were tried with the protections available in American civilian courts. This should underline the need for protecting constitutional rights. And if due process is systematically denied to accused al-Qaeda members, one likely consequence is that other categories of accused persons—drug dealers, mass murderers, child molesters, etc.—will be labeled as similarly undeserving. Unfortunately, civil liberties particularly need defense in circumstances that involve the most loathsome defendants. The next time, it may be too late.

∝◈∾

Proponents of human rights have been divided over the tribunals. Harvard Law School's Laurence Tribe more or less endorses tribunals—invoking, without attribution, Justice Robert Jackson's line that the Constitution is not a suicide pact —but he wants the objectionable features of Bush's order regulated by Congress. Yale Law School's Harold Koh, who served with distinction as assistant secretary of state for human rights in the Clinton administration, calls for trials in American federal courts of alleged terrorists, wherever they are arrested. "Why not show," Koh writes, "that American courts can give universal justice?"

Unfortunately, no momentum has developed for another solution: trial before a special international court such as those established to deal with former Yugoslavia and Rwanda. Indeed Harold Koh, who labels such a court a "more benign approach than President Bush's military tribunals," nevertheless rejects it as "slow and expensive."

Koh is no doubt right that international trials would be costly and cumbersome; but it is not clear that those disadvantages outweigh the value of proceeding in a manner that has a better chance to gain broad international acceptance than entirely American courts, especially a military court set up in Guantánamo or some other military base. Deferring to such an international court could strongly advance American interests. Despite the slow pace with which they have proceeded, the worldwide credibility achieved by the tribunals for ex-Yugoslavia and Rwanda is very high. For the US, achieving such credibility is second in importance only to convicting the guilty.

Human rights advocates who have supported international tribunals in other circumstances did not press for them after September 11, believing that any such effort was doomed to be rejected by the Bush administration. In the immediate aftermath of the attacks, as the administration courted other governments to build an alliance against terrorism, some commentators suggested that the administration was abandoning its strongly proclaimed unilateralism. In fact, however, the administration's quick success in Afghanistan has reinforced those in the White House and the Defense Department who believe that America is better off going it alone. Renunciation of the ABM treaty is an obvious example. With the rapid triumph of the US, any faint prospect evaporated that the administration would accept multilateral participation in trials of alleged al-Qaeda members.

What then is to be done about the military tribunals? A first step is to narrow the range of those who may be tried before them. A judicial process should be available to distinguish prisoners of war from unlawful combatants. The authority of the tribunals to try permanent residents of the United States should be eliminated. The trials should be required to observe standards of due process that include, at least, rights to a public trial; to counsel of the defendant's choice; to call and cross-examine witnesses; to be convicted only upon proof beyond a reasonable doubt; to appeal to an independent and impartial court; and, in the case of aliens arrested in the United States, to have an opportunity to challenge the jurisdiction of such tribunals by *habeas corpus*.

Finally, human rights groups should be provided the opportunity to establish a presence in Guantánamo or wherever else the trials are held, and to monitor all proceedings and to circulate their findings. Whatever the facilities provided to such groups, they will, of course, study the trials as best they can. Their conclusions about the tribunals are likely to matter to the United States, and to other countries, almost as much as the verdicts of the tribunals about the defendants who appear before them.

POSTSCRIPT

Should Terrorist Suspects Be Tried by Military Tribunals?

While objecting to military tribunals, at least in their present form, Neier seems receptive to the idea of special international courts such as the Nuremberg tribunals used to try Nazi leaders and the more recent international trials of those accused of atrocities in Yugoslavia and Rwanda. The suggestion is worth exploring, though it raises some questions. How would the members of an international tribunal be selected? Would judges from Islamic countries be included? If so, would they be able to function impartially amid pressures from the "Arab street" and their own home governments? Is there a danger that such tribunals would become occasions for anti-American diatribes? Typically, international tribunals are used in cases where no viable state exists in the region where the atrocities occurred. In this case the atrocities occurred in the midst of the world's most powerful nation—a nation reluctant to cede any of its sovereignty to an international tribunal.

Almost from the day of President Bush's executive order establishing them in November 2001, military tribunals became the subject of vigorous debate in newspapers and periodicals. Columnist Nat Hentoff condemned what he called "drumhead tribunals" in "Assault on Liberty," *The Village Voice* (November 21–27, 2001), while Peter J. Wallison, of the American Enterprise Institute, wrote "In Favor of Military Tribunals," *The Christian Science Monitor* (January 3, 2002). Former Appeals Court judge Robert H. Bork anticipated some of Wallison's arguments in "Having Their Day in (a Military) Court," *National Review* (December 17, 2001). Books related to military tribunals include Barbara Olshansky, *Secret Trial and Executions: Military Tribunals and the Threat to Democracy* (Seven Stories Press, 2002), which discusses the historical use of such courts, and, more generally, *All the Laws but One: Civil Liberties in Wartime* by Supreme Court justice William H. Rehnquist (Vintage, 2000).

As of this writing, it is not clear that military tribunals will be used in the present conflict. President Bush wants them as an "option," an available tool for dealing with certain Al Qaeda leaders, particularly those captured in Afghanistan. John Walker Lindh, the American caught fighting with the Taliban in Afghanistan, is being tried in a civilian court because he is an American citizen, yet Zacarias Moussaoui, the so-called 20th hijacker, is also being tried under civilian auspices, though he is a French national. So, at this point, the question remains unresolved: will all this debate turn out to be anything more than a classroom exercise?

Contributors to This Volume

EDITORS

GEORGE McKENNA is a professor of political science and chair of the Department of Political Science at City College, City University of New York, where he has been teaching since 1963. He received a B.A. from the University of Chicago in 1959, an M.A. from the University of Massachusetts in 1962, and a Ph.D. from Fordham University in 1967. He has written numerous articles in the fields of American government and political theory, and his publications include *American Populism* (Putnam, 1974) and *American Politics: Ideals and Realities* (McGraw-Hill, 1976). He is the author of the textbook *The Drama of Democracy: American Government and Politics,* 3rd ed. (Dushkin/McGraw-Hill, 1998).

STANLEY FEINGOLD, recently retired, held the Carl and Lily Pforzheimer Foundation Distinguished Chair for Business and Public Policy at Westchester Community College of the State University of New York. He received his bachelor's degree from the City College of New York, where he taught courses in American politics and political theory for 30 years, after completing his graduate education at Columbia University. He spent four years as Visiting Professor of Politics at the University of Leeds in Great Britain, and he has also taught American politics at Columbia University in New York and the University of California, Los Angeles. He is a frequent contributor to the *National Law Journal* and *Congress Monthly,* among other publications.

STAFF

Theodore Knight   List Manager
David Brackley   Senior Developmental Editor
Juliana Gribbins   Developmental Editor
Rose Gleich   Administrative Assistant
Katherine O'Connell   Editorial Intern
Brenda S. Filley   Director of Production/Design
Juliana Arbo   Typesetting Supervisor
Diane Barker   Proofreader
Richard Tietjen   Publishing Systems Manager
Larry Killian   Copier Coordinator

AUTHORS

MARY FRANCES BERRY, author of seven books, is a prominent social scholar and historian and is currently the Geraldine R. Segal Professor of Social Thought at the University of Pennsylvania, where she teaches history and law. Berry has served as the Civil Rights Commission chairwoman under a number of different administrations.

CARL T. BOGUS is an associate professor at Roger Williams University School of Law in Bristol, Rhode Island. He is also a contributor to *The American Prospect.*

ROBERT H. BORK is a senior fellow and scholar of legal/constitutional studies and political philosophy/ethics at the American Enterprise Institute for Public Policy Research. He has been a partner at a major law firm, taught constitutional law as the Alexander M. Bickel Professor of Public Law at the Yale Law School, served as solicitor general and as acting attorney general of the United States, and served as a U.S. Court of Appeals judge.

STEPHEN G. BREYER is an associate justice of the U.S. Supreme Court. He received his A.B. from Stanford University in 1959, his B.A. from Oxford University in 1961, and his LL.B. from Harvard University in 1964. A former U.S. Circuit Court of Appeals judge, he was nominated to the Supreme Court by President Bill Clinton in 1994.

PATRICK J. BUCHANAN is founder of the American Cause, an educational foundation dedicated to the principles of freedom, federalism, limited government, traditional values, and a foreign policy that puts America first. He was a senior adviser to three American presidents before he challenged President George Bush for the 1992 Republican presidential nomination. He has been a nationally syndicated newspaper columnist, cohost of CNN's *Crossfire,* and host of Mutual Radio's *Buchanan & Co.*

LINDA CHAVEZ is president of the Center for Equal Opportunity, a nonprofit public policy research organization in Washington, D.C. She also writes a weekly syndicated column that appears in newspapers across the country, and she is a political analyst for FOX News Channel.

CHRISTOPHER C. DeMUTH is president of the American Enterprise Institute for Public Policy Research.

ERIC M. FREEDMAN is a professor of law in the School of Law at Hofstra University. He chairs the Committee on Civil Rights of the Association of the Bar of the City of New York and is a member of the association's Special Committee on Representation in Capital Cases. Freedman earned his M.A. at Victoria University of Wellington in New Zealand and his J.D. at Yale University. He is coauthor, with Monroe H. Freedman, of *Group Defamation and Freedom of Speech: The Relationship Between Language and Violence* (Greenwood, 1995).

ROBERT P. GEORGE is the McCormick Professor of Jurisprudence and director of the James Madison Program in American Ideals and Institutions at Princeton University. Recently, he was appointed by President George W.

Bush to the President's Council on Bioethics. He previously served on the U.S. Commission on Civil Rights and as a judicial fellow at the Supreme Court of the United States.

BERNARD GOLDBERG is an Emmy Award–winning broadcast journalist who has worked for three decades as a reporter and producer at CBS.

MARY GORDON is a novelist and short-story writer. She is the author of *Penal Discipline: Female Prisoners* (Gordon Press, 1992), *The Rest of Life: Three Novellas* (Viking Penguin, 1993), and *The Other Side* (Wheeler, 1994).

DANIEL T. GRISWOLD, associate director of the Cato Institute's Center for Trade Policy Studies, focuses on the movement of goods, services, capital, and people across international borders. He earned a master's degree in the politics of the world economy from the London School of Economics.

THOMAS HARRISON is a member of the editorial board of *New Politics.* He has written for *The Nation, Z Magazine, Labour Focus on Eastern Europe,* and *Peace & Democracy.*

JIM HIGHTOWER is a national radio commentator, writer, and public speaker, and he is the author of *If the Gods Had Meant Us to Vote They Would Have Given Us Candidates* (HarperCollins, 2000). He served as director of the Texas Consumer Association before running for statewide office and being elected to two terms as Texas agriculture commissioner (1983–1991).

DOUGLAS A. IRWIN is a professor of economics at Dartmouth College and a research associate of the National Bureau of Economic Research. He is the author of *Against the Tide: An Intellectual History of Free Trade* (Princeton University Press, 1996) and *Managed Trade: The Case Against Import Targets* (AEI Press, 1994).

ROBERT KAGAN is a senior associate of the Carnegie Endowment for International Peace as well as a cofounder of the Project for a New American Century. He is also a contributing editor to *The Weekly Standard,* a member of the Council on Foreign Relations, and the author of *A Twilight Struggle: American Power and Nicaragua, 1977–1990* (Free Press, 1996).

ROBERT D. KAPLAN is a contributing editor to *The Atlantic Monthly* and the author of several books, including *To the Ends of the Earth: A Journey at the Dawn of the Twenty-First Century* (Vintage Books, 1997).

ANTHONY KING is a professor of political science at the University of Essex and the author of *Running Scared: Why America's Politicians Campaign Too Much and Govern Too Little* (Martin Kessler Books, 1997).

WILLIAM KRISTOL is editor of *The Weekly Standard,* cofounder of the Project for a New American Century, and a former leader of the Project for the Republican Future, which produced the 1994 Republican congressional victory. He also served as chief of staff to Vice President Dan Quayle during the Bush administration and to Secretary of Education William Bennett under President Ronald Reagan.

PAUL KRUGMAN is a professor of economics at the Massachusetts Institute of Technology. He is the author of many books, including *Pop Internationalism*

(MIT Press, 1996) and *The Accidental Theorist: And Other Dispatches From the Dismal Science* (W. W. Norton, 1998).

DAVID M. LAMPTON is the George and Sadie Hyman Professor of China Studies and director of China studies in the School of Advanced International Studies at Johns Hopkins University in Washington, D.C. He is a former president of the National Committee on U.S.-China Relations and a former director of the China Policy Studies Program at the American Enterprise Institute. His many publications include *Same Bed, Different Dreams: Managing U.S.-China Relations, 1989–2000* (University of California Press, 2001). He received his Ph.D. in political science from Stanford University.

CHARLES R. LAWRENCE III is a professor in the School of Law at Georgetown University in Washington, D.C. He is coauthor, with Mari J. Matsuda, of *We Won't Go Back: Making the Case for Affirmative Action* (Houghton Mifflin, 1997) and *Affirmative Action* (Houghton Mifflin, 1997).

CHRISTOPHER LAYNE is an associate professor of international and comparative studies at the University of Miami and a former visiting fellow in foreign policy studies at the Cato Institute.

DANIEL LAZARE is a political analyst who has written for the *Wall Street Journal,* the *New York Times, Village Voice, Harper's, Dissent, Le Monde diplomatique,* and *New Left Review.* He is the author of *The Frozen Republic* (Harcourt Brace, 1996) and *America's Undeclared War: What's Killing Our Cities and How We Can Stop It* (Harcourt Trade Publishers, 2001).

ROBERT W. LEE is a contributing editor to *The New American* and the author of *The United Nations Conspiracy* (Western Islands, 1981).

JOHN R. LOTT, JR., earned his Ph.D. in economics from the University of California, Los Angeles, in 1984. He served as a senior research scholar at the Yale University Law School (1999–2001) and taught at the University of Chicago Law School as the John M. Olin Visiting Law and Economics Fellow (1995–1999).

MICHAEL McFAUL is the Peter and Helen Bing Research Fellow at the Hoover Institution. He is also an associate professor of political science at Stanford University and a nonresident associate at the Carnegie Endowment for International Peace. He received his M.A. in Slavic and East European studies from Stanford University in 1986. McFaul was awarded a Rhodes scholarship to Oxford University, where he completed his Ph.D. in international relations in 1991, and he is the author of *Russia's Unfinished Revolution: Political Change From Gorbachev to Putin* (Cornell University Press, 2001).

DAVID MORRIS is cofounder and vice president of the Institute for Local Self-Reliance. He is also the editor of the institute's publications, including *The New Rules* and *The Carbohydrate Economy.*

LIAM MURPHY is a professor of law and philosophy at the New York University School of Law. He earned his Ph.D. from Columbia University in 1991.

THOMAS NAGEL is a professor of law and philosophy at the New York University School of Law. His many publications include *Equality and Partial-*

ity (Oxford University Press, 1991), *Other Minds* (Oxford University Press, 1995), and *The Last Word* (Oxford University Press, 1997).

ARYEH NEIER is the president of the Soros Foundations and Open Society Institute. For many years he was also the national director of the American Civil Liberties Union and the executive director of Human Rights Watch. He is the author of *War Crimes: Brutality, Genocide, Terror, and the Struggle for Justice* (Random House, 1998).

NORMAN PODHORETZ is a senior fellow at the Hudson Institute, an editor-at-large of *Commentary,* where he served as editor-in-chief for 35 years, and a member of the Council on Foreign Relations. He earned a master's degree in English from Cambridge University, where he was a Fulbright Scholar and a Kellett Fellow.

SAMUEL L. POPKIN is a professor of political science at the University of California, San Diego. He has been an active participant in and an academic analyst of presidential elections for over 20 years, and he served as a consultant to the Clinton campaign in 1992, for which he worked on polling and strategy.

RICHARD POSNER is a senior lecturer in law at the University of Chicago Law School. In 1981 he was appointed a judge of the U.S. Court of Appeals for the Seventh Circuit and was chief judge of the court from 1993 to 2000. He is the author of *Public Intellectuals: A Study of Decline* (Harvard University Press, 2001).

PIERRE-RICHARD PROSPER is the ambassador-at-large for war crimes for the U.S. Department of State. Prior to his appointment as ambassador, he served as special counsel and policy adviser in the Office of War Crimes Issues, and he served as a war crimes prosecutor for the United Nations International Criminal Tribunal for Rwanda.

LUCIAN W. PYE is the Ford Professor of Political Science Emeritus in the Center for International Studies at the Massachusetts Institute of Technology in Cambridge, Massachusetts. He was also the president of the American Political Science Association in 1998–1999. His research focus has been in the field of comparative politics with special emphasis on Asian political cultures and development, and he is the author of *The Spirit of Chinese Politics,* 2d ed. (Harvard University Press, 1992).

JONATHAN RAUCH is a writer for *The Economist* in London and the author of *Kindly Inquisitors: The New Attacks on Free Thought* (University of Chicago Press, 1993).

WILLIAM H. REHNQUIST became the 16th chief justice of the U.S. Supreme Court in 1986. He engaged in a general practice of law with primary emphasis on civil litigation for 16 years before being appointed assistant attorney general, Office of Legal Counsel, by President Richard Nixon in 1969. He was nominated by Nixon to the Supreme Court in 1972.

JOHN SAMPLES is the director of the Center for Representative Government at the Cato Institute. He is also an adjunct professor in the Public Policy Institute at Georgetown University. Prior to joining Cato, Samples served eight years as director of Georgetown University Press and, before that, as vice president of the Twentieth Century Fund.

BENJAMIN SCHWARZ is a correspondent for *The Atlantic Monthly* and a former executive editor of *World Policy Journal.* He was the 1999 recipient of the Nona Balakian Citation for Excellence in Reviewing.

AMITY SHLAES is an editorialist on tax policy at the *Wall Street Journal.* Her writing has also been published in *Commentary* and *The New Yorker,* and she is the author of *Germany: The Empire Within* (Farrar, Straus & Giroux, 1991).

CASS R. SUNSTEIN is a professor of jurisprudence at the University of Chicago Law School as well as a member of the political science department. He earned his law degree from Harvard Law School in 1978, and he is the author of *Designing Democracy: What Constitutions Do* (Oxford University Press, 2001).

PAUL D. WELLSTONE is the Democratic U.S. senator for Minnesota. He earned his Ph.D. in political science from the University of North Carolina in Chapel Hill in 1969. He accepted a teaching position at Carleton College in Northfield, Minnesota, and taught there for 21 years before being elected to the Senate.

Index

On the Internet . . . DUSHKIN ONLINE

Student Voices: School Vouchers

This site has been erected by New York City Student Voices, which is part of the National Student Voices Project, an initiative of the Annenberg Public Policy Center of the University of Pennsylvania. It provides numerous links to news and journal articles on various aspects of the school voucher issue.

http://student-voices.org/newyork/links/vouchers.php3

Democratic Congressional Campaign Committee

The Democratic Congressional Campaign Committee is dedicated to achieving or maintaining a Democratic majority in the House, offering campaign news responses to Republican tactics, and links.

http://www.dccc.org

PART 5

Bonus Issues

*T*he two debates presented in this part represent issues that have become especially contentious since the publication of the 13th edition of this book. They are particularly important in that they are shaping public policy that is being considered today. The first debate stems from the 2002 Supreme Court decision regarding Cleveland's school voucher program and how it might affect future interpretations of the establishment clause of the First Amendment. The second issue presents an analysis of the two political parties and tries to determine which one is more in line with postindustrial America.

- Are School Vouchers Compatible With the First Amendment?

- Is There an Emerging Democratic Majority?

ISSUE 21

Are School Vouchers Compatible With the First Amendment?

YES: William H. Rehnquist, from Majority Opinion, *Susan Tave Zelman, Superintendent of Public Instruction of Ohio, et al. v. Doris Simmons-Harris et al.*, U.S. Supreme Court (June 27, 2002)

NO: David Souter, from Dissenting Opinion, *Susan Tave Zelman, Superintendent of Public Instruction of Ohio, et al. v. Doris Simmons-Harris et al.*, U.S. Supreme Court (June 27, 2002)

ISSUE SUMMARY

YES: Supreme Court chief justice William H. Rehnquist, in his majority opinion, maintains that Ohio's program of school vouchers offers a true private choice of schools and is neutral with respect to religion.

NO: Supreme Court justice David Souter, dissenting from the Court's opinion, argues that Ohio's program offers an unparalleled and unconstitutional degree of support for religious schools.

The United States spends roughly $500 billion annually on public education. Yet studies have shown serious deficiencies in the educational achievements of America's children. The problems are particularly severe in the inner cities.

What is wrong with American education, and what can be done about it? To some the real problem stems from inadequate and inequitable school funding. Teachers' salaries in general are low compared to those of other professions, and lower still are the salaries of inner-city teachers, whose additional hardships include large class sizes, dilapidated buildings, and a lack of adequate equipment and support.

Others diagnose the problem differently. From their perspective, the problems have less to do with inadequate funding than with the cultural atmosphere of public schools: stifling bureaucracies, mindless rules, educational fads, anarchical classrooms, and schoolyards filled with drugs and fighting, particularly in the inner cities. For these critics, the best way to reform education in America is to give parents alternatives to the public schools in their neighborhoods.

A number of alternatives to public schools do exist. Probably the least controversial is magnet schools, which have been around for more than 20 years. Magnet schools have specially trained teachers, modern facilities, and enriched curricula, with the object of bringing students from different races and social classes together for a meaningful educational experience. Another alternative is charter schools, which are publicly funded yet are largely free of direct bureaucratic control by the government.

One of the most controversial school choice programs is school vouchers, which are certificates or cash payments provided by the government for a fixed amount that a student can present to a private school—secular or religious—to cover part or all of the cost of his or her education. Economist Milton Friedman first proposed the use of vouchers in his 1962 book *Capitalism and Freedom* (University of Chicago Press). In it, Friedman argued that state governments "could require a minimum level of schooling financed by giving parents vouchers redeemable for a specified maximum sum per child per year if spent on 'approved' educational services."

Friedman advocated vouchers for all children. Later supporters of vouchers sharply modified this view, arguing that vouchers should only be available to poor families in order to provide an alternative to overcrowded schools and the system's failure to provide an adequate education for the most disadvantaged children. Limited voucher programs won the support of many poor families, Christian conservatives, and others who saw vouchers as a way to stimulate competition and improve public education. Vouchers were opposed by teacher organizations, suburban whites who had invested in communities with more highly regarded schools, and others who feared that vouchers would reduce both public funding and public support for improved public schools.

Voucher programs were soundly defeated in California and Michigan in 2000. However, they have been adopted in Florida; Cleveland, Ohio; and Minneapolis, Minnesota. In these areas, limited sums of money are given to parents to be used to pay tuition fees to participating schools that the parents choose for their children. In 2001, however, an educational reform law was adopted by Congress that does not include federal money for vouchers.

In June 2002 the U.S. Supreme Court decided the case *Zelman v. Simmons-Harris,* in which the constitutionality of Cleveland's school voucher program —specifically as it relates to the separation of church and state mandated by the First Amendment—came into question. In a 5–4 decision, the Court upheld the constitutionality of school vouchers as employed in Cleveland to pay for the enrollment of inner-city children in private secular and parochial schools. Both the majority and the minority acknowledged the failure of that city's public schools, in which more than 90 percent of the students fail to meet basic proficiency standards. In the following excerpts from the decisions, Chief Justice William H. Rehnquist, delivering the majority opinion, maintains that Cleveland's voucher program, in which all private schools may participate, offers a true private choice that is neutral with regard to religion. Justice David Souter, dissenting, argues that the program offers an unparalleled and unconstitutional degree of support for religion in that more than 96 percent of the participants are enrolled in church-related schools.

411

Majority Opinion

Zelman *v.* Simmons-Harris

Chief Justice Rehnquist delivered the opinion of the Court.

The State of Ohio has established a pilot program designed to provide educational choices to families with children who reside in the Cleveland City School District. The question presented is whether this program offends the Establishment Clause of the United States Constitution. We hold that it does not.

There are more than 75,000 children enrolled in the Cleveland City School District. The majority of these children are from low-income and minority families. Few of these families enjoy the means to send their children to any school other than an inner-city public school. For more than a generation, however, Cleveland's public schools have been among the worst performing public schools in the Nation. In 1995, a Federal District Court declared a "crisis of magnitude" and placed the entire Cleveland school district under state control. Shortly thereafter, the state auditor found that Cleveland's public schools were in the midst of a "crisis that is perhaps unprecedented in the history of American education." The district had failed to meet any of the 18 state standards for minimal acceptable performance. Only 1 in 10 ninth graders could pass a basic proficiency examination, and students at all levels performed at a dismal rate compared with students in other Ohio public schools. More than two-thirds of high school students either dropped or failed out before graduation. Of those students who managed to reach their senior year, one of every four still failed to graduate. Of those students who did graduate, few could read, write, or compute at levels comparable to their counterparts in other cities.

It is against this backdrop that Ohio enacted, among other initiatives, its Pilot Project Scholarship Program. The program provides financial assistance to families in any Ohio school district that is or has been "under federal court order requiring supervision and operational management of the district by the state superintendent." Cleveland is the only Ohio school district to fall within that category.

The program provides two basic kinds of assistance to parents of children in a covered district. First, the program provides tuition aid for students in

From *Susan Tave Zelman, Superintendent of Public Instruction of Ohio, et al. v. Doris Simmons-Harris et al.*, 536 U.S. ___ (2002). Notes, references, and case citations omitted.

kindergarten through third grade, expanding each year through eighth grade, to attend a participating public or private school of their parent's choosing. Second, the program provides tutorial aid for students who choose to remain enrolled in public school.

The tuition aid portion of the program is designed to provide educational choices to parents who reside in a covered district. Any private school, whether religious or nonreligious, may participate in the program and accept program students so long as the school is located within the boundaries of a covered district and meets statewide educational standards. Participating private schools must agree not to discriminate on the basis of race, religion, or ethnic background, or to "advocate or foster unlawful behavior or teach hatred of any person or group on the basis of race, ethnicity, national origin, or religion." Any public school located in a school district adjacent to the covered district may also participate in the program. Adjacent public schools are eligible to receive a $2,250 tuition grant for each program student accepted in addition to the full amount of per-pupil state funding attributable to each additional student. All participating schools, whether public or private, are required to accept students in accordance with rules and procedures established by the state superintendent.

Tuition aid is distributed to parents according to financial need. Families with incomes below 200% of the poverty line are given priority and are eligible to receive 90% of private school tuition up to $2,250. For these lowest-income families, participating private schools may not charge a parental co-payment greater than $250. For all other families, the program pays 75% of tuition costs, up to $1,875, with no co-payment cap. These families receive tuition aid only if the number of available scholarships exceeds the number of low-income children who choose to participate. Where tuition aid is spent depends solely upon where parents who receive tuition aid choose to enroll their child. If parents choose a private school, checks are made payable to the parents who then endorse the checks over to the chosen school.

The tutorial aid portion of the program provides tutorial assistance through grants to any student in a covered district who chooses to remain in public school. Parents arrange for registered tutors to provide assistance to their children and then submit bills for those services to the State for payment. Students from low-income families receive 90% of the amount charged for such assistance up to $360. All other students receive 75% of that amount. The number of tutorial assistance grants offered to students in a covered district must equal the number of tuition aid scholarships provided to students enrolled at participating private or adjacent public schools.

The program has been in operation within the Cleveland City School District since the 1996–1997 school year. In the 1999–2000 school year, 56 private schools participated in the program, 46 (or 82%) of which had a religious affiliation. None of the public schools in districts adjacent to Cleveland have elected to participate. More than 3,700 students participated in the scholarship program, most of whom (96%) enrolled in religiously affiliated schools. Sixty percent of these students were from families at or below the poverty line. In the 1998–1999 school year, approximately 1,400 Cleveland public school students received tutorial aid. This number was expected to double during the 1999–2000 school year.

The program is part of a broader undertaking by the State to enhance the educational options of Cleveland's schoolchildren in response to the 1995 takeover. That undertaking includes programs governing community and magnet schools. Community schools are funded under state law but are run by their own school boards, not by local school districts. These schools enjoy academic independence to hire their own teachers and to determine their own curriculum. They can have no religious affiliation and are required to accept students by lottery. During the 1999–2000 school year, there were 10 start-up community schools in the Cleveland City School District with more than 1,900 students enrolled. For each child enrolled in a community school, the school receives state funding of $4,518, twice the funding a participating program school may receive.

Magnet schools are public schools operated by a local school board that emphasize a particular subject area, teaching method, or service to students. For each student enrolled in a magnet school, the school district receives $7,746, including state funding of $4,167, the same amount received per student enrolled at a traditional public school. As of 1999, parents in Cleveland were able to choose from among 23 magnet schools, which together enrolled more than 13,000 students in kindergarten through eighth grade. These schools provide specialized teaching methods, such as Montessori, or a particularized curriculum focus, such as foreign language, computers, or the arts.

In 1996, respondents, a group of Ohio taxpayers, challenged the Ohio program in state court on state and federal grounds. The Ohio Supreme Court rejected respondents' federal claims, but held that the enactment of the program violated certain procedural requirements of the Ohio Constitution. The state legislature immediately cured this defect, leaving the basic provisions discussed above intact.

In July 1999, respondents filed this action in United States District Court, seeking to enjoin the reenacted program on the ground that it violated the Establishment Clause of the United States Constitution. In August 1999, the District Court issued a preliminary injunction barring further implementation of the program, which we stayed pending review by the Court of Appeals. In December 1999, the District Court granted summary judgment for respondents. In December 2000, a divided panel of the Court of Appeals affirmed the judgment of the District Court, finding that the program had the "primary effect" of advancing religion in violation of the Establishment Clause. We granted certiorari and now reverse the Court of Appeals.

The Establishment Clause of the First Amendment, applied to the States through the Fourteenth Amendment, prevents a State from enacting laws that have the "purpose" or "effect" of advancing or inhibiting religion. ("[W]e continue to ask whether the government acted with the purpose of advancing or inhibiting religion [and] whether the aid has the 'effect' of advancing or inhibiting religion" (citations omitted)). There is no dispute that the program challenged here was enacted for the valid secular purpose of providing educational assistance to poor children in a demonstrably failing public school system. Thus, the question presented is whether the Ohio program nonetheless has the forbidden "effect" of advancing or inhibiting religion.

To answer that question, our decisions have drawn a consistent distinction between government programs that provide aid directly to religious schools and programs of true private choice, in which government aid reaches religious schools only as a result of the genuine and independent choices of private individuals, *Mueller* v. *Allen* (1983); *Witters* v. *Washington Dept. of Servs. for Blind* (1986); *Zobrest* v. *Catalina Foothills School Dist.* (1993). While our jurisprudence with respect to the constitutionality of direct aid programs has "changed significantly" over the past two decades, our jurisprudence with respect to true private choice programs has remained consistent and unbroken. Three times we have confronted Establishment Clause challenges to neutral government programs that provide aid directly to a broad class of individuals, who, in turn, direct the aid to religious schools or institutions of their own choosing. Three times we have rejected such challenges.

In *Mueller,* we rejected an Establishment Clause challenge to a Minnesota program authorizing tax deductions for various educational expenses, including private school tuition costs, even though the great majority of the program's beneficiaries (96%) were parents of children in religious schools. We began by focusing on the class of beneficiaries, finding that because the class included "*all* parents," including parents with "children [who] attend nonsectarian private schools or sectarian private schools," the program was "not readily subject to challenge under the Establishment Clause." ("The provision of benefits to so broad a spectrum of groups is an important index of secular effect"). Then, viewing the program as a whole, we emphasized the principle of private choice, noting that public funds were made available to religious schools "only as a result of numerous, private choices of individual parents of school-age children." This, we said, ensured that " 'no imprimatur of state approval' can be deemed to have been conferred on any particular religion, or on religion generally." We thus found it irrelevant to the constitutional inquiry that the vast majority of beneficiaries were parents of children in religious schools, saying:

> "We would be loath to adopt a rule grounding the constitutionality of a facially neutral law on annual reports reciting the extent to which various classes of private citizens claimed benefits under the law."

That the program was one of true private choice, with no evidence that the State deliberately skewed incentives toward religious schools, was sufficient for the program to survive scrutiny under the Establishment Clause.

In *Witters,* we used identical reasoning to reject an Establishment Clause challenge to a vocational scholarship program that provided tuition aid to a student studying at a religious institution to become a pastor. Looking at the program as a whole, we observed that "[a]ny aid . . . that ultimately flows to religious institutions does so only as a result of the genuinely independent and private choices of aid recipients." We further remarked that, as in *Mueller,* "[the] program is made available generally without regard to the sectarian-nonsectarian, or public-nonpublic nature of the institution benefited." In light of these factors, we held that the program was not inconsistent with the Establishment Clause.

Five Members of the Court, in separate opinions, emphasized the general rule from *Mueller* that the amount of government aid channeled to religious institutions by individual aid recipients was not relevant to the constitutional inquiry. Our holding thus rested not on whether few or many recipients chose to expend government aid at a religious school but, rather, on whether recipients generally were empowered to direct the aid to schools or institutions of their own choosing.

Finally, in *Zobrest,* we applied *Mueller* and *Witters* to reject an Establishment Clause challenge to a federal program that permitted sign-language interpreters to assist deaf children enrolled in religious schools. Reviewing our earlier decisions, we stated that "government programs that neutrally provide benefits to a broad class of citizens defined without reference to religion are not readily subject to an Establishment Clause challenge." Looking once again to the challenged program as a whole, we observed that the program "distributes benefits neutrally to any child qualifying as 'disabled.'" Its "primary beneficiaries," we said, were "disabled children, not sectarian schools."

We further observed that "[b]y according parents freedom to select a school of their choice, the statute ensures that a government-paid interpreter will be present in a sectarian school only as a result of the private decision of individual parents." Our focus again was on neutrality and the principle of private choice, not on the number of program beneficiaries attending religious schools. Because the program ensured that parents were the ones to select a religious school as the best learning environment for their handicapped child, the circuit between government and religion was broken, and the Establishment Clause was not implicated.

Mueller, Witters, and *Zobrest* thus make clear that where a government aid program is neutral with respect to religion, and provides assistance directly to a broad class of citizens who, in turn, direct government aid to religious schools wholly as a result of their own genuine and independent private choice, the program is not readily subject to challenge under the Establishment Clause. A program that shares these features permits government aid to reach religious institutions only by way of the deliberate choices of numerous individual recipients. The incidental advancement of a religious mission, or the perceived endorsement of a religious message, is reasonably attributable to the individual recipient, not to the government, whose role ends with the disbursement of benefits. As a plurality of this Court recently observed:

> "[I]f numerous private choices, rather than the single choice of a government, determine the distribution of aid, pursuant to neutral eligibility criteria, then a government cannot, or at least cannot easily, grant special favors that might lead to a religious establishment."

... We believe that the program challenged here is a program of true private choice, consistent with *Mueller, Witters,* and *Zobrest,* and thus constitutional. As was true in those cases, the Ohio program is neutral in all respects toward religion. It is part of a general and multifaceted undertaking by the State of Ohio to provide educational opportunities to the children of a failed school district. It confers educational assistance directly to a broad class of individuals defined without reference to religion, *i.e.,* any parent of a school-age child who resides in the Cleveland City School District. The program permits the participation of *all* schools within the district, religious or nonreligious. Adjacent public schools also may participate and have a financial incentive to do so. Program benefits are available to participating families on neutral terms, with no reference to religion. The only preference stated anywhere in the program is a preference for low-income families, who receive greater assistance and are given priority for admission at participating schools.

There are no "financial incentive[s]" that "ske[w]" the program toward religious schools. Such incentives "[are] not present... where the aid is allocated on the basis of neutral, secular criteria that neither favor nor disfavor religion, and is made available to both religious and secular beneficiaries on a nondiscriminatory basis." The program here in fact creates financial *dis*incentives for religious schools, with private schools receiving only half the government assistance given to community schools and one-third the assistance given to magnet schools. Adjacent public schools, should any choose to accept program students, are also eligible to receive two to three times the state funding of a private religious school. Families too have a financial disincentive to choose a private religious school over other schools. Parents that choose to participate in the scholarship program and then to enroll their children in a private school (religious or nonreligious) must copay a portion of the school's tuition. Families that choose a community school, magnet school, or traditional public school pay nothing. Although such features of the program are not necessary to its constitutionality, they clearly dispel the claim that the program "creates... financial incentive[s] for parents to choose a sectarian school."...

There also is no evidence that the program fails to provide genuine opportunities for Cleveland parents to select secular educational options for their school-age children. Cleveland schoolchildren enjoy a range of educational choices: They may remain in public school as before, remain in public school with publicly funded tutoring aid, obtain a scholarship and choose a religious school, obtain a scholarship and choose a nonreligious private school, enroll in a community school, or enroll in a magnet school. That 46 of the 56 private schools now participating in the program are religious schools does not condemn it as a violation of the Establishment Clause. The Establishment Clause question is whether Ohio is coercing parents into sending their children to religious schools, and that question must be answered by evaluating *all* options Ohio provides Cleveland schoolchildren, only one of which is to obtain a program scholarship and then choose a religious school.

Justice Souter speculates that because more private religious schools currently participate in the program, the program itself must somehow discourage the participation of private nonreligious schools. But Cleveland's preponderance of religiously affiliated private schools certainly did not arise as a result of the program; it is a phenomenon common to many American cities. Indeed, by all accounts the program has captured a remarkable cross-section of private schools, religious and nonreligious. It is true that 82% of Cleveland's participating private schools are religious schools, but it is also true that 81% of private schools in Ohio are religious schools. To attribute constitutional significance to this figure, moreover, would lead to the absurd result that a neutral school-choice program might be permissible in some parts of Ohio, such as Columbus, where a lower percentage of private schools are religious schools, but not in inner-city Cleveland, where Ohio has deemed such programs most sorely needed, but where the preponderance of religious schools happens to be greater. Likewise, an identical private choice program might be constitutional in some States, such as Maine or Utah, where less than 45% of private schools are religious schools, but not in other States, such as Nebraska or Kansas, where over 90% of private schools are religious schools.

Respondents and Justice Souter claim that even if we do not focus on the number of participating schools that are religious schools, we should attach constitutional significance to the fact that 96% of scholarship recipients have enrolled in religious schools. They claim that this alone proves parents lack genuine choice, even if no parent has ever said so. We need not consider this argument in detail, since it was flatly rejected in *Mueller*, where we found it irrelevant that 96% of parents taking deductions for tuition expenses paid tuition at religious schools. Indeed, we have recently found it irrelevant even to the constitutionality of a direct aid program that a vast majority of program benefits went to religious schools. The constitutionality of a neutral educational aid program simply does not turn on whether and why, in a particular area, at a particular time, most private schools are run by religious organizations, or most recipients choose to use the aid at a religious school. As we said in *Mueller*, "[s]uch an approach would scarcely provide the certainty that this field stands in need of, nor can we perceive principled standards by which such statistical evidence might be evaluated."

This point is aptly illustrated here. The 96% figure upon which respondents and Justice Souter rely discounts entirely (1) the more than 1,900 Cleveland children enrolled in alternative community schools, (2) the more than 13,000 children enrolled in alternative magnet schools, and (3) the more than 1,400 children enrolled in traditional public schools with tutorial assistance. Including some or all of these children in the denominator of children enrolled in nontraditional schools during the 1999–2000 school year drops the percentage enrolled in religious schools from 96% to under 20%. The 96% figure also represents but a snapshot of one particular school year. In the 1997–1998 school year, by contrast, only 78% of scholarship recipients attended religious schools. . . .

Respondents finally claim that we should look to *Committee for Public Ed. & Religious Liberty* v. *Nyquist* (1973), to decide these cases. We disagree for two reasons. First, the program in *Nyquist* was quite different from the program challenged here. *Nyquist* involved a New York program that gave a package of benefits exclusively to private schools and the parents of private school enrollees. Although the program was enacted for ostensibly secular purposes, we found that its "function" was "*unmistakably* to provide desired financial support for nonpublic, sectarian institutions." Its genesis, we said, was that private religious schools faced "increasingly grave fiscal problems." The program thus provided direct money grants to religious schools. It provided tax benefits "un-related to the amount of money actually expended by any parent on tuition," ensuring a windfall to parents of children in religious schools. Id., at 790. It similarly provided tuition reimbursements designed explicitly to "offe[r] . . . an incentive to parents to send their children to sectarian schools." Indeed, the program flatly prohibited the participation of any public school, or parent of any public school enrollee. Ohio's program shares none of these features.

Second, were there any doubt that the program challenged in *Nyquist* is far removed from the program challenged here, we expressly reserved judgment with respect to "a case involving some form of public assistance (*e.g.*, scholar-ships) made available generally without regard to the sectarian-nonsectarian, or public-nonpublic nature of the institution benefited." That, of course, is the very question now before us, and it has since been answered, first in *Mueller,* then in *Witters,* and again in *Zobrest.* To the extent the scope of *Nyquist* has remained an open question in light of these later decisions, we now hold that *Nyquis* does not govern neutral educational assistance programs that, like the program here, offer aid directly to a broad class of individual recipients defined without regard to religion.

In sum, the Ohio program is entirely neutral with respect to religion. It provides benefits directly to a wide spectrum of individuals, defined only by financial need and residence in a particular school district. It permits such individuals to exercise genuine choice among options public and private, sec-ular and religious. The program is therefore a program of true private choice. In keeping with an unbroken line of decisions rejecting challenges to similar programs, we hold that the program does not offend the Establishment Clause.

The judgment of the Court of Appeals is reversed.

It is so ordered.

Dissenting Opinion of David Souter

Justice Souter, with whom Justice Stevens, Justice Ginsburg, and Justice Breyer join, dissenting.

The Court's majority holds that the Establishment Clause is no bar to Ohio's payment of tuition at private religious elementary and middle schools under a scheme that systematically provides tax money to support the schools' religious missions. The occasion for the legislation thus upheld is the condition of public education in the city of Cleveland. The record indicates that the schools are failing to serve their objective, and the vouchers in issue here are said to be needed to provide adequate alternatives to them. If there were an excuse for giving short shrift to the Establishment Clause, it would probably apply here. But there is no excuse. Constitutional limitations are placed on government to preserve constitutional values in hard cases, like these....

The applicability of the Establishment Clause to public funding of benefits to religious schools was settled in *Everson* v. *Board of Ed. of Ewing* which inaugurated the modern era of establishment doctrine. The Court stated the principle in words from which there was no dissent:

> "No tax in any amount, large or small, can be levied to support any religious activities or institutions, whatever they may be called, or whatever form they may adopt to teach or practice religion."

The Court has never in so many words repudiated this statement, let alone, in so many words, overruled *Everson*.

Today, however, the majority holds that the Establishment Clause is not offended by Ohio's Pilot Project Scholarship Program, under which students may be eligible to receive as much as $2,250 in the form of tuition vouchers transferable to religious schools. In the city of Cleveland the overwhelming proportion of large appropriations for voucher money must be spent on religious schools if it is to be spent at all, and will be spent in amounts that cover almost all of tuition. The money will thus pay for eligible students' instruction not only in secular subjects but in religion as well, in schools that can fairly be characterized as founded to teach religious doctrine and to imbue teaching in all subjects with a religious dimension. Public tax money will pay at a systemic level for teaching the covenant with Israel and Mosaic law in Jewish schools, the

From *Susan Tave Zelman, Superintendent of Public Instruction of Ohio, et al. v. Doris Simmons-Harris et al.*, 536 U.S. ___ (2002). Notes, references, and case citations omitted.

primacy of the Apostle Peter and the Papacy in Catholic schools, the truth of reformed Christianity in Protestant schools, and the revelation to the Prophet in Muslim schools, to speak only of major religious groupings in the Republic.

How can a Court consistently leave *Everson* on the books and approve the Ohio vouchers? The answer is that it cannot. It is only by ignoring *Everson* that the majority can claim to rest on traditional law in its invocation of neutral aid provisions and private choice to sanction the Ohio law. It is, moreover, only by ignoring the meaning of neutrality and private choice themselves that the majority can even pretend to rest today's decision on those criteria.

❧❦❧

... In the period from 1947 to 1968, the basic principle of no aid to religion through school benefits was unquestioned. Thereafter for some 15 years, the Court termed its efforts as attempts to draw a line against aid that would be divertible to support the religious, as distinct from the secular, activity of an institutional beneficiary. Then, starting in 1983, concern with divertibility was gradually lost in favor of approving aid in amounts unlikely to afford substantial benefits to religious schools, when offered evenhandedly without regard to a recipient's religious character, and when channeled to a religious institution only by the genuinely free choice of some private individual....

[I]t seems fair to say that it was not until today that substantiality of aid has clearly been rejected as irrelevant by a majority of this Court, just as it has not been until today that a majority, not a plurality, has held purely formal criteria to suffice for scrutinizing aid that ends up in the coffers of religious schools. Today's cases are notable for their stark illustration of the inadequacy of the majority's chosen formal analysis.

❧❦❧

Although it has taken half a century since Everson to reach the majority's twin standards of neutrality and free choice, the facts show that, in the majority's hands, even these criteria cannot convincingly legitimize the Ohio scheme.

Consider first the criterion of neutrality. As recently as two Terms ago, a majority of the Court recognized that neutrality conceived of as evenhandedness toward aid recipients had never been treated as alone sufficient to satisfy the Establishment Clause. But at least in its limited significance, formal neutrality seemed to serve some purpose. Today, however, the majority employs the neutrality criterion in a way that renders it impossible to understand....

In order to apply the neutrality test, it makes sense to focus on a category of aid that may be directed to religious as well as secular schools, and ask whether the scheme favors a religious direction. Here, one would ask whether the voucher provisions, allowing for as much as $2,250 toward private school tuition (or a grant to a public school in an adjacent district), were written in a way that skewed the scheme toward benefiting religious schools.

This, however, is not what the majority asks. The majority looks not to the provisions for tuition vouchers but to every provision for educational opportunity: "The program permits the participation of *all* schools within the district, [as well as public schools in adjacent districts], religious or nonreligious." The majority then finds confirmation that "participation of *all* schools" satisfies neutrality by noting that the better part of total state educational expenditure goes to public schools, thus showing there is no favor of religion.

The illogic is patent. If regular, public schools (which can get no voucher payments) "participate" in a voucher scheme with schools that can, and public expenditure is still predominantly on public schools, then the majority's reasoning would find neutrality in a scheme of vouchers available for private tuition in districts with no secular private schools at all. "Neutrality" as the majority employs the term is, literally, verbal and nothing more. This, indeed, is the only way the majority can gloss over the very nonneutral feature of the total scheme covering "*all* schools": public tutors may receive from the State no more than $324 per child to support extra tutoring (that is, the State's 90% of a total amount of $360), whereas the tuition voucher schools (which turn out to be mostly religious) can receive up to $2,250.

Why the majority does not simply accept the fact that the challenge here is to the more generous voucher scheme and judge its neutrality in relation to religious use of voucher money seems very odd. It seems odd, that is, until one recognizes that comparable schools for applying the criterion of neutrality are also the comparable schools for applying the other majority criterion, whether the immediate recipients of voucher aid have a genuinely free choice of religious and secular schools to receive the voucher money. And in applying this second criterion, the consideration of "*all* schools" is ostensibly helpful to the majority position.

The majority addresses the issue of choice the same way it addresses neutrality, by asking whether recipients or potential recipients of voucher aid have a choice of public schools among secular alternatives to religious schools. Again, however, the majority asks the wrong question and misapplies the criterion. The majority has confused choice in spending scholarships with choice from the entire menu of possible educational placements, most of them open to anyone willing to attend a public school. I say "confused" because the majority's new use of the choice criterion, which it frames negatively as "whether Ohio is coercing parents into sending their children to religious schools," ignores the reason for having a private choice enquiry in the first place. Cases . . . have found private choice relevant under a rule that aid to religious schools can be permissible so long as it first passes through the hands of students or parents. The majority's view that all educational choices are comparable for purposes of choice thus ignores the whole point of the choice test: it is a criterion for deciding whether indirect aid to a religious school is legitimate because it passes through private hands that can spend or use the aid in a secular school. The question is whether the private hand is genuinely free to send the money in either a secular direction or a religious one. The majority now has transformed this question about private choice in channeling aid into a question about selecting from examples of state spending (on education) including direct spending on magnet and community public schools that goes through no private hands and could never reach a religious school under any circumstance. When the choice test is transformed from where to spend the money to where to go to school, it is cut loose from its very purpose.

Defining choice as choice in spending the money or channeling the aid is, moreover, necessary if the choice criterion is to function as a limiting principle at all. If "choice" is present whenever there is any educational alternative to the religious school to which vouchers can be endorsed, then there will always be a choice and the voucher can always be constitutional, even in a system in which there is not a single private secular school as an alternative to the religious school. And because it is unlikely that any participating private religious school will enroll more pupils than the generally available public system, it will be easy to generate numbers suggesting that aid to religion is not the significant intent or effect of the voucher scheme.

That is, in fact, just the kind of rhetorical argument that the majority accepts in these cases. In addition to secular private schools (129 students), the majority considers public schools with tuition assistance (roughly 1,400 students), magnet schools (13,000 students), and community schools (1,900 students), and concludes that fewer than 20% of pupils receive state vouchers to attend religious schools. (In fact, the numbers would seem even more favorable to the majority's argument if enrollment in traditional public schools without tutoring were considered, an alternative the majority thinks relevant to the private choice enquiry).... If the choice of relevant alternatives is an open one, proponents of voucher aid will always win, because they will always be able to find a "choice" somewhere that will show the bulk of public spending to be secular....

It is not, of course, that I think even a genuine choice criterion is up to the task of the Establishment Clause when substantial state funds go to religious teaching... it is not. The point is simply that if the majority wishes to claim that choice is a criterion, it must define choice in a way that can function as a criterion with a practical capacity to screen something out.

If, contrary to the majority, we ask the right question about genuine choice to use the vouchers, the answer shows that something is influencing choices in a way that aims the money in a religious direction: of 56 private schools in the district participating in the voucher program (only 53 of which accepted voucher students in 1999–2000), 46 of them are religious; 96.6% of all voucher recipients go to religious schools, only 3.4% to nonreligious ones. Unfortunately for the majority position, there is no explanation for this that suggests the religious direction results simply from free choices by parents. One answer to these statistics, for example, which would be consistent with the genuine choice claimed to be operating, might be that 96.6% of families choosing to avail themselves of vouchers choose to educate their children in schools of their own religion. This would not, in my view, render the scheme constitutional, but it would speak to the majority's choice criterion. Evidence shows, however, that almost two out of three families using vouchers to send their children to religious schools did not embrace the religion of those schools. The families made it clear they had not chosen the schools because they wished their children to be proselytized in a religion not their own, or in any religion, but because of educational opportunity.

Even so, the fact that some 2,270 students chose to apply their vouchers to schools of other religions might be consistent with true choice if the students "chose" their religious schools over a wide array of private nonreligious options, or if it could be shown generally that Ohio's program had no effect on educational choices and thus no impermissible effect of advancing religious education. But both possibilities are contrary to fact. First, even if all existing nonreligious private schools in Cleveland were willing to accept large numbers of voucher students, only a few more than the 129 currently enrolled in such schools would be able to attend, as the total enrollment at all nonreligious private schools in Cleveland for kindergarten through eighth grade is only 510 children, and there is no indication that these schools have many open seats. Second, the $2,500 cap that the program places on tuition for participating low-income pupils has the effect of curtailing the participation of nonreligious schools: "nonreligious schools with higher tuition (about $4,000) stated that they could afford to accommodate just a few voucher students." By comparison, the average tuition at participating Catholic schools in Cleveland in 1999–2000 was $1,592, almost $1,000 below the cap.

Of course, the obvious fix would be to increase the value of vouchers so that existing nonreligious private and non-Catholic religious schools would be able to enroll more voucher students, and to provide incentives for educators to create new such schools given that few presently exist. Private choice . . . would then be "true private choice" under the majority's criterion. But it is simply unrealistic to presume that parents of elementary and middle schoolchildren in Cleveland will have a range of secular and religious choices. . . . And to get to that hypothetical point would require that such massive financial support be made available to religion as to disserve every objective of the Establishment Clause even more than the present scheme does.

There is, in any case, no way to interpret the 96.6% of current voucher money going to religious schools as reflecting a free and genuine choice by the families that apply for vouchers. The 96.6% reflects, instead, the fact that too few nonreligious school desks are available and few but religious schools can afford to accept more than a handful of voucher students. And contrary to the majority's assertion, public schools in adjacent districts hardly have a financial incentive to participate in the Ohio voucher program, and none has. For the overwhelming number of children in the voucher scheme, the only alternative to the public schools is religious. And it is entirely irrelevant that the State did not deliberately design the network of private schools for the sake of channeling money into religious institutions. The criterion is one of genuinely free choice on the part of the private individuals who choose, and a Hobson's choice [a choice that appears to be free when there is no real alternative] is not a choice, whatever the reason for being Hobsonian.

I do not dissent merely because the majority has misapplied its own law, for even if I assumed *arguendo* that the majority's formal criteria were satisfied on the facts, today's conclusion would be profoundly at odds with the Constitution. Proof of this is clear on two levels. The first is circumstantial, in the now discarded symptom of violation, the substantial dimension of the aid. The second is direct, in the defiance of every objective supposed to be served by the bar against establishment.

The scale of the aid to religious schools approved today is unprecedented, both in the number of dollars and in the proportion of systemic school expenditure supported. Each measure has received attention in previous cases. On one hand, the sheer quantity of aid, when delivered to a class of religious primary and secondary schools, was suspect on the theory that the greater the aid, the greater its proportion to a religious school's existing expenditures, and the greater the likelihood that public money was supporting religious as well as secular instruction. . . .

On the other hand, the Court has found the gross amount unhelpful for Establishment Clause analysis when the aid afforded a benefit solely to one individual, however substantial as to him, but only an incidental benefit to the religious school at which the individual chose to spend the State's money. When neither the design nor the implementation of an aid scheme channels a series of individual students' subsidies toward religious recipients, the relevant beneficiaries for establishment purposes, the Establishment Clause is unlikely to be implicated.

The Cleveland voucher program has cost Ohio taxpayers $33 million since its implementation in 1996 ($28 million in voucher payments, $5 million in administrative costs), and its cost was expected to exceed $8 million in the 2001–2002 school year. These tax-raised funds are on top of the textbooks, reading and math tutors, laboratory equipment, and the like that Ohio provides to private schools, worth roughly $600 per child.

The gross amounts of public money contributed are symptomatic of the scope of what the taxpayers' money buys for a broad class of religious-school students. In paying for practically the full amount of tuition for thousands of qualifying students, the scholarships purchase everything that tuition purchases, be it instruction in math or indoctrination in faith. . . . [T]he majority makes no pretense that substantial amounts of tax money are not systematically underwriting religious practice and indoctrination.

It is virtually superfluous to point out that every objective underlying the prohibition of religious establishment is betrayed by this scheme, but something has to be said about the enormity of the violation. Jefferson described [freedom of conscience] as the idea that no one "shall be compelled to . . . support any religious worship, place, or ministry whatsoever," even a "teacher of his own religious persuasion," and Madison thought it violated by any " 'authority which can force a citizen to contribute three pence . . . of his property for the support of any . . . establishment.' " Madison's objection to three pence has simply been lost in the majority's formalism.

... [T]o save religion from its own corruption, Madison wrote of the " 'experience... that ecclesiastical establishments, instead of maintaining the purity and efficacy of Religion, have had a contrary operation.' " In Madison's time, the manifestations were "pride and indolence in the Clergy; ignorance and servility in the laity[,] in both, superstition, bigotry and persecution" in the 21st century, the risk is one of "corrosive secularism" to religious schools, and the specific threat is to the primacy of the schools' mission to educate the children of the faithful according to the unaltered precepts of their faith....

The risk is already being realized. In Ohio, for example, a condition of receiving government money under the program is that participating religious schools may not "discriminate on the basis of... religion," which means the school may not give admission preferences to children who are members of the patron faith; children of a parish are generally consigned to the same admission lotteries as non-believers. This indeed was the exact object of a 1999 amendment repealing the portion of a predecessor statute that had allowed an admission preference for "[c]hildren... whose parents are affiliated with any organization that provides financial support to the school, at the discretion of the school." Nor is the State's religious antidiscrimination restriction limited to student admission policies: by its terms, a participating religious school may well be forbidden to choose a member of its own clergy to serve as teacher or principal over a layperson of a different religion claiming equal qualification for the job. Indeed, a separate condition that "[t]he school... not... teach hatred of any person or group on the basis of... religion" could be understood (or subsequently broadened) to prohibit religions from teaching traditionally legitimate articles of faith as to the error, sinfulness, or ignorance of others, if they want government money for their schools.

For perspective on this foot-in-the-door of religious regulation, it is well to remember that the money has barely begun to flow. Prior examples of aid, whether grants through individuals or in-kind assistance, were never significant enough to alter the basic fiscal structure of religious schools; state aid was welcome, but not indispensable. But given the figures already involved here, there is no question that religious schools in Ohio are on the way to becoming bigger businesses with budgets enhanced to fit their new stream of tax-raised income. (Of 91 schools participating in the Milwaukee program, 75 received voucher payments in excess of tuition, 61 of those were religious and averaged $185,000 worth of overpayment per school, justified in part to "raise low salaries"). The administrators of those same schools are also no doubt following the politics of a move in the Ohio State Senate to raise the current maximum value of a school voucher from $2,250 to the base amount of current state spending on each public school student ($4,814 for the 2001 fiscal year). Ohio, in fact, is merely replicating the experience in Wisconsin, where a similar increase in the value of educational vouchers in Milwaukee has induced the creation of some 23 new private schools, some of which, we may safely surmise, are religious. New schools have presumably pegged their financial prospects to the government from the start, and the odds are that increases in government aid will bring the threshold voucher amount closer to the tuition at even more expensive religious schools.

When government aid goes up, so does reliance on it; the only thing likely to go down is independence.... A day will come when religious schools will learn what political leverage can do, just as Ohio's politicians are now getting a lesson in the leverage exercised by religion.

Increased voucher spending is not, however, the sole portent of growing regulation of religious practice in the school, for state mandates to moderate religious teaching may well be the most obvious response to the third concern behind the ban on establishment, its inextricable link with social conflict. As appropriations for religious subsidy rise, competition for the money will tap sectarian religion's capacity for discord....

Religious teaching at taxpayer expense simply cannot be cordoned from taxpayer politics, and every major religion currently espouses social positions that provoke intense opposition. Not all taxpaying Protestant citizens, for example, will be content to underwrite the teaching of the Roman Catholic Church condemning the death penalty. Nor will all of America's Muslims acquiesce in paying for the endorsement of the religious Zionism taught in many religious Jewish schools, which combines "a nationalistic sentiment" in support of Israel with a "deeply religious" element. Nor will every secular taxpayer be content to support Muslim views on differential treatment of the sexes, or, for that matter, to fund the espousal of a wife's obligation of obedience to her husband, presumably taught in any schools adopting the articles of faith of the Southern Baptist Convention. Views like these, and innumerable others, have been safe in the sectarian pulpits and classrooms of this Nation not only because the Free Exercise Clause protects them directly, but because the ban on supporting religious establishment has protected free exercise, by keeping it relatively private. With the arrival of vouchers in religious schools, that privacy will go, and along with it will go confidence that religious disagreement will stay moderate.

⋅⊶⊙⊷⋅

If the divisiveness permitted by today's majority is to be avoided in the short term, it will be avoided only by action of the political branches at the state and national levels. Legislatures not driven to desperation by the problems of public education may be able to see the threat in vouchers negotiable in sectarian schools. Perhaps even cities with problems like Cleveland's will perceive the danger, now that they know a federal court will not save them from it.

My own course as a judge on the Court cannot, however, simply be to hope that the political branches will save us from the consequences of the majority's decision. *Everson's* statement is still the touchstone of sound law, even though the reality is that in the matter of educational aid the Establishment Clause has largely been read away. True, the majority has not approved vouchers for religious schools alone, or aid earmarked for religious instruction. But no scheme so clumsy will ever get before us, and in the cases that we may see, like these, the Establishment Clause is largely silenced. I do not have the option to leave it silent, and I hope that a future Court will reconsider today's dramatic departure from basic Establishment Clause principle.

POSTSCRIPT

Are School Vouchers Compatible With the First Amendment?

In their opinions, Rehnquist and Souter cite different precedents. Rehnquist asserts that the controlling precedents are *Mueller v. Allen* (1983, which focused on tax deductions for private school tuition), *Witters v. Washington Dept. of Servs. for Blind* (1986, tuition aid to a student studying at a religious institution to become a pastor), and *Zobrest v. Catalina Foothills School Dist.* (1993, salaries of sign-language interpreters assisting deaf children in religious schools). Souter considers the 1973 case *Committee for Public Education and Religious Liberty v. Nyquist,* which struck down a program of tuition grants and tax deductions for parents who send their children to religious schools, more to the point. He also considers the 1947 case *Everson v. Board of Ed. of Ewing* to be foundational. Even though the *Everson* Court upheld bus transportation to parochial schools, it insisted that this was aid to the *families of children,* not to the schools. According to the Court, no such tax-supported aid "can be levied to support any religious activities or institutions." It appears that the disputants on both sides of the voucher issue can select from a rich menu of precedents.

In "Are School Vouchers Un-American?" *Commentary* (February 2000), Gary Rosen concludes that vouchers that permit lower-income parents to pay for private schools for their children will raise achievement levels without causing any of the harmful effects that opponents of vouchers have attributed to them. Joseph P. Viteritti provides an excellent summary of the background to the *Zelman* decision in "Vouchers on Trial," *Education Next* (Summer 2002). Also see Viteritti's defense of vouchers in *Choosing Equality: School Choice, the Constitution, and Civil Society* (Brookings Institution Press, 1999). Opposing vouchers, Judith Pearson, in *Myths of Educational Choice* (Praeger, 1993), contends that school choice violates the basic principle of equity because it benefits some schools and children at the expense of others. In *The Market Approach to Education: An Analysis of America's First Voucher Program* (Princeton University Press, 2000), John W. Witte examines the strengths and weaknesses of a voucher program in Milwaukee, Wisconsin, and reaches the conclusion that although it seems to be working there, it would be dangerous to implement universally, at least at the present time. Voucher proponent Terry M. Moe has proposed that a lottery should be established to determine voucher admissions so that schools do not take the best students only and that schools that accept students with vouchers should be required to conduct tests to ensure that their curricula is high quality.

The bitter division of the Supreme Court over *Zelman* is only the latest salvo in the continuing conflict over educational quality and equality and the intertwined conflict over church-state relations. It remains to be seen whether or not more states and cities will adopt voucher programs and whether or not more private schools will participate in them. An altered Supreme Court may be called upon to reexamine this decision. Even as it stands, intriguing questions are likely to be raised: May tax dollars be used to buy religious materials for schools? Will children who employ vouchers to attend church-affiliated schools receive higher scores on standardized tests? Will public schools improve as a result of competition spawned by voucher programs, or will they decline because of reduced funding? And can vouchers be used to send children to an anti-American, radical, Islamic fundamentalist school?

ISSUE 22

Is There an Emerging
Democratic Majority?

YES: John B. Judis and Ruy Teixeira, from *The Emerging Democratic Majority* (Scribner, 2002)

NO: Daniel Casse, from "An Emerging Republican Majority?" *Commentary* (January 2003)

ISSUE SUMMARY

YES: Social analysts John B. Judis and Ruy Teixeira argue that on key issues the Democratic Party is more in line with the values of modern, postindustrial America than the Republican Party is.

NO: Public communications director Daniel Casse contends that the Republicans occupy the middle ground on domestic issues, driving the Democrats to adopt less popular, extreme positions.

Since the election of Abraham Lincoln in 1860, there have been two—and only two—major political parties in the United States: the Republican Party and the Democratic Party. Throughout the nation's history, the major parties have played indispensable roles: presenting candidates, serving as convenient labels for differing views, getting out the vote, and providing "a place at the table" for previously disfranchised or neglected populations, such as the Irish in the late nineteenth century and African Americans in the twentieth.

For many decades after the Civil War the two major parties differed on major issues, but only in degree, so that one party could be characterized as more conservative or liberal on a particular issue. This was seen as desirable in order for the parties to make the broadest possible appeal to the largest number of voters. An example of this may be seen in the Democratic Party from the 1930s to the 1960s, which contained both the strongest supporters of federal civil rights, liberals and African Americans, and the strongest opponents, the southerners who had been the backbone of the party since the Civil War and who usually occupied key leadership positions in Congress.

Curiously, the most significant sign of the realignment of the parties occurred when each nominated a candidate who was identified as clearly ideological but who was perceived by many voters as out of the mainstream. This occurred when the Republicans nominated Senator Barry Goldwater, who unabashedly called himself a conservative, but was defeated in a landslide by President Lyndon Johnson in 1964. This was almost the political mirror image of what happened just eight years later, in 1972, when the Democrats nominated Senator George McGovern, who proudly defended his liberal principles and who was roundly defeated by President Richard Nixon.

Goldwater and McGovern were harbingers of a movement toward more ideologically polarized parties. That began to happen with the election of conservative Republican Ronald Reagan to the presidency in 1980 and culminated with the Republican capture of congressional majorities in 1994. The once "solid South" for Democrats became increasingly Republican, suburbs that were once safely Republican became more competitive, and the political map became more ideological. Voters can, by and large, expect Democrats to favor the right to abortion and Republicans to oppose it. Similarly, voters can expect most Republicans to support cutting taxes and most Democrats to spend more tax money on social programs such as Medicare and prescription drug coverage.

In 1969 political commentator Kevin Phillips wrote the book *The Emerging Republican Majority,* urging that Republicans adopt a "Southern strategy" that would require an increasing appeal to white conservatives and an abandonment of any effective appeal to the Northeast liberal establishment or African American voters. This is what happened, and race along with the issues that voters identify with race (including civil rights, affirmative action, and the rights of accused persons) became a dominant, if often unspoken, theme of American politics. Because of this strategy, no Democratic presidential candidate since Johnson has received a majority of the votes cast by white voters, not even in the three elections of Jimmy Carter and Bill Clinton. This is not to say that either party has not reached out to interests that have not been closely allied with it. Nevertheless, there has been a conspicuous ideological, racial, sectional, and economic class realignment of the parties.

As the prominence of a particular issue rises and falls, so do the fortunes of the major parties. Since 1995 Republicans have controlled the House for ten consecutive years and the Senate for only two years less (because of the defection of a Republican senator). Does this mean that an era marked by a Republican majority has begun? Or is it just an aberration? In the first decade of the twenty-first century, the prospect of either party controlling the presidency, the two houses of Congress, and over a period of time the federal judiciary depends on the movement of American politics in a more conservative (Republican) or a more liberal (Democratic) direction.

In the following selections, John B. Judis and Ruy Teixeira contend that the pendulum is swinging back to the Democrats and a greater role for government in dealing with the economic and social issues of a postindustrial economy. Daniel Casse argues that this viewpoint is contradicted by the election results in 2002 and the more favorable image that voters have of Republicans and of its more moderate image.

John B. Judis and Ruy Teixeira

 **YES**

The Progressive Center

These are turbulent and unusual times. In the 1990s, America saw its longest peacetime economic expansion, including a half decade of spectacular economic performance, led by computer automation and the Internet. Although superficially identified with twenty-something millionaires making a killing on dotcom stocks, the period presaged a postindustrial society in which advanced electronic technology would progressively liberate human beings from repetitive drudgery and toil; in which knowledge and intelligence would displace brute physical power as the engine of economic growth; and in which citizens could increasingly devote their lives to the pursuit of knowledge and happiness. The boom of the nineties was followed, of course, by a recession and by the onset of a war against radical Islamic terrorists who, if successful in their jihad, would have undermined the promise of postindustrial society and plunged the world back into the dark uncertainty and otherworldly fanaticism of the Middle Ages.

In the midst of these tumultuous times, the United States has been undergoing a significant political transition from a conservative Republican majority, which dominated American politics during the 1980s and maintains a weak grip on national power, to a new Democratic majority, which began to emerge during the Clinton presidencies of the 1990s. This new majority is intimately bound up with the changes that America began to go through in the last part of the twentieth century: from an industrial to a postindustrial society, from a white Protestant to a multiethnic, religiously diverse society in which men and women play roughly equal roles at home and at work, and from a society of geographically distinct city, suburb, and country to one of large, sweeping postindustrial metropolises.

The conservative Republican realignment of the 1980s was in large part a reaction to the turmoil of the sixties and seventies. It sought to contain or roll back the demands of civil rights protesters, feminists, environmentalists, welfare rights organizers, and consumer activists. It was also a reaction to the changes wrought in family structure, work, neighborhood, and ethnic composition by the transition to postindustrial capitalism. And it was a protest against government programs that cost too much and accomplished too little in the midst of a stagnating economy.

From John B. Judis and Ruy Teixeira, *The Emerging Democratic Majority* (Scribner, 2002), pp. 163–177. Copyright © 2002 by John B. Judis and Ruy Teixeira. Reprinted by permission of Scribner, an imprint of Simon & Schuster Adult Publishing Group. Some notes omitted.

Much of that political reaction was inevitable and understandable. Some government programs did waste resources and did little to promote better citizens and a better society. Welfare, as originally devised, did encourage family breakup; much public housing fostered ghetto crime. And the intersection of war and social protest gave the movements of the sixties an apocalyptic edge. The civil rights movement degenerated into ghetto riots and gun-toting militants; feminists ended up challenging the utility of the family and of marriage; consumer activists looked down upon the tastes and habits of average Americans; the counterculture championed drugs and mocked traditional religion in favor of fads and cults; and community organizers encouraged the poor to depend on government handouts.

But the conservative reaction has ranged to extremes of its own. It exploited white Southern resistance to racial desegregation; it denigrated single mothers and working women while stigmatizing homosexuals; it rejected any government intervention into the market and called for abolishing whole sections of the federal government; and it sought to impose the strictures of sectarian religion on education and scientific research. The emerging Democratic majority is a corrective to this Republican counterrrevolution—an attempt to come to terms with what was positive and enduring in the movements of the sixties and in the transition to postindustrial capitalism. It does not represent a radical or aggressively left-wing response to conservatism, but a moderate accommodation with what were once radical movements. Like the Republican realignment of 1896, it seeks to ratify and consolidate progressive views that increasingly dominate the center of American politics.

Security, Stability, and Free Markets

In the early twentieth century, Republican progressives pioneered the idea of a regulatory capitalism that stood between laissez-faire capitalism and socialism. This kind of public intervention through government attempted to reduce the inequities and instability created by private growth without eliminating the dynamism of markets. It preserved private ownership of farms, factories, and offices, but subjected them to regulation on behalf of the public interest. Franklin Roosevelt's New Deal expanded the scope of government regulation and intervention, creating a system that worked well for many decades. By the 1970s, however, the system was breaking down and became mired in a crippling stagflation that government seemed helpless to correct. Many liberal Democrats came to believe that measures like nationalization of the energy industry, the control of wages, prices, and even investments, and publicly guaranteed full employment were necessary to get the system back on track.

At that point, Republican conservatism provided a useful corrective, a reassertion of the importance of markets and entrepreneurial risk to economic growth. But the Republican support for markets became hardened into a laissez-faire dogma. By the midnineties, the economy was booming, aided by technology-driven productivity growth, but it was also generating new kinds of inequity, instability, corruption, and insecurity—problems that would become even more apparent during the downturn that began in late 2000. Yet

Republican conservatives continued to argue for reducing regulations and for cutting taxes for corporations and the wealthy even further. They were motivated partly by laissez-faire ideology, but also by alliances with business lobbies in Washington that heavily funded their campaigns.

By the nineties, the Republican approach put them at odds not only with public opinion, but with the demands that the new postindustrial economy was putting on Americans. For one thing, Republicans seemed oblivious to Americans' concern about their quality of life. Air pollution continued to pose a risk to public health and, through global warming, to the planet's future. But after winning the Congress in 1994, Republicans tried to virtually close down the EPA [Environmental Protection Agency]. When Democrats tried to toughen air standards in 1997, Republicans and their business allies blocked the new rules through a court suit. A decade before, Democrats had used the same legal tactics to block Republican attempts to weaken regulations. What was a sign of political weakness in the Democrats of the eighties was equally a sign of political weakness and desperation in the Republicans of the nineties.

When George W. Bush became president, he undid Clinton administration environmental regulations and pulled the United States out of negotiations for a global-warming treaty. Bush equally ignored popular concern about product quality and safety, appointing regulatory foes to head the Federal Trade Commission and the Consumer Product Safety Commission. Bush's moves were so controversial that he eventually had to back off on some of them, including the reduction of clean water standards. Mindful of potential public opposition, the administration resorted to eliminating regulations by quietly negotiating them away in response to industry suits that were brought against them.

Republicans also ignored public concerns with the corruption of the campaign finance system. In the aftermath of 1996 campaign finance scandals, Democrats and a few moderate Republicans, including John McCain, backed a modest measure—well short of public financing of elections—that would have eliminated unlimited "soft money" contributions by corporations, unions, and wealthy individuals to candidates. But conservative Republicans, led by Kentucky senator Mitch McConnell, blocked the legislation. After George W. Bush took office, a campaign finance bill passed the Senate over Bush's objection, but conservative Republicans were able to stop it in the House. Finally, in the wake of the Enron scandal, moderate Republicans in the House banded together with Democrats to pass the campaign bill and Bush, facing a public revolt, finally signed it, though with a conspicuous lack of enthusiasm.

Republicans seemed equally oblivious to the insecurities created by the postindustrial economy. In the older industrial economy, a blue-collar worker at an automobile or steel factory could expect to hold his job until he retired and to enjoy health insurance and a pension. So could a white-collar worker at a bank or insurance company. In the postindustrial economy of global competition and automation, these kinds of jobs declined in number and could also suddenly disappear as companies moved overseas or reorganized or automated at home. Many of the newer jobs in low-wage services and professions were without the kind of fringe benefits that American workers of the 1950s had enjoyed. From 1979 to 1998, the percentage of private sector workers with employer-provided health insurance went down 7.3 percent. The drop was the sharpest among the lowest-paid workers. Of those in the bottom fifth of wage earners, coverage went down by 11.1 percent. Americans also lacked the kind of job protections they had enjoyed earlier. Their sense of insecurity rose, even during a period of recovery. In 1978, 29 percent of workers believed they were in some danger of losing their job; by 1996, the percentage had risen 10.7 percent to 39.7 percent. During the recession, these figures rose still further. In 2001 alone, 1.2 million Americans lost their health insurance.

Democrats sought to respond to this new insecurity through a national health insurance program, but when the public balked at that level of government intervention, they began considering a series of incremental measures. These included extending medicare downward to Americans fifty-five years and older and to children under eighteen; providing prescription drug coverage as part of medicare; eliminating abuses by health maintenance organizations; making health insurance and pensions portable; and providing universally available retirement accounts that workers can use to increase their old-age pensions. By contrast, Republicans have insisted that Americans would be best off in the hands of private markets and with government removed entirely from the economy. "We do have an economic game plan," the House Republicans declared in *Restoring the Dream,* "and its central theme is to get bureaucratic government off of America's back and out of the way." They advocated turning medicare into a voucher system and partially replacing social security with private investment accounts. Only in the face of widespread public support for the Democratic programs did they sponsor their own version of a patients' bill of rights or medicare prescription drug coverage—and in both cases, their proposed alternatives were intentionally so full of loopholes as to be virtually ineffective.

The rise of postindustrial capitalism and the increase of global competition has also put a premium on educated workers. Over the last three decades, only workers with a four-year college degree or more have seen their real wages increase, while workers with less than a college degree have seen their real earnings actually decline. Workers with a high school degree, for instance, made $13.34 an hour in 1973 and $11.83 an hour in 1999 (in 1999 dollars). In the same period, workers with advanced degrees saw their income rise from $23.53 an hour to $26.44 an hour. The clear message to workers was to acquire more education. That message was reinforced by changes in the global economy in which manufacturing work—the most remunerative of noncollege occupations—increasingly shifted from the United States to less developed capitalist countries.

Democrats have advocated more money for job retraining and early childhood education and to allow every high school graduate to attend a two-year college. They have also called for more money for school buildings, science and computer equipment, and teacher salaries. By contrast, Republicans, after taking control of Congress in 1994, tried unsuccessfully to shut down the Department of Education. In many states, Republicans, led by the religious right, have promoted home schooling or exotic theories of education. Nationally, Republicans have made a special priority of vouchers—a program with particular appeal to some white Catholic and evangelical Protestant voters, but remarkably unpopular with much of the electorate. Republicans have deservedly criticized some Democratic efforts as merely "throwing money at problems" and correctly emphasized the need for high standards, but they have used these deficiencies in the Democrats' approach as an excuse to neglect needed spending. Even in a recession, the Bush administration cut funds for worker training—a key component of any education program—in the fiscal year 2002 budget.

Democrats, reflecting their New Deal heritage, have also tried to use government policy to reduce the income inequality created by the new postindustrial economy. In 1993, the Clinton administration dramatically raised the earned income tax credit (EITC) for low-wage workers, while raising the top rate for upper-income Americans. According to the Harvard political scientist Jeffrey B. Liebman, the increase in the EITC worked wonders for low-income workers: "As recently as 1993, a single-parent family with two children and a full-time minimum-wage workers made $12,131 (in today's dollars) with the EITC.... Because of the expansions of the EITC during the 1990s, that family now makes $14,188—a 17 percent boost above the poverty line. The Census Bureau estimates that the EITC lifts 4.3 million people out of poverty, including 2.3 million children."

By contrast, the Republican efforts of Reagan, the Republican Congresses of the 1990s, and the George W. Bush administration have widened income inequality by bestowing tax breaks disproportionately on the most wealthy and on corporations. In the Bush plan that Congress passed in August 2001, the tax cuts, phased in over ten years, will primarily benefit the top 10 percent of income earners. After 2001, they will receive 70.7 percent of the tax benefits, while the bottom 60 percent will get 6.5 percent of the benefits.

These broad differences between the parties became even more apparent after the September 11 terrorist attacks. With the economy slumping, Democrats wanted to give the bulk of money in a stimulus package to unemployed workers who would spend it immediately, with some extra money thrown in to help the newly jobless buy health insurance. By contrast, Republicans in the House, with the Bush administration's support, passed a bill that would primarily have provided tax benefits to corporations and wealthy individuals. Under the bill, almost three-quarters of the tax benefits would have gone to the top 10 percent of income earners, and incredibly, no benefits whatsoever would have gone to a typical family of four with an income of $50,000. In addition, *Fortune* 500 companies would have gotten a $25-billion windfall through the retroactive elimination of the corporate "alternative minimum tax." Almost all of the tax measures in the Republican bill would have taken effect too late to help the economy.

Democrats blocked the Republican stimulus package in the Senate, but in its 2002 budget, the Bush administration was back at redistributing the country's wealth to the wealthy. With deficits rising, the administration actually proposed accelerating when the ten-year tax cuts that Congress had passed would take effect. The administration also proposed making them permanent after ten years rather than subject to congressional review.

Race and Realignment

Republicans were the original party of racial equality. In the 1950s and early 1960s, leaders from both parties attempted to come to terms with the new Southern civil rights movement. But after 1964, the Democrats embraced, and the Republicans rejected, the cause of civil rights. The new conservative movement took root in opposition to the federal civil rights acts of 1964 and 1965. It gained a wider following and credibility in the 1970s and 1980s—attracting many whites without any animus toward black civil rights—because of the extremes to which some black militants, such as New York's Reverend Al Sharpton, the author of the infamous Tawana Brawley hoax, went and because of the corruption and venality of some black Democratic officials, such as Washington, D.C.'s Marion Barry. The backlash was also sustained by white voters' frustrations with 1970s stagflation and by the utter inadequacy of many of the civil rights remedies proposed by liberal Democrats. School busing, for instance, often had the effect of encouraging white flight rather than integrating schools. Some public housing programs put the entire onus of integration on working-class white neighborhoods. But Republicans used the corruption of the black officials and the inadequacy of these programs to stigmatize the Democrats and to avoid offering any constructive remedies of their own.

Republicans, particularly in the South, sought to build a new majority by wooing the white who had backed segregationist George Wallace in 1964 and 1968. South Carolina Republican Hastings Wyman, a former aide to Strom Thurmond, recalled the tactics by which Republicans built this new majority in the South: "I was there, and I remember denouncing the 'block vote'; opposing busing so long and so loud that rural voters thought we were going to do away with school buses; the lurid leaflet exposing 'the integrationist ties' of our Democratic opponents—leaflets we mailed in plain white envelopes to all the white voters in the precincts that George Wallace had carried.... Racism, often purposely inflamed by many Southern Republicans, either because we believed it, or because we thought it would win votes, was a major tool in the building of the new Republican Party in the South."

In 1980, when the realignment finally occurred, it was based to some extent on disenchantment with Democratic economics and foreign policy. But opposition to the civil rights movement and to a cluster of race-based or race-identified policies was particularly important in the South and in the ethnic suburbs of the Midwest and Northeast. In many of those areas, the two parties became identified with their different racial compositions—the Republicans as the "white party" and the Democrats as the "black party." Such an identification was inimical to the cause of racial reconciliation. It created a dynamic by which the Republicans, to maintain their majority, sought to divide whites from blacks. It also created an incentive for Republicans to ignore black economic inequality in their policy proposals and legislation.

Some Republican politicians, such as former congressman Jack Kemp, tried to develop a multiracial Republican Party and strategy, but they were ignored. (Kemp was popular among Republicans because of his outspoken advocacy of tax cuts, not because of his support for racial equality.) Most Republican politicians were swept away by the racial logic underlying the Republican majority. Faced with the prospect of defeat at the hands of a Democratic opponent, Republicans from Jesse Helms to the elder George Bush used racial wedge issues to win over erstwhile white Democrats. And while Bush's son avoided these sorts of tactics in his own run for president, as recently as fall 2001 two other Republicans—both of whom, interestingly, had reputations for racial reconciliation—pulled out the race card once they found themselves trailing in the polls.

Early on in his run for the governorship of Virginia, Republican attorney general Mark Early had boasted of his membership in the NAACP and vowed that he would not ignore the black vote. But by the summer's end, Early was trailing Democrat Mark Warner by 11 percent in the polls. Warner was even ahead in Southside Virginia, where small-town white voters had deserted the Democrats for Wallace in 1968 and had subsequently backed Republican presidential candidates. To win back Southside whites, who were drawn to Warner's message of encouraging high-tech growth, Early and the Virginia Republican Party ran radio ads and passed out leaflets in the area accusing Warner and the Democratic candidates for lieutenant governor and attorney general of supporting gun control, same-sex marriage, and the abolition of capital punishment. The charges were false, and without foundation. And they grouped together the candidates in spite of the fact that they had been nominated separately, disagreed on a range of issues, and were running entirely separate campaigns. What was most striking about the leaflets, however, was not what they said about the candidates' positions, but what they showed: a photograph of Warner with that of attorney general candidate Donald McEachin. Warner is white and McEachin is African-American. Such a technique, pioneered by Helms's political machine in North Carolina, was designed to demonstrate to these white Southside voters, who had a history of racial voting, that Warner was the candidate of the "black party."

In New Jersey, Republican Bret Schundler had captured the mayor's office in Jersey City twice, winning substantial black votes each time. But, as he fell far behind Democrat Jim McGreevey in the race for governor, Schundler increasingly resorted to issues with a strong racial component. In New Jersey, these issues pivot around the differences between the primarily black cities and primarily white suburbs. In his first debate with McGreevey, Schundler, without any prompting, raised his opposition to the New Jersey Supreme Court's Mount Laurel decision. This 1975 decision forced developers in affluent suburbs to devote a "fair share" of their new properties to affordable housing. Schundler said he wanted to "get rid of" the decision because it increased "suburban sprawl." Although people tend to worry about suburban sprawl because they're concerned about pollution or want to ease congestion on the roads, the link to the Mount Laurel decision made it obvious that Schundler had something other than the environment or traffic in mind: Schundler was proposing to curb the movement by the poor—overwhelmingly black and Hispanic—into more affluent, mostly white suburbs.

In the closing months of his campaign, Schundler also highlighted his plan to provide vouchers. Some conservatives have advocated vouchers so that ghetto children could afford to go to private schools as an alternative to failing public schools. But in his campaign, Schundler brazenly appealed to Catholic and religious right parents who already send their children to private schools. He attacked spending on public education as a subsidy to urban—that is, minority—schools and presented vouchers as a way of rewarding suburban parents who send their children to private schools. Schundler charged that McGreevey, who opposes vouchers, "wants to just throw more money into urban school districts and cut money for suburban and rural school districts." McGreevey, in Schundler's coded words, was guilty of favoring primarily black cities over primarily white suburban and rural school districts.

Early and Schundler, like the elder Bush, showed no sign of personally being racist. But as Republicans, they inherited a coalition and a strategy that divided the parties along racial lines and that encouraged Republicans, when in trouble, to stress their opposition to race-based or race-identified programs. In the seventies and early eighties, these tactics frequently worked. But as Democrats abandoned programs like busing, and as a new generation of black leaders, including Washington, D.C., mayor Anthony Williams and Detroit mayor Dennis Archer, replaced the old, race-baiting began to backfire on Republicans, particularly among professionals and women voters who were raised in the sixties ethos of racial tolerance. In Virginia's 1989 gubernatorial race, African-American candidate Douglas Wilder's standing in the Washington, D.C., affluent suburbs shot up after a Virginia Republican attempted to paint Wilder as a black militant. And in the 2001 Virginia and New Jersey races, Republicans had no success whatsoever using these kinds of tactics.

Stem Cells, Gay Rights, and the Religious Right

In 1980, when Ronald Reagan called on Americans to affirm the values of "family, work, and neighborhood," he was drawing a distinction between these values and those that the extremes of the sixties counter-culture had embraced. Republicans became the party opposed to the drug culture, bra burning, sexual promiscuity, teenage pregnancy, and the New Age denigration of religion. And they won elections on this basis. But in the 1980s, as Republicans embraced the religious right of Falwell and Robertson, they went well beyond repudiating the most extreme movements of the sixties. They rejected the new values and social structure that postindustrial capitalism is creating and nourishing.

Most important among these are women's equality at home and at work. The transition to postindustrial capitalism has profoundly altered family structure and the role of women, as the public sector and private industry have increasingly absorbed tasks at home that women traditionally performed. The imperative to have large families has disappeared. Women, no longer consigned to the home, have entered the workforce and many have taken up professional careers. The numbers of divorced women and single mothers have risen; so has the number of college-educated women professionals. *Father Knows Best* has given way to *An Unmarried Woman*. Modern feminism arose in response to these changes. Like other political movements, it included apocalyptic and utopian extremes, but at its core, it represented an attempt to remove the contradiction between an older patriarchal ideology and the growing potential for equality between men and women.

The Republicans, prodded by the religious right and by conservatives who sought its support, rejected the Equal Rights Amendment and the right of women to have an abortion. They balked at federal money for child care and held up the older ideal of the family. (Pat Robertson stated the case in 1992: "I know this is painful for the ladies to hear, but if you get married, you have accepted the headship of a man, your husband. Christ is the head of the household and the husband is the head of the wife, and that's the way it is, period.") Republicans highlighted the most extreme aspects of the women's movement in order to reject the whole. By contrast, Democrats absorbed the mainstream of the new feminist movement, exemplified by the abortion rights organizations and the National Organization for Women. Democrats also advanced proposals for child care and paid family leave to accommodate the reality that so many others were not working outside the home.

Democrats and Republicans have similarly parted ways on encouraging sexual education among teenagers and on preventing discrimination against homosexuals in housing or employment. Like the controversies about prohibition in the 1920s, these seem peripheral to the heart of politics, but in fact arise directly from the transition from one way of life to another. Prohibition was the cause of the small town against city, the ordered life of the farmer and craftsman against the chaos and squalor of the factory city, and of Anglo-Saxon Protestants against ethnic immigrants. Similarly, the Republicans, goaded by the religious right, have become the defenders of the mores of Middletown against those of the postindustrial metropolis.

Republicans, as the party of the religious right, have upheld the older ideal of sexual abstinence and of family life as not merely the norm, but as a moral imperative. They have opposed sexual education, if not sex itself, for teenagers. In December 1994, congressional Republicans forced the Clinton administration's surgeon general, Jocelyn Elders, to resign because she responded favorably to an off-the-cuff question at a press conference about the advisability of discussing masturbation as part of sexual education. Republicans have also adopted the religious right's attitude toward homosexuals as purposeful sinners who represent a threat to public morals. They opposed not only Clinton's unpopular proposal to allow gays to serve openly in the military, but also began to mount initiative campaigns to deny gays protection from discrimination in housing and employment. In Congress, Senate Republicans even refused to confirm a Clinton administration choice for ambassador to Luxembourg because he was a homosexual. They have also indicted homosexuals for causing the AIDS epidemic. In Virginia's 2001 contest for lieutenant governor, the Republican candidate, Jay Katzen, declared that AIDs "is the product, sadly, in most cases of a choice that people have made. . . . We recognize that homosexuality is a choice. It's a lifestyle with public health consequences."

These Republican attitudes were common, of course, fifty and a hundred years ago, but they have lost ground in postindustrial America. Americans today see sex not simply as a means to procreation, but as a source of pleasure and enjoyment. Many still cringe at the sight or prospect of homosexuality, but recognize it as a possibly inherited form of sexual expression that, if denied and closeted, could prevent a person's pursuit of happiness. They may not want gays to be honest about their sexual preference in the military, but they see conservative attempts to punish and stigmatize gays as bigotry and intolerance.

Conservative Republicans and Democrats also part ways on the relationship of religion to science. Here, there was little provocation by the Democratic left or even from the counterculture, unless the arch-Victorian Charles Darwin is seen as representative of the left-wing counterculture. In search of votes, the conservative Republicans of the 1980s made a devil's pact with religious fundamentalists that entailed their indulgence of crackpot religious notions. While Democrats have opposed the imposition of sectarian religious standards on science and public education, the Republicans have tried to make science and science education conform to Protestant fundamentalism. Throughout the South and the Midwest, Republicans have promoted teaching creationism instead of or in competition with the theory of evolution. Creationists hold that the Bible is the literal truth and that the world began several thousand rather than billions of years ago. One leading creationist, for instance, holds that dinosaurs roamed the earth in the twentieth century.

Prominent Republican politicians and intellectuals, including Irving Kristol, William Bennett, and Robert Bork, have refused to repudiate these notions. Instead, they have sanctioned the idea that creationism and Darwinian evolution are merely two competing theories. In the 2000 presidential campaign, George W. Bush endorsed this view: "I believe children ought to be exposed to different theories about how the world started." Later Bush's official spokeswoman said, "He believes both creationism and evolution ought to be taught. He believes it is a question for states and local school boards to decide but he believes both ought to be taught."

The Republican rejection of modern science reached an apogee during Bush's first year in office when he became embroiled in a controversy over whether the government should fund stem-cell research. Stem cells were finally isolated and reproduced for research purposes in 1998 by a University of Wisconsin scientist. These cells could provide the basis for a new "regenerative medicine" that would aid, and even cure, victims of Parkinson's, Alzheimer's, heart disease, stroke, diabetes, and some forms of cancer by replacing or regenerating cells. Stem cells have been garnered from embryos at fertility clinics. Some one hundred thousand embryos are currently frozen and, if not used, will eventually be discarded. Scientists want to use them for scientific research, and the Clinton administration agreed to fund research on new stem cells.

But Republicans sided with the religious right who argued that these embryos are living beings that cannot be "murdered" for the sake of scientific research.[1] This notion of life prompted journalist Michael Kinsley to ask in *Time* magazine, "Are we really going to start basing social policy on the assumption that a few embryonic cells equal a human being?" But Bush, after claiming to spend months pondering the issue of life in a petri dish, finally announced in a nationwide address that researchers could only use stem cells that had already been created from embryos. They could not use new embryos. Such a decision bore out the degree to which conservative Republicans had become hostage to the religious right's campaign against modernity and postindustrial America.

On many of these economic and social issues, conservative Republicans initially won support by standing resolutely against excesses of the sixties and of post–New Deal liberal Democrats. But clearly they have gone to extremes of their own. They are putting forth remedies for problems that no longer exist and ignoring problems that do. They are fighting the future on behalf of the past. In the meantime, Democrats, chastened by defeat during the eighties, have repudiated their own extremes and moved to the political center, which itself has gravitated in a broadly progressive direction. Ironically, the party that the Democrats most clearly resemble is the one that Bush and Rove claim for themselves—the progressive Republicans of the early twentieth century. Like the progressive Republicans, today's Democrats stand between the extremes of right and left and at the gateway at the end of one era of capitalism and the beginning of another. They are the new party of progressive centrism.

Today's Americans, whose attitudes have been nurtured by the transition to postindustrial capitalism, increasingly endorse the politics of this progressive centrism. They want government to play an active and responsible role in American life, guaranteeing a reasonable level of economic security to Americans rather than leaving them at the mercy of the market and the business cycle. They want to preserve and strengthen social security and medicare, rather than privatize them. They want to modernize and upgrade public education, not abandon it. They want to exploit new biotechnologies and computer technologies to improve the quality of life. They do not want science held hostage to a religious or ideological agenda. And they want the social gains of the sixties consolidated, not rolled back; the wounds of race healed, not inflamed. That's why the Democrats are likely to become the majority party of the early twenty-first century.

Note

1. Bush also solicited the views of the pope and other Catholic leaders on whether to fund stem-cell research. Bush was not similarly concerned about Catholic views on capital punishment or on government aid to the poor. His interest in Catholic views seemed to flow from the interest of his political adviser Karl Rove in winning votes for 2004.

NO ↵

Daniel Casse

An Emerging Republican Majority?

By the time Al Gore conceded the presidency to George W. Bush in December 2000, there was widespread agreement that the razor-close election they had just fought, and the fractious litigation that followed it, had exposed a disturbingly deep fissure in our national politics. In newspapers and magazines and on television, brightly colored maps showed a country divided almost exactly in half into red (Republican) and blue (Democratic) voting patterns. "There are now two distinct Americas," proclaimed *Business Week* in a typical cover story, "split along geographic, social, religious, and racial lines." So disparate were the tastes and attitudes of the people inhabiting those two different Americas, the story continued, as to "demand entirely different things from government."

Not only was the country said to be fractured, it was also said to be, on that account, ungovernable—and certainly ungovernable by George W. Bush. Wherever the new President turned, averred the political scientist Walter Dean Burnham, he was bound to find himself crippled by severely "limited opportunities" to forge a consensus behind his policies.

It was in this very circumstance, indeed, that some in the still-smarting Democratic party saw a sign of hope. Although the Democrats had lost not only the presidency but, as it then seemed, both houses of Congress, opportunity lurked in Bush's irreparable weaknesses. The new President, after all, was woefully inexperienced, especially in foreign affairs. The Republican coalition that had supported him—an unlikely mix of business groups, social conservatives, and libertarians—remained as fragile as ever. Only through the tie-breaking vote of the Vice President could the GOP expect to hold its majority in the Senate. And, as if these difficulties were not enough, the new administration was facing the first serious downturn in the national economy after eight years of remarkable prosperity presided over by a Democratic executive.

As the 2000 results were further digested, Democratic strategists took particular comfort in their reading of the red-blue map. The blue metropolitan clusters that had gone for Al Gore were composed disproportionately of educated professionals, women, and minorities—groups that were projected to grow more quickly than the rural and suburban voters who had pulled the lever for Bush. These demographic trends, along with the swooning stock market and other economic woes, suggested that Democrats might be well positioned to

From Daniel Casse, "An Emerging Republican Majority?" *Commentary* (January 2003). Copyright © 2003 by The American Jewish Committee. Reprinted by permission of *Commentary* and the author.

mount a fresh challenge to the GOP as early as the mid-term election of 2002. The party's prospects brightened further when, in June 2001, Senator James Jeffords announced that he was bolting the GOP and would henceforth vote as an independent—thus giving Democrats a majority in the Senate. In July, for the first rime since Bush's inauguration, a Zogby poll showed a majority of Americans disapproving of his performance. Around Washington, "Re-Elect Gore" bumper stickers began to appear.

But then came September 11, followed by the war in Afghanistan and the budding confrontation with Saddam Hussein—events whose political importance served to boost George W. Bush's popularity to once-unimaginable levels and make the Gore defeat fade into memory. [The 2002] mid-term campaign, on which the Democrats had pinned so much hope, became instead a months-long exercise in frustration; by November 5, the actual results left in tatters the party's dream of a public backlash against an "accidental" President and of its own quick reemergence in American politics. In fact, its fortunes today are lower than they were in November 2000. Two years after the country seemed split down the middle, it is George W. Bush's Republicans who look to be on the verge of creating a new and wholly unexpected political majority.

⋆◈⋆

To get a sense of the magnitude of the Democratic defeat, it helps to bear in mind that only twice since 1862 has the party not holding the White House failed to gain seats in the House of Representatives in a mid-term election, and seldom has it failed to gain in the Senate. As November 5 approached, however, candid Democratic leaders were already admitting they had little hope of winning the House (though none foresaw the loss of fully seven Democratic seats). As for the Senate, eleven races were still deemed to be toss-ups through the final weekend before the balloting. Stunningly, the Republicans went on to win all but one of them. At the end of the balloting, the President enjoyed larger majorities in both houses of Congress than on the day he took office.

The morning after the voting, the line from the Democratic National Committee (DNC) was that the party's losses in Congress were offset by significant gains in gubernatorial races, including in such former Republican strongholds as Michigan, Pennsylvania, Wisconsin, Kansas, and Arizona. But this was spin. Not a single elected Republican governor lost on November 5. Most of the Democratic victories occurred in states where Republicans had held the governor's mansion for twelve years or more, making it relatively easy for Democratic candidates to call for a change. Moreover, many of the victorious Democrats had campaigned on explicitly conservative platforms, and in Tennessee, Kansas, and Arizona they had vigorously opposed tax increases. The one notable exception was Mark Fernald in New Hampshire, who advocated an increase in state taxes and lost to the Republican candidate by 21 points.

Democratic gubernatorial victories also have to be seen against even more surprising wins by the GOP. Sonny Perdue became the first Republican governor to be elected in Georgia since Reconstruction. Robert Ehrlich, a graduate of Newt Gingrich's congressional class of 1994, defeated Kathleen Kennedy

Townsend in Maryland, a state widely viewed as the most Democratic in the nation. And Jeb Bush, the President's brother, resoundingly upset the prediction of DNC chairman Terry McAuliffe that he would soon be "gone," defeating his challenger by thirteen points.

There were other significant reverses at the state level as well, where Democrats lost control of seven legislatures. Republicans now control 21 state capitols nationwide, compared with only seventeen still in the hands of Democrats. (Another eleven are split.) This marks the first time since 1952 that Republicans have enjoyed such a majority. In Texas, the state House of Representatives is ruled by Republicans for the first time since 1870; in Missouri, for the first time since 1955.

⌒

From one perspective, of course, the results of the November election were not so astonishing. Ever since September 11, President Bush's approval rating had stood at historically high levels, and in most polls a majority of Americans were saying that the country was on the right track. In the new era of patriotism and national unity, the deep political chasms that separated Bush voters and Gore voters had become less meaningful.

The mid-term election reflected this changed mood in more ways than one. Although many Senate races were closely contested, and there were many tight gubernatorial races, none was a pitched ideological battle. In no contest did abortion, the death penalty, gun control, race, or class warfare play a major role. With the exception of the late Paul Wellstone, no candidate for the U.S. Senate actively argued against disarming Saddam Hussein or removing his regime from power. Even on the economy, which remains worrisome to most voters, the campaigns produced no clear party-line disagreements that might have tipped the balance one way or another in the hundreds of local races.

If the country was no longer so bitterly torn, however, Democratic activists failed to notice it—or so their campaign strategy would suggest. Many in the party's leadership appeared to believe that Bush's post-September 11 popularity was ephemeral, and that the lingering wounds of the "stolen" election of 2000 would be enough in themselves to excite the Democratic base. "We must never, ever forget what happened" in 2000, intoned Ralph Neas, president of People for the American Way. Donna Brazile, Gore's former campaign manager, advised activists to "go out and say, 'Remember what happened in Florida.'"

It may well have been this mistaken assumption of a generalized desire for payback that lay behind the failure of the party's elites to present a genuine challenge to Bush's Republicans. That failure, at any rate, was the burden of much post-election analysis. The Democrats, lamented Peter Beinart, the editor of the *New Republic,* had "fought this election from the meek and cynical center." Two former Clinton advisers, Tom Freedman and Bill Knapp, sounded a similar note in the *New York Times,* complaining that the Democrats had "ended up arguing over seemingly esoteric differences [and] let bigger national trends, like the war on terrorism, dominate."

But what all such Monday-morning criticisms ignore is that, from the very start of the election year, Democrats in Congress had in fact tried to seize upon every possible issue by which to create a clear distinction between their own priorities and those of the White House. In every instance, however, they found themselves outmaneuvered by a President who seemed determined not to let them get the upper hand on any contentious matter.

Thus, early in 2002, Democrats proposed a reconsideration of the Bush tax cut, only to be waylaid by a White House gleefully reminding reporters of the many Democrats who had initially supported the cut. When, soon thereafter, congressional Democrats joined Senator John McCain's call to rid election campaigns of soft money, they found the President suddenly willing to sign a campaign-finance bill even if it was patently defective and constitutionally suspect. Democrats hoping to tie a cascade of corporate scandals to Republicans and their business donors came up against a White House that welcomed bipartisan legislation to contain corporate fraud. On government-financed prescription-drug benefits—a winning Democratic issue according to every poll—the GOP produced a plan that to the casual eye was indistinguishable from the Democrats'. And so it went.

In short, the Democratic problem in 2002 was not just the failure to win a fight but the inability even to pick one. Politically, the war on terror was off-limits—even John Ashcroft, Bush's attorney general and the Democrats' nemesis, was given a relatively free hand to implement his controversial measures for detaining and investigating suspected terrorists. And in the meantime, again and again, domestic issues that had once seemed the exclusive preserve of the Democratic party were being quietly co-opted by a President riding a crest of popularity and a White House enjoying a unique moment of immunity to complaints from the Right that it was pandering to liberals or selling out its own political base.

◦◦◦

So what has happened to the red and blue map, with its supposedly hard-line divisions between Democratic and Republican voters? Few analysts of American politics could have been more confounded by the electoral transformation wrought by Bush than John Judis and Ruy Teixeira. Ever since the 2000 election, these two authors had been arguing tirelessly that the demographic facts signified by that famous map augured well for the Democratic party. In a book bearing the now-embarrassing title *The Emerging Democratic Majority*—a play on Kevin Phillips's prescient book of 1969, *The Emerging Republican Majority*—Judis and Teixeira drew a profile of the new, winning coalition. Its members are the educated professionals, working women, minorities, and middle-class Americans who live in large metropolitan areas—"ideopolises," in the authors' coinage —and are affiliated with the technology sector, universities, social-service organizations, and government.

Today it still seems indisputable that these urban clusters will be increasingly important in national elections—and also that, as Judis and Teixeira demonstrate, they are growing faster than the older suburbs and rural areas in the South and West where Republicans have dominated. But the core of the Judis-Teixeira argument rests less on shared demographics than on shared ideas. What has drawn this particular group of voters together, they contend, is a new kind of politics, or rather a new combination of political attitudes, to which they give the collective name "progressive centrism."

If the name sounds somewhat oxymoronic, that is for a reason. On the one hand, the authors write, these voters

> do not subscribe to the [Republican] gospel of deregulation and privatization. They want to supplement the market's invisible hand with the visible hand of government.... They want to strengthen social-insurance programs... [and they] reflect the outlook of the social movements that first arose during the 60's.... They oppose government interference in people's private lives... [and] support targeted programs to help minorities that trail the rest of the population in education and income.

But, on the other hand, this is not your father's brand of progressivism. Although these voters may indeed "flavor government intervention," they do not, "except in very special circumstances," favor

> the government's supplanting and replacing the operation of the market.... They want incremental, careful reforms that will substantially increase health-care coverage.... They want aid to minorities, but they oppose the large-scale imposition of quotas or the enactment of racial reparations.

And so forth. Judis and Teixeira are quite deliberate in defining what is to their mind this winning combination of fiery Democratic populism with the tempered incrementalism of "New Democrat" politics a la Bill Clinton. This "new synthesis," they believe, accurately reflects the transformation of America into a post-industrial society characterized by large, diverse metropolitan centers; it speaks to the interests and preferences not only of the blue (Democratic) states but of most denizens of "ideopolises" who are hungering for a new political brew. And it is the natural property of the Democratic party, its two components having been clearly if separately at work in, respectively, Clinton's 1992 centrist appeal and Gore's populist defiance of corporate power in 2000. The successful amalgam of these two strategies is what, in their view, will help usher in the new era of Democratic dominance.

After the divisive election of 2000, it was surely not unreasonable to suggest that a new brand of politics would emerge. But Judis and Teixeira's analysis, shaped by hopes as much as by facts, was out of date even as they were writing it, and is at odds with the current disposition of both political parties.

⋅❧⋅

Concerning the Republicans, Judis and Teixeira are stuck in the year 1994, the year of Newt Gingrich's Contract with America. Their straw man is a GOP supposedly rife with racial hatred, disdainful of single mothers and homosexuals, hostile to all government programs, and eager to infiltrate religious orthodoxy into every nook and cranny of American fife. This overheated caricature prevents them from recognizing a lesson that in retrospect can be seen emerging out of their own reading of the 2000 election data. Two years later, not only had major parts of the agenda of "progressive centrism" been seized by a Republican President, but the party he led was no longer, if it ever had been, the party of their imagining.

Judis and Teixeira are hardly the only observers who thought the Republicans were heading for the precipice in the mid-1990's. As Christopher Caldwell wrote in the *Atlantic Monthly* in 1998, the party had allowed itself to be captured by a Southern voting bloc that socially and culturally was far to the Right of the rest of the country, and as a result it had lost the confidence of the electorate. But if voters once told pollsters that they trusted Democrats more on everything from education to the economy to crime and taxes, that is surely not the case today.

In a Gallup survey conducted a few days after November's mid-term elections, respondents consistently held a much more positive image of Republicans than of Democrats, and regarded them as better equipped to lead the country by a margin of 57 to 47 percent. To be sure, those findings reflected the afterglow of a Republican electoral triumph, and would undergo revision in later surveys. But the fact remains that, thanks largely to Bush, Republicans have become more palatable to a majority of Americans, and they have done so by moving away from some of the defining themes of late-20th-century Republicanism.

I have already mentioned a number of signposts from last year, but the shift really goes back to the fall of 2001. It was then, in the weeks immediately following the attacks of September 11, that Bush sent a signal of things to come by adroitly acquiescing in Democratic demands to federalize airport security workers. The shift could be seen again last spring when he announced the imposition of tariffs on imported steel, a stunning retreat from the free-trade principles he himself had advocated during his campaign for the presidency. Since then, he has signed a massive expansion of farm subsidies, reversing a market-driven policy instituted just a few years earlier; agreed to a corporate-accounting law that includes a high level of new regulation and a considerable expansion of federal intrusiveness; and created a $37-billion Department of Homeland Security that may augment and consolidate federal power to a breathtaking degree.

One can defend each of these initiatives on its merits, or at least try to explain why it has been politically necessary. But that is beside the point. Nowhere in this list can one find the themes—limited government, reduced spending, local empowerment—that preoccupied Republican leaders only a few election cycles ago.

As those themes have faded, so, too, have the cultural hot buttons that gave the GOP such strength among social and religious conservatives. As the columnist John Podhoretz has pointed out, it was only three years ago that prominent conservative spokesmen, notably including Lynne Cheney, appeared before Congress to condemn the violence purveyed in rap lyrics by stars like Eminem. But when Eminem's semi-autobiographical movie *8 Mile* opened to large crowds recently, not a syllable of conservative criticism was to be heard. Of course, rap singers in general and Eminem in particular have somewhat moderated the raw brutality of their message in recent months; but it is also true that, in the age of terrorism, the battle against the liberal culture has faded as a key component of Republican politics.

If once high-profile conservative causes are losing their punch, the same can be said of certain high-profile conservative spokesmen. Jerry Falwell may have permanently lost his place in acceptable conservative circles when, on the heels of the September 11 attacks, he appeared to place the blame on America's "tolerant" culture. More recently, the Bush White House has distanced itself from both Falwell and his fellow Christian broadcaster Pat Robertson for antagonistic remarks about the Muslim religion.

Nor are conservative Christian activists the only ones out of favor with the White House. In the lead-up to the mid-term elections, it was widely reported that Karl Rove, the President's top political strategist, was discouraging openly ideological candidacies. In California's GOP primaries, Richard Riordan, the former mayor of Los Angeles, known as a moderate, was said to be favored by the White House over the conservative activist Bill Simon. In Minnesota, the majority leader of the state House of Representatives was reportedly dissuaded by Vice President Richard Cheney from challenging Democrat-turned-Republican Norm Coleman in the primary. Both stories, if true, reflect an effort to shape the public face of GOP challengers, and in retrospect the political judgment involved is hard to fault: Coleman's victory in Minnesota relied in part on his ability to attract Democratic voters, while Bill Simon, who won the Republican primary in California, went on to be trounced by the incumbent Gray Davis in a race that many thought Riordan would have won.

⋅⦿⋅

This is hardly to say that George W. Bush is out to create a Republican party in the mold of a James Jeffords or even a John McCain. After all, he pressed for and signed the largest tax-cut package in more than a decade and is now seeking to make those cues permanent. He has consistently selected bona-fide conservatives as his nominees to the federal bench. He fought, successfully, to keep the new Homeland Security Department exempt from federal-employee union rules. He is a strong opponent of human cloning, and has severely restricted the use of stem cells in federal medical research. His administration has proposed privatizing thousands of government jobs. In his personal style, and in his religious faith, he appears genuinely conservative. And this is not even to mention his vigorous stance in foreign policy, clearly reminiscent of Ronald Reagan and clearly distinct from the typical Democrat of today.

But there is also no mistaking the fact that Bush is prepared to offer voters something different from Reaganism and Gingrichism, something that goes beyond even the "compassionate conservatism" he introduced in his campaign for the presidency. What he and his advisers—and his party—appear to have grasped is that mustering the kind of bipartisan support required by a wartime Republican President depends on the ability to stand in or near the Center, and so turn to advantage the same demographic and cultural trends that, a mere two years ago, seemed so threatening to the GOP's future. The question is whether the palpable successes of Bush and the new GOP as measured in the mid-term elections are an artifact of the moment, or whether they can be molded into something more permanent, and more meaningful.

That will depend in large measure on the Democrats, and on how they play the hand they have now been dealt. So far—and here again is where Judis and Teixeira go wrong—there are abundant signs that they will play it not by sticking to "progressive centrism" but by moving Left. For all the alleged changes that the Democratic party underwent during the Clinton years, it now appears that its congressional wing is retreating to a familiar form of interest-group populism. Despite all the attempts to create a coalition of the Center, the party as a whole remains hostage to public-employee unions, trial lawyers, and organized lobbyists of every kind.

The choice of the unreconstructed liberal Nancy Pelosi to lead the minority caucus in the House, together with the emergence of Senator Hillary Rodham Clinton in a leadership role in the Senate, is a clear indication of the Left's determination to claim for its own the shreds of the party's fortunes....

If this pattern continues, one can safely predict that on the road to the next presidential campaign, even as Republicans continue to downplay their "wedge" issues, Democrats will be more and more likely to emphasize theirs —especially in such areas as environmental protection and guaranteed health insurance, already emerging as favored themes. So far, faced with challenges on these or similar issues—the Patient's Bill of Rights, protection of the domestic steel industry—Bush Republicans have tended to respond with their now-standard "me, too." But a more left-wing, populist Democratic party may render this strategy, unworkable by robbing Bush of any chance of compromise.

That will be a testing moment for the GOP—and, conceivably, an opportunity to define itself for the foreseeable future. If it is to hold on to its edge, the party may be driven to articulate a more consistent and more truly conservative approach to issues of policy, if not to evolve a true conservative philosophy of governance. This does not mean veering sharply Right in a move mirroring the Democrats' turn to the Left. It does mean, in the broadest terms, developing a constantly reiterated commitment to the virtues of limited government over expanded entitlements, to market incentives over command-and-control regulation, to competition in place of entrenched bureaucratic monopolies, to economic growth over austerity, to conservation over radical environmentalism.

Such an exercise has much to recommend it, and not just in order to reassure doubting conservatives that Republican politics is about more than winning elections from Democrats. There is, in fact, a real danger in the strategy being pursued by the White House. In the hands of a less gifted, or less convincing, politician than Bush, and in circumstances other than wartime, it may represent less a blueprint for future political dominance than a reversion to an older and thoroughly failed Republican role. I am thinking, of course, of the long decades after the New Deal when the GOP was defined primarily by its efforts to slow the inexorable march of liberal ideas—not by substituting better ones but by accommodating them and sanding down their sharper edges. This is essentially a defensive form of politics, and it is a losing proposition. By contrast, making the case for limited government in a consistent and serious and positive manner could actually increase the appeal of the GOP in the eyes of many centrist and/or traditional Democratic voters wire have been drawn to it in the months since September 11.

⋅⊰❂⊱⋅

Over the last three decades, the GOP has gone through a number of minor revolutions in an effort to reinvent itself. Kevin Phillips chronicled the start of the process in *The Emerging Republican Majority,* where he forecast a GOP majority based in the new entrepreneurial communities of the South and West rather than in the old WASP business elites. Ronald Reagan transformed the political face of the party, combining supplyside economics and anti-big-government themes at home with internationalism abroad. Fifteen years later, Gingrich shook up the party once again, demanding the reform of Congress and a shifting of power from Washington to state governments.

Today, Bush's mix of aggressive foreign policy, expanded government in the interest of domestic security, and a willingness to find a middle ground on domestic issues long owned by the Democrats has given him strengths that have defied almost every prediction of how his presidency would evolve. To be sure, he is a beneficiary of extraordinary circumstances. Nor do we yet know whether the brand of politics he has practiced is ultimately driven by expediency or by principle. But it is certain to set the terms of political debate for the balance of his first term, inform his reelection bid two years hence, and just possibly determine whether his party will emerge unexpectedly as a new political majority.

POSTSCRIPT

Is There an Emerging Democratic Majority?

Judis and Teixeira concede that on some issues, such as welfare and civil rights, the Democrats once went too far and provoked a majority backlash, while Casse is willing to admit that some of the old Republican positions on "hot button" issues no longer appeal to the majority. But both sides insist that their parties have learned from their past mistakes and now occupy the true "center." This suggests that a reputation for centrism is highly valued by the leaders of America's major parties, a preoccupation that distinguishes them from many parties in other countries.

An understanding of the changing fortunes of America's political parties can be gained from studies of electoral behavior over the past quarter century. The title of Ronald Radosh's book *Divided They Fell: The Demise of the Democratic Party, 1964–1996* (Free Press, 1996) reflects the author's view that the Democrats have been badly hurt (but not destroyed) by racial and rights issues, coercive and redistributive government tax policies, and Vietnam and antiwar protests. *The Rise of Southern Republicans* by Earl Black and Merle Black (Belknap Press, 2002) is an analysis of how southern politics has been transformed from the solidly Democratic South from the 1930s through the 1970s to a highly competitive area in which the Republicans have enjoyed a clear majority. A different southern perspective is offered in Alexander P. Lamis, ed., *Southern Politics in the 1990s* (Louisiana State University Press, 1999), which describes the movement of so-called New Democrats to oppose the welfare system and to favor the death penalty. Stanley Greenberg and Theda Skocpol, eds., *The New Majority* (Yale University Press, 1997) contains essays that examine strategies that the Democrats might follow in order to achieve future success. In *They Only Look Dead* (Simon & Schuster, 1996), E. J. Dionne supports a resurgence of Democratic Party power. Judis, in *The Paradox of American Democracy* (Pantheon, 2000), and Teixeira, in *The Disappearing American Voter* (Brookings Institution Press, 1992), both write about recent changes in public support. Teixeira states that skilled professionals (who constitute only 15 percent of the electorate, but who have the highest turnout rate of any occupational group) have moved largely from Republican to Democratic support since 1988. Dan Balz and Ronald Brownstein, in *Storming the Gates: Protest Politics and the Republican Revival* (Little, Brown, 1996), contend that the parties have become so polarized that they have alienated moderate voters.

Evaluating the arguments of Judis/Teixeira and Casse is difficult at this time because events are moving quickly and their outcomes are quite uncertain.

A stable, intact, and reasonably democratic Iraq coupled with a clear economic recovery in the United States could ensure a Republican majority for years to come, but the Republicans' failure to achieve these ends could set the stage for a lasting Democratic majority. By now, the reader may be in a better position to judge the outcome than either protagonist in the debate presented here.